The Corporate Social Challenge
Cases and Commentaries

The Irwin Series in Management and the Behavioral Sciences

The Corporate Social Challenge
Cases and Commentaries

Frederick D. Sturdivant

Senior Vice President
The MAC Group, Inc.

James E. Stacey
Ithaca College

Fourth Edition

Homewood, IL 60430
Boston, MA 02116

Associate publisher: Martin F. Hanifin
Developmental editor: Elizabeth J. Rubenstein
Project editor: Jane Lightell
Production manager: Bette K. Ittersagen
Designer: John Rokusek
Compositor: Better Graphics
Typeface: 10/12 Century Schoolbook
Printer: R. R. Donnelley & Sons Company

Library of Congress Cataloging-in-Publication Data

The Corporate social challenge/[edited by] Frederick D. Sturdivant.
James E. Stacey.—4th ed.

    p.   cm.

Includes index.

ISBN 0-256-07044-X (pbk.)

1. Industry—Social aspects—United States—Case studies.

2. Corporations—United States—Case studies.   I. Sturdivant,
Frederick D.   II. Stacey, James E.

HD60.5.U5C688   1990

302.3′5—dc20
                                       89–30502
                                         CIP

Printed in the United States of America
2 3 4 5 6 7 8 9 0 DO 6 5 4 3 2 1

Preface

One of the most important lessons over the years since *The Corporate Social Challenge* has appeared is that business cannot afford to be complacent. While one group may look to the "golden past" and another to a "utopian future" for solace, most business people are firmly rooted in a turbulent present. As soon as one challenge is disposed of, another awaits in the wings. Anyone in business who expected the social and political environment to settle down in the later years of the Reagan administration was to be sadly mistaken. Although many economic indicators such as inflation and unemployment improved during the Reagan years, others, such as family income, remained stagnant or declined while the national debt was tripled.

Many business commentators applauded the continuation and broadening of deregulation activities begun under President Carter. Others felt that these efforts either went too far or reduced protective mechanisms for socially responsible businesses and the environment. "Privatization" presented businesses with new opportunities along with new performance expectations by stakeholders. The federal government cut social programs and asked business to pick up the slack through philanthropy, and American business responded that the burden was too heavy for them to bear. As unionization efforts declined and government hammered away at legislation protecting workers' rights, commentators warned that we might be returning to working conditions reminiscent of the late 19th century.

With the start of the Bush administration, enormous challenges for business remained. With a questionable economic recovery taking place, the nation was faced with a massive national debt and a corporate debt level that was rapidly climbing as the result of a dramatic increase in large leveraged buyouts. A debate raged over whether these leveraged buyouts were helping or hurting the economy. The purported escalation in the use of drugs in American society and the workplace, the plight of the homeless, and the state of the educational system were major issues touching business operations. Lurking everywhere was the specter of AIDS. This deadly disease raised new discrimination, privacy, and insurance issues that business leaders had to face. In all of these areas, people turned to business as the culprit to blame or the savior to ask for help. The interest and controversy surrounding the issues of ethics and morality in government and in business surpassed that of the Watergate era.

Although the early 1980s may have seemed more turbulent than any other time since the Great Depression, the late 1980s were full of equally important challenges to business. Business, as one of the central institutions in this society, faced the challenge of remaining economically viable while meeting the often conflicting expectations of its various stakeholders for jobs, community support, quality products and services, nondiscrimination in hiring and promotion, ethical conduct, and a clean environment.

It is with a sense of déjà vu that the authors complete this fourth edition of *The Corporate Social Challenge.* Although we would not subscribe to a deterministic "history repeats itself" theory, enough old problems have resurfaced to become major themes once again. Many issues, such as the marketing of infant formula in underdeveloped countries, have a nasty habit of reemerging just when business may have thought that they were disposed of once and for all. The historical perspective has also demonstrated that we would be seriously misled in interpreting many of the cases in this book as isolated and unique instances of malfeasance or misfeasance on the part of a company. Time after time, companies involved in an industrial accident have been found to have a history of problematic or antisocial behavior. On the other hand, other companies have a long track record, even under adverse circumstances, of socially responsible behavior. Finally, we notice that technological development presents extraordinary challenges and opportunities to management. Some of these challenges call into question our ability to train management and workers for the ethical and managerial challenges they face.

The cases and commentaries in the fourth edition of *The Corporate Social Challenge* are designed to stimulate discussion of some of the most important issues in contemporary society. As was true of the earlier editions of this book, the materials are organized to parallel the structure of the companion volume, *Business and Society: A Managerial Approach.* Most of the cases provide the reader the opportunity to wrestle with the challenges of managing complex situations. In a limited number of instances, the cases are retrospective, but most require the reader to make decisions without knowing the outcome.

While there are no hard and fast rules about how to derive the best results from cases, we offer the following advice to our students: In order to derive maximum benefit from the case method, it is essential that you mentally "get inside" the case situation. Do not approach a case as you would a chapter in a book or an article in a magazine. You are not an observer but a participant. If a case centers on a decision that needs to be made, put yourself in the shoes of the decision maker. Feel the frustration he or she feels with respect to data limitations. Feel the pressures he or she feels with respect to difficult trade-offs, limited resources, and political conflicts. Do not try to find out prior to analysis how some of the cases have been resolved. Doing so eliminates your opportunity to struggle with the issues and challenges that the original manager confronted. Please do not call the companies involved since many of them have already given generously of their time. It would not be fair to burden them with additional requests. When you are in class, share your ideas with others as you and your peers work jointly to resolve the issues.

In preparing a case, it is recommended that your first reading be a relatively quick one. Who and what is involved here? What seem to be the *major* questions or issues? With your second and much more thorough reading of the case, test your preliminary conclusions from the first reading concerning the major problem(s) and key players. Begin sifting through the facts in the case and sorting them out in terms that are useful to you in analyzing and resolving the major issues. Keep in mind that case facts are presented in a more orderly fashion than they tend to be in the real world, but you should not assume that they are all equally useful or that they are properly and fully related as presented in the case. A statement on one page when combined with the data in a table found on another page may be of great significance. There may also be factual gaps which you will need to fill with reasonable assumptions. Perhaps most important, you should keep in mind that the mere collection and recitation of case facts is unlikely to be much of a contribution. It should be assumed that everyone in the classroom will be quite familiar with the facts of the situation. Thus, the problem is not one of citing facts, but of identifying problems and engaging in analysis that offers insights with respect to the nature of the problems and their solution. A third careful reading of the case should enable you to test your earlier analysis and modify it or enhance it with data or insights that may have been overlooked in the first two readings. Certainly, we have been using many of the cases for many years, yet they are so powerful that they continue to raise new issues and insights into the social responsibility of business.

The commentaries are usually not specifically related to a given case. In short, the "answers" to the cases are not to be found in the commentaries. The commentaries were selected to shed light on a range of issues confronting corporations. Some were chosen because they illustrate other dimensions of issues covered in a case. They tend to be relatively brief, thought-provoking, and sometimes controversial. The commentaries come from sources that are both "pro" business and "anti" business. Some are objective; others will strike the reader as biased. They were not selected from scholarly sources, so they should not be viewed as the product of careful and thorough research. Again, they are there to provoke your thinking and broaden your scope of awareness of the social issues that confront managers.

We are indebted to many people who helped with this venture: Roy Adler and Claudia Hutchinson, charter members of "Fort Riklis," researched and drafted some of the enduring cases in this volume: Farah Manufacturing, United Brands, and McDonnell Douglas and the DC-10. Others who recently played a similar role include Harry Levins (International Harvester and SCA Corporation); Dane Roberts, Jerry Sayre, and Richard Watman (Illinois Power/60 Minutes); Bob Davidson, Greg Green, Art Reine, and Jim Simler (Adolph Coors Company); Kalyani Balachandran, Kirthi Govindarajan, Amy Hanna, and Leigh-Ann Williams (Johnson & Johnson/Tylenol); Julie Richards (Pacific Lumber Company's Last Stand); Randy Jenny (National Savings & Loan and the Specter of AIDS); and Alexandra Novy (Abbott Laboratories). Appreciation is also expressed to Michael Lovdal (Mead Corporation), George

C. Lodge and Joseph Badaracco (Allied Chemical), Donna M. Randall (A Management Dilemma: Regulating the Health of the Unborn), Arthur Sharplin (Union Carbide), John A. Pearce II and Julio O. DeCastro (Goodyear Tire and South Africa), John A. Seeger (Arthur D. Little and the Toxic Alert), and Neil H. Snyder (A. H. Robins and the Dalkon Shield), for granting permission to include their excellent cases in this collection. Special thanks are due Joe Chevarley of Northeastern University for his indispensable help on the Pacific Lumber Company's Last Stand, the National Savings & Loan, and the Specter of AIDS cases.

A substantial debt is also owed to those companies which cooperated in allowing us to have access to records and members of management. In those instances (Abbott Laboratories, SCA Corporation—disguised, National Savings & Loan Association—disguised, Illinois Power, and Armco Steel), the results are all the richer for their efforts.

Frederick D. Sturdivant
James E. Stacey

Contents

PART I
Managing Social Responsiveness, 1

Cases

Farah Manufacturing Company, 5

Abbott Laboratories: Similac (A), 20

The Mead Corporation (A), 40

Commentaries

1. Rating America's Corporate Concience, Council on Economic Priorities, 67
2. A Score Card for Rating Management, Edward McSweeney, 72

PART II
Ideology and Ethical Responsibility, 77

Cases

McDonnell Douglas Corporation: The DC-10, 81

Equity Funding Corporation of America, 99

A Management Dilemma: Regulating the Health of the Unborn, 113

Commentaries

3. Ethics and the Corporation, Irving Kristol, 128
4. Businesses Are Signing Up For Ethics 101, John A. Byrne, 132
5. Ethical Conduct and the Bottom Line, Robert V. Krikorian, 135
6. Small-Business Jungle, Michael Allen, 140
7. Sears Has Everything, Including Messy Fight Over Ads in New York, Robert Johnson and John Koten, 141

PART III
Social/Political Responsiveness, 147

Cases

The American Ship Building Company, 151

International Harvester: Plant Closing (A)/Fort Wayne versus Springfield, 161

Arthur D. Little, Inc., and the Toxic Alert (Revised), 204

Commentaries

8. Avco Corp. Makes Judicious Use of Gifts to U.S. Congressmen, Brooks Jackson, 233

9. Banker Who Battled Urban Blight in Chicago Takes on New Economic Challenges in Arkansas, David Wessell and Alex Kotlowitz, 238

10. Shift of Auto Plants to Rural Areas Cuts Hiring of Minorities, Jacob M. Schlessinger, 241

11. California Growers Rail against Efforts to Stem Flow of Illegal Aliens, Marilyn Chase, 245

12. States' Watchdogs Sharpen Teeth on Big Business, Nancy Mullen, 250

PART IV
International Management, 255

Cases

Goodyear Tire and Rubber Company (South Africa), 259

Union Carbide of India, Limited, 277

United Brands, 302

Commentaries

13. Dollar$ for Apartheid, James Carson and Michael Fleshman, 319

14. Defense Spending Is So High U.S. Falters on World Markets, Knight-Ridder News Service, 324

15. A Code of Worldwide Business Conduct—Caterpillar Tractor Co., 327

PART V
Human Investment, 339

Cases

Manville Corporation, 343

J. P. Stevens & Co., Inc., 380

SCA Corporation, 395

National Savings & Loan and the Specter of AIDS, 412

Commentaries

16. Worker's Hands Bound by Tradition, Peter F. Drucker, 420

17. Firefighters' Questionable Minority Status Went Unchallenged 10 years, Associated Press, 423

18. Workers Go Back to the Basics, Meghan O'Leary, 425

19. More Concerns Set Two-Tier Pacts with Unions, Penalizing New Hires, Roy J. Harris, Jr., 429

20. The AIDS Commission's Hidden Tax, Richard A. Epstein, 433

PART VI
Openness of the System, 435

Cases

Illinois Power Company and "60 Minutes," 439

Adolph Coors Company, 456

Massachusetts Mutual Life Insurance Company, 477

Pacific Lumber Company's Last Stand (A), 497

Commentaries

21. Privacy, Business Week, 508

22. Legal Challenges Force Firms to Revamp Ways They Dismiss Workers,
     Joann S. Lublin, 514

23. Tobacco Titans Get Tough, Bonnie Liebman, 519

24. Talking Business with Smith of Interfaith Center: Companies Face
     the Social Issues, Barnaby J. Feder, 521

PART VII
Consumer Welfare, 523

Cases

Johnson & Johnson/Tylenol (A): "Death in a Bottle," 525

A. H. Robbins and the Dalkon Shield, 547

Commentaries

25. Debate Rages over Marketing and Alcohol Problems, Kevin Higgins, 573

26. Solved: The Riddle of Unintended Acceleration, John Tomerlin, 578

27. "All-Terrain" Vehicles Spark Debate As User Deaths and Injuries Mount,
     John R. Emshwiller, 587

28. Why More Corporations May Be Charged with Manslaughter, Business Week,
     590

PART VIII
The Environment and Energy, 593

Cases

Armco Steel Corporation: The New Miami Coke Plant, 597

Metropolitan Edison Company: Three Mile Island Nuclear Plant, 606

Allied Chemical Corporation (A), 628

Commentaries

29. Utilities Face a Crisis over Nuclear Plants; Costs, Delays Mount,
     Geraldine Brooks, Ron Winslow, and Bill Richards, 648

30. Corporate Donors Embrace Free-Market Environmentalism, Jo Ann Kwong, 653

31. Industry is Going on a Waste-Watcher's Diet, Eric Jay Dolin, 656

32. SEE NO EVIL: Can $100 Billion Have 'No Material Effect' On Balance Sheets?, Amal Kumar Naj, 658

Bibliography, 663

Index, 685

PART ONE

Managing Social Responsiveness

Business is one of the major institutions in American society. As such it is part of the social, legal, political, and economic structure that defines and helps to shape the nature and character of the nation. As business changes, so do the underlying values of society. In order to exist, business must enjoy the trust and support of broad segments of society. In an increasingly educated and relatively progressive society, the old 19th century justifications for business activities are inadequate. No longer shielded by the primacy of property rights and a political philosophy based on laissez-faire, business increasingly finds itself at the vortex of change. Government agencies from the federal to the local level, social activists, concerned consumers, and investigative reporters all play a role in the conduct of business.

Corporate social performance has become central to the task of managing a modern business. However, management has generally been slow to recognize the centrality of business/society relationships, due in part to a belief that such an orientation conflicts with the "bottom line." Nevertheless, it is a myth that being responsive to social demands will necessarily hurt a company's long-run economic performance and profit objectives. Executives with a broad definition of the role of business in society tend to deal effectively with the demands and expectations of the firm's various stakeholders, while not sacrificing corporate economic performance.[1]

It is a central theme of this book and its companion volume, *Business and Society*, that companies should be managed in such a way that they are responsible to the legitimate expectations of their stakeholders (those who have a "stake" in the exchanges). The importance of being attuned to stakeholder needs has achieved strong support across the curriculum of schools of management and business and in many industries and firms.

The period between the late 1960s and late 1980s witnessed rapidly changing expectations in the performance of business and other major institutions. Indeed, public confidence in these institutions declined sharply over that period. Business institutions were forced to consider a wide range of new issues. Answers had to develop within the context of a competitive environment. As social values changed with respect to such issues as the role of

---

[1] Frederick D. Sturdivant, James L. Ginter, and Alan G. Sawyer, "Management Conservatism and Corporate Performance," *Strategic Management Journal* 5, no. 4 (October–December 1984).

women, marriage, and corporate accountability, the concept of corporate social responsiveness tended to supplant the older notion of social responsibility. No longer was simply "not breaking the law" sufficient. During this period, the activities of business were subjected to closer public scrutiny and criticism than in any other time of our nation's history. Some of the activities were illegal, unethical, and immoral, and served to raise additional questions about the role of business in American society.

Increasingly, business became a participant in the political arena. Some observers suggested that large corporations, in fact, dominated the political system. Others saw business as but one special interest group contending within a pluralistic process. Whatever the perception of the political power of business, it was clear that the role of the federal government in economic life had expanded dramatically. Even with the dramatic deregulation of certain industries, such as airlines and trucking, federal agencies and regulatory bodies monitored, evaluated, and sometimes controlled management activities.

A less traditional adversary, the media, emerged as a major contender for social influence, and as a more businesslike industry in its own right. In the latter part of the 1980s, with the economy still in questionable shape, the media focused on ethical issues such as takeover battles and insider trading. Many executives expressed the view that national magazines, newspapers, and especially the television networks were antibusiness. Even those in business who were less suspicious of the press and electronic media often felt that business was not well understood by reporters. They felt that reporting too often reflected an ignorance of basic economic facts. Investigative reporters found the traditional private preserves of the corporate world especially alluring during the period of widespread revelations of corporate bribes and payoffs in the wake of Watergate. During the sharp and lengthy recession of the early 1980s, the media focused on management failures, which had resulted in plant closings, layoffs, and numerous bankruptcies.

Religious groups, social activists, shareholders, and labor unions declared that they had a significant stake in the decisions made by managers. The often-conflicting expectations of these and other stakeholder groups caused some companies to recognize the need for treating social responsiveness in a systematic fashion. Others tried a more traditional approach and proclaimed that their decisions were private, economic matters, not social/political ones.

Since so many corporate policies and practices have intended or unintended social consequences, it is essential that social responsiveness be an integral part of a company's strategic plan and organizational design. A major test of managerial success is the degree to which a company is compatible with its environment. Since the environment houses the economic, social, political, and technological threats and opportunities available to a firm, the success of the enterprise is closely linked to its ability to anticipate change and to position itself to be responsive to new environmental forces. To do so, a company needs to know its own nature and purpose (mission), its objectives, and its strategies for achieving those objectives. Even the best of plans are of little value, of course, unless they are effectively implemented. The organization must be structured as well as motivated to facilitate the implementation of the plan.

Once a company has decided that social responsiveness is to be central to its plan, it still faces the challenge of deciding where responsibility for social performance is to be housed in the organization. It may reside with the chief executive officer, staff specialists ("vice president of public affairs") and their departments, or with operating management. Responsibility probably should be shared by all three.

As in any traditional functional area of business, if social responsiveness is to be managed effectively, there must be "a systematic attempt to identify, analyze, measure (if possible), evaluate, and monitor the effect of an organization's operations on society."[2] Such a method need not be a so-called social audit that was tried by a number of companies in the 1970s and generally proved unworkable. There simply needs to be a systematic approach to the assessment of corporate social performance in selected areas of the company's operations.[3]

In order to achieve a systematic approach to social responsiveness, the manager should not perceive the economy as something set apart from society. Economic activities do not represent a separate entity. The manager can no longer focus exclusively on the economic activities of the business and industry and assume that they can be isolated from society. For example, in our increasingly high-tech and/or service-oriented society, the manager needs to understand the long-term relationship between the society's educational institutions and business' ability to obtain properly trained workers and managers. A systems view of the complex interrelationships between society and economic activities is needed in order to manage the firm responsively.

The cases and commentaries in this section offer sharp contrasts in the definition of the scope of management and the evaluation of corporate performance. The Farah Manufacturing Company case reviews the account of a relatively small and previously little-known company that suddenly found itself thrust into the national limelight in a confrontation with a union, the Catholic Church, the news media, and a number of national political figures. The response to this situation contrasts sharply with the approach taken by the management of Abbott Laboratories when its marketing of infant formula became a matter of controversy. In the third case in this section, the Mead Corporation attempts to anticipate and forestall such problems through the creation of a Corporate Responsibility Committee, including not only directors

---

[2] David H. Blake, William C. Frederick, and Mildred S. Myers, *Social Auditing: Evaluating the Impact of Corporate Programs* (New York: Praeger Publishers, 1976), p. 3.

[3] See, for example, Frederick D. Sturdivant and Heidi Vernon- Wertzel, *Business and Society: A Managerial Approach*, 4th ed. (Homewood, Ill.: Richard D. Irwin, 1990).

but employees as well. In all three cases, managing social responsiveness proves to be a major challenge.

The commentaries offer a look at different approaches to measuring the internal and external performance of a firm in social issues areas. The reading from the Council on Economics Priorities (CEP), *Rating America's Corporate Conscience*, gives an indication of the types of information services that concerned consumers have been looking for. In addition to CEP's book, a number of socially responsible and ethical investing firms have developed to give consumers an opportunity to express their ethical values through investment. In the context of a firm's search for internal performance data, Edward McSweeney, the author of "A Score Card for Rating Management," suggests a number of criteria for evaluating the social and ethical performance of management. This is only a continuation of trends established earlier in the social auditing movement. We expect these trends to continue and to develop more sophisticated measures of social performance.

CASE

Farah Manufacturing Company

Kenneth Farah walked briskly out to greet the plane taxiing toward the Farah hangar at the El Paso International Airport. Each of the two company jets had been used for some time to shuttle apparel buyers into El Paso for firsthand inspections of Farah's operations and facilities. This series of flights in May 1973 were believed to be the widest use yet made of company aircraft for "customer calls," as opposed to calls by salespeople to the retailers' place of business.

After brief introductions, Mr. Farah led the businesspeople through the hangar toward waiting company automobiles. On the way, Mr. Farah stopped to point out the restoration of a silver twin-engine aircraft on one side of the hangar. The plane was an A-20 Havoc, an American attack bomber that had seen extensive action in the early years of World War II. This particular aircraft had been flown during the war by William F. Farah, Kenneth's father and the president of the Farah Manufacturing Company.

The A-20 was the second such restoration project. The first was a silver B-26, completed in the late 1950s at the cost of several thousand work-days effort. His father had spent many enjoyable hours flying that plane on weekends in the 1960s, when the company was setting annual growth and earnings records. Kenneth now wondered privately if his father would ever be able to fly the A-20.

For the last year, William F. Farah had been the central figure in one of the most controversial and significant labor-media events in the history of the country. The Farah strike, which began May 3, 1972, had not been exceptionally long or violent. A nationwide boycott, which began June 19, 1972, however, was the first time a labor organization had used that tactic to organize a work force. Kenneth's father defiantly resisted unionization.

The publicity surrounding the conflict was destroying the company that William Farah had built. The customer flights were a desperate measure to present Farah's side of the story to its customers.

This case is not intended to provide a precise account of the thinking or behavior of the parties involved.

WILLIAM F. FARAH

William F. ("Willie") Farah was a modern American success story. His father, Mansour Farah, was a Lebanese immigrant who ran a small dry goods company in El Paso and began a small garment manufacturing plant in 1920. When his father died in 1937, Willie Farah left college at the age of 18 to help his mother and brother James run the company. The company's growth was accelerated by military clothing production during World War II, and in 1947 the company was incorporated.

The corporation went public in 1967, but the Farah family retained control of about 41 percent of the 5.9 million shares of outstanding stock as of 1969. Mr. Farah personally owned about 10 percent of the shares and controlled another 18 percent as the executor of his brother's estate.[1] James had died at the plant in 1964. As president and chief executive officer of the company, Willie Farah gained a reputation as a tough and stubborn executive. The business in which Farah was engaged made these requisite qualities.

THE APPAREL INDUSTRY

Farah was one of the nation's major producers of men's and boys' casual slacks, shorts, and jackets. Although most manufacturers were, like Farah, specialized in one or two product lines, the clothing industry as a whole was highly competitive because of the ease with which new firms could enter. The 22,000 clothing firms already existing in the industry scrambled after low profit margins and had a higher rate of business failures than most industries. Because of the high degree of competition, pricing within the industry was very competitive, and the penalty for incorrectly anticipating consumer demand for given styles was severe. By 1970, Farah had established a prominent place among the many thousands of manufacturers in the industry. The company earned over $8 million that year on about $136 million in sales, and the stock split two-for-one (see Exhibit 1).

The Farah plants of 1970 were not typical trouser manufacturing plants. The industry was highly labor intensive, and limited economies of scale could be achieved with larger-sized plants. As a consequence, there were thousands of relatively small, 100- to 200-employee plants, located primarily in the southern United States. The largest volume manufacturer, Levi Strauss & Co., had about 50 such plants located in small towns from Knoxville, Tennessee, to El Paso, Texas, and had contracts with an additional 50 independent producers in the same general area.

Each of these small plants used essentially the same manufacturing procedure. Large cylindrical bales of cloth were received by truck or rail from mills generally located in North Carolina. Higher quality producers checked

---

[1] Deborah DeWitt Malley, "How the Union Beat Willie Farah," *Fortune* 90, no. 2 (August 1974), p. 165.

EXHIBIT 1 Farah Manufacturing Company 10-Year Financial Highlights
(in thousands of dollars except per share data)*

	1974	1973	1972	1971	1970
Operating results					
Net sales	$126,447	$132,125	$155,606	$164,570	$136,293
Cost of sales and expenses	129,853	131,821	169,324	151,514	119,031
Operating income (loss)	(3,406)	304	(13,718)	13,056	17,262
Other income, net	1,016	839	37	313	132
Interest expense	1,557	1,706	2,462	1,790	1,037
Earnings (loss) before income taxes	(3,947)	(563)	(16,143)	11,579	16,357
and extraordinary credit	(1,907)	(606)	(7,619)	5,550	8,065
Income taxes					
(credits)					
Earnings (loss) before extraordinary credit	(2,040)	43	(8,524)	6,029	8,291
Extraordinary credit	—	—	248	—	—
Net earnings (loss)	$ (2,040)	$ 43	$ (8,276)	$ 6,029	$ 8,291
Financial position					
Current assets	$ 75,079	$ 63,775	$ 73,221	$ 83,325	$ 53,718
Property, plant and equipment, net	28,482	27,082	27,549	26,682	21,328
Other assets	1,551	497	467	629	1,201
Total assets	$105,112	$ 91,354	$101,237	$110,636	$ 76,247
Current liabilities	$ 25,179	$ 9,385	$ 20,075	$ 26,574	$ 16,527
Long-term debt	22,954	24,073	23,984	16,892	16,913
Other liabilities	3,571	2,448	1,773	1,522	1,227
Stockholders' equity	53,408	55,448	55,405	65,648	41,508
Total liabilities and stockholders' equity	$105,112	$ 91,354	$101,237	$110,636	$ 76,247
Current ratio	3.0 to 1	6.8 to 1	3.6 to 1	3.1 to 1	3.3 to 1
Per share information†					
Weighted average shares outstanding	5,983,277	5,983,277	5,983,277	5,653,866	5,444,964
Earnings (loss) per share before					
extraordinary credit	$ (0.34)	$ 0.01	$ (1.42)	$ 1.07	$ 1.52
Net earnings (loss) per shares	(0.34)	0.01	(1.38)	$ 1.07	$ 1.52
Book value per share based on shares					
outstanding at balance sheet dates	8.93	9.27	9.26	10.97	7.64
Cash dividends per common share‡	—	—	0.34	0.44	0.40

* Years 1970–74 taken from 1974 Annual Report; years 1965–69 taken from 1972 Annual Report.
† Includes the effect of a two-for-one stock split in the form of a 100 percent stock dividend distributed in January 1971 and
  5 percent stock dividend distributed in January 1970.
‡ Includes the effect of a two-for-one stock split in the form of a 100 percent stock dividend distributed in January 1971.

the shading or slight variations in color for the bales, which usually were 48 inches long and often four feet in diameter, weighing 500 to 600 pounds.

Bales that passed the shading test were sent to the cutting room to be "spread." Spreading consisted of mounting the bales on a movable carriage that traveled on rails for the length of a cutting table. The cutting table was often 100 feet long, with longer tables being more efficient. The job of the spreaders was to spread the fabric down smoothly on the table until about 160-

EXHIBIT 1   *(concluded)*

	1969	1968	1967	1966	1965
Operating results					
Net sales	$118,250	$ 92,137	$ 73,913	$ 61,346	$ 48,100
Cost of sales and expenses	104,424	79,073	66,142	54,384	43,266
Operating income (loss)	13,826	13,064	7,770	6,962	4,834
Other income, net	95	107	217	140	50
Interest expense	983	476	544	452	228
Earnings (loss) before income taxes	12,938	12,695	7,443	6,649	4,655
and extraordinary credit	6,626	6,428	3,474	3,078	2,176
Income taxes (credits)					
Earnings (loss) before extraordinary credit	6,312	6,267	3,969	3,078	2,479
Extraordinary credit	—	—	—	—	—
Net earnings (loss)	$ 6,312	$ 6,267	$ 3,969	$ 3,571	$ 2,479
Financial position					
Current assets	$ 47,922	$ 35,297	$ 27,592	$ 19,688	$ 15,019
Property, plant and equipment, net	16,702	14,688	11,087	8,439	7,209
Other assets	—	—	—	—	—
Total assets	—	—	—	—	—
Current liabilities	$ 13,736	$ 13,764	$ 6,506	$ 5,763	$ 5,335
Long-term debt	16,250	6,650	7,550	7,150	5,250
Other liabilities	—	—	—	—	—
Stockholders' equity	34,927	29,789	24,391	15,090	11,675
Total liabilities and stockholders' equity	—	—	—	—	—
Current ratio	3.5 to 1	2.6 to 1	4.2 to 1	3.4 to 1	2.8 to 1
Per share information†					
Weighted average shares outstanding	—	—	—	—	—
Earnings (loss) per share before					
extraordinary credit	$ 1.16	$ 1.15	$ 0.76	$ 0.76	$ 0.52
Net earnings (loss) per shares	1.16	1.15	0.76	$ 0.76	$ 0.76
Book value per share based on shares outstanding at balance sheet dates					
Cash dividends per common share‡	0.38	0.37	0.29	0.03	0.03

ply (or about five to six inches) of fabric had been spread on the table. Spreaders usually walked 8 to 10 miles a shift.

"Markers" then laid a paper pattern over the fabric. They were judged on how economically they could utilize fabric in order to minimize "fallout," or waste. Ninety-eight percent usage was a good standard.

"Cutters" then used vibrating electric knives to cut through 160-ply of fabric to make parts for 80 pairs of one size of pants. Cutting was hard work, and experienced cutters developed extremely strong wrists and biceps.

After the parts were cut, they were tied together, and the entire bundle of parts was placed on a "bundle cart." The bundle cart was then moved to the first sewing station. A pair of pants required about 50 sewing operations, each accomplished at a separate station. Each station consisted of a seated operator, typically female, and a type of specialized sewing machine. The operator was usually surrounded by partially complete bundles and allowed about six square feet of personal floor space.

"Bundle boys" moved carts from one operation to the next. At the end of the 50-operation line, a complete bundle of 80 trousers of one size had been produced out of parts that were on the same ply before they were cut.

In order to ensure high productivity, operators were paid on a modified piece-rate system. It was not unusual to pay a base minimum wage, with a performance standard that allowed the operator to earn about double the base rate for reaching standard. An elaborate operator accounting system was developed to record production against standard. To reach standard, many skilled operators performed their tasks literally faster than the eye could follow. Some plants placed spreaders and cutters on incentive, as well.

Industry working conditions were generally not pleasant. Factories were housed in old, low-rent structures. Scrap cloth and lint from operations was ever-present. Operators often spiked their fingers with sewing needles, but when manufacturers provided needle guards they generally found that employees disposed of them because they felt that the guards slowed down production.

The eight Farah plants did not fit this mold.[2] The Farah plants were new and extremely modern. The company noted that they "provide a clean, airy, healthy environment that has a beneficial effect upon the happiness and productivity of all of our people."[3] Leonard Levy, vice president of the Amalgamated Clothing Workers of America concurred that "a cockroach needs a special invitation to get into the place."[4]

Within the industry, Mr. Farah was recognized as a production genius. In 1970, the company reported that "further advances in technology of production were accomplished with the successful, innovative design of new machinery, utilizing advanced electronics and unique mechanisms developed by our own engineers."[5] These advances, however, were not patented because Mr. Farah feared the ideas would be stolen by competitors.[6]

Plant security was extremely strong, but some insiders reported seeing elevated sewing stations that relieved the operator of her typically claustrophobic situation, an overhead system of bundle delivery that eliminated the typical floor congestion of bundle carts, and small packages and bundles being delivered from one end of the plant to another by bundle boys on bicycles. Mr.

---

[2] Four Farah plants were located in El Paso, including the Gateway plant, which was by far the largest. Two small plants were located in San Antonio, one in Victor, Texas, and one in Las Cruces, New Mexico.

[3] Farah Manufacturing Company, 1969 Annual Report.

[4] Homer Bigart, "Classic Labor-Organizing Drive Splits El Paso," *New York Times,* September 11, 1972, p. 58.

[5] Farah Manufacturing Company, 1970 Annual Report.

[6] Malley, "How the Union Beat Willie Farah," p. 166.

Farah stated with obvious pride that "our people, both production and supervision, are producers without peer. . . . They realize our success as manufacturers and merchandisers is the sole factor that provides them with employment security and opportunities for advancement."[7]

By industry standards, the fringe benefits that Mr. Farah provided his employees were unparalleled. Employees and their familes were given free medical, hospital, and dental care, including an annual physical exam and free eyeglasses, if needed. Free bus transportation to and from the plants was provided, as were free coffee and doughnuts during morning and afternoon breaks. Hot lunches on the premises were subsidized. Profit-sharing and pension plans were in effect.

Wages were generally on a par with the rest of the industry, but the question of wages merits the additional perspective gained through the analysis of the unique location of Farah manufacturing facilities.

THE CITY OF EL PASO

The vast majority of Farah employees worked in El Paso, a city almost ideally situated for the manufacturing requirements of men's garments. Located in the westernmost corner of Texas, El Paso was directly across the Rio Grande river from Juarez, Mexico. The combined metropolitan population of the two cities was over 1 million people, with about 360,000 on the El Paso side. About 58 percent of the El Paso population was of Mexican descent, [8] and an estimated 80 percent of the residents were bilingual.

El Paso was not highly industrialized, with primary employment being in government and service industries. The largest component of the city's nonservice economic base was the garment industry, with the four Farah plants, four Levi Strauss plants, a large Billy-the-Kid plant, and 32 smaller firms located in the city. In 1970, Farah was the largest single industrial employer, hiring about 14 percent of the local work force.[9] About 95 percent of Farah's work force was of Mexican ancestry.[10]

The median family income for El Paso in 1970 was $7,792 compared with a national median of $10,474.[11] The cost of living in El Paso, however, was unusually low. The low living costs were attributed to the extremely mild weather, the ease of shopping for low-cost goods and services on both sides of the border, and the low wage rates in Mexico. At a time when the U.S. minimum wage was $1.60 per hour, the minimum wage in Mexico was $2.40

---

[7] Farah Manufacturing Company, 1969 Annual Report.

[8] Jean Caffey Lyles, "The Fight at Farah," *The Christian Century* 90, no. 8 (September 26, 1973), p. 935.

[9] Bigart, "Classic Labor-Organizing Drive Splits El Paso," p. 57.

[10] Rex Hardesty, "Farah: The Union Struggle in the 1970s," *American Federationist* 80, no. 6 (June 1973), p. 10.

[11] Ibid.

per *day*.[12] In 1970, El Paso was the last American city where a family earning $10,000 per year could afford a full-time maid.[13]

The opportunities in El Paso drew many "green card" workers, who were Mexican citizens with permits to work in the United States. While many companies considered this an excellent source of cheap labor, Farah did not. Farah would hire only American citizens, a policy which was upheld by a federal court decision in 1972.

Unionism in Texas was not strong, chiefly because the closed union shop was illegal. Only 2,200 of El Paso's 20,000 clothing workers were covered by a union contract, and they worked primarily for Billy-the-Kid, which had been unionized since 1944.[14] Late in 1969, the Amalgamated Clothing Workers of America (ACWA) had begun a drive to organize Farah, with some incidents but without significant results.

TROUBLE IN THE EARLY 1970s

In October of 1970, however, the National Labor Relations Board (NLRB) held an election among the cutters and spreaders in the cutting room of the large "Gateway" plant in El Paso. The union won by a vote of 109 to 73, but the company objected that the small group of employees (about 7 percent of the plant total) was an "inappropriate unit" for collective bargaining purposes.

In order to go to court with that argument, the company then had to refuse to bargain with the ACWA as a representative of the inappropriate unit. The case was not heard for nearly two years, and during that time, the ACWA used Farah's "refusal to bargain" as a persuasive organizing tool.

At this point, however, ACWA organization attempts were not the key concern of top management. In 1970, knit slacks were introduced for men's casual wear. Farah evaluated the style, but thought that the tendency of knit, fabrics to snag would cause disappointment among the customers that tried them. Farah concluded that they would be accepted only for limited use activities, such as golfing. The success of Farah's operation was built on high-speed production, and knits provided an additional problem in this regard. After being spread, knit fabrics would have to be allowed to contract on the cutting table in order for patterns to be cut the right size. Converting to knits would penalize Farah's production more than it would affect less efficient manufacturers.

For these reasons, Farah did not add knits to its line. By the 1971 spring selling season, the success of knits had become clear. The company, however, had about $27 million in orders for woven fabrics. These orders could have been canceled, thereby passing the loss to Farah suppliers, but Farah considered that this would be an unethical business practice. The result was a $20 million inventory write-down that largely contributed to an $8.3 million loss

---

[12] Ibid., p. 12.
[13] Bigart, "Classic Labor-Organizing Drive Splits El Paso," p. 57.
[14] Ibid.

for 1972. Shares of common stock which in 1970 had sold at 49½ were, by the end of August 1971, selling at 11. It was clear that Farah was no longer a glamour stock.

THE WALKOUT

While Farah executives struggled to return the business to its former position in the industry, Paul Garza, a Farah production worker, was fired for lying about an illness in order to be absent from work. Freely admitting his guilt, he took several other employees with him to see his supervisor in order to ask for reinstatement. The supervisor told Mr. Garza that the company no longer wanted him and asked the other employees either to return to work or leave the plant. Six mechanics, who had been active in the ACWA organization campaign, turned in their tools and left the plant.

The ACWA strengthened its organizing attempts against the company, and the results surprised even the union. By the end of the week, 500 workers had walked off their jobs. Two weeks later, over 2,000 workers had struck.[15] The issues were the workers' rights to provide input to management regarding production quotas, job security, termination policies, and the fundamental right to unionize if desired. About 4,500 workers remained at their jobs.

The union quickly picked up the "Chicano theme," which was already familiar to the public because of Cesar Chavez's farm workers' struggle. Picket signs lettered in Spanish and Farah's close-to-minimum wages made good copy, and Willie Farah's enthusiastic support of traditional American values made him an unusually useful foil for union purposes. An outspoken patriot, he told visitors:

> It's the worst form of treason for the American businessmen to use foreign labor to the detriment of American labor. Our responsibility is to the American worker. This country gives us everything, and we're gratified to live here.
>
> Everything we buy is American-made. We could go offshore and save thousands of dollars a week. We have only one piece of equipment from overseas, a German cut-off machine . . . . There are two billion foreigners out there willing to work for 10 cents an hour. We've got to whip 'em with American know-how and the will to work.[16]

It was said that when Mr. Farah found Japanese-made nails at the site of the construction of his new home, he had a partially completed wall removed and rebuilt with American nails.[17] He was convinced that unionization of a company paying competitive wages and providing model working conditions was morally wrong, and vowed not to capitulate. The union believed that the major issue was the right for employees to unionize, if they so chose.

---

[15] Malley, "How the Union Beat Willie Farah," p. 167.

[16] Bigart, "Classic Labor-Organizing Drive Splits El Paso," p. 58. Copyright 1972 by The New York Times Company, Reprinted by permission.

[17] Hardesty, "Farah: The Union Struggle in the 1970s," p. 7.

Mr. Farah's intransigence, the "refusal to bargain," news pictures of the high chain-link fences surrounding the plant, and reports of the continued use of guard dogs after the strike began gained little sympathy for the company position. The union additionally claimed the company was guilty of discharging workers for union activities, personal intimidation and coercion, using court orders to bar legal picketing, and obtaining arrest warrants for picketers that were served in the middle of the night. The company charged that workers were beaten by strikers, tires were slashed, and shots were fired through plant windows.[18] No one was seriously hurt by these incidents.

Given the scenario of Chicano strikers and Anglo management in confrontation, the citizens of El Paso remained remarkably unconcerned with the strike. If the company was to be unionized, additional help would need to be enlisted.

THE BOYCOTT

On July 19, 1972, a national boycott of Farah products was called. Organized by the ACWA, the boycott was supported by the AFL–CIO Executive Council and a number of Democratic politicians. Among them were presidential candidate George McGovern, his running mate Sargent Shriver, Senator Edward Kennedy, New York Mayor John Lindsay, and Senator Gaylord Nelson, who headed a National Citizen's Committee for Justice to Farah Workers.

In mid-August, the NLRB held that the firing of Paul Garza, the incident causing the initial walkout, had been legal. By this time, however, the issue of the right to organize and the drama of the national boycott had dwarfed all earlier issues.

Getting media play for the nationwide boycott proved to be relatively easy, once the Chicano theme had been established. Mass picketing became a "natural" for TV news coverage, which in turn made it easier to recruit more pickets. Picketing became so intense in the New York area that retailers quit advertising Farah slacks. On December 11, 1972, "Don't Buy Farah Day," 175,000 pickets marched nationwide.[19]

On February 14, 1973, the ACWA placed full-page ads in newspapers in the 13 largest advertising markets to call attention to what it called unfair labor practices at Farah. Included in the ad was a letter "to all Catholic Bishops in the United States" from the Most Reverend Sidney M. Metzger, bishop of El Paso.[20] The letter recommended a boycott of Farah slacks and was to have a profound effect on the success of the boycott (see Exhibit 2).

---

[18] Bigart, "Classic Labor-Organizing Drive Splits El Paso," p. 57.

[19] Malley, "How the Union Beat Willie Farah," p. 238.

[20] The 70-year-old bishop had been educated at the Gregorian University in Rome and held doctorates in both theology and canon law. A personal friend of Pope John XXIII, he had been bishop of El Paso since 1942.

EXHIBIT 2   The "Bishop's Advertisement" Supporting the Boycott from the Bishop of El Paso to the Catholic Bishops of the United States

What follows occurred when a member of the Catholic hierarchy addressed a letter of inquiry to the bishop of El Paso concerning the strike of Mexican-American employees against the Farah Manufacturing Co. The bishop of El Paso addressed his reply to all Catholic bishops in the United States.

1012 North Mesa Street
El Paso, Texas

Your Excellency:

Recently one of our bishops sent me a letter through his diocesan office asking for information concerning the strike at the Farah Manufacturing plant in El Paso. Because of a nationwide boycott of Farah products by the Amalgamated Clothing Workers of America the strike has assumed nationwide importance and its effects are felt in a number of cities throughout the nation. The Bishop's Office wrote that he needed some guidance from people on the scene as to the problems. The following questions were asked in the letter:

1. Do you feel the company is acting in an unjust manner in this strike? Can you point out specific and verified instances of this?
2. Has anyone toured the plants of Farah? What were the conditions?
3. Is the Farah pay scale equitable with other plants in the area? Is the pay adequate to live on?
4. How is this issue defined by the people concerned in regard to the dignity of each party—the strikers and the company?
5. Is the case strong enough that you recommend the Bishop make a formal request to a retail outlet not to reorder?

My answer to these questions is contained in the following. If you are asked about the merits of the strike I hope this information may be useful.

Yours in Christ,

S. M. Metzger
Bishop of El Paso

Dear Father:

In reply to your letter I must give you pertinent information concerning the Farah situation in El Paso, which is difficult and complicated.

Farah finds it well nigh impossible to be objective and to recognize that the worker has the right to collective bargaining and join a union. The company is convinced that it is doing wonders for the worker and that a union would be detrimental to the worker and to the company. I feel that the company is acting unjustly in denying to the workers the basic right to collective bargaining. We know that these matters are decided by means of federally sponsored representational elections and the Farah Company uses all possible means to block such elections in their plants. Let the workers decide if they want a union or not. If all is so beautiful and ideal as the company publicly proclaims why should they fear an election?

EXHIBIT 2 *(continued)*

I know that for the past five years complaints were made by Farah workers to their parish priest. This you will understand when you realize that nearly all Farah workers are humble Mexican-Americans who must earn their bread by hard work and who often have a way of coming to their parish priest with personal problems.

There were complaints about the drastic demands for production. This was explained by a worker who has been with the company 14 years. She explains that the great majority of workers make $69 per week, which is take-home pay after deducting Social Security, etc. At the present moment her assignment is to sew belts on the finished slacks. The quota amounts to 3,000 belts per day; in an eight-hour workday this means the girls have to sew on 6 belts per minute, and even this would amount to only 2,880 belts per day. The girls say that it is physically possible to sew on only five belts per minute, even with the modern machines they operate. As long as they cannot sew on six belts per minute they cannot get a raise and their wages are frozen at that point. While the quota of 2,760 belts is tolerated the company will dismiss a worker who in their opinion falls too far below 2,760. It has been said that the production demands can be set by the company as high as they want them and they can fire the worker who cannot stand the strain physically. Workers have said that they are treated as production machines and not as human beings. They also said that wages increase only when and if the company wants. Women have also complained that the maternity benefits were far from adequate and that when they returned to work they would lose their position on the pay scale and start as beginners.

It seems to me that there are some flagrant defects in the Farah plants as they are presently operated. Perhaps the most flagrant is that there is no job security; the company can fire anyone anytime and the worker has no appeal. A second very serious defect is that there are no negotiated production standards so that the workers can have a say how much they can produce and are not treated like machines. There should also be negotiated wage increases according to a definite schedule. There should be better maternity insurance and negotiated leaves for illness, etc. and workers should be able to return to their same jobs and same rate of pay.

Farah Company has an impressive list of benefits which look good on paper. At closer scrutiny however, these like the maternity insurance are tokens. I have before me a photocopy of "Your Retirement Benefits" addressed to a worker. It states "This is a total monthly retirement income of $234.50." which looks fine. But $214.50 comes from an estimated amount of Social Security and the monthly retirement check from Farah amounts to $20.00. Nothing is explained about what the actual retirement age is or how many years of work with Farah are required for retirement benefits.

I hope I am not in error when I say that job security for the workers, negotiated production standards, negotiated wage increases according to a definite schedule, adequate maternity insurance, and leaves for illness are all in accord with the principles of social justice. All these are lacking in the present Farah Company and these serious defects can be remedied by collective bargaining.

However, it should also be noted that without job security and with the high production demands, workers live in fear of being dismissed and left without a job if their output falls short of their production quota. Also the company exercises constant supervision to be sure the workers do not complain to others but say the right thing when outsiders visit the plant. This brings me to question whether lower pay than clothing workers are listed under a catch-all listing as "others," although clothing is El Paso's number one industry. In comparison, Chamber of Commerce statistics show that

EXHIBIT 2   *(concluded)*

petroleum workers earn an average of $7,500 yearly, metal workers earn $7,200 yearly, food-processing employees average $6,100. The Amalgamated Clothing Workers of America who are seeking a contract with Farah have contracts with three apparel manufacturers in El Paso. These three are Levi Strauss, Hortex Incorporated, and Tex-Togs. Levi Strauss is national but Hortex Incorporated and Tex-Togs are small local companies, much smaller than Farah. Work for which workers at Farah receive $69 per week take-home pay, union workers receive $102 per week take-home pay, which sounds more like a living wage. If these smaller plants can live with a union contract and prosper why is it so impossible for gigantic Farah to do the same?

When you ask is the annual pay of $3,588 at Farah adequate to live on the answer is decidedly no in these days of high prices. A single person can get by on this amount, but a married person with a family simply cannot adequately support the family with this amount. It about puts bread on the table. Some of our Mexican people have large families and they have serious problems. In terms of social justice $3,588 is not an adequate living wage in our day for a family in El Paso.

Farah apparently wasn't aware or didn't want to be aware that resentment was growing. But the fact that today over 3,000 workers are on strike is evidence that both grievances and resentment are real. And by listening to the people over the years one gradually became aware that things at Farah were not actually as they were made to appear.

"Is the case strong enough that you would recommend the bishop to make a formal request to a retail outlet not to reorder?" I answer: Yes, from my knowledge of the case here, I think it is strong enough to recommend to His Excellency that he make a formal request to a retail outlet not to reorder. The strike has assumed national importance and is supported by persons of national prominence. Our own "little people" in El Paso would be crushed if it were not for this national support. His Excellency will of course weigh what I have written and decide what he deems best.

> With every good wish and blessing, I am,
> Sincerely Yours in Christ,
>
> S. M. Metzger
> Bishop of El Paso

You Can Help the Farah Workers by Not Buying Farah Slacks

U.S. Representative Herman Badillo
Ramsey Clark, Esq.
Michael Harrington, Author
Dorothy Height, President,
    Council of Negro Women
Professor Irving Howe,
    City University of New York

Mayor John V. Lindsay
Commissioner Bess Meyerson,
    Dept. of Consumer Affairs,
    The City of New York
U.S. Representative Ogden Reid
A. Philip Randolph, President,
    A. Philip Randolph, Institute
Rabbi Henry Siegman

Amalgamated Clothing Workers of America/15 Union Square/New York, N.Y. 10003

The bishop had been involved in labor affairs since 1941,[21] and had tacitly approved of the strike since the beginning. Mr. Farah was not impressed with the bishop's endorsement of the strike, because he thought him ignorant of conditions at the plant. Neither the bishop nor members of his staff had ever been there.[22] Mr. Farah also characterized the bishop as "lolling in wealth" and belonging "to the rotten old bourgeoisie."[23] Bishop Metzger was supported locally in his efforts by Rev. Jesse Munoz, the 32-year-old pastor of El Paso's largest parish. Rev. Munoz was called the "spark" of the strike,[24] and characterized opponents of the strike, such as the editor of the *El Paso Times* and nationally syndicated religious columnist Daniel Poling, as "pimps of the establishment."[25] Munoz believed that "the basic reason [my parishioners] are supporting the strike with such dedication is that they are so determined to change the future of El Paso, mostly for their children, that they will go to any lengths to achieve the goal."[26] Company advertising director Kenneth Farah responded to the boycott by asserting that in some markets it has "even strengthened our position, because it has focused attention on our products." When asked if Farah would present its case through national advertising, he said, "No. We're in the pants business. We're not in the business of arguing."[27] The 1973 advertising budget was approximately double 1972 expenditures, and the customer flights to El Paso had begun.

In late March, the NLRB had censured both Farah and the ACWA for various illegal strike activities. On May 14, the NRLB made the significant ruling that Farah's "refusal to bargain" position that it had assumed since the original cutting room elections of October 1970 was not correct. The NLRB then ordered Farah to bargain. Farah refused in order to take the case to the U.S. Court of Appeals.

Throughout the rest of 1973 a stalemate existed, but media support of the boycott continued. For many church groups, particularly Roman Catholics, the Farah struggle became a moral crusade. Cardinal Mederios of Boston reflected the views of many churchmen when he said "the internal affairs of business become the concern of religious leadership when violations of social justice and human dignity are at stake."[28] The *Christian Century* concluded an article with the hope that "the concern expressed . . . may indicate that at least some of El Paso's upper-middle-class Anglo citizens are beginning to feel uncomfortable living in a city where middle class affluence is built on the

---

[21] Hardesty, "Farah: The Union Struggle in the 1970s," p. 5.

[22] "Farah Says Strike Is Not Hurting Promotions Much," *Advertising Age,* March 12, 1973, p. 38.

[23] Bigart, "Classic Labor-Organizing Drive Splits El Paso," p. 57.

[24] Hardesty, "Farah: The Union Struggle in the 1970s," p. 6.

[25] Jean Caffey Lyles, "The Fight at Farah," p. 936.

[26] "A Boycott Begins to Hurt at Farah," *Business Week,* June 2, 1973, p. 56.

[27] "Farah Says Strike Is Not Hurting Promotions Much," pp. 38–39.

[28] Malley, "How the Union Beat Willie Farah," p. 167.

poverty of underpaid Chicano workers."[29] The Farah manufacturing company made the annual list of the 10 worst performing companies in the social responsiveness area.[30]

Mr. Farah felt that he would only demean the company by replying to what he regarded as extreme propaganda. His nonresponse was used by his opponents as proof of his arrogant and uncaring attitude.

Fiscal year 1973 ended October 31, 1973, with sales of $132 million, down $23 million from the previous year. A negligible profit was shown. The stock price, which had been near 50 in 1971, was below 8. In November, Mr. Farah bowed to board of directors' pressure and closed the four small outlying plants. Of the 3,000 employees who had walked out over the previous 18 months, about half remained on strike. The ACWA had spent an estimated $15 million on the strike and boycott.[31]

Very early in 1974, Farah asked the NLRB to hold representation elections in the plants that were still open. The union refused, claiming that a climate of fear prevented the holding of a fair representative election. In actuality, the union had chosen the more time-consuming but less risky course of organizing smaller segments of workers.[32]

In late January, NLRB Judge Walter H. Maloney ruled that the company had pursued "a policy of flouting the NLRB Act and trampling on the rights of its employees as if there was no Act, no Board, and no Ten Commandments."[33] The Maloney Decision rules that all strikers be rehired, that the original six mechanics who walked out be reinstated with back pay plus 6 percent interest, and that the union be given access to employees. Farah asked for an immediate review of the decision by the NLRB, but its request was refused. The "public relations impact of the decision was devastating" to Farah.[34]

Still, no elections could be held with the litigation pending. The break in the deadlock finally occurred on February 5, when El Paso Mayor Fred Hervey suggested that an informal poll be conducted among current employees, strikers, and those laid off by plant closings. The ACWA would be permitted to campaign and solicit pledge cards from employees in favor of union representation. Both sides agreed.

The result of the poll showed that 62 percent of 7,703 workers supported representation.[35] As a result, Farah agreed to recognize the union as the bargaining agent for his employees. On February 24, 1974, the national boycott was lifted, and on March 8, the agreement was ratified. Willie Farah had surrendered.

---

[29] Jean Caffey Lyles, "The Fight at Farah," p. 936.

[30] Milton Moskowitz, "Social Responsibility Portfolio 1973," *Business and Society* 7, no. 1 (January 15, 1974), p. 1.

[31] "A Texas Pants Maker Loses to a Boycott," *Business Week,* March 2, 1974, p. 25.

[32] Jean Caffey Lyles, "The Fight at Farah," p. 935.

[33] *Monthly Labor Review* 97, no. 4 (April 1974), pp. 73–74.

[34] Farah Manufacturing Company, 1974 Annual Report, p. 5.

[35] *Monthly Labor Review,* p. 73.

FINDINGS AFTER THE SETTLEMENT

Although the union had achieved its objectives, two appeals by the company were still pending. The first, decided on March 21, 1974, in the U.S. Court of Appeals, affirmed Farah's position that the initial union election in 1970 among cutting room employees was with an inappropriate unit for collective bargaining purposes. What this meant, from Farah's viewpoint, was that:

> The company was right from the beginning. It was right in October 1970 when it protested that election, in September 1972 when it refused to bargain, and in May 1973 when it refused to obey the NLRB's order that it bargain. And most importantly, the company was wronged by the politicians, prelates, and others who unthinkingly parroted Amalgamated's line and solemnly denounced its "refusal to bargain" with the union.[36]

Seven months later, the NLRB review of the Maloney Decision also supported the company. The board reversed Judge Maloney's decision regarding the reinstatement of the six mechanics and found merit in the company's contention that Judge Maloney's ". . . numerous characterizations of the employer were unwarranted and injudicious. . . . Accordingly, the board disavows and repudiates the section of the judge's decision entitled 'Farah and the Board: The Past as Prologue' and those comments throughout his decision that intemperately characterized the employer."[37]

---

[36] Farah Manufacturing Company, 1974 Annual Report, p. 5.
[37] *Labor Law Reports,* Case Number 15, 113 (Commerce Clearing House, Inc., 1974).

Abbott Laboratories: Similac (A)

On January 3, 1980, David O. Cox, president of the Ross Division of Abbott Laboratories, sat listening to the taped proceedings of a public meeting held on October 8, 1979, the day previous to a World Health Organization (WHO) conference convened in Geneva. This so-called informational meeting was jointly sponsored by two activist organizations—the Interfaith Center on Corporate Responsibility (ICCR) and the Infant Formula Action Committee (INFACT)—who were extremely critical of the marketing practices of the infant formula industry. The "informational meeting" had been widely publicized as a forum for the discussion of the alleged wrongdoings of the infant formula industry with interested parties, the press, and industry representatives invited by the organizers. As Mr. Cox listened to the tapes, he reflected on the basic issues addressed at the WHO conference.

THE BASIC CHARGES

By the end of 1979, a substantial number of charges had been leveled against the use of infant formula in developing, or Third World, countries. Many of them were overlapping or directly related to others, so a clear differentiation between charges could not be made. Perhaps the clearest objections were based on economic and environmental grounds.

Economic objections were given on both the macro and micro levels. It was charged that the nonutilization of breast milk led to economic waste at the macro level. For example, the annual loss of breast milk in Kenya was estimated at $11.5 million. For the developing world as a whole, the cost of wasted human milk was estimated at more than three quarters of a billion dollars. On the micro level, unnecessary usage of formula was seen as a waste of scarce family resources. The cost of sufficient formula to feed a three-month-old child for a day in the United Kingdom was 2 percent of the minimum daily wage, but in India the cost was 23 percent, in Nigeria 30 percent, and in Egypt 41 percent. For older infants, the costs were higher.[1] One way for the mother to lower costs was to dilute the formula, thereby reducing the baby's calorie intake.

---

[1] Mike Muller, "The Baby Killer." (London: *War on Want*, March 1974), p. 7.

Environmental objections hinged on two factors: lack of facilities and usage proliferation. In an environment where a large part of the population lacked fuel for heating, clean water to wash bottles or mix formula, cleaning brushes, spare bottles, or refrigeration in which to store excess formula, the chances of product misuse were very high.[2] Even if promotion was not directed toward that segment, however, critics predicted that product usage would diffuse to the poor. It was alleged that the poor might even consider it more attractive because it would be, in a sense, forbidden. Since the poor could not properly use the product, any sales in developing countries should therefore be prohibited. According to Christian activist Leah Margulies, socially enlightened individuals in developed countries should "help countries decide their real priorities."[3]

The greatest number of specific charges were related to what were seen as predatory advertising practices. The very fact that formula manufacturers worked with native hospital personnel was regarded as a powerful force to legitimize formula in the eyes of mothers. Colorful posters used for decoration in the hospitals, even those that boldly stated that breast milk was best, and the booklets on other aspects of mothercraft that were provided free by formula manufacturers were condemned because they carried pictures of formula products. The traditional Western practice of providing a going-home formula for new mothers was seen as a ploy to cause premature reduced lactation in mothers.

The use of "milk nurses" was especially criticized. Milk nurses were usually trained medical personnel employed by formula manufacturers to teach "mothercraft" techniques, such as bathing babies and selecting nutritious foods. In some countries, the only medical guidance for new mothers came from mothercraft personnel because of the shortage of doctors. Milk nurses, however, performed their tasks dressed in uniforms and were alleged to trade on their identification with hospitals to promote formula usage. Two examples supported these allegations: (1) milk nurses had been paid on a sales related (commission) basis by some companies and (2) retail market share seemed to be remarkably correlated with the number of nurses a company employed. For example, the most extensive mothercraft activities in the Far East took place in the Philippines. Wyeth, Mead Johnson, and Nestle had an estimated total of 160 mothercraft nurses and a combined market share of 92 percent in 1975. Each mothercraft nurse corresponded to between 0.4 and 0.7 share points for the three companies.

---

[2] Liquid formula, indeed, single serving containers, had been available for some time in the U.S. and European markets. Abbott and other infant formula manufacturers had not introduced the product in this form in the Third World because of the high costs associated with the product, its packaging, and its shipment.

[3] Leah Margulies, "Baby Formula Abroad: Exporting Infant Malnutrition," *Christianity and Crisis,* November 10, 1975, p. 267.

Perhaps the major target for criticism was the use of mass media advertising that, critics believed, led poorly educated mothers to think of formula as a type of wonder drug. Nestle was especially active in using billboards, idiomatic radio, newspapers, popular magazines, and sound trucks to sell their products. Other companies were less aggressive, but their distributors occasionally placed media advertisements. Abbott Laboratories did no consumer advertising and was particularly adamant in insisting that this type of promotion had no place in the industry.

The critics also saw aggressive sales promotion practices as a fundamental issue. Of special concern was the mass media advertising campaigns undertaken by many of the non-U.S. based producers and some of the Third World distributors of the American formula companies. U.S. infant formula producers were not free of this criticism. For instance, during the "informational meeting," Leah Margulies, an activist member of ICCR, noted the following passage from the Ross Laboratories' training manual for its *domestic* sales force as evidence of what she termed "the misguided behavior of the infant formula industry":

> Hospitals represent one of the most important markets for the sale of infant formula . . . there is a 93 percent brand retention. . . . Another point worth remembering is that if nurses are sold and serviced properly they become like extra sales people. . . . The salesman should remember to make occasional calls on the second and third shift nurses as well since their influence on mothers is also important.[4]

While not all of the above examples were true as a general rule, responsible industry executives agreed that there were at least some elements of truth in all of the charges.

INDUSTRY REACTIONS

By early 1975, it had become clear that an industrywide response was required to combat the charges of industry irresponsibility. Representatives of nine manufacturers, including Abbott, therefore met in Zurich in April of that year for discussions, which led to the formation of the International Council of Infant Formula Industries (ICIFI). ICIFI became an official body on September 1, 1975, with the implementation of an official code of conduct governing industry members. The largest members in terms of formula sales were Nestle Alimentana, Unigate Foods, American Home Products, Glaxo, and Dumex. These corporations held over half of the world market for infant formula. Key factors of the international code were that (1) manufacturers agreed as a matter of policy that breast milk from healthy mothers was best for infants; (2)

---

[4] *Infant Formula Sales Training Manual, United States,* Ross Division of Abbott Laboratories, Inc., undated, p. 30.

"milk nurses" or other industry personnel would be paid on a noncommission basis; and (3) formula proportions of powder to water would be standardized among manufacturers in order to decrease the opportunity for incorrect preparation.

Having been a prime mover in the formulation of ICIFI, Abbott Laboratories had an important decision to make regarding acceptance of the code. Abbott's own prototype, International Code of Marketing Ethics (see Exhibit 1), was stronger than the ICIFI code. The ICIFI code did not outlaw direct promotion to the customer and, therefore, in the opinion of Abbott management, did not deal with the central issue. In November 1975, Abbott formally implemented its own code and decided not to join ICIFI. By doing so, Abbott believed it would be free to work for a stronger industry code in general.

EXHIBIT 1 Abbott Laboratories' Code of Marketing Ethics for Developing Countries with Reference to Infant Feeding

Because good nutrition is essential to proper health care, we believe supervision of the infant's diet should be the responsibility of medical and allied personnel whose knowledge of nutritional science and understanding of local needs best quality them to provide this guidance. We attempt to conduct our business as an adjunct to local health personnel, supporting their efforts through the provision of appropriate health care products and services. We believe that this alliance is especially important in developing countries, where delivery of primary health care to major segments of the population is complicated by unfavorable living conditions. Within this context we are keenly aware of the responsibilities of Abbott Laboratories and Ross Laboratories to make a positive contribution to the health and well-being of infants in developing countries.

In marketing our products in these countries, the management, employees, and authorized representatives of Abbott are directed to observe the following guidelines for ethical behavior:

1. Breast milk of healthy, well-nourished mothers is the best feeding to meet nutritional needs of the infant from birth through four to six months of age, and should continue to be fed thereafter, together with appropriate foods, for as long as possible. Mothers in general—and especially those in the lower income and non-money sectors of the economy—should be encouraged to feed their infants at the breast as long as quantity and quality of milk remain adequate.

2. We believe our nutritional products have a valid place in the economy of developing countries, yet we want to restrict their use to feeding infants of relatively affluent parents when breast feeding is not chosen, or to infants of working mothers who cannot breast feed because of separation from their infants, and to infants of mothers who cannot breast feed for any other reason. We recognize that true need for substitute feedings exists in segments of the population not able to purchase them. Government sponsored programs or public assistance in some form is the best way to aid mothers who can neither breast feed nor afford a suitable replacement.

EXHIBIT 1 *(continued)*

3. For those infants who will not or cannot be fed at the breast or who need supplemental nutrition, we offer SIMILAC® infant formulas, which are patterned as closely after the nutritional qualities of human milk as current knowledge and technology permit. In presenting these products to the medical and allied professions, our goal is to promote awareness and acceptance of physiologic nutrition as the most desirable alternative when breast feeding is not available.

4. We cooperate in every way possible with local health authorities to prevent misuse of our products because of ignorance, poverty, or lack of proper hygienic conditions. We do not encourage use of our products where private purchase would impose a financial hardship on the family, or where inadequate facilities for preparation constitute a hazard to infant health.

5. Our product label carries a statement that breast milk is the preferred feeding for young infants, and emphasizes proper proportions in mixing formula.

6. We work with professional and government agencies, and industry to bring about standardized instructions for mixing all powdered nutritional products, i.e., one scoop (provided in tin of product) of each powder product to a standardized quantity of water, with each scoop individually designed to provide the proper caloric density set by the manufacturer for his product. Such standardization can assist educational efforts of public health personnel to create parental awareness of proper mixing of formula.

7. We believe that promotion of infant feeding products directly to mothers unjustly impels them to make decisions concerning the care and nutrition of their babies for which they lack adequate medical and nutritional knowledge. Therefore, we do not advertise our products through general circulation magazines, directories, newspapers, radio, television, billboards, and other public mass media. In addition, we do not offer special inducements which encourage mothers to use our products independently of professional advice. We terminate a distributorship when it violates these constraints. Further, we believe that no communication to the general public should encroach in any way on the responsibility of health care professionals to provide guidance as their judgment and experience dictate.

8. We direct our resources toward increasing the effectiveness of qualified local health personnel through communications on current health care development and by providing them with service literature for distribution to mothers to *(a)* promote good nutrition; *(b)* encourage breast feeding; *(c)* improve infant and child care; *(d)* improve sanitation, and *(e)* stress proper preparation of infant formula when recommended by health authorities.

9. We represent accurately the cost of proper infant feeding and use of our products so that professional personnel can better advise mothers according to their economic status.

10. Our advertising is directed to medical and other allied professionals (physicians, midwives, nurses, nutritionists, etc.). It seeks to provide better understanding of the proper role for our products, of their proper preparation, and of our willingness to assist medical personnel in their practice. We attempt to influence use of our products through the presentation of scientific information and the offering of aids to medical practice.

EXHIBIT 1 *(concluded)*

11. Whenever possible, we choose as representatives, experienced, allied medical personnel who understood local needs. They are thoroughly taught the preference and value of breast feeding, the knowledge and proper application of our products, and the influence of social pressures that can lead to unwise purchases and practices by those who cannot afford to buy infant formula. They are schooled to perform their duties in a professional manner and with integrity. Deception and other unethical practices are expressly forbidden.

12. The activities of our representatives are coordinated with those of medical professionals responsible for infant and mother care. We want them, with the supervision of clinic personnel, to furnish genuine mothercraft outreach services where practical, in support of instructions and counsel received in clinic. Our mothercraft nurses will make home visits only when specifically requested by appropriate authorities.

13. These mothercraft nurses are reimbursed through adequate salary, with monetary incentive given only for true service rendered to the customer and not directly derived from measurement of sales impact. Their functions are to develop product understanding, to render services that facilitate application of our products, and to make available other health care aids, without attempt to incur obligation for services.

14. We want medical and governmental health professionals to advise industry on training its representatives and on establishing the range of mothercraft activities.

15. We recognize the variation that exists between countries as to state of development, economic resources, and availability of trained health personnel, and work to assure that our activities in all countries conform to the spirit of this code.

Abbott's position then became one of activism. Management made the decision not to keep a low profile, and line managers met a number of times with their chief critics. These meetings required managers to accept the unusual role of being the object of direct criticism and were taxing both emotionally and in terms of the time away from the operational aspects of the business. However, Abbott's personnel continued to meet with their critics in hopes of resolving the controversy.

Abbott's Ross Laboratories personnel thought their approach to be quite positive. By late 1976, they had set up a "Third World Team" consisting of a coordinator, a nutritionist, a market researcher, and a pediatrician. As of the fall of 1979, this team had grown to a department of approximately 15 people. Along the way, five strategies were identified by Ross for responding to the problems at hand: (1) to create a board of advisors composed of pediatricians and nutritionists who could make and defend policy in the area; (2) to stress the positive accomplishments of Ross Laboratories in peripheral activities, such as medical education and solving past nutritional problems; (3) to strengthen further the Abbott Code of Marketing Ethics; (4) to stress the development of a prenatal food for mothers; and (5) to attempt an extensive program of well-controlled, cross-cultural research.

Although none of these strategies had been fully implemented, Ross nevertheless felt its position was eminently defensible and very proactive. Yet a senior member of the ICCR staff suggested in Geneva that Ross's position had become less responsive during the previous year. In addition, Ross had always believed the U.S. market, in which they held the largest market share, was well served. David Cox was therefore concerned, if not surprised, when he heard Leah Margulies state in Geneva that the ICCR research effort was expanding to the domestic market in the belief that infant formula constituted a health hazard in the less affluent areas of the United States.

BACKGROUND ON ROSS AND ABBOTT

Ross Laboratories considered itself to be a collection of evangelists for good health care. The organization was founded in 1903 as the Moores and Ross Milk Company in Columbus. By 1924, the company had expanded into a variety of dairy products, but that same year one of the founders, Stanley Ross, met Alfred Bosworth, a famous milk chemist. Bosworth had developed a usable infant formula while working at the Boston Floating Hospital, a pioneering effort at inner city pediatric care. Ross began to produce a formula for Bosworth called *Similac*.

In 1928, the profitable ice cream and milk processing operations were sold to the Borden Company. M&R Dietetic Laboratories, the successor company, grew through the Depression, won service awards during World War II, and thrived during the baby boom of the 1950s. Iron was added to Similac in 1959, and new plants were opened in the early 1960s, including one in the Netherlands to serve the Common Market. Similac had become the preeminent infant formula in the United States by the mid-1960s.

In 1964, Ross merged with Abbott Laboratories. Like Ross, Abbott had always been concerned with service to the medical profession. Abbott had been founded in 1888 by Wallace Calvin Abbott, a Chicago physician. Frustrated by the erratic availability of quality medication—particularly alkaloidal granules—he proceeded to make and sell his own. By the turn of the century, the Abbott Alkaloid Company consisted of a modern multistory laboratory and manufacturing facility. Through the first half century of the company's existence it was headed by physicians, and this gave the company a unique orientation. There was extreme emphasis on quality control, advertising was remarkably restrained for the period, and a free medical information service was provided to physicians apart from the drug selling function.

During the first half of the 20th century, Abbott research led to improved products, especially in the field of anesthetics (Butyn, Nembutal, and Pentothol Sodium were created by Abbott scientists), vitamins, and other synthetic chemicals. Later research concentrated on nutritional supplements,

EXHIBIT 2   A Partial Listing of Professional Services Sponsored
by Ross Laboratories*

1. *Ross Conference on Pediatric Research.* These conferences, attended by 30 to 40 medical educators, were paid for by Ross and run by prestigious medical schools. The proceedings of a conference typically contained about 15 papers concerned with an important pediatric problem, totaled 90 to 100 pages, and were distributed free to all pediatricians in the United States. At the end of 1979 there had been 77 Ross Conferences.

2. *Ross Conference on Obstetric Research* and *Ross Roundtable on Critical Approaches to Common Pediatric Problems.* These conferences, similar in design to those described above, were held less frequently, but each generally contained more papers.

3. *Perinatology, Neonatology, Pediatric Nutrition "Currents"* was an abstracting service published monthly in conjunction with the *Excerpta Medica* and distributed to pediatricians.

4. *Ross Timesaver* was a bimonthly newsletter on current topics. There were actually seven different series under the *Timesaver* name, each published every two months and distributed free to subscribing pediatricians.

5. *Distinguished papers* on children and nutrition was a series of 11 comprehensive papers on classic infant problems, available free upon request.

6. *The Ross Audio Visual Library* contained about two dozen films designed for both professional and lay education and available rent free to physicians.

7. *Ross Laboratories Clinical Education Aids* were a series of pamphlet-slide show packages designed for use in medical schools.

8. *Patient information.* In addition to the above professional materials, Ross published dozens of pamphlets on the parent-child relationship for the physician to hand out to his patients. These pamphlets were in both Spanish and English, were typically 12 to 20 pages in length, and contained no more than three pages of advertising.

* Unless otherwise noted, topics covered are of general pediatric interest and *not* limited to the topic of infant feeding.

of which Sucaryl was probably the best known. In addition, the benefits of Ross's research were extended through the publication of a variety of medical service pieces, a number of which are noted in Exhibit 2.

By 1979, total sales for Abbott Laboratories were approximately $1.7 billion, about 3.7 times the amount recorded in 1971. Net earnings in 1979 were approximately $179 million, 7.6 times the total recorded in 1971. About 34 percent of sales were in foreign markets. A more detailed breakdown of the financial data is presented in Exhibit 3.

As a division of Abbott Laboratories, Ross continued to concentrate on the production of Similac and other more specialized infant formulas. Ross accounted for about 20 percent of Abbott's total sales and nearly all the parent firm's pediatric sales volume. Most of the sales were in the well-penetrated

EXHIBIT 3   Abbott Laboratories Selected Financial Data, 1978 ($ millions)

Year	Sales	Aftertax Earnings	International Sales	Pediatric Sales	International Pediatric Sales
1978	$1,445.0	$148.6	$499.1	n.r.*	n.r.
1977	1,245.0	117.8	408.8	n.r.	n.r.
1976	1,084.9	92.5	375.9	$222.9	$56.4
1975	940.7	70.7	335.4	192.4	47.8†
1974	765.4	55.0	280.1	165.2	37.8
1973	620.4	46.0	219.2	141.0	31.3
1972	521.8	39.4	173.7	124.4	23.7
1971	458.1	23.4	145.9	114.5	18.9
1970	457.5	40.0	128.8	101.3	14.6
1969	403.9	35.2	n.r.	n.r.	n.r.
1968	356.1	32.1	n.r.	n.r.	n.r.
1967	311.1	28.6	n.r.	n.r.	n.r.
1966	275.2	27.5	n.r.	n.r.	n.r.

* n.r. = not reported.
† The casewriter estimated that less than 25% of Abbott's international pediatric sales were of Similac products in developing countries.

U.S. market where Similac was the dominant brand. Control of international sales was maintained by Abbott International, the corporate international marketing division. About one fourth of Abbott's pediatric sales were made overseas, but this total included both nutritional and pharmaceutical products. Ross Laboratories' records indicated that an estimated 20 percent of their infant formula sales were the result of international transactions. A roster of the major multinational corporations marketing infant formula throughout the world is included as Exhibit 4.

Although the dollar value of the international component of Ross's infant formula sales increased drastically during the 1970s, as a percentage of total sales the volume remained relatively stable. In each year, international infant formula sales represented approximately 20 percent of the total infant formula sales, and even if the international sales had been totally eliminated for each year, Ross's infant formula sales volume would still have increased by approximately 20 percent over each previous year.

However, eliminating the international component of their infant formula sales was not considered a viable alternative by Ross's management. They believed very strongly in the need for infant formula in the Third World. Management believed Ross knew more about infant nutrition than any other company and that the failure to pass on that knowledge would be ethically unconscionable.

As he reviewed the history of infant feeding practices, David Cox had once summed up Ross's position on the question of infant formula sales to the Third

EXHIBIT 4 Major Multinational Corporations Marketing Prepared Infant Formula, 1979

Corporation	Subsidiary	Nationality	Major Brand Name	Membership in ICIFI?	Estimated Share of World Market*
Nestle Alimentana	—	Swiss	Lactogen (and 26 others)	Yes	35–40
Unigate Foods	Cow and Gate	U.K.	Cow and Gate	Yes	10–15
Glaxo	Oystermilk	U.K.	Oystermilk	Yes	5–10
American Homes Products	Wyeth	U.S.A.	SMA	Yes	10–15
Mead Johnson	Bristol Myers	U.S.A.	Enfamil	No	10–15
Abbott Laboratories	Ross Laboratories	U.S.A.	Similac	No	4–8
Dumex	—	Dutch	Dumex	Yes	5–10

* "World market share" treats total market share outside the United States as 100 percent. These estimates were compiled from secondary sources by the casewriter and are not necessarily reflective of estimates by various corporations.

World by stating: "What posture do we take when the child is in the very helpless state of having no breast milk available, and no formula substitute is available?"

BACKGROUND ON INFANT NUTRITION

Since the beginning of human existence, babies have been fed what has been called "the original convenience food"—mother's milk. Portable, sanitary, preserved at correct temperatures, nutritious, and possessing yet-unduplicated immunizing agents, human breast milk from healthy mothers has always been universally considered the ideal food for normal infants. Breast feeding has also had some apparent contraceptive aspects and has been economical in terms of total mother-child nutrition as well.

In the event that mothers were unable to feed their own infants, a wet nurse—often a relative—was the traditional answer. Cow's milk and goat's milk were excellent supplements for older children, but poor substitutes as an infant food because of unfavorable nutritional composition and curd tension (a term relating to the strength of protein bonds in the chemistry of milk). Gail Borden's development of evaporated milk in the late 19th century helped reduce curd tension, but the problems of nutrition and potential milk allergy remained. In the early 1920s, infant formulae were developed in the United States by several companies, including Ross, both from cow's milk and from a variety of vegetable bases. With increasing urbanization and the assumption of more than motherhood roles by many women, the popularity of formula feeding grew. By the late 1950s, about 75 percent of all American babies were fed infant formula at some time during their first year.

As prosperity returned to Europe following World War II, and newly independent Third World nations began their drive toward development, many of the same conditions that had been present in the United States arose internationally. With increasing urbanization, mobility, ability of women to supplement family income, and familiarity with powdered milk through foreign aid programs, infant formula grew in popularity. Those firms that had been selling infant formula internationally expanded their markets.

In the United States, infant formula products had been positioned as a medical specialty requiring the intervention of health care personnel. In developing countries, however, infant formula had been positioned as a food. Promotion had been aimed directly at mothers, and it was not unusual to hear a radio jingle or to see a billboard promoting infant formula in developing countries.

Some formula manufacturers worked closely with what local medical personnel there were. Promotion practices included donations or sales at cost to maternity hospitals, sampling of new mothers through "gift packs," and the provision of extensive literature to hospitals regarding proper infant care. The use of milk nurses—women employed by formula manufacturers to educate mothers in all aspects of mothercraft—was generally welcomed in developing countries where medical personnel were in extremely short supply. Many of the medical personnel had been educated in countries where the use of infant formula was widespread.

There was agreement among virtually all informed observers that the extent of breast feeding had declined worldwide concurrent with the introduction of infant formula. It was difficult to generalize from specific studies, however, because of lack of consistent category definitions. A mother who fed formula to her infant 10 percent of the time, for example, would be classified as "breast feeding," "formula feeding," or "both," depending on which of three commonly used criteria were employed for a specific study. Furthermore, different studies used varying ages to set the limits of infancy. As might be expected, the percentage of babies fed formula in the first year of life was greater than the percentage fed formula in the first three months.

It was also difficult to ascertain the role that sales promotion played in winning formula converts. Pediatrician Bo Vahlquist, a strong proponent of breast feeding, observed that "a steady decline in breast feeding is taking place also in communist countries where promotion from private industry does not occur."[5]

There was some debate over the length of time that healthy mothers should nurse their children and when weaning foods should be introduced. Most authorities agreed that four to six months after birth was a reasonable time to begin weaning. A few medical personnel endorsed some native practices of breast feeding for periods of up to several years after birth. Infant formula could be started at any time after birth, but the use of formula tended to be addictive, in that, when the mother's milk was not used, the supply diminished and more formula was needed to make up for the lack of breast milk.

THE RELATIONSHIP BETWEEN INFANT FORMULA AND INFANT MORTALITY/MORBIDITY

Perhaps ironically, questions about the propriety of using infant formula products in developing countries had arisen at a time when trends in infant mortality had been declining at an impressive rate (Exhibit 5). This trend reinforced David Cox's belief that the producers of infant formula products had a responsibility to provide their products to meet the "special needs" of many infants. These *special needs* referred to the dietary requirements that breast milk cannot satisfy due to malabsorption problems, lactose intolerance, milk allergy, inborn errors of carbohydrate metabolism or amino acid metabolism, low birth weight or immaturity, and intestinal resection during early infancy.[6]

---

[5] Bo Vahlquist, "Environmental Children's Health," *Clinical Pediatrics* 15, no. 2 (February 1976), p. 180.

[6] "The Infant Formula Marketing Practices of Bristol-Myers Company in Countries Outside the United States," an unpublished monograph by the Bristol-Myers Company, August 7, 1975, p. 4.

EXHIBIT 5 Trends in Infant Mortality: Developed and Developing Countries

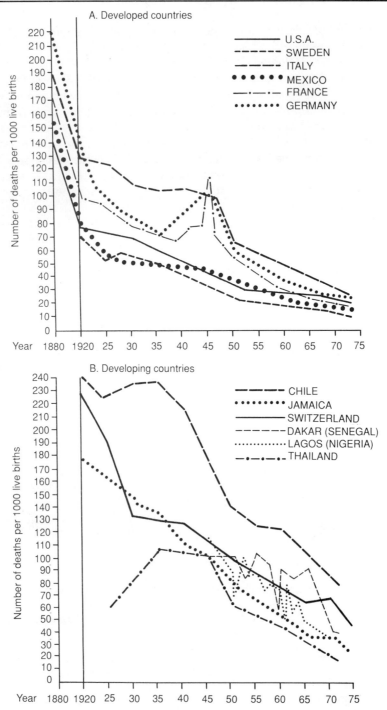

Note: *Infant* is defined as being in the first year of life.

SOURCE: Dr. H. R. Müller, "Nutrition and Infant Mortality," unpublished monograph distributed by Nestlé Alimentana, November 28, 1976, p. 6; data from *Demographic Yearbook,* United Nations.

The feeling of the industry, as expressed by Mr. Cox, was that without formula products the magnitude of Third World infant mortality and morbidity would be greatly increased. Nevertheless, researchers continued to suggest a link between formula use and infant health based on several factors, including these:

1. Low levels of sanitary conditions leading to disease.
2. Shortages of and distance from medical facilities.
3. Shortage of nutritious foods for mothers and infants.
4. Ignorance regarding the importance of nutritious foods.

These four factors led to several of the direct causes of infant mortality. Low birth weight and the insufficiency of mother's milk were two of these causes. The connection between these two factors and infant mortality had been documented by many studies, and it has been suggested that perhaps 40 percent of the babies in developing countries weighed less than the international standard of 2,500 grams (6 pounds, 11 ounces) at birth.[7] In addition, a large number of studies had indicated that mothers in developing countries often did not secrete more than 400–500 milliliters of milk per day.[8] Normal babies require approximately 500 milliliters of breast milk at birth, about 700 milliliters at one month, and about 1,000 milliliters at three to four months.

The exact nature of the relationship between infant formula use and infant mortality/morbidity had been investigated by a number of studies. Unfortunately, scientific controls that could isolate the specific cause and effect relationships were not employed. The research undertaken often failed, for example, to specify whether a sick baby had been switched to formula after becoming sick or had been fed infant formula continuously since birth.

The resulting malnutrition was not always attributed by mothers to a lack of good food. One study of infant feeding in Nigeria found that the cause of malnutrition is attributed to "an inevitable phase in childhood" by 23 percent of mothers, "an act of God" by 56 percent, and "an evil spirit evoked by wicked people" by 7 percent. Only 20 percent believed that it was due to a lack of good food.[9]

---

[7] Dr. H. R. Muller, "Nutrition and Infant Mortality," an unpublished monograph distributed by Nestle Alimantana, November 28, 1976, p. 6.

[8] Ibid., p. 10. A total of 15 studies establishing the insufficiency problem are cited in Dr. Muller's paper.

[9] Olikoye Ransome-Kuti, "Some Cultural and Social Aspects of Infant Feeding in Nigeria," *Modern Problems in Pediatrics* 15 (1975), p. 123. The percentage did not sum to 100 because of multiple attributions.

The interactions among maternal ignorance, maternal malnutrition, unsanitary conditions, disease, and medical shortages clearly made the question of infant nutrition in developing countries very complex. Furthermore, the lack of reliable data on virtually all of these variables led to a great deal of speculation and uncertainty. The reason for the general decline in mortality was in itself a topic of speculation.

In spite of the multiple potential interpretations of studies, it was clear that the wider availability of infant formula in developing nations might profoundly modify feeding practices. This prospect attracted the attention of the Protein Advisory Group (PAG) of the United Nations in the early 1970s. At the suggestion of that organization, the World Health Organization (WHO) and UNICEF sponsored a conference on the subject in Bogota, Colombia, in November 1970. The purpose of the conference was to focus discussion on the issue of consumer misuse of foods for infants in developing countries. The conference began with some hostility toward the industry for what was seen as aggressive marketing practices toward those consumers who were almost prevented by lack of education and income from properly using the product. By the end of the conference, some accommodation had been reached between representatives of industry, nutritionists, and government officials.

THE DEVELOPMENT OF INFANT FORMULA FEEDING AS A PUBLIC ISSUE

Although a number of questions had been raised earlier about the product and the marketing practices of the producers, the question of infant formula sales in underdeveloped countries seemed to emerge as a serious public controversy with the Protein Advisory Group conference. This conference was the first forum for the critics and the manufacturers to interact. The publicity generated by the sessions undoubtedly helped propel the issue forward as a matter of public concern.

After the initial conference, the International Pediatrics Association met in Vienna in 1971 to discuss the same issue. Subsequent PAG conferences were then held in Paris in June 1972, in Geneva in December 1972, and in New York in June of 1973. The tangible outcome of this series of meetings was PAG Statement No. 23, "Promotion of Special Foods (Infant Formula and Processed Protein Foods) for Vulnerable Groups," dated November 1973. The statement contained seven specific recommendations for governments, five for pediatricians, and six for industry (see Exhibit 6).

While the above conference had raised the public's consciousness concerning the sale of infant formula in the Third World, a publication titled "The Baby Killer" raised the interest in the issue to an emotional pitch. This pamphlet was published in March 1974 by War on Want, a London-based political action group devoted to making poverty a major social issue. "The

EXHIBIT 6   PAG Statement No. 23 (abridged)

PROMOTION OF SPECIAL FOODS
(INFANT FORMULA AND PROCESSED PROTEIN FOODS)
FOR VULNERABLE GROUPS
18 July 1972, Revised 28 November 1973

Summary

The statement emphasizes the critical importance of breast feeding under the sociocultural and economic conditions that prevail in many developing countries. Infants of more affluent socioeconomic groups in industrialized and developing countries, in the absence of breast feeding, suffer no nutritional disadvantage when fed properly constituted and hygienically prepared processed commercial formulas. These infants usually receive sufficient formula, and the diet is also supplemented with baby foods. However, the early abandonment of breast feeding by mothers among lower socioeconomic groups can be disastrous to infants, particularly when this occurs without adequate financial resources to purchase sufficient formula and without knowledge of and facilities to follow hygienic practices necessary to feed infants adequately and safely with breast milk replacements. Under such circumstances, and where animal milk and other supplementary protein resources are expensive or in short supply, an important function of the food industry, in close cooperation with governments and physicians, should be the development and marketing of relatively low-cost, nutritionally equivalent protein foods that can be used to supplement breast feeding.

To assist the various interests concerned with these problems in dealing with them objectively and effectively, the PAG proposes three sets of coherent recommendations: one for governments and United Nations agencies, a second for nutritionists and physicians caring for children, and a third for the food and infant formula industries.

Recommendations to Industry

*1. Food industry leaders should be involved constructively in the solution of the special nutritional problems of vulnerable groups, particularly in developing countries.

*2. The importance of breast feeding should be stressed in employee training, and personnel should be instructed to avoid sales and promotional methods that could discourage appropriate breast feeding in any way.

*3. Industry should train its personnel adequately in matters concerning local public health norms, needs, and regulations in the implementation of national food and nutrition policies.

 4. Industry should recognize and emphasize that the immediate postpartum period and the hospital nursery are not appropriate for any promotion of infant foods directed at other than professional personnel.

*5. To minimize misuse, industry should give special attention to the importance of unambiguous and standard directions for reconstituting formulas from dry or liquid preparations for feeding young infants. The needs of illiterate as well as

EXHIBIT 6   *(concluded)*

literate persons should be considered in designing labels. Labels and product literature should foster hygienically oriented practices such as the use of boiled water and the proper cleaning of utensils.

6. Industry should give active consideration to the development and production of supplementary foods and infant formulas that do not require reconstitution or can be rendered palatable by boiling only.

* Recommendations implemented by the industry.

SOURCE: "Promotion of Special Foods (Infant Formulas and Processed Protein Foods) for Vulnerable Groups," PAG Statement No. 23, July 18, 1972, revised November 28, 1973.

Baby Killer" accumulated information from personal and published sources to form a powerful indictment of the international infant formula industry. The publication began with the following summary (abridged):

> Third World babies are dying because their mothers bottle feed them with western style infant milk. Many that do not die are drawn into a vicious cycle of malnutrition and disease that will leave them physically and intellectually stunted for life.
>
> The frightening fact is that this suffering is avoidable. The remedy is available to all but a small minority of mothers who cannot breast feed. Because mother's milk is accepted by all to be the best food for any baby under six months old.
>
> Although even the baby food industry agrees that it is correct, more and more Third World mothers are turning to artificial foods during the first few months of their babies' lives. In the squalor and poverty of the new cities of Africa, Asia, and Latin America, the decision is often fatal.
>
> The baby food industry stands accused of promoting their products in communities that cannot use them properly, of using advertising, sales girls dressed up in nurses' uniforms give away samples and free gimmicks that persuade mothers to give up breast feeding. . . .
>
> Where there is no choice but squalor, the choice of an artificial substitute for breast milk is in reality a choice between health and disease. . . .
>
> The results can be seen in clinics and hospitals, the slums and graveyards of the Third World. Children whose bodies have wasted away until all that is left is a big head on top of the shriveled body of an old man. Children with the obscene bloated belly of kwashiorkor.
>
> Why are mothers abandoning breast feeding in countries where it is part of the culture? Are we helping to promote the trend? What is the responsibility of the baby food industry? What are we doing to prevent avoidable malnutrition?
>
> These questions are being raised by doctors and nutritionists throughout the Third World. War on Want believes that by opening the subject to public debate a solution may be found faster than through silence.[10]

---

[10] Muller, "The Baby Killer," p. 1.

In the months following the publication, dozens of articles paraphrasing portions of "The Baby Killer" appeared in the popular press under such titles as "The Milk of Human Unkindness," "Shrivelled Children, Swollen Profits," and "Formula for Malnutrition." One of the most extreme examples was a German interpretation published in Switzerland by the Third World Action Group titled "Nestles Kills Babies." Because the document allegedly deleted many of the qualifying statements of the original work and singled out Nestle as the major villain in the controversy, Nestle promptly sued the organization and its 13 members for libel. The defendants were fined $120 each, and the judge, in delivering his verdict, suggested that the company ought to reconsider its advertising policies.

Not all of the publications to appear during this period were solely popular press pieces. Exhibit 6 lists some of the scientific statements made regarding the question of infant formula sales in the Third World. Perhaps the most quoted medical critic of bottle feeding in the less developed parts of the world was Derrick Jelliffe, professor of pediatrics and public health at UCLA. With over 30 years of service in Third World countries and several hundred published articles to his credit, Dr. Jelliffe's views on "commerciogenic malnutrition" became well known. He attributed well-financed, steamroller marketing techniques to the infant formula industry in their attempts to sell what he believed to be totally unaffordable and inappropriate foods for impoverished communities. Dr. Jelliffe believed the industry's claim that they were attempting to take a leadership role in the improvement of child nutrition especially offensive. Not all medical professionals completely agreed with Professor Jelliffe, but he was not alone in his beliefs.

Two very significant works appeared during 1975 that further fueled both the scientific and the emotional criticisms of infant formula. The first was the publication of the "Cornell Report," a monograph written by Ted Greiner, a graduate research associate.[11] Assistance was provided by the aforementioned Dr. Jelliffe; author Robert Choate, whose exposés of the breakfast-cereal industry had been widely read; and nutritionist Michael Latham, whose view was that "placing an infant on a bottle might be tantamount to signing the death certificate of the child."[12] The monograph reviewed infant food advertising practices back to the 1920s and summarized many of the charges that had been made up till that time.

The second piece was a German film documentary by Peter Kreig titled *Bottle Babies*, which described various marketing practices that allegedly result in the death of many infants. The most powerful scene was of an infant graveyard outside Lusaka, Zambia, where baby bottles and cans of infant

---

[11] Ted Greiner, "The Promotion of Bottle Feeding by Multinational Corporations: How Advertising and the Health Professions Have Contributed," Cornell University Monograph, 1975.

[12] "Third World Death Warrant," *The Washington Star*, February 20, 1976.

formula had been placed by a mother on her child's grave in the belief "that the magic qualities of the formula would carry to the grave and beyond."[13]

During 1976 the infant formula issue received additional publicity from a stockholder suit filed against the Bristol-Myers company. The suit alleged certain untruths were contained in the firm's proxy statements. The complaint regarded Bristol-Myer's claim that they had discontinued advertising in those markets where chronic poverty existed. The legal action was settled out of court where certain modifications of the proxy statements were agreed upon.

The years 1975 and 1976 were also the gestation period of the infant formula division of the ICCR. Leah Margulies stated during the 1979 information day proceeding before the WHO Geneva Conference that the project actually dated from a 1975 Consumer's Union publication, "Hungry for Profits."

The year 1977 saw the birth of a second major critical organization, INFACT. Acccording to Douglas Johnson, head of the INFACT organization, the group began with four local committees in January 1977. What was originally developed as a Minnesota-only organization for the boycott of Nestle products "quickly became out-of-hand." By January of 1978, Douglas Johnson indicated that 135 local boycott groups existed, while one year later 400 such groups had been formed.

In 1978, additional publicity was generated by a public hearing held by the U.S. Senate Health and Science Research Subcommittee. Chaired by Senator Edward Kennedy, the committee called a number of industry, professional, and critical experts to testify. At one point during the hearings, the president of Nestle's Brazilian subsidiary was roundly criticized for suggesting that the intent of the critics was the overthrow of the capitalistic system. This statement and the response to it seemed to characterize the emotional nature of the proceedings.

The major infant formula event in 1979 was the Geneva Conference called by WHO and UNICEF. The major purpose of this conference was to bring together all interested parties to discuss once again the appropriateness of the present marketing practices of the infant formula industry in the Third World. The major outcome of the meeting was an agreement that all promotion should be halted in the Third World.

During 1979, "The Baby Killer Scandal" by War on Want was published as well.[14] This sequal to "The Baby Killer" updated the charges made by the earlier work, adding additional fuel to the emotional nature of the infant formula question.

The infant formula question also was addressed within the U.S. government by the 96th Congress. During May of 1979, Congressmen Dellums and Miller, both of California, introduced the Infant Nutrition bill of 1979 in the

---

[13] Quoted in "Bottle Babies," *CNI Weekly Report,* February 20, 1976.

[14] Andy Chetley, *The Baby Killer Scandal* (London: War on Want, 1979).

House of Representatives. As reported in the May 16, 1979, issue of the *Congressional Record*, the bill suggested that the increased promotion and availability of infant formula had resulted in a decrease in breast feeding, causing escalating infant morbidity and mortality.

In an effort to rectify the problem perceived by the congressmen, the Infant Nutrition bill of 1979 sought to (1) ban all proprietary promotion; (2) require graphic instructions for product use; and (3) require a license to export, sell, or otherwise distribute infant formula in any developing country. To meet the requirements of the proposed legislation, the Federal Trade Commission would also be charged with processing and approving all license applications. In order to have a license approved, the bill would require all companies selling infant formula to submit sufficient data produced through tests or studies to establish that the use of infant formula in each Less Developed Country would not contribute to infant morbidity or mortality among any specific set of consumers. The data presented would have to include, but not be limited to the following:

1. Adequacy and availability of sterilization and refrigeration techniques.
2. Water quality.
3. Epidemiological studies of gastrointestinal, respiratory, nutritional, and dental diseases in infants.
4. Life expectancy and infant mortality rate and causes.
5. Cost of infant formula vis-à-vis family incomes.
6. Literacy levels among target groups of consumers.

CASE

The Mead Corporation (A)

The Mead Corporation was one of 35 U.S. companies with board-level committees dealing with questions of corporate social responsibility. Mead's Corporate Responsibility Committee (CRC) was unique, however, in that it included company employees along with outside directors as regular members. The Committee had been formed in 1972, at the recommendation of a special board committee and Mead's chairman and chief executive officer, James W. McSwiney. The hope was that by bringing together representatives of two groups—directors and employees—who seldom had an opportunity to share ideas, and by giving them the freedom to choose their own agenda, the flow of "unorthodox" and "unconventional" ideas could be encouraged and stimulated throughout the organization. McSwiney believed that this opening up of communication between the bottom of the organization and the top was essential to Mead's continued health in a society that was demanding that corporations be more responsive to social needs.

In April 1976, Warren Batts, Mead's president and chief operating officer—with the encouragement of McSwiney—was attempting to evaluate the effect of this four-year experiment and to determine whether, at this point, the company would benefit from having management establish more formal links with the Committee. He had just received a paper prepared by an employee member of CRC recommending that Mead establish an ombudsman function with companywide responsibility. In formulating his response to the issues raised in the paper for the next CRC meeting, scheduled for May 27, 1976, Batts was considering whether operating management should become a more active participant in CRC's deliberations.

THE MEAD CORPORATION

The Mead Pulp & Paper Company was founded in Dayton, Ohio, in 1846 by Daniel E. Mead and several partners. Mead's grandson, George H. Mead, became president of the corporation in 1910, served as chairman of the board from 1937 to 1948, and was honorary chairman until his death in 1963. Between 1910 and 1963, the Mead Corporation (renamed in 1930) added 37 plants and mills to its two original paper mills in Dayton and Chillicothe, Ohio. Mead's product line, originally limited to magazine paper, expanded under George Mead's leadership to include a wide variety of paper products.

In the 1960s, the company determined to grow and broaden its base, and by 1976, largely as a result of acquisitions, it was producing such products as furniture, school and office products, rubber products, precision castings, and coal, as well as pulp and paper.[1] The company owned operating units in 30 states and 23 foreign countries and was 1 of the 10 largest paper manufacturers in the United States.[2] It owned or managed more than 1.5 million acres of timberland in North America. In 1976, forest products (paper, paperboard, packaging, containers, and pulp) accounted for 56 percent of Mead's sales; school, office, and home products, 28 percent; and industrial products (castings, coal, rubber parts, and piping), 13 percent.

Mead's sales reached the $1 billion mark for the first time in 1969, with record net earnings. (See Exhibit 1 for a financial history.) In 1970, however, net earnings dropped substantially because of national declines in the housing market, rising pulp costs, reduced demand for white papers, and strikes at a number of Mead plants. In 1971, earnings showed improvement, but this was followed by a sharp decline in 1972 when wildcat strikes closed plants in Atlanta, Georgia, and Anniston, Alabama.[3] These were the first major walkouts the company had experienced since the 1940s.[4]

---

[1] Between 1960 and 1974 Mead acquired 40 companies. The largest, in terms of sales volume, were the Woodward Corporation, manufacturers of castings, and coal, rubber, and iron products; Chatfield & Woods, paper merchants; Westab, Inc., producers of educational and consumer products; and Stanley Furniture Company, Inc.

[2] Mead was usually compared with the following companies: Boise-Cascade, Champion, Crown Zellerbach, Georgia Pacific, Great Northern Nekoosa, Hammermill, International Paper, Kimberly Clark, Potlatch, Scott, St. Regis, Union Camp, Westvaro, and Weyerhaeuser.

[3] The following description of strike issues appeared in Mead's 1972 Annual Report: "Several hundred employees of Mead Packaging and Containers plants in Atlanta, in response to a local civil rights group that was attempting to organize a citywide minority union, staged a 55-day wildcat strike. Though illegal, it did focus attention on some real problems: minority promotional opportunities, a dust condition, and blocked communications. The dust problem was soon dealt with, a representative council formed to survey employee feelings more directly, and a new presupervisory training program for blacks and females instituted. A 10-day wildcat strike in Anniston, Alabama, revealed several misunderstandings. New Anniston management has stepped up information-sharing with employees; meetings to answer questions about pensions have proved especially helpful."

[4] Among Mead's 26,200 employees, 16,000 were represented by unions in 1976. The largest (in terms of number of Mead employees represented) were the United Paper Workers International, the Printing Specialists Union, and the United Steel Workers.

EXHIBIT 1 Financial History, 1970–1976

	1976	1975	1974	1973	1972	1971	1970
Net sales (millions)	$1,599	$1,245	$1,526	$1,299	$1,129	$1,056	$1,038
Net earnings (millions)	$ 89	$ 53	$ 82	$ 49	$ 18	$ 23	$ 20
Return on sales	5.6%	4.2%	5.4%	3.8%	2.3%	2.2%	2.0%
Return on equity	14.9%	9.9%	16.2%	10.9%	5.9%	5.2%	4.5%
Per common share							
Net earnings (fully diluted)	$ 2.94	$ 1.78	$ 2.72	$ 1.59	$ .57	$ .91	$ .70
Dividends	$ .89	$ .80	$ .60	$ .43	$ .40	$ .67	$ .67
Book value	$24.34	$22.05	$20.80	$17.71	$15.97	$15.86	$15.92
Capital expenditures (millions)	$ 76	$ 64	$ 124	$ 77	$ 40	$ 61	$ 44
Total assets (millions)	$1,227	$1,091	$1,057	$ 941	$ 862	$ 865	$ 861
Number of employees	26,200	24,000	27,000	32,000	32,000	34,000	34,200
Number of stockholders	29,525	31,197	31,372	32,164	30,119	30,555	30,924

SOURCE: Information supplied by the Mead Corporation.

Mead's sales and earnings reached record highs in 1974. But in the next year, earnings were off because of the national recession and because more than 3,000 workers staged walkouts in Escanaba, Michigan (26 weeks), and Chillicothe, Ohio (11 weeks), in response to the company's determination to include Social Security offsets as part of its pension benefits. In addition, Mead's affiliates in British Columbia were closed by industrywide unrest in Canada. The company recovered rapidly, however, and expected a 76 percent rise in profits for 1976.

THE MEAD ORGANIZATION

In 1976, the Mead Corporation was organized into six operating groups and a corporate staff headed by a group vice president on a peer level with the heads of the operating groups. (See Exhibit 2 for an organization chart.) Originally a paper company with centralized management, Mead began to move toward a decentralized structure during its acquisition program. In 1976, Mead's Paper and Paperboard Groups were made up of the paper and paperboard mills that had previously been the cornerstone of the corporation, and the packaging and container plants that had been acquired and expanded. The four other groups consisted of all the remaining acquisitions.

The expansive phase of Mead's development had been engineered by James W. McSwiney, chairman of the board in 1976, who had joined Mead in 1934 at the age of 18. He had been president and chief executive officer between 1968 and 1971. When he became chairman in 1971, he retained his CEO position, and Paul Allemang (a group vice president since Mead acquired his company in 1966) became president and chief operating officer. Allemang was succeeded in 1973 by Warren Batts, 42, who had joined Mead as a group vice president in 1971. (Before joining Mead, Batts had been co-founder, president, and CEO of a small hand-tool company.)

Despite its substantial diversity in business, Mead's management at the corporate level was made up largely of people with backgrounds in the paper industry until the late 1960s. As new companies had been acquired, only one, the Stanley Furniture Company, had brought a "Mead man" into the ranks of its top management. Others, like the Industrial Products Groups (with the former Woodward Corporation as its core), were run exclusively by the acquired management. A senior executive commented: "Relations became strained during the acquisition program, which brought on board a lot of new people and businesses. The corporate staff was strictly paper-oriented and had real problems relating to foundries and coal mines."

A manager who had been with Mead since the 1950s described the paper industry as being high in capital investment, with slow growth and little chance for marketing innovation. "If you do everything right and your competitors do everything wrong," he said, "your market share might change a fraction of 1 percent." He went on, "It is not unusual for the average paper manager to ride with his subordinates; he is willing to accept less than

EXHIBIT 2 Organization Chart

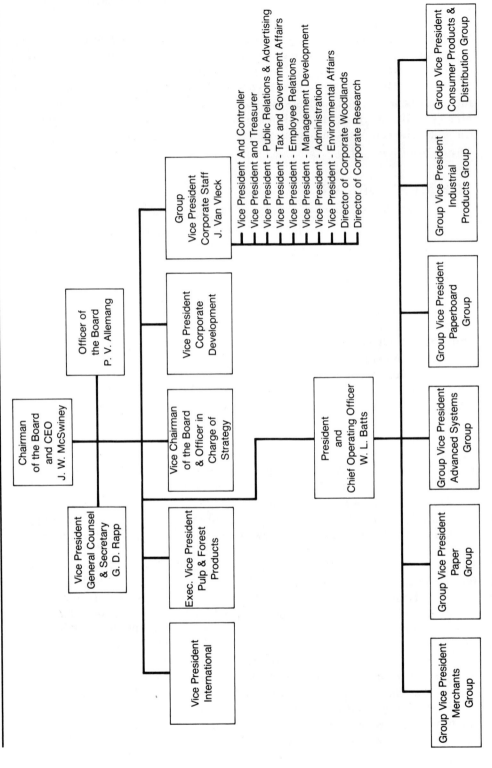

SOURCE: Information supplied by the Mead Corporation.

44

perfection. Personal relations always played a major role in the company. The old Mead Paper was almost as much a social organization as a business. When I came with the company, it seemed like a family."

When Batts became president in 1973, the company was examining the fruits of its acquisition phase and beginning to divest itself of 22 operations that did not fit into its long-range plans. In 1975, Batts began the process of integrating Mead's product groups, while strengthening the decentralized management structure. He described Mead's previous structure and its current direction:

> It took time for McSwiney's philosophy of organization and planning to take on meaning. In some groups decentralization was taken to mean that a group vice president was a prince with a moat around his division and his people. You came across his drawbridge at his pleasure.
>
> Now, we have gotten to the point where decentralization means that the group vice presidents are totally responsible for choosing the right people to run their businesses, for seeing problems and opportunities, and for presenting alternatives. But the corporate officers make the final selection among alternatives. We share the responsibility with the group vice presidents for results.

Early in 1974, Batts established the Operating Policy Committee (OPC), which he chaired and which included William Wommack (vice chairman of the board and officer in charge of strategy) and all the group vice presidents. He explained why:

> In order to maximize the results from a decentralized organization there had to be a vehicle for: (1) building common beliefs and goals into the company while recognizing critical differences among units; (2) establishing corporate policies; and (3) strengthening the position of the group vice presidents.
>
> In the past, many people felt—and it was true in some instances—that if someone on the corporate staff had an idea, it was fired right down to the plant managers, without the group vice presidents being consulted. Now the OPC serves as a buffer. Sometimes it takes 15 drafts to get an idea in shape. But by the time OPC signs off on it, each group vice president and his people are committed to getting it through the system.

In addition to developing better "top-down" communication, the OPC served as a vehicle for the divisions to exchange ideas. For example, in early 1976 the OPC was considering a program for improving internal communications that had been developed by the Paper Group. This program consisted of employee attitude surveys, management seminars, and management-employee councils. Batts intended that all the group vice presidents would eventually adopt a similar type of communications program, as a result of OPC discussions. Still, he was aware that such adoption would best be voluntary: "Given our organizational philosophy, each group vice president should have final authority in operational matters. I would rather persuade than order them to establish a particular program for internal communications."

The change in the management structure was in some ways a function of the difference in style between McSwiney and Batts and in the role of president and chief operating officer. A group vice president made this comparison:

> McSwiney is more likely to say something and then assume it will come out the way he wants it to. He is a powerful man, magnetic, very difficult to say no to, even when you know you should say no. I still have a tendency to think he can't do anything wrong. As CEO, he has the ability to see things that the rest of us, wrapped up in the day-to-day issues, don't think about. He never lets us get too satisfied with ourselves.
>
> When McSwiney was president, he knew all the details and had a compulsion to make all the decisions. Batts likes to know the sequence of steps involved, but he is more willing to give the group vice presidents independence. Still, he is very structured and wants to know how things are likely to turn out.

Since 1971, 5 of 6 group vice presidents and 19 of 24 division presidents had been changed—mostly replaced with people from within the company.

THE MEAD BOARD

During most of the Mead Corporation's history, many of its directors were members of the Mead family and officers of the corporation. As it acquired new businesses in the 1960s, Mead added top officers of the merged companies to the board. (Exhibit 3 lists the members of the board in 1976.)

In September 1970, James McSwiney became concerned about the board's composition. He was especially interested in achieving a better balance between inside and outside directors. (At that time, Mead's 22-member board included only six directors who were not associated with the Mead family or the company.) With the board's approval, McSwiney appointed a special committee consisting of four outside directors to study the board's functions, size, and composition. Alfred W. Jones, who would retire at the end of 1972 after 33 years as a Mead director, was named chairman of the committee. In its final report the "Jones Committee" recommended that:

> An effective number of directors for a company the size of Mead should be between 12 and 15, with inside directors not to exceed one third—Outside directors should be chosen for breadth of experience and interest, and the balance they can bring to the Board's deliberations.

The committee also described the type of person who should be considered for board membership in the future—namely, heads of companies similar to Mead in size; owners of large amounts of Mead stock; one or more people "oriented to minority, ethnic, or other social concerns," and individuals with the ability to ask critical questions. Finally, the Jones committee analyzed the functions of existing board committees and recommended that the board establish a "Corporate Responsibility Committee," to provide the company with a "means of responding to salient social and environmental aspects of the world."

EXHIBIT 3   Board of Directors (April 1976)

Vernon R. Alden (1965)*
Chairman of the Board
The Boston Company, Inc.
Boston, Mass.
Common shares owned: 600

Ivan Allen, Jr. (1971)
Chairman of the Board
Ivan Allen Company
Atlanta, Ga.
Common shares owned: 200

Warren L. Batts (1973)
President and Chief Operating
Officer
Mead Corporation
Common shares owned: 1,100

George B. Beitzel (1973)
Senior Vice President
International
Business Machines Corporation
Armonk, N.Y.
Common shares owned: 200

William R. Bond (1968)
Chairman of the Board
Cement Asbestos Products
Company
Birmingham, Ala.
Common shares owned: 7,500

Newton H. DeBardeleben (1968)
Vice Chairman of the Board
First National Bank
Birmingham, Ala.
Common shares owned: 720

James W. McSwiney (1963)
Chairman of the Board and
Chief Executive Officer
Mead Corporation
Common shares owned: 102,801

H. Talbott Mead (1946)
President
Mead Investment Company
Dayton, Oh.
Common shares owned: 48,244

* Date of appointment to Board.

Nelson S. Mead (1959)
Vice President, International
Mead Corporation
Common shares owned: 28,408

Paul F. Miller, Jr. (1963)
Partner, Miller Anderson &
Sherrerd
(Investment management firm)
Philadelphia, Penn.
Common shares owned: 1,000

George H. Sheets (1963)
Executive Vice President
Mead Corporation
Common shares owned: 13,736

William M. Spencer III (1968)
Chairman of the Board
Motion Industries, Inc.
Birmingham, Ala.
Common shares owned: 26,648

Thomas B. Stanley, Jr. (1970)
Investor
Stanleytown, W.V.
Common shares owned: 172,400

C. William Verity (1966)
Chairman of the Board and
Chief Executive Officer
Armco Steel Corporation
Middletown, Oh.
Common shares owned: 2,232

John M. Walker, M.D. (1957)
Consultant
White, Weld & Co., Inc.
New York, N.Y.
Common shares owned: 5,715

William W. Wommack (1968)
Vice Chairman of the Board and
Officer in Charge of Strategy
Mead Corporation
Common shares owned: 9,404

SOURCE: The Mead Corporation.

In keeping with the Jones Committee's recommendations, the board began to meet six times each year, with meetings averaging three hours in length. In addition, the executive committee met with outside directors four times a year. Five other board committees—Finance, Compensation, Audit, Corporate Responsibility, and Corporate Objectives (formed in 1975)—also met periodically throughout the year. In 1976, outside directors received compensation of $10,000 per year, plus $600 for each executive committee meeting and $400 for meetings of other board committees.

In 1974, at McSwiney's suggestion, Mead's board appointed another directors' task force, composed of outside directors and chaired by Vernon Alden, to reexamine the board and to bring the original Jones Report up to date. (See Exhibit 4 for excerpts from this group's report.)

EXHIBIT 4   Excerpts from Directors' Task Force Report, 1974

Board Responsibilities and Expectations of Mead Directors

In the legal corporation framework the Mead Board has ultimate *responsibility* for the management of the corporation. The board discharges this responsibility by delegating the executive function to management and by holding management accountable. In a broad sense, the board holds a *charter of trust* for the corporation. In this perspective, it stands between the Mead organization and the outside environment, including shareowners, customers, public, etc.

In operational terms, the board reviews and approves or rejects recommendations of Mead management on certain major decisions. . . . Final decisions on such matters as declaration of dividends, mergers, and disposition of principal assets constitute *reserved powers* and require formal action by the board. In addition to these formal actions, directors are expected to counsel management on decisions . . . of major importance . . . such as . . . the charging of business strategy with regard to particular products or markets and major employment fluctuations (growth or curtailment).

One way to sharpen the definition of what the board does might be to distinguish between the board's role and function and the role and function of Mead management. In the functioning of the board organization, directors should review, consider, contribute, formulate, and advise; operating and staff managers should propose, implement, operate, account for, and assist. . . .

Audit and Accountability: The Board Agenda

In the discharge of its duties to audit the operation and to hold management accountable, the Mead board needs access to information. The board's effectiveness is based upon the capability of Mead directors to ask the right questions and their ability to receive prompt and responsive answers. The quality and efficiency of discussions and decisions at Mead board meetings is thus determined by the *quality of information* that the board members receive. It is the responsibility of the chairman of the board to ensure the adequacy of information services to Mead directors. In all cases, board

EXHIBIT 4 *(concluded)*

members should have the opportunity (and should take the initiative) to seek information which they need, in addition to regular reports by management. . . .

Corporate Responsibility

Corporate responsibility is an emergent but not well defined function of corporate boards in their role as trustee, standing between the corporation and society. Corporations in general have not demonstrated a clear sense of how to articulate this function in operational terms (i.e., who in the board should do what, when). Fiscal accounting is precise and financial audits are feasible because measurement standards apply universally across divisional and corporate boundaries. No such universal means of measurement are available for corporate responsibility.

The Mead board has an opportunity to serve in this area, by virtue of the emphasis placed by the chief executive officer, by directors, and by the response throughout the corporation to the establishment and the work to date of the Corporate Responsibility Committee of the board. *We believe and recommend that the board should continue to regard corporate responsibility as one of its major concerns.*

McSwiney often referred to the Mead Corp.'s board as a "working board." The president of Mead, Warren Batts, offered his perception of the board:

> We have a core of outside directors who are truly tough-minded businessmen. They know that the job of a director is basically to protect the shareholder—first, foremost, and always. The board's role is to review and approve corporate objectives and to review management's actions but not to meddle in operations. Among our directors, however, there is a wide spectrum of opinion about the board's role in corporate responsibility. This is the most nebulous area for the board and one that we have to make more concrete.

INITIATION OF THE CORPORATE RESPONSIBILITY COMMITTEE

In March 1972, the full board of directors accepted the Jones Committee's recommendation to form a Corporate Responsibility Committee. McSwiney described his thinking:

> At the time there were several issues. Blacks were very vocal about the rights of minorities, and equal opportunity for women was also in the spotlight. The term *corporate responsibility* was the new buzz word, and some people thought it was simply a fad. But I took the idea very seriously. I thought a Corporate Responsibility Committee, with both directors and employees as members, could provide a way to send unfiltered information to the top of the organization.

I have a feeling that if you can't stand unfiltered information in an organization, or if you don't get it, you probably are going to make a lot of erroneous assumptions. I saw this committee as a mechanism for encouraging dialogue, and for breaking through the walls that surround managers at the top of the company.

Although he was instrumental in the formation of CRC, McSwiney felt very strongly that he himself should not be a member. He explained why:

I didn't feel the committee would make a real contribution if the chief executive meddled with it. The resolution of critical or sensitive issues, especially those that involve prestigious positions and talented people, can seldom be achieved by edict. Only when those people who are affected are involved in the process of working out their own solutions is the process likely to become an ongoing part of the system.

A CEO must not become so insecure that he blocks communications—sometimes accurate, sometimes inaccurate, but always believed by those in the system—from reaching the outside directors.

Consistent with this philosophy, McSwiney met with CRC on only two or three occasions after its initiation. However, he and the full board regularly received formal and informal reports from the committee's chairman and secretary on the work and functioning of CRC.

McSwiney chose Gerald D. Rapp, general counsel and vice president for human resources, to chair the committee and he asked three outside directors to serve as members. These four then took responsibility for recruiting three employee members. In their early discussion, the directors mentioned wide outside interests, college background, and youthful thinking as criteria for selection of employee members. One director argued that hourly workers should be represented; another felt that no one should be chosen simply to represent the union point of view. No definite criteria for employee membership emerged from these discussions.

Notices announcing openings for employee membership on CRC were posted at all Mead facilities in the United States. Rapp interviewed every candidate (nearly 100) and his or her supervisor. Next, 10 finalists, with their husbands and wives, were invited to meet with the CRC director members in July 1972. On the night they and their spouses arrived for scheduled interviews, finalists were asked to write essays on corporate responsibility and, at dinner, to speak informally about themselves and their goals. One of the finalists described the experience: "It was not enjoyable. You yank someone out of the bottom of the organization and bring him to the Plaza in New York City to meet the directors of the company and it produces some bizarre behavior." Three employees were finally chosen for CRC membership and the committee was introduced to the company in a newsletter. (See Exhibit 5.)

Nine months later, a decision was made to recruit an hourly paid employee for the Committee. Most of the applicants for committee membership were nominated by their supervisors. After employee members narrowed the list of applicants down to 10 finalists, all CRC members, in teams of two, conducted interviews and chose two new members: Quepee Gates, a railroad

EXHIBIT 5   These Employees and Outside Directors Will Serve on the New Corporate Responsibility Committee

Randy Evans has just been promoted to manager of Customer Service for Mead Paperboard Products' Western Region. He has worked with Mead since 1968.

Annabel Clayton (Mead Packaging) sells convenience packaging to the industrial market in New York. She joined Mead in 1966.

Bobby Bullock started his Mead career in 1962 as an hourly worker at Durham and worked his way up to general foreman of Mead Containers' Spartanburg plant.

G. D. Rapp, Mead's Assistant General Counsel, has been appointed chairman of the new Corporate Responsibility Committee.

W. Walker Lewis, Jr. is General Counsel for Mead. He serves as the Corporate Responsibility Committee's secretary.

Ivan Allen, Jr. is Chairman of the Board of the Ivan Allen Company in Atlanta, which merchandises office supplies and equipment. He served two terms as mayor of Atlanta from 1962 to 1969. He was elected to the Mead board in 1971.

Vernon R. Alden is Chairman of the Board at The Boston Company. He was President of Ohio University from 1962 to 1969, a period characterized by strong student unrest. He has been a Mead director since 1965.

N. H. DeBardeleben is President of the First National Bank of Birmingham. He joined the Mead Board of Directors in 1968.

THREE EMPLOYEES CHOSEN FOR DIRECTORS' COMMITTEE

A three-month search for three employees to fill out the Mead Board of Directors' new Corporate Responsibility Committee has resulted in the selection of a saleswoman, a general foreman, and a customer service manager to serve with three outside directors. The three were chosen from a panel of ten — narrowed down from a field of nearly 80 candidates from all parts of the company — for the contribution each can make to the committee's work.

The board created the committee to help Mead keep abreast of its changing responsibilities — toward the environment, the communities it operates in, its customers and employees — and to see that it is developing sound ways to deal with them. Chairman J. W. McSwiney says that it should "provide a means for unorthodox, unexpected, unconventional — perhaps unwelcome — ideas to emerge and find their way to top level attention."

A small task force is already accumulating fresh data on such topics as Mead woodlands policies, employment practices, and environmental quality programs. The committee expects to draw upon the ideas of all 80 original nominees and welcomes the input of any interested employee. Direct your comments to the committee's chairman, G. D. Rapp, The Mead Corporation, 118 W. First Street, Dayton, Ohio 45402.

HERE ARE THE OTHER FINALISTS WHO VIED FOR COMMITTEE MEMBERSHIP

Grady A. Roberts, Jr. came to Montag in Atlanta in 1971 to help with training for disadvantaged employees. He also works in the Cost Department.

Young Kim, controller for Westab at Sunnyvale, Calif., came to the U.S. for an education and liked it so well he stayed. He joined Mead in 1971.

Ronald Sedenquist, an electrician at Mead Publishing Papers' Escanaba mill, takes an active role in his union. His service began in 1957.

Owen L. Gentry (Board Supply division) is superintendent of the Sylva, N.C. mill. He has been with Mead since 1960.

Mike Noonan, who joined Mead in 1968, is general sales manager for Mead Packaging division in Atlanta.

Howard Hughes is special projects manager with Murray Rubber in Houston, Texas. He came to Mead in 1968.

Lester (Bill) Reed is general manager of Woodward's Chattanooga Coke and Chemical division. He came to Mead in 1966.

SOURCE: The Mead Corporation.

conductor from a Mead facility in Woodward, Alabama, and Warden Seymour, a pipe fitter and union official from a paper mill in Chillicothe.

EARLY COMMITTEE ACTIVITIES

In the summer of 1972, the Corporate Responsibility Committee began to carry out the duties assigned by the full board—duties which represented the CRC's original charter:

> Examine and report on the attitudes of all levels of management toward social and environmental responsibilities and concerns.

> Examine and recommend specific issues for Board and management consideration and determine their relative priority.

> Determine and recommend policy related to priority issues.

> Project potential new areas of social responsibility and involvement.

> Recommend where duties and responsibilities lie throughout the various levels of the company.

To help the committee select its priorities, Rapp, at the direction of the committee, formed a task force to study Mead's performance in pollution control, equal opportunity, and land management, and to analyze the attitudes of outside groups (e.g., the National Council of Churches and the Environmental Protection Agency) toward industry. Research assistants to the task force were four recent college graduates who were about to enter graduate school. These researchers gave Mead managers their first inkling of what CRC might be up to. One recalled:

> Their three-month escapade certainly didn't help the credibility of the committee. CRC was brand new from the chairman of the board, so people knew it was important. The next thing they saw were these college kids—"Rapp's Raiders" as they came to be known—marching through their doors, telling them their EEO performance was lousy, their contributions budgets all wrong. And reporting to top management.
>
> One manager got fired. He should have been fired, but there was a direct link between the exposure these kids gave him and his dismissal. He happened to be a highly regarded—incompetent—guy. That he got fired scared a lot of people. Some people quietly let their stomachs churn. Others became outwardly hostile to the committee.

At the conclusion of their studies, the students made several recommendations to CRC. The primary ones were that the company use incentives to reward and punish managers for pollution control and equal opportunity performance and that the company establish a multiple-use strategy for its forests. Within a year, corporate staff reported to CRC that Mead had begun a systematic expansion of hunting, fishing, and hiking rights in its forests, as part of a multiple-use program. By April 1976, however, the company had not formally implemented the researchers' first recommendation.

REACHING THE EMPLOYEES

The employee members of the CRC felt strongly in 1972 that contact with Mead employees was needed to communicate priorities to the committee. To help in this process, Rapp arranged to have Randy Evans released from his regular job and assigned to the human resources staff for three months to coordinate regional meetings. Under Evans's supervision, 140 employees were chosen, from names submitted by supervisors and general managers, to attend two-day conferences. The conferees included 56 hourly and 84 salaried workers from 48 operating units. Forty-six of the employees were members of minority groups; 38 were women. Evans described the employee meetings:

> Initially, a lot of people were uncertain about the purpose but as things started unfolding on the first evening, they began to see that we were serious. By and large, a feeling of sincerity was communicated, and people said, "Well, if this is real, how can we make it worthwhile?"
>
> The interchange that began happening was just beautiful. One salesman said that salespeople have no job satisfaction. A black hourly worker said: "I'm not concerned with job satisfaction. I don't even know what you're talking about. I've got four children and I'm happy to have a job. And let me tell you what it's like to work in a foundry." This kind of exchange started going on.

Most of the employees who had spent two days discussing what was "right" and what was "wrong" with the Mead Corporation seemed to leave the meetings with good feelings. For many, the opportunity to share information and experiences, at meetings sponsored by the company itself, elicited a positive attitude toward management. One participant wrote to the organizer of a California meeting: "I think we all felt a little proud of Mead and the CRC for this opportunity. We may eventually let a little 'we' creep into our thinking, instead of the ominous 'they.'" In a report prepared for the directors, Evans wrote:

> Employees wanted the existing communications channels to work. They did not want the Corporate Responsibility Committee to do an "end run" around management. Rather, they wanted the CRC to fix the system so that a mutual listening and trust relationship could be developed between the employee and his immediate supervisor.

CRC IN 1973—REPORTING TO MANAGEMENT

Mead's group vice presidents had their first formal contact with CRC early in 1973 at a Hueston Woods, Ohio, retreat, where CRC employee members reported on the 1972 employee meetings. One group VP described the presentation:

> All of us were impressed with the eloquence of the people describing the problems they found in Mead. They were obviously words from the heart. We went down skeptical, but came away really impressed. The issues were pretty clear—better

information-sharing and communication and a need to make the system work more effectively.

After the Hueston Woods meeting, the employee members of CRC and a few employees who had attended the 1972 regional conferences met with managers throughout the company. Robert Richards (a manager chosen for CRC membership in 1975) recalled a story he had heard about a 1973 CRC plant visit:

> I heard about the visit from the plant manager. Some CRC people toured his place, a lovely old brick building surrounded by trees. He asked one CRC member how he liked the plant, expecting the usual praise. Instead, the CRC person said: "I don't see any blacks working here. Haven't you hired any?" The manager told him that no blacks lived in that area. In that case, the CRC member said, the manager should be recruiting blacks throughout the state. The manager told me that, in his opinion, CRC was out to manufacture issues where it couldn't find them.

After a year of management meetings, the employee members of CRC expected the organization to respond in some way. But nothing seemed to happen. A senior manager offered this explanation: "After the early meetings, there was an air of endorsement and enthusiasm among the operating managers, but it was not their role to pick up the responsibility for making things happen."

In addition to holding meetings for management and recruiting new committee members in 1973, CRC also heard reports from corporate staff on EEO performance, corporate contributions, programs for employees with drug and alcohol problems, and a placement effort for employees who were laid off when Mead closed a facility in Anniston, Alabama. Exhibits 6 and 7 are examples of the kind of data the Committee received in these reports.

EXHIBIT 6   Equal Opportunity Percentages, 1974–1976*

Category	April 1, 1976	April 1, 1975	April 1, 1974
Executives, officials, and managers	4.2/4.4	3.0/4.0	2.2/3.7
Professionals	15.3/3.6	12.0/3.4	9.9/3.5
Technicians	9.4/7.1	7.0/4.3	6.7/5.5
Sales workers	11.5/4.4	8.1/4.4	5.4/2.9
Office and clerical	75.9/9.8	72.1/9.4	71.0/8.7
Skilled crafts	1.1/12.3	.9/11.8	1.4/11.6
Semiskilled operatives	14.7/27.7	12.7/26.6	11.8/27.1
Unskilled laborers	29.2/28.9	24.9/27.5	20.8/33.0
Service workers	9.9/37.9	9.6/32.4	8.9/31.1
Total work force	19.6/19.7	18.1/18.6	16.9/20.7

* All females/all minorities (male or female).

EXHIBIT 7   Corporate Gifts, 1969–1975

Year	Net Gifts ($000)	Gift as Percent of Earnings before Tax	
		Mead	All Industry
1969	$624	1.07%	1.24%
1970	496	1.51	1.08
1971	408	1.06	1.03
1972	440	1.51	.95
1973	453	.90	.86
1974	514	.34	.83
1975	492	.96	n/a

In preparation for the last CRC meeting of 1973, Jerry Rapp, committee secretary, sent several recommendations for the next year's agenda to Chairman Vernon Alden:

> Our basic task now is to see how Mead could institutionalize this process of employee communication. Next, we might consider new major projects that we should undertake ourselves or encourage other Mead people or groups to take on. From the employee meetings, we have identified problems falling into six clusters . . . equal employment opportunity; job satisfaction; communications; the external human environment; the external physical environment; and personal services for employees, such as counseling for retirees, day care centers, and clean working conditions.

NEW DIRECTORS JOIN CRC

In April 1974, two new director members were appointed. These were C. William Verity, chairman of the board of Armco Steel Company, and George B. Beitzel, senior vice president and director of IBM. (As a means of familiarizing directors with the company, the board rotated membership on CRC.) In the years that followed, members of CRC often referred to this April meeting as a turning point for the committee. It brought two issues into focus: the frustration and disappointment that employee members were experiencing after the intensity of CRC's start-up years, and the difference between director and employee members' perception of the role of CRC within the company.

All the employee members were angry about the corporation's failure to deal with the problems discussed at the employee conferences in 1972 and reported to management in 1973. At the April meeting, they argued that, if it did nothing else, CRC should at least respond to the most widespread complaint voiced at the employee meetings—dirty rest room facilities in plants and mills throughout the company. Both new director members expressed their surprise at the nature of the issue and the manner in which it had been uncovered. One recalled the meeting:

> It was hard to get a definition of what the committee was and what it should be doing. At my first meeting, somebody mentioned that the men's rooms were very dirty and said the committee ought to do something about that. I argued that it was not the committee's responsibility. If the company's policy was to keep the men's rooms clean, that was the responsibility of the plant managers.
>
> I didn't think CRC should have been asking employees what was on their minds. That was management's job. I told them that the committee should not be a lightning rod for employee grievances. The only people CRC should be talking to is management, asking them questions about policy.

The employee disagreed. One of the committee members described the April meeting as "the most intense we'd ever had." For all five employee members, it was a disheartening experience. One commented:

> Beitzel and Verity came on the committee and pretty much refuted the prior posture of the CRC as a committee that would go out and *do* things. They were most vocal in saying: "This is a committee of the board; you are to ask questions of management and let them respond." They felt actually going into the organization and holding employee meetings was something that management should do, not the members of CRC.
>
> You know, we had put our hearts and souls into this and there were these new members coming in and scaring the hell out of you just by sitting there, and then downgrading everything you'd been doing for the last year and a half.

As a result of this meeting, Jerry Rapp and consultant Constantine Simonides, an MIT vice president, worked together to fashion an agenda for CRC. They spoke with chief executive officers and other top management and staff people from companies all around the country with records of achievement in the area of corporate responsibility. In October 1974, they made a presentation to CRC. Their primary recommendations were that CRC should turn its attention to the world outside Mead and pass the responsibility for employee-oriented programs to management.

Specifically, they recommended that Mead's president and group vice presidents take responsibility for improving communications between managers and employees, that corporate staff plan career development and personal service programs for employees and work more closely with supervisors on equal opportunity planning, and that CRC begin to assess the company's contributions policy and programs for involving Mead employees in the affairs of their communities. Rapp described the meeting: "Our recommendations fell on deaf ears. The employee members were just more interested in internal issues. Our discussion of what other companies were doing, what was going on in the outside world, made no impact at all."

A few weeks before Rapp made this presentation to CRC, employee member Warden Seymour had written a letter to Mead's chairman, expressing his concern about the committee's lack of activity:

From the time you informed me I had been selected for the committee, I have believed in the good it can do for all the employees and for the corporation. Recently though I have become very discouraged with the lack of activity by the committee. I feel the chairman of the board has a very deep sense of responsibility to all the employees, but I feel people under you are reluctant to accept the changes recommended by this body. I feel the only way the committee can survive is with very strong support from you and Mr. Batts.

McSwiney responded to Seymour early in November and emphasized his continued support of the committee:

I also could be discouraged when I think of all the things that have not been accomplished. The existence of the Corporate Responsibility Committee in some ways may aid in raising expectations beyond what can realistically be accomplished; but that is a risk I am willing to live with so long as we can have open dialogue throughout the company about the expectation level and the measures of performance (or lack of performance) about these expectations. . . .

During 1975, I would urge you and other committee members to consider contact with fellow employees and others in the context of the committee's responsibility of monitoring progress within the company on the key corporate responsibility issues, with results to be reported to the board and corporate management.

In November 1974, the employee members came together to discuss the issues they felt the whole committee should tackle in the coming year. They put together a list of 35 objectives to pursue in 1975 (see Exhibit 8).

EXHIBIT 8 CRC Priorities for 1975 (recommendations from employee members)

1. Examination by board of Mead's policy on involuntary separations, layoffs, terminations, and early retirements (equality of treatment with respect to notices and placement and committee audit).
2. Bring together board and employee members of committee.
3. Board examination of Mead's policy and performance regarding corporate contributions.
4. Board examination of Mead's policy regarding educational assistance, including leave policy and family assistance.
5. Meetings:
   a. Full day.
   b. Operating locations.
   c. Outside contributors.
   d. Times other than board meetings.
   e. Six meetings per year.
   f. Workshop meetings.
   g. Annual meeting with board by full committee with report by employee members.
   h. Routine receipt of reports.
   i. Outsider take minutes.

EXHIBIT 8   *(continued)*

6. Audit personal services effort.

7. Inquire, examine, or investigate policy or method of communications to employees, i.e., *Progress Report* (ask Mead people *and* outsiders to review for committee).

8. Board agenda to include CRC report and, perhaps, questions regarding employee concerns.

9. Board examine Mead's policy concerning handicapped people: ex-offenders, physically handicapped, Vietnam veterans, hard-core unemployed, etc.

10. Policy and performance at Mead regarding career planning.

11. Board examine Mead's policy concerning managerial rewards and punishments with respect to EEO performance.

12. Quarterly report to board by management of EEO performance.

13. Board require management to report routinely in advance on actions that impact Mead constituencies—employees, community, suppliers, customers.

14. Individual access to and control of information.

15. Recommend that Mead should have policy with respect to an individual nonunion employee appeals process.

16. Ask for policy on employee recognition.

17. Ask for policy concerning assistance to families of employee who dies.

18. Policy affecting contact with retired employees also disabled.

19. Ask for policy on age discrimination.

20. Ask what is company policy regarding minimum physical standards for Mead employee facilities.

21. Policy on CRC membership turnover.

22. Deal with personal problems of members due to CRC service.

23. Decision on staff support to committee.

24. Determine interest, policy, and posture regarding "external" concerns.

25. Decision regarding employee meetings—recommend to management.

26. Examine management efforts to place black males in *top* line positions—what are goals?

27. Company should address attention to determining concerns of middle managers.

28. Company policy regarding response to recent pension legislation.

29. What impact expected from "inflation management" concept and procedures.

30. What attempt and results of management efforts to improve quality of communication between supervisors and subordinates.

31. Connect 1975 CRC agenda with the past two years.

32. Examine the effect of attitude surveys and assessment mechanisms on employees.

33. Board emphasize performance measurement beyond financial results.

EXHIBIT 8   *(concluded)*

34. Ask for Mead's policy on the company's participation in the community.
35. Big external issues—work with other institutions:
    a. ZEG/ZPG impact on Mead.
    b. Cooperation versus competition with respect to unions, competitors, government communication.
    c. Conservation.
    d. How people relate to company and what are new ways of relating.
    e. Impact of future technology and discoveries on Mead and its constituencies.

SOURCE: The Mead Corporation.

NEW EMPLOYEES JOIN CRC

In 1975, three employee members left the committee, and Rapp and Paul Allemang managed the recruitment process for replacements.[5] CRC discussed at great length the problems of recruiting new members because employee members believed that few in the company understood the committee's function. In response to a director's recommendation, Rapp and Allemang prepared a proposal for recruiting new members and discussed it with Warren Batts. They suggested that the group vice presidents select a panel of employees (managers, staff, and hourly workers) to screen candidates from groups other than their own. The candidates so chosen would then be interviewed by all the members of CRC. This would be an annual process.

Batts invited Allemang and Rapp to discuss the proposal at an April 1975 meeting of the group vice presidents. He described what happened at the meeting:

> I thought that Paul and Jerry's proposal for getting new members for CRC was sound since it got management involved. So they met with the group vice presidents to discuss the recruitment process. The response from the group vice presidents was not what I expected. They were upset. "We're closing down and selling plants and laying off many in the work force," they said, "and now we're going to have all this song and dance, at great expense." At their insistence, the process of selecting new members was toned down.

In July of 1975, Randy Evans (one of the retiring employee members) made a 10-day trip around the country to interview applicants for CRC, most of whom had been nominated by their supervisors and general managers. Evans

---

[5] When Paul Allemang stepped down as president, chief operating officer, and director of Mead in 1973, he was appointed to the position of officer of the board. His main responsibility was to help coordinate CRC activities.

chose 10 finalists, who were then interviewed by committee members. The four new employee members were Robert Richards, a marketing manager; Robi Love, coordinator for college employment; David Hubbard, a sales representative in California; and Ister Person, who worked in the order processing department of a paper merchant unit. All four had been nominated for CRC membership; only Person had been unaware of the committee's existence before receiving word of her nomination.

In August 1975, Jerry Rapp sent a memorandum to James McSwiney on the future of CRC. He made four recommendations:

1. Strengthen the leadership and active participation of director members.

2. Balance the employee membership by including middle management and clarify the selection process by involving local operating management.

3. Beef up the staff support to the committee in order to provide more information to members, and to communicate the committee's concerns and activities to corporate staff and operating management.

4. Broaden the CRC agenda to include not only employee concerns, but also the concerns of external groups such as customers, shareholders, government agencies, suppliers, and communities in which plants are located.

In October, the new employee members attended an orientation meeting, and in December, their first regular committee meeting. By their second meeting, in February 1976, they were expressing doubts about CRC's ability to get things done. One new member was especially concerned about the employee members' isolation from the directors, and the committee's isolation from the company:

> What bothered me from the first was that all the employee members had suggestions for the agenda, issues we felt were important, but we didn't get a chance to discuss them with the directors. We rely on the directors for leadership, and without more direct communication with them, we probably won't have much of an impact on the company. What also bothered me was that we had no formal means of communicating with the organization. We seemed to be operating in a closet.

In a speech delivered at this time, McSwiney offered his views on the committee's progress:

> After three years' experience with the Mead Corporate Responsibility Committee, I have found the process in our company both rewarding and frustrating. Things that needed to be said to or about the organization have often been much more effectively stated without my direct participation . . . and this is, of course, a pleasant surprise! When a director, for instance, asks an officer, "Are you humane?" I assure you the penetration and subsequent attitudinal change is much different than if the same question were asked by the CEO. . . .
> Gaining the understanding and support of middle managers is a crucial step in the effectiveness of a corporate responsibility effort. At Mead, we have not done as well as we would like in this area. We have learned, sometimes painfully, that we must take special care not to threaten middle managers by our anxiety to institute

new programs and changes quickly. The understanding and cooperation of middle management is a vital part of making progress in this as well as in any other area that affects operations. We must not allow corporate responsibility to appear as the esoteric mental exercise of top management.

PLANT CLOSING POLICY

At the same time that CRC was recruiting new members in 1975, it was giving its attention to a policy issue that both director and employee members agreed was of major importance to the corporation. This was the company's plant closing policy and the question of management's responsibility to employees who lost their jobs when Mead closed or sold an operating unit. The issue gave the president of the company, Warren Batts, his first direct encounter with the committee.

Following the development and implementation of its strategic plan, between 1973 and 1976, Mead closed 22 of its operating facilities and dropped 8,500 employees from its payroll. The 1973 Annual Report explained:

> We made a searching classification of all our businesses in 1971-72. Then we projected each ahead to 1977 and took a look at where they—and the corporation as a whole—would be. That indicated clearly which businesses we should cultivate and which we should move out of to give us the soundest portfolio for the long haul. . . .
>
> We've been acting on the analysis, moving out of businesses no longer viable for us and zeroing in on opportunities of special promise. . . . To put it simply, we expect to fund businesses with strong growth potential aggressively and to withdraw from those that offer neither growth nor cash.

During CRC's early years, employee and director members occasionally discussed the need to learn whether Mead management had developed a formal companywide policy for dealing with employees affected by plant closings. In December 1974, they raised the issue with Robert Schuldt, vice president of employee development (who was present to report on EEO performance), after employee member Quepee Gates told the committee that he had lost his job in Mead's Woodward, Alabama, foundry that month. Gates was 60 years old and had worked at the foundry for 35 years. What especially troubled him, he said, was that management had notified him at 3:00 P.M., on what he thought was a normal working day, that the plant was closing at the end of the shift.

Two months later, in March 1975, Warren Batts attended a CRC meeting to discuss the company's plant closing policy. Batts reported that a total of 1,825 employees had been laid off in 1974 as a result of 11 plant closings. In most cases, the employees had been notified of the closings from four days to three weeks ahead of time. One hundred and fifty employees had chosen to retire, and Mead had helped another 500 to find jobs in other plants or with other companies. The balance chose to remain on unemployment compensation until their eligibility ran out. Batts explained that within the framework of Mead's policy of management decentralization, each division had its own

closing policy. This accounted for the disparity in notification dates and severance pay. However, by edict each division followed a standard practice including help from a corporate task force in finding employment for those who
wished to work. Progress was monitored by a regular reporting process, and
managers were rewarded for finding jobs for displaced employees.

In January 1976, Batts reported that a policy statement on plant closings
had been officially adopted. One outside director commented: "The one concrete thing CRC did was to get management to put together a policy on how
we're going to handle people when we shut down a location. Had the committee
not raised the question, we might still not have a policy." CRC members felt
that the committee had at last been able to influence the company.

THE OMBUDSMAN ISSUE

In 1976, the employee members of the CRC suggested that the committee
begin to study Mead's grievance procedures for nonunion employees. Mead had
no companywide procedures for handling such problems since the Human
Resources staff in each group had this responsibility. Some divisions had set up
employee councils that met several times a year to discuss problems directly
with management. Others had letter-writing programs, with staff assigned to
investigate employees' complaints. One employee member commented on the
problem:

> I've worked at a number of locations and know the concerns of white-collar
> workers and middle managers. They're the unheard segment of the company. They
> perceive, rightly or wrongly, that the unions have a very effective grievance
> mechanism and that the top management group takes care of itself but that
> nobody looks out for them.

> Robert Richards, who felt strongly that Mead needed change in this area,
> volunteered to prepare a paper on an "ombudsman function"[6] as a basis for
> committee discussion at the CRC meeting scheduled for May 27, 1976. In this
> paper, Richards wrote: "Without a mechanism whereby ideas, complaints, and
> suggestions are freely discussed, many white-collar workers will be functioning in
> an atmosphere of anxiety, apprehension, and fear." (Excerpts appear in Case
> Appendix.)

THE PRESIDENT'S DILEMMA

Warren Batts had had no formal contact with the full CRC until attending
the meeting in March 1975 to discuss plant closing policy. In the years since
becoming president, however, he had found that few people understood the

---

[6] An *ombudsman* is a person to whom aggrieved parties (e.g., consumers, hospitalized patients,
employees) take their complaints. The ombudsman makes an investigation, prepares a report, and
attempts to achieve a fair settlement. Traditionally, the ombudsman function was used to protect
individuals from abuse by government agencies. The first U.S. corporations to appoint ombudsmen
were Xerox Corp. in 1972, and General Electric Company and Boeing Vertel Company in 1973.

reason for the committee's formation, and he had heard numerous complaints about its activities:

> There was never any kind of message from the corporate level that explained why directors thought that Mead needed a CRC. Some managers inferred that either the board felt they were not acting in a responsible manner or else someone in the system was chasing the latest corporate fad at their expense.

An operating manager who had been with Mead for 30 years confirmed this view when he summed up his impressions of CRC:

> The general feeling has been that CRC was imposed from the top. It has little or no support or credibility with operating managers. It serves no genuinely constructive purpose. It's a corporate gimmick. The real job of transmitting information, handling two-way communications, and dealing with employee problems should be at the operating level, not the corporate level.
>
> I suppose the intent is to provide the top echelon with grassroots sentiments on what has to be done. But I question whether employee representatives can speak for anyone but themselves. Many things are important at the local level and should be handled locally, not escalated. CRC is kept in place because McSwiney wants it, with the endorsement of the board. But it doesn't enjoy prestige or status with the rest of the company.

A group vice president described his managers' reactions to the committee: "The basic problem is that CRC is seen as a complete bypass of management. Whenever employees can talk directly to directors, there is bound to be trouble."

Mead's chairman was aware of the hostility to CRC, but he continued to support it in discussions with board members and management. He made these observations about the company's response to the committee:

> There were various types of management reaction to CRC: concern, fear, admiration, pride. But, in general, there was an avoidance of integrating the system into the company. The group vice presidents—their natural inclination reinforced by the negative attitude of some of their managers—constantly sent darts at the people who supported the committee. There were two reasons for this. First, CRC did make some mistakes. It focused solely on employee issues, because this was what mattered to the employee members, as would be expected. But the board and the company had expected the committee to deal with external issues as well. Second, some senior managers wanted to test whether CRC would be eliminated if they criticized it long enough.
>
> I realized from the first that if a new development were to be creative, it was likely to destroy something that already existed. That's the nature of creativity. And if something is destroyed, there is bound to be a certain amount of tension. The main thing is to keep the tension healthy, or at least contained within certain parameters. What has finally happened is that the president of the company has begun to realize that the issues being raised by CRC are real and that all of us are hearing things faster and more directly than we would through the usual channels. He is beginning to see that the full potential for CRC is not being realized because it is outside the system.

I've always believed in the validity of the premise on which CRC was founded, and the whole organization and the board saw that I wanted it to stay. Otherwise, it might have been eliminated. I still think the organization can absorb it. As we move forward, I think CRC will be helpful to Mead, no matter what form it ultimately takes. It could turn out to be a superb thing. The final decision is still out.

Batts, who had to formulate a response to Richards' paper for the next CRC meeting, had a number of questions about the committee and the proposal:

On the ombudsman question—it's true that there's always been a massive communications gap in companies from the division level down to the foreman level. Where we don't get good marks is with the nonexempt salaried people, the first- and second-level supervisors, and professional staff. But despite our problems, we've found from attitude surveys that Mead always scores higher than average as a good place to work. We have very little turnover at these levels. So we have to be careful about overreacting.

The fact that the CRC has become more and more of a concern to more and more of the operating people is what really bothers me. This is something that has to be wired into the organization; it has to be made into a positive force for the company instead of being a peripheral activity. One of my real questions is: Will CRC be a directors' committee, like all other committees of the board, or will it be an employees' grievance committee?

The chairman thought there were two basic questions about the Corporate Responsibility Committee:

First, how secure must an organization be in order to incorporate such a vehicle into its normal operations? Second, what other alternatives do we have to the "filtering out process" of the pyramid organization?

Appendix: Excerpts from Richards' Background Report

WHY THE NEED AT MEAD FOR AN OMBUDSMAN-TYPE FUNCTION

Without exception, there is a feeling of frustration in all sectors of the white-collar work force that they are squeezed between the unions and top management. They contend that there is no effective way to bring their complaints, concerns, or frustrations to the decision makers without the fear of possible disciplinary action. Some of the concerns I have heard are as follows:

SOURCE: The Mead Corporation.

1. There is no effective mechanism to protect an individual from unjustly being fired.

2. The company makes arbitrary decisions on work hours, retirement, and other fringe benefits without explaining why they made the change, how they arrived at the decision, and so forth.

3. Bitterness is arising over the differentials in wage/salary policy between union and unrepresented employees. I have had managers with titles such as director, comptroller, and general manager complain that the differentials, as they have existed over the past few years, have created an almost untenable labor environment. They ask, "Does Mead really believe they are treating our employees fairly? How much longer do they expect the nonrepresented employees to accept merit salary increases substantially below union settlements? We're headed for unionization faster than we think."

In the eyes of many nonrepresented white-collar employees, such problems are being managed through a philosophy of benign neglect. The frustrations being voiced are not from radicals, drug users, or troublemakers. They are from some of the outstanding, conservative, and loyal members of this company. Without a mechanism whereby ideas, complaints, and suggestions are freely discussed, many white-collar workers will be functioning in an atmosphere of anxiety, apprehension, and fear.

POSSIBLE OPTIONS

While it is not the role of the Corporate Responsibility Committee to develop solutions, I have taken the liberty to scope out some possible options which could be investigated by the directors.

1. *Personnel Council*—This is a monthly forum where representatives of management and employees sit down to discuss mutual problems and opportunities. This is done on the sectional, departmental, and divisional level, with the main council serving as the top tribunal.

    It is a two-way communication. Employees voice their complaints and suggestions to their elected council representatives who bring them to management's attention at the regular meetings. Management, at the same time, communicates its policies and ideas to employees. Some discussions bear on companywide matters of significance. Others cover irritations that, if allowed to fester, could cause unpleasant consequences.

2. *Corporate Ombudsman*—This function could entail an individual or a number of individuals who serve as intermediaries between employees and the various departments that frequently make up the corporate staff such as the Benefits Department and Salary Administration.

3. *Grievance Committee*—It has been suggested that a formal grievance committee be set up. Its functions would be a cross between a judge/jury

system and an arbitrator. There are several concerns I have with this move. First, this step could lead to very legalistic approaches by some employees and could weaken management's ability to manage properly. Second, it could be too radical a step in solving potential problems that basically arise out of misunderstandings on both sides and therefore might not be as productive as desired.

4. *The Inspector General*—The role of the inspector general within the military is well known by most of us, and the use of this concept could have some decided merits. This office could function similar to the way our internal audit department works. It would work with the various divisions, departments, and managers to see that the corporate policies, benefits, and other services are properly explained and carried out. It would also function somewhat as an intermediary between the employees and the many aspects of the corporation which would affect the employee. This type of function should not impinge upon the managerial prerogatives of management, yet it should help to bring about positive results.

SUMMARY

If the Mead Corp. were to establish a form of ombudsman-type function, I believe the following benefits could arise:

1. It would serve as an early warning system (a DEW line) for top management, alerting them of potentially serious problems which might arise.

2. It could alert corporate officials to those areas or individuals whose human skills need improving.

3. Serve as a safety valve on issues that might otherwise create explosive situations.

4. It should help sharpen management to think out decisions affecting people without hindering their ability to manage. The old adage, "It's not what you say but how you say it," applies here.

5. This system should be a preferable alternative to unionization without being viewed as an antiunion movement.

Commentaries

1. Rating America's Corporate Conscience

For years, companies have been evaluated by assessing their financial performance—sales, profits, assets. Their brand-name products have been advertised and promoted using packaging, reliability, price, or a catchy slogan. But it has been virtually impossible to compare companies on their social performance—policies and activities on key issues of social responsibility.

The charts in *Rating America's Corporate Conscience* (see Exhibit 1 for a sample) will help you cast an economic vote on corporate social responsibility when you shop—whether you're buying toothpaste, a typewriter, or an airline ticket. (*Rating America's Corporate Conscience* rates corporate social performance by analyzing comparable data and presenting them in a practical format. For those actively concerned with social issues, *Rating America's Corporate Conscience* provides a new lever for social change. For those in the business community—from chief executive officers to middle managers to analysts and investors—*Rating America's Corporate Conscience* provides a compelling look at an intriguing array of corporate programs and policies.) By referring to the product charts and company profiles you can become more fully informed as an effective consumer, investor, worker, or manager.

Assessing a company's overall social record is not the same as determining its profitability; there is no clear-cut bottom line. One cannot successfully average positive performance in one area and negative performance in another. Sometimes the choices may be easy. For instance, few would have trouble distinguishing Polaroid's superior performance from A. H. Robins's, which we consider to be dismal. More often, however, a company's performance may be outstanding in one category, unsatisfactory in another, and mixed in yet another. How does one characterize IBM, for example? Here is a company that has taken noteworthy creative steps in job training for disadvantaged

Lyndenberg/Marlin/Strub, *Rating America's Corporate Conscience,* Copyright 1986 by Council on Economic Priorities. Reprinted with permission of Addison-Wesley Publishing Co., Inc., Reading, Massachusetts.

youth, provided child-care support for its employees, and exhibited innovative leadership in many other areas. But IBM is also a major military weapons contractor, and by virtue of its sales of computers in South Africa, it could be considered to be a supporter of apartheid.

In assessing a company's record, the issues you feel most strongly about may clearly dictate your choices. For some, the fact that Philip Morris aggressively promotes smoking, despite the well-documented adverse health effects of that habit, may override the company's substantial commitment to minority development or its patronage of the visual arts. We present the facts and indicate our own preferences as an additional guide to evaluating the data. After reviewing the product charts, company charts, and profiles, you will be able to make an overall appraisal. Of course the judgment and final decision is yours—to buy or not to buy.

Over the past decades many companies have taken substantial strides. Amoco, for example, has developed an outstanding program of economic support for community revitalization and minority- and women-owned businesses. Avon's corporate policies have focused on women, minorities, and the poor for almost a decade. The company profiles in this book reveal many other significant corporate initiatives.

But there is a long way to go. Disasters such as Love Canal and other toxic waste disposal controversies demonstrate the issues of arguable corporate irresponsibility and ineptitude are still with us. Less drastic but no less dramatic, many companies in the conduct of their day-to-day business supply oil to the South African government or manufacture nuclear-armed weapons. The implications of corporate behavior can have far-reaching and potentially dangerous repercussions.

Rating America's Corporate Conscience is only a beginning. Since it was necessary to limit the scope of the book, we excluded financial services, retail stores, and supermarket chains due to regional differences and the sheer number of companies. We considered including small, "alternative" companies, such as worker-owned cooperatives, organic food producers, or companies owned and run by minorities or women. However, space and time considerations forced us to exclude these as well. We hope a sequel to *Rating America's Corporate Conscience* will permit further explorations of these and other companies now covered here.

Product safety and quality are obviously important issues for consumers. For the most part we've left these assessments to organizations that already provide this information, such as Consumers Union; other resources are listed in Appendix C. However, where a company's record shows a dramatic commitment to public welfare (e.g., Johnson & Johnson's expensive voluntary recall of its drug Zomax), or where a company was involved in a controversy of an exceptionally serious nature (e.g., A. H. Robins's handling of the Dalkon Shield controversy), we have included this information within the company's profile. We have also noted, briefly, debates over the harmfulness of such products as cigarettes, alcoholic beverages, and highly processed foods.

We have reluctantly kept our discussions of environmental issues and labor relations to a minimum, due to a lack of comparable data. However, we have reported major problems in these areas, as well as particularly positive actions taken by companies (respectively, Dow Chemical's battle over the toxic pollutant dioxin and People's Express's innovative worker ownership and job rotation programs).

Social responsibility has become an accepted and broadly interpreted concept by many in the corporate community. Some managers of major corporations take the position that financial and social concerns cannot be separated and that a company's sense of social responsibility and its long-term profitability are ultimately linked.

James E. Burke, chairman of Johnson & Johnson, states that "There's an important correlation . . . between a corporation's public responsibility and its ultimate financial performance. Although public service is implied in the charter of all American companies, public responsibility—in reality—is a company's very reason for existing."

This contrasts with the more conventional wisdom that profitability is a company's only rationale for existence. But Johnson & Johnson's ability to survive the Tylenol crises of 1982 and 1986 demonstrated one way in which the reputation of commitment to the public good can become immediately relevant to a company's financial stability. The company's response to the first of these tampering incidents was swift and sure. When cyanide-laced Tylenol capsules resulted in seven deaths in Chicago in 1982, Johnson & Johnson immediately opted for an expensive nationwide recall of the pain reliever, even though the poisonings were in no way Johnson & Johnson's fault and despite the fact that there was no evidence of tampering elsewhere. It then reintroduced Tylenol in tamper-resistant packages, but kept the name—a calculated gamble that proved successful. Again, in the face of renewed tamperings and a second poisoning incident in 1986, the company took the potentially costly step of ceasing to market Tylenol in capsule form as the measure most clearly in the interest of public safety.

Johnson & Johnson was able to weather these crises in the face of intense efforts by the competition to capitalize on them. This was due partly to its solid reputation for commitment to the public good. As Burke put it, "The Tylenol situation dramatically proved that serving the public good is what business is all about."

A business operating with various commitments to social responsibility can do so profitably, as a number of studies have demonstrated. In the area of employee relations, Franklin Research and Development found that the stock of those companies included in the book *The 100 Best Companies to Work for in America* dramatically outperformed the Standard & Poor's 500 stock price average over a 10-year period.

The stocks rose from a value of just over 100 in 1975 to 700 in 1985, compared with a rise to just over 200 for the Standard & Poor's 500. A similar study, reported in Rosabeth Kanter's book, *The Change Masters,* asked human resources experts from the business community to come up with a list of companies most progressive in their relations with employees. The 47 companies chosen by these experts were then compared to similar firms of the same size within their industries. It was found that the "progressive" companies were more profitable and fostered greater growth over 20 years than did their counterparts.

Positive performance on environmental issues has also been shown to be beneficial. In 1972 a study by Joseph Bragdon and John A. Marlin that used five different measures of financial performance concluded that the companies within the pulp and paper industry that had the best record on pollution control and the environment were also the most profitable.

Of course, one cannot claim that social responsibility assures profits, or that all profitable companies are socially responsible. Polaroid, a company with one of the best social records, has encountered loss of market share in recent years. American Brands, which in our opinion has a poor social record, has been a consistently profitable company, largely because of its sale of cigarettes. Because numerous factors determine a company's performance, it would be naive to attribute financial success or failure to a single one.

Nevertheless, social considerations are slowly but surely becoming one of the many aspects of running a company well. The role of the chief executive officer in the integrations of social accountability issues into the corporate structure cannot be overestimated. A recent study by Michael Useem and Stephen I. Kutner of the Boston University Center for Applied Social Science confirms the conclusion reached by many other studies: The greatest influence on the size and nature of a company's charitable giving program is its CEO. Experts who have studied other social issues, such as employee-involvement and child-care programs, agree that a forceful commitment from top management is essential if meaningful long-term initiatives are to be institutionalized.

PRODUCT PROFILES

The product charts (for a sample product chart, see Exhibit 1) permit a quick comparative overview of how we rated different manufacturers on specific social issues.

Note that the product charts (see Exhibit 1) do not comment on or recommend the products themselves. For many products, ranging from vitamins to automobiles, you will want to give careful consideration to issues of safety, reliability, and appropriateness to your needs.

By glancing across the columns in the product charts, you can obtain an approximate idea of the degree to which we believe a company is committed to charitable contributions, women and minorities among directors and top offices, disclosure of social information, involvement in South Africa, and conventional- or nuclear-arms contracting.

Please see *Rating America's Corporate Conscience* (Lyndenberg et al., 1986) for a more complete discussion of how the Council on Economic Priorities determined these figures and their significance.

EXHIBIT 1 Infant and Baby Food

INFANT FORMULA

Size of Charitable Contributions	Women Directors and Officers	Minority Directors and Officers	Social Disclosure	Brand Name	Company (Profile Page)	Involvement in South Africa	Conv. Weapons-Related Contracts	Nuclear Weapons-Related Contracts	Authors' Company of Choice
$	🧍	No	No	Similac Isomil	Abbott Labs (p. 202)	Yes B	No	No	
*	🧍🧍	No	✍✍✍	S-26 SMA Nursoy Promil	American Home Products (p. 406)	Yes A/B	No	No	
$$$	🧍🧍	?	✍✍✍	Enfamil ProSobec	Bristol-Myers (p. 208)	Yes B	No	No	✔
$$$	🧍🧍	🧍	No	Gerber	Gerber (p. 137)	No	No	No	
$$$	🧍	No	✍✍	Heinz	Heinz (p. 138)	No	No	No	
*	No	?	No	Beech-Nut	Nestlé (p. 150)	Yes ?	No	No	

*= See company Profile
? = No information available
Single figure ($, 🧍) = Minimal
Double figure ($$, 🧍🧍, ✍✍, 🧍‍🧍) = Moderate
Triple figure ($$$, 🧍🧍🧍, ✍✍✍, 🧍‍🧍‍🧍) = Substantial

No = No involvement or participation
Yes = Involvement or participation. A, B, C in the South African column reflect the degree of compliance with Sullivan Principles and/or involvement in strategic industries.

See Chapter 4 for a detailed discussion of chart symbols.

SOURCE: Council on Economic Priorities, *Rating America's Corporate Conscience,* (Addison-Wesley, 1987).

2. A Score Card for Rating Management

Edward McSweeney

One myth about corporate directors is that they select the top man who runs the company. They almost never do. But an even bigger myth is that directors operate a business in the best interests of the owners (stockholders). This is what the law says they should be doing, but the responsibility is so vague, so poorly defined, that directors, particularly those drawn from outside the company, normally don't even try to find out what they should be doing.

If the statutes mean anything, they mean that an outside director should be monitoring top management and scoring it just as carefully as management itself is trying to score its subordinates. Yet in all my years of serving as an outside director on dozens of corporate boards, I have never once heard anyone talk about that task seriously, and never once have I heard any reference to the most critically important aspect of that task: removing a chief executive officer who is falling down on the job.

Why should this be? The answers are known to any experienced director. The outside director is supposed to be independent, but, in fact, he is not much better off than the inside director, whose future depends on compatibility with the chief and who is not about to criticize something the chief has done poorly.

Almost always, the outside director has been selected personally by the chief executive or recommended by a close mutual friend or dominant stockholder. He is chosen on the basis of friendship and loyalty. He becomes a member of a private club. The loyalty of such a group is especially intense when critics question the way the business is being run. Like the old frontiersmen, they wheel their wagons into a circle and prepare to shoot it out.

In most cases, moreover, the outside directors are at the mercy of a top man, who may be the chairman of the board or a dominant stockholder. If he is in the chief executive officer's corner, the outside director will be only as effective as the board chairman wants. If he appears to be a troublemaker, if he is in the wrong camp on an issue, the chairman can find ways to kill him off as a disloyal board member.

THE FRUSTRATIONS

Despite all this, the Penn Central case makes it plain that the Securities and Exchange Commission is going to hold outside directors responsible for monitoring management. Like it or not, they will have to be effective. And I

SOURCE: Reprinted from the June 8, 1974, issue of *Business Week* by special permission, Copyright 1974 by McGraw-Hill, pp. 12, 15.

am convinced that the typical outside director will like it very much. I have never talked with any outside director who has given serious thought to the functions, duties, and responsibilities of a director who was not also thoroughly disillusioned and frustrated. This frustration, in my opinion, is largely responsible for the decline in accepting directorships, even more significant than the growing fear among directors of the risk of facing liability suits.

I am not minimizing the liability suits. They are a great nuisance. They have become a way of life for some hungry lawyers and stockholders who, like vultures, swoop down on directors who didn't realize that they were guilty in approving questionable contracts, for example. All of a sudden, a director finds his responsibility driven home by a stockholder suit, and he says, "Holy smoke, how did I get in this spot?"

Sometimes a director goes to jail, but most have some liability insurance. In any case, actual convictions are uncommon. What really scares directors is that the suit will be publicized and, guilty or not, they will become suspect.

The combination of frustration and fear of lawsuits has made it increasingly hard for companies to get qualified outsiders to serve on their boards. Some companies are reverting to the old system of inside boards composed almost entirely of company officers who are completely subservient to the chief executive. Others are selecting their outside directors from the ranks of the lawyers, consultants, and investment bankers, who usually manage to make money out of their directorships. This is unfortunate. It is simply naive to expect an investment banker, who may gain a fat underwriting commission on a new stock issue, to be objective in all instances about the performance of the chief executive and his staff.

I can readily appreciate why many of my colleagues on boards shy away from the task of monitoring top management. But before we outside directors surrender, we ought to at least make a serious effort to be more effective. There is a function for us to perform. We should make a determined, good-faith attempt to perform it.

The basic question, of course, is: How? What means have we for checking on the performance of a chief executive?

THE AUDIT COMMITTEE

One answer has been to set up an audit committee of the board. A good audit committee can eliminate most of those big surprises that pop up when management hasn't let the board know about operating problems until the damage is done. This is certainly a step in the right direction.

A strong chief executive, however, doesn't like even the idea of an audit committee, and he can block its work, slow it down, or minimize its effectiveness in various ways. Most top executives these days know how to take care of themselves, and circumstances force them to concentrate their attention on the short run. They want to see the company's stock rise so that they can cash their stock options and secure their future with a handsome

EXHIBIT 1   General Scoreboard

General Scoreboard			
	Good	*Fair*	*Poor*
Return on stockholders' equity			
Return on sales			
Management of stockholders' assets			
Development of sound organizational structure			
Development of successors			
Development of proprietary products			
Development of organization morale			
Development of corporate image			
Development of growth potential			
Percentage of industry by segments			
Divestments			
Acquisitions			
Application of research and development			
Application of engineering and technology			
International			

retirement or a consulting contract. This is simply a fact of executive life that an experienced director has to accept. In any case, auditing the company's operations cannot really provide a reliable measure of the chief executive's performance.

That is why, some years ago, I began working on a method for scoring top management on their job performance. Eventually, I wound up with a score card that covers the most significant factors an outside director should try to measure. (See Exhibit 1 for the General Scoreboard.) This scoring system represents my conclusions after many years of studying the functions and responsibilities of top management. It is still experimental, and it will have to be adapted to each individual company. In some cases, it will not be necessary to score all the factors listed. Also, weighting of factors undoubtedly will vary from company to company.

Nevertheless, if outside directors will use even part of such a score card, or make up their own score cards, they should be able to do a far better job than they are now doing—which is practically no job at all so far as monitoring the chief executive goes. If 10 or 12 outside directors pool their score cards, the net judgment is likely to be accurate, regardless of individual variations.

The score card has two parts: general factors and personal factors. In my experience, a chief executive has to be seen from both sides. His performance as shown by financial and operating results must be interpreted in the light of his personal impact on the company and on the world in which it operates.

Most of the items on it lend themselves to an objective, quantitative approach. Directors should be able to compare return on investment and on sales with similar figures for competitive companies. They can often tell whether the corporate image is good or bad by the company's access to the financial community. If they have doubts about organization morale, an employee-attitude survey, designed to protect the identities of the respondents, will provide a better picture than any number of plant visits.

The personal score card necessarily is more subjective, but it is vitally important. It can detect trouble in the making long before anything shows up in the financial and operating statements.

I would suggest that the personal score card cover these topics and ask these questions:

Corporate Citizenship.   What does the chief executive give back to the community? Does he overdo it? Does he make a reasonable contribution of time and effort to community and government work without overcommitting himself?

Interlocking Directorships.   Is he sitting on too many boards to make a real contribution to any of them? Is he risking conflict of interest?

Outside Business Activities.   What percentage of his time should he give to the company that is paying him $100,000 or more?

Health.   Is the chief executive watching his physical condition? Is he trying to handle everything himself to the point of exhaustion? Is a periodic medical report available? Is there any question about his use of alcohol?

Builder of Human Resources.   Is he seriously trying to develop his subordinates as their coach, teacher, and counselor? Or is he aloof, expecting others to perform this task? Does he keep an eye on promising young managers and let them know he is watching them?

Decisiveness.   How does the chief executive meet and solve problems? Does he depend on committees? Postpone action on a problem that might go away? Does he make major decisions arbitrarily—without consulting even the board? Can he live with his decisions? Does he develop tensions and anxiety when things turn out poorly?

Trading in Company Stock.   Is he behaving like a speculator rather than a manager? Is he asking for trouble with the SEC under the insider trading rules? This is something the board should watch closely.

Outside directors are not used to throwing their weight around. It is small wonder that they are reluctant to assume the critical responsibility of evaluating the chief executive's performance and of removing him if he doesn't measure up.

But the fact remains that the outside directors are the only real safeguard the stockholders have against incompetent management. And I honestly think that nearly all those decent guys serving on boards would very much like to be more effective than they have been. The main trouble is that there has been no procedure for them to follow in monitoring the top man so that they would have solid facts and fair evidence that he is—or is not—doing his job.

That's why I am suggesting a score card. It may stir some directors into trying something they should have been doing all along.

PART TWO

Ideology and Ethical Responsibility

Ethics emerged in the late 1980s as the dominant issue in the business community. Business leaders, business academics, and elements of the lay public formed a chorus decrying the purported decline in ethics in business and called for new efforts on the part of business and other professional schools to incorporate ethics into the curriculum. This development occurred at the end of the Reagan administration and amidst a period of intense corporate take-over activity and emerging scandals associated with insider trading and other questionable business practices. The Reagan administration was notable in terms of having more high-level officials either indicted or convicted than any other administration since President Grant. Many felt that the administration was giving the business community a message of unrestrained greed through its deregulatory actions and its questionable ethics. Indeed the archetypal symbol of the period, the YUPPY (Young Urban Professional) exhibited a moral system based on maximizing income and self-definition in terms of the corporation. Family, church, state, and friendship were subservient to a push to get on a "fast track" to success irrespective of the costs. On the other hand, this was a period in which business ethics courses across the nation were in great demand and corporations were running ethics seminars for their employees.

What seemed to be happening during this period was an undercurrent of reaction to the dominant business ideologies and institutions of the period. Student activism over a variety of issues began to reemerge on American campuses. Although this activism was less intense than that of the later 1960s and early 1970s, it was growing at the time we were writing this book. That activism seemed to be attracting business students as well. That it would be attracting business students should not be surprising since business schools were growing explosively during the 1980s. Brighter students who might have gone into sociology, political science, and other humanities areas were attracted to business schools because of what they perceived to be better career opportunities.

Because of this intense interest in ethics and the continued emergence of business as the dominant institution in American society, it is important to examine the values and beliefs of managers and the ethical basis for business decision making. This section includes cases and commentaries that treat issues involved in assessing the "rightness" or "wrongness" of specific managerial decisions, viewed from an ethical perspective.

Business leaders are clearly a diverse group, with differing values and beliefs. Nonetheless, it is useful to consider what is business ideology, and its importance to American economic and democratic institutions. *Ideology* is defined by University of Detroit professor Gerald Cavanaugh as "a coherent, systematic, and moving statement of basic values and purpose. It is a constellation of values generally held by a group, and those in that group tend to support one another in that ideology."[1] An ideology is similar to the sociological definition of *myth:* something which gives meaning to an action and that the myth may or may not be true or partly true is often beside the point. As long as people believe in the myth or ideology and act on it *as if* it were true, then the myth or ideology is important. The ideology of business at the beginning of the 20th century was, of course, much different from the common views held by executives in the 1980s. The earlier view centered on the preeminence of the stockholders, as high-lighted by the quote often attributed to Cornelius Vanderbilt: "The public be damned, I work for my stockholders." The ideology of the time focused on the right of the owner to do with property as he saw fit. The ideology was antiunion and antigovernment. It was believed that the individual, whether business executive or employee, customer or competitor, should be unrestrained in freedom to act within the confines of the Constitution as interpreted by the courts.

That this was a late-19th-century, early-20th-century ideology and not that of the Founding Fathers, and the Constitution was ignored as the new ideology and myths helped explain, gave authority and legitimacy to, and helped pave the way for the new industrial organization of that period. For example, one of the dominant myths of that time tried to define the United States as a free market system wherein government intervention in the economy was severely limited and businesses and whole industries rose or fell depending on their ability to attract and hold customers. Those customers, through the market mechanism, were able to chose among products depending on their price. That this was not an accurate picture of the period's history has been pointed out by many for some time.[2] However, it is a measure of the power of an ideology or myth in that it can survive and remain robust despite evidence to the contrary.

The so-called managerial ideology described above recognizes the existence of a variety of stakeholders whose self-interest is intertwined with that of the private corporation. It also recognizes the modern reality that while a

---

[1] Gerald F. Cavanaugh, *American Business Values in Transition* (Englewood Cliffs, N.J.: Prentice-Hall, 1976), p. 13.

[2] Robert Lively, "The American System: A Review Article," *Business History Review* 29, no. 1 (1955), pp. 81–96.

large corporation may be "owned" by the stockholders, effective control resides in management; and it recognizes that corporations are creatures of the state and consequently must serve social goals as well as traditional economic goals. The critical task for managment is viewed as balancing the needs of all stakeholders.

Business ethics is concerned with the "right" and "wrong" in "good" and "evil" dimensions of business decision making. It is often difficult to evaluate a given decision as ethical or unethical without knowing details of the motivations and expectations of decision participants. For instance, low expectations followed by low performance does not necessarily represent unethical conduct, as noted by Professor Robert Bartels, "Simply to make an untrue statement about a product is in itself not unethical, nor to make a shoddy product—that may be bad management, but it is not necessarily unethical."[3] Likewise, a manager who makes a basic moral commitment to do what is right will seldom face charges of unethical behavior.

Ideologies evolve over time as realities force change in basic beliefs. Thus, in the 1980s, business leaders viewed their role quite differently from their predecessors. Perhaps one of the clearest descriptions of contemporary business ideology has been proposed by the Committee on Economic Development:

> The modern professional manager also regards himself, not as an owner disposing of personal property as he sees fit, but as a trustee balancing the interests of many diverse participants and constituents in the enterprise, whose interests sometimes conflict with those of others. The chief executive of a large corporation has the problem of reconciling the demands of employees for more wages and improved benefit plans, customers for lower prices, government for more taxes, stockholders for higher dividends and greater capital appreciation—all within a framework that will be constructive and acceptable to society.[4]

The cases in this section focus on both ethical dilemmas and clear instances of fraudulent behavior. Illegal and unethical behavior by the leaders of any institution poses a threat to the very existence of that institution. Therefore, a number of people have expressed alarm about the future of the American business system in light of the revelations of questionable decisions, corruption, and misconduct.

In the *McDonnell Douglas Corporation: The DC–10* case the design of the DC–10 aircraft represents a profound ethical issue. No aircraft can be made 100 percent safe, but who determines the appropriate level of risk? Who is responsible for enforcement? Who is responsible for revealing unethical conduct? The *Equity Funding Corporation of American* case involves blatant fraud. It is intriguing to consider how something of this magnitude could occur

---

[3] Robert Bartels, "A Model for Ethics in Marketing," *Journal of Marketing* 31, no. 1 (January 1967), p. 21.

[4] Committee for Economic Development, *Social Responsibilities of Business Corporations* (New York, 1971), p. 22.

and how it could go undetected for so long in a highly regulated and visible industry. The case also illustrates the role of small decisions that build up to major ethical dilemmas and the impact of these issues on middle-level personnel. The third case, *A Management Dilemma: Regulating the Health of the Unborn,* Bunker Hill Co.'s decision to exclude fertile women from toxic work environments, presents the manager with an excruciating moral dilemma with ramifications for other areas of technology and management.

The McDonnell Douglas and Bunker Hill Co. cases help to illustrate the current predicament of the high-tech manager: our increasing knowledge and increasingly sophisticated technology often does not mean that legal, moral, and ethical issues melt away. Indeed, just the reverse seems to occur—our moral dilemmas seem to increase not only in number but also in complexity.

The commentaries in this section begin with a thoughtful essay, "Ethics and the Corporation," by Irving Kristol. Then John Byrne discusses recent trends in business ethics education. Robert Krikorian's essay discusses the relationship between ethical conduct and the bottom line. Robert Krikorian was CEO of the Rexnord Corp. where he implemented a business ethics training program. The pieces by Michael Allen, Robert Johnson, and John Koten illustrate some common ethical proble s in small-business operations and advertising.

McDonnell Douglas Corporation: The DC-10

On the evening of June 12, 1972, American Airlines Flight 96 took off from Detroit Metropolitan Airport with 56 passengers aboard. About five minutes later, the plan had reached 11,500 feet over Windsor, Ontario, when suddenly there was a loud bang. Air rushed through the cockpit and the passenger cabin. Part of the rear of the cabin floor collapsed, and dust, ceiling panels, hatch doors, and baggage flew through the air, some of them hitting the passengers. The captain, Bryce McCormick, and his crew were able to regain control of the airplane and fly it back to the Detroit airport for an emergency landing. No one was seriously hurt.[1]

The cause of the near-crash was soon discovered: The rear cargo door had not been completely latched. The switch that turned off the cockpit's warning light had nevertheless been pushed by the mechanism, indicating to the crew that the door was safely closed. In the investigation, which began the following morning, the baggage handler who had closed the door, William Eggert, testified that after shutting the cargo door electrically he had attempted to pull down the manual handle, but it would not go down. Unable to see inside the door, and sure that he had followed correct procedure so far, Eggert pulled harder on the handle, using his knee for extra leverage, and the handle went down into the locked position. Noticing that the vent door was still slightly crooked, he lifted the handle and pushed it down again to make sure it was closed. The vent door remained crooked, but an American Airlines mechanic indicated that this was not an unusual problem with DC-10 vent doors. The investigation showed that the latches had missed going over center by one third of an inch. When Eggert pushed on the exterior handle, one of the bars in the locking pin linkage had broken under the pressure.

Part of the reason the plane had been saved may have been the fact that it carried relatively few passengers (the DC-10 was built to carry 380 people). Under the weight of the full load, more of the floor might have collapsed, and the control cables and hydraulics could have been cut. After the incident, the

---

[1] "No Bomb on Plane; Cargo Door Opened Explosively in Flight," *Los Angeles Times,* June 13, 1972, p. 1.

plane's captain, Bryce McCormick, was asked by McDonnell Douglas to advise the company as to what action it ought to take. McCormick suggested that they tell all DC-10 pilots what would happen in the event of an explosive decompression and explain the flying techniques he and his crew had used to land the plane safely. The company did not follow his suggestions.

Fifteen days after the Windsor incident, F. D. Applegate, director of product engineering for the Convair Division of General Dynamics Corporation of San Diego, California, wrote a memorandum expressing his frustration with the handling of the DC-10 cargo door problems (see Exhibit 1). He recommended that Convair, a subcontractor on the DC-10 project, contact McDonnell Douglas "at the highest management level" to convince the company to correct the door design.[2] Applegate's immediate superior, J. B. Hurt, sent the memo to the Convair vice president in charge of the DC-10 project, M. C. Curtis, along with his own comment on it (see Exhibit 2). Hurt indicated that if Convair approached Douglas about the difficulties, they should realize that it would probably mean Convair would have to pay the costs of fixing the faulty door. He referred to the matter as "an interesting legal and moral problem."

EXHIBIT 1 The Applegate Memorandum

27 June 1972

Subject: DC-10 Future Accident Liability.

The potential for long-term Convair liability on the DC-10 has caused me increasing concern for several reasons.

1. The fundamental safety of the cargo door latching system has been progressively degraded since the program began in 1968.

2. The airplane demonstrated an inherent susceptibility to catastrophic failure when exposed to explosive decompression of the cargo compartment in 1970 ground tests.

3. Douglas has taken an increasingly "hard-line" with regards to the relative division of design responsibility between Douglas and Convair during change cost negotiations.

4. The growing "consumerism" environment indicates increasing Convair exposure to accident liability claims in the years ahead.

Let me expand my thoughts in more detail. At the beginning of the DC-10 program it was Douglas' declared intention to design the DC-10 cargo doors and door latch systems much like the DC-8s and -9s. Documentation in April 1968 said that they would be hydraulically operated. In October and November of 1968 they changed to electrical actuation which is fundamentally less positive.

---

[2] Paul Eddy, Elaine Potter, and Bruce Page, *Destination Disaster* (New York: Quadrangle/The New York Times Book Co., 1976), p. 185.

EXHIBIT 1 *(continued)*

At that time we discussed internally the wisdom of this change and recognized the degradation of safety. However, we also recognized that it was Douglas' prerogative to make such conceptual system design decisions whereas it was our responsibility as a subcontractor to carry out the detail design within the framework of their decision. It never occurred to us at that point that Douglas would attempt to shift the responsibility for these kinds of conceptual system decisions to Convair as they appear to be now doing in our change negotiations, since we did not then nor at any later date have any voice in such decisions. The lines of authority and responsibility between Douglas and Convair engineering were clearly defined and understood by both of us at that time.

In July 1970 DC–10 Number Two was being pressure-tested in the "hangar" by Douglas, on the second shift, without electrical power in the airplane. This meant that the electrically powered cargo door actuators and latch position warning switches were inoperative. The "green" second shift test crew manually cranked the latching system closed but failed to fully engage the latches on the forward door. They also failed to note that the external latch "lock" position indicator showed that the latches were not fully engaged. Subsequently, when the increasing cabin pressure reached about 3 psi [pounds per square inch] the forward door blew open. The resulting explosive decompression failed the cabin floor downward rendering tail controls, plumbing, wiring, etc. which passed through the floor, inoperative. This inherent failure mode is catastrophic, since it results in the loss of control of the horizontal and vertical tail and the aft center engine. We informally studied and discussed with Douglas alternative corrective actions including blow out panels in the cabin floor which would provide a predictable cabin floor failure mode which would accommodate the "explosive" loss of cargo compartment pressure without loss of tail surface and aft center engine control. It seemed to us then prudent that such a change was indicated since "Murphy's Law" being what it is, cargo doors will come open sometime during the 20 years of use ahead for the DC–10.

Douglas concurrently studied alternative corrective actions, in-house, and made a unilateral decision to incorporate vent doors in the cargo doors. This "Band-Aid fix" not only failed to correct the inherent DC–10 catastrophic failure mode of cabin floor collapse, but the detail design of the vent door change further degraded the safety of the original door latch system by replacing the direct, short-coupled and stiff latch "lock" indicator system with a complex and relatively flexible linkage. [This change was accomplished entirely by Douglas with the exception of the assistance of one Convair engineer who was sent to Long Beach at their request to help their vent door system design team.]

This progressive degradation of the fundamental safety of the cargo door latch system since 1968 has exposed us to increasing liability claims. On June 12, 1972, in Detroit, the cargo door latch electrical actuator system in DC–10 number 5 failed to fully engage the latches of the left rear cargo door, and the complex and relatively flexible latch "lock" system failed to make it impossible to close the vent door. When the door blew open before the DC–10 reached 12,000 feet altitude the cabin floor collapsed disabling most of the control to the tail surfaces and aft center engine. It is only chance that the airplane was not lost. Douglas has again studied alternative corrective actions and appears to be applying more "Band-Aids." So far they have directed us to install small one-inch diameter, transparent inspection windows through which you can view latch "lock-pin" position, they are revising the rigging instructions to increase lock-pin engagement and they plan to reinforce and stiffen the flexible linkage.

EXHIBIT 1   *(concluded)*

It might well be asked why not make the cargo door latch system really "fool-proof" and leave the cabin floor alone. Assuming it is possible to make the latch fool-proof this doesn't solve the fundamental deficiency in the airplane. A cargo compartment can experience explosive decompression from a number of causes such as: sabotage, mid-air collision, explosion of combustibles in the compartment and perhaps others, any one of which may result in damage which would not be fatal to the DC–10 were it not for the tendency of the cabin floor to collapse. The responsibility for primary damage from these kinds of causes would clearly not be our responsibility; however, we might very well be held responsible for the secondary damage, that is the floor collapse which could cause the loss of the aircraft. It might be asked why we did not originally detail design the cabin floor to withstand the loads of cargo compartment explosive decompression or design blow out panels in the cabin floors to fail in a safe and predictable way.

I can only say that our contract with Douglas provided that Douglas would furnish all design criteria and loads (which in fact they did) and that we would design to satisfy these design criteria and loads (which in fact we did). There is nothing in our experience history which would have led us to expect that the DC–10 cabin floor would be inherently susceptible to catastrophic failure when exposed to explosive decompression of the cargo compartment, and I must presume that there is nothing in Douglas's experience history, which would have led them to expect that the airplane would have this inherent characteristic or they would have provided for this in their loads and criteria which they furnished to us.

My only criticism of Douglas in this regard is that once this inherent weakness was demonstrated by the July 1970 test failure, they did not take immediate steps to correct it. It seems to me inevitable that, in the 20 years ahead of us, DC–10 cargo doors will come open and I would expect this to usually result in the loss of the airplane. [Emphasis added.] This fundamental failure mode has been discussed in the past and is being discussed again in the bowels of both the Douglas and Convair organizations. It appears however that Douglas is waiting and hoping for government direction or regulations in the hope of passing costs on to us or their customers.

If you can judge from Douglas's position during ongoing contract change negotiations they may feel that any liability incurred in the meantime for loss of life, property, and equipment may be legally passed on to us.

It is recommended that overtures be made at the highest management level to persuade Douglas to immediately make a decision to incorporate changes in the DC–10 which will correct the fundamental cabin floor catastrophic failure mode. Correction will take a good bit of time, hopefully there is time before the National Transportation Safety Board (NTSB) or the FAA ground the airplane which would have disastrous effects upon sales and production both near and long term. This corrective action becomes more expensive than the cost of damages resulting from the loss of one plane load of people.

F. D. Applegate
Director of Product Engineering

EXHIBIT 2   The Hurt Memorandum

3 July 1972.

To: M. C. Curtis

From: J. B. Hurt.

Subject: DC–10 Future Accident Liability.

Reference: F. D. Applegate's Memo, same subject, date 27 June 1972.

I do not take issue with the facts or the concern expressed in the referenced memo. However, we should look at the "other side of the coin" in considering the subject. Other considerations include:

1. We did not take exception to the design philosophy established originally by Douglas and by not taking exception, we, in effect, agreed that a proper and safe philosophy was to incorporate inherent and proper safety and reliability in the cargo doors in lieu of designing the floor structure for decompression or providing pressure relief structure for decompressions or providing pressure relief provisions in the floor. The Reliance clause in our contract obligates us in essence to take exception to design philosophy that we know or feel is incorrect or improper and if we do not express such concern, we have in effect shared with Douglas the responsibility for the design philosophy.

2. In the opinion of our Engineering and FAA experts, this design philosophy and the cargo door structures and its original latch mechanism design satisfied FAA requirements and therefore the airplane was theoretically safe and certifiable.

3. In redesigning the cargo door latch mechanism as a result of the first "blowout" experience, Douglas unilaterally considered and rejected the installation of venting provisions in the floor in favor of a "safer" latch mechanism. Convair engineers did discuss the possibility of floor relief provisions with Douglas shortly after the incident, but were told in effect, "We will decide and tell you what changes we feel are necessary and you are to await our directions on redesign." This same attitude is being applied by Douglas today and they are again making unilateral decisions on required corrections as a result of the AAL Detroit incident.

4. We have been informally advised that while Douglas is making near-term corrections to the door mechanism, they are reconsidering the desirability of following-up with venting provisions in the floor.

I have considered recommending to Douglas Major Subcontracts the serious consideration of floor venting provisions based on the concern aptly described by the reference memo, but have not because:

1. I am sure Douglas would immediately interpret such recommendation as a tacit admission on Convair's part that the original concurrence by Convair of the design philosophy was in error and that therefore Convair was liable for all problems and corrections that have subsequently occurred.

EXHIBIT 2   *(concluded)*

2. Introducing such expression at this time while the negotiations of SECP 297 and discussion on its contractual justification are being conducted would introduce confusion and negate any progress that had been made by Convair in establishing a position on the subject. I am not sure that discussion on this subject at the "highest management level" recommended by the referenced memo would produce a different reaction from the one anticipated above. We have an interesting legal and moral problem, and I feel that any direct conversation on this subject with Douglas should be based on the assumption that as a result Convair may subsequently find itself in a position where it must assume all or a significant portion of the costs that are involved.

J. B. Hurt
Program Manager, DC–10 Support Program.

THE McDONNELL DOUGLAS COMPANY

The Davis-Douglas Aircraft Company was founded in 1920 in Long Beach, California, by Donald Douglas with $600 of his own capital and $40,000 from a fellow aviation enthusiast, David R. Davis. Douglas, 28, had studied aeronautical engineering at MIT and had worked for an aircraft company, Glenn L. Martin, for five years. The company's name was changed to the Douglas Aircraft Company in 1921, and in 1928 a new company with the same name was organized in Delaware to take over the assets of the California company. Three hundred thousand shares of stock were issued, of which Donald Douglas received 200,000.

Initially, Douglas built military planes. Its first commercial airplane, the DC–1, appeared in 1933. The plane's designer, Arthur Raymond, felt that for Douglas to be a success with commercial aircraft, the company would have to "build comfort and put wings on it."[3] The DC–1 was quieter and more luxurious than any other planes built at that time. Its successor, the DC–3, appeared two years later and proved to be one of the most successful airplanes ever built. Over 10,000 DC–3s were built for use as transport planes during World War II, and a number of DC–3s were still in service in the 1980s.

Until the mid-1950s, Douglas remained the unchallenged leader in commercial aviation. However, while Douglas abandoned the idea of building a pressurized aircraft in 1940, the Boeing Corporation of Seattle, Washington, and the Lockheed Corporation of Burbank, California, continued to work on pressurized planes. In 1940 Boeing developed the first pressurized passenger airliner, the Model 307 Stratoliner, which carried 33 passengers and traveled

---

[3] Ibid., p. 35.

at 20,000 feet (the DC-3 could carry 20 passengers and flew in the comparatively turbulent air at 11,000 feet). Douglas finally produced a pressurized airplane, the DC-6, in 1946, but only one year later Boeing entered the jet era with the XB-47 bomber. The DC-3 remained an extremely popular airplane, however. In 1950, two thirds of all the aircraft on scheduled service in the noncommunist countries had been built by Douglas, and in 1955 the figure was 50 percent.[4] It was after the appearance of the Boeing 707 in 1957 that Douglas sales began to fall. In 1956 Douglas sold 106 airplanes; in 1957 it sold 167; in 1958 it still sold more planes than Boeing, Convair, Lockheed, and Fairchild together; but in 1959 the company sold only 22 airplanes, while Boeing sold 73 of its 707s.[5]

In the first generation of commerical jet airliners, there were three classes: long-range, mid-range, and short-range. In the long-range category the competitors were the Boeing 707 and the Douglas DC-8. The 707 was a commercial derivative of a military aircraft—the KC-135—for which the government had paid most of the development costs. The development cost of the DC-8 had been paid by Douglas, so the DC-8 always had difficulty being price competitive with the 707. Nevertheless, the DC-8 program was successful. It had a production run of 556, reportedly well above break-even. In the short-range class, the DC-9 was a clear winner over the Boeing 737. However, the Boeing 727 had the crucial mid-range class all to itself and became the biggest money-maker in commercial jet transport history. Douglas's inability to compete with the highly popular 727 contributed to a $75 million loss in 1966, the year in which the company was taken over by the McDonnell Aircraft Company.

The McDonnell Aircraft Company had been founded in St. Louis, Missouri, in 1938, nearly 20 years after the Douglas Company. Its founder, James S. McDonnell, was, like Donald Douglas, a graduate of MIT and had spent a number of years working for other aircraft companies. He started his own company with $165,000 in capital and received no orders for the entire first year of the company's existence. In 1939 McDonnell began making parts for military aircraft, and in 1940 the firm received a contract from the U.S. government to research the use of jet propulsion in military airplanes. Beginning in 1946, McDonnell produced an extremely successful line of fighter planes for the military, including the Phantom jets and the Banshee, Voodoo, and Demon fighters, which were used extensively during the Korean War. By the mid-1960s McDonnell Aircraft was a very successful and profitable company.

In 1963 James McDonnell bought 200,000 shares of stock in the Douglas Aircraft Company but failed to gain control of the company and subsequently sold the stock. In 1966, however, with Douglas facing bankruptcy, McDonnell

---

4 Ibid., p. 41.
5 Ibid., p. 42.

was able to present the most attractive of several offers to take over the company. Under new McDonnell management, production of the DC-8 and DC-9 airplanes at the Long Beach plant continued, and plans started to be developed for the new DC-10 "air-bus." The Douglas plant delivered 195 planes in 1967 and 302 in 1968. Production time was reduced, and Douglas's debts began to be repaid. By July of 1970, *Forbes* could call McDonnell Douglas "perhaps the healthiest major [airplane manufacturing] company."[6] By 1971, the company ranked 45th on the Fortune 500 with sales of $2.1 billion and a net income of $81 million.[7]

THE BUILDING OF THE DC-10

Douglas had begun work on a long-range airliner to carry 400 people in 1965, but when the Boeing 747 was announced in 1966, Douglas decided to slow down its development of the DC-10. The plane was rescheduled to be completed in 1974 or 1975, and Douglas indicated that it hoped waiting would enable the company to build a better airplane. Then in September 1967 Lockheed presented detailed specifications for its L-1011 (later named the TriStar), a wide-bodied, three-engined jumbo jet for short-range to medium-range travel. Realizing that it was going to lose its opportunity in the wide-bodied jet market to the L-1011 and the 747, McDonnell Douglas promptly announced two months later that it would produce the DC-10. The development of the DC-10 and the L-1011 progressed at about the same rate.[8]

Then there was the problem of selling the DC-10 to the airlines, which by 1967 flew primarily Boeing jets. Lockheed and McDonnell Douglas engaged in stiff competition for orders from the major U.S. airlines. Each company tried to present a more favorable package, and concessions were made to the airlines concerning such matters as higher payloads, lower prices, more luxurious interior design, and easier financing.

One concession made by McDonnell Douglas to American Airlines concerned the cargo doors of the DC-10. McDonnell Douglas had planned to use a hydraulic system to close the doors—something the company had used before successfully—but American wanted a door closing mechanism with fewer working parts. The airline's engineers suggested an electrically driven system, and McDonnell Douglas agreed to the change.

American Airlines agreed to buy the DC-10s for $15.3 million each. Then Lockheed announced a price cut to $14.4 million each for its TriStars; and Eastern Airlines, Trans World Airlines, Delta Airlines, and a British corporation named Air Holdings Ltd. announced that they would buy the TriStar. The

---

6 "From Underdog to Top Dog," *Forbes,* July 1, 1970, p. 31.

7 "The Fortune Directory of the 500 Largest Industrial Corporations," *Fortune* 85, no. 5 (May 1972), p. 190.

8 Douglas J. Ingells, *The McDonnell-Douglas Story* (Fallbrook, Calif.: Aero Publishers, 1979), ch. 12.

remaining major American airline, United, finally chose the DC–10 after Douglas lowered the price by $500,000. Considerable pressure was apparently put on United by the other airlines to buy the TriStar; the argument was that if two airbuses were built, both manufacturers would have difficulty remaining financially healthy. Indeed, had United decided to buy the TriStar, the DC–10 program would have ended; the costs were simply too high to continue developing a plane for which there were few orders. However, one of the reasons United's president George Keck gave for choosing the DC–10 was that he felt it would be bad for the industry if McDonnell Douglas were forced out of the commercial airplane business.

Development costs for the TriStar and the DC–10 appeared in 1967 to be about $1 billion for each company.[9] Boeing had committed 90 percent of its net worth, $750 million, to the development of the 747. The 747 had been well received as a long-distance aircraft. In order to succeed, the DC–10 and the TriStar had to prove that they would be efficient at shorter distances. After the United decision, Lockheed had sold a total of 168 TriStars, and McDonnell Douglas had sold 86 DC–10s. Both of the companies faced a 500 unit break-even requirement. By the mid-1970s, due to the tremendous increase in fuel costs and the fact that air passenger traffic did not increase as had been predicted in the 1960s, it was estimated that it would take 15 to 20 years for the giant airplanes to become profitable.

While the TriStar and the DC–10, as they developed, were roughly equivalent in interior and exterior appearance, there were several major design differences. Large aircraft used hydraulic systems to enable the pilot to operate the controls easily. They employed "redundant" hydraulic systems: That is, while only one system was actually necessary to operate the airplane's controls, one or two parallel systems were installed to enable the plane to function in the event that one or even two of the systems stopped working. The pilot of a smaller jet such as the DC–9 might possibly be strong enough to manipulate the controls of that plane if all three hydraulic systems failed, but this was not the case with the jumbo jets. If their hydraulic systems did not work, the pilot had no way of operating the plane's controls. For this reason, both Boeing and Lockheed decided to install four hydraulic systems in the 747 and the TriStar. Indeed, the crash of a 747 in San Francisco in June 1971 was averted by the fourth hydraulic system when the other three were severed during a takeoff mishap. However, McDonnell Douglas decided to put only three hydraulic systems in the DC–10.

One of the major dangers to any of the wide-bodied jets was "explosive decompression." This problem was associated with the fact that these aircraft, like other jets, flew at 20,000 feet and above, where the atmosphere was extremely thin. Since passengers could not breathe the air at that height, jets that traveled there had to be pressurized—that is, the atmosphere inside the

---

9 Ibid., p. 81.

plane had to be similar in pressure and oxygen content to that near the ground. Thus, when a plane reached the higher atmosphere above 11,000 feet, the pressure inside the plane was considerably greater than that outside it. Normally this was no problem, as the aircraft's hull was built to withstand the pressure, which in the case of a wide-bodied aircraft was about 20,000 tons, or seven and one half to nine pounds per square inch. But problems arose if a hole developed in the fuselage. This could happen in a number of ways: Two airplanes could collide, a bomb might go off in a plane, or a door could come off; in fact, birds had even been known to crash through the pilot's windows. A small hole could be tolerated without difficulty—the air pressure was simply turned up to compensate for the leak. However, if a large hole appeared suddenly in the fuselage, the air inside the plane would rush out at tremendous speed to equalize the pressure inside and outside the plane. This was called "explosive decompression." Internal panels and floors, not as strong as the hull of the airplane, would collapse under the pressure of the escaping air.

A further complication was the fact that the 747, TriStar, and DC–10 all had their vital hydraulic tubes running under the floor of the passenger cabin. Beneath the passenger area was the baggage compartment with its cargo doors. Should one of the cargo doors come off or a bomb of moderate size explode, at least part of the cabin floor would collapse as the air from the passenger cabin above rushed down and out, and some of the hydraulic systems could be severed. In the case of the 747, there were two hydraulic systems on either side of the floor close to the hull wall, and that part of the floor was reinforced by braces. It was unlikely that both sides of the floor would collapse except in the case of a large explosion which, Boeing reasoned, would probably destroy the hull as well. Furthermore, the 747's control cables ran through the plane's ceiling, so that even if only one hydraulic system remained, the plane's controls would function. The TriStar and the DC–10, however, ran both control cables and hydraulic systems under the floor, so that a floor collapse could easily sever all controls and prove disastrous.

An obvious solution to the problem was to make the floors of the wide-bodied jets strong enough to withstand a sudden depressurization, or to vent them so that air could rush through without crushing the floor. However, the weight of a sufficiently reinforced floor would have meant reducing the number of passengers the jets could carry by about 12, and McDonnell Douglas felt this would be unacceptable to the airlines. Placing enough vents in the floor to withstand loss of pressure was also a problem. Passengers and luggage could block the vents, and it was questionable whether such a vented floor would be strong enough to support the passengers.

Another way of making the floor collapse unlikely was to make the cargo doors "fail-safe"—that is, to make it impossible for them to come off. The ideal door for this purpose was a "plug" door. This type of door opened into the airplane and was larger than its frame. When closed, the internal pressure pushed the door tighter against its frame, making it impossible for the door to come open. Passenger doors on the wide-bodied jets were of the plug type. There were, however, disadvantages to the plug door: it was heavy, it had to open into the cargo hold, and it had to be very rigid, which meant that it did not bend in response to stress during flight with the rest of the aircraft's frame. Weight had to be kept to a minimum in large aircraft. The airlines wanted to carry as many passengers as possible, and that meant minimizing the weight of parts such as doors. The airlines were also unenthusiastic about doors that opened into the plane and took up valuable cargo space. So a door that opened outward was highly desirable.

The TriStar's solution to the dilemma was a "semi-plug" door, which had been used successfully on the Boeing 727. It opened outward from hinges at the top. Along the sides of both door and frame were a series of steel "teeth." When the door was closed (by an electric motor), the teeth of the door passed between those on the frame. Once the door's teeth had passed the ones on the frame, the motor moved the door down several inches until the teeth of the door were directly behind those on the frame. In this position, the door would act as a plug: The pressure inside the door would push it more tightly closed.

The DC–10's cargo door opened outward like those of the 747 and the TriStar. However, it relied on its latching system to hold it in place. It used a series of "over-center" latches, which required a certain amount of pressure to push them down and around a latching bar at the bottom of the door frame. Once past the center of their arc, the latches could not be pushed back except with a pressure equal to that which had pushed them down to begin with. (The principle was similar to that of a light switch.) Thus, the latches could not slip back and open. However, they *had* to move the correct distance around the latching bar in order to stay closed. If they or the motor or the door itself were out of adjustment, it would be possible for the door to appear to be latched when in fact the latches had not gone completely around the bars. Furthermore, the person closing the door had no way of seeing the latching system, which was located inside the door. For this reason, it was necessary to have a back-up system to detect whether or not the latches had gone all the way around the latching bars. The DC–10 used a series of locking pins that were supposed to slide into position only after the latches were properly locked. The baggage handler, whose job it was to close the door, had to press an electric switch, which shut the door, then one to latch it. Finally, he manually pushed down a lever to send the locking pins into place. The locking pin mechanism hit a switch as it went down, and this turned off a warning light in the pilot's cabin, indicating that the door was locked. Unfortunately a torque tube in the linkage between the lever that the baggage handler pushed and the locking pins was weak and could be bent rather easily. Thus, the lever could be pushed all the way down even if the latches were not over center, and the locking pins would not go all the way down. The light could go off in the cockpit, making the crew think the door was closed. The plane could then take off with an improperly closed door and with a real possibility of explosive decompression.

CONVAIR

Since a vast number of parts were needed for an aircraft such as the DC–10, many of them were made by subcontractors, and one such subcontract went to the Convair Division of General Dynamics Corporation. General Dynamics had experienced serious financial problems in recent years. Indeed, the company's performance in 1971 earned it the dubious distinction of being labeled as one of the 10 worst performers on the Fortune 500. The St. Louis–based firm had a net income of $22 million in 1971 on sales of $1.9 billion. As the 41st-ranked company on the Fortune 500 list in 1970, General Dynamics had also been one of the worst performers with losses of $6.5 million on sales of $2.2 billion.[10]

Convair was to do the detail design of the fuselage and doors of the DC–10 according to McDonnell Douglas specifications. The original contract between McDonnell Douglas and Convair called for a hydraulic system to close the cargo door latches. The doors were also to have a manual locking system designed so that the handle or latch lever could not be stowed unless the door was properly closed and latched. However, in November 1968 McDonnell Douglas told Convair that electrical rather than hydraulic actuators were to be used for the door latching system. This, McDonnell Douglas said, would make each door 28 pounds lighter, and American Airlines had requested the electric system because they felt it would be easier to maintain. The hydraulic system was preferred by the Convair engineers because its fluid maintained a constant pressure on the latches while the door was closed, rather than having its power shut off like an electric current as soon as a switch was released. In addition, in the hydraulic system, unlike the electrical one, the latches could slide back if they were not completely around the latching bars, allowing the door to open as soon as moderate pressure developed inside the aircraft.

In mid-1969, Convair wrote up a "Failure Mode and Effects Analysis" (FMEA) for the DC–10 cargo door to indicate how likely the door was to fail and what the consequences would be. FMEAs would be given to McDonnell Douglas regarding the safety of all major systems of the plane, and McDonnell Douglas would likewise send FMEAs to the Federal Aviation Administration in Washington before the plane could be certificated for flight. Convair warned that there were several ways in which the cargo door might not be closed properly and could subsequently come open during flight. It classified this as a "Class 4 hazard," meaning one involving danger to the lives of the passengers and the possible crash of the plane. The FMEA indicated that the warning light in the cockpit might go off because of problems in the circuit regardless of whether the door was closed and that ground crews could, after visually checking the position of the manually operated door handle, mistakenly think it was in the closed position when it was not. When FMEAs were finally submitted to the Federal Aviation Administration by McDonnell Douglas,

---

10 The Fortune Directory of the 500 Largest Industrial Corporations," p. 190 and p. 172.

however, they did not discuss the possibility that serious hazards were associated with the cargo doors. General Dynamics was forbidden by its contract with McDonnell Douglas to discuss any DC–10 problems with the Federal Aviation Administration.

In May 1970 the air conditioning system of "Ship 1," the first DC–10 to be completed, was tested at the Douglas plant in Long Beach. This meant that the plane was pressurized. When the pressure reached about four pounds per square inch, the forward lower cargo door blew out. The escaping air caused part of the passenger cabin floor to collapse. The mishap was blamed on a mechanic who, the company said, closed the door incorrectly. Nevertheless, McDonnell Douglas decided to modify the cargo door and install a small vent door in it. The purpose of this smaller door was to serve as a check as to whether the cargo door was properly closed. The vent was closed by the handle, which pushed down the locking pins. When the handle moved all the way down, the vent door closed. But, as was mentioned earlier, the locking pin linkage could bend, and the pins would not go down. The handle, however—and therefore the vent door—could reach their closed position without indicating anything about the condition of the locking mechanism. Boeing had used a similar check on its 747 door (which used a hydraulic system to operate the latches), but their vent doors were closed by the locking pin mechanism and could not close if the pins did not reach their correct position.

An argument between McDonnell Douglas and Convair ensued over who would pay for the installation of vent doors. McDonnell Douglas argued that the vent door was a normal design change, which Convair should have expected; it was Convair's fault that the floor had collapsed. There was a flaw in the floor design, and Convair had not told McDonnell Douglas about it as required by their contract. Therefore, Convair should pay for the vent doors. Convair, on the other hand, maintained that the door design was satisfactory, and if Douglas insisted upon modifying it, there were better ways of doing so. Vent doors were installed, but the disagreement over who should pay was not resolved.

Despite the seriousness of the door problem, the DC–10 was completed and certified as airworthy by the Federal Aviation Administration on July 29, 1971. Shortly thereafter, delivery of the planes to their buyers began.

THE ROLE OF THE FEDERAL AGENCIES

The Federal Aviation Administration (FAA) was established by an act of Congress in 1958 and was responsible for the regulation of safety standards in American aviation and the promotion of its commercial success. It licensed pilots and airports and operated air traffic control systems. It had to approve each step in the designing and manufacturing of all American aircraft, and it certificated them as "airworthy" when they were completed. It had the power to inspect any aircraft manufacturing plant whenever it chose.

The FAA did not, it claimed, have enough personnel to carry out all the inspections necessary for the certification of an airplane. Therefore, the FAA appointed "Designated Engineering Representatives" (DERs) who were engineers employed by the aircraft manufacturers. It was the responsibility of the DERs to inspect the parts of a plane as they were built and make sure that they complied with FAA regulations. Of the 42,950 inspections conducted on parts of the DC-10 as it was built, about one fourth were done by FAA inspectors, and the remainder were carried out by McDonnell Douglas engineers in their capacity as DERs.

The National Transportation Safety Board (NTSB) was responsible for the investigation of accidents. However, if its investigation revealed the need for some change in an aircraft or its manner of operation, enforcing the change was the job of the FAA. The FAA had the right to order that the change be made by issuing an airworthiness directive, which had the force of a federal law.

In the case of the Windsor incident, the NTSB—after an initial refusal by McDonnell Douglas to disclose any information on cargo door problems—examined the company's records and found that there had been about 100 reports of problems with the closing of DC-10 cargo doors. The electric actuators sometimes failed to drive the over-center latches all the way around the latching bars. McDonnell Douglas had first tried lubricating the latching bars. When that did not work, the company sent out a service bulletin to all purchasers of DC-10s, recommending that the airlines install heavier gauge wire in the power supply to the actuators to increase their power. The airlines involved (United, American, National, and Continental) had been in the process of making this alteration at the time of the Windsor mishap, but the rewiring had not yet been done on the plane involved in that incident.

The NTSB investigators recommended that it be made "physically impossible" to close the cargo doors improperly. The FAA did not want to ground all the DC-10s, because a large number were involved, and because air traffic during the summer of 1972 was particularly heavy.

The western regional office of the Federal Aviation Administration, headed by Arvin O. Basnight, began drafting the first of a series of airworthiness directives, which Basnight assumed would be used to enforce modifications to the DC-10 cargo door. The first airworthiness directive would make mandatory the rewiring of the doors, which had been recommended in the McDonnell Douglas service bulletin. Subsequently, the installation of a peephole in the doors would be required. The peephole would be one-inch square and would be placed over one of the locking pins. This would enable the person closing the door to look in and actually see that one of the pins had moved to its proper position—eliminating the major problem that the baggage handler had no way of seeing whether the door was closed.

But the airworthiness directives were never issued. On the morning of June 16, 1972, Mr. Basnight received a telephone call from the president of McDonnell Douglas' Douglas Division, Jackson McGowen. McGowen told Basnight that he had talked the previous evening with John H. Shaffer, the new administrator of the FAA appointed by president Richard M. Nixon. Shaffer had indicated that since McDonnell Douglas had been so cooperative with the FAA, there would be no need for the issuance of airworthiness directives against the company. Instead, McDonnell Douglas and the FAA would make a "gentlemen's agreement" that the required work would be done. Basnight and his colleagues in the western division did not feel that such an agreement would be a sufficient remedy, nor that the rewiring would resolve the door closing problem, but their opinion was overruled by the Washington office. Arvin Basnight wrote an account of these events in a "Memorandum to File" dated June 20, 1972, which is reproduced in Exhibit 3.

EXHIBIT 3 The Basnight Memorandum to File

On Friday, 16 June 1972, at 8:50 A.M., I received a phone call from Mr. Jack McGowan [sic], president, Douglas Aircraft Company, who indicated that late on Thursday, 15 June, he had received a call from Mr. Shaffer asking what the company had found out about the problem about the cargo door that caused American Airlines to have an explosive decompression.

Mr. McGowan [sic] said he had reviewed with the Administrator the facts developed which included the need to beef up the electrical wiring and related factors that had been developed by the Douglas Company working with FAA.

He indicated that Mr. Shaffer had expressed pleasure in the finding of reasonable corrective actions and had told Mr. McGowan that the corrective measures could be undertaken as a product of a Gentleman's Agreement thereby not requiring the issuance of an FAA Airworthiness Directive.

In light of this data, I consulted with Dick Sliff[a] as we were already preparing an airworthiness directive and Mr. Sliff advised that several steps seemed advisable to prevent future explosive decompression on the DC–10 cargo door and the Air Worthiness Directive Board was reviewing what we considered an appropriate airworthiness directive.

Mr. Sliff also indicated that earlier in the week when FAA engineers contacted the Douglas Company, the company people had not made available any reports indicating problems encountered by the operating airlines with the cargo doors. Mr. Sliff stated that he had raised a fuss because they had not produced the information and on the following day (which was about Wednesday) the company had produced data showing that approximately 100 complaints had been received by the company indicating that the airlines using the DC–10 had noted and reported to the company mechanical problems in locking the bulk cargo doors. Mr. Sliff was disturbed by the company's attitude and felt they had not performed well in that their cooperation with the FAA in considering this data had been unresponsive.

With Mr. Sliff present, I called Mr. Rudolf, FS–1,[b] and reviewed with him what we were doing, the background data available to me and informed him our Airworthiness Board was in session and asked his guidance as to their continuing this effort. He suggested we continue what we were doing and wanted a copy of our draft air

---

[a] Richard Sliff, then Chief of the Aircraft Engineering Division, Western Region, FAA.
[b] James Rudolph, director of Flight Standards Service, FAA, Washington, D.C.

EXHIBIT 3   *(continued)*

worthiness directive, which Mr. Sliff had already furnished the Washington office by telecopier.

Later in the day, I received a call from Ken Smith, DA-1,[c] and reviewed basically the same background information, the action of our Airworthiness Board, our judgment as to the appropriateness of issuing an airworthiness directive and was asked by Mr. Smith why our MRRs[d] had not made known the problem of the DC-10 bulk cargo doors so that we were as well informed as to their proper function at the Douglas Company. My response was the reporting system had not disclosed this type of data, the reason for which I would research and advise him.

Mr. Smith queried particularly why the Douglas Company's attitude might be one of not revealing the record of difficulty with the cargo doors to the FAA. Mr. Smith indicated that he concurred with our judgment that an airworthiness directive should be issued and that he would consult with the Administrator.

The Airworthiness Board continued to meet and refine the earlier drafted directive, and I continued to expect some advice from Washington as to a directive being issued. Quite late in the day, having received no advice, we called Mr. Rudolph again and were advised that they had had difficulty locating Mr. Shaffer, but Mr. Smith and Mr. Rudolph together discussed the matter with me. They were planning to have a conference by telephone with the Douglas Company and the three airlines using the DC-10 equipment to assure that the objectives for effective operation of the DC-10 cargo doors sought by our proposed draft of an airworthiness directive were accomplished.

Additional time passed and we had no further advice so I again called Mr. Rudolph as we had learned through the Douglas Company that the Telecon had taken place and that steps were being taken to accomplish the objective of the proposed airworthiness directive.

Significance of this action includes the fact the drafted airworthiness directive was upgraded by the Airworthiness Directive Board based on data our engineering personnel had worked out with the Douglas Company to add an additional provision that would require drilling the fuselage near the lock bolts on the cargo door to allow a visual inspection of the locking mechanism after the doors were closed.

We so informed Mr. Rudolph at this time and asked him if it would be possible to include this provision in what we then understood to be the message transmitted by the deputy administrator to the Douglas Company and the three airlines involved.

Mr. Rudolph indicated that it was then after office hours in Washington. The message containing basically our draft phraseology had been released by Mr. Smith and since it was over the deputy administrator's signature, Mr. Rudolph could not modify the language and suggested we work the problem on Monday, but indicated he agreed with our proposed amendment.

Early on Monday, 19 June, I received a phone call from Joe Ferrarese, Acting FS-2,[e] who stated that present with him was Mr. Slaughter, chief, engineering and manufacturing division, FS-100, and that they were calling to advise that the teletype

[c] Deputy Administrator, FAA, Washington, D.C.

[d] MRR—Mechanical Reliability Reports, regularly sent to the FAA by the airlines.

[e] Mr. Rudolph's deputy.

EXHIBIT 3 *(concluded)*

message signed by Mr. Smith and transmitted by Mr. Rudolph relating to the DC–10 cargo doors had been distributed to the three regions where the DC–10s are in primary use and that he was acting on instructions to ask that we destroy all but one copy of this message.

I then told Mr. Ferrarese that I had not seen the message, but would conform with his instruction. Shortly thereafter, the message came in a sealed envelope through our Duty Officer in three copies. I discussed the matter with Messrs. Blanchard and Sliff. We then called Mr. Ferrarese back, told him we had the message, were destroying all but one copy and reviewed with him Mr. Smith's inquiry regarding the MRRs.

I explained I had not engaged in trying to gain Mr. Smith's understanding of the scope of MRRs on Friday, but that I was sure he [Ferrarese] appreciated that the MRRs were designed to cover what was then considered to be significant safety factors involving maintenance and reliability and had not included items such as cargo doors which in earlier forms of aircraft were not judged to be critical to the equipment safety. Therefore, the MRRs available to us could not reasonably be expected to include data in this subject area.

There are other reports called Maintenance Information Summaries which include data of this category in abbreviated form which had surfaced some 10 entries indicating such matters as AAL's N105 Trip 96/11 being delayed 18 minutes at Los Angeles on account of difficulty in locking the bulk cargo door.[f] This data normally is processed with a 30-day time delay and our FAA processes would not normally have surfaced a significant problem with the cargo door from this source of information, but that is retrospect, our personnel concentrating on scanning numerous entries of this nature had disclosed these 10 entries.

I gave the original of the message signed by Mr. Smith and transmitted by Mr. Rudolph to Mr. Sliff for his Aircraft Engineering records and destroyed the other two copies in the presence of Messrs. Blanchard and Sliff.

Signed

ARVIN O. BASNIGHT
Director, Western Region
20 June 1972

---

[f] An American DC–10 flight from Los Angeles to New York, via Chicago.

The FAA sent a request to all the airlines asking that they complete the wiring modifications in the McDonnell Douglas Service Bulletin and install warning placards telling baggage handlers not to use more than 50 pounds of pressure in closing the cargo doors. McDonnell Douglas then sent out several additional Service Bulletins. An "Alert" Service Bulletin—meaning that the modification involved safety—asked the airlines to install the peephole, as well as a decal showing what the baggage handler should see if the locking pin was in its proper position. A second routine Service Bulletin instructed the airlines to place a support plate on the torque tube which was likely to bend if too much pressure was applied in closing the cargo door. This would mean that 440 pounds of pressure would have to be used in closing the door—more than a human being could exert. The locking pins were also to be adjusted so that they would have to travel one quarter of an inch further, which would make it more obvious if the mechanism jammed against latches which were not over center.

Then in February of 1973, after President Nixon had fired John Shaffer and replaced him with Alexander Butterfield,[11] the FAA wrote to all three jumbo jet manufacturers and asked them to reassess their designs in light of the Windsor incident. Specifically, the FAA wanted the manufacturers either to strengthen the floor and add vents to combat the effects of explosive decompression, or reroute the control and hydraulic systems away from the passenger cabin floor. Boeing and Lockheed responded indignantly that their doors were not the same as those of the DC–10, and Boeing pointed out that its control cables did not run under the floor. McDonnell Douglas maintained that the possibility of a door coming open in flight was 'extremely remote.'[12] This time, the Washington office of the FAA asked the Western Region office to obtain more information, and the Western Region office responded:

> We are aware of no subsequent service difficulties [since Windsor] which would constitute a basis for recertification [of the DC–10 floor]. In the light of the above, we feel that an investigation of the detailed nature presented in the memo of 30 May 1973 would be premature.[13]

---

[11] Butterfield was later to gain a degree of fame as the Watergate witness who revealed the existence of the secret recording system in the Oval Office during the Nixon presidency.

[12] Eddy et al., *Destination Disaster,* pp. 162–63.

[13] Ibid., p. 163.

Equity Funding Corporation of America

Ronald Secrist was worried. Even at the last minute he debated about whether he should go through with his plan. The former administrative officer of Equity Funding Life Insurance Company, a subsidiary of Equity Funding Corporation of America, sat next to the telephone in his empty home. His wife was at work, and their three children had left for school. What about their safety? Shouldn't that concern him more than the shady dealings he knew were going on at Equity Funding? If the people at the company had the power to keep a fraud of such magnitude a secret for so many years, what retribution might await the person who exposed it? There had been rumors of Mafia connections at the company; indeed, one officer had told Secrist that he could get a contract on the life of anyone who talked. What if the authorities didn't believe him? He was still not sure he had enough information to make a case that they would investigate. But this dilemma had been eating away at him for three years. He had felt he would have to say something eventually, but he had to have a job; he had to provide for his family. After all, changing companies four times in the last 12 years did not look good on a resume. So he had gone along with the Equity Funding scheme, all the while plotting ways to expose it. Now that the company had fired him and he had another job, he decided the time was finally at hand. He picked up the receiver and dialed the number of the New York Insurance Department. When that was over, he made another call.

Raymond Dirks, vice president of Delafield Childs, a Wall Street research firm, had found Ron Secrist's story difficult to believe. The New York securities analyst had received a call from Secrist one morning in early March 1973. The man had been fired from his job at Equity Funding Corporation of America, and now he wanted to tell the world that the company was a fraud. An obvious attempt at revenge, it appeared. But there had been rumors about Equity Funding before, and frankly Dirks had never thought much of this "go-go" company himself. The insurance industry, he felt, was generally un-

---

This case drew heavily on Raymond L. Dirks and Leonard Gross, *The Great Wall Street Scandal* (New York: McGraw-Hill, 1974), for details related to the Equity Funding scandal.

99

ethical—and why had Equity Funding prospered during years when so many other insurance companies had gone under? Dirks decided to do some investigating on his own. He talked to present and former employees of Equity Funding, a number of executives of organizations that were clients of his firm, and everyone else he could think of who might have information on Equity Funding. Gradually he developed a picture of what had gone on. Partly because of his efforts, Equity Funding Corporation was exposed as one of the most spectacular frauds in the recent history of American business. On March 27, 1973, the New York Stock Exchange suspended trading in the company's stock, and a full investigation was undertaken.

But during his inquiry into the activities of Equity Funding, Raymond Dirks had gotten himself into serious trouble with the New York Stock Exchange and the Securities and Exchange Commission. In the process of corroborating what he had learned with several of his firm's large institutional clients, Dirks had let them know that something was apparently wrong at Equity Funding. Some of them had sold large blocks of their Equity Funding stock. The other institutions and companies that had purchased that stock and had been left holding it when trading was suspended were now suing Dirks for millions of dollars. The Stock Exchange and the SEC accused Dirks of passing inside information to the institutions that "dumped" their stock. Not so, maintained Dirks. The people from whom he had obtained his leads had not been insiders. The insiders had been busy covering everything up. In fact, had he *not* told his clients and thus caused the stock price to drop suddenly, the scandal might have taken much longer to expose.

THE BEGINNINGS

The company, which was to become Equity Funding, was established in 1960 as Tongor Corporation, and a year later the name was changed to Equity Funding Corporation of America. One of the company's founders, Gordon McCormick, leading salesman in the United States for the Keystone mutual fund, had an idea for selling a package combining life insurance and mutual funds, which he felt would be extremely attractive to buyers of insurance. Equity Funding Corporation was organized to sell McCormick's package, which became known as the *Equity Funding concept*. As the program was sold, the customer signed up for both life insurance and mutal fund shares. He first bought a certain number of shares in the mutual fund, and these could then be used as collateral for a loan from Equity Funding Corporation to pay the premium on an insurance policy. Each year for 10 years the customer would buy more shares and borrow against them to pay his annual insurance premium. In recent years the purchaser had to pay a minimum of $300 per year for insurance and purchase at least $750 worth of mutual fund shares annually. At the end of 10 years, the customer sold enough shares to pay off the loans from Equity Funding. If the mutual funds had performed well during this time, the customer would have enough shares to repay his debt, have a nice profit in excess shares, and own a valuable life insurance policy as well. In addition, if the shares had not depreciated in value, he would have had 10 years of free life insurance. The salesman who talked the client into buying the package received a double commission.

This was an ideal time to be in the life insurance business. An average life insurance stock rose 100 percent during 1961,[1] and Equity Funding prospered. The major thrust of the company's business was not selling to people who had no life insurance, but rather convincing people who already had policies to cancel them and switch to the insurance-mutual funds combination. Insurance companies called this *twisting,* but Equity Funding referred to it as *restructuring.*[2] Customers were attracted by the prospect of a considerably higher return on their investments, but, at the same time, the practice did not endear Equity Funding Corporation to the rest of the insurance industry. While twisting was a relatively common practice in the industry, it had never before been used as the basis for a company's existence.

Equity Funding went public in 1964, and it was soon after this event that the fraudulent activities began. Shortly after the company's founding, Gordon McCormick's shares in it had been purchased by his four associates in the venture: Stanley Goldblum, Michael Riordan, Eugene Cuthbertson, and Raymond Platt. Platt died in 1964, and Cuthbertson quit the company the following year, leaving Goldblum and Riordan in control.

Michael Riordan was an outgoing Irishman whose favorite song was "The Impossible Dream." His father was vice president of Abraham and Strauss and owned a controlling interest in Stern's Department Store. Riordan was a great promoter, was excellent with the sales force, and had a personality that seemed to magnetize people. He was also a heavy drinker and a ladies' man. As chairman of the board of Equity Funding, it was he who thought up new ventures and maintained contact with Wall Street, where he had many close friends. He also provided much of the drive behind the company's sales force.

Stanley Goldblum had worked in a meat-packing plant, rose rapidly to plant supervisor, and then quit to sell insurance. He was variously described by people who knew him as cold, standoffish, authoritarian, arrogant, offensive, untrustworthy, and a loner who had little appreciation for other people's time. One insurance analyst told a *Wall Street Journal* reporter, "If you wanted to describe a man in the insurance business as someone you wouldn't want to do business with, you described him as another Stanley Goldblum."[3] Yet Glodblum's few close friends described him as warm and generous. He made substantial contributions to charity and political campaigns, including over $30,000 worth of Equity Funding stock to the Nixon reelection campaign,

---

[1] Raymond L. Dirks and Leonard Gross, *The Great Wall Street Scandal* (New York: McGraw-Hill, 1974), p. 29.

[2] Dirks and Gross, *Great Wall Street Scandal,* p. 30.

[3] Hal Lancaster and G. Christian Hill, "Stanley Goldblum Is a Man of Many Facets—But What Are They?" *The Wall Street Journal,* April 27, 1973, p. 17.

and he constantly gave money out of his own pocket to his brother and other people. Goldblum enjoyed high living. An athletic man, he had a $100,000 gym built onto his $300,000 home. He drove two Rolls Royces and a Ferrari, owned a 35-foot racing yacht, and was a knowledgeable art collector. By the early 1970s he was estimated to be worth $30 million. As president of Equity Funding Corporation, Goldblum managed the company and stayed in the background, leaving dealings with the public to Riordan. Ironically, Goldblum was often characterized by acquaintances and employees as straight-laced and puritanical. He became chairman of the National Association of Securities Dealers' business conduct committee during his tenure at Equity Funding. In that capacity he meted out harsh penalties in cases that came before him and was especially concerned with irregularities in the insurance industry. "I was completely taken in by Stanley Goldblum," said Lawrence Williams, vice president for Compliance at Equity Funding and former enforcement officer at the Securities and Exchange Commission. "He [Goldblum] gave the impression that if he caught somebody stealing he wanted him *out*. He seemed so upright."[4]

Stanley Goldblum now appears to have been the major force behind the Equity Funding fraud, which seemingly stemmed from his obsession with keeping the price of Equity Funding's stock continually on the rise. If the stock price could be kept high, Equity Funding would be able to make acquisitions by trading valuable stock for the assets of other companies. The earnings of the companies thus acquired could be added in with those of the parent company, making Equity Funding appear to be increasing earnings when, in fact, it was losing money. The high stock price was also important in convincing banks to lend money to the company and in compensating the company's sales force, which was done largely by giving the salespeople stock options.

THE RISE OF EQUITY FUNDING

Through 1965, Equity Funding Corporation sold insurance and mutual funds as an agent for other companies—principally Pennsylvania Life Insurance Company of Philadelphia and the Keystone mutual funds organization in Boston—and most of its income came from commissions. It did begin to finance some program loans of its own in 1964, however. In 1966, according to a later Equity Funding prospectus, the company sold $226.3 million worth of insurance policies, mostly those of Pennsylvania Life. In addition, while mutual fund sales dropped substantially in that year nationally, Equity Funding reported a 47 percent increase in profits and a 58 percent increase ($6 million)

---

[4] Wyndham Robertson, "Those Daring Young Con Men of Equity Funding: The Full Story of an Incredible Fraud," *Fortune* 88, no. 2 (August 1973), p. 85.

in program loans, $4 million of which it had financed itself.[5] With this kind of rise in the company's earnings, its stock price went steadily upward.

It was in November of that profitable year that Equity Funding received permission to list its common stock on the American Stock Exchange. In the November/December issue of its publication *American Investor,* the American Stock Exchange noted the following progress being made in its operations:

> *Listing Standards.* Twice since 1962 standards have been raised or supplemented. More important, companies that exceed the higher standards are being attracted to the Exchange. The average newly listed common stock in 1965 represented a company with net tangible assets of more than $6 million (the criterion is $1 million). Similarly, standards for net income, number of shares publicly held, and number of shareholders are being exceeded by wide margins.
>
> Establishment of delisting criteria has resulted in removal of more than 100 issues.[6]

It was also in 1966 that Equity Funding Corporation started its own mutual fund, Equity Growth Fund of America, and the following year it rapidly began to acquire other companies. The year 1967 saw the purchase of Presidential Life Insurance Company of America, a Chicago-based firm. During 1968 and 1969, Equity Funding acquired Bankers National Life Insurance Company of Parsippany, New Jersey; Northern Life Insurance Company of Seattle; a savings and loan association; a mutual funds company; and Investors Planning Corporation, the domestic assets of a Swiss firm called Investors Overseas Services. (Investors Overseas Services was soon to become embroiled in a scandal of its own that involved the transference of millions of dollars of the company's assets to other companies controlled by IOS's chairman of the board Robert Vesco. Also implicated in this far-reaching scheme were a nephew of Richard Nixon, a son of the late Franklin D. Roosevelt, the president of Costa Rica and his son, and a former Cuban foreign minister.)

Equity Funding also entered the oil and gas exploration and cattle breeding businesses. All the while, the corporation's stock continued to soar. By 1969, the stock, which had started out at $6 a share in 1964, was selling for $80 a share.

But 1969 was a significant year for Equity Funding in other ways. It saw the death of Michael Riordan in a mudslide that engulfed his home, and there were problems with retraining the low-caliber sales force of Investors Planning Corporation and meeting rapidly increasing expenses. Despite these setbacks, Equity Funding reported an earnings increase of nearly 40 percent. Program loans funded by the company had jumped from $19.9 million to $29.5

---

[5] Ibid., p. 120.

[6] "Time of Change," *American Investor* 2, no. 10 (November–December 1966), p. 10.

million.[7] Perhaps the most significant event of all was an agreement entered into by Presidential Life Insurance Company (the Equity Funding subsidiary) with Ranger National Life Insurance Company, whereby Ranger National would reinsure a large amount of Presidential's business. (Presidential also had reinsurance arrangements with other companies.) Reinsuring, a widespread practice in the insurance industry, meant that Ranger National purchased for a substantial sum policies that Presidential sold. Presidential thus acquired needed cash, and Ranger National was promised most of the future premiums from the policies it bought. The details of the deal were later described in *Fortune* as follows:

> The new agreement provided that Ranger would take on all of Presidential's business not [re]insured elsewhere in the second half of 1969, and would also get certain other new business through 1973. Over the entire four-and-a-half-year period, Ranger would [re]insure business represented by a maximum of $15 million in first-year premiums. At the end of 1972, Ranger held some $835 million of insurance in force that had been ceded from the Equity Funding subsidiary.
>
> There was one peculiar aspect to the deal. Presidential, whose name was changed to Equity Funding Life Insurance Company (EFLIC) in 1970, *guaranteed* a "persistency rate" of 85 percent in the second year. That is, it guaranteed that policyholders representing 85 percent of the first-year premiums would also pay in the second year—or EFLIC would make up the difference. This unusual provision served as a "kicker" that enticed the [re]insurers to pay more than they normally would have for the business. Under most [re]insurance agreements, the [re]insurer pays around 100 to 120 percent of the first-year premium (which is a bit less than what it would have cost the [re]insurer to write the business itself). But the persistency guarantee assured the [re]insurer of getting back most of its cash outlay by the second year; in addition, the guarantee strongly implied that EFLIC viewed the policyholders as loyal. For these reasons it was able to get 180 percent—and, in some recent agreements, 190 percent.
>
> In practice, this meant that EFLIC would keep the first-year premium and receive an additional 80 percent (or 90 percent) in cash from Ranger. The arrangement naturally did a lot for EFLIC's profits. The costs charged against the [re]insured business in the first year showed up as a little less than the amount of the first-year premium. Hence EFLIC netted a little *more* than the [re]insurance payment. In 1969, thanks to several such [re]insurance agreements, EFLIC contributed significantly to Equity Funding's profits. Altogether, it accounted for about 20 percent of the parent's reported aftertax earnings.[8]

Apparently this arrangement and others like it provided the setting for a major part of the scandal at Equity Funding, which was centered in the Equity Funding Life Insurance Company subsidiary. But the fraud had its beginnings much earlier.

---

[7] Robertson, "Those Daring Young Con Men," p. 22.

[8] Ibid., p. 122.

THE FALL

As events have been reconstructed, the fraud at Equity Funding Corporation began with overstatement of assets. While Equity Funding's prospectus of May 25, 1967, indicated that "the greater part" of its $226.3 million worth of life insurance sold in 1966 had been policies of Pennsylvania Life Insurance Company, Pennnsylvania Life's own prospectus, dated June 22, 1967, reported that "a total of $58.6 million of face amount of life insurance was sold by Equity Funding agents." No one caught the discrepancy until Alan Abelson of *Barrons* wrote in his "Up and Down Wall Street" column on April 16, 1973:

> Circumstantial evidence . . . indicates that Equity Funding might have been cooking its books a lot earlier than anyone has yet suggested. The possibility was raised to us by a keen-eyed reader with a long memory. And, with the help of our colleague Steve Anreder, we secured a couple of old prospectuses and did a little sleuthing, all of which tends to confirm the suspicion.[9]

Abelson then went on to describe the difference in figures noted above. Apparently earnings were inflated every year after 1966. Of the $6 million in program loans reported sold in 1966, $4 million appear never to have existed. Loans were simply invented and then counted as assets. Nevertheless, in March 1968, Equity Funding's auditors issued an unqualified certification of the company's 1967 financial statement. In later years, the company listed nonexistent bonds and securities as assets and even went so far as to print counterfeit securities. In 1972, the company listed in its year-end statement a purchase of commercial paper worth $8 million. But when investigators later tried to trace the sale, the bank had no record of it. The paper had never existed. By the time the fraud was exposed in April 1973, over $110 million of the assets Equity Funding Corporation claimed to possess were fictitious. Funded loans totaling $62.3 million supposedly made to Equity Funding policyholders simply had never been made. Fictitious bonds amounted to $24.6 million.[10]

In 1970, Equity Funding Life Insurance Company (formerly Presidential Life Insurance Company) began to invent insurance policyholders. Business was slow, and something had to be done to prevent the company from showing a loss, which would have caused the price of Equity Funding Corporation stock to drop. So imaginary policyholders were dreamed up and their policies then reinsured with Ranger National. The cash thus obtained was an excellent boost for profits. But problems arose the following year when 90 percent of the premiums on the reinsured policies had to be turned over to Ranger. To get the money, EFLIC invented still more policies, reinsured *them,* and paid the previous year's premiums with the present year's income. So year by year, the

---

[9] Alan Abelson, "Up and Down Wall Street," *Barrons,* April 16, 1973, p. 1.
[10] Robertson, "Those Daring Young Con Men," p. 84.

need for more policies mushroomed, until *Fortune* estimated that in the 10th year of the fraudulent operation, Equity Funding would have had to reinsure over $3.7 billion worth of phony insurance policies to pay all the premiums on previous nonexistent policies.[11] In spite of the incredible speed with which the costs of the fraud mounted, Equity Funding's top officials evidently believed that the phony business could eventually be phased out and the company made completely legitimate.

Nor was financing the only problem with the reinsurance scheme. In order to fool the auditors, EFLIC had to have files on all of its imaginary policyholders, complete with all the information the company would normally obtain on such people noted on the proper forms. Creating these was a time-consuming process, and in addition to hiring clerks who scored particularly low on the company's intelligence test (so they wouldn't wonder why they were forging forms) to perform the tedious work, the executives reportedly had evening "manufacturing parties" at which they gleefully made up names and filled out forms with details on imaginary customers. The invented customers were generally variations of real ones. Information on extant policyholders was altered slightly to form new policies, and these were then scattered throughout various policy number blocks in the computer records to prevent the similarities from being discovered. Ronald Secrist reported receiving letters from the company's internal auditors for Ronald Secret and Ronald Crist, which he was expected to sign confirming that those two men had loans from Equity Funding.[12] For the sake of realism, a policyholder had to be "killed off" occasionally. Equity Funding would arrange for the claim to be paid to an employee's address, and apparently this money was sometimes pocketed by the recipient.

In addition, the company's computers had to be programmed in such a way that the auditors could obtain some information—but not too much—on the phony business, identified as *Department 99*. The auditors would not check every policy, but would take a sampling of policy files and check the contents with premium receipts and policy reserve information. If files that the auditors requested on imaginary policyholders were incomplete or had not yet been made up, Equity Funding employees would say that these files were temporarily unavailable and then write up the missing documents so that they would be ready the next day. Each insurance policy had a five-digit identification number, but the printout that was given to the auditors contained only the last three digits of that number. In this way, numbers could easily be repeated without causing suspicion. Equity Funding explained the tremendous amount of activity in Department 99 by saying that this represented mail-order sales. It puzzled employees of the computer section that no bills were ever sent to any of the vast number of mail-order customers listed under Department 99.

---

[11] Ibid., p. 124.
[12] Dirks and Gross, *Great Wall Street Scandal,* p. 79.

In still another aspect of the scheme, Equity Funding Corporation, which had begun its spectacular rise with an idea for using the same money more than once, put that knack to considerable use transferring funds back and forth from the parent company to its subsidiaries to make it appear that its growing nonexistent assets really were there. *Fortune* described the situation with EFLIC, the site of most of the phony business:

> Beginning in 1970, it appears, the parent would "lend" money to bogus program participants (creating assets for Equity Funding) and credit EFLIC through an intercompany account with similar amounts of money in premium income. EFLIC in turn paid out sales commissions to the various marketing subsidiaries of Equity Funding, and these payments were debited against the intercompany account. The premiums credited to EFLIC exceeded the commissions it paid out, however, so the parent owed money to its life-insurance subsidiary at the end of the year. To clear this account, the parent transferred securities, rather than cash, to the life company. Those securities—in this case $24.6 million in bonds—are the ones that don't exist.[13]

While the policies reinsured in 1969 had apparently been genuine, "by 1972 virtually all the business reinsured—represented by over $7 million in first-year premiums—was phony."[14] EFLIC was now reinsuring policies with Kentucky Central Life, Great Central Life, and Connecticut General Life, as well as Ranger National.

In 1970, Equity Funding applied for permission to list its common stock on the New York Stock Exchange. Permission was granted in October 1970, but the Stock Exchange insisted that Equity Funding enlarge its board of directors and replace its present outside auditor with a larger firm.

Equity Funding Corporation was at that time being audited by the firm of Wolfson, Weiner, Ratoff and Lapin. The man in charge of Equity Funding's daily auditing was an auditor with Wolfson, Weiner named Sol Block. He was not a certified public accountant. He had an office on the executive floor of Equity Funding's corporate headquarters. The auditors of Equity Funding's largest subsidiary, Equity Funding Life Insurance Company, were Haskins & Sells. In 1972, after the New York Stock Exchange's decision, Wolfson, Weiner merged with the larger accounting firm of Seidman and Seidman. Seidman and Seidman then became the auditors of the parent corporation as well as the subsidiary, replacing Haskins & Sells at EFLIC. The same individuals who had conducted the Wolfson, Weiner audits now audited Equity Funding for Seidman and Seidman.

In further compliance with the Stock Exchange's ruling, four new directors were named to Equity Funding's board in 1972. They were Fred Levin, executive vice president, Insurance Operations and Marketing, Equity Fund-

---

13 Robertson, "Those Daring Young Con Men," p. 124.
14 Ibid.

ing; Gayle Livingston, vice president of the Professional Services and Equipment Group of Litton Industries, Inc.; Samuel B. Lowell, executive vice president, Corporate Operations and Finance, Equity Funding; and Judson Sayre, a retired industrialist who had developed the first automatic home washing machine while at Bendix Corporation and had later been a vice president of Borg-Warner Corporation. Other members of the board included Yura Arkus-Duntov, executive vice president, Investment Management Operations, Equity Funding; Robert Bowie, director, Institute of International Relations, Harvard University; Herbert Glaser, executive vice president, Real Estate and International Operations, Equity Funding; Stanley Goldblum, president and chairman of the board, Equity Funding; and Nelson Loud, one of the founders of New York Securities Company, a director of several other companies, and a trustee of the Union Dime Savings Bank of New York.

Other parties were keeping their eyes on Equity Funding. During the early 1970s, the company was researched by such prominent brokerage firms as Burnham and Company, Lehman Brothers, Edwards and Hanly, Wertheim and Company, and Adams, Harkness and Hill. The firms' reports ranged from favorable to glowing, and all recommended purchase of Equity Funding's stock. On February 9, 1973, Wertheim and Company reported that Equity Funding was "unlikely to be 'impacted' by [the 'Truth in Insurance' hearings opening in Washington at that time] and that it seemed 'most attractive at about nine times fully diluted earnings'."[15] A group of institutional analysts chose Equity Funding in 1972 as its favorite stock out of the many finance and financial services securities.[16] In the February 1973, issue of *Institutional Investor,* two of five analysts whose opinions were featured in an article on life insurance companies said that Equity Funding would be one of 1973's star performers.[17] A report was issued by Hayden, Stone, Inc., on March 26, 1973, stating that "several rumors have been circulating which have affected Equity Funding's stock; we have checked these rumors, and there appears to be no substance to them." Hayden, Stone had checked with the insurance departments of Washington, Illinois, and New Jersey (states in which insurance companies owned by Equity Funding were licensed) and "each man told us that he is not conducting an investigation of Equity Funding or any of its subsidiaries, had no present intention of conducting an investigation, and knows of no other insurance department that is conducting such an investigation."[18] A spokesman for Ranger National Life Insurance Company told *Barrons* columnist Alan Abelson that his company had run spot checks on Equity Funding policies and had "never uncovered an instance of fictitious

---

[15] The Spreading Scandal at Equity Funding," *Business Week,* April 14, 1973, p. 84.

[16] Ibid.

[17] Dirks and Gross, *Great Wall Street Scandal,* p. 258.

[18] Robert J. Cole, "Anatomy of an Insurance Scandal," *The New York Times,* April 15, 1973, sec. 3, p. 9.

insurance."[19] Indeed, in 1970 the president of Anderson, Clayton—Ranger National's parent company—asked the accounting firm of Peat, Marwick, Mitchell to conduct a special review of EFLIC. The review was begun, and the management of Equity Funding was kept quite busy dreaming up schemes to fool the investigators. But when the men from Peat, Marwick came back for a third visit, they were told management was simply too busy to provide them with the information they needed. The auditors left and did not return.[20]

On March 6, 1973, Ronald Secrist made his telephone calls to Raymond Dirks and the New York State Insurance Department. Both Dirks and the Insurance Department began investigating. Meanwhile, the Illinois and California insurance departments sent in examiners to conduct a surprise audit of the company. Equity Funding executives tried a last-ditch effort to cover up the fraud—including bugging the room in which the examiners were working to find out what they were uncovering—but it was no use. At a board of directors' meeting on April 1, 1973, Stanley Goldblum and two other top executives who had helped him organize the scheme were forced to resign. They protested, asserting that they were entitled to severance and vacation pay, and they offered to run the company as consultants for $200 an hour. Finally, one of the directors ordered them off the premises. The California Insurance Department seized Equity Funding's plush offices on the top floors of 1900 Avenue of the Stars in Century City, changed all the locks on the doors, and installed guards with clubs and pistols to prevent anything from being removed and to keep out the deposed executives.

The company filed for reorganization the following Thursday under Chapter 10 of the Federal Bankruptcy Act. Normally the assets of a bankrupt company would have been sold and the proceeds used to pay its creditors. But under Chapter 10, Equity Funding could continue to exist. A trustee, Robert Loeffler, formerly a lawyer with Investors Diversified Services, was appointed by the court to take over the company and try to straighten out the mess.

Touche Ross and Company began an audit of Equity Funding to find out exactly what was there. Equity Funding Corporation in its 1972 annual report had listed assets of $737.5 million and a net worth of $143.4 million. The audit found the actual assets to be $488.9 million and set the net worth at a *negative* $42 million.[21] The company had never had any genuine profits, and in fact had suffered huge losses each year. The auditors found the accounting at Equity Funding to be "chaotic," and they could not reconstruct an accurate statement of Equity Funding's profits and losses. Millions of dollars of the company's funds could not be found. There was no evidence of embezzlement except of

---

[19] Alan Abelson, "Up and Down Wall Street," *Barrons,* April 2, 1973, p. 25.
[20] Robertson, "Those Daring Young Con Men," pp. 127–128, 132.
[21] "Criminal Trial in Equity Funding Case Starts Today for Two Former Officers," *The Wall Street Journal,* October 1, 1974, p. 16.

some phony death claims, and it was concluded that the missing money—some $80 million—went to cover the ever-increasing operating costs.

In February 1974, Robert Loeffler, the court-appointed trustee, described the company he was attempting to reorganize as "virtually a fiction concocted by certain members of its management, a fiction enlarged upon year by year, until Equity Funding Corporation of America [was] proclaimed the fastest growing diversified financial company in *Fortune's* list."[22] In November of that year he filed a 239-page report on his findings regarding the fraud with a Los Angeles federal court. In his report, Loeffler characterized the fraud not as the carefully calculated, well-organized scheme some had thought it to be, but rather as a haphazard, frantic series of attempts to cover up each successive fraud with a bigger one, held together by the "lies, audacity, and luck"[23] of Goldblum and his associates.

Loeffler felt that the company could be successfully reorganized, probably as a holding company based on a couple of its subsidiaries, which had been healthy at the time of the collapse. Twenty-two former officers of the company and three auditors had been indicted by federal and state grand juries on charges including conspiracy, mail fraud, stock fraud, filing false bank statements, interstate transportation of counterfeit securities and securities obtained by fraud, falsifying financial statements, and illegal wiretapping. Eighteen of the former officers, including Stanley Goldblum, had so far pleaded guilty, and the trials of others were in progress. As of December 1974, trading had still not been resumed in Equity Funding's stock.

In the meantime, lawsuits totaling in the millions of dollars had been filed against Equity Funding Corporation. It was not known whether the worthless stock now owned by prominent universities including Princeton, Amherst, Antioch, and Sarah Lawrence, and other institutional investors such as the Ohio State Teachers Retirement System, Salomon Brothers, the Ford Foundation, and the New World Foundation, as well as numerous individuals, would ever regain any value. In addition, those companies that had bought Equity Funding stock in the last frantic days of trading were now suing to force the companies that had sold it—because they knew about the fraud, said the suits—to take back the stock and the losses. It was estimated that these legal actions would take years to complete.

AFTERTHOUGHT

Probably one of the most unusual aspects of the Equity Funding fraud was the fact that it was not a closely guarded secret. It is now believed that over 100 people within the organization were aware of the fraud's existence to some

---

22 William E. Blundell, "Equity Funding's Worth Is $185 Million Less Than Firm Had Claimed, Trustee Estimates," *The Wall Street Journal*, February 22, 1974, p. 6.

23 William E. Blundell, "Equity Funding Trustee Calls the Fraud Inept, and Assails the Auditors," *The Wall Street Journal*, November 4, 1974, p. 4.

extent. The very nature of the fraud necessitated its rapid expansion and the involvement of more and more people. As the fraudulent activities filtered down from top management to subordinates, it created what trustee Robert Loeffler called a "a climate of moral decay."[24] There were numerous cases of individuals embezzling relatively small amounts of money. Some billed the company for personal expenses; others stole money or checks. When these people were caught, they were not fired but were instead set to work assisting in the fraud. Those who had falsified death claims and pocketed the money now did the same thing for the company. Offenders were even given financial assistance to help them repay what they had taken.

Many employees who were not involved in embezzlement or even directly in the fraud itself nonetheless knew about some aspects of it. Some examples follow.[25]

Early in 1972, Ron Ronchetti, a specialist in computer systems employed by Equity Funding Life Insurance Company, requested a list of Equity Funding's funded insurance policies to resolve a problem regarding sales commissions. The printout he received listed 18,000 policies; Equity Funding's 1971 annual report had listed 41,121. Shortly thereafter, Ronchetti was fired. He decided not to say anything about his discovery, since his word alone would mean nothing.

Frank Majerus, controller of Equity Funding Life Insurance Company, was ordered by a company official to write up a phony insurance file. Majerus had become increasingly suspicious that something unsavory was going on at Equity Funding, and this confirmed his fears. He was so upset that he went to his minister for advice. The minister told him that his first duty was to protect his job for the sake of his family. Still, Majerus was dismayed at the way Equity Funding was being run, and some months later, in October 1971, he resigned. He wanted desperately to tell someone about what he knew, even if it meant implicating himself, but he did not trust the authorities. He was sure he could not convince them to investigate.

Bob Ochoa ran an Equity Funding print shop in Santa Monica. One day Fred Levin, executive vice president for Marketing of Equity Funding, and three other company officials came in to see him. They showed him pictures of securities certificates of a number of leading American companies and asked him to make plates and run copies of them for a presentation they were preparing on retirement programs. The executives insisted on taking everything with them after each evening printing session. Scrap materials had to be put through a paper shredder. Ochoa had done a bit of investing himself. He knew what the securities certificates were, and he was surprised, to say the least. But these men were at the highest levels of the corporation—they must know what they were doing, so why ask questions?

In July 1971, Pat Hopper, administrative officer of Equity Funding Corporation, went to the office of Jim Banks, an attorney and assistant secretary of EFLIC, to

---

[24] Ibid.

[25] For more detailed descriptions of these individuals and situations, see Dirks and Gross, *Great Wall Street Scandal.*

approve a letter, which had been requested by the New Jersey Insurance Department, containing information on Beneficial National Life, a company that underwrote policies for Equity Funding. Finding the letter to be satisfactory, Hopper told Banks he would send it to the president of Beneficial for his signature. "No," Banks told him, he would take care of it. And with that he pulled out a form containing the Beneficial president's signature and traced it onto the letter. Hopper was speechless.

Several months later, Hopper was made Vice President for Investments of Bankers National Life Insurance Company, Equity Funding's recently acquired subsidiary in New Jersey. In December 1971, he received a phone call from Lloyd Edens, secretary-treasurer of EFLIC. Edens wanted Hopper to send $3 million from Bankers National to the EFLIC offices in California. Edens would keep it three hours and then return it to Hopper. That way, with the time difference between California and New Jersey, the $3 million would be on the books of both companies at the close of business on December 31. This was the most recent in a series of such requests, all of which Hopper had refused. Arthur Lewis, EFLIC's actuary, informed him that he was costing the company 14 cents a share on its earnings report for the year by his continued refusal to cooperate. Hopper resigned in disgust. He was now convinced that Equity Funding was a fraud, but he knew also that he would say nothing because he had no proof. He was simply relieved to be out of the mess.

A Management Dilemma: Regulating the Health of the Unborn

One of the top 10 mining production areas in the world is in northern Idaho's panhandle. The area, appropriately called the *Silver Valley,* is a 30-mile stretch of land lying between two small Idaho towns, Cataldo and Mullan, and following the South Fork of the Coeur d' Alene River. The Silver Valley is a major U.S. supplier of lead, silver, zinc, and cadmium. To date, nearly $4 billion worth of mineral wealth has been extracted from the area.

The Bunker Hill Company, founded in 1887, was one of the first mining companies established in the Silver Valley. The main entrance to the underground mine, the famous Kellogg Tunnel, was constructed between 1893 and 1902. In May 1891 the Bunker Hill concentrator (which crushes the ore and separates the metal from waste rock), at the time the largest in the world, sent out its first trainload of ore to be smelted (i.e., melted and refined). The company built its own lead smelter in 1916.

With its lead industry expanding rapidly, the Bunker Hill-Sullivan Company (renamed after a merger) began to develop its zinc operations in 1926. The company completed construction of a zinc plant and began refining zinc in 1928. Throughout the 1930s and 1940s the company continued to expand. A research laboratory was added to the complex, and the lead smelter was enlarged. By the early 1950s the company had grown to one of the largest mining operations in the country. In 1956 the company officially changed its name from Bunker Hill-Sullivan to the Bunker Hill Company.

Bunker Hill's growth pattern attracted the interest of a number of investors. In 1968 Gulf Resources, a small sulfur company based in Houston, bought

Written by Donna M. Randall and reprinted with permission from the Fall 1985 issue of the *Journal of Management Case Studies* by special permission, Copyright 1985 Elsevier Scientific Publishing Co., Inc.

For a fuller discussion of the issues involved in the Bunker Hill controversy, see Donna Randall, "Women in Toxic Work Environments: A Case Study and Examination of Policy Impact." In *Women and Work, An Annual Review,* eds. L. Larwood, A. Stromberg, and B. Gutek (Beverly Hills: Sage, 1985).

Bunker Hill for $80 million. The purchase proved a wise investment. The chairman of Gulf Resources, Robert Allen, claimed that Bunker Hill was one of his best and largest acquisitions. In fact, Bunker Hill was larger than Gulf Resources when purchased.[1] According to Gulf Resources President Frank Woodruff, revenues from the Bunker Hill Company exceeded $1.8 billion between 1968 and 1977.[2] In 1980 the Bunker Hill Company contributed 66 percent of Gulf Resources's operating profits and 50 percent of Gulf Resources's sales. With the revenue from Bunker Hill, Gulf Resources was able to develop into a large, diversified resources concern with $700 million in revenue.[3]

In the early 1980s the Bunker Hill Company produced 20 percent of the nation's primary refined silver, lead, and zinc. The company owned wholly, or in part, four major silver and lead mines: the original Bunker Hill mine, the Crescent mine, the Pend Oreille mine, and the Star mine. The largest of the mines, the Bunker Hill mine, is considered one of the world's largest underground lead, zinc, and silver mines. In addition to the mines, lead smelter, zinc plant, and research laboratory, the Bunker Hill Company operated three sulfuric acid plants that converted sulfur dioxide gas to liquid sulfuric acid; a tree farm located 3,000 feet underground in the Bunker Hill mine that produced seedlings; the Silverhorn Ski area in the mountains above Kellogg; and, in a joint venture with Stauffer Chemical Company, a plant to produce phosphoric acid and dry ammonium phosphate fertilizer.

The Bunker Hill Company, with about 1,700 hourly workers and 4,090 salaried workers, was not only the Kellogg area's largest employer (approximately 40 percent of the local population worked for the company) but also drew employees from all neighboring communities. Almost one half of the employees in Idaho's Shoshone County employed in mining and smelting worked for Bunker Hill. Moreover, the company was the largest employer in the northern half of Idaho.[4]

PROBLEMS AND CONTROVERSIES

The Bunker Hill Company has been beset by a variety of labor problems and embroiled in a number of controversies with regulatory agencies within the last decade over air and water pollution regulations and health and safety standards within the workplace. A major controversy erupted in 1974 when the Center for Disease Control revealed that the Bunker Hill lead smelter was the cause of elevated blood lead levels in approximately 1,000 school children. In 1977 a serious labor dispute resulted in Bunker Hill's operations being closed for over four months. In 1981 the company was named a defendant in a $20-million lawsuit in which the parents of nine children alleged their chil-

---

[1] A. Bagamery, "Subtle Charms," *Forbes* 128 (1981), pp. 171–172.

[2] "Kendrick, Woodruff Testify," *Kellogg Evening News,* October 21, 1981, p. 1.

[3] Bagamery, "Subtle Charms," p. 172.

[4] L. Young, "Big Mine Firm Plans to Close; *Spokesman Review,* August 26, 1981, p. A1.

dren suffered physical and mental damage by living near Bunker Hill's lead smelter.

Of these controversies, one of the most significant and far-reaching concerns an employment policy for women working in toxic work areas.

BUNKER HILL'S EXCLUSIONARY POLICY

Few women had been hired by Bunker Hill to work in production positions. Because of labor shortages during World War II, women were hired as production workers at the company, but immediately after the war all but two of the women who had been hired by the company discontinued their work. Employment opportunities for women in production remained limited for the next 20 years.

In 1972 a major change in Bunker Hill's hiring practices took place. Bunker Hill began to accept applications from women to work in production in response to pressure from the Equal Employment Opportunity Commission (EEOC). Over the next few years about 45 women were hired as production workers. Thirty of these women were placed in the lead smelter, the remaining 15 in the zinc plant. While both locations involved exposure to the toxic substance lead, there was little concern at the time about the possible negative health effects on women working in environments where they would be exposed to lead.

In early April 1975, however, Bunker Hill executives became very concerned about the possible consequences of exposing women to lead. One of the physicians on contract with Bunker Hill had attended a lead industries conference in Florida where he was advised by a number of nationally known lead experts to encourage the company to remove women employees from the smelter because of potential harm to the unborn fetus.[5]

Upon his return to Kellogg, Idaho, the physician alerted the president of Bunker Hill at the time, James Halley, of the possible dangers of lead exposure to fertile women. Halley met with his lawyers and executive staff to consider what action the company should take. After a lengthy conference, Halley decided the company had no choice but to exclude all female workers who could become pregnant from areas of the plant where they would be exposed to lead. On the morning of April 14, 1975, Halley invited local union representatives to meet with him and his staff. At the meeting, union representatives of the United Steelworkers of American were informed that the company intended to exclude all fertile women from workplaces with lead exposure and would do so immediately.

In the afternoon of the same day, company management met with the 29 women currently employed in the lead smelter and the upper part of the zinc

---

[5] C. Tate, "Women Shifted From Bunker Hill Smelter Jobs," *Lewiston Morning Tribune*, April 17, 1975, p. A1.

plant (where exposure to lead is the greatest). These women were informed they could no longer work in the lead smelter and zinc plant because of the possible harmful effects of lead on the health of the fetus. They were told that medical evidence had revealed women to be particularly susceptible to the effects of lead. In addition, the women were told that other firms had adopted similar policies that removed fertile women from working around lead.

The women were advised that an "exclusionary" policy had been put into effect. According to the policy set forth by the company, fertile women would no longer be permitted to work in the lead smelter and zinc plant. Those women desiring to maintain their jobs in the smelter and zinc plant would have to show proof of sterilization from their physicians before they could return to their jobs. No other form of birth control would be viewed as acceptable to the company.

The women were informed that they could report back to the lead smelter and zinc plant only to clear out their lockers and that they would be temporarily reassigned to the mine yard crew (maintenance work) until permanent positions could be found for them in "safer" areas of the plant. Because they were being transferred from their departments, the women were informed that their departmental seniority would immediately end. Finally, they were told that if they disagreed with the exclusionary policy they would be fired.

The women affected by the policy were taken by total surprise when it was announced and were quite uncertain what to do. For some, the course of action was clear. At least six of them had previously undergone sterilization; they simply obtained a letter from their physicians attesting to their operation and were able to return to their jobs in the lead smelter and zinc plant shortly afterward.

The decision was much more difficult for those women who had not been previously sterilized. Some of them underwent sterilization in order to return to their former jobs.[6] Where the precise number of women who sought sterilization solely to keep their jobs is unknown, a female physician sent by Occupational Safety and Health Administation (OSHA) in 1980 to investigate the policy determined that at least three women obtained sterilization procedures within two to three months after the policy was enacted. These women informed the physician that they had consented to the operation solely to be allowed by the company to return to their former jobs. In total, 17 of the 29 women originally employed in the smelter and zinc plant returned to their former jobs.

The unsterilized women remained on the mine yard crew while the company attempted to place them in "safe" areas of the plant. However, the company had great difficulty finding areas of the plant without lead exposure. As the lead smelter and a major portion of the zinc plant were no longer open to

---

[6] J. Accola, "Women: Company Officials Told Us To "Get Fixed," *The Idaho Stateman,* September 28, 1980, p. A1.

fertile women, the women could be transferred only to the melting and purification plants, which had a limited number of openings. In an effort to place women in permanent positions, the company began to recruit women to work underground as miners in mid-September 1975.[7]

Despite the company's efforts to relocate the women, many of the women affected by the exclusionary policy were very upset about it and its effect on their lives. As a result, several women decided to take action to protest the company's policy. They first complained to their United Steelworkers of America (USWA) local. While the union was clearly sympathetic to the plight of the women, it did not have medical evidence to refute the company's policy, and its efforts to protest the treatment of the women had little effect.

One woman filed a complaint with the Idaho Human Rights Commission (IHRC), which drew up a "Memorandum of Understanding" between the company and the women affected by the policy change. The document set forth an agreement about the use of exclusionary policies at Bunker Hill. Unfortunately, the approach was ineffectual as some of the company executives reportedly refused to sign the agreement.

Finally, 18 of the 29 women affected by the policy filed sex discrimination charges with the EEOC. An EEOC investigator met with each of the women and successfully negotiated individual monetary settlements. By mid-March 1976, all charges filed by the women with the EEOC were dropped, but not all the women were satisfied with the settlement. Some felt they had been "bought out" by the company and would have preferred for the EEOC to have made a policy decision on the legality of exclusionary policies.

The controversy over Bunker Hill's exclusionary policy did not end with EEOC's settlement. In April 1980, OSHA responded to a request by the union for an intensive investigation of health and safety conditions at Bunker Hill. On September 11, 1980, OSHA issued a citation against Bunker Hill for 108 violations of occupational safety and health regulations discovered during the inspection. One of those violations was for the maintenance of what OSHA called a *sterilization* policy. The proposed fine for this violation alone was $10,000.

Bunker Hill was not the first company to be cited and fined by OSHA for maintenance of an exclusionary policy. On October 9, 1979, OSHA had cited American Cyanamid for maintenance of a similar policy and had also proposed a $10,000 fine for the violation. After Bunker Hill was cited for the violation, OSHA's case against American Cyanamid was decided by the Occupational Safety and Health Review Commission (OSHRC). On April 28, 1981, the OSHRC determined the policy did not lie within OSHA's jurisdiction and the impact of the company's policy was outside the reach of the Occupational Safety and Health Act. OSHA lost its case against American Cyanamid.

---

[7] J. Kuglin, "Women Take Plunge To Work At Bunker Hill," *Lewiston Morning Tribune,* January 27, 1977, p. 3A.

Because of the similarity of the Bunker Hill controversy to the American Cyanamid case, OSHA lawyers decided to drop the citation for the sterilization policy against Bunker Hill. On July 21, 1981, the citation against Bunker Hill for the exclusionary policy was officially dismissed.

THE AFTERMATH

Despite the attempts by the women, their union, IHRC, EEOC, and OSHA to change Bunker Hill's exclusionary policy, the policy remained in force. However, because of subsequent events at Bunker Hill, it is unlikely that the controversy over the policy will ever be reopened. On August 25, 1981, Gulf Resources, the owner of Bunker Hill, announced that it planned to close the plant owing to falling metal prices, the unavailability of ore to process, and the rising costs of labor, supplies, and meeting federal regulations. Bunker Hill had lost $7.7 million in the first six months of 1981, and the economy offered little hope of improvement. Today the plant is under the new ownership of Bunker Ltd. Partnership and currently remains closed.

While the controversy was finally resolved at Bunker Hill by the closure of the plant, the issue of whether exclusionary policies are an acceptable industry practice has not been settled. To understand fully the complex issues raised by the use of such policies, it is desirable to present various viewpoints on their use.

CONFLICTING VIEWPOINTS ON THE CONTROVERSY

The Company's Viewpoint

Bunker Hill maintained that its policy was defensible on medical, technological, and moral grounds. Top management felt that medical evidence clearly warranted exclusion of the female worker. Bunker Hill's president at the time, James Halley, claimed recent studies indicated, "There appears to be some physiological difference between a man and a woman that makes women more susceptible to the effects of lead in general."[8] Similarly, Jack Kendrick, president of Bunker Hill during the OSHA investigation, explained, "The simple truth is that medical research, based on animal studies, has indicated prolonged exposure to chemicals or heavy metals may adversely affect a fetus."[9]

The company also justified its policy on technological grounds. A company executive explained the difficulty in improving working conditions in the plant:

---

[8] Tate, "Women Shifted from Bunker Hill Smelter Jobs," p. A1.

[9] J. Kendrick, "Smelter Safety Insured," *The Idaho Stateman,* November 15, 1980, p. 1A.

The plant was constructed in the early 1920s, and much of the original equipment and facilities still in use is not in the best physical condition. Maintenance dollars in many instances have been diverted to buy and install pollution control equipment. Expansion of production capabilities over the past 50 years has been achieved by adding equipment within existing plant areas or by modification of processes within processes. This has resulted in a plant layout which makes good housekeeping and maintenance most difficult. Thus, the company is faced with the requirement of revising old plants, equipment, and processes to meet the working area environmental standards expected of modern facilities and which can only be readily incorporated into a plant at the original design stage.[10]

Top management felt that the technology simply did not exist that would make the work place safe for unborn children.[11] As an executive explained,

People want an environment safe for males, females, and young children, too. That's impossible. You can't have a lead smelter and do that. Like you can't have Montana air in Los Angeles.[12]

Finally, Bunker Hill defended its policy on moral grounds. Gulf Resources chairman, Robert H. Allen, charged that OSHA's use of "catchy buzzwords" like *sterilization* make for great headlines in the press. But, he asked, would anyone "reasonably suggest that these employees should be allowed, under some bizarre concept of freedom of choice, to continue in a position where there is a known risk to their health?"[13] Similarly, Halley felt that the moral course of action for Bunker Hill was to protect the health of the fetus:

So am I supposed to put those women in the plant, or am I supposed to keep them out of the plant? Which is the more moral thing to do? If we don't put women in the smelter, that's going to mean fewer jobs for women. If we put a woman in the smelter, and she gets pregnant, we're liable to have a mentally retarded person born who otherwise would have been normal.[14]

Despite management's belief that the exclusionary policy was justified on these grounds, management also recognized the controversial nature of the policy. After the citation was dropped by OSHA, Bunker Hill management fully expected to be challenged again on its exclusionary policy by new female applicants or other federal agencies.[15] A vice president of the company summarized the situation: "The issue is a political football and, therefore, it will not die."[16]

---

[10] "Fact File," *The Bunker Hill Company,* February 14, 1975, pp. 8–9.

[11] "OSHA confronts Bunker Hill," *Idaho Miner,* September 25, 1980, p. 1.

[12] Interview. Corporate Official.

[13] B. Schlender, "Sterilization Is Main Issue In OSHA Suits," *The Wall Street Journal,* December 9, 1980, p. I125.

[14] C. Tate, "American Dilemma of Jobs, Health In An Idaho Town," *Smithsonian* 12 (1981), p. 79.

[15] Interview. Corporate Official.

[16] Interview. Corporate Official.

Industry's Viewpoint

Industry has an obvious economic interest in the health of unborn children of its work force. "When we remove a woman it is not to protect her reproductive capacity, but to protect her fetus," explained Bruce W. Karrh, medical editor of E. I. du Pont de Nemours & Company.[17] Industry may face legal liability if a female employee gives birth to a deformed child. Whereas some women may be willing to take the risk of pregnancy, industry representatives maintain that the women cannot legally waive the rights of the unborn children to sue for damages in the future. A child born with defects or diseases caused by parental exposure to toxic chemicals may bring personal injury actions against a company. Moreover, the media exposure and adverse publicity arising from a lawsuit involving a deformed child may be devastating to a company's image. After weighing the risks, Dr. Norbert J. Roberts, medical director of Exxon, concluded, "I would rather face an EEOC inspector than a deformed baby."[18]

The chemical companies and manufactuers of toxic substances contend that they have no choice but to remove women to protect them from toxic exposures. Like Bunker Hill management, industry representatives maintain that the technology does not presently exist to make workplaces, such as lead smelters, completely safe for either worker or fetus and that offering women affected by exclusionary policies equitable transfers to safer areas of the corporation is simply not economically feasible.[19]

Furthermore, industry representatives claim that federal regulatory agencies have not given them sufficient guidance in the area of reproductive health and have actually placed them in the middle of a legal dilemma. Should the employer conform with the Occupational Safety and Health Act of 1970 (in which workers are given a right to a safe and healthy workplace) or with Title VII of the Civil Rights Act of 1964 (in which workers are given a right to equal employment opportunities)? Industry representatives contend if the employer seeks to conform to OSHA's laws, the fertile female would be excluded from the work place to protect the fetus, and equal employment laws would be violated. On the other hand, if the employer seeks to conform to EEOC's laws, the health of the fetus would be endangered and OSHA's standards would be violated. Hence industry representatives complain that industry has been left with a task of complying with conflicting regulations.

---

[17] P. Shabecoff, "Industry And Women Clash Over Hazards In Workplace," *New York Times,* January 2, 1981), p. 1.

[18] D. Pauly, "Women's Work?," *Newsweek* (June 28, 1976), pp. 56–58.

[19] N. Stillman, "The Law in Conflict: Accommodating Equal Employment and Occupational Health Obligations," *Journal of Occupational Medicine* 21 (1979), pp. 599–606.

Women Employees' Viewpoint

The 29 women removed from their jobs in the lead smelter and zinc plant at Bunker Hill were very dissatisfied with the change in corporate policy for a variety of reasons. They were most upset at losing their department seniority. Seniority, as a union representative explained, is the "backbone of the system." It is the recognized way for an employee to advance in the company and to obtain more interesting, better-paying positions. By losing their departmental seniority, the women would lose all the rights and privileges they had worked to build up.

A number of the women were upset at the abrupt manner in which they were informed of the policy; they were informed of the new policy and removed from their jobs on the same day. Many felt the temporary work on the mine yard crew was demeaning. Removed from responsible positions, they were assigned to pick up gum wrappers and paint signs. Others enjoyed the work in the smelter and zinc plant and did not want to leave. These women felt they had worked hard to obtain their positions, had proven themselves, and had earned a right to stay in their jobs.

Many of the women transferred to the mine yard crew were upset with their new work schedules. Specifically, these women could no longer work evenings and nights to meet their families' schedules as they could in the smelter and zinc plant. The women were required to work from 8 o'clock to 5 o'clock, five days a week. Moreover, work on the mine yard crew lacked night and holiday work, overtime opportunity, and incentive earnings offered in the lead smelter and zinc plant.

Other female employees felt their privacy was being invaded with the exclusionary policy. These women complained that in returning to the lead smelter and zinc plant, they were subjected to derogatory comments from their male co-workers. Women in other companies have voiced similar concerns, maintaining that an exclusionary policy

> subjects all women to special scrutiny about their childbearing intentions, sexual activities, and birth control methods and, thus, operates to invade their personal privacy in a most sensitive area. Any woman who remains in a restricted job is forced, per se, to publicly reveal her sterility. Men, on the other hand, are not asked if or when they intend to have children, even though their exposure to toxic substances could also result in injury to a future child.[20]

Finally, economic concerns were central to many of the women workers. About one half of the women employed at Bunker Hill were single parents. Jobs were scarce in the Silver Valley, and Bunker Hill was the largest employer. Women employees could have been replaced easily by men and could

---

[20] C. Clauss and J. Bertin, *Brief of the American Civil Liberties Union Women's Rights Project, et. al., Amici Curiae* (New York: American Civil Liberties Union Foundation, 1981), p. 22.

apply for only a limited number of openings as waitresses, bartenders, nurses, clerks, secretaries, teachers, and beauticians. All these positions meant substantial wage cuts from production work. For those women faced with a significant cut in income, a sterilization procedure that would allow them to keep their high-paying job became very attractive.

Women employees in other companies with exclusionary policies report similar economic pressure to consent to sterilization. A woman who applied to the Pittsburgh & Midway Coal Mining Company explained the economic pressure to get sterilized:

> It seemed that you could have a tubal ligation in a very short period of time. It cost about $800, and it seemed to be less than what one would pay for an employment agency to find you a job.[21]

Women's Advocates' Viewpoints

Women's advocates maintain that widespread use of policies such as that adopted by Bunker Hill would significantly diminish women's employment opportunities in the lead industry. Hricko estimated that if women of childbearing age were not allowed to work where there was lead exposure, almost two of every three female applicants for an estimated 1.3 million jobs would be turned away.[22] Women's advocates point out that females can be easily discriminated against during periods of high unemployment and that they have been chosen by corporations to be economic scapegoats.[23] Furthermore, exclusionary policies are perceived by some to be full employment for men.[24]

While industry maintains that the technology does not presently exist to make workplaces such as lead smelters completely safe for either worker or fetus, Ann Trebilcock, an attorney for the United Auto Workers (UAW), asserts that the technology does exist to make the workplace safe for the fetus, but employees would rather hire "superworkers" who can withstand toxic exposure instead of going to the expense of cleaning up the workplace.[25] Women's advocates insist that exclusionary policies are female workers. "The costs of such a policy," Win-O'Brien points out, "are borne by the women who must leave their jobs in order to protect their ability to have children or the women who'll never be hired into these workplaces."[26]

---

[21] "A New Twist to Exclusionary Policies: The Case of Synfuels," *Coalition for the Reproductive Rights of Workers Newsletter* 1, no. 1 (1981), p. 7.

[22] A. Hricko, "Social Policy Considerations Of Occupational Health Standards: The Example Of Lead And Reproductive Effects," *Preventive Medicine* 7 (1978), p. 400.

[23] S. Krekel, "A Worker's Viewpoint," In E. Binham (ed.), *Proceedings: Conference on Women and the Workplace* (Washington D.C.: Society for Occupational and Environmental Health, 1977), p. 125.

[24] "Do Protective Laws Hinder Women on Job?, *The Idaho Stateman,* 1980, p. 1.

[25] J. Hyatt, "Work Safety Issue Isn't as Simple as It Sounds," *The Wall Street Journal,* August 1, 1977, p. 1.

[26] M. Win-O'Brien, "Law In Conflict: Another View," *Journal of Occupational Medicine* 22 (1980), p. 509.

To support their claims of discrimination, women's advocates point to the different manner in which the issue of reproductive health is treated in hospitals, dental offices, beauty parlors, and the textile industry. In these areas where most of the employees are female, the employment of fertile women is unregulated although chemicals such as ionizing radiation are known to be dangerous.[27] In addition, women have been barred from heavy industrial jobs entailing lead exposure, but not from lower-paying jobs in certain industries, such as pottery work, which also entail lead exposure.[28]

Many women advocates feel that current medical research does not warrant exclusion of only women from the workplace and point to research evidence which indicates that both male and female reproductive abilities are damaged by exposure to lead.[29] According to available research evidence, occupational exposure of male workers to high levels of lead can lead to reduced sexual drive, impotence, decreased ability to produce normal sperm, and sterility.[30] Occupational exposure of females can lead to abnormal ovarian cycles, menstrual disorders, sterility, premature birth, miscarriage, and stillbirth.[31] Lead can also affect the nervous system of the developing fetus, resulting in learning disorders and psychological impairments. However, the precise nature of harm to the fetus and level of lead exposure at which such damage occurs cannot be determined with certainty. Only limited medical research has been conducted on the effects of lead on male and female reproductive systems.

Despite the medical evidence indicating the susceptibility of both male and female reproductive systems to lead, women advocates complain that only women have been the objects of exclusionary policies and that the policies ignore the threat of damage to unborn children of male workers. Such policies assume that the future children of female workers are at a greater health risk than the unborn children of male workers.

Moreover, exclusionary policies are perceived to reject the female worker as a person with options. Surgical sterilization is required by the policies regardless of whether the female has chosen not to have a family, her sex partner has a vasectomy, or she is using another form of birth control.[32]

The impact of such policies may go beyond sex discrimination. Burnham has pointed out that a policy that excludes one sex may also be used to exclude

---

[27] J. Stellman, *Women's Work, Women's Health* (New York: Pantheon Books, 1977), p. 183.

[28] Ibid., p. 178.

[29] See U.S. Department of Labor, "Lost in the Workplace: Is There an Occupational Disease Epidemic?," *Proceedings from a Seminar for the News Media* (Washington, D.C.: U.S. Government Printing Office, 1979), p. 186–187.

[30] R. Gold, "Women Entering Labor Force Draw Attention to Reproductive Hazards for Both Sexes," *Family Planning/Population Reporter* 10 (1981), p. 10.

[31] A. Hricko and M. Brunt, *Working for Your Life: A Woman's Guide to Job Health Hazards* (Berkeley: Labor Occupational Health Program and Public Citizen's Health Resource Group, 1976), pp. C7–C8.

[32] Win-O'Brien, "Law in Conflict: Another View," p. 509.

certain races from the workplace.[33] Lead may pose special health problems for blacks who might have sickle cell disease. Therefore, if fertile women can be excluded from toxic work environments on inconclusive medical evidence, the same type of evidence may be used in the future to exclude blacks.

Union's Viewpoint

The United Steelworkers of America (USWA) local sought to help the women affected by the exclusionary policy, but the local union did not possess enough personnel, medical expertise, and technological information to help the women. The local union consisted of 14 officers; only two (the president and financial secretary) were hired full-time. The union had no medical evidence to prove that lead could harm male reproductive systems nor did it envision a technological solution to the dilemma. The officers believed it was impossible to clean up the workplace to the point where it would be safe for fertile women.

However, the local union did offer some support to the women. They protested the company's failure to consider the wages, seniority, and benefits of the transferred women, assisted the women in filling out complaints to both EEOC and IHRC, tried to obtain medical research on the health effects of lead, and contacted the international headquarters of the USWA in Pittsburgh, Pennsylvania, for advice and information.

The efforts of the international union to protest the treatment of the women also had little effect. The international office could not maintain that a financial burden had been placed upon the women because the women had eventually been reimbursed by the company for lost wages. The union was also fearful of antagonizing Bunker Hill because the union wanted the company to continue to hire females as production workers. Moreover, Bunker Hill had decided that "it was easier to deal with union protests over the exclusion of women than with a damages trial in 1990 where a jury would be confronted by a horribly deformed human being."[34]

The international office of the USWA had filed a grievance against Bunker Hill for the sterilization policy. However, OSHA's dismissal of the citation against American Cyanamid and Bunker Hill destroyed the union's arguments. Several factors entered into the USWA's decision to withdraw its grievance against the company for the exclusionary policy: (1) the factual evidence was not that strong that the women at Bunker Hill were sterilized solely to keep their jobs, (2) the union would have legal problems in a suit since lead has not been proven to be a real hazard to the reproductive abilities of

---

[33] D. Burnham, "Rise in Birth Defects Laid to Job Hazards," *New York Times,* March 14, 1976, p. 42.

[34] G. Robinson, "The New Discrimination," *Environmental Action* 10 (1979), p. 4.

men, and (3) even the USWA's own doctors advised that pregnant women should not work around lead.[35]

Other unions are resisting the transfer of women workers from hazardous jobs unless those transferred suffer no economic penalties. For instance, the United Auto Workers filed grievances against the General Motors Corporation, which barred fertile women from holding battery plant jobs where they may be exposed to lead in the air. Both the UAW and USWA are insisting that women and other workers removed from certain jobs must not suffer loss of pay or seniority.

EEOC's Veiwpoint

After EEOC "settled" the Bunker Hill controversy in 1976, the agency began to receive complaints of exclusionary policies from female employees in other companies. About 50 women filed complaints to EEOC that they were being involuntarily transferred from their jobs because of corporate exclusionary policies. The EEOC was uncertain about how to proceed with the new complaints; the agency had still not developed a policy to handle exclusionary policies and could deal with them only on a case-by-case basis. In fact, the year before the Bunker Hill controversy arose, EEOC had tacitly approved a similar corporate exclusionary policy maintained by the National Lead Industries.[36] However, the EEOC has warned employers that efforts to bar all women from certain jobs could violate federal civil rights legislation.

OSHA's Viewpoint

Bunker Hill is very visible in regard to environmental problems. By citing Bunker Hill, OSHA sought to pressure other companies into reducing lead levels in the workplace.[37] OSHA believed its actions would give an incentive for companies to reduce lead exposure to safe levels and would discourage other companies from employing exclusionary policies. As Susan Fleming, a spokeswoman for OSHA, explained:

> Bunker Hill, like a lot of other firms, refuses to allow women who can bear children to work at lead smelting operations. OSHA is discouraging this policy. Employers should know that we're going to pressure them on the issue, and employees should know they needn't put up with this policy.[38]

---

[35] Interview: International Union Official.

[36] Freedom of Information Act: OSHA Investigative File.

[37] W. Harris, "OSHA Fines Bunker Hill on Sterility Policy," *Metals Daily*, September 16, 1980, p. 1.

[38] Ibid., p. 1.

While Bunker Hill officials view OSHA's accusations as an abuse of government power, OSHA sees its actions as incentives to industry to develop the necessary technology to reduce lead levels and maintains that the task is feasible.[39]

OSHA claimed that Bunker Hill could not legally seek to eliminate the health hazards lead presents to female employees "by compelling them to choose between their jobs and sterilization, thereby incurring serious and irreversible impairment to their reproductive systems."[40] The company's policy struck Marshall Saltzmann, who prepared OSHA's case, as "odious." "It seems so wrong," he said, "that it just has to be a violation of something."[41]

Eula Binham, former head of OSHA during the Carter administration, maintained that industry must clean up the workplace to make it safe for the fetus. "This business of having people go out and be sterilized—and I would feel the same way if it were men—to me it's like saying you're going to work on this machine and you might get your hand cut, so to prevent our liability, you'd better go and have your hand amputated."[42] Moreover, OSHA's area director in Boise, David M. Bernard, contended that there was a basic human right in question at Bunker Hill. He insisted, "Whether or not you want to limit your reproductive capabilities is your business. We don't feel it should be made a condition of employment."[43]

OSHA continues to be interested in exclusionary policies despite its failure to extend jurisdiction over the issue of exclusionary poilicies. OSHA officials do not believe the controversial issues raised by such policies will be resolved in the near future.[44] One OSHA official describes the issue of exclusionary policies to be "a shaggy dog: it'll go on and on," and predicts that exclusionary policies will become one of the major regulatory issues in the 1980s.[45]

Some question whether EEOC and OSHA should be involved in the regulation of reproductive hazards in the first place. Williams observes, "To date the state has not prohibited women of childbearing capacity or pregnant women from smoking, drinking coffee or alcohol to excess, or taking aspirin—any one of which poses a greater hazard to fetal health than most jobs from which women have been excluded by protective employers."[46]

---

[39] "OSHA Confronts Bunker Hill," p. 1.

[40] "OSHA Proposes $82,765 Penalty for Alleged Health Violations at Bunker Hill Company," *U.S. Department of Labor News,* September 12, 1980, pp. 1-2.

[41] Schlender, "Sterilization Is Main Issue in OSHA Suits," p. I125.

[42] Tate, "American Dilemma of Jobs, Health, in an Idaho Town," p. 80.

[43] Accola, "Women: Company Officials Told Us to "Get Fixed," p. A1.

[44] Interviews: OSHA Officials.

[45] Interview: OSHA Official.

[46] W. Williams, "Firing the Woman to Protect the Fetus: The Reconciliation of Fetal Protection with Employment Opportunity Goals under Title VII," *Georgetown Law Journal* 69 (1981), p. 652.

Agreement on the rights and responsibilities of government, top management, industry, the union, and the female employee in the regulation of reproductive health does not exist. That some agreement be reached is critical, because it is highly likely that exclusionary policies will become common throughout industry. To prevent possible fetal damage, a number of major corporations have implemented corporate policies preventing female employees of childbearing age from working in positions where they would be exposed to lead. Among these corporations are the General Motors Corporation of Canada and the United States; the DuPont Corporation of Wilmington, Delaware; the Olin Corporation of East Alton, Illinois; and St. Joe's Mineral Corporation of Monoco, Pennsylvania. Exclusionary policies will undoubtedly be developed by other corporations not only to deal with lead but with a host of other toxins including benzene, beryllium, mercury, cotton dust, vinyl chloride, and ionizing radiation.

Dr. Corn of the National Institute of Occupational Safety and Health (NIOSH) identified the importance of this issue to Congress by observing, "We are in an area of social regulation, if you will, that has enormous ramification."[47]

---

[47] U.S. Congress, House Committee on Education and Labor, Subcommittee on Manpower, Compensation, and Health and Safety, 94th Congress, 2nd Session, Part 2. Statement of Dr. Morton Corn, Assistant Secretary, Occupational Safety and Health Administration (Washington D.C.: U.S. Government Printing Office, 1976), p. 411.

Commentaries

---

3. Ethics and the Corporation

Irving Kristol

At a time when the reputation of business in general is low, when the standing in popular opinion of the large publicly owned corporation is even lower, and when there is a keen post-Watergate concern for probity among officials of all organizations, public or private—at such a time one would expect corporate executives to be especially sensitive even to appearances of conflict of interest, or to the mildest deviations from strict standards of fiduciary behavior. Yet this seems not, on the whole, to be the case.

I do not wish to be misunderstood. The majority of corporate executives are certainly honest and honorable men. This, however, is rather like saying that the majority of New York City's police officers are honest and honorable men. Of course they are. But the statement itself implies that a not altogether insignificant minority are less than that, and the presence of such a minority is fairly taken to constitute a rather serious problem. In the case of the corporation, the situation is worsened by the fact that, whereas honest cops will usually express open indignation at corrupt ones, corporate executives almost never criticize other corporate executives, even when these latter are caught *in flagrante delicto*. No one seems to be "read out" of the corporate community—which inevitably leads the outsider to wonder whether this community has any standards of self-government at all.

But to talk in terms of "corruption" is misleading. Problems of corporate ethics only rarely arise out of illegal actions by corporate executives. Such illegal actions are doubtless more frequent than they ought to be, and the response of the business community certainly is far more lethargic than it ought to be, but in the end such illegalities are quite efficiently disposed of by law enforcement officers. The more common and significant issues in corporate ethics arise from practices which are not illegal, but which seem to reveal a shockingly naive unconcern both for the interests of stockholders and the good opinion of the public. Too many corporate executives seem to be under the

---

The Wall Street Journal, April 16, 1975, p. 18. Reprinted with permission of Irving Kristol, the John M. Olin Professor of Social Thought at New York University and Co-editor of *The Public Interest*. Copyright Dow Jones & Company, Inc., 1975. All rights reserved.

illusion that they *are* the corporation. The problem here is rarely one of wicked motives but rather of a bland self-righteousness which does not even perceive an abuse of power for what it is.

GOING PRIVATE

Take, for instance, a rather extreme and somewhat marginal case: the recent efforts of several smaller corporations which, having gone public during the boom years of the 1960s, now wish to "go private." When such a corporation originally went public, the controlling stockholder sold a portion of his shares at a price substantially higher than the present market price. Now, disillusioned by the contemptuous way the stock market treats "his" firm, he uses his power to have the corporation repurchase, *with corporate funds,* that "public" stock. He ends up, if successful, owning the corporation all over again—*and* with a substantial capital gain from the original sale of his stock. However innocent the intentions of the controlling stockholder, the whole operation really amounts to a way for a privately held corporation to use the mechanism of "going public" in order to trade profitably in its own stock.

Apparently, if incomprehensibly, this procedure is perfectly legal. All right: the law will have its loopholes. But is this way of doing business *ethically acceptable* to the financial and corporate communities? There is no doubt that the public which originally purchased this stock is now under the distinct impression that it has been fleeced. That is certainly undesirable—especially since these stockholders usually own stock in other corporations, too, and their indignation is all too likely to spill over and touch all corporations. So why does one not observe the boards of directors of the New York and American Stock Exchanges denouncing such a procedure and taking what actions they can to discourage it? Why does one not hear the heads of major Wall Street houses similarly come to the defense of the shareholders? Why don't corporate executives, individually or collectively, put themselves on record? Don't they care?

One supposes they do care—indignant and resentful stockholders are what the financial and business communities least need these days. But apparently they do not regard it as a matter that directly concerns them. Every executive assumes that so long as he personally behaves in a way that is above reproach, he has discharged his moral obligations. This is a fateful error. Precisely because there is never enough individual moral sensitivity to go around, every profession must protect its good name with a measure of collective self-discipline. And it should be clear that if the business community makes so little effort to discipline itself, then the government will step in and do the disciplining for it. That is the least desirable but most predictable outcome.

More directly affecting the large corporations, and therefore with a clear consequence for the good reputation of "big business" generally, is the way in which several firms are fiddling around with stock options for their executives. The officers of a major corporation, for instance, are voting themselves the right to borrow money from the firm so that they will not have to sell out their positions in the company's stock—positions they acquired through stock options financed in turn by bank loans. Because of the decline in the value of a firm's stock, these executives are faced with margin calls from the banks. They stand to lose a lot of money if they cannot answer these calls. So they are transferring these loans to the company, and are justifying this action by the assertion that they will be able to do their job better if they are not distracted by personal financial worries.

It is all very odd, to put it mildly. To begin with, what kind of relief do these executives obtain by virtue of going into debt to "their" corporation rather than to the banks? A debt is a debt, after all. Why should a corporate executive be less "distracted" if he owes money to his employer instead of to a bank or a brokerage house or a personal loan company? If he does achieve greater peace of spirit, it can only be because there exists in the back of his mind the notion that, at some point, the corporation will be a more indulgent creditor. But this in turn raises even more serious questions about the ethical status of this arrangement.

Besides, many of the 40,000 stockholders of this corporation are, or have been, in exactly the same situation as these executives, and the corporation certainly never did anything to help *them* cope with margin calls. Is it really the company's view that it is wrong for its executives to lose money in the company's stock but a matter of indifference to it if anyone else does? If a company does badly, and its stock falls, are executives a privileged group to be "made whole" through the use of company funds? The company would surely repudiate both of these propositions. Yet its actions in effect assert them.

Or take the case of another large corporation. Its shares, too, have gone way down, thereby making the stock options of its executives worthless. So the company has simply reduced by 50 percent the price at which these options may be exercised. Again, the assumption seems to be that, even though all stockholders are suffering, corporate executives must not lose money in the company's stock—or, in this case, must not fail to make money in the company's stock. But the conventional argument in favor of stock options is that it offers executives an incentive for superior performance. What kind of incentive is it that rewards good and poor performance indifferently?

DISGRUNTLED STOCKHOLDERS

Now, the case of these two corporations has been amply reported in *The Wall Street Journal* and elsewhere. (Since I am interested in making only a general point, there is little to be gained by naming them accusingly.) What I find most interesting is the reaction within the business community to it. Or, to be exact, the absence of any discernible reaction. Why, for example, hasn't one of the prestigious organizations of businessmen thought it proper to suggest a code governing the use and abuse of stock options? It seems to have occurred to no one. Instead, the stock exchanges are mute, the major brokerage houses are mute, the corporate community is mute. Is it surprising, therefore, that there are thousands of stockholders out there whose loyalty to the corporation as an institution has been subverted? And is it surprising that these stockholders should infer from their experiences that more rather than less government regulation of corporations is desirable?

There are just too many other current instances of questionable behavior on the part of corporate executives. For instance, I am struck by the fact that one major company seems to be having considerable difficulty in divesting itself of a large and profitable subsidiary, as required by the Federal Trade Commission. I am willing to think, on general principles, that the FTC is being unreasonable in the conditions it is attaching to the divestiture. But there is an easy way out for the company, one which the FTC could not possibly object to—i.e., spinning off the subsidiary to the company's shareholders. The company has rejected this possibility on the grounds that it is not in the "best interests" of these stockholders.

But why isn't it? It is hard to see why, and I rather imagine that if those shareholders were given the chance to vote on the issue, they might well decide that a spin-off is decidedly in their best interests. They will not, of course, be given any such opportunity. For it is obvious that life would be more interesting—and presumably in the end more profitable—for the company's executives if *they* had $800 million dollars or so to play with, rather than seeing all this money vanish into the pockets of its stockholders. Perhaps these executives will indeed invest this money more wisely than the stockholders could, and to the stockholders' ultimate benefit. But, on the other hand, perhaps not. What does seem clear is that the executives do not even seem to realize that they are involved in a situation that suggests a potential conflict of interests, and that there is an ethical aspect to their decision to which attention should be paid.

THE CORPORATE CLUBHOUSE

And then there are those recurring reports of corporate executives who, having brought their corporations to the brink of ruin, and their stockholders to the brink of despair, "resign" with huge cash benefits. One notes that an executive of such a corporation recently departed with a $2 million cash payment to console him for the loss of his position. Nor is his case so unusual. It is a fact that the corporate community often more nearly resembles a corporate club, in which the genial spirit of "clubbiness" ensures that everyone is adequately provided for. Nonmembers, of course—stockholders and employees—must learn to cope with the harsh rigors of free enterprise.

It might be said that all this is little more than the froth on the surface of corporate life, of no great significance to the basic economic mission of the corporation, and only remotely relevant to its success in accomplishing that mission. That is true—but somewhat beside the point. The point is that American corporations do have a critical problem with public opinion, and to cope with this problem spend tens of millions of dollars a year on "public relations." Yet a number of these corporations then proceed to behave in such a way as to offend and outrage the corporation's natural constituency: the stockholders. More important, the business community as a whole remains strangely passive and silent before this spectacle. This disquieting silence speaks far more eloquently to the American people than the most elaborate public relations campaign. And it conveys precisely the wrong message.

4. Businesses Are Signing Up for Ethics 101

John A. Byrne

Item: *Rockwell International Corp. has been indicted by a federal grand jury for defrauding the Air Force.*

Item: *Hertz Corp. has overcharged consumers and insurers $13 million for repairs to damaged rental cars.*

Item: *Ocean Spray Cranberries Inc. has been indicted by a federal grand jury for pollution in Middleboro, Mass.*

Fraud. Price-gouging. Pollution. All these allegations made headlines in a recent week. It's not exactly the kind of image American business likes to project. Yet the frequency of such stories is leading many to wonder if American management is suffering a crisis in ethics.

The result: Corporations are rushing to adopt codes of ethics. Business schools are scrambling to add ethics courses. And hundreds of consultants are being hired to put "integrity" into corporate cultures. Kenneth Blanchard, author of *The One Minute Manager,* is coming out with a breezy book on ethical management cowritten by none other than Norman Vincent Peale.

Elements of a full-blown management fad in the making? "The market is full of hucksters, promoting quick-fix ethics programs," says Mark J. Pastin, director of the Lincoln Center for Ethics in Tempe, Arizona. "I wonder where all these qualified people in ethics have come from."

The issue has also attracted attention from the Business Roundtable, composed of the chief executive officers of 200 major corporations. It has just completed a landmark study of how big business deals with such questions. Andrew C. Sigler, chairman of Champion International Corp., helped initiate the effort, and the Roundtable set up a task force that included five ethicists and consultants. The group studied ethics programs at 10 companies. "I've read so much on this subject by so-called experts who have never set foot in the

Reprinted from the February 15, 1988, issue of *Business Week* by special permission, Copyright 1988 by McGraw-Hill, Inc., pp. 56–57.

real business world," says Sigler. "All we're trying to do here is lay out what companies are really doing."

It turns out some companies are doing a lot. The question is whether it's working. One rather disquieting lesson: Even companies that have long emphasized ethics can't guarantee that they will be immune from a lapse in judgment. Take Boeing Co. Since 1964 the aircraft maker has had an ethics committee that reports to the board. Besides "ethics advisers" in subsidiaries, Boeing has a corporate office for employees to report infractions. Training in ethics is done by line managers, not consultants. Yet in 1984 a Boeing unit illegally used inside information to gain a government contract.

"Sitting up here in Stamford," explains Sigler, "there's no way I can affect what an employee is doing today in Texas, Montana, or Maine. Making speeches and sending letters just doesn't do it. You need a culture and peer pressure that spells out what is acceptable and isn't and why. It involves training, education, and follow-up." The Roundtable report makes several recommendations: greater commitment of top management to ethics programs, written codes that clearly communicate management expectations, programs to implement the guidelines, and surveys to monitor compliance.

High-level corporate involvement seems essential. At Chemical Bank, for example, some 250 vice presidents have taken part in two-day seminars on corporate values that begin with an appearance by the chairman. Managers work through 12 case studies of such issues as loan approvals, staff reductions, branch closings, and foreign loans.

MUTUAL TRUST

Strict enforcement of codes is also important. Chemical Bank, the report says, has fired employees for violations of the company's code of ethics even when there are no violations of the law. Xerox Corp. has dismissed employees not only for taking bribes but also for fairly minor manipulation of records and petty cheating on expense accounts.

Executives at several corporations, including Xerox and General Mills Inc., believe that active civic involvement is a critical part of a corporate ethics campaign. As one General Mills executive told a Roundtable researcher: "It's hard to imagine that a person who reads to the blind at night would cheat on his expense account."

Another issue: striking the right balance between centralized management controls and giving employees enough autonomy to build mutual trust critical to maintaining a value system. Johnson & Johnson is seen as a model. With some 150 units, J&J emphasizes individual autonomy and initiative. Yet its one-page statement of values, known as its Credo, is an exception to decentralization. "The Credo is a unifying force that keeps the individual units marching together," declares CEO James E. Burke.

J&J's Credo addresses the need for business to make a sound profit while also acknowledging the need to respect employees as individuals and to make high-quality products. Burke credits the statement for helping to guide the company through its product-tampering crises with Tylenol in 1982 and 1986.

CHALLENGE MEETINGS

The Credo has become a central part of J&J's corporate culture. In 1975, Burke began "challenge meetings" for top managers to explore whether the 30-year-old statement was still valid. For three years more than 1,200 managers attended two-day seminars of 25 people to challenge the Credo. Burke or President David R. Clare presided at each session. J&J has been through two other major follow-ups since, and challenge meetings are now held twice a year for new top managers.

Some experts feel such an ongoing approach is essential. "You have to keep renewing the effort," says Laura L. Nash, a Harvard University ethicist who studied J&J. Unfortunately, though, such an extensive program is unusual in Corporate America. Stanford University's Kirk O. Hanson, an authority on ethics, figures only 1 in 10 companies is doing it the right way: via a continuing program that works at all corporate levels.

And there's some question just how important an issue ethics is, given the host of other problems confronting American business today. "If you asked the members of the Business Roundtable to list the five major issues they confront today, I don't think many of them would list ethics," says Paul J. Rizzo, former vice chairman of International Business Machines Corp. That may be so, but ethics seems to be moving up the corporate priority list.

EXHIBIT 1   How Some Companies Attack the Ethics Issue

Boeing

CEO involvement, line managers lead training sessions, ethics committee reports to board, toll-free number for employees to report violations

General Mills

Guidelines for dealing with vendors, competitors, customers; seeks recruits who share company's values; emphasizes open decision making

Johnson & Johnson

A credo of corporate values integral to J&J culture, companywide meetings to challenge the Credo's tenets, and surveys to ascertain compliance

Xerox

Handbooks, policy statements emphasize integrity, concern for people; orientation on values and policies; ombudsman reports to CEO

SOURCE: Business Roundtable.

EXHIBIT 2   Hertz Is Doing Some Body Work—On Itself

Frank A. Olson, chairman of Hertz Corp., is wishing that he could handle the current scandal at the giant car-rental company the way Lee Iacocca managed Chrysler Corp.'s odometer follies last year. Through candor and charisma, Iacocca allayed concerns over Chrysler's practice of spinning back odometers on cars used by executives and later sold to consumers.

"People believe him," says Olson. "He said, 'We did it, we were dumb, it won't happen again.' But I'm not Lee. It's devastating."

Hertz isn't Chrysler either. The car-rental company admitted overcharging motorists and insurers $13 million for repairs. Hertz has an ethics code and requires its employees to sign a compliance statement, but it didn't seem to make a difference.

Olson says senior management discovered the problem in 1985, when a U.S. Postal Service inspector, acting on complaints by car insurers, found that a Boston office was creating damage estimate reports from nonexistent body shops. An internal audit, Hertz says, pointed to the company's national accidents control manager.

Claims poured in from 13 zones, all of which reported to manager Alan Blicker, five levels below the chief executive officer. Blicker claims that he is being made a scapegoat. Olson charges that Blicker was the "architect" of several fraudulent practices that led to a grand jury probe. Olson fired Blicker, cast out 18 others, and centralized control.

Retail costs.   As much as 80 percent of the $13 million in overcharges from 1978 to 1985 resulted from charging the retail cost of fixing cars—though Hertz received volume discounts on the repairs. Senior management approved this practice on the advice of in-house legal counsel, who pointed out that such competitors as Avis, Budget, and Alamo followed a similar practice. Unlike the competition, however, Hertz failed to disclose to customers that they would pay for damages at "prevailing retail rates."

Olson ended that policy in 1985. Now the company charges the actual repair costs. Hertz has also refunded more than $3 million to customers and insurers so far. What about the future? Vows Olson: "If I catch one guy billing at something other than cost, I'll throw him out the window myself."

5. Ethical Conduct and the Bottom Line

Robert V. Krikorian

I want you to consider two quotes that I think bear on the subject of Ethical Conduct and the Bottom Line.

In the late 1960s, an observer of business wrote this in the *Harvard*

An address before the Tax Executive Institute Tri-State Tax Conference, Milwaukee, Wisconsin, April 16, 1984. Reprinted by permission of Robert V. Krikorian.

Business Review, "No one should think any the worse of the game of business if its standards of right and wrong differ from the prevailing tradition of morality in our society." The second quote comes from a conference on ethics more recently held at Marquette University. The authors of a paper said, "When you have a competitive situation and unethical marketing practices, the advantage in the marketplace falls to the unethical firm."

To both of these statements, I must ask, why? *Are we to assume that the most effective business practices are per se unethical? Or even worse, are unethical business practices per se effective? I don't believe that; I never have and I never will.* That just isn't the way business works. The authors of that last quote did admit that they were speaking of the short term, not the long term. But I still don't buy it. If you build your business on return customers or clients, how many are going to return after they find out that you aren't trustworthy all the time?

To me, the authors of those two quotes were speaking from their own personal assumptions and not from much experience in the world of business. I would much rather consider a simple bit of informal research conducted recently by a businessman who wanted to know this: Do companies with written, codified principles stating a central belief in serving the public in an ethical manner perform better or worse in the marketplace than other companies? In other words, is there a relationship between conducting business according to ethical principles and the bottom line?

The answer was a very definite yes. He surveyed 15 companies which had written commitments to serve the public and found they averaged 11 percent earnings growth compounded over 30 years, three times the growth in GNP. Thirty thousand dollars invested equally in these companies 30 years ago would be worth more than $1 million today.

The businessman who had this research done is the chairman of Johnson & Johnson, and I'm sure many of you know how that company's commitment to serve the public also served the company very well during the tragic incident involving Tylenol, one of Johnson & Johnson's leading products. Now I don't suggest that such a small sample and such an informal procedure make a firm correlation possible. But based on many years of business experience, I can tell you that the result doesn't surprise me.

Our business system depends on the application of ethical values and the trust that is the natural result of these values. After all, who wouldn't rather do business with someone who can be trusted? Or to put it in the words of business, ethical conduct does affect the bottom line—positively.

I'm afraid that many people in and out of business just don't understand this simple premise. They somehow believe that ethical conduct makes it tougher to do business. Unfortunately, this attitude is very widespread. Dishonest and unethical business dealings are assumed to be normal by much of the media, for example—certainly by the people who write television scripts—by many college professors, and I would guess by all critics of business. Even some people in business seem to go along with this attitude. For some reason they accept the myth that unethical behavior can somehow help them in their business. I am convinced that it is a myth—but it's a myth that dies hard.

Several years ago, Fred T. Allen, then head of Pitney-Bowes, said something that is worth hearing again and again. He said, "We must learn to sacrifice what is immediate, what is expedient, if the moral price is too high. What we stand to gain is precious little compared to what we can ultimately lose." What we can ultimately lose, it seems to me, is a continuing erosion of trust in us by our customers, employees, the general public—in short, just about everybody who is important to our success. And that adds up to bottom line effect.

When we business people think of the bottom line, we tend to think only of profits. This is understandable. We were practically raised that way. That's what we learned in our college business courses. That's what many of us learned on the job. And that's what we read in the press and in many annual reports. In fact, the press, many investors, and lots of business people seem obsessed with short-term bottom line results. But I think that the attitude about the overriding importance of the bottom line is giving way to a deeply felt but harder to articulate belief, that there are more bottom lines than just profits. The profit bottom line will always be with us, of course, as it should. After all, in business, profit means survival and provides for the future health of the organization. But there are other bottom lines which can carry us far beyond survival. Let's take a look at a few:

1. Satisfied, returning customers.
2. Employees who are motivated, enthusiastic, supportive, and productive.
3. A reputation for integrity and a credible voice.
4. Reduced risk when faced with a crisis or catastrophe.
5. Good relations with our communities and the government.

I hope you will agree that these results, these other bottom lines, are not only desirable but necessary for a company to achieve superior results in our modern world. Business people still have a tough time understanding how to achieve these highly desirable goals. Business schools certainly didn't teach us how, and long experience as business managers often didn't either. Many business people feel inadequate tackling such problems as eroding employee loyalty and long-term commitment, growing public antagonism and increasing government regulations that are the result of such feelings. We've been busily looking for answers, studying other management systems, sending managers to seminars, examining other countries and cultures. We've been trying to find a variety of ways to solve these problems.

Superior performance is based on many factors, and seminars and studies of other cultures can be useful. But to me, one of the key levers to pull is labeled with some familiar, enduring ideas:

1. Ethical conduct.
2. And shared value systems.

These factors that once seemed intangible, at best only incidental to the marketplace and management, are now widely recognized as critical in such areas as productivity, self-regulation, quality, dependability, public acceptance, team effort, and employee motivation.

Let me digress for a moment to tell you why I feel so strongly about this. I am the son of an American immigrant who fled for his life to America to escape from the tyranny of an all-powerful central government. As my father did, I see the United States of America as a nation of opportunity, individual liberty and freedom—in constant struggle to develop a more just and equitable society. As a child, I recall how little our family had, compared with our friends and neighbors. Yet, my father considered himself a rich man, as an American citizen. He had a roof over his head, some wholesome food for his family, schooling for his children, and freedom to worship. All of that was more than enough for him.

As many children do, I would often complain about not having more of the material things my friends and neighbors had. Whenever I did, my father would remind me that now was the time for me to develop good work and study habits and concentrate on getting a good education. He would continually remind me that my whole life was ahead of me and that there was plenty of time for the material things later. But most importantly, he told me that no matter what I would ever acquire later in life, nothing I could ever own would be of more value than my personal integrity and my word. I've never forgotten his advice. It seems to me that our American socio-economic system depends on the kind of trust that my father talked about—trust in each other and in our insitutions. Certainly you who are concerned with taxation understand this.

It also seems to me that in the area of taxation, much of this trust is being lost. For years, we in the United States had a tax system that was considered by other countries to be a model: a voluntary system that was reasonably fair. In other countries, tax evasion was a national pastime, but not here. But catch-22 started to be felt. As the system got more complex and ate up more and more of our wages, abuses increased partly because simplicity and the sense of fairness decreased. To curb the abuses, Congress and the IRS continue to write even more complex tax laws probably leading to more abuse.

The U.S. Census Bureau tells us that the untaxed underground economy is now more than $200 billion and growing. Judging from past performance, Congress and the IRS will try to solve this problem by further complicating the system leading to entirely predictable results.

I hope we can agree that adherence to the enduring ideas of ethical conduct and shared values systems is an essential ingredient in running our businesses. The remaining question, then is this: What can we as business people do to encourage such adherence? I would like to suggest five actions.

> **First,** we can make a major effort to integrate ethics in all levels and functions of our operations. Strong support from the Board of Directors and top management is an absolute must.

Second, we can make sure all our communication with the public states all the facts clearly, accurately, and fairly.

Third, we can take great care to treat all our employees as trusted, valuable individuals who are given the opportunity to realize their full potential and the satisfaction of participating in a worthwhile enterprise.

Fourth, we can place the utmost emphasis on serving our customers—making sure our products and services do what we say they will and standing behind them when they don't. If our employees take personal responsibility for our customers, they, and we, will be well served.

Fifth, we can do everything possible to assure that all our activities follow a written code of conduct that fits as tightly at the top of the organization as at the bottom. This code must be clearly and simply written and communicated internally to all employees of the organization. Key managers should certify in writing that they and their subordinates understand the Code of Conduct and are abiding by it. And finally, such a code must be enforceable—and enforced. If it isn't, it is worth less than the paper it is written on.

Some companies are taking a lead in making ethical conduct an integral part of the way they manage their operations. A list of companies that have been particularly successful in integrating ethics into their organizations would have to include Allied Corporation, Cummins Engine, Hewlett-Packard, Johnson's Wax, Norton Company, and J. C. Penney, to mention just a few. There are many more, of course.

For those of you who don't operate with a code of conduct or need to revise the one you have, I want to tell you that there is help available from the Ethics Resource Center, headquartered in Washington, D.C. The staff at the Center has recently made available a Business Services Package, which includes a rather complete kit entitled "Creating a Workable Company Code of Ethics." The kits can be obtained by contacting the Center (1730 Rhode Island Avenue, NW, Washington, D.C. 20036).

I would like to sum up what to me are the two most important points that I have made today. *First, doing business in an honest, ethical manner is a necessary ingredient to success as a business*—as necessary as quality products, excellent people, and growing markets. Ethical behavior does have a positive bottom line effect. And *second, by expecting ethical conduct and following a system of shared values, we can help achieve the superior results that American business will require in the rest of this century.*

I firmly believe, as my father did, that the American system of laws and limited government is the best system ever devised to serve the people. If the ultimate test of any national system is how well it can and does serve the people—then ours is superior to any other. It's up to us to make sure we keep it.

In closing, let me share with you what the founder of Ethics Resource Center, Ivan Hill, had to say about ethics. "One of the basic tenets of ethics is the principle of cooperation and sharing. And one of the most precise measurements of the maturity of an individual or of a society is a concern for those who come after us. It is our ethical obligation to do our best to enable those who follow us in life's relay to have as good a chance to win as we had when the baton was passed along to us."

6. *Small-Business Jungle*

Michael Allen

Owners say the lack of clear rules makes it tough to toe the ethical line.

Is it harder to walk the straight and narrow on Main Street than it is on Wall Street?

A recent national survey by Arthur Andersen & Co. suggests that it is. A whopping 39 percent of the small-business executives queried felt their companies had been hurt by "questionable business practices," especially bribes, kickbacks, price collusion, and conflicts of interest. The smaller the company, the higher the incidence; those with fewer than 25 employees were affected at twice the rate of those with over 300.

Analysts say that little companies are more subject to such transgressions for several reasons. For one, they don't have the legal responsibility of full disclosure that tends to keep large, publicly owned outfits in line. For another, they often lack a system of internal controls that would tend to make potential chiselers think twice. In small businesses, people frequently get a broad range of authority, and can use it unethically with little risk. "Sometimes key employees are the check *and* balance, and so there's greater potential for wrongdoing," says Domenick Esposito, an assistant managing partner at Grant Thornton, the accounting firm.

Analysts also point out that while large companies have the resources to weather minor business setbacks, little ones frequently don't. This makes their owners particularly vulnerable to extortion by corrupt public officials. Professor William Baxter of the Stanford Law School notes that for such owners, delayed building permits for failed sanitation inspections can be "life-threatening events" that make them cave into bribe demands. By contrast, he adds, "The local manager of Burger King is in a much better position" to tell these people to get lost. A good many small-business owners *offer* bribes, too, particularly when they are slugging it out with multiple competitors. A police investigation into Miami's cutthroat construction industry led to 24 bribery arrests last year, including some of the trade's most prominent local figures. "A lot of people here believe this is just a cost of doing business," says Alex Ramirez, a police officer who posed as a building inspector to nab them.

An executive of a small privately owned food-processing company agrees that there is more sleaze in small business. This executive, who previously worked at big public companies, says most of the sleaze amounts to "stupid stuff someone shouldn't jeopardize his job for," such as selling a used company car to a customer for a big discount.

But he thinks there is no point to tattling to the authorities about petty ethical breaches by a competitor. The amount involved is too small and the law too vague. Besides, he adds, "You run the risk of putting yourself on the number-two list with other potential suppliers if they think you're going to wave the flag every time somebody leans on you."

Bob Kilpatrick, an adviser to minority small-business owners in the Los Angeles area, says that a little guy competing with a bigger firm may feel that he simply has to offer cash to get the business, he lacks the clout, and the access to the customer, that his competitor often has, and a bribe is his way of offsetting the disadvantage. "His bigger competitor may play a better golf game," says Mr. Kilpatrick, "or the competitor's wife may go to the same PTA meetings that the customer's wife goes to."

What to do? Accounting consultants advise small businessmen to adopt uniform, strictly enforced pricing and purchasing policies; to divide sensitive responsibilities (never let anyone writing checks do the bookkeeping, for example); and to draw up a code of ethics to be read and signed by all employees.

The experts also note that if small businesses have inherent weaknesses that make them more prone to ethical problems, they also have one strength that any owner-boss ought to capitalize on—the intimacy that comes with a small operation. Mr. Esposito of Grant Thornton says: "In these places the CEO is walking around the shop saying, 'How are we doing today?' instead of sitting, aloof, in corporate headquarters dictating memos about policy and procedures. The small-businessman can come straight to his employees and say, 'Hey—it's my integrity on the line here.'"

---

7. Sears Has Everything, Including Messy Fight over Ads in New York

Robert Johnson and John Koten

Is one of the nation's most trusted retailers deceiving its customers? And why is it trying to torpedo New York's consumer-protection law?

The questions arise in a bizarre legal battle between Sears Roebuck & Co.

The Wall Street Journal, June 28, 1988, p. 1, 17. Copyright Dow Jones & Company, Inc. All rights reserved.

and the New York City Department of Consumer Affairs. The city wants Sears to stop certain forms of advertising it considers misleading under New York law and is suing Sears in state court. One disputed practice involves promoting a discounted price, say "30 percent off," without explaining whether the markdown is based on the regular price of the merchandise.

Instead of changing its advertising and perhaps avoiding bad publicity, Sears is fighting back. Earlier this month, it sued New York City in federal district court, contending that it should be able to advertise as it sees fit. Besides, Sears says, its ads are accurate and are protected by the First Amendment. The company also asserts that New York is trying to interfere with its right to engage in interstate commerce.

The giant retailer has another big stick to wave. In a press release distributed June 16, it warned that its only alternative, should it lose its fight with New York, is to "virtually discontinue advertising in New York City, including national publications and network broadcasts in that market."

A VERY BIG ADVERTISER

That's no small threat. Sears has the third-largest promotion budget among U.S. corporations, spending $1.17 billion a year to tout its 819 stores and the products they sell. Its advertising circulars are a staple of Sunday newspapers all over the country. Sears won't say how much it budgets for advertising in New York City.

Yet, considering what it spends bolstering one of the most enviable reputations in American business, industry watchers find it surprising that Sears would risk any damage to its good name.

"Sears has the strange idea that they should abide by the lowest common denominator of consumer-protection behavior," says Susan Kassapian, a consumer advocate in the Department of Consumer Affairs. Regulators also are now concerned about the potential effect Sears could have on advertising in New York if it succeeds in its lawsuit to have the city's consumer-protection laws declared unconstitutional.

Angelo J. Aponte, New York's consumer-affairs commissioner, says his office has negotiated advertising changes with more than 100 retailers since the laws in question took effect 20 years ago. All the others have complied when contacted, he says, and Sears is the only retailer to offer serious resistance.

"ETHICAL MARGINS"

Even some people in the advertising business are wincing. "It's a sad commentary on what's happening in marketing these days," says Paul Koenigsberg, the vice president of marketing strategy at Management Horizons, a retail consulting firm. "Years ago, companies weren't cutting their ethical margins so close."

Sears is being accused, among other things, of advertising clothing discounts without explaining where prices started; promoting a tire sale without saying how much its more expensive tires sell for; and saying that a carpet-cleaning bargain is about to end when, actually, the promotion is going to go on and on for months.

Stanley Lipnick, an outside attorney whom Sears has assigned to the case, says the company believes that its advertising hasn't misled any customers. "It's truthful," he says. W. Stan Knipe, a regional manager for Sears in New York, adds that the battle with New York regulators should do no harm to the company's image. "Our reputation for dealing with the American public is 100 years old. Our policies haven't changed: The phrase 'Satisfaction Guaranteed or Your Money Back' is still over the door at every store." Senior executives at Sears declined repeated requests for interviews.

SEARS AND "THE PUBLIC"

The battle already has gotten messy. "We were trying to show their 'public be damned' attitude," says Gary Walker, the public-information director of the city's consumer agency. Shortly after Sears filed its lawsuit, the city issued a press release that sought to embarrass the company by quoting from a heated exchange between Sears's attorney, Mr. Lipnick, and Mr. Aponte. At one point, Mr. Aponte asked whether Sears was concerned about hurting its reputation with customers. The attorney responded: "I don't care what the public thinks." (Sears doesn't deny its lawyer said that but says the quotation was taken out of context.)

Consumer officials in California and Florida have begun studying the New York charges and are reviewing Sears's ads. James Musselman, an attorney at the Center for Study of Responsible law, a consumer group in Washington, says he will lobby for tougher consumer-advertising laws in other states. He scoffs at Sears's claims that the Constitution protects the way it advertises. "The First Amendment doesn't give you the right to lure people into your store under false pretenses," he says. Sears reiterates that its ads are accurate.

The dispute between Sears and New York actually began last year when city officials spotted in Sears's advertising what they now allege are violations of local law. For example, in its carpet-cleaning ads that ran in certain New York newspapers last September, Sears promised a $34.98 "Fall Savings Spectacular." It exhorted readers: "Hurry! Call by Sept. 26."

But the very next month, it made the same offer, except for the date: "Hurry! Call by Oct. 25." The same urgent pitch, with yet another expiration date, appeared on October 25.

"This is the sort of thing you might expect from some small-time schlock operator," says Mr. Aponte, the consumer commissioner. "It's deceptive to imply this is some special offer when it goes on month after month."

Since health clubs, travel agents, and car dealers in New York do this sort of thing all the time and continue to do so, year after year, one has reason to wonder how common the abuse is and how consistent the law enforcement. The consumer-affairs department says it has ordered more than 100 merchants to stop such practices in the past 10 years. But the department concedes that problems persist. The agency is going after Sears because the huge retailer affects substantial numbers of consumers. Sears's alleged violations, which it denies, have yet to be established in court; the company has never been found in violation of New York consumer laws.

"AND AS HIGH AS"

Another Sears newspaper ad under fire in the city's lawsuit touted Sears's Guardsman Radial Tires for "as low as $34.99." New York City law prohibits advertising offers of this sort that don't also cite the prices of similar but more expensive items. Such prices must be published in a type size "at least as tall and broad as the lowest price stated," according to the law.

Mr. Lipnick, the Sears attorney, says the tire ads aren't deceptive. "What about the car ads that say payments are from $95 a month without explaining how much higher they go?" he wonders.

Another fundamental Sears ad style that is questioned by the city's suit is the promotion of a "percent off" discount without specifying the everyday price of the advertised product. Sears's May 15, 1987, ad in the *New York Daily News* said, "Save 15% to 30% on selected apparel." The everyday, prediscount price isn't stated.

Mr. Aponte asserts in an interview that, besides misleading the consumer about the true discount involved, such advertising also can be a form of bait and switch. "This isn't just a technical violation," he says, referring to an allegation in the city's suit. "Customers go to Sears thinking they'll get 30 percent off and they're told, 'Oh no, not on this rack. Only those over there'."

A BIG DRAW

Sears's advertising does say that only selected merchandise is on sale. But Mr. Aponte thinks that ads draw people into the store believing that more is on sale than actually is. Sears says that, with its huge inventory, it's hard to list exactly all the items discounted in a major sale.

Mr. Aponte says Sears is the largest and most consistent consumer-law breaker in New York, the city whose laws, he says, are the toughest in the nation. The ordinances Sears is charged under are 20 years old, and, Mr. Aponte says, every other major retailer has complied with them, sometimes after receiving warnings from city officials. Sears was first warned nearly a year ago and hasn't been cooperative, he says. "They just think they can thumb their nose at New York City laws," he says.

One reason for Sears's resistance: Ads of the sort being challenged in New York are a mainstay of the company's national advertising and could easily enough be contested elsewhere. The company spends most of its billion-dollar promotion budget on print and television ads—known in the trade as "door-busters"—that promote special prices.

In a statement, Sears asserts that the advertising practices disputed in New York are "used by retailers across the country, comply with federal advertising laws, and are recognized as truthful, accurate, and nondeceptive everywhere except New York City."

People in advertising say that discount promotions are crucial to Sears for a variety of reasons. "For one thing," says Thomas Flynn, a former advertising executive who investigates consumer complaints, "they are a cheap way to compete on price. You mark things down, but you don't kill yourself discounting everything."

The ads also are designed to persuade people to go shopping. They create a sense of urgency in consumers' minds. Leo Shapiro, a Chicago market researcher, notes that boasting discounts is an important line of defense for Sears against the advancing tide of discount stores catering to shoppers looking for bargains. More than 80 percent of the items that retailers sell today are at discounted prices, he says. Through advertising discounts on selected items—instead of offering prices on its whole inventory low enough to compete with the growing competition of discount chains—Sears can capitalize on its reputation as a quality retailer to convince customers that they can have the best of both worlds—quality and price—at Sears. "These ads create the attitude, 'I better check at Sears'," says Mr. Flynn.

Rather than contract the work out to its advertising agency, Ogilvy & Mather, Sears does all the work on its price-oriented advertising in-house. A company official says that even though the ads look fairly simple, more than 100 workers—copywriters, artists, layout experts, and marketing specialists—are involved in the preparation. There are also "people who do nothing but check over all the things that other people do to make sure we do nothing to offend a customer, violate our ad policies, or Federal Trade Commission rules," says Thomas Morris, the vice president of the company's merchandise group.

CAST OF CHARACTERS

Many of the ads are prepared a year in advance, when marketing officials pick items that will go on sale around the country. An artist's pencil draws up to five versions of the ad, with different print and photo sizes. Copywriters draft the words. That process sometimes takes weeks. Ultimately, attorneys check the ads, and Mr. Morris approves them. Most of these ads are "national," in that common ad styles are sent to newspapers and magazines across the country. Sometimes, Sears will send out a newspaper ad to different areas of the country, advertising perhaps a 30 percent discount on coats—even though its stores might not stock exactly the same styles.

This isn't the first time Sears has been in hot water over discounts. In 1983, California sued the company, alleging that it used misleading discount pricing in some of its promotions. Sears was charged in a civil lawsuit by the California attorney general's office with misrepresenting an artificially inflated price on certain items as the regular, or everyday, price. Sears agreed as part of a settlement to refrain from making untrue representations in ads; it also paid California $55,000.

New York City's civil suit in state court is seeking $500 for each alleged violation by the company. It also is asking the court to issue a permanent injunction against Sears to prohibit consumer-law violations of the sorts alleged. Sears, meanwhile, is asking the federal court to declare the city's consumer laws unconstitutional.

One securities analyst says he believes Sears management is showing bad judgment in fighting consumer laws. "This is bureaucratic management rigidity, not good business sense," says Edward Weller of Montgomery Securities. "You'd think Sears would say. 'You're right. Let's get on the consumer side of this thing.' Instead, they seem to want to get dragged kicking and screaming into losing market share." But Sears, insisting that its ads are accurate, says altering them might drive up its retail prices.

PART THREE

Social/Political Responsiveness

There is an intricate web that links business and government with the rest of society. Business is vitally concerned with the actions of government at all levels (federal, state, and local) and in all branches (executive, legislative, and judicial). Often business seeks governmental action on its behalf. In recent years, for example, Lockheed and Chrysler have secured loan guarantees from the federal government to avert bankruptcy. Virtually each of the 50 states and thousands of cities seek to attract or retain businesses via tax concessions and other devices. Industries lobby the administration and the Congress for protective trade barriers while other industries plead for free trade. It is important to note that governmental intervention in the economy is not an aberration of our modern era either in the form of regulation or incentives. The partnership of American business and government extends back to and before the founding of this country. Even in the late 19th century, the supposed heyday of free-market capitalism, there was hardly a single major industry or firm that rose to prominence without the aid of government.[1] But this partnership is ever changing with participants whose demands often conflict.

Government contributes to the confusion and uncertainty of the political/legal environment by giving conflicting messages to the business community. Government breaks up American Telephone & Telegraph Company, while at the same time drops its decade-long antitrust suit against IBM. Government approves the merger of Texaco and Getty Oil only to turn around and oppose the combination of G. Heileman Brewing Company and Schlitz. The federal government, on the one hand, deregulates the airlines, allows the restrictions of the Banking Act to erode, but becomes increasingly aggressive in regulating public utilities (especially those constructing and operating nuclear power plants) and petroleum companies. During the 1980s two major factors have been changing the business-political relationship. On the one hand, more companies have become multinationals, thereby making it more difficult for-

---

[1] Robert Lively, "The American System: A Review Article," *Business History Review* 29, no. 1 (1955), pp. 81–96.

any one nation to be able to control their actions. Indeed, many of the largest multinationals have budgets and resources larger than many countries. On the other hand, one effect of the Reagan administration's federal deregulation efforts was an increase in state regulatory actions. For many businesses this increased the number of regulations with which they had to contend, since in many cases federal regulations preempted state and local regulations. If this continues to be a burden for a significant portion of the business community, then the trend toward re-regulation will increase, leading to additional conflicts within the business community.

Government in a free society provides a major mechanism for the exercise of the people's will. Government is complex, however, and not always quick to respond to the public mood. Indeed, the notion of "the public" is misleading in a diverse, pluralistic society. Some groups push for equal employment and affirmative action programs, while others complain of reverse discrimination. Some members of society argue that American companies should not be allowed to do business in South Africa because of the racist policies of the government of that country. Others argue for U.S. business involvement there as a means of improving conditions for blacks and other minorities in that country. The government does not and cannot resolve all such questions with legislation or executive orders. Thus, while the debates continue, managers must make decisions which are not fully guided by law but rather by judgment and conscience. Perhaps the most important lesson for business people, particularly those managing small- to medium-sized firms, is not to depend on the government for survival and to expect constant change in laws and regulations. What is legal or unregulated today may be illegal or regulated tomorrow. When an activity is regulated, a businessperson may find frequent and significant changes occurring in the regulations, consequently raising or lowering costs. One of the best ways to deal with this is for business people to get involved politically. Of course, many businesses, business people, and industry associations are politically active, yet more could be done, particularly in areas that would lead to improved social responsibility by adding additional protection for socially responsible firms.

The cases in this section provide insights about certain social issues and relationships at all three levels of government. The American Ship Building Company case focuses on illegal contributions to the campaign committee for former President Nixon. The International Harvester case involves management choosing between two states and the citizens of two cities who are struggling to retain their truck assembly plants and the jobs and economic benefits associated therewith. Arthur D. Little and the Toxic Alert highlights the issues of local government control and autonomy, high-tech research in toxic chemicals and biomedical research, and the general welfare.

The commentaries in this section emphasize a number of issues touching on community/political responsiveness issues: campaign contributions and lobbying by companies and trade organizations, states' competition for companies, business responsibility to provide minority employment and improve local economics, and the rise in state regulatory activities in response to the Reagan administration's deregulation efforts. The issues selected are diverse, but that is intentional. Business people regularly confront multiple challenges with often conflicting expectations from the community and the political system. The fact that so many business people succeed, and succeed in a legal, moral, and ethical manner, in the face of great challenges is a statement of their fortitude.

The American Ship Building Company

On August 30, 1974, George M. Steinbrenner, chairman and chief executive officer of The American Ship Building Company, was fined $10,000 by Judge Leroy J. Contie in the Cleveland (Ohio) Federal District Court on felonious charges of illegally contributing to the election campaigns of former President Richard M. Nixon and several members of Congress. In addition, Steinbrenner was fined $5,000 for violation of federal campaign laws, involving participation (in an accessory capacity) after the fact of the violation. The court's actions were taken a week following guilty pleas by American Ship and Steinbrenner to the charges. The company was fined $20,000 for its role in the violations. Although this was the eighth firm and related officer to confess to federal election violations, it was the first case in which Watergate investigators had filed felonious charges.

THE AMERICAN SHIP BUILDING COMPANY

American Ship Building Company was incorporated in 1899; its main lines of business were construction, conversion, and repair of ships; construction of barges; and the supplying of building materials. Divisions of the company included the following: (1) Amship Division: ship building and repair; (2) Tampa Division: ship repair; (3) Nabrico Division: bridge and towboat construction; (4) Building Products Division: metal fabricating and building materials; and (5) Transportation, Cargo, and Material Handling Division.

American Ship was one of the nation's leading independent ship repair, conversion, and construction firms. Historically, the firm had been quite active and successful in the Great Lakes region and had expanded aggressively into the Gulf Coast area through its Tampa Division. In the fall of 1974, discussions were initiated with the Netherlands Antilles island of Curacao in an attempt to broaden the company's market via joint ventures. By serving governmental agencies as well as the private sector, American Ship played an important role in the delivery of many power-related materials, such as oil and iron ore, to U.S. ports of entry and inland waterways.

Annual sales for the firm had increased from $38 million in 1969 to $95 million in 1973; net income also increased during this period from $1.5 million in 1969 to $4.2 million in 1972—fiscal 1973 net income dropped to $2.3

million, due partly to unrecovered excess costs incurred on a government contract. Part of the firm's success during the 1970s came about as a result of the creation of its Tampa and Nabrico Divisions in 1972 and 1969, respectively. Although revenues generated from federal government contracts did not represent a significant percentage of American Ship's annual totals, a working relationship had been established with federal agencies. One government contract had been initiated in 1965 and another in 1966; both projects, which involved the construction of ships for several agencies, were completed in 1970. In 1974, a project was undertaken with the U.S. Corps of Engineers; the contract called for the repair of government "dredge vessels."[1]

GEORGE M. STEINBRENNER III

Mr. Steinbrenner, despite his relatively young age of 43, had become a significant figure in the shipping industry. After a short career in college football coaching at Northwestern and Purdue universities, Steinbrenner returned to his family's shipping firm, Kinsman Marine Transit Company. In 1968, while serving as Kinsman's president, he became part of a group organized by Roulston and Co., a Cleveland brokerage house that bought a large block of American Ship Building stock. To avoid a proxy fight within the company, American Ship officials appointed George Steinbrenner chief executive officer. That same year the family's business also became part of American Ship.

Although Mr. Steinbrenner maintained a hectic schedule as top man in the American Ship organization, he was quite active in community affairs. He became involved with the Cleveland Urban Coalition and served as vice chairman of the Greater Cleveland Growth Corporation. In 1968, the Cleveland Press Club named Steinbrenner "Man of the Year" for his civic and philanthropic efforts. Many underprivileged youngsters in the Cleveland area were able to attend college as a result of Mr. Steinbrenner's donation of personal funds. In 1974, he gave $10,000 for the benefit of out-of-work reporters and editors who were on strike against two daily newspapers; the only requirement attached to the funds was that each individual would participate in a lecture series on journalism.

Sports had always been a part of George Steinbrener's life. He participated in several sports during his high school and college years. After leaving coaching for a career in business, Steinbrenner became involved in several investments in sporting organizations. He took an interest in a local industrial league basketball team, the Cleveland Pipers, that later joined a professional league; through a partnership he bought the team for an undisclosed amount of cash. The team eventually filed bankruptcy with liabilities totaling $125,000. Although Mr. Steinbrenner was not legally obligated for the organi-

---

[1] This is a vessel used for scraping the bed of a body of water.

zation's liabilities, he worked for three years to pay off creditors and investors. In 1972, Steinbrenner joined a group that bought the National Basketball Association's Chicago Bulls, and in 1973 he became major owner and chief executive officer of the New York Yankees.[2] With the Yankees, he often attended important games and other team activities where he entertained prominent guests.[3] Other financial interests in sports included horse racing and breeding; to enhance this interest, Mr. Steinbrenner bought 800 acres of land near Ocala, Florida, and built a thoroughbred farm, the Kinsman Stud Farm.

The large financial interests and civic activities also enabled George Steinbrenner to involve himself with many political figures, particularly members of the Democratic party. In 1969 and 1970, he organized the Democratic Congressional Dinner and was able to raise $803,000 and over $1 million, respectively, for these two events.

Steinbrenner originally became involved with politicians and government representatives in 1968 when he became an executive of American Ship Building. "From the start I knew the secret for American Ship was to get the Great Lakes included in the maritime act to get the Great Lakes in there so they could get their share of assistance . . . I saw that the whole Great Lakes fleet had to be rebuilt, and the only way this could be done was with help."[4] Coincidentally, Congress had begun considering the amendment of the Merchant Marine Act of 1936 in the same year that Steinbrenner joined American Ship. He then began a three-pronged effort, meeting with politicians and industry officials and lobbying on Capitol Hill. When the act was finally amended, the construction of Great Lakes vessels qualified for tax benefits.

Despite all of his contacts among politicians and governmental agencies, George Steinbrenner discovered that the 1972 presidential campaign would witness an uprecedented amount of pressure on big business to contribute funds to the reelection of the incumbent president, Richard Nixon.

POLITICAL-BUSINESS CLIMATE OF CAMPAIGN 1972

Federal election campaigns were always expensive, and the presidential campaign of 1972 was no exception. This campaign did, however, offer something new for raising campaign funds—the Committee for the Re-Election of the President (CREEP). CREEP was comprised of 500 full-time workers, including 100 volunteers, devoted to the goal of reelecting a president who had become one of the most popular to serve in the White House and who was

---

[2] In January 1973, a group of business people headed by Mr. Steinbrenner purchased the Yankees from the Columbia Broadcasting Company for $10 million.

[3] For the Yankees' opening game of the 1974 season, Steinbrenner's guests were Sen. Edward Kennedy, D-Mass., and his son, Edward, Jr.

[4] Everett Groseclose, "Quick Comeback: George Steinbrenner, Hit by Nixon Scandal, Barely Misses a Stride," *The Wall Street Journal*, June 25, 1975, p. 16.

virtually a sure winner for the 1972 election (as per popularity polls and surveys). What made CREEP different from past reelection committees was that it had no formal relationship with the political party of the president, the GOP; instead, it was answerable only to its own leadership. Two members of the CREEP leadership, Maurice Stans and John Mitchell, had served in Nixon's cabinet as secretary of commerce and attorney general, respectively, prior to joining the committee. Another individual who played a leading role in CREEP was President Nixon's personal attorney, Herbert Kalmbach.

By concentrating on wealthy individuals and the business community, CREEP was able to raise an unprecedented $60 million for the 1972 election campaign. There was great emphasis on obtaining most of these funds prior to April 7, 1972, the effective date of the Federal Election Campaign Act of 1971. This new election campaign law required all candidates for federal office to report the name, business address, and occupation of donors who contributed in excess of $100. In effect, the new legislation was designed to require full disclosure of all contributions. Corporate contributions, disallowed even under previous laws, had been overlooked in many earlier campaigns; but it became evident that under the Federal Election Campaign Act of 1971, the guidelines barring corporate contributions would be enforceable.

Although the new legislation did not take effect until April of 1972, corporate contributions prior to this time were eventually investigated, charges were filed, and convictions were handed down against some corporations and/or officers of these firms. Prior to the revelation of American Ship's political contribution, executives of seven major companies admitted to illegal contributions. The companies and the amounts contributed were as follows:

American Airlines	$ 55,000
Ashland Oil	100,000
Gulf Oil	100,000
Goodyear Tire and Rubber	40,000
Minnesota Mining and Manufacturing	30,000
Phillips Petroleum	100,000
Braniff Airways	40,000

The chairman of American Airlines, George Spater, came forward and confessed to authorizing illegal contributions to the Nixon campaign. According to Spater's testimony before the Senate Watergate Committee, American Airlines "was solicited by Herbert W. Kalmbach, who said that we were among those from whom $100,000 was expected."[5] The company then decided to contribute $75,000; of this amount, $20,000 was contributed by company officials and $55,000 was taken from corporate funds. "I knew Mr. Kalmbach to be both the president's personal counsel and counsel for our major com-

---

[5] Michael C. Jensen, "The Corporate Political Squeeze," *New York Times,* September 16, 1973, pp. F1–F2.

petitor (United Airlines),"[6] stated Mr. Spater. He said that many corporations gave funds to the Nixon campaign because they feared government reprisals against them or the advantages that would be gained by competitors. The latter fear was based on statements made by campaign fund-raisers that competitors had already pledged funds. The method used for channeling the funds from American Airlines to CREEP involved a false payment to an agent in Lebanon who then brought the money back to the company in cash; the cash was then forwarded to the committee's headquarters.

Another company that confessed to illegal contributions, Gulf Oil, ordered cash ($100,000) from subsidiaries based in the Bahamas.[7] Ashland Oil entered a nonexistent corporate expenditure on the books of a subsidiary, Gabon Corporation; the funds ($100,000) were then deposited in a Swiss bank account, returned to company headquarters, and finally forwarded to CREEP.[8]

As a result of their illegal contributions, the companies were charged with misdemeanor violations. Mr. Spater was not charged with any violation because he was the first to confess; however, officials of Ashland and Gulf were charged with misdemeanors. Each firm was fined $5,000, the maximum penalty for the violation. A vice president of Gulf, Claude C. Wild, Jr., was fined $1,000 for authorizing the company's contibution; chairman Orkin E. Atkins of Ashland was also fined $1,000. The maximum penalty for corporate officials was $1,000 in fines and one year imprisonment.

THE CASE OF AMERICAN SHIP BUILDING

On April 5, 1974, a federal grand jury in Cleveland returned a 15-count criminal indictment against Mr. Steinbrenner and American Ship; the charges stemmed from Watergate investigators' findings that illegal contributions had been made to President Nixon's campaign as well as to various Democratic and Republican congressional campaigns. Committees that received funds from American Ship were as follows:

1. September 1970: $5,000 to a committee supporting the reelection of Rep. Charles A. Mosher, R-Ohio.

2. October 1970: $2,000 to the Democratic Congressional Campaign Committee.

3. October 1970: $500 to the committee for the reelection of Rep. Frank T. Bow, R-Ohio.

4. October 1970: $1,000 to the committee for the reelection of Sen. Vance Hartke, D-Ind.

---

[6] Ibid.

[7] Gulf also made contributions to the campaigns of Sen. Henry Jackson (D-Wash.) and Rep. Wilbur Mills, D-Ark; both were Democratic hopefuls for their party's nomination.

[8] Ashland also bought a $10,000 ad in the Republican National Convention magazine.

5. October 1970 and February 1971: $11,000 to the National Democratic Congressional Dinner.

6. February 1972: $14,000 to the Senate-House Majority (Democratic) Dinner.

7. April 1972: $25,000 to CREEP.

8. November 1972: $6,200 to unnamed committees for President Nixon's re-election.

9. July 1973: $500 to the reelection committee for Sen. Daniel K. Inouye, D-Hawaii.

Two top officials of the firm were also named in the indictment; however, they had been granted immunity from prosecution because of their testimony given before the Senate Watergate Committee. Robert Bartlome, company secretary, and Matthew Clark, company purchasing director, testified before the committee in November of 1973, describing a bogus bonus plan for themselves and six other company employees (see Exhibit 1). Bartlome testified that as early as 1970 plans were formalized for channeling political contributions to both Republican and Democratic interests. He stated that Steinbrenner instructed him to "make a list of loyal employees"[9] who could carry out the necessary instructions that would enable the firm to funnel the contributions; the justification for such action was that Steinbrenner was being pressured for the contributions. The source of this pressure was not mentioned.

The plan devised by Steinbrenner involved the following: (1) each employee on the list was to receive a $5,000 bonus, which resulted in an average net amount of $3,700 after taxes; (2) they were then instructed to write two separate checks, in the amounts of $3,000 and $100, from their personal

EXHIBIT 1   American Ship Building Employees Who Received Bonus Payments

Name	Title
Robert Bartlome	Secretary
Matthew Clark	Purchasing director
Stanley Lepkowski	Treasurer
Gordon Stafford	Executive vice president
Daniel Kessell	Treasurer for company's fleet of cargo ships
Ian Cushenan	President, transportation, cargo, and material handling
Robert Dibble	Employee
Roy Walker	Employee

---

[9] Monroe W. Karmin, "American Ship Building Gift to Nixon Drive Concealed as Bonuses, Employees Say," *The Wall Street Journal,* November 14, 1973, p. 4.

accounts to the designated organization; (3) finally, the remaining $600 was to be returned to the company's petty cash fund.[10]

According to Bartlome, the eight employees received approximately $97,000 during the period 1970–72. Steinbrenner also received a bonus in October 1970 for $75,000.[11] The final bonus for the eight employees was issued on April 6,1972; on this day, an unnamed corporate vice president was sent to Washington to deliver $100,000 in cash—$75,000 from Steinbrenner's personal funds and $25,000 from the employees—to the CREEP headquarters.[12]

When questioned about the last minute bonuses and their timing, Steinbrenner told Bartlome that the payments needed no elaboration. Corporate treasurer Stanley Lepkowski questioned Mr. Steinbrenner's actions and was told that "many corporations in the United States do it in this manner."[13] As a result of these final bonuses, Bartlome felt it was necessary to legitimize Steinbrenner's actions in the corporate records. In January of 1973, he composed a memo authorizing the bonuses and backdated the memo one year; the memo was then placed in the company's official records.

In August 1973, Clark, Bartlome, and the six other employees signed sworn affidavits before FBI investigators stating that the bonuses were proper and all contributions were personal in nature. Bartlome said the false information was the result of extensive pressure they had received from Steinbrenner and company general counsel John Melcher.[14]

When the Watergate grand jury subpoenaed the eight employees, they decided to tell the real story behind the bonuses and the company's illegal contributions. As Clark put it, "All I could see was me standing behind bars and [the corporate lawyer] telling me not to worry about it."[15] Upon hearing of the employees' decision to confess, Bartlome said Steinbrenner laid his head on the desk, moaning that he and the company were ruined, and mentioned something about jumping off a bridge. He then told Bartlome to "have a good weekend" with his family and handed him an envelope with some cash in it.[16]

George Steinbrenner chose not to testify before the Watergate committee; he told investigators that he would plead the Fifth Amendment. Consequently, it was not until April 5, 1974, that Steinbrenner made a public statement.

---

[10] The company's petty cash fund was also used for campaign contributions, according to Bartlome's testimony.

[11] Eileen Shanahan, "2 Tell of Scheme To Hide Nixon Gift," *New York Times*, November 14, 1973, p. 32.

[12] According to Bartlome, this vice president was not aware of the contents of the delivery package (addressed to Herbert Kalmbach).

[13] Karmin, "American Ship Building Gift to Nixon Drive Concealed As Bonuses, Employees Say," p. 4.

[14] *The Wall Street Journal*, September 16, 1973, p. 1.

[15] "Mr. Nixon Comes Out Fighting," *Newsweek*, November 26, 1973, p. 34.

[16] Shanahan, "2 Tell of Scheme To Hide Nixon Gift," p. 32.

Through a Cleveland public relations consultant, he said that the Watergate prosecutors offered him the option of pleading guilty to a criminal charge of willful conspiracy to violate election laws, carrying with it a maximum penalty of a $10,000 fine, two years imprisonment, or both. "There was no way I could plead guilty . . . because I just am not guilty of any such violations. I feel it is very important that I state publicly why I have chosen to fight, and it is also equally important to ask the public to remember that an indictment is not a conviction."[17]

By August 1974, Steinbrenner agreed to confess on two counts: (1) illegally contributing to election campaigns of Nixon and several members of Congress and (2) participating (in an accessory capacity) after the fact (of illegally contributing to the Nixon campaign).

Despite his confession, George Steinbrenner felt that his actions were the result of extensive pressure from government authorities. American Ship Building was at that time involved in four different actions with the federal government.

> They included a government oceanographic-survey ship called the *Researcher,* on which American Ship was negotiating a settlement on a $5.4 million overrun of contract costs; Justice Department antitrust interest in American Ship's acquisition of Great Lakes Towing Co., the largest tug-boat company on the Great Lakes; a Labor Department investigation of American Ship's working conditions and safety standards after a fire on a huge iron-ore carrier called *The Roger Blough* in which four workmen died; and Justice Department objections to American Ship's purchase of Wilson Marine Transit Co., and a shipyard at Erie, Pa., both owned by Litton Industries.[18]

Prior to the solicitations for donations to Nixon's reelection, Steinbrenner apparently felt that American Ship was insulated from such pressures because of his friendship with Thomas Evans, who attended college with him and had also served as a director of American Ship. Evans, a former law partner of Nixon's, was deputy chairman of finance for the presidential campaign, but eventually fell from favor with the reelection committee. However, the numerous actions mounted by federal agencies against his company made it appear that earlier warnings from Steinbrenner's Democratic friends in Washington about Nixon's vindictiveness were well founded. According to Steinbrenner, he felt that he had no choice but to give CREEP the requested amount of funds.[19]

Governmental action against American Ship and Mr. Steinbrenner was not over, however; they also had violated regulations governing financial reports filed with the Securities and Exchange Commission (SEC).

---

[17] *Cleveland Plain Dealer,* April 6, 1974, p. 32.

[18] Groseclose, "Quick Comeback: George Steinbrenner, Hit by Nixon Scandal, Barely Misses a Stride," p. 16.

[19] Ibid.

SEC ACTION AGAINST AMERICAN SHIP AND STEINBRENNER

As a result of the false entries made in the company's financial records for the employee bonuses, in October of 1974 the SEC filed charges against the company: (1) American Ship tried to conceal illegal contributions via ordinary business expenses and (2) the company failed to disclose to its stockholders that company funds were being used for political contributions and that certain officers who were standing for election as directors were participating in these activities. In view of the above, the SEC recommended that George Steinbrenner be required to refund the company all unauthorized funds used for political purposes, and that a review committee be created, by the company's board of directors, to determine the exact amount that Steinbrenner authorized for political purposes. The company and Steinbrenner agreed to cease the filing of any further false financial reports and agreed to create a review committee, which would then report back to the board of directors; however, American Ship and its chairman admitted or denied nothing.

The review committee was comprised of two outside directors (company directors not employed by American Ship), Messrs. James Nederlander and Arnold Sobel, and a nondirector, Mr. Allan Shaw. Mr. Shaw was appointed chairman of the committee.[20]

The review committee's report was completed in May of 1975 and submitted to the firm's board of directors.[21] Of the $97,000 taken from the corporate treasury for political contributions, the committee recommended that George Steinbrenner repay approximately $42,000. In response to the committee's recommendation, Steinbrenner released the following statement:

> I stand ready to reimburse the corporation in line with the committee's recommendations. Right or wrong, the buck stops here. Contributions were made in 1972, we cannot argue that. And while they were made in the full belief that they were legal, I will honor the committee's recommendations and will comply with any action taken by the board with respect to the requirements.[22]

The amount recommended by the committee was linked to the employee bonuses of April 6, 1972. In addition to this liability of $42,000, the committee found only one other irregularity, a $500 contribution to Sen. Daniel Inouye,

---

[20] Mr. Nederlander, who was president of the Nederlander Theater Corporation, was also Steinbrenner's business partner in several theatrical productions, such as *Applause, Seesaw, Funny Girl, On a Clear Day, George M.,* and other theatrical ventures. Mr. Sobel was executive vice president of Material Service Corporation. Mr. Shaw was a former executive vice president of the Cleveland Trust Company, one of American Ship's registrars.

[21] American Ship's board was chaired by Steinbrenner during the review of the committee's recommendations.

[22] *Cleveland Plain Dealer,* May 8, 1975, p. 6-A.

D-Hawaii, a member of the Senate Watergate Committee. This contribution was traced to the company's petty cash fund.

POST LITIGATION PERIOD

On February 20, 1975, George Steinbrenner was replaced as chief executive officer by Francis W. Theis. In a quarterly report to stockholders, Steinbrenner stated that "The selection of Mr. Theis concludes an intensive search for a new top man qualified to serve as president and to succeed me in the role of chief executive officer. Mr. Theis has served as president and chief executive officer of Hooker Chemical Corporation."[23]

As a result of Mr. Steinbrenner's guilty plea and conviction, baseball commissioner Bowie Kuhn suspended him from participating in any Yankee activities for a period of two years.[24]

After stepping down as chief executive officer, George Steinbrenner moved his family to Florida and began working out of the company's Tampa office. He then began devoting most of his time to his interests in horse racing, theatrical ventures, and the Kinsman marine Transit fleet of ships (bought back from American Ship along with an associate). He also returned to fund-raising activities for the Democratic party. Indeed, at the 1975 Democratic Congressional Victory Dinner, Speaker Carl Albert presented Steinbrenner with an engraved plaque for his services to the party. The audience of prominent political figures gave the "businessman, sports lover, political fund-raiser, and felon" a lengthy ovation.[25]

---

[23] American Ship Building Company, *Second Quarter Report to Shareholders,* March 31, 1975.

[24] The commissioner had the authority to take any action he deemed necessary for the best interests of the sport. In the past, any convicted felon who owned shares in a professional sports organization was ordered to sell his interest in that organization.

[25] Groseclose, "Quick Comeback: George Steinbrenner, Hit By Nixon Scandal, Barely Misses a Stride," p. 1.

International Harvester: Plant Closing (A) / Fort Wayne versus Springfield

The headlines of the July 29, 1982, Fort Wayne, Indiana, evening newspaper plaintively told its residents, "Our IH Plant's in Jeopardy." The Springfield, Ohio, newspaper carried a similar message. International Harvester Company, the major employer in each city, had decided to close a truck-making plant in one of the two communities (by October 31, 1983).[1] The closing was part of a massive International Harvester restructuring of its operations designed to cut costs by $1 billion and save the company from bankruptcy. Exhibits 1 through 5 provide financial data on International Harvester (IH or Harvester) from 1977 through 1982.

Part of Harvester's problem and an added reason for concern by the two communities was the national economy during the early 1980s. From 1980 to 1982 the United States suffered one of the worst economic downturns since the Great Depression of the 1930s. The recession hit manufacturing—and the automotive industry in particular—especially hard.[2] National unemployment stood near 10 percent in mid-1982; among nonwhites, it was 16 percent. In Fort Wayne and Springfield, both primarily manufacturing towns, the unemployment rates were 11.9 percent and 13.5 percent, respectively. The average prime rate charged by banks peaked over 20 percent in late 1980 and averaged 18.87 percent during 1981. The consumer price index jumped 13.5 percent from 1979 to 1980 and another 10.4 percent from 1980 to 1981.

The prime criterion for the plant closing was the minimization of manufacturing costs. But the decision was a decidedly human one. It would ultimately be made by one man, Donald Lennox, IH's president and chief operating officer. Donald Lennox was an operations expert who had spent most of his career at Ford and Xerox. Starting as a part-time consultant to IH, he became a full-time special assistant to Harvester's president in 1979. In 1980 he was appointed senior vice president in charge of IH's operations staff and

---

[1] IH had actually announced that it intended to close one of its three North American truck-making plants, the third being located in Chatham, Ontario. But Harvester could not close that plant without paying a 15 percent tariff on trucks it shipped into Canada, which accounted for 15 percent of its 1981 truck sales. Privately, IH officials indicated that Chatham was not a candidate for closure.

[2] Manufacturing employment dropped 12 percent and capacity utilization reached a post–World War II nadir from 1980 through 1982. During the third quarter of 1980, the automotive industry was losing money at a rate of $13.3 billion a year.

EXHIBIT 1

INTERNATIONAL HARVESTER
Income Statement and Per Share Data
1977–1982
($ millions)

	1977	1978	1979	1980	1981	1982
Sales and other revenues:						
Sales	$5,975.1	$6,664.3	$8,392.0	$6,311.8	$7,040.9	$4,292.3
Other income	27.6	34.1	34.4	30.3	(22.8)	29.6
Total revenues	6,002.7	6,698.4	8,426.4	6,342.1	7,018.1	4,321.9
Cost and expenses:						
Cost of sales	4,924.7	5,454.5	6,904.4	5,700.1	6,406.8	4,118.7
Marketing and administrative	593.7	659.8	769.3	811.9	739.5	501.1
Interest expenses	114.9	126.8	148.4	283.9	376.7	345.3
Exchange (gain) loss		107.2	(20.9)	30.0	(86.1)	(23.2)
Other expenses	118.5	157.3	245.9	407.7	447.1	299.6
Total costs and expenses	5,751.8	6,504.7	8,047.2	7,233.7	7,884.1	5,241.5
Income of consolidated group:						
Income before taxes	250.9	193.7	379.2	(891.6)	(866.0)	(919.5)
Taxes	116.6	85.4	116.1	(387.3)	(98.7)	(54.2)
Net income of consolidated group	134.3	108.3	263.1	(504.3)	(767.3)	(865.3)
Income of nonconsolidated companies:						
Income before taxes	125.9	146.0	190.9	217.6	230.2	116.0
Taxes	58.9	67.6	84.4	82.9	98.7	73.1
Net income of nonconsolidated companies	67.0	78.4	106.5	134.7	131.6	42.8
Income (loss) from continuing operations	201.3	186.7	369.6	(369.6)	(635.7)	(822.4)

EXHIBIT 1 *(concluded)*

	1977	1978	1979	1980	1981	1982
Unusual item: Provision for operational restructuring costs						(443.9)
Income (loss) from discontinued operations:						
Construction equipment (sold 1982)						
Operating loss, net of tax benefit						(13)
Loss on sale						(326)
Solar (sold 1981)						
Operating income, net of taxes on income					4.8	
Gain on sale					275.7	
Wisconsin Steel (sold 1977)						
Operating income, net of taxes	2.4				(5.1)	
Valuation adjustment, net of tax benefit				(27.7)	(32.9)	(55)
Net income (loss) from discontinued operations	2.4			(27.7)	242.6	(393.7)
Extraordinary income						21.8
Net income (loss)	$ 203.7	$ 186.7	$ 396.6	$ (397.3)	$ (393.1)	$(1,638.2)
Income (loss) per common share:						
Continuing operations	$ 6.84	$ 6.14	$ 12.01	$ (12.02)	$ (20.44)	$ (39.88)
Discontinued operations	.08			(.89)	7.54	(12.19)
Extraordinary income						.68
Net income (loss) per common share	$ 6.92	$ 6.14	$ 12.01	$ (12.91)	$ (12.90)	$ (51.39)
Dividends per common share	$ 1.85	$ 2.10	$ 2.35	$ 2.50	$ .30	-0-

Note: IH's fiscal year ran from November 1 through October 31 of the following year.

SOURCE: Annual reports.

EXHIBIT 2

INTERNATIONAL HARVESTER
Balance Sheet
1977–1982
($ millions)

	1977	1978	1979	1980	1981	1982
Assets						
Current assets:						
Cash	$ 17.2	$ 27.3	$ 25.2	$ 137.1	$ 185.6	$ 40.7
Receivables	537.7	682.6	805.5	768.8	555.4	305.5
Inventories	1,729.5	1,892.9	2,342.9	2,331.7	1,634.4	646.8
Other current assets	39.8	45.9	92.1	189.9	296.6	663.2
Total current assets	2,324.2	2,648.7	3,265.8	3,427.4	2,672.0	1,656.2
Investments and long-term receivables	666.7	755.4	910.2	1,097.2	1,246.9	978.6
Property	771.2	889.7	1,039.1	1,277.2	1,360.8	965.6
Other assets	26.0	22.3	32.4	41.6	66.4	98.3
Total assets	$3,788.1	$4,316.1	$ 5,247.5	$5,843.5	$5,346.1	$3,698.8

EXHIBIT 2 *(concluded)*

Liabilities and Stockholders Equity	1977	1978	1979	1980	1981	1982
Current liabilities:						
Notes payable	$ 248.6	$ 305.5	$ 411.4	$ 808.9	$ 441.8	$ 153.3
Accounts payable	411.6	609.9	943.6	984.7	712.3	423.5
Accrued liabilities	344.0	449.3	487.8	587.7	573.5	511.2
Current maturities of 1-t debt	43.8	74.2	30.6	51.5	80.5	47.3
Total current liabilities	1,048.0	1,438.9	1,873.4	2,432.8	1,808.2	1,135.2
Noncurrent liabilities:						
Long-term debt	926.3	932.5	948.2	1,327.1	1,985.0	2,015.3
Deferred income taxes	80.0	68.5	226.9	139.7	5.8	
Other noncurrent liabilities				47.4	65.5	515.6
Total noncurrent liabilities	1,006.3	1,001.0	1,175.1	1,519.1	2,056.3	2,530.9
Preferred stock	50.0	50.0	50.0	200.0	196.7	400.0
Common stockholders' equity:						
Common stock	591.2	607.2	622.9	644.2	653.9	723.1
Capital in excess of par	12.4	22.0	36.2	42.4	45.2	
Retained earnings	1,093.1	1,211.6	1,504.8	1,024.3	599.9	(1,078.0)
Less: Common stock in treasury and receivables	12.9	14.6	14.8	14.4	14.1	12.2
Total common stockholders' equity	1,733.8	1,826.1	22,149.1	1,696.5	1,285.0	(367.1)
Total liabilities and stockholders' equity	$3,788.1	$4,316.1	$ 5,247.5	$5,843.5	$5,346.1	$3,698.8

SOURCE: Annual reports.

EXHIBIT 3 Key Statistics, 1977–1982 (millions)

	1977	1978	1979	1980	1981	1982
Sales by product group:						
Trucks	$2,701	$3,211	$3,966	$2,701	$3,318	$2,428
Agricultural equipment	2,334	2,348	3,069	2,507	2,980	1,864
Construction equipment	731	852	1,000	760	743	†
Turbo machinery	208	253	356	343	*	
Total	$5,975	$6,664	$8,392	$6,312	$7,041	$4,292
Sales by geographic area:						
United States	$4,315	$4,836	$6,100	$4,124	$4,908	$3,065
Canada	459	493	717	603	679	409
Europe, Africa, and						
Mideast	868	1,006	1,159	1,140	983	732
Latin America	25	37	55	68	78	43
Pacific	309	293	362	376	393	43
Total	$5,975	$6,664	$8,392	$6,312	$7,041	$4,292
Net income:						
Amount	$ 203	$ 187	$ 370	(397)	(393)	(1,638)
Percent of sales	3.39%	2.8%	4.4%	—	—	—
Return on equity	12.38%	10.36%	18.34%	—	—	—
Other:						
Capital expenditures	$ 168	$ 210	$ 285	$ 384	$ 325	$ 108
Long-term debt as a per-						
cent of capitalization	36%	33%	30%	41%	57%	98%
Current assets to						
current liabilities	2.2-1	1.8-1	1.7-1	1.4-1	1.5-1	1.5-1

* On July 31, 1981, after fiscal year 1981 sales of $280.2 million, International Harvester sold its turbo machinery business to Caterpillar Tractor Company for approximately $505 million in cash.
† On November 1, 1982, after fiscal year 1982 sales of $433 million, International Harvester sold substantially all of its construction equipment business to Dresser Industries, Inc., for approximately $83 million.

SOURCE: Annual reports.

executive vice president of the Components Group. As the result of a 1981 reorganization, he was named president of IH's new Manufacturing Group. And in a May 1982 management shake-up, he was promoted to president and chief operating officer of the company.

Donald Lennox's decision would terminate the jobs of thousands of long-time workers in the losing community. The effect on that community would be severe. (Exhibit 6 compares the two cities, while Exhibit 7 describes how a plant closing would affect each city.) To understand the complexity of Lennox's decision, it is necessary to look at Harvester's long relationship with both communities and the origins of its financial crisis.

EXHIBIT 4

INTERNATIONAL HARVESTER
Quarterly Financial Information
($ millions)

	1979				1980				1981				1982			
	1st	2nd	3rd	4th	1st	2nd	3rd	4th	1st	2nd	3rd	4th	1st	2nd	3rd	4th
Sales	$1,610	$2,205	$2,082	$2,495	$1,008	$1,160	$1,823	$2,321	$1,549	$2,117	$1,598	$1,777	$891	$1,264	$1,158	$979
Gross profit	288	394	362	444	(73)	(55)	351	388	185	226	114	110	(32)	175	121	10
Income (loss):																
Continuing operations	59	95	68	148	(222)	(230)	62	20	(105)	(77)	(166)	(288)	(283)	(166)	(108)	(265)
Unusual item																(444)*
Discontinued operations						(27)			8	(2)	268	(31)	(16)	(32)	(22)	(324)†
Extraordinary income																22
Net income (loss)	$ 59	$ 95	$ 68	$ 148	$ (222)	$ (257)	$ 62	$ 20	$ (96)	$ (79)	$ 101	$ (319)	$(299)	$ (198)	$ (130)	$(1,011)

* Operational restructuring excluding the disposal of the construction equipment business, including a $197 million charge for the writedown of net assets to realizable value and $247 million relating to operating costs, administrative expenses, and additional pension and other employee-related costs to be incurred in connection with the sale or liquidation of the noncore business and consolidation of the remaining core business facilities.
† Mostly due to the disposal of the construction equipment business.

SOURCE: Annual reports.

EXHIBIT 5   Stock Price, 1979–1982 (last sale or bid price on last day of month)

	1982	1981	1980	1979
January	7.75	24.125	32.75	36.75
February	6.5	18.625	31.125	37.625
March	5.25	20.125	26.5	39.375
April	4.625	17.5	27.125	38.125
May	3.375	16.375	26.25	38.125
June	4.25	15.875	28.125	39.25
July	4.125	14.75	31.0	40.375
August	4.5	10.625	32.0	43.0
September	4.5	10.125	33.125	41.25
October	3.75	8.25	30.125	36.5
November	4.0	8.25	30.75	36.875
December	4.25	7.125	26.625	39.125

June 1932—record low stock price of 1.75.
April 1966—record high stock price of 52.875.
October 1979—13-year high of 45.5; one month before the beginning of the 172-day UAW strike.
September 1981—43-year low of 7.25 after announcement of IH's third quarter earnings.
May 1982—1982 low of 2.625 amidst rumors of bankruptcy and after announcement of IH's second
   quarter loss.

SOURCE: Standard & Poor's Corporation *Security Owners' Stock Guide.*

HISTORY AND DESCRIPTION OF FORT WAYNE, INDIANA

General "Mad" Anthony Wayne built a fort at the confluence of the St. Joseph and St. Mary's Rivers in 1794. The military abandoned the fort in 1819 as the danger from Indians shifted west and the first settlers arrived. Fort Wayne's industrialization began with locomotive servicing and construction after the arrival of the first railroad in 1852.

IH executives announced in November 1919 that they were looking for a site to build a $5-million truck plant that would initially employ 5,000 people and produce 30,000 trucks a year. Fort Wayne outbid 27 other cities (including Springfield, Ohio) for the plant. The new plant opened in 1923; IH closed its small Akron plant and moved its truck-making operations to Fort Wayne in 1925. Fifty years later the plant was still turning out 30,000 trucks a year; Fort Wayne had become the "heavy duty truck capital of the world."

In the late 1970s, Fort Wayne had over 20 industrial firms, each of which employed more than 500 people, but Harvester was easily the largest. It employed 10,500 people in its heavy duty truck, International Scout, and truck axle and transmission factories; a parts distribution center; a truck engineering and design center; and other facilities. General Electric and Magnavox each employed several thousand workers and were the next largest employers. While definitely a manufacturing town, Fort Wayne was also the base for

EXHIBIT 6 Comparison of Fort Wayne and Springfield (1982 data except where noted otherwise)

	Fort Wayne		Springfield	
	City	SMSA	City	SMSA
Population (1)				
1960	161,776	306,330	78,181	161,154
1970	177,671	361,984	81,926	187,606
1980	172,196	382,961	72,563	183,885
U.S. ranking, 1980	80	101		183
Urbanized area, 1980	236,479		86,742	
Households (occupied housing units) (2)	67,200	138,800	27,400	66,500
Homeowner households (2)		101,900		47,000
Median income in 1979 dollars (1)				
Per household	$16,038	$18,862	$13,541	$16,767
Per family	19,580	21,732	16,778	19,340
Total retail sales (millions) (2)	$ 967	$ 1,784	$ 251	$ 718
Total effective buying income (millions) (2)		$ 3,390		$ 1,450
Percent of total U.S. buying power (2)		.17%		.07%
Large manufacturing plants (3)	67*	104	34*	43
Total manufacturing plants (3)	216*	312	111*	133
Chamber of Commerce operating budget: 1982 (4)	$270,000		$350,000	
1983 (5)	$220,000		$400,000	
Land area (square miles) (1)	52.6	1,732	18.1	827

* Entire country.

SOURCES:
(1) U.S. Bureau of the Census, *1980 Census of the Population.*
(2) "1982 Survey of Buying Power," *Sales and Marketing Management* 129, no. 2 (July 27, 1982).
(3) "1982 Survey of Industrial Purchasing Power," *Sales and Marketing Management,* 128, no. 6 (April 26, 1982).
(4) *Fort Wayne News-Sentinel,* April 28, 1982.
(5) *Springfield News & Sun,* September 24, 1982.

several large service-related companies such as Lincoln National Life Insurance Company.

In November 1979, the first of a series of economic misfortunes hit Fort Wayne. The city's economy lost $100 million during the six-month United Auto Workers (UAW) strike against Harvester. By the time the strike ended in April 1980, the auto industry slump was forcing cutbacks in working hours and layoffs in the many Fort Wayne businesses that supplied parts to that industry (such as B. F. Goodrich and the Dana Corporation). In November 1980, IH shut down its International Scout division and laid off 2,500 workers, 500 of them permanently. The city's unemployment rate doubled to 11 percent. And flooding devastated the city in March 1982. A 1981 *New York Times* News Service article described Fort Wayne as one of America's medium-size indus-

EXHIBIT 7   Impact of a Plant Closing on Fort Wayne and Springfield
(data and projections as of July 1982)

	Fort Wayne	Springfield
Number of IH truck plant employees	2,500	2,200
Total number of IH employees in area	4,300	3,200
Percentage of the area work force	2.1%	4.0%
Weekly truck plant payroll	$2.2 million	$2 million
Total direct contribution to the local economy*	$200–300 million	$154 million
Percentage of the area economy	7%	—
Current unemployment rate	11.5%	12.6%
If the city lost:		
Projected unemployment rate	20%	—
State liability for unemployment benefits	$15 million	$25 million
Other effects	71% (1,570) of the hourly truck plant workers were between the ages of 40 and 55—the age group hardest to reemploy	Real estate values were expected to drop 10–12%
If the city won:		
Number of new IH manufacturing jobs	1,800	1,700
Total employment gain†	4,800–6,300	4,500–6,000
Effect on unemployment rate	Drop of 4%	Significant drop

Note: In July 1982, the average IH worker earned $25,000 a year.
* Economists estimated that each dollar directly spent on goods and services would be respent 2.7 to 7 times as it circulated through the local economy.
† Each new manufacturing job created 1.67 to 2.5 additional jobs.

SOURCES: *Fort Wayne News-Sentinel* and *Springfield News & Sun.*

trialized cities "gripped by a trend of . . . postindustrial decline but unable to effectively deal with it."[3] By July 1982, Harvester employment in Fort Wayne had dropped to 4,300 workers with 3,500 others on indefinite layoff. The area's unemployment rate was 11.5 percent (Exhibit 8).

HISTORY AND DESCRIPTION OF SPRINGFIELD, OHIO

The first settlers arriving in the Springfield area in 1799 named it for the thousand freshwater springs bubbling everywhere out of the ground. Over the next century Springfield developed into an industrial center. Following the

[3] Reginald Stuart, "Fort Wayne—One of America's Medium-Size Cities," *Fort Wayne Journal-Gazette,* March 16, 1981.

EXHIBIT 8   Unemployment Rates, 1979–1982: Fort Wayne and Springfield SMSAs

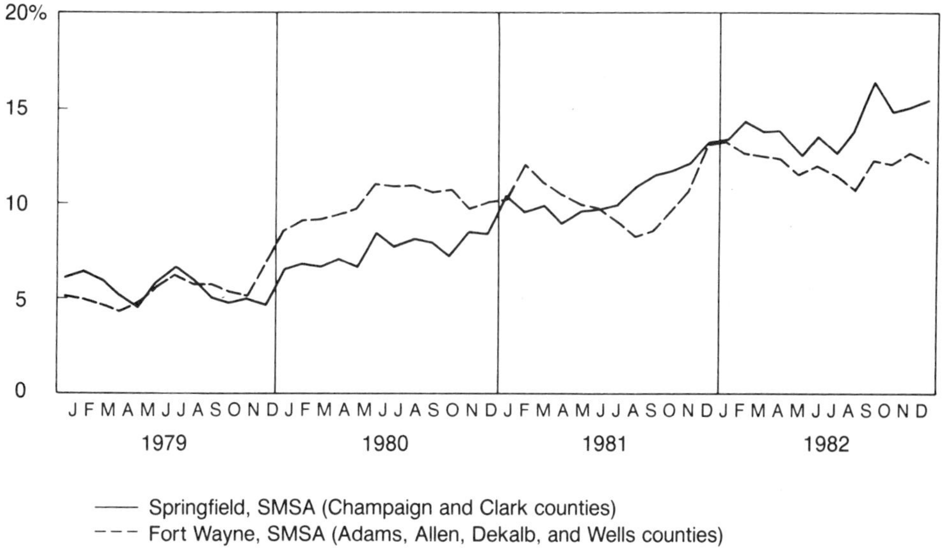

SpringField, SMSA (Champaign and Clark counties)
Fort Wayne, SMSA (Adams, Allen, Dekalb, and Wells counties)

SOURCES: Fort Wayne: U.S. Department of Labor, Bureau of Labor Statistics, *Employment and Earnings,* January 1979 through December 1982. Springfield: Monthly "Ohio Labor Market Information" pamphlets by the Ohio Bureau of Employment Services.

Civil War, it challenged Chicago for primacy as the world's largest farm equipment manufacturing center. In the 1880s, one Springfield factory (owned by a competitor of Cyrus McCormick and reputed to be the world's second largest industrial facility under one roof) produced 170,000 reapers annually, more farm machines than all the factories in Chicago put together. The plant burned down in 1902, however, and control of the business passed to the International Harvester trust in Chicago. In 1920, IH switched production at the site from agricultural equipment to trucks. IH's Lagonda Works (which became Springfield's truck cab fabrication plant) and the Crowell-Collier publishing plant became the city's two largest employers.

The Crowell-Collier plant was shut down in 1957, but Harvester retooled its old Lagonda works and built a new two-million-square-foot plant north of town in 1965. By 1979, Springfield and the surrounding Clark County had 200 manufacturing firms, but only four employed more than 500 people. Harvester employed 5,500 of the 22,000 manufacturing workers who lived in the community.

In the late 1970s, Springfield worked hard to strengthen and diversify its economic base. The city attracted 50 new manufacturers from 1979 through 1982 and won a national award for industrial development. In 1976, voters approved an income tax increase to rebuild their downtown, but the dismal economy halted urban renewal efforts in the early 1980s. In July 1982, IH employed 3,200 workers in Springfield with 2,300 others on indefinite layoff.

Peak Harvester employment had been 7,470 workers in 1973. The area's unemployment rate was 12.6 percent (Exhibit 8).

DESCRIPTION OF THE INTERNATIONAL HARVESTER COMPANY

In July 1982, the International Harvester Company was engaged in three core businesses: heavy duty and medium duty trucks, agricultural equipment, and construction equipment. Exhibit 9 describes the financial aspects of each of IH's three businesses. IH also owned finance and insurance subsidiaries. Harvester was seeking a buyer for its construction equipment business, which had been losing money for several years. It was also disposing of other assets

EXHIBIT 9   Operations by Product Group ($ millions)

Product Group	Sales	Operating Profit (loss)	Identifiable Assets	Capital Expenditures
Truck:				
1978	$3,211	$ 245	$1,365	$ 82
1979	3,966	303	1,745	102
1980	2,701	(153)	1,579	104
1981	3,318	15	1,364	101
1982	2,428	(12)	766	36
Agricultural equipment:				
1978	2,348	290	1,387	102
1979	3,069	442	1,549	136
1980	2,507	(1)	1,739	229
1981	2,980	69	1,677	198
1982	1,864	(269)	1,174	62
Construction equipment (sold in 1982):				
1978	852	55	507	16
1979	1,000	53	646	31
1980	760	(119)	698	33
1981	743	(17)	580	18
1982	433	(13)		10
Turbo machinery (sold in 1981):				
1978	253	20	240	10
1979	357	29	288	16
1980	344	11	305	18
1981	286	6		8

SOURCE: Annual reports.

and planning to restructure its operations to concentrate on trucks (production in the United States and Canada) and agricultural equipment (production in the United States, Canada, and Western Europe).

The Truck Industry

Trucks were usually segmented by weight. The eight different weight classes were grouped into light duty trucks, such as pickups and vans (90 percent of all U.S. truck sales in 1981); medium duty trucks (2.5 percent); and heavy duty trucks (7.4 percent). Medium duty trucks were used for intracity delivery, while heavy duty trucks were used to haul trailers long distances and for a variety of off-highway applications. While heavy duty trucks accounted for only 7.1 percent of the truck and bus market in 1982, they had a far larger share in terms of dollars; the price of a fully equipped, top-of-the-line, heavy duty model could approach $100,000, while the price of a small truck only approximated or slightly exceeded that of a large passenger car. Exhibit 10 describes the three truck classifications and provides data on truck sales in the United States between 1973 and 1982.

The truck market was also segmented by buyer. Fleet operators purchased both medium and heavy duty trucks, basing their decisions on price. Private owner-operators purchased mainly heavy duty trucks; they bought on the bases of service, features (customization), and brand loyalty.

Generally, manufacturers of trucks were not backward integrated. They assembled parts purchased elsewhere: the truck's cab, frame, axles, driveshaft, transmission, and engine. The truck's ultimate owner purchased the body or trailer separately. IH was in the process of selling the component manufacturing plants that it did own as part of its ongoing operational restructuring.

Harvester had been the industry leader in the North American medium duty and heavy duty truck markets since the 1930s; its 1981 U.S. market shares were 35 percent and 25 percent, respectively. In the heavy duty market, IH was strongest in the fleet-only segment. Major competitors were Ford and GM. PACCAR, which produced Peterbilt and Kenworth trucks (the Rolls Royces of trucking), was the leader in the owner-operated segment of the heavy duty market. Other companies focusing on the owner-operator market were Mack,[4] Freightliner, and White.[5] Exhibit 11 describes market shares in the U.S. heavy duty truck market.

In medium duty trucks, GM and Ford were IH's only major competitors in the North American market. However, foreign manufacturers were attempting to enter the market. Exhibit 12 describes market shares in the U.S. medium duty truck market.

---

[4] In 1982 Mack Trucks, Inc. was 45 percent owned by Renault of France.

[5] In 1981, following its bankruptcy in 1980, White Motor sold its heavy duty truck operation to AB Volvo of Sweden.

EXHIBIT 10   U.S. Truck and Bus Factory Unit Sales, 1973–1982

	Light Duty Trucks—Group 1–3 (under 14,000 lbs)	Medium Duty Trucks—Groups 4–6 (14,000–26,000 lbs)	Heavy Duty Trucks—Groups 7–8 (over 26,000 lbs)
1982	2,257,335	45,194	127,942
1981	1,970,114	54,031	161,344
1980	2,217,085	66,282	193,410
1979	3,103,310	151,426	213,074
1978	3,297,044	190,457	218,738
1977	3,069,846	183,365	188,310
1976	2,660,185	176,282	143,009
1975	1,959,840	185,929	126,391
1974	2,277,401	241,888	208,024
1973	2,541,850	229,718	208,120

SOURCE: Motor Vehicles Manufacturers Association.

Harvester was uniquely positioned as the only major producer specializing in a full line of trucks as a major business. It had a powerful reputation as a manufacturer for fleet buyers. Its strengths were its established market leadership; the quality of its products (including the least-cost-of-ownership vehicles in the industry); its broad warranty program; and its extensive dealer, service, and sales network. Its network of over 1,100 dealers and 25 used truck centers comprised the largest truck retail organization in the industry. Exhibit 13 provides data on IH's North American dealer network. However, in the fleet

EXHIBIT 11   Percentage of U.S. Market Share, Heavy Duty Trucks (groups 7 and 8 trucks only: over 26,000 lbs)

	1977	1978	1979	1980	1981	1982
Ford	18.59%	19.72%	17.68%	23.89%	21.11%	23.59%
International	24.26	26.35	30.91	20.78	25.13	22.47
GMC	10.39	9.59	9.55	15.02	13.99	15.87
Mack	14.70	14.28	13.73	10.89	11.25	10.61
Chevrolet	2.61	2.95	2.90	8.28	6.33	5.94
Kenworth (PACCAR)	7.88	7.38	6.99	5.77	6.43	5.74
Freightliner	6.35	6.11	6.40	5.41	5.64	5.70
Peterbilt (PACCAR)	6.04	4.93	4.08	3.62	4.12	4.52
White	5.51	5.54	4.29	2.57	1.77	2.09
Others	3.67	3.05	3.46	3.77	4.17	3.48
Total market (units)	156,421	191,837	213,174	193,410	161,344	127,942

SOURCE: 1978–1983 annual "Market Data Book Issues" by *Automotive News*.

EXHIBIT 12   Percentage of U.S. Market Share, Medium Duty Trucks (groups 4, 5, and 6 trucks only: 14,000–26,000 lbs)

	1977	*1978*	*1979*	*1980*	*1981*	*1982*
International	22.52%	18.14%	17.98%	25.01%	35.14%	37.94%
Ford	32.89	33.92	35.56	30.54	27.30	28.76
Chevrolet	20.61	21.91	24.22	22.55	16.29	12.38
GMC	14.12	15.57	17.19	15.77	12.90	12.01
Mack	0	0	0	1.04	2.87	4.47
Dodge	9.06	9.41	3.26	0.29	0	0
Others	.80	1.05	1.79	4.80	5.50	4.43
Total market (units)	170,805	165,196	151,426	66,282	54,031	45,194

SOURCE: 1978–1983 annual "Market Data Book Issues" by *Automotive News*.

market, where price was important, IH could not match GM or Ford on price; in the owner-operated market, where perceived reputation, product quality, and customization were important, price was IH's biggest selling point.

In 1981, sales for the truck group were $3.3 billion, or 47 percent of total IH sales (Exhibit 9). The truck group's operating profit was $15 million, following an operating loss of $153 million in fiscal year 1980 (a 172-day UAW strike against IH occurred during this period). By way of comparison, PAC-CAR's 1981 operating income as a percentage of revenues was 6.5 percent.

Because of the economic downturn, which began in 1980, 1982 North American truck industry sales were the lowest in two decades. Truck production was running at less than 40 percent of 1979 levels, and all major competitors were heavily discounting inventories. A rebound in the truck market

EXHIBIT 13   North American Dealerships (as of October 31)

	Trucks	*Agricultural Equipment**	*Total†*	*Worldwide Total*
1982	1,105	1,648	2,275	4,100
1981	1,299	1,746		5,400
1980	1,503	1,821		
1979	1,638	1,884		

* International Harvester attributed the decline in the number of its agricultural equipment dealerships to the prolonged depression in that industry, low-growth market projections for the near to mid-term future, attrition resulting from the failure of financially weak dealers, and its planned program for decreasing the number of dealers while increasing the size of the remaining dealerships (which was in line with the trend toward fewer but larger farms in the United States).
† Some dealerships handled both trucks and farm equipment.

SOURCE: Annual reports.

EXHIBIT 14   North American Truck Production by IH, 1978–1982

	1st Quarter	2nd Quarter	3rd Quarter	4th Quarter	Total
United States:					
1978	28,736	34,332	26,093	33,962	123,123
1979	38,771	37,870	25,377	13,435	115,453
1980	–0–	23,818	24,557	17,835	66,210
1981	19,349	18,591	15,210	9,711	62,861
1982	12,852	13,900	8,646	9,716	45,114
Canada:					
1978	5,533	6,333	3,314	1,398	16,578
1979	5,560	5,785	4,127	4,660	20,132
1980	3,160	4,949	4,458	3,472	16,039
1981	3,189	3,084	2,349	2,130	10,752
1982	3,071	3,248	1,795	2,780	10,894

SOURCE: 1979–1983 annual "Market Data Book Issues" by *Automotive News.*

was not expected until 1984. Exhibit 10 provides data on U.S. truck and bus sales from 1973 through 1982, while Exhibit 14 gives data on Harvester's North American truck production from 1978 through 1982.

Although they accounted for 47 percent of IH's sales in 1981, trucks had only recently eclipsed agricultural equipment as IH's most important business.

The Agricultural Equipment Industry

The agricultural equipment industry included combines, tractors, and a wide range of attachments for crop production and harvesting. Tractors represented over 50 percent of industry sales and were used as a barometer of market trends. The manufacturers were usually vertically integrated, purchasing few parts from outside sources. Product quality and service determined purchase decisions. Competition centered on the strength of the dealer network.

In 1982, Harvester was the second largest producer and distributor of tractors and combines in North America behind Deere & Company. Deere, the industry's low-cost producer, had 2,200 North American dealers and the finest customer base (the top 5 percent of U.S. farmers who enjoyed over 80 percent of the nation's net farm income). Other major competitors included Massey-Ferguson Ltd., Allis-Chalmers Corp., the J. I. Case division of Tenneco, and Ford's tractor division.

In the major European markets, IH ranked among the top three producers and distributors of tractors, and among the top four for combines. IH's major competitors in Europe were its North American competitors plus Claas, Fiat, and Sperry New Holland. Both the North American and European markets were highly competitive.

Harvester's strengths included the quality of its products, an effective parts distribution system, and a strong dealer and sales network. Deere had 300 more North American dealers than IH, but IH had 500 more than the next closest competitor. Exhibit 13 describes Harvester's North American dealer network. In its principal European markets, IH had more dealers on an aggregate basis than any other single competitor.

In 1981, sales for IH's agricultural equipment group were $3 billion, or 42 percent of total IH sales (Exhibit 9). The operating profit was $69 million, following a 1980 operating loss of $1 million. By way of comparison, Deere's 1981 operating income as a percentage of revenues was 11.1 percent.

The worldwide agricultural equipment business was not only highly seasonal (most sales occurring in the spring and fall), but also highly cyclical. Sales depended on numerous factors, including commodity prices, the weather, the general state of the economy (as reflected in interest rates), land values (which helped determine a farmer's borrowing and purchasing power), and political actions (such as federal agricultural policies and embargoes). In 1980, President Carter embargoed grain sales to Russia, and interest rates topped 20 percent. These and other factors, such as the worldwide depression, led to the collapse of the North American and European agricultural equipment markets. Sales fell to their lowest levels in two decades. In 1982, sales of farm wheel tractors fell 45 percent below 1978's peak. By mid-1982, the farm equipment industry was operating at about 50 percent of capacity. Manufacturers were heavily discounting their machines to reduce inventories. A rebound for agricultural equipment sales was not expected until 1984.

As a result of this prolonged depression in agricultural equipment sales, all of the industry participants except Deere and Company had experienced severe financial distress. Combined industry losses in 1982 were expected to exceed $1 billion.

Together, trucks and agricultural equipment accounted for 90 percent of IH's sales in 1981; construction equipment accounted for the remaining 10 percent.

The Construction Equipment Industry

The worldwide construction equipment market was dominated by Caterpillar Tractor Co. (50 percent of the market) with over $9 billion in worldwide sales. Komatsu (Japanese, 17 percent of the world market), and IBH Holding (West German, 7 percent of the world market) followed. Other major contenders were Harvester (4.5 percent of the world market), the J. I. Case division of Tenneco, Fiat-Allis (a joint venture between Fiat and Allis-Chalmers), Deere, Clark Equipment, Massey-Ferguson, and Ford. Caterpillar maintained a price umbrella and followed a full product line strategy. IH also offered a full product line.

IH's strengths included a worldwide network of 900 dealers and strong crawler dozer and large capacity dump truck product lines. The IH construction equipment group's major weakness was capital starvation in a capital-intensive industry. Sales of the group in 1981 were $743 million (10.6 percent of total IH sales), which generated an operating loss of $17 million. The group had suffered a 1980 operating loss of $119 million. Its performance compared poorly with Caterpillar's 1981 operating income as a percentage of revenues of 14.8 percent. Company insiders had been urging sale of the division since 1979, but IH had delayed while waiting for an economic recovery. In July 1982, the company was attempting to sell the division to IBH Holding, Dresser Industries, and other companies.[6]

HISTORY OF HARVESTER, 1833–1980

In 1831, 22-year-old Cyrus McCormick invented the mechanical reaper, which mechanized the harvesting of grain and eventually greatly improved farm labor productivity. However, he was not an instant success. McCormick began advertising the machine in 1833. But because his first prototypes were not equal to the rigors of their intended use, he was not able to sell any for nine years. Bankrupt in 1837, McCormick was able to keep his patents only because his creditors thought they were worthless. McCormick kept struggling to improve the machine and sold his first reaper in 1843. In 1845 he sold 50. And in 1847 he opened a factory in the frontier town of Chicago and sold 800.

In 1848 the patents on the reaper expired. Within two years there were more than 30 competitors selling reapers based on McCormick's patents. So McCormick focused on outselling his competitors. In so doing, he became a pioneer of modern marketing. His aggressive and innovative marketing included initial sales at cost; extensive distribution of both reapers and spare parts (by exclusive distributors); a standard price; careful instructions to dealers and buyers; a written, money-back guarantee; illustrated advertising; testimonials; field demonstrations; extended credit; and a direct marketing newsletter, "Farmer's Advanced."

The McCormick Harvesting Machine Company prospered. By 1900 it offered a full line of agricultural equipment and implements. In 1902 it merged with four competitors to become the International Harvester Company. Cyrus McCormick's son became the first president. IH introduced its first tractor in 1906 and its first trucks and buses in 1907.

World War I stimulated the development of both motorized tractors and nonfarm trucks; IH became the leading producer of both in the 1920s. At the

---

[6] Exhibit 15 compared Harvester's overall performance in 1981 with the performance of a major competitor of each of its three core businesses.

EXHIBIT 15 1981—Comparative Statistics and Ranking within the Fortune 500

	IH Amount	IH Rank	PACCAR Amount	PACCAR Rank	Deere Amount	Deere Rank	Caterpillar Amount	Caterpillar Rank
Sales (millions)	$ 7,327	46	$ 1,735	216	$ 5,447	65	$ 9,155	37
Assets (millions)	$ 5,346	51	$ 848	287	$ 5,684	44	$ 7,285	33
Sales/assets	1.37	n.a.	2.05	n.a.	0.96	n.a.	1.26	n.a.
Net income (millions)	$ (393)	487	$ 85	210	$ 251	77	$ 579	30
Equity (millions)	$ 1,285	112	$ 602	214	$ 2,450	49	$ 3,857	28
Number of employees	65,640	51	10,529	331	60,900	58	83,455	34
Net income/sales	—	—	4.9%	223	4.6%	244	6.3%	131
Net income/equity	—	—	14.1%	232	10.2%	359	15.0%	206
Earnings per share	$ (12.90)	—	$ 9.39	—	$ 3.79	—	$ 6.64	—
10-year growth rate in EPS	—	—	13.4%	213	13.5%	207	16.0%	158
Total return to investors (percent)	(71.03)%	469	18.7%	125	(21.98)%	387	(0.2)%	234
Total return: 10-year average (percent)	(7.98)%	441	13.6%	118	14.8%	97	9.1%	211
Sales per dollar of equity	$ 5.70	n.a.	$ 2.88	n.a.	$ 2.22	n.a.	$ 2.37	n.a.
Sales per employee	$112,000	n.a.	$165,000	n.a.	$89,000	n.a.	$110,000	n.a.
Assets per employee	$ 81,000	n.a.	$ 81,000	n.a.	$93,000	n.a.	$ 87,000	n.a.

SOURCE: "Fortune's Directory of the 500 Largest Industrial Corporations," *Fortune* 105, no. 11 (May 3, 1982), pp. 258–96.

same time, Harvester began making construction equipment. IH did not let a single worker go during the Great Depression. By 1950 IH employed 90,000 people and had a reputation for quality, service, and good employee relations.

Post–World War II Deterioration

From its position of strength after World War II, IH began a long decline. The Caterpillar Tractor Co. had prospered as a result of the world war—developing a reliable product line, emphasizing the largest sizes of construction equipment, and gaining a strong international distribution network. IH's attempts to catch up to Caterpillar and its postwar diversification strategy led to relative neglect of research and development in its core agricultural equipment business. At the same time, some of its farm equipment competitors, particularly Deere, made large investments to improve their products. Poor product and market decisions coupled with several severe strikes (one for 10 weeks, another for four months) further contributed to IH's deteriorating market position.

Poor leadership hastened the decline. Fowler McCormick, Cyrus's grandson, was ousted as CEO in 1951. His successors presided over disastrous decisions on labor work rules. For example, in the early 1950s, while Deere and Caterpillar had interpreted their UAW labor contracts to require overtime when necessary, IH had decided that its (similar) UAW contract made overtime voluntary for assemblyline workers, a significant disadvantage in times of high demand.

In 1971, Brooks McCormick, great-grandnephew of Cyrus, became president of Harvester. While he stopped the deterioration of the 1950s and the 1960s and improved the company's performance, in 1977 the company was still "a fat, sluggish, overextended giant running well ahead of its principal competitors in sales and far behind them in profits."[7] Exhibit 16 provides data on IH's financial performance from 1910 through the 1970s. In 1976 a Booz Allen consulting study recommended that IH bring in a new president from outside the company to "sweat it into shape."

Archie McCardell

Archie McCardell, president and number two man at Xerox, became president and chief operating officer of IH in September 1977. Brooks McCormick had wanted someone with financial, international, and automotive experience, all of which McCardell had acquired in 17 years at Ford. He had joined Xerox in 1966, where he became known as a "tiger" on costs. He became

---

[7] "Fighting to Save Harvester's Jobs," *Newsweek* 101, no. 10, "Fiftieth Anniversary Issue," Spring 1983, p. 145.

EXHIBIT 16 Historical Performance ($ millions)

Year	Sales	Net Income	Return on Sales	Equity	Return on Equity	Debt-to-Equity Ratio*	Capital Expenditures
1910	$ 102	$ 16	15.8%	$ 156	10.3%		
1920	225	17	7.4	218	7.6		
1930		26		317	8.1		
1940	248	23	8.4	338	6.9		
1945	622	25	3.9	397	6.2		
1950	943	67	7.1	615	10.9		
1955	1,166	56	4.8	761	7.3		
1960	1,683	54	3.2	1,021	5.4	12%	$ 63
1965	2,337	98	4.2	1,089	9.2	16	120
1966	2,583	110	4.3	1,092	10.1	20	99
1967	2,542	93	3.7	1,130	8.5	19	94
1968	2,542	75	3.0	1,152	6.7	21	102
1969	2,653	64	2.4	1,155	5.5	21	99
1970	2,636	52	2.0	1,147	4.5	26	89
1971	2,930	45	1.5	1,150	3.9	27	63
1972	3,413	87	2.5	1,198	7.4	28	61
1973	4,092	112	2.7	1,269	9.1	28	107
1974	4,864	123	2.5	1,347	9.4	32	181
1975	5,246	80	1.5	1,378	5.7	40	173
1976	5,488	173	3.2	1,514	11.6	37	168
1977	5,975	203	3.4	1,681	12.4	36	168
1978	6,664	187	2.8	1,826	10.4	33	210
1979	8,392	370	4.4	2,149	18.3	30	285
1980	6,312	(397)	—	1,697	—	41	384
1981	7,041	(393)	—	1,285	—	57	325
1982	4,292	(1,638)	—	(367)	—	98	108

* This debt-to-equity ratio is long-term debt to capitalization.

SOURCE: Annual reports.

president of Xerox in 1971 at the age of 45. He took the job at Harvester for three reasons: "More money, the immediate chance to run a multi-billion dollar corporation, and the challenge of improving the performance of one of the stodgiest companies in the industry."[8] His compensation package included an annual base salary of $460,000 (later raised to $525,000); annual bonuses (for example, $300,000 in 1979); a onetime, up-front payment of $1.5 million; and a $1.8 million loan (at a 6 percent interest) from IH to buy stock in the company. IH promised to cancel the loan if the company's financial ratios were brought up to the average level of six of its competitors during the seven years of McCardell's employment contract.

---

[8] "McCardell Starts Things Moving at International Harvester," *Dun's Review*, April 1978, p. 28.

McCardell identified high production costs as IH's main problem. They sapped earnings, which crimped capital spending, which in turn hurt earnings more because old machines were not as productive as new ones. The average age of IH's tooling in 1977 was 23 years versus the industry standard of 10 years. Labor work rules also kept production costs high. McCardell lived up to his reputation and successfully trimmed costs. By 1979, sales had grown 40 percent, and net income had risen 60 percent over 1977 levels. McCardell was named CEO in January 1978 and chairman and CEO in June 1979.

The Strike.   In the fall of 1979, McCardell decided to take on the United Auto Workers Union in order to change work rules that gave workers the right to refuse overtime and to transfer from job to job without limitation. Both Deere and Caterpillar, two of Harvester's biggest competitors and also UAW companies, had the right to impose overtime and to limit transfers. At Harvester, "horror stories"—no-shows for Saturday overtime, 28,000 job transfers in one year at a plant employing 4,500, and thousands of temporary transfers (based on seniority) by remaining employees during temporary layoffs—abounded. But the company had buckled on such issues throughout the 1950s, 1960s, and 1970s, and the workers now considered them "rights."

On November 1, 1979, 35,000 members of the UAW went on strike against IH. The strike ended 172 days later, the longest national strike in UAW history. They had won; the company gained only a few restrictions on transfer rights. But the workers, whose average weekly paycheck had dropped from $380 to $60 in strike pay, were angry. Despite a 1980 first half loss of $480 million, the company expressed satisfaction at the outcome. Said one executive, "At least they'll know next time that we're serious."[9] The UAW had also struck Deere and Caterpillar, but they had settled quickly and cut into IH's market share. Following the strike, IH regained its market share but only by discounting heavily. It earned second half profits of $82 million for a net loss of $397 million for 1980.

The Loan.   International Harvester's 1979 financial ratios topped—but just barely—the average of those of the six competitors named in McCardell's 1977 compensation package (Exhibit 17). Some United Kingdom tax credits had given Massey-Ferguson, one of the six, a small profit. Without the tax credits, Massey would have posted a loss and been omitted from the calculations (as stipulated by the terms of the loan agreement). With Massey, the six competitors averaged 9.15 percent; without, 10.39 percent. IH scored 9.55 percent. Harvester's score was also helped by the United Kingdom tax credits and by dealer stockpiling of inventory in anticipation of the strike.

---

[9] Carol J. Loomis, "The Strike That Rained on Archie McCardell's Parade," *Fortune,* no. 10 (May 19, 1980), p. 99.

EXHIBIT 17   IH and Competitor Profitability Ratios, 1977–1980 (used to determine forgiveness of Archie McCardell's $1.8 million loan)

	1977	*1978*	*1979*	*1980**
International Harvester:				
Return on assets	5.38%	4.33%	7.04%	—
Return on equity	11.80	10.00	17.20	—
Return on sales	3.41	2.80	4.40	—
Average†	6.86	5.71	9.55	—
IH's six competitors‡:				
Return on assets	9.00%	10.18%	8.00%	7.63%
Return on equity	17.22	18.82	14.88	13.47
Return on sales	5.28	5.80	4.58	4.82
Average†	10.50	11.60	9.15	8.64

* Ford, GM, and Massey-Ferguson were removed from the calculations in 1980 because each posted a loss. International Harvester posted a loss of $397 million in 1980.
† The arithmetic average of the three ratios.
‡ Caterpillar, Deere, Ford, GM, PACCAR, and Massey-Ferguson.

SOURCE: Carol J. Loomis, "Archie McCardell's Absolution," *Fortune* 102, no. 12 (December 15, 1980), p. 90.

In August 1980, IH's board forgave the entire loan as a reward for McCardell's "spectacular performance" during 1979. In February 1981, they forgave a $973,000 loan granted under a similar arrangement to IH's president, Warren Hayford. IH workers, still bitter about "McCardell's strike" and the closing of Fort Wayne's International Scout plant in October 1980, were furious. "Morale is zero," said one. "We see [Chrysler Corporation Chairman] Lee Iacocca working for a dollar a year. The general feeling is that our top guys are lapping up the gravy."[10] McCardell conceded, "It looked terrible; the timing couldn't have been worse." He considered refusing the benefit, but "There was a question whether I would have had to pay income tax on the money without actually getting it."[11]

THE ECONOMIC DOWNTURN

Traditionally, when one of IH's three principal markets (trucks, agricultural equipment, and construction equipment) was down, at least one and often both of the others were up. But in the spring of 1980 President Carter's "credit crunch" began. While interest rates remained relatively moderate

[10] "Harvester Says Loan of $973,438 to Hayford Is Forgiven by Board," *The Wall Street Journal,* January 26, 1981, p. 26.
[11] Paul Ingrassia and Steve Weiner, "Grim Reaper: Harvester Is Tackling Its Problems Head-on, But Bankers Are Wary," *The Wall Street Journal,* June 12, 1981, p. 2.

during the summer and fall, they soared to 21 percent by December and stayed near 20 percent throughout 1981. The high interest rates squeezed the company by simultaneously depressing sales in all three of its markets and pushing up interest rates on the huge debt that IH had taken on during the strike. (Exhibits 1, 2, and 3 provide data on IH's interest expenses and debt load from 1977 through 1982.) Sales of heavy duty and medium duty trucks in the United States dropped 30 percent from 1979 to 1980 and 17 percent from 1980 to 1981 (Exhibit 10). IH's truck sales dropped accordingly. Agricultural equipment sales plunged 25 percent, and construction equipment sales dropped 15 percent over the same period. And IH's interest payments ballooned from $148 million in 1979 to $377 million in 1981. At the same time, agricultural commodity prices plummeted, reducing farm income and farm equipment sales. To make matters worse, agricultural equipment sales in Europe had been weak since 1979. By the end of its 1981 fiscal year, IH's inventories were estimated at one year of sales. Fierce discounting in all three of its markets pared profits on the equipment it did manage to sell.

Cost Cutting

The company remained optimistic, nevertheless. It kept its common stock dividend intact throughout 1980 at a cost of $20 million. Dividends were reduced by 50 percent during the first quarter of 1981 and eliminated for the second quarter.

On January 1, 1981, IH cut the salaries of its top 26 corporate officers by 20 percent and froze the salaries of 30,000 other white-collar workers. It also initiated Project 200, designed to cut costs $200 million in 1981. The company even banned personalized Harvester stationary for executives and reduced the number of college recruits by 33 percent from 1980 levels.

On July 31, 1981, Harvester sold its Solar Turbines division to Caterpillar Tractor Co. for $505 million (2½ times Solar's book value). Solar had a bright future and had earned IH profits of $11 million on sales of $344 million in 1980—one of IH's few profitable operations that year. In September IH announced plans to fire 2,000 salaried employees, reduce its five operating divisions to three, and eliminate overcapacity in its factories, all of which would save another $100 million. It discontinued production of heavy duty trucks at the Wagoner, Oklahoma, facility (which it had opened in the summer of 1980) and in Great Britain; it also closed a foundry in Memphis, Tennessee. Harvester also began buying more components from outside suppliers. It cut the number of suppliers for each component in order to increase order sizes and earn volume discounts. And it asked its suppliers for price reductions. By October IH had laid off 10,000 of its 50,000 hourly workers and cut inventories by $500 million. Exhibit 18 provides Harvester employment figures from 1979 through 1982.

EXHIBIT 18 Employment

| | Worldwide | | | United States | | | Fort Wayne | Springfield |
	Wage	Salaried	Total	Wage	Salaried	Total		
October 31, 1979	n.a.	n.a.	93,358	n.a.	n.a.	n.a.	10,500	5,500
October 31, 1980	50,600	31,600	83,244	n.a.	n.a.	n.a.	7,300	n.a.
October 31, 1981	38,933	26,707	65,640	21,420	17,600	39,020	5,500	3,600
April 30, 1982	n.a.	n.a.	n.a.	n.a.	n.a.	n.a.	4,900	3,200
July 31, 1982	n.a.	n.a.	54,000	n.a.	n.a.	n.a.	4,300	3,200
October 31, 1982 (projected)	25,100	18,200	43,300	13,100	10,900	24,000	4,000*	3,200

n.a. = information not readily available.
* At this point International Harvester dropped from first place to become Fort Wayne's second largest employer.

SOURCES: Annual reports, *Fort Wayne News-Sentinel* and *Springfield News & Sun.*

At the end of November, IH reported a net loss of $393 million: a loss from continuing operations of $635.7 million and of $32 million valuation write-down of assets it intended to sell, offset by a gain of $276 million from the sale of Solar Turbines (Exhibits 1 and 4).

Debt Restructuring

Early in 1981, IH asked eight of its biggest creditors, led by Continental Illinois National Bank, to reorganize its loans from 193 banks into a single package with easier payment terms. Harvester owed the banks $3.4 billion. It wanted to convert its $1.5 billion short-term debt and its credit subsidiary's $1.9 short-term debt into term loans. It also wanted the bankers to buy $750 million of IH receivables. As a spur, the company suspended all repayment of principal pending completion of the restructuring. Since Harvester's assets were worth only $2.4 billion in liquidation, the banks had considerable incentive to cooperate. The negotiations dragged on throughout 1981; the last two banks agreed to a refinancing two days before the "drop-dead date" of December 23.

In addition to granting IH term loans of $3.4 billion (expiring at the end of 1983) and purchasing $750 million in receivables, the banks agreed to defer some cash interest payments. IH suspended dividend payments on its preferred stock for two years. At the same time, IH acknowledged that it would not be able to repay the loans in 1983. Instead, it hoped to refinance them in more favorable circumstances (lower interest rates and recovered markets for its products).

IH returned to its bankers twice during the first half of 1982 to ask for waivers of two of the agreement's covenants: that IH would maintain a minimum net worth of $1 billion and a maximum ratio of liabilities to tangible net worth of 4.0. In May 1982, Harvester asked for a second major renegotiation of its debt structure in order further to reduce cash interest payments. At that time IH management promised to present a new operating plan to the bankers at the end of July. In June, Agriculture Secretary John Block rejected the idea of federal intervention to help Harvester.

More Cost Cutting

IH's debt restructuring problems and the continued depression in all three of its principal markets heightened the need to cuts costs even further. But additional write-downs of assets (with the intention of selling them) would have driven IH's net worth dangerously close to zero. Thus, the company had reason to emphasize concessions from its lenders, employees, and 5,000 suppliers and to delay further corporate surgery.

Nevertheless, in its 1981 annual report issued in January 1982, Harvester said it intended to consolidate operations around its core businesses, reduce the number of plants, outsource more component production, dispose of assets not needed by the core businesses, reduce inventories another 12 percent, and reduce the number of salaried employees by another 7,000. IH expected these measures to save $650 million during 1982. IH also asked its suppliers for price cuts of up to 5 percent. In February it sold a joint venture in construction equipment to Komatsu, its joint venture partner. It disposed of two iron mines located in northern Michigan, put several more noncore businesses on the market, and began pursuing potential buyers of its construction equipment business.

Renegotiation of the UAW Contract

In November 1981, Harvester asked the UAW for contract concessions that would have saved the company $100 million through October 1, 1982, the expiration date of the UAW's existing contract with IH. IH wanted union members to give up a combination of wages and benefits worth $2.50 an hour per employee.

In January 1982, the UAW indicated a willingness to negotiate if IH addressed several of the union's concerns, including job security, reimbursement of any concessions, and limitations on outsourcing of parts and components. The union also criticized the "outrageously high salaries" of senior IH officials and called for "equality of sacrifice" among all Harvester employees.[12] The next week, IH awarded $6 million in bonuses (approximately $1,800 each) to 3,300 managers who had cut inventories $500 million during 1981 and maintained the company's liquidity. The bonuses followed a three-to-four-week shutdown of 19 plants, which had cost UAW members an estimated $10 million. Union members were outraged.

But the union was alarmed by IH's worsening financial position; IH had lost another $300 million during the first quarter of 1982 and expected similar losses in the second quarter. Harvester also announced a cut in pay and benefits for all salaried workers and the elimination of most management bonuses and incentives for 1982. In addition, the board stated that it was going to reverse the controversial forgiveness of personal loans to McCardell and Hayford if it could do so without harming the company. The union responded by sidestepping the IH request for interim concessions but agreed to open talks on a new contract immediately instead of in August. On May 3, the UAW approved a new contract, which would run through October 1, 1984. It agreed to give up wages and benefits worth $200 million over the next 2½ years in return for IH assurances regarding job security.

---

[12] "Harvester Receives Demand from UAW on Bid to Cut Job Cost," *The Wall Street Journal*, January 14, 1982, p. 22.

Manufacturing Facility Overcapacity

IH first announced that it intended to eliminate the overcapacity in its factories in order to cut costs in September 1981. It had already closed the ultramodern truck assembly plant it had opened the year before in Wagoner, Oklahoma. Inventory levels were still at one year of sales, and IH did not expect demand to rebound until 1983. The company's facilities were operating at 40–50 percent of capacity, causing severe pressure on manufacturing costs. Cost of sales had risen from 83 percent in 1979 to 91 percent in 1980 and in 1981 and was expected to be much higher in 1982. In December, IH shut down 19 plants for three or four weeks in order to bring inventories in line with the low levels of demand; all three truck plants were among those closed. In February 1982, IH closed the Fort Wayne facility for two more weeks.

The 1981 annual report, issued in January 1982, stated that, "Virtually every part of the company's manufacturing system has to be consolidated with few plants with higher levels of utilization." At its annual meeting in February, IH officials reiterated their intention to "rationalize" facilitites. President Hayford stated that IH had "a great deal more truck capacity than we need" at its three North American truck plants and that IH was "taking a long look" at what to do about the problem.[13] He indicated that Harvester would decide within 90 days on which, if any, of the truck plants would be closed or downsized.

THE BIDDING WAR

Fort Wayne officials had already read the handwriting on the wall. In December 1981, Indiana Governor Robert Orr and Lieutenant Governor John Mutz met with Archie McCardell to try to convince him to keep IH jobs in Indiana. They pledged the state's financial support in the form of tax abatements, money for retraining programs, and loan guarantees. Orr said, "It is imperative we do everything we can to ensure the company's continued operation and growth."[14] Mutz stated that Indiana would "pull out all the stops" in an attempt to halt movement of even a portion of IH's manufacturing operations from Fort Wayne. He said that the state had encouraged IH "to consult with us and give us a chance to put together a package before they do anything that would cost us jobs."[15]

In January 1982, U.S. Representative Clarence Brown, whose district included Springfield, Ohio, called Dennis Shere, the publisher of the *Spring-*

---

[13] Alan Johnson, "IH Forecasts Profits," *Springfield News & Sun*, February 19, 1982, p. 5.

[14] Gary Penner, "IH Begins Another Round of Layoffs; Orr, McCardell Confer," *Fort Wayne News-Sentinel*, December 5, 1981, p. 3A.

[15] Roger Metzger, "Truck Builder, Others Work to Reach Bottom Line—Rescuing Jobs, Income," *Fort Wayne News-Sentinel*, December 12, 1981, p. 4A.

field News & Sun and chairman of the Springfield Area Chamber of Commerce's industrial development committee. Brown told Shere that his contacts at IH had warned him that "people in Fort Wayne" were pushing hard for the company to close the Springfield plant and consolidate its truck production in Fort Wayne. Springfield immediately dispatched its own delegation to IH's Chicago headquarters. It was at this meeting that a purchase-leaseback of the Springfield plant was first suggested.

The Springfield Chamber of Commerce immediately began working to pull together a $60 million financial package (later negotiated down to $30 million) to purchase the truck assembly plant from IH and then lease it back to the company. In February, Ohio Governor James Rhodes sent IH a telegram pledging state aid (tax abatement, tax-free bonds, or a guaranteed, low-interest loan) to keep the Springfield facilities operating. The governor and Springfield officials followed that up with a trip to Chicago in early March. Both state and local officials felt that it would be cheaper to advance money to keep the plant open than to pay unemployment benefits after it closed.

Fort Wayne Mayor Winfield Moses had suggested that the state of Indiana excuse IH from paying taxes on its inventory, which would have saved Harvester several million dollars a year, but Governor Orr vetoed the plan as unconstitutional. This was the first of many clashes between the Republican governor and the Democratic mayor over how to best help Fort Wayne keep its truck plant. Governor Orr was considering offering a guaranteed loan package to IH. For its part, Fort Wayne agreed to cut $50,000 from the amount IH paid for fire protection.

The Telegram

On March 30, IH sent a telegram to the governors of Indiana and Ohio and to the mayors and executive directors of the Chamber of Commerce in Fort Wayne and Springfield. In that telegram, Manufacturing Group President and executive Vice President Donald Lennox stated that IH would "seriously consider" keeping both plants open if "a meaningful package of concessions by the union and incentives from the state and local community can be developed." The telegram explained that, "Further significant cost reductions would be necessary" if the ailing manufacturer was to keep both plants open. Exhibit 19 contains the full text of the telegram sent to the mayor of Springfield. An IH spokesman said that the telegram was sent in response to a proposal by the Springfield Area Chamber of Commerce for a $60 million purchase-leaseback agreement for Springfield's truck assembly plant. He called allegations that IH was encouraging a competitive bidding war between the two cities and states for the right to retain Harvester operations "grossly unfair." Donald Lennox followed up his telegram with visits to both Fort Wayne and Springfield the following week.

EXHIBIT 19 Text of Donald D. Lennox's March 30, 1982, Telegram to Springfield Officials

As you are well aware, International Harvester has been engaged in some very extensive marketing and manufacturing studies that will affect the future of the manufacturing activities at the Springfield, Ohio, assembly plant.

This is part of a recently announced program to achieve, through consolidation, every manufacturing efficiency consistent with our intention of concentrating on core businesses, including heavy and medium duty trucks.

In light of these objectives, our truck manufacturing studies are examining all possible actions, including maintaining the two U.S. truck manufacturing plants in some mode.

Because of the enormous implications of closing one of these plants in terms of many long-time and valued employees as well as the communities in which they reside, it is our intention in the immediate future to fully evaluate the possibility of maintaining core manufacturing operations at both Fort Wayne and Springfield, assuming the current cost structures of these operations can be dramatically altered.

Further significant cost reductions would be necessary to make this possible.

The remainder of the necessary cost savings will depend on local unions as well as community and state participation. In our minds this would principally include: (1) revisions of some local union procedures and (2) any special efforts of the state and local community to assist us (we are familiar with the conventional state economic development programs).

In this regard, some unique ideas have been suggested in Ohio, including a sale/lease-back proposal for the Springfield plant. We are ready to discuss the possibilities of this proposal further.

If a meaningful package of concessions by the union and incentives from the state and local community can be developed, I can assure you it will be very seriously considered in our final deliberations.

I stand ready to meet with representatives of the community and state to discuss these matters further.

SOURCE: *Springfield News & Sun,* March 30, 1982.

Both Fort Wayne and Springfield were encouraged by IH's apparent willingness to consider keeping both plants open. The chairman of the Fort Wayne Area Chamber of Commerce said that it was important for both cities to help IH remain in business. He added, "We don't look at it as a competitive sort of thing. I don't want us to get into a bidding war. Neither of us can afford to lose Harvester, but we don't want to pay through the nose to keep it here."[16] Springfield Mayor Roger Baker, however, felt that IH was pitting Fort Wayne against Springfield and seeking "the best possible packages from both places.

---

[16] Alan Johnson, "Cities' Officials Don't See IH 'Bidding War,'" *Springfield News & Sun,* March 31, 1982, p. 4.

If I were in their position, I would do the same thing."[17] Springfield Area Chamber of Commerce Executive Director Larry Krukewitt also felt that the telegram would start a bidding war between the two cities: "I don't view this as one community against another, but we are dealing with the single largest employer in both towns."[18]

In early April, *Fortune* magazine reported that Harvester had told its bankers back in February that it intended to raise capacity use in its truck operations from 44 percent to 77 percent during 1982. Since demand for trucks was not expected to rise in 1982, reaching that goal required "jettisoning a lot of truck capacity."[19]

McCardell's Ouster

On May 3, 1982, McCardell was fired. Donald E. Lennox, 63, was named president and COO. He was an operations expert whom McCardell had worked with at Ford and Xerox. Louis W. Menk, 64, a Harvester director, former chairman of Burlington Northern, Inc. and a "capable and strong-willed" operations man, took over as CEO. William G. Karnes, 71, former chairman of Beatrice Foods Co. and a past director of Continental Illinois Corporation (Harvester's biggest creditor), was made a director and given the chairmanship of the board's finance committee.

Harvester's bankers had not been impressed with McCardell's performance. One said, "What Harvester needed was a crisis manager used to competition. What it has is someone from a one-product company with few labor problems."[20] Although IH already had a heavy debt load and a union contract that put IH at a competitive disadvantage when he arrived, McCardell had made several spectacular mistakes: the 172-day UAW strike, his misjudgment of the economy in 1980, and a series of optimistic—but wrong—financial forecasts. After his resignation, McCardell related that his biggest regret was that he had not had an additional one or two years to streamline the company's operations before the slump hit in 1980.

McCardell had been reluctant to shrink company assets because the huge write-offs would plunge IH's equity below zero. Lennox had no such "psychological block."[21] He intended to get rid of nonperforming assets. First on his list was the construction equipment business. Next were noncore businesses

---

[17] Ibid.

[18] Keither Streitenberger, "Chamber, IH to Confer," *Springfield News & Sun*, March 31, 1982.

[19] Geoffrey Calvin, "International Harvester's Last Chance," *Fortune* 105, no. 8 (April 19, 1982), p. 108.

[20] Maurice Barnfather and Lisa Gross, "The Bankers' Partner," *Forbes* 128, no. 11 (November 23, 1981), p. 43.

[21] "Can Don Lennox Save Harvester?" *Business Week*, August 15, 1983, p. 82.

such as the manufacture of truck axles and transmissions, airplane tow trucks, and off-highway haulers; life insurance; and mining. Also on the list were the corporate research and development operations (not vital for short-term survival) and excess plant capacity. The May 17, 1982, *Business Week* stated that, with McCardell gone, "Management is now expected to . . . consolidate manufacturing in its underutilized U.S. plants."

In late May, IH announced a 1982 second quarter loss of $198 million, bringing the first half net loss to $497 million, almost the full amount of the loss McCardell predicted for the entire year. Because of continued high interest rates, low commodity prices, severely depressed demand for Harvester's products, and chronic price discounting, Chairman Menk announced that IH had "realistically revised its previous estimate": Harvester's 1982 losses would exceed $900 million; profitability was not expected until 1984.[22]

The Bidding War Continues

At the same time it announced its second quarter loss, IH indicated that it was still considering proposals by private sector and state and local government agencies in Fort Wayne and Springfield that would enable it to maintain truck production in both cities. It also announced that it would present a new operating plan and financial restructuring program to its bankers in late July.

During the next two months, both communities worked to pull together their economic incentive packages. The state of Indiana, Allen County, and the city of Fort Wayne offered to guarantee a $9.2 million loan (later reduced to $8.7 million when the state reduced its share by $2 million and the city could only add another $0.15 million) to a private investor who would buy IH's parts distribution center in Fort Wayne and then lease it to a newly formed redevelopment commission. The commission would then sublease the center to IH. In return, Indiana wanted IH to promise to manufacture trucks in Fort Wayne for the duration of its sublease—10 years. State and local government and business leaders were also working on other packages involving other IH facilities in Fort Wayne.

Springfield continued to work on its $30 million purchase-leaseback of the local IH truck plant. Ohio banks would put up $20 million, half guaranteed by the state and the other half covered by ownership of the plant itself. The Ohio Department of Economic Development would contribute the other $10 million at an interest rate of 2 percent. On July 18, the Springfield Area Chamber of Commerce ran a full-page advertisement in the *Springfield News & Sun* to explain the Chamber's role in the proposal and to show why the truck plant was so important to the community. A reproduction of the ad appears in Exhibit 20.

---

22 Paul B. Carroll, "Harvester Posts 2nd Period Loss of $198.4 Million," *The Wall Street Journal,* May 21, 1982, p. 3.

EXHIBIT 20 International Harvester: Why It Is Critical to Our Local Economy

Since January, representatives of the community working through the Springfield Area Chamber of Commerce have been attempting to construct a purchase-leaseback plan for the IH assembly plant in Springfield . . . here are some facts and figures surrounding that proposal and an explanation of why we feel it is extremely important to the economic well being of this community and surrounding area.

WHY WE BECAME INVOLVED

Following International Harvester's huge debt restructuring last November, it became apparent that if the company were to survive, major alterations to its existing operations would be necessary. On the strength of a report that IH was considering consolidating truck production at one location, probably Ft. Wayne, representatives of the local community met with IH officials in Chicago in January to see if there was anything we could do to protect IH operations in Springfield.

That meeting produced several suggestions. Among those was the possibility of the community purchasing and leasing back to IH the assembly facility on Route 68 North.

The senior IH official attending that meeting was Donald D. Lennox, who has since been named president and chief operating officer. He indicates a purchase-leaseback would be a major consideration when deciding which plants remained open and which closed.

In subsequent discussions with IH, it became apparent that the company intended to close or mothball the assembly plant on Route 68. We believe the interest shown by representatives of the community—and our willingness to pursue the purchase-leaseback arrangement—helped to keep the plant open this long.

We should emphasize our primary purpose was, always has been and remains to protect local jobs, not bail out IH.

WHY PURCHASE THE PLANT IF IH IS BROKE?
WHAT'S IN IT FOR THE COMMUNITY?

International Harvester as a corporation has experienced some serious losses; however, throughout that period, the truck division has remained surprisingly strong, controlling approximately 35 percent of the world truck production.

Financial analysts indicate if Harvester is to survive as a corporation, it will do so as a scaled-down operation, built around its truck division. Under our proposal, as a condition of the deal, as long as IH produces trucks it would be required to build the lion's share in Springfield.

In the event International Harvester does not survive, we would gain control of the assembly plant on 68 North, and the local community and state could immediately begin marketing the facility and maintain the current job levels. The economic impact and recovery from such a blow can be determined by the time that elapses before the lost jobs can be replaced. In the case of IH, every day the plant sits idle, the community would lose more than $400,000 in wages.

If we own the plant, we would be able to control our own destiny and be in an excellent position to quickly entice a new manufacturer to resume production and capture the void created by IH's departure from the truck market.

Legal advice has indicated that without such control, if IH were to go bankrupt, the local plant could be tied up in legal proceedings for three to five years . . . three to five years during which the community would be hamstrung in any attempt to recover those lost jobs!

The assembly plant is recognized as one of the most modern, efficient in the world. Under our proposal the community, through the Chamber of Commerce, would own it for approximately 20 percent of its replacement cost.

WHY SHOULD THE STATE OF OHIO HELP IH?

In the event IH should close . . .

The State of Ohio would lose $2.5 million in taxes annually.

EXHIBIT 20   *(continued)*

The State of Ohio has a MANDATORY liability in excess of $25 million . . . just in unemployment benefits.

Add to these direct costs, all of the indirect costs . . . such as retraining and finding jobs for displaced workers . . . and you can quickly see if International Harvester closes the state could lose in excess of $30 million.

HOW PURCHASE PRICE CHANGED FROM $60 MILLION TO $30 MILLION

Initially, IH told us the book value of its assembly plant was about $60 million. During negotiations it was determined this figure included the Lagonda stamping plant. We felt that conditions on the purchase of the assembly plant could be structured in such a manner to effectively control the future of Lagonda production without a direct purchase of those facilities. This reduced the price to $48.6 million. Further negotiations eliminated a hi-rise warehouse portion of the assembly plant, reducing the price to $33–34 million. Final proposed purchase price for the building and land on 68 North property is $30 million.

"I DON'T WORK AT IH . . . IT DOESN'T AFFECT ME"

The economic impact of International Harvester touches each and every one of us. International Harvester has an annual payroll of $104 million. Add to this the additional $50 million it spends in our areas for direct services, and you will see the total economic effect amounts to more than $400,000 a day. That's a lot of money spent every day in local stores, on local services, in local restaurants, with local banks, etc. Take that amount out of the local economy, during this current recession, and add 2,000 to 2,500 more unemployed to our already high (14 percent plus) unemployment . . . and the economic stress is simply too much. You don't have to look further than the home you own, the schools your children attend or the services you receive from the city or county governments to determine IH's direct effect on you and everyone else.

- Housing Values

  Conservative estimates have suggested that real estate in Springfield/Clark County would lose 10–12 percent of its value if we lost that number of manufacturing jobs. (For example, if you now live in a home currently worth $50,000—it would be worth between $44,000 and $45,000.)

- Government Services

  The City of Springfield would lose $650,000 in employment taxes (nearly $1 for every $40 of the city's total budget) at a time when the financial viability of the city is in question. Such a loss would result in reduced services and/or charges for services now being delivered. Similar problems would surface at all levels of government.

- Local Schools

  The Northeastern school district would be bankrupt and probably closed. More than 400 jobs would be lost in that district alone. The Superintendent's office of the City Schools has submitted the following projections on the effect on city schools:
  "We would have to go to the state for money immediately to stay open.
  "We would have to close at least one elementary school, and perhaps as many as three.
  "We would be forced to close at least one middle school.
  "We would be forced to terminate 150–200 positions in our system.
  "We would not be able to pass any form of tax levy for operations for years and years."

EXHIBIT 20 *(concluded)*

• Other Jobs

The more than $400,000 per day being spent in the local economy serves as a base for many other jobs throughout the community. Statistics show a dollar will be spent and respent seven times before it leaves a community. Using that multiplier, we are talking about almost $3.5 million each day in our local economy to pay other people's wages. Virtually, everyone is affected . . . everyone is touched. The Chamber of Commerce has conservatively suggested such an economic loss would have a 15 percent trickle down effect throughout the economy.

Whatever the category . . .

number of jobs lost . . .

payroll lost . . .

retail sales lost . . .

property tax lost . . .

use a multiplier of 115 percent to reach true figures. (Example: Every 1,000 jobs lost through IH would result in an additional 150 in support-type operations.)

Our proposal has been subject to some criticism. The purchase-lease-back proposal now being considered involves funds from the State of Ohio and from the banks. It is a complex deal with some risks. It requires all of the parties involved to view the transaction, first, in light of what the loss of International Harvester operations in Springfield would mean to the community. We hope these facts and figures will provide you with a better understanding of the situation. All Clark and surrounding county residents need to recognize how important this project is to our economic well-being and to rally around this community effort . . . we need your help and support.

We believe if this proposal is accepted, our local economy will get a much-needed boost. If it fails, and the local plant is jeopardized, we will try to meet that challenge in other ways.

We are not trying to bail out IH. We are trying to save our community's economic base, local jobs, and the quality and standard of life we all enjoy in Springfield and Clark County.

Springfield Area Chamber of
Commerce Board of Directors

SOURCE: *Springfield News & Sun,* July 18, 1982, p. 12A.

IH'S ANNOUNCEMENT OF A DOWNSIZING OF ITS OPERATIONS

On July 29, 1982, IH announced a massive plan to consolidate its operations around its truck and agricultural equipment businesses and to restructure its bank debt with the objective of eliminating interest payments and converting part of the debt to equity. The plan would cut costs by $1 billion and return the company to profitability by 1984. IH also announced that it expected to lose $925 million by the end of 1982.

Specifically, Harvester intended to terminate its truck-making partnerships with German, Spanish, and Swedish firms, and to narrow its manufacturing operations to production of heavy duty and medium duty trucks in North America and production of agricultural equipment in North America and Europe. It would continue to market both worldwide. Harvester also intended to sell its construction equipment business and close 23 of its 41 plants (27 of which were in North America) by the end of 1984. IH terminated operations at its Louisville, Kentucky, and Memphis, Tennessee, plants and put up for sale the idle Wagoner, Oklahoma, truck plant and two other plants in Ohio and Illinois. Finally, Harvester intended to reduce employment from 54,000 in July 1982 (Exhibit 18) to 36,000 by October 1984.

Most significantly for the residents of Fort Wayne and Springfield, among the 23 plants to be closed would be one of IH's three North American truck plants located in Chatham, Ontario; Fort Wayne; and Springfield.

The Banks' Reaction.   The bankers were impressed; the company had "finally presented a business plan that appears conservative and rational."[23]

Springfield's Reaction.   Springfield reacted with confidence. In June the *Washington Post* had quoted a Harvester official as saying that Springfield's proposal was "a rather key factor" in the company's restructuring plan. Larry Krukewitt stated, "It's really sad that this had to come down to an either-or situation. But we knew that if it did come down to a contest, we'd give it our best shot. That's what we did, and we can't see how we can lose. Logically, we're the choice. We hoped it wouldn't come to this. Sorry, Fort Wayne."[24] He later reiterated that, "It was not our intention, nor Fort Wayne's intention, that it would come down to this. We have been negotiating for several months with the stipulation that both plants remain open."[25] The president of UAW Local 402 in Springfield said that the workers were "immensely concerned" about their jobs. He added that if only one of the two plants remained open, "I'm hoping like heck that it'll be us."[26]

Fort Wayne's Reaction.   Fort Wayne was shattered. Springfield's financial aid package was three times larger than Fort Wayne's. Mayor Moses lamented, "We're in serious trouble. Very serious trouble."[27] The *Fort Wayne Journal-Gazette* compared Fort Wayne to South Bend, where Studebaker had shut down a plant without warning in 1963, throwing 7,000 people out of work.

Chatham's Reaction.   The Chatham workers were not concerned. The Auto Trade Agreement between Canada and the United States prevented IH from selling trucks in Canada at competitive prices without making them

---

[23] "Harvester's Pruning: Too Late to Bear Fruit?" *Business Week,* August 16, 1982.

[24] Jim Quinn, "Springfield Says: Sorry, Fort Wayne," *Fort Wayne News-Sentinel,* July 29, 1982, p. 1A.

[25] Alan Johnson, "Purchase-Leaseback Plan Could Be the Key: Krukewitt Is Optimistic on Outcome," *Springfield News & Sun,* July 30, 1982, p. 1.

[26] Ibid., p. 5.

[27] "IH Events of Week Reviewed," *Fort Wayne News-Sentinel,* August 1, 1982.

there. IH would have to add a 15 percent excise tax to the price of any vehicles it exported to Canada without importing the same dollar value from Canada. Since Chatham accounted for 15 percent of IH's North American production in 1981 (Exhibit 14), it was inconceivable that they would close the plant. Jack Reilly, IH vice president for manufacture, stated, "We have a much larger market share in Canada than we do in the United States. It's a high volume market. Canada is very important to us."[28] In addition, IH's labor costs in Canada were $5 per hour less than in the United States. And Canada's national health care program reduced IH's cost of a worker's health care premium to $45 per month versus $200 in the United States. The costs of pension and unemployment benefits were also lower in Canada. In July 1982, the Chatham plant employed 800 people, down from a high of 2,000. IH was the major employer in that city of 40,000.

Plant Closing Criteria

IH would decide which plant to close—Fort Wayne's or Springfield's—using the following criteria, as abstracted from various published sources. Exhibit 21 compares the two plants.

1. *Size of the aid package offered by state, county, and local community officials.* Springfield was working to finalize its $30 million purchase-leaseback deal, while Fort Wayne was working to increase its offer to match or top Springfield's.

2. *Plant efficiency.* The Springfield plant, built in 1965, was a model of industrial efficiency, while most of the Fort Wayne complex had been built in 1923. The Springfield location would lower IH's production costs and save the company money in the long run.

3. *Production capacity.* See Exhibit 21.

4. *Cost of consolidation.* It would cost twice as much to move Fort Wayne's heavy duty equipment to Springfield as it would to move Springfield's medium duty gear to Fort Wayne. The Springfield plant would require at least $10 million in modifications if operations were consolidated there. Little information on the costs of a Fort Wayne consolidation was available.

5. *Resale value.* The smaller, modern Springfield plant was much more salable than the old, sprawling Fort Wayne complex. If IH needed the cash badly enough, it might sacrifice the Springfield facility. But there was not much demand for manufacturing buildings of two million square feet.

6. *Proximity to other IH operations.* One other IH plant was located in Springfield, while a number of other IH facilities were located in Fort Wayne. Exhibit 21 lists those facilities.

---

[28] Ron Carter, "Indiana Must Hurry to Complete IH Package," *Springfield News & Sun,* August 10, 1982, p. 3.

EXHIBIT 21   Comparison of Truck Plants in Fort Wayne and Springfield, July 1982

	Fort Wayne		*Springfield*
Truck plant only: Size	1,500,000 ft²	heavy duty truck plant	2,000,000 ft²
	600,000 ft²	machinery/ forging plant	
	600,000 ft²	axle and trans- mission plant*	
	345,000 ft²	warehouse	
	87,000 ft²	warehouse	
	3,132,000 ft²		
Reputation	World's largest truck plant, earning Ft. Wayne the title "Heavy Duty Truck Capital of the World"; most profit-able of IH's 3 truck plants		The second most modern and efficient truck plant in the world
Year built	1923		1965
Appraisal value (building & grounds)	—		$30 million
Replacement value	—		$237 million
Production: Capacity	200 heavy duty trucks/day		600 light and medium duty trucks/day or 400 me-dium/day
July 1982	90 heavy duty trucks/day		140 medium duty trucks and buses/day

7. *Labor costs.* The higher the average number of years of employment, the higher the labor costs: no Fort Wayne hourly worker had less than 10 years seniority. On the other hand, Springfield's less senior labor force could be terminated with much lower pension funding costs.

8. *Long-standing relationships.* Three generations of workers had worked at the Fort Wayne truck plant; 71 percent of the truck plant workers were between the ages of 40 and 55—the most difficult group to reemploy. On the other hand, Fort Wayne's militant UAW Local 57 had a reputation as having a "difficult personality." It was the UAW's largest bargaining unit within Harvester, representing 9,000 Fort Wayne workers at the time of the 1979–80 strike. IH's relationship with most Springfield workers was much newer; while the Lagonda Avenue works (employing 1,000) dated back to 1902, the truck plant had been built in 1965. In either case, the effects of a

EXHIBIT 21 *(concluded)*

	Fort Wayne	*Springfield*
Number of trucks in 1981	21,911	40,619
Features	11-year old assembly lines, which are among the most modern in the world; $13 million automated warehouse completed in 1980	Modern, semiautomated assembly lines; wholly robotized warehouse
Situated on	215 acres	44 acres
Location	Southeast of Fort Wayne	8 miles north of downtown
Employees	2,500	2,200
Area: Total number of IH employees	4,300	3,200
Other facilities	Axle and transmission plant† Truck engineering and design center Parts distribution center Materials management center Product reliability center Truck proving ground 560,000 ft^2 light duty truck plant (closed 1980)	Truck body (cab fabrication plant employing 1,000)

* The axle and transmission plant was completely surrounded by the heavy duty truck plant.
† The axle and transmission plant employed about 500; the parts distribution center, 900; the materials management center, 200; and the other facilities, 100.

SOURCES: *Fort Wayne News-Sentinel* and *Springfield News & Sun.*

plant shutdown on the local economy and the residents of each city would be severe. Exhibit 7 details those effects.

One security analyst summed up the decision: "Springfield is the most efficient plant. And all things being equal, it is the Fort Wayne plant that is in more danger than the Springfield plant. But the bottom line is Harvester has to survive short term. Nothing else matters. Short-term considerations will weigh as much, if not more, than long-term considerations."[29] An Ohio banker stated, "The Fort Wayne offer is going to end up, short term, several million dollars better. But if Harvester is willing and able to look farther into the future, Springfield's offer will be far in the lead."[30]

---

[29] Mike Seemuth, "Many Factors Influencing IH Decision," *Springfield News & Sun,* August 15, 1982, p. 1A.
[30] Ibid., p. 7A.

International Harvester said it would announce by the end of August which plant it would close.

AUGUST 1982

The day IH announced its decision to close a plant in one of the two cities, Springfield Area Chamber of Commerce Executive Directory Larry Kru- kewitt's statement, "Sorry, Fort Wayne," made front-page headlines in Fort Wayne. Fort Wayne's dismay turned to anger, then determination. As its business leaders, led by Mayor Winfield Moses, worked to match Springfield's $30 million offer, the people of the city displayed the same spiritedness that had made national headlines in March when river waters flooded the city. Full-page ads urging residents to write letters to IH Chairman Louis Menk appeared in the August 7 newspapers and were reprinted daily. Fort Wayne's citizens responded with tens of thousands of letters. On August 11 Menk wrote an open reply to the city, acknowledging that the plant consolidation was "both an economic and a people decision" and assuring Fort Wayne's residents that their "voices are being heard."[31] The highlight of the city's campaign was "Sign a Letter Day," an all-city, all-day pep rally, including a visit by a hot air balloon and songs by The Lettermen. The August 13 *Fort Wayne New-Sentinel* trumpeted, "Harvester, Here We Come!" and carried an open letter to the officers and directors of Harvester offering the company both cash and "tough partners and rock-solid assets"—the people of Fort Wayne. On August 17, a delegation of city officials presented Donald Lennox with a symbolic 50 letters of the 101,000 signed by area residents. Lennox promised a decision within two weeks.

Fort Wayne's Financial Aid Package.   On August 19, Indiana's gover- nor and lieutenant governor and Mayor Moses presented a $31 million finan- cial aid package to IH officials in Chicago. It consisted of three separate deals plus two smaller offers of assistance. First, Fort Wayne would pay $18.5 million in cash for IH's axle and transmission plant and other related assets. IH would lease the plant for 10 years, at which time ownership would revert to Harvester. The $18.5 million would come from five local banks ($8 million), the state ($3.5–4 million in state Community Development Block Grants funds), and the city ($6.5 million of its Community Development Block Grant funds). Second, the city and Allen County would buy the International Scout plant (idle since 1980) for $3.5 million and lease it back to IH for 10 years. Harvester would not pay rent for the first two years, and they would repay the loan at 11 percent interest during the final eight years. Third, a private firm would borrow $9 million from Lincoln National Corporation, buy IH's parts distribution center, and lease it back to Harvester. IH would be required to buy back both the Scout plant and the parts distribution center upon expiration of

---

[31] "IH's Letter to City," *Fort Wayne News-Sentinel,* August 11, 1982, p. 1A.

the 10-year leases. Fourth, Fort Wayne offered IH $2.9 million in the form of a five-year tax abatement on new machinery and federal aid for retraining workers rehired by the company. Fifth, 60 area businesses volunteered $2.4 million of discounts on services such as moving, lodging, and construction (to help relocate Springfield workers to Fort Wayne and to renovate the old Fort Wayne plant).

Springfield's Financial Aid Package.   On August 23, Springfield finalized its offer. Ohio's package had not changed. Eleven local banks and the state's Department of Economic Development would loan $20 million and $10 million, respectively, to the Springfield Community Improvement Corporation, which would buy the truck plant and lease it to IH. The state would guarantee half of the bank's loan money. The 2 percent interest rate on the state's share of the money would cost Ohio taxpayers more than $15 million in forgone interest over the life of the agreement.

In the meantime, Larry Krukewitt and Winfield Moses had debated each other on the "McNeil-Lehrer Report," a nationally broadcast public television program. Journalist Neal Pierce challenged the two: "International Harvester is trying to hornswoggle these two communities. The culmination of either of these deals would be an outrageous abuse of these taxpayers."[32] Pierce argued that the cities should diversify their industrial bases and retain their workers instead of trying to save a dying giant. Another guest on the show, a stock analyst for Paine-Webber, suggested that Fort Wayne and Springfield were being asked to pay for IH's past management mistakes.

Fort Wayne's high-profile campaign contrasted sharply with Springfield's low-key approach. Dennis Shere, publisher of the *Springfield News & Sun,* observed: "Bells and whistles may be therapeutic, but I've got to believe IH will make a cold and calculated decision based on economics. I think we have the edge."[33] Krukewitt concurred: "The decision will be made in a board room by bankers, not by a bunch of letters."[34] Krukewitt called Fort Wayne's offer "almost insignificant. Our package, from its inception, had been structured as a bankable business deal. It is structured in the best interests of everybody— the community, the banks, the state, and IH." He said Fort Wayne's recent frantic attempts to pull together even larger deals to top Springfield's "would seem to me to underscore the frustration and panic, if you will, that the community is feeling."[35]

---

[32] Judy Rakowsky, "Krukewitt, Moses Face Off on National TV," *Springfield News & Sun,* August 21, 1982, p. 1.

[33] William Hershey and Michael Cull, "IH Drama Provides Another Tale of Two Cities," *Springfield News & Sun,* September 2, 1982, p. 3.

[34] Fred Knapp, "The Grim Reaper: How International Harvester Held Two Towns Hostage," *The Progressive* 48 (January 1984), p. 30.

[35] Alan Johnson, "Krukewitt: Springfield's Deal Is Best," *Springfield News & Sun,* August 21, 1982, p. 1.

IH was also receiving offers of aid from other cities. The state of Illinois and the city of Rock Island gave IH $7 million to help move axle and transmission production from Louisville, Kentucky, to Rock Island. Memphis, Tennessee, workers pledged to take a $3-an-hour pay cut (from $12.85 to $9.85) to reverse IH's announced decision to close their agricultural equipment factory.

In mid-August Harvester reported a 1982 third quarter loss of $125.9 million, its narrowest loss in five quarters. It also announced the sale of its 29 percent stake in profitable Steiger Tractor Co. to a West German firm and the pending sale of its construction equipment business to Dresser Industries. Although the construction equipment business had a book value of $500 million, analysts estimated that IH would receive only $100 million for the ancient plant and equipment.

SEPTEMBER 1982

While IH officials carefully reviewed the two packages, residents of both cities remained apprehensive. Three hundred and twenty more Fort Wayne truck plant workers were laid off indefinitely, and daily heavy duty truck production dropped from 70 to 57, down from 90 earlier in the summer.

On September 13, Ohio modified its package to allow the Springfield Community Improvement Corporation (CIC) to repay its $30 million debt over 20 years instead of 10. On September 16, the 11 banks who were loaning $20 million to CIC discovered that IH could not grant them a clear lien on the truck plant because of outstanding debentures on the property. The bankers balked, and it looked like the deal was dead. But Governor Rhodes intervened and convinced the appropriate state officials to raise the state's loan guarantee from 50 percent to 85 percent. On September 22, Ohio announced that the price of the purchase-leaseback package had been dropped to $27.6 million as a result of three independent appraisals and deletion of some equipment previously included. This lowered the banks' share to $18.4 million and the state's share to $9.2 million (and the forgone interest over the term of the state loan to $14 million).

Fort Wayne and Indiana officials were irritated and concerned by the changes. IH had given them a firm "no changes" deadline back in August, yet it was allowing Ohio to adjust its package a month later. Further, IH sent representatives to Columbus to work out details of the Ohio plan, while Indiana representatives had to travel to Harvester's headquarters in Chicago at their own expense to present their package. They felt that these actions indicated a clear preference by IH for consolidation in Springfield; IH was apparently postponing its decision while Ohio worked out snags in its package. But on September 20, Harvester officials told Indiana's Lieutenant Governor Mutz that a decision had not been made yet.

On September 15, to spur a decision in Fort Wayne's favor, Fort Wayne Future, Inc. bypassed the UAW Local and took a wage deferral plan directly to the workers. The local civic group asked the workers to use newspaper coupons to make pledges to defer 15 percent of their wages (which would be repaid with interest). A week later the group announced that 831 workers, 20 percent of IH's Fort Wayne work force, had pledged to defer a total of $9.3 million over three years. On September 24 Fort Wayne added another $8 million in incentives: a private sector commitment to construct a $6 million paint facility for IH; $1 million in city utility improvement grants; and a $1 million city facilities improvement loan. Democratic Mayor Moses, whose term expired at the end of 1983, lashed out at the Republican governor and lieutenant governor for not doing enough for Fort Wayne:

> Here in Indiana we cities are on our own. The state is not prepared to compete for jobs. The state has no money to invest in struggling industries. And they make no exceptions to their senseless rules. Fort Wayne took on Harvester alone. We took on the state of Ohio alone. We found the money, we wrote the documents, we negotiated the financing . . . and when the pressure became great enough, the state came along for a share of the credit.[36]

In Indianapolis, Mutz accused Moses of looking for a scapegoat in case Fort Wayne lost the Harvester contest.

Meanwhile, Harvester continued to deal with its financial morass. In mid-September it reached a tentative agreement with its bankers to lower or defer interest payments and to convert up to $350 million of deferred interest and debt principal into equity, giving the banks ownership of as much as 40 percent of the company. The proposal was predicated on Harvester's winning $50 million in concessions from its suppliers, $20 million from its 2,800 dealers, and $75 million from debenture holders. At the same time, Harvester sharply widened its estimate of 1982 losses from $925 million to between $1.5 to $1.6 billion, indicating that it was close to bankruptcy. Shareholder equity would be wiped out by October 31. The two major factors in the revised estimate were a $325–375 million charge against the sale of its construction equipment business and the drastically reduced estimate of the gain from conversion of part of its debt into equity.

On September 24, *The Wall Street Journal* quoted a Harvester spokesperson as saying that the Springfield and Fort Wayne packages were "in place" and that a decision would be made "within a week to 10 days."

---

[36] Kevin Leininger, "Fort Wayne Boosts IH Offer," *Fort Wayne News-Sentinel,* September 24, 1982, p. 1A.

Arthur D. Little, Inc.
and the Toxic Alert (Revised)

We who are associated with Arthur D. Little, Inc., are indeed fortunate in that, in the course of serving our personal, professional, and corporate interests, we serve society as well. Our central function, that of bridging the gap between the development of new knowledge and its practical application by business and government, has never been more important. We do this by developing new products and processes based on emerging technologies, like genetic engineering or artificial intelligence, and other consulting assignments; we also transfer know-how to developing economies through the ADL Management Education Institute programs. In pursuing our professional work for our clients, the relationship of our activities to the societies in which we operate is a matter of daily, overriding concern.

John Magee, President, 1984

Arthur D. Little, Inc. (ADL), an internationally known consulting firm, was founded in Boston in 1886 and moved to neighboring Cambridge in 1917, a year after MIT made the same move. The company thus became the first research-oriented commercial organization in a city which later would be home to hundreds of high-tech firms. By 1984 ADL employed over 2,600 people and had offices in 14 countries. Sales volume for 1984 exceeded $200 million.

More than 1,400 ADL employees worked in the extensive network of laboratories and office buildings at Acorn Park, the company's 40-acre headquarters campus in North Cambridge. The research, engineering, and management consulting services offered by ADL involved disciplines ranging from strategic management to hazardous waste management to forensic economics. Thirty-seven corporate vice presidents served as "professional services officers" in charge of various technical specialties. Twenty-nine more vice presidents and senior vice presidents oversaw geographic offices or administrative

This case was prepared by John A. Seeger, associate professor of management at Bentley College, Waltham, Massachusetts, to serve as a basis for class discussion. It was presented at the annual meeting of the Case Research Association, 1985. Permission to republish should be obtained from CRA and the author. Copyright 1986 by John A. Seeger.

functions. Ten independently organized "complementary business units," each with its own president and staff, offered a wide range of services such as systems management, opinion research, and property valuation. Five of these units were headquartered at Acorn Park; two more were located in nearby Lowell.

Arthur D. Little had experienced consistent growth in revenues for the past decade, from $81 million in sales in 1975 to $213 million in 1984. Net income had grown from $3.1 million in 1975 to $6.1 million in 1983 but fell to $3.6 million in 1984. Disappointing results in three of the complementary business units accounted for the drop, according to the 1984 annual report. (See Exhibit 1 for a 10 year summary of the firm's financial highlights. Exhibits 2 and 3 summarize 1984 financial results.)

Until 1969, ADL was wholly owned by the Memorial Drive Trust, a deferred compensation profit-sharing plan whose beneficiaries were past and present employees of the firm. Thirty percent of ADL's stock was sold to the public in 1969, but two thirds of that had been reacquired by individual employees or by the Employees Investment Plan. In 1985 about 10 percent of ADL's stock was held by the public, while 78 percent was controlled by the trustees of the trust and the plan. The company had contributed to these plans (and charged to operations) about $9 million in each of the past three years.

CONSULTING OPERATIONS

ADL dealt with an average of 1,000 clients and undertook about 4,000 to 5,000 individual assignments annually, according to Senior Vice President and General Manager of Professional Operations Alfred E. Wechsler. Some three quarters of ADL's clients were repeat customers.

New projects and activities at ADL went through a formal acceptance procedure, usually beginning with a prospective client contacting a professional staff member, who would draft a proposal for the work. The proposal was submitted to a 10-member management group composed of 5 permanent members of the senior staff and 5 junior ADL professionals who rotated every three months. The management group met every morning to evaluate all potential assignments according to a four-question formula.

The four questions were:

Is the work something that ADL would be happy to do?

Will the work create a conflict of interest with other work ADL is doing?

Can the client pay the bill?

Does ADL have the staff on hand to do the job?

Upon acceptance of the project, a budget was established and an ADL professional was given the task of assembling a team to do the job, drawing from whatever disciplines were needed. The team leader did not have to get approval from department managers for the use of their people.

EXHIBIT 1 Ten-Year Summary of Financial Highlights (dollars and shares in thousands, except per share data)

(dollars and shares in thousands, except per share data)	1984	1983	1982	1981	1980	1979	1978	1977	1976	1975
Operating results for the year										
New contracts, net	$174,420	$158,268	$132,972	$144,755	$136,911	$116,063	$129,963	$96,566	$75,777	$67,353
Index	259	235	197	215	203	172	193	143	113	100
Professional service income, net	$161,097	$147,580	$141,174	$137,119	$127,463	$116,099	$99,098	$87,585	$70,908	$64,621
Index	249	228	218	212	197	180	153	136	110	100
Royalties and venture income	$ 1,421	$ 1,619	$ 1,344	$ 3,104	$ 3,434	$ 2,340	$ 1,772	$ 3,113	$ 2,038	$ 1,595
Index	89	102	84	195	215	147	111	195	128	100
Revenues	$213,363	$192,478	$181,398	$175,600	$163,215	$141,036	$120,879	$106,619	$86,221	$80,827
Index	264	238	224	217	202	174	150	132	107	100
Salaries, wages, and other employment costs	$112,999	$102,598	$97,483	$94,298	$86,900	$79,922	$67,419	$60,189	$49,753	$45,016
Index	251	228	217	209	193	178	150	134	111	100
Income from operations	$ 9,063	$ 10,724	$ 11,086	$ 12,651	$ 10,826	$ 11,080	$ 10,344	$ 11,082	$ 6,529	$ 6,080
Index	149	176	182	208	178	182	170	182	107	100
Income before taxes on income	$ 7,456	$ 11,088	$ 10,496	$ 12,800	$ 10,975	$ 10,984	$ 10,545	$10,834	$ 6,971	$ 6,257
Index	119	177	168	205	175	176	169	173	111	100
Net income	$ 3,611	$ 6,070	$ 5,510	$ 6,740	$ 5,793	$ 5,777	$ 5,300	$ 5,578	$ 3,574	$ 3,142
Index	115	193	175	215	184	184	169	178	114	100
Cash flow from operations	$ 8,728	$ 10,988	$ 9,976	$ 10,257	$ 8,832	$ 8,388	$ 7,460	$ 7,226	$ 4,628	$ 4,217
Index	207	261	237	243	209	199	177	171	110	100
Revenues per share	$ 84.47	$ 76.57	$ 72.17	$ 69.86	$ 64.93	$ 56.11	$ 48.09	$ 42.42	$ 34.30	$ 31.91
Income before taxes on income per share	$ 2.95	$ 4.41	$ 4.18	$ 5.09	$ 4.37	$ 4.37	$ 4.20	$ 4.31	$ 2.77	$ 2.47
Earnings per share	$ 1.43	$ 2.41	$ 2.19	$ 2.68	$ 2.30	$ 2.30	$ 2.11	$ 2.22	$ 1.42	$ 1.24
Dividends declared per share	$ .70	$ .70	$ .70	$ .60	$ .50	$ .48	$ .44	$ .37	$ .23	$ .17

EXHIBIT 1 *(concluded)*

(dollars and shares in thousands, except per share data)

	1984	1983	1982	1981	1980	1979	1978	1977	1976	1975
Financial position at year end										
Cash and cash equivalents	$ 10,301	$ 14,337	$ 8,380	$ 14,554	$ 12,550	$ 11,841	$ 12,912	$ 17,622	$ 11,945	$ 4,993
Index	206	287	168	291	251	237	259	353	239	100
Accounts receivable and unbilled services	$ 56,209	$ 49,707	$ 45,414	$ 38,487	$ 36,823	$ 31,328	$ 27,633	$ 24,589	$ 20,448	$ 22,744
Index	247	219	200	169	162	138	121	108	90	100
Working capital	$ 27,761	$ 28,001	$ 24,906	$ 24,226	$ 24,353	$ 21,677	$ 19,521	$ 22,888	$ 19,077	$ 17,237
Index	161	162	144	141	141	126	113	133	111	100
Total assets	$107,520	$102,575	$ 91,442	$ 87,142	$ 79,333	$ 71,321	$ 65,860	$ 60,119	$ 49,904	$ 37,784
Index	285	271	242	231	210	189	174	159	132	100
Long-term and capital lease obligations	$ 3,617	$ 3,488	$ 3,830	$ 4,212	$ 4,624	$ 4,972	$ 5,212	$ 6,952	$ 7,944	$ 1,220
Index	296	286	314	345	379	408	427	570	651	100
Shareholders' equity	$ 61,197	$ 58,865	$ 54,555	$ 50,805	$ 45,573	$ 41,037	$ 36,479	$ 32,291	$ 27,634	$ 24,647
Stockholders' equity per share	$ 24.16	$ 23.42	$ 21.70	$ 20.21	$ 18.13	$ 16.33	$ 14.51	$ 12.85	$ 10.99	$ 9.81
Other data										
Return on average stockholders' equity	6.0%	10.7%	10.5%	14.0%	13.4%	14.9%	15.4%	18.6%	13.7%	13.4%
Net income as percent of revenue	1.7%	3.2%	3.0%	3.8%	3.6%	4.1%	4.4%	5.2%	4.1%	3.9%
Average number of shares outstanding	2,526	2,514	2,514	2,514	2,514	2,514	2,514	2,514	2,514	2,534
Number of employees at year end	2,606	2,424	2,330	2,340	2,394	2,529	2,308	2,078	1,821	1,798
Index	145	135	130	130	133	141	128	116	101	100

EXHIBIT 2

ARTHUR D. LITTLE, INC.
Consolidated Balance Sheets at December 31
(dollar amounts in thousands)

	1984	1983	1982
Assets			
Cash and cash equivalents	$ 10,301	$ 14,337	$ 8,380
Receivables and unbilled services	56,209	49,707	45,414
Prepaid and other current assets	3,957	4,179	4,169
Total current assets	70,467	68,223	57,963
Land	2,301	2,241	2,241
Buildings and leasehold improvements	33,002	30,591	29,428
Equipment, furniture, and fixtures	31,447	27,498	23,369
Less: Accumulated depreciation	(33,840)	(28,834)	(24,442)
Total net fixed assets	32,910	31,496	30,596
Investments and other assets	4,143	2,856	2,883
Total assets	$107,520	$102,575	$ 91,442
Liabilities and Equity			
Accounts payable	$ 4,145	$ 6,446	$ 4,304
Accrued expenses	24,850	19,835	16,350
Accrued income taxes	3,398	4,471	2,860
Advanced payments from clients	10,313	9,470	9,543
Total current liabilities	42,706	40,222	33,057
Long-term debt	1,487	1,199	1,394
Capital lease obligations	2,130	2,289	2,436
Total liabilities	46,323	43,710	33,057
Common stock and paid-in capital	4,908	4,427	4,427
Retained earnings	56,289	54,438	50,128
Total stockholders' equity	61,197	58,865	54,555
Total liabilities and equity	$107,520	$102,575	$ 91,442

A 10-year graph in ADL's 1983 annual report showed billings to U.S. federal government–sponsored projects ranging between $25 million and $27 million per year from 1979 to 1983, while U.S. state and local government revenues were $10 million to $13 million per year. No similar graph was included in the 1984 annual report, but tabulated results showed federal billings rose by $3.2 million in 1984, while state and local government business dropped by $3 million.

EXHIBIT 3

ARTHUR D. LITTLE, INC.
Consolidated Income Statements for Years Ended December 31
(dollar amounts in thousands)

	1984	1983	1982
Revenues	$213,363	$192,478	$181,398
Employment costs	112,999	102,598	97,483
Other operating expenses	40,456	35,877	33,949
Client reimbursable costs	50,845	43,279	38,880
	204,300	181,754	170,312
Income from operations	9,063	10,724	11,086
Income from short-term investments	884	1,038	1,902
Other income (charges)	(2,491)	(674)	(2,492)
Income before taxes	7,456	11,088	10,496
Provision for income taxes	3,845	5,018	4,986
Net income	$ 3,611	$ 6,070	$ 5,510

COMPANY POLICIES

The founder of ADL, Dr. Arthur Dehon Little, was deeply committed to the idea that science and technology were the keys to progress. He felt that positive thinking and a "can do" attitude could successfully apply new ideas to the problems of industry and government. In 1921, the 35th anniversary of ADL's founding, Dr. Little found a symbolic representation of his credo and a lasting beacon for his firm: He decided not only that it *should* be possible to make a "silk purse from a sow's ear," but that his people *would* do it. Starting with 1,000 ears, his staff boiled up a gelatinous goo, spun a thread from it, and produced a purse, which is now on display at the Smithsonian Institution.

The same sense of irreverence for dogma was shown again 56 years later, when the firm set out to debunk another platitude of impossibility, the old cliche "It went over like a lead balloon." Anthony Baldo, writing in the *Cambridge Chronicle,* reported, "for ADL staffers, this provided a weighty challenge. . . . In fact, three very differently designed lead balloons were created. Curiously, the winning entry was so buoyant that it tore away from where it was tied. 'It was last seen going over the Atlantic,' said Alma Triner, ADL's vice president for public relations."

ADL attempted to provide its staff with an intellectual climate to encourage free thinking as well as bottom-line results, wrote Baldo. Staff members were not required to work on a specific quota of projects. Staff members set their own goals. Nobody was required to work on a project found personally objectionable. No dress code existed, and personnel were free to decorate their offices any way they liked. "I think we have a lot of respect for each other as individuals," the *Chronicle* quoted ADL President John F. Magee. "We have a respect for individual tastes and idiosyncrasies."

"Humor, too, has a place within ADL's corporate structure," continued the *Chronicle*. "It starts at the top with the firm's chairman of the board, Robert K. Mueller, who has written a book called *Behind the Boardroom Door*. While the book is about corporate rivalries and politics, Mueller, according to an ADL release, mostly concludes that 'too few businessmen, and hardly any directors, have the ability to laugh at themselves.' "

At the corporate level, a set of governing policies reinforced the firm's fundamental regard for people and the communities within which it operated. For example, ADL supported the "Sullivan Principles"[1] and conducted evaluations of the equal rights provisions of those principles for corporations maintaining offices in South Africa. As a corporate policy, ADL donated 2.5 percent of its pretax income to projects and institutions "designed to improve the quality of life in our communities throughout the world." Corporate policy also prohibited development work on weapons systems.

Additionally, company-paid staff time was contributed to a variety of public interest programs, and staff members were encouraged to contribute their own personal time to education, social programs, and political service. Senior Vice President D. Reid Weedon, Jr., was a prime example of the kind of community involvement found in the ADL staff; he served as a life member of the MIT Corporation, a life trustee of the Boston Museum of Science, and board chairman of the Winchester Hospital.

The company also carefully preserved its links with the university community. In 1984, the presidents of MIT, Smith College, and the Woods Hole Oceanographic Institution—Paul E. Gray, Jill Ker Conway, and Paul M. Frye—were members of the Arthur D. Little board of directors. So was C. Roland Christensen, university professor at Harvard University and one of the country's leading authorities in the field of business policy.

In the spring of 1984, Arthur D. Little, Inc. was justifiably proud of its standing as a socially involved and concerned pillar of the community.

By the spring of 1985, however, some residents of Cambridge, Arlington, and Belmont were referring to Arthur D. Little and its officers as arrogant, hypocritical, lying, avaricious outlaws—unwelcome intruders in the community and threats to the safety and security of all. The president's letter to the stockholders in the annual report published in March 1985 noted,

---

[1] In 1978, the Reverend Leon Sullivan proposed a list of voluntary guidelines, which have become the accepted standard of ethical and moral behavior for American employers in South Africa. These principles seek improvement in the economic, educational, and social life of South African workers, through full integration, equal benefits, fair and equal pay at the workplace, and through employee assistance outside of work as well.

Over the years we have taken considerable pride in the manner in which our pursuit of our professional and corporate objectives serves the interest of society as well.

Ironically, during the past year the company has been plagued by activist community opposition to certain research that we consider of vital importance to the defense of the United States, its military personnel, and civilian population against chemical warfare agents. The purpose of this research, performed in a safe, secure laboratory built in our Cambridge, Massachusetts, headquarters, is to develop better protective materials and methods of detecting and detoxifying chemical agents. This work is important, and the chemicals are handled in a manner that assures the safety of our staff and our neighbors. It is worth noting that, although safety is the expressed concern, opponents of our research for the U.S. Department of Defense appear to be unconcerned about nondefense-related research with substances of comparable hazard. I am saddened, however, by the strain in the fine relations we have enjoyed with Cambridge since the early days of this century.

THE TOXIC ALERT

Chief among ADL's critics was a loosely knit community organization called the North Cambridge Toxic Alert Coalition (later shortened to Toxic Alert). Key members of the organization as of August 1985 are described in Exhibit 4. Charlie Rose, a professional organizer and one of Toxic Alert's founders, described the conditions which led to its formation:

> People in North Cambridge already had a strong feeling they were being dumped on. For years, W. R. Grace and the Dewey and Almy chemical company had left chemical wastes standing in ponds. They often spilled naphthalene and left whole neighborhoods smelling like mothballs; that frightened people, and when the managers denied spilling anything it made people mad. The old city dump caught fire occasionally. The subway construction over the past five years threatened a lot of changes. There was a growing awareness. John O'Connor and I had seen the changes. We had scoped out an organizing plan for W. R. Grace a year earlier.
>
> Then the discovery that ADL was testing nerve gas came as the last straw. Things crystallized. We sat down and planned it. There were already good people in the neighborhood. We brought in skilled, professional, paid organizers beginning in the summer of 84

As New England codirector of the Clean Water Action Project, Charlie Rose had resources available. CWAP employed door-to-door canvassers who spent half their time soliciting funds (on commission). Their remaining time was spent studying and applying community skills in Rose's "Organizing School." "Canvassers should get people involved," said Rose. "It's not enough just to let people pitch money into the hat." One CWAP canvasser, Hillary Frank, became a mainstay of the Toxic Alert.

Toxic Alert operated through meetings of subcommittees, a steering committee, the membership at large, and meetings planned as media events for the whole population. The group had a volunteer treasurer but no other

EXHIBIT 4 Key Members of the Toxic Alert

Ed Cyr—age 28; native of North Cambridge; studied economics at University of Massachusetts, now studying planning at University of Massachusetts at Boston; former organizer for Cambridge Economic Opportunity Commission and North Cambridge Planning Team; executive director, Cambridge Committee of Elders.

John O'Connor—age 31; professional organizer; coordinator of the National Campaign against Toxic Hazards, an umbrella organization with affiliates in 28 states; travels and speaks extensively, concentrating in 1985 on the superfund law; studied sociology and journalism at Clark University.

Charlie Rose—age 27; New England codirector of the Clean Water Action Project; professional organizer, beginning in 1977 as a Volunteer in Service to America (VISTA); the only Toxic Alert worker not resident in Cambridge.

Sharon Moran—age 27; three-year resident; involved with Toxic Alert from its founding; B.A. in chemistry, Boston University; paralegal worker with an environmental law firm.

Wendy Baruch—pretzel salesperson at public events, known near Fenway Park for her singing pretzel call; teaches home construction skills; with Dan Grossman, led the ADL balloon release project and was interviewed on "20/20" and other programs; major interest: waste cleanup at W. R. Grace.

Hillary Frank—on leave from studies at Harvard University; employed by CWAP, on loan to Toxic Alert; ran first canvass for TA; keeps member records, does the telephone and mail work to encourage meeting attendance and committee work.

Dan Grossman—age 27; MIT Ph.D. candidate, political science; Cambridge resident since 1977; Toxic Alert representative to the health care task force of the Massachusetts legislature.

Michael Kanter—owner/manager of Cambridge Natural Foods store; 12 years in Cambridge; B.A. in history, University of Buffalo.

Steve Schnapp—age 39; eight-year resident; professional organizer on Boston's North Shore; studied organization at Boston University; chairperson, Cambridge Peace Commission.

Richard Durling-Shyduroff—director, Cambridge Institute of the Arts and Sciences; provided sound systems and space for membership meetings and fund-raising events in his headquarters building.

---

officers. There were no elections; anyone with the initiative to find the steering committee meetings could attend. Members of the steering committee took turns chairing the larger membership meetings which might see 25 to 40 attendees.

Originally the steering committee was made up of representatives of other neighborhood organizations, who generally listened to and agreed with the ideas of the professional organizers. By August of 1985 many of its members were local residents who took initiative and carried out programs without the organizers' involvement.

Between meetings, organizers and volunteers knocked on doors and made telephone calls, sought business support, wrote and distributed newsletters and publicity flyers, met with government officials, and maintained liaison with the press.

Ed Cyr, another Toxic Alert founder and a professional organizer, reported spending one hour per week at the *Cambridge TAB* and two hours at the *Cambridge Chronicle* (both weekly newspapers). "The *Boston Globe* never did catch on with the story," Cyr said. "It was really a television-type story." Cyr succeeded in bringing ABC's "20/20" to one communitywide meeting. "It's not hard to get coverage when you have a sexy issue," he said. "You just find an assignment editor four days ahead of the event, and then visit with them every day." Contacts with local radio and television stations were handled by Charlie Rose.

A CHRONOLOGY OF CONTROVERSY

Before a partisan audience and a battery of cameras at a community meeting sponsored by the Toxic Alert in March of 1985, Reid Weedon reviewed the events of the previous two years.

In January of 1983, he said, Arthur D. Little informed the Cambridge police and fire departments that work in a planned new laboratory facility "would involve highly toxic materials of particular interest to the Department of Defense." Specific information on chemical names, structures, and toxicities was not requested by the city officials, Weedon said. In a series of meetings, Cambridge police and fire officials reviewed the design. Several modifications were made at their suggestion.

Construction proceeded with an investment of approximately $800,000. In September of 1983 the building was ready for operation, and ADL again met with Cambridge fire and police officials, this time with instructions on handling public safety in the event of fire or intrusion into the facility.

In the event of fire, the laboratory should be allowed to burn to the ground. In the event of unauthorized entry into the laboratory, police should surround it and allow nobody to leave, but under no circumstances should they attempt to enter it themselves. The laboratory, it was explained, was engaged in testing highly toxic materials, including Department of Defense "surety agents." ADL technical people would respond to any alarm; nobody should enter without their assessment of the hazards involved. Furthermore, it was required in the interest of security that the city authorities make no public announcements that would call attention to the laboratory.

TA:

> See there? "Surety agents," they call them. That's nerve gas and blister agents—the most deadly stuff ever invented for killing people. And ADL wanted the city authorities to lie about it for them.[2]

---

[2] Throughout this case, inserts like this are used to interject points of view of the Toxic Alert (TA) or Arthur D. Little managers (ADL).

ADL:

> We didn't want or ask anyone to lie about anything. It was in the best interests of the public and our employees not to advertise that we had chemical warfare materials here. It was in the interest of maximizing safety.

Cambridge officials, under reciprocal public safety agreements with neighboring towns, asked ADL to inform the authorities in Arlington and Belmont. After touring the laboratory, the town manager of Arlington informed ADL that he could not, in good conscience, comply with the request for confidentiality; he would raise the issue at the next meeting of the selectmen, October 17.

"On that same day," wrote Sheldon Krimsky later, "ADL issued a news release announcing the opening of a high-security laboratory for the testing and analysis of toxic materials. The news release was skillfully written and avoided any mention that the facility would be handling chemical warfare agents or that the research under taken there would be defense related."[3]

ADL:

> There was nothing secret about the work. We sent memos to literally hundreds of staff members, because we were concerned about staff reaction. We held a reception for the lab's dedication; that's what the press release was for. It just never occurred to us that this would be a safety concern to the community. We made the assumption, perhaps naively, that it *was* safe, people would recognize that.

A *Boston Globe* story on the Arlington selectmen's meeting was noticed by Nancy Cyr in Cambridge; her calls to Cambridge city hall resulted in the issue's appearance on the City Council agenda that same night. The council asked the city's commissioner of health and hospitals, Dr. Melvin Chalfen, to inspect the new laboratory. He did so on October 19.

The council also asked for a hearing with Arthur D. Little's officers, who appeared on October 24. They reported that the Levins Laboratory (it was named to honor Dr. Philip L. Levins, the senior ADL officer who had advocated the facility's construction, who had died in a swimming accident before its completion) was the safest conceivable facility for its purpose, and that its purpose was in the public interest. ADL's contracts with the Department of Defense dealt with detecting chemical nerve agents, with neutralizing them, and with developing improved protective clothing.

TA:

> All very well, but it doesn't explain why we should welcome nerve gas in one of the most densely populated cities in the country. Put the laboratory in the desert or on some military post where it can be properly guarded, and those arguments make sense. Not here.

---

3 Sheldon Krimsky, "Local Control of Research Involving Chemical Warfare Agents," in *Science and Technology in a Democracy: Who Should Govern?*, ed. Malcolm L. Goggin (Knoxville: University of Tennessee Press, 1986).

ADL:

> The words *nerve gas* have a frightening connotation. They show a deliberate
> attempt to misdescribe the situation. We don't receive gas. We don't store gas. We
> use these agents in liquid form, in minute quantities. It's not easy to disperse these
> materials. Even when it's used on the battlefield, this material isn't a gas, by and
> large. It's an aerosol. This talk about "gas" is designed purely to heighten people's
> anxieties.

The Cambridge City Council had faced a similar issue before. In 1976 a
substantial public debate erupted over the dangers and propriety of genetic
research, in which DNA molecules might be modified to create new life
forms—in the worst-case scenario to create an "Andromeda strain" of lethal
bacteria. After a great deal of poliltical gesturing and scientific consideration,
Cambridge became the first city in the country to regulate genetic research. Its
new ordinance, based on federal guidelines developed by the National Institute
of Health, became a model for other cities facing the same problem.

Following its meeting with Arthur D. Little management, the Cambridge
City Council called for creation of a Scientific Advisory Committee "to advise
the City Council and the commissioner of health and hospitals on issues of
public health and safety related to the environmental hazards of ADL's research with chemical warfare agents." Arthur D. Little had already received
its first consignment of nerve agents and begun testing.

In the fall of 1983 and winter of 1984 several individual city councillors
attempted to stop the ADL work or to gain a moratorium while the Scientific
Advisory Committee (SAC) was organized and deliberating. ADL officials
responded that the terms of their contracts with the Department of Defense
imposed a schedule which could not be interrupted. ADL offered a 30-day
moratorium on initiation of new contracts and offered to cooperate with any
committee, but would not interrupt work already begun. Finally, on March 13,
1984, Dr. Chalfen issued an emergency order barring the testing of five
specified nerve and blister agents until the SAC rendered its report.

ADL:

> A moratorium would have removed any incentive for the council to appoint the
> committee or for the committee to act. Dr. Chalfen had previously told us he
> considered the laboratory to be safe. He issued his order under pressure from the
> city council, not on the basis of his professional judgment.

On March 16, Arthur D. Little went to court, claiming that no city action
could legally infringe on Department of Defense work, since federal regulation
(in this case, by DOD) took precedence over regulation by local authorities.
Superior Court Judge Robert Hallisey granted an injunction to restrain the
city from enforcing the commissioner's order. Tests continued at the Levins
Laboratory.

On April 12, 1984, the Scientific Advisory Committee held its first meeting. Dr. Sheldon Krimsky, a former member of the panel which had drawn up
the city's regulations on DNA research, served as chairman. The names,

EXHIBIT 5 Membership of the Cambridge Scientific Advisory Committee

Sheldon Krimsky (chair)—associate professor of urban and environmental policy. Tufts University; Ph.D. in philosophy of science.

Ann Hochberg (vice chair)—fisheries specialist, New England Fishery Management Council; B.A. in biology, M.S. in oceanography.

Frederick Centanni, Jr.—Cambridge resident; business element manager, EG&G Wakefield.

Edmund Crouch—research fellow in energy and the environment, Harvard University; Ph.D. in high-energy physics.

Edward Cyr—Cambridge resident; executive director, Cambridge Committee of Elders.

Lou DiBerardinis—industrial hygienist. Department of Environmental Health and Safety, Harvard; B.S. in chemical engineering, M.S. in industrial hygiene.

Joseph Fantasia—Cambridge resident and restaurant owner, active in Chamber of Commerce affairs; Cornell University.

Paul Fennelly—Arlington resident; group scientist and manager, Environmental Measurements Department, GCA Technology Division, GCA Corporation; Ph.D. in physical chemistry.

Richard Goldstein, M.D.—Department of Microbiology and Molecular Genetics, Harvard Medical School; Ph.D. in biology.

Jack Martinelli—Cambridge resident and Volkswagen mechanic; Ph.D. in chemistry; former student of Judith Harris.

Henry Mautner—chairman, Department of Biochemistry and Pharmacology, Tufts University School of Medicine; Ph.D. in medicinal chemistry.

John O'Connor—Cambridge resident; coordinator, National Campaign against Toxic Hazards.

David Ozonoff, M.D.—chief, Environmental Health Section, Boston University School of Medicine; former president, Massachusetts Public Health Association.

Placido John Paula—radiation technologist, Office of Environmental Health and Safety, Harvard University.

John J. Malone—Belmont resident; director, Belmont Department of Public Health; member, Governor's Hazardous Waste Council.

Ralph Wolfe—Cambridge resident; technical coordinator, Skidmore, Owings & Merrill; M.Arch. degree; son of a chemist.

occupations, and institutional affiliations of the SAC members are shown in Exhibit 5.

In May, the city's legal department attempted to end the temporary restraining order on the basis of a technical consulting report. The court ruled for ADL and continued the preliminary injunction barring enforcement of the city's health regulation. Cambridge retained a prominent Boston law firm, Palmer and Dodge, to continue the case.

For the next five months, the Scientific Advisory Committee worked to

EXHIBIT 6 "Ground Zero" Map of ADL Area

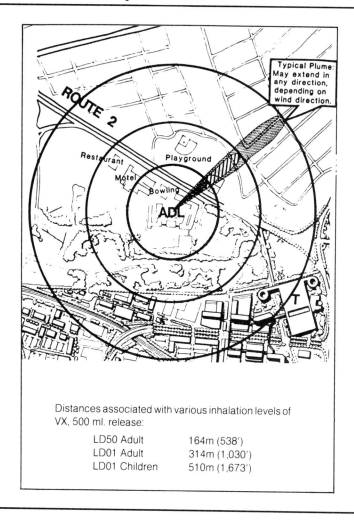

Distances associated with various inhalation levels of VX, 500 ml. release:

LD50 Adult	164m (538′)
LD01 Adult	314m (1,030′)
LD01 Children	510m (1,673′)

define and resolve the complex issues of technology and values which underlay the risk and benefit arguments of ADL and the city. Subcommittees were set up to investigate the physical and chemical properties of nerve agents, the various scenarios which could result from releases at ADL, and comparable risks presented by other chemicals in general use. Exhibit 6 shows one of many graphic representations presented in the SAC report. It is a "ground zero" map of the ADL area, showing the "zone of lethality" for the plume of gas emanating from a postulated half-liter spill of the agent "VX," with a southwesterly wind.

In September 1984, the committee issued its final report. The risks involved in transporting and processing chemical warfare agents in densely populated areas were not justified, the SAC concluded. Even though the risk might be very small, as ADL contended, the consequences if an accident did occur were such that the ADL work should not continue. The SAC found no discernible benefit to the city from the work's location in Cambridge; a majority of members saw no benefit in the work regardless of its location.

ADL:

> That report is incompetent. It was not written by a group of scientists. To call that a "Scientific" Advisory Committee was absurd! The representation on that committee of anyone who knew anything about risk analysis and these materials was essentially nil. There were some scientists, but what kind? There was one man, from MIT, who had direct working experience with this kind of issue. But he was the only one, and he quit the Committee—in disgust.[4]

Judge Hallisey called a meeting to hear attorneys' arguments on the federal "supremacy" issues. He would rule separately on the reasonableness of Cambridge's action, if the local regulation were found to be valid. Pending those decisions, the court continued its restraining order against Dr. Chalfen's regulation. The testing continued.

TA:

> And it's *still* going on. ADL still says it's their own job to decide whether it's safe enough, and nobody else's opinion counts for beans. They'll appeal this forever, and the courts will always give them another restraining order. We thought the SAC decision would decide something. Are we going to stand for this?

Impatient residents of the North Cambridge area were already concerned over another environmental issue—the location and disposal of chemical wastes on a 17-acre W. R. Grace site scheduled for industrial development. This was fertile ground for dissent, and the "nerve gas" issue was both threatening and compelling. SAC members Ed Cyr, John O'Connor, and Ralph Wolfe decided to organize, and O'Connor asked Charlie Rose for help. The North Cambridge Toxic Alert coalition [NCTAC] took shape with a community meeting in October 1984.

"We were surprised at the turnout," Ed Cyr said later. "It showed again the basic law of organizing: The number of bodies at a meeting depends on the hours of dirty work done before." Toxic Alert workers had blanketed North Cambridge with three different flyers, had knocked on doors and rung telephones to build grass roots communications. "After the October meeting, it was like a tidal wave," Cyr continued. "People signed up. We had 40 or 45 people helping plan the next steps."

Loudly, NCTAC challenged both W. R. Grace and Arthur D. Little to appear at a public meeting on November 29, 1984. W. R. Grace countered by

---

[4] Members of the Scientific Advisory Committee expressed substantial surprise at this comment by a high ADL official. They reported the chairman of MIT's Department of Nutrition and Food Sciences, Dr. Gerald N. Wogan, had contributed greatly to the subcommittee on toxicity before international commitments forced his resignation from the SAC for lack of time. When asked for clarification, Dr. Wogan commented, "In disgust? That certainly is not the case."

holding a series of small neighborhood meetings of its own, announcing it would not attend the NCTAC affair. ADL made no comment on the NCTAC challenge and was not expected to attend either.

"We saw no benefit in appearing at a meeting where we had no idea of the agenda, the structure, the process," said ADL's John Magee later. "There was no assurance of an opportunity to do anything but be pilloried."

Television crews did attend the November meeting, and so did the managers of the W. R. Grace division concerned with the real estate development. Patently obvious to the viewers of the evening news was the empty chair labeled *Arthur D. Little.* Speakers included Ed Cyr and John O'Connor, Dr. Sheldon Krimsky, Cambridge City Manager Robert Healy, a city councillor, and two technical consultants on environmental pollution. At the close of the meeting an angry Ed Cyr called for the city to retaliate against the absent Arthur D. Little by freezing building permits, refusing permission to park on public land, or shutting off water and sewer connections until the firm agreed to talk. The following day at 3 P.M., he announced, the Toxic Alert would meet on the highway outside ADL to release a cloud of black balloons, demonstrating how the wind could carry particles from Acorn Park to the neighboring blocks of densely packed two- and three-family houses. Television crews were invited to the demonstration; an ABC News "20/20" crew working on the story filmed the launching the next day. Cameras in pursuit, the Toxic Alert balloon people then strode into the Arthur D. Little reception area, demanding a meeting with President John Magee. The negotiation process for defining a forum for public debate began.

TA:

> So we win a round. But we still don't have Weedon and Magee out where people can see them. People have to hear ADL's arguments firsthand, to recognize how blind these guys are. They're still testing nerve gas next door. We have to get them out in the open.

Four days after the NCTAC meeting, on December 3, 1984, the Bhopal tragedy in India made poison gas a common topic and a more credible threat. ABC Television, which had filmed the Cambridge meeting without a specific production schedule, aired the ADL segment on "20/20" the following week. Toxic Alert members continued to organize.

On December 14, 1984, superior court Judge Robert Hallisey ruled in favor of the city of Cambridge on the "supremacy" question, establishing the right of the local government to regulate activities on DOD [Department of Defense] work at Arthur D. Little. ADL requested reconsideration of the issue. On January 14, Judge Hallisey issued a supplemental decision reconfirming his stand. Still to be heard were arguments over whether Cambridge's actions were reasonable. In the meantime, the testing continued.

Negotiations also continued between Toxic Alert leaders and ADL management about the timing and format of a public meeting in which each side could present its views. On several occasions, steering committee members visited ADL to demand that a date be set. After each meeting, local TV crews

EXHIBIT 7 Excerpts from John Magee's Letter of January 28, 1985

Dear Neighbor,

You probably have heard about some research being conducted in one of our analytical chemistry laboratories on highly toxic substances, referred to in the press as "nerve gases." . . . Although as liquids these agents are no more volatile than water, we realize the term *nerve gas* causes reasonable people to wonder whether the existence of such substances in the neighborhood should be cause for concern.

Because we value your good opinion and the friendship of our community, I would like to share with you the reasons we consider this research so important and why we are doing it here in Cambridge rather than in some isolated area. . . . We believe something must be done to reduce the threat of uncontrolled toxic chemicals in the environment. . . . Before our Levins Laboratory was constructed, we had to turn down community requests, including one from the Commonwealth of Massachusetts, for work involving dioxins and other contaminants. We did not like having to refuse to help our home state.

The research . . . is for defensive and protective purposes only . . . to develop better methods of detecting minute quantities . . . and safer, more effective means of destroying them on a large scale. We also are working to develop better protection, including clothing, for people who might be exposed to these substances.

We are doing the work here in Cambridge because this kind of chemical analysis cannot be performed in isolation. . . . Moving the laboratory to a remote location would mean moving much of our technical work out of Cambridge. This we do not want to do. . . . We have a record as good citizens of the community and a major investment here.

We invested nearly a million dollars . . . worked closely with the Cambridge city manager and the relevant public safety officials. . . . The result, experts concur, is a laboratory that advances the state of the art for the safe handling of hazardous substances.

If you have any comments or questions . . . I would appreciate your sending those to: Mr. D. Reid Weedon, Jr., senior vice president. We are interested in your views.

Sincerely,

/s/   John F. Magee, President and Chief Executive Officer

---

with minicameras were waiting to interview participants, often for the live 5:30 news. Finally, March 7 was selected.

At the end of January 1985, 61,000 residents in North Cambridge, Arlington, and Belmont received by first-class mail a package of materials including a three-page letter from ADL President John Magee, a four-page specification on the Levins Laboratory, and a four-page reproduction of a *Cambridge Chronicle* story describing Arthur D. Little's history, strengths, and virtues. Exhibit 7 contains excerpts from this letter and enclosures.

TA:

Will you look at this! We've been trying to smoke him out and here he comes, all by himself! Comparing nerve gas to water, for God's sake! Valuing our good opinion!

So sorry they had to turn down this work before! And so very, very safe! That lab has enough nerve gas on hand to kill 300,000 people, but we should have confidence because it's so very safe. This letter is a Christmas present from Magee to the Toxic Alert!

Reaction to ADL's communication was not limited to NCTAC activists. Weekly newspapers in all three affected communities took note of the mailing, and their readers responded with a barrage of letters to the editors, printed in mid-February. Three of these letter are excerpted in Exhibit 8. Exhibit 9 shows segments of a *Cambridge Chronicle* editorial of March 14.

"Public reaction was either moderately supportive or 'ho-hum,'" said John Magee later. "There are a lot of people in those communities and very few in the newspapers. A substantial number of people called or wrote in support, and of course those people don't write to the papers. When you look at the demonstrations and think of the numbers of people involved—why, I've almost gotten to know them on a first-name basis, because it's always the same small group."

On February 26, 1985, superior court Judge Hallisey ruled that the Cambridge regulation prohibiting chemical warfare agent work was valid and enforceable under the law. In an addendum to the decision, called "remarkable" by both parties and the press, the judge expressed reservations about his decision, thinking it unfair but unavoidable under the law. The next day he removed the restraining order which prevented the regulation's enforcement. The testing stopped.

In preparation for the March 7 public meeting, Toxic Alert wrote to the directors of ADL, inviting them to attend the meeting in order to inform

EXHIBIT 8   Excerpts from Letter to the Editors, *Cambridge Chronicle* and *Arlington Advocate,* March 7 and 21, 1985 (ellipses omitted)

Do you know what "the arrogance of power" is? It's a large corporation deciding to do something extremely dangerous to others and using its money and influence to steamroll over the local opposition. It's writing a patronizing letter to the locals afterward, saying, essentially, "If you only knew the facts you'd understand," as if we're too ignorant or misguided to realize what's really in our best interest. It's writing us a letter and saying, at the end, that if we have a reply, we should send it to someone else. Who is D. Reid Weedon, Jr., and why do I care whether he reads my reply to your letter?

Anyone who would build a lab for testing nerve gas in one of the most heavily populated urban areas in the United States is clearly beyond the reach of rational protest.

As ADL's neighbors we cannot accept this risk. Magee never wanted to know whether his neighbors feel safe. He never wanted us to know the lab exists. His newfound concern is insulting and absurd.

This is one resident who doesn't give a hoot about how many safety precautions they've taken. That just proves how lethal the stuff is. Testing those chemicals in our highly populated area is damn poor policy from a company that I've come to expect good judgment from.

EXHIBIT 9   Excerpts from a *Cambridge Chronicle Editorial,* March 14, 1985
               (ellipses omitted)

There are times when it is prudent to recognize that most lead balloons do not, in fact, fly. Now is the proper time for the Arthur D. Little Company to recognize that the best way to remain [a] "good neighbor" is to give up its quixotic battle against the city's ban on nerve agent testing.

ADL has handled the nerve agent issue with rather surprising stupidity, first attempting to stonewall its residential neighbors and city hall, then, belatedly, attempting to patch things up with a deceptively reassuring mass mailing (which included, for the record, a reprint from the *Chronicle.* It is not likely the firm will ask for reprint permission on this editorial.)

ADL has not come up with any particularly convincing arguments on its own behalf. Above all, company officials have stressed that the facilities where the nerve agents are stored and tested are "state-of-the-art" safe.

The one fact which inevitably weakens any defense of ADL's positon is that what's at issue here is a substance to which exposure can mean instant death, pure and simple. The city's ban is not an effort to restrict research, and it is not yet another attempt to overregulate business. Instead, the ban is the proper execution of the city's responsiblity to its people.

---

themselves, independently of management, on the issues and the potential impact on the company's good name. The letter also appealed for formation of a board-level committee on social responsiveness. It noted that ADL's relationships with its neighbors had always been so positive that board inputs to management had not been necessary. Now the inputs were needed, the letter said, but "it seems unlikely such a committee would be organized at Mr. Magee's own request, given his level of commitment to continued testing." One director responded to the Toxic Alert letter; none attended the March 7 meeting.

"Some directors asked my advice—what would management prefer they do about the invitation," John Magee recalled. "My reaction was, 'Do what you please.' In their view, it wouldn't have been appropriate to attend as board members."

MARCH 1985: THE PUBLIC FORUM

Television crews, reporters, and some 300 citizens attended the March 7 meeting in the auditorium of the Fitzgerald School in Cambridge. Moderator Anthony Cortese gave a brief chronology of events, noting that testing operations were now stopped due to the recent court decision, and outlined the rules of the program: Each side would have 30 minutes, 45 minutes would be allowed for questions from the floor, and each side would have 5 minutes for summarizing. Cortese introduced D. Reid Weedon, Jr., John Magee, ADL Vice

President for Chemical and Food Sciences Judith Harris, and Safety Officer R. Scott Stricoff. Weedon presented the ADL case.

THE ARTHUR D. LITTLE POSITION

Arthur D. Little, he said, had two concerns—one with the hazards of their work and another with the hazards of banning research. Safety for ADL staff and the community had always been uppermost in their minds, in all their work on pesticide wastes, PCBs, dioxin, and chemical warfare agents such as nerve gas, "or, really, nerve agents since they're not gases." All authorities who had seen the Levins Laboratory had praised it as representing the state of the art in safety. Indeed, ADL was now doing design work for the U.S. Centers for Disease Control. Weedon quoted expert authorities to vouch for the lab's safety and noted the health and hospitals commissioner had delayed five months between inspecting the lab and issuing his regulation—hardly the behavior of someone concerned about public health perils.

Weedon described the precautions taken in transporting nerve agents under armed escort and showed the audience a gray steel canister, called a *pig,* which had withstood drops from an army helicopter onto concrete without damage to the flame-sealed glass vials packed inside it. A pig could carry five 20-milliliter (mL) vials of liquid. On arrival at the laboratory, each vial was opened and its contents transferred to 1-mL vials. Since most experiments required less than 1 milliliter, any risk of spilling was minimized by working with the smaller standard quantity.

Near the end of the SAC deliberations, ADL had announced it would limit its inventory to a maximum of 40 milliliters of any of the three most hazardous nerve agent concentrates: Sarin (BG), Soman (GD), and VX. Additionally, the combined inventory of all three would not exceed 100 milliliters, although larger quantities of Mustar (HD) and Lewisite (L), up to a combined inventory of 500 milliliters, might be on hand at one time. Weedon referred to ADL's self-imposed limit of $1/10$ of a liter as a primary safeguard against the kind of accidental spills postulated in the SAC report.

Further, said Weedon, ADL used mostly dilute concentrations and would never leave a spill to evaporate. Household bleach was an effective decontaminating agent. The SAC report scenario showing a "puff" of gas, as from an explosion, could not happen because the agents decomposed in temperatures over 500 degrees. Besides, the injury and fatality counts deemed possible by the SAC assumed none of the injured received medical treatment—again, an assumption without credibility. Any accidents in any of the 14 laboratories doing this kind of work in America had resulted in injuries successfully treated; no testing-related fatalities had ever been reported. The assumptions used in the SAC report, Weedon said, were totally unrealistic. It was not fair to postulate impossible risks.

Weedon went on to describe the need for knowledge about chemical warfare agents, which were in current use in the Iran-Iraq war and might pose a threat to American military forces at any time. There was need, too, for research using these agents for medical applications. Hodgkin's disease had been found by an Army lab to respond to a nerve agent, and Alzheimer's disease was thought to be a prospective target. But if there could be no research, he said, there might be no cures.

"We're often asked, 'Why locate chemical warfare work in Cambridge?'" Weedon said, "The appropriate answer is, 'Because it is safe, and Arthur D. Little is here.' Usually the larger part of the work in an assignment does not use toxic materials and therefore is done outside the toxic materials laboratory. The next question is, 'Why not locate just the toxic materials laboratory elsewhere?' We do not have, nor do we expect, sufficient volume of work on chemical warfare agents to justify full-time staff in such a laboratory.

"Furthermore, a separate location would require medical personnel whenever people were in the laboratory, full-time guard service, and immediate-response technical and maintenance support services. All of these services are in place at our Acorn Park facility, and duplication, while possible, would price us out of the competition," Weedon said.

He went on to enumerate a list of toxic chemicals, many similar to the nerve agents, which were widely used in medical schools and were available from lab supply houses with no regulation at all. "A typical hardware store or garden center will have on its shelves a quantity equivalent to more than 100 lethal doses of the pesticide Malathion in concentrated form, in totally unventilated spaces. This pesticide acts on the human nervous system by exactly the same biochemical mechanisms as do the DOD chemicals GD, GB, and VS. . . . True, ounce for ounce, Malathion is less toxic than the chemical warfare agents. But because use and storage of Malathion is totally uncontrolled and the available quantities are so large, I submit that the risk of exposure to this nerve agent is much greater than the risk of exposure to similar chemicals safely stored within the Levins Laboratory."

Weedon concluded the ADL presentation with an appeal for the city to establish standards and regulations for *all* toxic agents, rather than banning a certain class of them based on their purpose as weapons of war. Arthur D. Little, he volunteered, stood ready to use its substantial talents to help the city in this effort.

"Arthur D. Little has been a part of Cambridge since the early days of this century," Weedon concluded. "We love this city. We're proud of it. The city we love is a world-class city, which provides an environment that encourages and supports scientific talent in a spirit of research and investigation. We trust you also wish, as we do, to protect that very special environment that is Cambridge."

THE TOXIC ALERT PRESENTATION

Five speakers shared the presentation and summary of the Toxic Alert position. The moderator introduced Ed Cyr, Sharon Moran, John O'Connor, and Steve Schnapp, all of the Toxic Alert, and David Ozonoff, M.D., a

Cambridge resident and SAC member. Steven Schnapp began the presentation.

Responding to ADL's many assurances of safety, Schnapp said, "It seems to me we've heard this kind of corporate reassurance before." As the house lights dimmed and a slide of a bushy-whiskered sea captain appeared on the screen, Schnapp continued:

> Captain Edward J. Smith said, "I cannot conceive of any kind of vital disaster happening to this vessel. Modern shipbuilding has gone beyond that." On April 12, 1912, Captain Smith's ship, the *Titanic,* struck an iceberg and sank with a loss of 1,500 lives. *John Magee says there is no credible danger in nerve gas testing at ADL. The risk is vanishingly small.*

The captain's picture changed to a slide showing a newsboy hawking papers with the headline "Titantic Lost!" and then to a handful of capsules. Schnapp continued,

> "We have firmly established the safety, dosage, and usefulness of Kevidon," said Frank Gettman, the president of William S. Merrill Company in 1960. "There is still no positive proof of a causal relationship between the use of thalidomide during pregnancy and malfunctions in the newborn." But in 1962 the drug was pulled off the market. More than 8,000 children suffered grave birth defects. *John Magee says, "There are more risks in the kitchens of Cambridge than in the laboratories of Arthur D. Little."*

The slide switched to a view of Niagara Falls.

> "When you come right down to it," said an ad of Hooker Chemical Company in the 1940s, "you would be hard pressed to find any group of people who care as much about the environmental well-being of Niagara Falls as the people at Hooker." In 1979, 239 families were evacuated from the Love Canal neighborhood. *Arthur D. Little cares just as much for Cambridge.*

The slide showed a refugee family leaving Love Canal and then the ominous cooling towers of a nuclear power plant.

> "Do you think I'd work here if it was dangerous?" said William Metzger, a Three Mile Island employee, shortly before the catastrophic near-meltdown of March 29, 1979. *"If this lab weren't safe," said Alma Triner, vice president for public relations at Arthur D. Little, "I wouldn't be working here."*

The slide changed again to show a chemical plant and then a *Newsweek* photograph of the Bhopal disaster.

> "A factory is not a small stone that can be shifted elsewhere," State Labor Minister Tarasingh Viyogi told the provincial assembly of Madhya Pradesh in India. "There is no danger to Bhopal, nor will there be." *Arthur D. Little, working with compounds 50 to 100 times more toxic than methyl isocyanate, is just as certain of their safety.*

"All of those assurances came from highly trained, competent people who most probably believed what they were saying," Schnapp said. "Will Cambridge be next on the 11 o'clock news?"

Sharon Moran told of attending the first Cambridge City Council meeting on the topic, in October of 1983. She described how Mr. Weedon "spent 10 minutes telling the council there wasn't any nerve gas at ADL. There were chemical surety agents, he said. It came out later these were liquids, which would explode into a shower of tiny droplets called an aerosol when a chemical warfare shell detonated. *That* was nerve gas, and ADL didn't have any. Later the SAC received a letter saying ADL would vaporize the liquid agents. Tonight again they say they don't."

Moran told of hearing "evasive answers" on what agents were at the laboratory and what tests and end results were expected. "What can you believe?" she asked. "What disturbs me is that, in spite of all their professional expertise, they couldn't—or maybe they didn't want to—be clear and coherent and forthcoming about what substances they were using. Confusing us with technical jargon is too often the trick of the arrogant scientist—not the kind of behavior I expect from a company with a commitment to be a good neighbor, as ADL has told us they have."

"Left out of tonight's presentation," said Moran, "was information about the agents themeslves. They were invented with one purpose: killing people. One 100th of a drop of agent VX will kill you, if it touches your skin or if you inhale it. These chemicals affect the nervous system, causing all bodily processes to go haywire. The victim sweats intensely, and vomits and defecates uncontrollably. Finally, the person becomes completely paralyzed and unable to take a breath; death follows by asphyxiation. Nerve agents are awesomely lethal, compared to compounds like Malathion. That is why I find it disturbing when Mr. Magee minimizes their danger by telling us that greater danger exists in the average kitchen.

"Also disturbing," said Moran, "was ADL's discounting of the SAC's findings. This was a group of professionals, not a bunch of radicals, and they found that an accidental release *could* happen. It is not impossible. Further, however small the risk, it was unacceptable in so densely populated an area. The only group that likes the idea of ADL's work is ADL. This kind of work should be done in remote military installations." Morgan concluded, "Commercial companies have too much at stake to be the sole judges of whether their work is acceptable."

David Ozonoff introduced himself as a physician with a bias in favor of public health. "The issue here," he said, "is not freedom of inquiry as Mr. Weedon would have the audience believe. The testing of nerve gas has about the same relationship to science as pornography has to photojournalism. Nor is the issue about trading one risk for another. There is a perfect way to have no risk at all from nerve gas in the city of Cambridge, and that is not to do this work in the city. Nor is the issue about regulation; Cambridge can and should regulate ADL, because otherwise they would be regulated only by the Department of Defense—reputed to be the worst polluter in the country.

"In fact," Ozonoff said, "everybody knows what the issue is about: It's the Willie Sutton principle. You may remember that, when somebody asked the late bank robber Willie Sutton why he robbed banks, he said, 'Because that's where the money is.' EPA money has dried up, and consultants are turning to where the money is—the Department of Defense."

Ozonoff concluded, "This controversy is about risk and the notion of what is acceptable. Some risks are unacceptable even though their numeric measurements are very, very small; examples are the presence of dangerous chemicals in drinking water, asbestos in schools, and cyanide in Tylenol capsules. The Levins Laboratory risks are also very small, but they are real, and they have been judged unacceptable by everyone in the community except ADL."

Ed Cyr took the platform next to argue that this was not a question for scientists or managers to answer. "This is too important to be left to experts, businessmen, or scientists because they are unable to deal with being wrong, and that makes them dangerous," Cyr said. "Informed citizens," he went on, "have a basic right to full information about all the risks they are exposed to. More importantly, they have a right to decide for themselves what risks they will take.

"I will not fall into the scientists' trap of trying to prove how an accident could happen," Cyr said. "instead, I look at why I am afraid in this case the stage has been set for one." Claiming that public officials and businesses normally keep accidents secret until they get out of hand, Cyr said, "We must judge the people who would run the facility as well as the facilty itself. ADL planned the lab in secret, with no public consideration in siting, design tradeoffs, or security considerations. ADL went to great lengths to make sure we were *not* informed until contracts were in hand; they asked our police and firefighters to lie for them.

"It would be good if I could tell you that, when the story broke, ADL saw the folly in their approach and came clean. At least then we would know they were capable of admitting a mistake. But no. At every meeting, ADL has downplayed the danger and played us for fools. They paint themselves as victims, even after 16 weeks of hearings at the SAC. No Cambridge project has ever been looked at as thoroughly as this one.

"Can you trust ADL to safely manage this lab, when they worked so very hard to avoid telling you about it in the first place? . . . Can you trust a company that regularly, in forum after forum, compares these incredibly deadly chemicals to *water?* to *backyard pesticides?* and to things that are commonly found in your *kitchen?*

"Do *you* believe the Department of Defense intends to kill a million Russians with 2 gallons of Liquid Plumber?"

DISCUSSION AND SUMMARIES

John O'Connor summarized for the Toxic Alert, calling the ADL public relations campaign a "snow job" to cover the main reason for ADL's involvement—to make money. "The community has the right to say no to nerve gas testing," he said, demanding that ADL drop its appeal, renounce nerve gas forever, and move present stocks out of Cambridge. "The one person with power to do that is Mr. Magee," O'Connor continued. "We are angry, frightened—and also on the move to ensure that not one dime of taxpayer money will be used to support a corporation that is chemically trespassing on our city. If need be, we will take to the streets like the founders of our country, to demand that our rights as citizens to be free from toxic hazards be recognized."

Mr. Magee summarized for Arthur D. Little, voicing appreciation for the audience's courtesy. He held up a quarter-teaspoon to demonstrate how small the quantity involved at any one time was, and how hard it would be to make that quantity reach beyond ADL's property. He quoted a recent visitor as saying the facility was "superb." Cambridge officials had been kept informed from the beginning, he said, adding, "We've continued to stay in touch with the city, and *not once* have city officials, even yet, expressed concern to us about the safety of our laboratory!"

"That's not true," said a voice from the back of the hall.

"That is true," Magee replied.

"I was in the laboratory, and I told Mr. Weedon at the time I examined it that I wasn't impressed with. . . ."

Magee interrupted, "Who are you?"

"My name is Tom Danehy, and I'm a city councillor, and I live in Cambridge, not in Wellesley."

"I must admit I was speaking specifically of the fire, police, and public health officials," said Magee.

"Those aren't the ones we elect," Danehy concluded.

Magee resumed his talk with an attack on what he called the bias of Dr. Ozonoff. Magee said Ozonoff, as director of a group called the Committee for Responsible Genetics, had taken a position against *any* defensive research on chemical or biological warfare agents. "That political stand has nothing to do with neighborhood safety," Magee said, "and we shouldn't let that point of view be imposed on the community under the disguise of a concern for neighborhood safety." He urged all who were "really concerned with safety" to join with ADL to help the city develop comprehensive regulations for all toxic substances, wherever they were used.

As the crowd left the auditorium, members of the Toxic Alert took an "exit poll," asking whether nerve gas work should be done in Cambridge. Four people said it should; 127 said no. Recognizing the possible bias in the population, the poll takers also asked whether respondents were members of Toxic Alert or employees of ADL. Seven were ADL workers, while 39 were Toxic Alert members.

TA:

See that? Seven employees here, but only four votes for the testing. Do you suppose three sevenths of ADL's own people are on our side? Think what we could do with that!

ADL:

We got a stronger reaction from staff members to raising the price of tuna sandwiches in the cafeteria than to this issue.

SPRING AND SUMMER 1985: THE DEBATE CONTINUES

Commenting in the *Cambridge Chronicle* on the impact of the interruption in testing, laboratory manager Dr. Judith Harris said that ADL was currently committed to several DOD contracts and had "several million dollars" in proposed contracts under consideration. "If we are forced to close down for some time, I think there's going to be a serious problem," she said, noting that if the ban on research held, ADL would have to subcontract its work to some other downtown area," she said, noting that most of the other labs were in densely populated areas like Birmingham, Alabama, or Columbus, Ohio.

In the weeks after the public forum, the *Cambridge Chronicle* took a strong editorial stand against nerve agent testing, and other local groups also took public positions on the issue. In a March 20 letter to ADL, the presidents of the Cambridge, Arlington, and Belmont Leagues of Women Voters supported the ban on testing. Alma Triner, ADL's vice president for public relations, told the *Chronicle* that the leagues' position was "very disappointing" to the company, which had contributed funds to league projects in the past. The league "has lost credibility in the eyes of ADL" as a result of its stand, Triner said.

While gaining local support, however, the movement lost ground in the courts. On March 12, ADL asked the state appeals court for a stay of Judge Hallisey's order; three days later Judge John Greaney complied, reinstating the injunction against enforcing Dr. Chalfen's regulation. Cambridge attorneys at once asked State Supreme Judicial Court Justice Paul Liacos to remove the case from the Appeals Court and hear it directly at the Supreme Court level, short-cutting one step of the appeals process. The case was heard by the Supreme Judicial Court on April 4, but no immediate finding was expected. Although no formal announcements were made, it was assumed by Toxic Alert members that testing had resumed in the Levins Laboratory.

On March 30, 1985, the new Boston subway station next door to ADL was opened. Toxic Alert members took advantage of the large crowds to picket with the message that the entire station was inside the "zone of lethality." On April 5, a group called the *Boston Committee for No Business as Usual* held a "twitch-in" rally in front of ADL's offices. On April 12, at the annual meeting of Arthur D. Little stockholders, pickets walked the sidewalks in front of the

Harvard Club in Boston, passing out leaflets questioning the ability of management to view the situation objectively.

ADL:

> The "twitch-in" was a demonstration by about six people who called themselves the *Revolutionary Communist Youth Brigade* and operate out of an office at MIT. The *Globe* covered the annual meeting but didn't do a story because the demonstration was a nonevent involving the usual 8 to 10 people.

On April 19, State Representative Thomas Gallagher introduced a bill which would ban the testing of chemical warfare agents within a mile of any home, business, or public road. For the next two months the scope of possible regulations was debated in the Joint Legislative Committee on Health Care, whose chairman toured the ADL laboratory and said he was much impressed. On June 12, ADL's Dr. William Augerson testified to the committee on the need for regulating *all* highly toxic chemicals, not just those designed as weapons. He named 16 "relatively common chemicals" whose toxicity, he said, equaled that of the agents prohibited in Cambridge. The list included strychnine, parathion, phosgene, arsine, and methylisocyanate. A special task force was eventually set up by the legislature, to report back in the fall. At the same time, Cambridge's Scientific Advisory Committee continued to work on drafting an ordinance to control toxic substances in general.

On May 28, 1985, the Army's undersecretary of research and development, Amaretta Hoeber, met with ADL and Toxic Alert representatives in the offices of Senator Edward Kennedy to reiterate the nation's needs for this research and the Army's confidence in its safe conduct at Acorn Park. On June 3, the Cambridge City Council okayed a referendum question for the November ballot, asking voter opinion on the ADL testing work.

As the summer passed, both sides awaited the ruling of the Supreme Judicial Court. The Supreme Court of the United States would be the next legal step if the Massachusetts loser decided to appeal further. Toxic Alert members wondered about their own next steps, and expected Arthur D. Little again to avoid complying with the health and hospitals regulation. How, they pondered, could they most effectively raise the cost of ADL to the point where testing would be abandoned? In the meantime, testing continued at the Levins Laboratory.

Publisher Russell Pergament of the *Cambridge Tab* summarized the situation on July 23:

> The story is simple. ADL says they don't plan to manufacture these deadly nerve gases, a thimbleful of which can kill thousands. No sir. They plan to study ways of making these gases inert. That reminds me of the guy who was arrested for stealing hubcaps. When the police collared him, he said, "But, officer, I wasn't stealing them, I was putting them back on." And so it is with ADL, who have double talked, double dealed, and deceived the city's health department since day one about their plans here. They never played straight with the city, and so they rate no special considerations, especially in view of the great danger their work puts local families in.

ADL:

> Quoting a Russ Pergament editorial from *The Tab* as a voice of local opinion is like quoting *The National Enquirer* as an authority on national mores.

John Magee was unaware of the Pergament column and did not recall the local editorials. "Those things have no impact, really," he said. "Oh, we receive the papers, and of course we have a clipping service. And we recognize they have an impact on other people. But do they cause us to stop and ask ourselves whether we're doing the right thing? No."

Most ADL people, Magee said, believed the company's standing in the community had not been damaged by the controversy. "There may be some circles where our standing is diminished," he said, "and that may be true with some of our staff as well. But in other circles we've received sympathy—where people say, 'They got to you, just like they've gotten to Harvard or MIT or Polaroid in the past'. Still other circles have expressed substantial admiration for our willingness to stand up and fight."

Magee speculated on how he and his managers formed their impressions of the people arrayed against them. "When it becomes difficult to engage these people in a discussion of the technical issues," he said, "then you begin to consider the question, are there other issues that are driving them? We look for what brings them together. We know Ozonoff and Krimsky are very active in antimilitary political activity.

"Ozonoff has been quoted as making some outlandish statements concerning the level of risk involved. The idea that one drop of this stuff could kill 10,000 people or whatever . . . that we have enough to kill . . . I don't know. . . . Anybody who is a serious student of the risks involved with toxic materials and dispersal issues *has* to see that as not being a factual estimate. It assumes people line up to get precisely the right dose. So there's got to be some kind of motivation here, to put out that kind of number. It's not put out as a factual analysis.

"We don't use gas at all. *We're* not the ones who are using misnomers or clouding the issue with semantics." Reminded that ADL's contracts included work on detection of gas, which seemed to imply the presence of gas, Magee paused. "I don't think we're generating any aerosols," he said. "I'd have to check."

Had the testing been pursued up to now as a matter of principle? "Well, there are principles and principles," said Magee. "If the principle is one of essential ethics, then you press it. But if it's a matter of being allowed to do something we think we ought to be allowed to do, then there is a practical limit to how far you want to press it, because there are alternatives. For example, if this is saying to us that Cambridge is no longer a healthy community for an organization like ours, then we have options. We have to address the issue of principle in that context."

Commentaries

---

8. Avco Corp. Makes Judicious Use of Gifts to U.S. Congressmen

Brooks Jackson

WASHINGTON—When Rep. Joseph Addabbo changed his mind about encouraging the Army to buy M1-tank engines from a second supplier, he surprised his liberal colleagues. But he delighted Avco Corp., which had just donated $5,000 to his 1984 reelection campaign.

The New York Democrat's defection on a crucial House vote last July helped save Avco from losing its profitable monopoly on the 1,500-horsepower gas-turbine engines. But "the campaign contributions didn't make up my mind," he says.

Mr. Addabbo was just one of a number of lawmakers to receive Avco money while being lobbied on the tank-engine issue. During the fight, the company's political-action-committee donations surged sharply to a total of more than $60,000 to 92 Senate and House members. The Greenwich, Connecticut, company also paid several $2,000 fees to lawmakers for appearances at Avco weapons plants.

Avco doesn't have the biggest political fund among weapons makers. It was outspent in the 1982 elections by at least a dozen other big Pentagon contractors and placed 64th in a ranking of all corporation-sponsored Political Action Committees (PACs) in 1982 campaign contributions.

LOTS OF ALLIES

But Avco places its money well. And it had no shortage of influential allies in Congress when its engine monopoly was threatened. The more prominent Avco backers included Rep. Nicholas Mavroules, a Massachusetts Democrat, who was given a $1,000 campaign gift the day after he voted in subcommittee to protect Avco; Rep. Dan Daniel, a Virginia Democrat, who was paid a $2,000

The Wall Street Journal, October 13, 1983, p. 1. Copyright Dow Jones & Company, Inc. All rights reserved.

speaking fee the day after the Army formally opened the tank-engine work for bids; Rep. Bill Dickinson of Alabama, the ranking Republican on the House Armed Services Committee, to whose campaign Avco made but a $1,000 campaign check the day before House debate began; and Rep. Bill Chappell of Florida, the second-ranking Democrat on the military-appropriations subcommittee, who received $8,000 in speaking fees from Avco last year and $5,500 in 1982 campaign donations.

All of these lawmakers, like Mr. Addabbo, say the donations didn't influence their positions on the tank-engines issue.

But Mr. Addabbo's turnabout stands out. For one reason, his $5,000 is the most Avco has given to any lawmaker this year. For another, Mr. Addabbo was among the first to prod the Army to seek a second supplier—the military-appropriations subcommittee he heads last December ordered a study of such an action. Avco for years had plagued the Army with higher-than-expected costs, tardy deliveries, and defective engines.

LOWER BID MADE

Even so, some were surprised when the Army actually sought bids from prospective competitors. And even though the Army says the low bidder offered to make the engine for $10,000 per unit less than Avco's best offer (and 21 percent under its current selling price), Mr. Addabbo on July 20 supported an amendment that *prevents* the Army from buying the engines from anybody but Avco. Congress passed the measure on September 15 and has frozen Army efforts to obtain competition for the engines.

During the tank-engine fight, Avco lobbyists repeatedly made contact with Mr. Addabbo. John B. Kelley, the company's top Washington hand, says he paid two or three visits to the congressman and sent numerous letters. An Avco consultant who used to work for Mr. Addabbo's subcommittee, Leonard Killgore, also came by to plead the company's case, Mr. Addabbo says.

Avco gave only token support of $500 to Mr. Addabbo's 1982 campaign. But after the Army advertised for bids on the tank engines, it gave him $5,000 in two equal installments, on April 13 and May 10. Mr. Kelley says he urged the tenfold increase to Mr. Addabbo. "I think he's a fine subcommittee chairman," the lobbyist says. "Some people think Joe is not for a strong defense, but I know he is." Mr. Addabbo says he needs the money because he is facing a tough primary fight next year and may have to spend $500,000 to be reelected.

HEAVY LOBBYING

During the tank-engine battle, Mr. Kelley was scurrying. "That's over a billion-dollar program, and I certainly wanted to make certain that it didn't become in jeopardy," he says. He and his staff made contact with about 150 Senate and House members on the subject, some of them several times. His message: Avco has cured its quality problems and is bringing production up to the promised numbers.

His arguments found fertile ground. On May 2, before the Army had evaluated the first tentative bids from potential Avco competitors, the House Military Procurement Subcommittee (not to be confused with Mr. Addabbo's appropriations panel) unanimously adopted a measure to block any new supplier.

Panel members were familiar with Avco. All but one of the 14 had received 1982 campaign donations from the company. The total exceeded $10,000. One of the biggest sums, $2,250, went to Mr. Mavroules of Massachusetts, who later championed Avco's cause on the House floor.

The day after the subcommittee action, Avco made out new checks for four of the subcommittee members, including another $1,000 for Mr. Mavroules. Avco's Mr. Kelley says that the timing was "absolutely a coincidence" and that the company was responding to requests for funds that the lawmakers had submitted in April. "There's no relationship at all," he says, between the money and the tank-engine vote.

A spokesman for Rep. Mavroules, the only New Englander on the procurement subcommittee, says he acted to save jobs at Avco's engine plant in neighboring Connecticut. "It's a pork-barrel issue," the aide says. "The contribution was not part of the equation."

The full House Armed Services Committee approved Avco's amendment a few days later. Twenty-four of its members have been given a total of $12,490 by Avco this year.

Often such narrow, special-interest amendments are passed by the House without challenge, but in this case a floor fight was staged by Rep. Norm Dicks, a Democrat from Washington state. He had fought hardest for the pro-competition amendment in the Addabbo subcommittee the previous December.

As the battle heated up, the Army evaluated results of preliminary offers received from three companies: Garrett Corp., a unit of Signal Cos.; the Pratt & Whitney Aircraft unit of United Technologies Corp.; and the Detroit Diesel Allison division of General Motors Corp. The Army also negotiated with Avco over the price for the engines after its current contract runs out.

For the Army, saving money was secondary. It had argued from the start that it would be worth paying more to a second supplier to provide capacity to produce tanks faster in time of crisis and to cut the risk that production could be halted by a single strike or act of sabotage.

Still, when the House began debate on June 16, Mr. Dicks said preliminary Army estimates were that $36 million could be saved over several years by using a second supplier.

Avco's allies counterattacked. Rep. Chappell argued that a second supplier would cost more, not less. "A new company would certainly have to spend at least $160 million just to get ready," he said. Rep. Mavroules said the extra cost was estimated at $109.8 million.

SAVINGS ESTIMATE

But by the time the second and final House debate took place July 20, the Army had produced figures contradicting Reps. Chappell and Mavroules. It had received "best and final" bids from Garrett and the others and had wrung price concessions from Avco during weeks of negotiatons. Garrett submitted a firm, fixed-price bid to make 1,170 engines for a unit cost to the Army of $341,500 each, according to Army documents submitted to Congress. That was $10,000 per engine below Avco's lowest offer, even though Garrett would be amortizing $32 million in start-up costs, the documents say.

The Army calculated that a total of $67 million would be saved in a few years by accepting Garrett's bid and giving it some additional work to make spare engines. Over the life of the M1-tank program, total savings could approach $300 million, the Army figured.

Did the money influence them? "The question is insulting," Rep. Dickinson says. "I don't look to where a campaign contribution comes from when I make a decision on what's best for the national defense." Rep. Daniel also says his objectivity is unimpaired.

Avco's Mr. Kelley also denies vote-buying. "Our competitors have bigger PACs, so that cancels out," he says. "We were outnumbered at all times." All of the companies competing for the tank-engine work gave campaign donations during the lobbying battle, but none gave as much as Avco or targeted their money as well, and none lobbied nearly as strenuously as Avco.

CONTRIBUTIONS RISE

Avco's political gifts surged markedly during the tank-engine fight. The $63,740 it gave through August nearly matched the $66,025 during all of 1982, an election year, and nearly doubled what it gave during the comparable seven-month period in 1981. The bulge caught the eye of the Project for Investigative Reporting on Money in Politics, a new Washington-based organization that first suggested a possible link to the tank-engine battle.

Not everyone who took Avco's money supported the company on the tank-engine issue. A total of 59 House members who received a total of $32,490 so far this year voted in Avco's favor, while 12 who got $4,050 voted against it. Indeed, Avco gave $500 to Mr. Dicks, the main supporter of a second supplier. But as Avco's Mr. Kelley notes, Rep. Dicks is supporting production of MX missiles, for which Avco makes reentry vehicles.

In addition to campaign gifts, Avco's Mr. Kelley says the company paid several speaking fees during the engine fight, but he won't say which lawmakers got the fees. Mr. Kelley says the fees are paid for speeches informing Avco executives about goings-on in Washington, not for votes.

"I think we've handled this in a very professional manner," Mr. Kelley says. "I think my integrity is intact. I'm proud of what I did."

But even one of Avco's staunchest defenders, Rep. Daniel, says he is uncomfortable with the rules allowing lobbyists to mix campaign donations, speaking fees, and requests for legislation.

"It *is* a rotten system, and I don't know how to correct it," Rep. Daniel says. "It's a nasty way to do business. . . . It doesn't look good to the public."

But Avco's allies stood firm, and Mr. Addabbo reversed positions. "I have been a prime mover for competition," he said on the House floor, "so it is with reluctance that I now rise to oppose" a second supplier. He objected to spending $32 million in start-up costs. When Mr. Dicks pointed out that this would be included in the price, Mr. Addabbo argued that the savings could prove to be ephemeral. "When I see a cost savings of only $10,000, I see how easy and fast that can dissipate," he said.

Everyone agrees Mr. Addabbo's conversion influenced a number of votes, though nobody can say how many. Mr. Dicks, interviewed while still stinging from his 241-to-187 defeat, said flatly, "I would have won the thing but for Joe Addabbo." Later, after reflection, he said the New Yorker's vote was "significant" but added: "I can't blame it all on Joe."

FINAL PASSAGE

Army officials hoped to nullify the vote in a House-Senate conference committee. But the Avco amendment was approved in the closed-door session and passed by Congress as part of the Pentagon authorization bill. The most vocal Senate critic of the Avco measure, Republican Sen. Barry Goldwater of Arizona, was hospitalized for surgery the day it was considered in conference. Avco this year has given a total of $14,500 to 9 of the 14 Senate conferees.

Top Army officials fumed after the conference adopted the Avco amendment. James Ambrose, the number two civilian official in the service, denounced the amendment at a news conference August 8. "The appearance is that it is special-pleading legislation," he said.

This in turn angered Reps. Dickinson and Daniel, who witnesses say had been among the most vocal defenders of Avco during the Senate-House conference. They signed a lengthy article in the September issue of the Armed Forces Journal attacking Mr. Ambrose by name. Army officials have since refused repeated requests for interviews on the tank-engine affair. The two Armed Services Committee members say in their article that Congress intervened to keep the Army from punishing Avco unfairly for its history of tardiness and defects, which they say now is behind it. "Congress said, in effect, that personal vendettas have no place in a rational procurement process," they wrote.

SPEAKING FEES

They devoted only five paragraphs to rebutting the Army's estimates of cost savings and misstated a key fact in the process. They said the Army's estimate of a $10,000 saving per engine was produced by comparing a final bid from Garrett with an "opening offer" from Avco. The Army documents, however, say Avco's offer was its third and lowest.

The Army's estimate of savings may indeed be overstated. An aide to Sen. Goldwater says an auditing team from the General Accounting Office, after reviewing the Army's figures at the senator's request, had raised some questions about the amount of savings. And Avco says its price is still subject to further negotiation. But second-source proponents argue that Avco offered to drop its price only when faced with possible competition, a threat that now has been outlawed.

Mr. Dickinson received a $1,000 speaking fee from Avco in 1981 and another $1,000 fee last year. He also received $2,000 in donations to his 1982 campaign in addition to the $1,000 donation he received the day before the House debate began. Mr. Daniel received $4,000 in speaking fees from Avco last year and says he got $2,000 more for speaking at Avco's tank-engine plant in Connecticut on February 9, the day after the Army advertised for bids. He also received a $1,000 donation to his 1982 campaign but nothing so far toward next year's election.

---

9. Banker Who Battled Urban Blight in Chicago Takes on New Economic Challenge in Arkansas

David Wessel and Alex Kotlowitz

ARKADELPHIA, Ark.—Sitting in the funeral home he owns here, Mayor James Williams delivers a eulogy for the local economy:

"Reynolds Metal, 425 jobs. Munsingwear, 140 jobs. Levi jeans, 225 jobs. Alco department store, 55 jobs. Fafnir, 457 jobs." The unemployment rate here in Clark County is 10 percent. The 300-acre industrial park has one working factory; most of the park is farmed.

In short, this seems a lousy place to buy a bank—unless you're Ronald Grzywinski, a hard-nosed yet soft-hearted banker from Chicago. Arkadelphia, a town of 10,000 people an hour's drive from Little Rock, is just what he has been looking for.

For 15 years, Mr. Grzywinski has been running a bank that helped arrest the decline of a blighted Chicago neighborhood by lending to residents who rehabilitated one apartment building after another. Now he heads a group of foundations and public-minded investors who last month bought

---

Arkadelphia's Elk Horn Bank & Trust Co. to try to resuscitate rural Arkansas by nurturing local entrepreneurs.

It is "the most radical experiment in rural economic development since the Tennessee Valley Authority," says David Osborne, author of a new book on state development strategies. Arthur White, a Connecticut consultant who invested $37,500 of his own money in the venture, describes Mr. Grzywinski and his staff as "extraordinary, if not unique, in their ability to understand the financial complexities of mobilizing capital to help the poorest of the poor in this period when the government does so little."

Like Chicago's South Shore Bank, Elk Horn is owned by a bank holding company that blends the spirit of political activism with the discipline of banking. Besides the banks, both parent companies also have for-profit lending subsidiaries and non-profit affiliates. "They said: 'We're not do-gooders. We want to make money. The difference is, we're not greedy'," says Steven Beck, Arkadelphia's city manager.

A START IN CHICAGO

South Shore Bank is a young rebel among Chicago's staid financial institutions. In the 1960s and early 1970s, whites moved out of the city's South Side, and property values dropped. The bank's previous owners prepared to move the bank downtown.

But Mr. Grzywinski and three others raised $800,000 from investors and borrowed $1.4 million to buy South Shore in 1973. The bank has been profitable since then, but none of the original financial "angels" has received any dividends. The profit has been plowed back into the bank, which has pursued its mission—to rebuild a decaying neighborhood—with a singular focus.

Three years ago, Zedie Hall and Janet Oliver tried to get a loan to rehabilitate a six-unit apartment building in the neighborhood. In a classic case of "red-lining," they couldn't find a bank that would lend them money— until they walked into South Shore. The bank loaned them $43,500, and the partners since have gone on to renovate four more buildings.

In 15 years, South Shore has provided loans for renovation of 22 percent of the neighborhood's rental units. The bank makes conventional loans that other banks won't. Other arms of the holding company make loans and equity investments deemed too risky for a bank, some of them subsidized. It sounds risky, but as Mr. Grzywinski says, "We don't own any empty offices in Houston or vacant land with great potential."

"In 1973 . . . the prediction was that in five years (the neighborhood) would be a slum," recalls Milton Davis, the bank's chairman and a former civil rights activist. South Shore's readiness to lend to its neighbors—the bank and its affiliates have invested $147 million in the community in 15 years—have encouraged other banks to follow suit.

Today, the South Side is no gold coast. An estimated 21 percent of the 78,000 residents are below the poverty line. But the bleeding has stopped.

Many of the turn-of-the-century red-brick tenements have been returned to their original charm. In 1975, 70 properties in the area had been tax delinquent for more than a year; 10 years later, only two were delinquent, according to Richard Taub, author of a book on the bank.

Zedie Hall and Janet Oliver's latest venture is a $400,000 renovation of a three-story building that had been a drug-trafficking center. In some apartments, the plumbing had been torn off the walls. Ceilings leaked. Roaches and mice infested the apartments. Today, they have a waiting list for the 26 apartments that should be ready by September. This is the third South Shore–sponsored renovation on the block.

But while this tree-lined street has flowered, just around the corner lies South Shore's biggest failure: its inability to revive the neighborhood's commercial strip. This once-vital boulevard is now a potpourri of bodegas, liquor stores, bars, and wig shops. Vacant stores outnumber active ones. Half of the businesses South Shore granted loans to in the 1970s failed. Commercial development "is a much harder nut to crack than any of us thought," Mr. Davis concedes.

SUMMONED BY FOUNDATION

Yet in Arkansas, lending to small local businesses is the bank's primary mission. Mr. Grzywinski and some of his Chicago staff came here at the behest of the Winthrop Rockefeller Foundation, a Little Rock–based philanthropic organization that had been frustrated in its attempts over the past decade to stimulate the state's economy.

The foundation kicked in $3 million and helped raise $10 million from others to finance the experiment. The idea was quickly embraced by Gov. Bill Clinton, who prodded one of the state's economic development agencies to invest $150,000. Bob Nash, the governor's economic development aide, says: "We can no longer look north and chant Sun Belt and expect a lot of these low-wage plants to arrive on a flatbed truck."

Less than two months after Elk Horn changed hands, about 60 businesses or prospective businesses have inquired about loans, says Jeff Doose, a lending officer. "I've got a backlog of appointments three weeks long," he says. One group has plans for bauxite tailings abandoned when big mining companies left. A musician from the local state college wants advice for a one-man business making marimbas and xylophones for orchestras.

But then, finding entrepreneurs who want money isn't the biggest challenge for Elk Horn's new owners. One question, raised even by South Shore Bank's admirers, is whether lessons learned in a crowded neighborhood in the shadow of Chicago's skyscrapers will transfer to small farm towns.

"Can you bring that same genius to a predominantly rural economy?" wonders Marlin Jackson, former Arkansas bank commissioner. "I hope so. (But) I have an intuitive feeling that the concentration of people had something to do with South Shore's success."

10. Shift of Auto Plants to Rural Areas Cuts Hiring of Minorities

Jacob M. Schlessinger

ANNA, Ohio—It's just a three-hour shot straight down Interstate 75 from Detroit to this tiny Midwestern town. But the two places are worlds apart.

Detroit's problems include murder, crack, and decay. In Anna (population 1,150), the big problem is the alleys. "Our alleys are pitiful. they're not paved; they're gravel!" says Harold Shue, the octogenarian mayor.

An equally stark contrast occurred last December, when General Motors Corp. mothballed two 70-year old factories in southwest Detroit while Honda Motor Co. cranked up a third shift at its spanking-new engine plant in Anna. The Detroit neighborhood is mostly black and Hispanic, like the GM workers. Anna is virtually all white, like the Honda workers.

It is a pattern cropping up all across industrial America. Optimists talk of "reindustrialization" by pointing to the spate of new plants, mainly Japanese, popping up in Rust Belt states such as Michigan, Ohio, Indiana and Illinois. But the new factories, unlike those they are supplanting, are mostly in small towns. So, rural whites are hitting the jobs jackpot, while urban minorities are hitting the streets.

FADED OPPORTUNITIES

In the 1960s, "all blacks could get was bus boy, car wash, or a job in the auto factory," says Joe Wilson, the black president of the United Auto Workers local for one of the two shuttered Detroit plants. Now, he says bitterly, "You can still get the bus boy, and you can still get the car wash. What's changed is you can't get anything in the auto industry."

Many blame that change on simple geography—and an effort to move away from unions. But some critics also accuse the Japanese companies of deliberately avoiding blacks. Honda and the U.S. Equal Employment Opportunity Commission settled a big racial-discrimination case last month.

Whatever underlies the change, "Blacks are being affected in a profound fashion," says Robert E. Cole, a University of Michigan professor who will publish a study on the subject this spring. "It's a major issue in terms of the future of American society and creating economic opportunities for all citizens."

MAJOR STEPPINGSTONE

That is especially so because the auto industry—more than other manufacturing sectors—has long been an important steppingstone for black
Americans into the middle class. For decades, thousands of poor Southerners,
including many blacks, headed north for low-skilled but high-paying auto jobs.
"Last night I went to sleep in Detroit City," Bobby Bare crooned in a 1963 song
celebrating this migration, "and I dreamed about the cotton field back home."

By the mid-1960s, blacks held one of every four U.S. auto-production jobs,
more than twice their share of the total work force. During the 1980 government hearings on whether to bail out Chrysler Corp., a critical fact swaying
support was that the number three auto maker alone provided 1 percent of
black income in the United States.

Thus, inevitably, the slump in manufacturing has especially damaged
minority-group members. Between 1979 and 1984, blacks lost 27 percent of
their manufacturing jobs, compared with a 19 percent drop for whites, a recent
Michigan State University study says. GM's major assembly-plant closings
over the past two years haven't hit just Detroit but also communities such as
Flint and Pontiac, Michigan and St. Louis, all 40 percent black.

SOME EXCEPTIONS

A few factories, however, are returning to urban areas. GM has built new
high-tech plants outside of Pontiac and in the inner Detroit city of
Hamtramck. Mazda Motor Corp. has resuscitated a closed Ford Motor Co.
plant in Flat Rock, Mich., near Detroit. The black share of Big Three hourly
jobs has held constant for the past two decades, although the black total has
dropped since 1979 to 140,000 from 180,000 as the industry has retrenched.

But the proportion of blacks may soon start to drop as well. GM's eight
plants built since 1981 also include sites such as Bowling Green, Kentucky,
and its high-profile new Saturn Corp. plant will open in Spring Hill, Tennessee. Prof. Cole estimates that, on the average, blacks constitute 15 percent
of the population in cities with Big Three plants that are either new or
renovated, while in cities with older plants blacks made up 20 percent of the
population. UAW-negotiated transfer agreements ensure that more blacks
will work in the new plants than otherwise might, but the location of those
plants may further dilute the minority work force.

And even if the percentage of black employment does hold constant at the
Big Three, it will probably drop for the auto industry. That's because Japanese
factories are providing a growing portion of those jobs, and they aren't setting
up near major black population centers. Of the seven new, major Japanese
assembly plants operating or planned for this country, none match the Big
Three in actual or potential black work forces.

Nissan Motor Co. comes the closest, with blacks making up 16.8 percent of
its production work force at Smyrna, Tennessee. But Fuji Heavy Industry Ltd.

and Isuzu Motors Ltd. will start making vehicles next year near Lafayette, Indiana, which is 1.7 percent black. Mitsubishi Motor Corp., in a joint venture with Chrysler, soon will begin making cars in the twin cities of Bloomington, Illinois and Normal, Illinois, which are 4 percent black.

Auto-assembly plants are highly visible, but the trend is far broader. Japanese auto-parts makers—and their U.S. rivals—are following their customers. Dana Corp. is shifting work away from its integrated manufacturing complexes in the North and doing some of it closer to the companies it supplies. It is making some Nissan truck drive shafts, formerly assembled near Philadelphia, in Gordonsville, Tennessee.

All this is reshaping the industrial landscape. The area of Detroit surrounding GM's now-silent Fleetwood and Clark Street factories that used to build Cadillacs is a stereotypical aging inner city. Anna, in contrast, is the last place one would expect an auto factory. Its downtown is a three-block stretch on Main Street whose only concession to the late 20th century is a tanning salon next to the barber shop.

FORSAKING THE FARM

For the Honda workers, the plant marks a new beginning. Jim Lemmon, a 25-year-old, had expected to spend his life on the family farm, but now he works on dies. He plans to stay at the Honda plant until he retires. "Farmers aren't too called for now," he says. "There's a lot more money here."

But the Detroit workers' future looks grim. "A third of the workers in this plant were women, most of them single parents," Mr. Wilson says. While the UAW official himself will have a job until GM officially leaves the plants later this year, his 27-year-old son was laid off from the Fleetwood plant in June and still hasn't found a job. Mr. Wilson's wife was laid off from GM's Hamtramck plant a year ago because the cars built there weren't selling well. He says, "The drug-selling lines in my neighborhood are getting longer. It used to be 20 guys, now it's 30. That's how they get their employment now."

Not surprisingly the people in Detroit and Anna explain their fates differently. "Economic violence" and "corporate greed" are phrases tumbling off Mr. Wilson's tongue. "They did it for selfish reasons. They did it for profit." A "No Foreign Cars" sign protects the local's parking lot. Since the plant-closing announcement, workers have sponsored rallies, news conferences, and trips to Washington to draw attention to their plight.

But to John Hofmann, senior manager of the Honda plant, success is simply a matter of hard work. "We don't have that problem [plant closings] at Honda, and the reason is the people here care about what they're doing," he says.

Auto makers say they aren't running away from blacks. Instead, they cite the advantages of rural locations. A big one is plentiful, and relatively cheap, land suitable for the sprawling, single-story factories such as Honda's yellow aluminum sided complex, which is next to a large field with a white farmhouse. Those are deemed far more efficient than the multistory structure that urban sites often require. Besides, Honda says it liked its site's proximity to a state automotive research and development center.

"We wanted easy access to potential suppliers, easy access to markets, available land and a supportive business climate," says J. J. "Bucky" Kahl, Nissan's director of human resources in Smyrna. He states flatly that the region's racial composition didn't play any role in site selection. He adds that the company has an active affirmative-action program, which includes about half-a-dozen summer internships for minority-group college students.

Another important factor in choosing a site seems to be avoiding organized labor. "Most Japanese companies are looking for areas of the state that are nonunion," says Bob Mason, Indiana's industrial-development specialist. Although most Japanese companies deny that this is an explicit factor, many clearly prefer a nonunion shop. Honda successfully beat back a UAW organizing bid, and Nissan is fighting to keep the union out. Those manufacturers pay roughly the same wages that Big Three factories do, but they apparently prefer the free rein to manage without dealing with a U.S. union.

Besides economic factors, other ones—including a lack of social consciousness at the least—may be at work. "The Japanese come in without that cultural background of minority hiring," says Michael J. Kane, who heads the fledgling U.S.-Japan International Management Institute at the University of Kentucky near Toyota Motor Corp.'s new Georgetown plant. "They're kind of economic animals, and we tend to be more social animals. They say a fact is a fact, and traditionally minorities have a low level of education."

THE HONDA CASE

Honda, the government alleged, was a case in point. Although many Japanese auto makers note their affirmative-action programs. Honda's hiring policies, in effect, screened out blacks. From the time it started hiring in 1979 (for its assembly complex in Marysville, Ohio, which began operations six years before the Anna engine plant), Honda had a strict rule that workers must live within 20 miles of the plant (later expanded to 30 miles).

"There's a fair amount of manufacturing in this area, and in the early 1980s many plants were either closing or laying off," Roger Lambert, a Honda spokesman, says. "The local residents said they hoped we'd hire from around here. . . . We were committed to deepening ties with the local community."

But the effect also was to exclude Columbus, which is 35 miles to the southeast and has the region's largest black population. The Urban League got seven complaints from black Columbus residents, most of whom worked at a nearby Rockwell International Corp. plant that was laying workers off after completing part of a B-1 bomber contract. "They even committed to move," says Samuel Gresham, the president of the civil-rights group's Columbus chapter. "Honda said move first. Who's going to take a chance like that?"

Last month, in its settlement with the EEOC, Honda agreed to give $6 million in back pay to 370 black and female employees that the government said should have been hired sooner. The company, which recently expanded its hiring area again to include Columbus, also agreed to change its promotion practices and recruit minorities more actively.

HONDA'S RESPONSE

Honda, which had argued that its 2.8 percent black work force merely reflected the portion of its applicants who were black, says it is unfair to generalize from that complaint about the social consciousness of the Japanese. Mr. Lambert says all those awarded damages were put on the payroll before the settlement, some as long as two years before. He argues that the auto maker had planned most of the actions outlined in the settlement anyway. Honda didn't admit any wrongdoing in the settlement, which it says it agreed to in order to avoid a lengthy court fight.

Mr. Lambert also notes tougher settlements by other U.S. institutions, including auto makers. In the early 1980s, Ford reached a $23 million settlement, both for discrimination against women and minorities.

Yet, as more Japanese companies move into the United States, some black leaders keep worrying about the possibility of a subtle, intentional racism. Blacks regularly cite the 1986 statement by then-Japanese Prime Minister Yasuhiro Nakasone that Japan's racial homogeneity made it a more "intelligent society" than the United States, "where there are blacks, Mexicans, and Puerto Ricans and the level is still quite low."

"If you look at the trend," says Porter G. Peeples, who heads the Lexington, Kentucky, Urban League, "The foreign car manufacturers are coming to rural areas here in the South." He praises Toyota's specific efforts to hire minorities in his area but adds that "one could easily assume under that trend that [the Japanese] are trying to avoid large numbers of black folks."

---

11. California Growers Rail against Efforts to Stem Flow of Illegal Aliens

Marilyn Chase

FRESNO, Calif.—As Mexican workers silently gathered the ripening boysenberries from the fields a few weeks ago, the air was thick with heat and dust—and charged with tension.

The workers were employed by Donald Rosendahl, one of this town's most prominent growers, and the tension wasn't without cause. Some 80 percent of

---

The Wall Street Journal, August 4, 1983, pp. 1, 15. Copyright Dow Jones & Company, Inc. All Rights reserved.

the harvesters were illegal aliens, making Mr. Rosendahl's operation vulnerable to a raid by the U.S. border patrol. The grower recalls that two years ago he lost a $100,000 berry crop when the border patrol ringed his fields at the height of the harvest; the crew vanished, and the sweet, dusky-purple berries withered on the vine.

On this more recent morning, the border patrol didn't appear. But Mr. Rosendahl has other continuing reasons for anxiety. He has other crops to be harvested throughout the year and has traditionally depended on illegal aliens for such work. So a raid by the border patrol is an ever-present threat. But of even greater consequence are the proposed changes in federal immigration laws that could dry up the supply of illegal aliens and therefore change the face of California agriculture.

OMINOUS PREDICTIONS

California's $14 billion agriculture industry—a cornucopia of fruits and vegetables for tables around the world around the year—owes its harvest to illegal labor almost as much as to sun and rain. The California Farm Bureau Federation says about 50 percent of the field hands on the state's 82,000 farms are illegal; the United Farmworkers of America, AFL–CIO, says the numbers run much higher. If this work force dries up, California growers are predicting shrinking acreage, skyrocketing overhead, and a surge in consumer prices of up to 100 percent for some of the most perishable fruit crops.

"More and more illegals do this work every year," Mr. Rosendahl says. "Local kids won't do it; they're getting better educated. The government is training legal farmhands to become welders and high-tech workers. And now Congress wants to pass a law saying we can't use illegal ones either. We're really caught."

The proposed changes in the law are embodied in parallel (although slightly different) bills introduced in Congress earlier this year by Republican Sen. Alan K. Simpson of Wyoming and Democratic Rep. Romano Mazzoli of Kentucky. The Simpson bill passed the Senate on May 18 by a vote of 76–18; the House hasn't yet acted on the Mazzoli bill.

Under the proposed legislation, aliens who have been in the United States since before a certain date would be accorded legal status—in effect freeing them to look for higher-paid nonfarm work. The bills also provide for the importation of seasonal workers from Mexico but would regulate their movement and require growers to pay for transportation and housing.

STIFF FINES, JAIL TERMS

What's more, the bills call for farmers who hire illegal aliens to face stiff fines and jail terms: $1,000 for each illegal worker on the first offense, $2,000 for each on the second offense, and a possible six-month jail sentence after that. Current laws don't penalize employers of illegal aliens.

If the bill becomes law, "It's going to be the biggest doggone scrambling mess you ever saw," Mr. Rosendahl says furiously. "There'll be crops destroyed and farmers bankrupt."

Whether California growers face doomsday, or merely disruption of their accustomed labor practices, is a point of debate. But one thing is clear, says Philip Martin, an economics professor at the University of California at Davis's School of Agriculture: "We're coming to the end of an era of cheap, plentiful labor."

Since the *bracero,* or Mexican guest-worker, program ended in 1964, "we've been forced to rely wholly on illegal labor," says Fresno raisin-rancher Earl Rocca. And Paul Chavez, the 26-year-old son of the Farmworkers' patriarch, Cesar Chavez, notes Mexico's sick economy has propelled millions of "economic refugees" north to California—many straight into a "marriage of convenience" with growers.

"I don't like using illegals. I don't even know how to talk to the darn fools," Mr. Rosendahl says. "But I don't have a choice."

DEFIANT WORDS

Mr. Rosendahl says further: "Our government's run out of guts. It's completely unfair to put the burden of enforcing immigration laws on us." Robert Brocchini, a vegetable grower in Ripon, California, agrees: "It's a lot easier for the government to enforce a few thousand miles of linear border than for us to enforce millions of square miles of interior."

One of the Napa Valley's largest private grape growers, Rennick Harris, admits his harvest crews are 80 percent illegal and declares: "If the choice is lose your crop or go to jail, I guess we'll go to jail."

The panic is more intense in northern California's fruit orchards and vineyards and in the strawberry fields of the south than it is in the state's "lettuce bowl" in the Salinas Valley. There, higher wages enable growers to hire a higher percentage of "legal" workers. Even so, by some estimates, the Salinas Valley may have up to 30 percent undocumented workers.

California growers have lobbied in Washington all year, arguing that provisions contained in the House and Senate bills are "unworkable" for their state. California, unlike single-crop states in the East, has 250 different crops, many perishable and each with a different harvest season. Such diversity makes a part-time, migrant work force essential, growers argue. "The problem with developing a stable, year-round, legal work force," Mr. Harris says, "is that we don't have stable, year-round work to offer."

The so-called amnesty provision legalizing millions of longtime aliens in this country is obviously appealing to undocumented workers and their advocates in the Farmworkers' union. But growers, who fear they will no longer be able to keep legalized Mexican field hands down on the farm, feel threatened.

"Like magic, when workers get their green cards, they leave the farm. As legal residents, they can work for $8 an hour," says Paul Murai, an Orange

County strawberry grower who argues that illegal aliens aren't only the most available but also the hardiest and best workers. "Documented workers have to be treated with kid gloves," he complains.

The proposed changes in the immigration laws would force California growers to get their seasonal help from the U.S. Department of Labor instead of through the alien-worker grapevine. For years, the government's H-2 program (named for a subsection of the Immigration and Nationality Act) has enabled farmers to apply 80 days in advance of harvest for foreign workers. The Simpson bill would relax that notification period to 50 days, but California farmers believe that is still too restrictive.

California Congressman Leon Panetta, a Democrat from the Carmel Valley, introduced an amendment to the Mazzoli bill that would allow growers of perishable crops to apply for foreign workers just 72 hours in advance and bring them in for 11 months; the amendment, passed by the House Agriculture Committee, was cheered by growers, but its fate before the full House remains uncertain.

Supporters of the immigration bills point out that the H-2 program long has been used by farmers around the country to meet their seasonal labor needs. "But California growers are so cynical they've never even tried it. They've always used illegals," says one proponent of the legislation.

California growers, however, maintain that with the state's multicrop economy, they need more flexibility than, say, apple growers in West Virginia or orange growers in Florida. They also contend that farm overhead would skyrocket under the H-2 program, with workers' transportation and housing costs adding up to 50 percent of current production costs. Growers must also pay a premium for legally imported Mexican labor, giving such workers 20 percent more than the prevailing local wage rate—in effect, a penalty on agriculture for the program's adverse effect on the U.S. labor market.

A BITTER JOKE

This "adverse-effect" wage rise is a bitter joke to growers. "There's no way we can recruit domestic people," Mr. Rosendahl says. "We tried a pilot program to recruit locals in 1979 through the state Employment Development Department. It was a disaster. Not enough workers came, and the biggest joke was that half were illegal aliens."

Henry Voss, the president of the California Farm Bureau Federation, forecasts that shrinking acreage and soaring prices will be the H-2 program's only real harvest. "I don't think growers will risk not having enough harvesters in time for harvest," he says. "That means considerably reduced acreage. That means short supply. And *that* means increased prices for perishable crops, especially berries, cherries, apricots and other soft fruits." He adds: "Depending on how severely growers react, it could mean up to a 100 percent price increase to the consumer."

Changes in California's farm-labor scene are likely to take years to evolve.

The Simpson bill would give growers three years to phase out their illegal workers—a concession that California's grower lobby rejoiced over but that others deplore as too lenient.

Even so, the bill is already advancing other long-range trends in California agriculture, such as mechanization and a thinning out of the state's rich crop diversity.

"I've been trying to reduce my labor needs because I've seen this coming," says Earl Rocca, whose Fresno raisin production now is largely mechanized. "I almost got out of farming. Then I learned about mechanical harvesting. It was $50,000 to buy a mechanical harvester, versus $100,000 to build a labor camp."

A PROBLEM OF PRIDE

The move to mechanization also will mean crops will be bred for hardiness more than for flavor or color. Vine-ripened tomatoes already have been supplanted by hard, green tomatoes that are mechanically harvested and then "ripened" with gas.

Many crops can't be mechanized, however. Machines bruise tender fruit and mangle vines. For growers, this is as much a problem of pride as economics, says Professor Martin of the University of California at Davis. "Most growers today pick their crop as if it were going to premium market, even though a juice lemon doesn't need to be as pretty as a fresh market lemon," he says."But it's hard to talk about that with farmers—they're bred to produce quality."

Some delicate, hand-harvested crops are being phased out in favor of hardier commodities. Growers are tearing out peaches and putting in almond trees. Rosendahl Farms is uprooting its boysenberry vines and replanting the fields with prunes, which can be machine-picked. "I've been growing boysenberries for 15 years and I'd love to continue, but I can't," Mr. Rosendahl says. "The boysenberry will be a rare and special thing in California."

Critics chide California growers for their "plantation mentality," and their struggle to preserve illegal Mexican farm labor, which could blind the industry to a more serious challenge arising from foreign competition in world markets. "I think we're going to see a real battle as international producers enter the U.S. market by 1990," says Prof. Martin of the University of California. "Right now, Brazil is the world's largest producer of juice oranges. Already, Turkish and Greek raisins are courting U.S. markets overseas. And Spanish and Israeli citrus fruits are coming on strong."

The Farm Bureau counters that changes in immigration laws that help to inflate produce prices will make it even tougher for U.S. producers to compete against foreign growers. But Prof. Martin says that may be missing the point: Growers should wean themselves of their dependence on cheap, illegal labor, mechanize selectivity, and pare their field crews to a smaller, professional corps of farm workers, he advises.

"Over the next 20 years, U.S. agriculture can't hope to compete on the basis of low wages," he says. "Our edge is technology. Immigration reform may nibble away at the industry—but it won't have nearly the bite that's coming from overseas competitors."

12. States' Watchdogs Sharpen Teeth on Big Business

Nancy Mullen

For some time, consumers had been complaining that they could not buy airline tickets at the advertised bargain fares because of restrictions not mentioned in the airlines' ads. Federal regulatory agencies, they said, were doing nothing in response.

So the National Association of Attorneys General decided it was time to police these ads. Early this year, NAAG issued its own set of national guidelines, which require the ads to spell out fare limitations. Rather than risk a court fight, the airlines began overhauling their advertising to comply with the guidelines.

Having cut their teeth on corporate giants like Coca-Cola and Kraft Inc., the state attorneys general seem to be ready to take on entire industries.

More recently, attorneys general in several states filed an antitrust suit against the nation's major insurance companies, which they say conspired to reduce or eliminate certain kinds of insurance coverage. The antitrust actions could force a restructuring of the insurance industry.

On a roll, the officials are now taking aim at car rental companies. NAAG has set up a committee to investigate two areas of complaint: hidden charges that can double the advertised rental rates, and collision damages waivers that cause renters to give up basic common law rights.

Not long ago, attorneys general would have concentrated on matters within their own state borders and left nationwide concerns like these to federal authorities. But in this era of deregulation, the states say, federal agencies have been ignoring consumer issues. Mounting complaints from individuals and frustrated consumer protection groups have propelled attorneys general into the national arena.

"With the withdrawal of federal enforcement authority in major areas, including consumer protection, there is a vacuum where perceived abuses are still occurring and where there's no effective remedial action forthcoming from the national level," says Oregon attorney general David Frohnmayer, who is president of NAAG.

STATES INTO THE BREACH

New York attorney general Robert Abrams claims that the laissez faire philosophy of the Reagan administration has "hurt consumers, and it's caused states to step into the breach." Agencies around New York State report that they are receiving 25 to 60 percent more consumer complaints now than in pre-Reagan years.

"People are concerned and are angered when the federal government continues to retreat from the historic role and responsibility of enforcing laws and making regulations to protect consumers," he says.

Mr. Abrams first got involved in national advertising in 1984, when the Center for Science in the Public Interest, a Washington-based consumer watchdog group, approached him about ads run by Coca-Cola, Pepsi-Cola, Seven-Up, and Royal Crown Cola. The group had filed a petition with the Federal Trade Commission, complaining that ads and labels for diet sodas proclaimed, "Now with NutraSweet," even though the products also contained saccharin. The FTC had not responded. So Abrams challenged the soft drink companies. Soon they changed their wording to "NutraSweet blend."

"There's really widespread deceptive advertising in the food industry, primarily involving health and nutrition claims," maintains Bruce Silverglade, legal director of the Center for Science. "The states brought a number of cases that we originally asked the Federal Trade Commission to bring, against Campbell's Soup, McDonald's, the National Coffee Association, Kraft Inc., Del Monte. We had alleged deceptive advertising on the part of all these companies, and the FTC acted practically in no situation. In only one situation did it bring a lawsuit. The states have resolved every one of these complaints."

Just the threat of a lawsuit in one state has been enough to force most companies to change their advertising nationwide. They don't want to risk the unfavorable publicity a court fight could generate, nor do they want the expense of tailoring ads for individual states.

FLEXING FOR THE VOTERS

Muscle-flexing by attorneys general may get quick results and win points with voters in their states (most of these officials are selected), but many people in business and government don't think it's fair.

"Is it fair for a resident of Iowa to receive only advertising that meets the standards of the New York State attorney general?" John O'Toole, vice president of the American Association of Advertising Agencies, asks in a recent commentary in *Adweek* magazine. He warns that ad regulation by the 50 states, even with a common set of guidelines, could become "a crazy quilt" of varying interpretations.

"National regulation should come from the national government," insists Daniel Oliver, chairman of the FTC. [State attorneys general] aren't elected to regulate national advertising. They are elected to deal with problems in their own states. And it's not as if there were no problems in their own states."

Mr. Oliver contradicts the view that the FTC had been lax in its responsibility to protect consumers. "You can always find a noisy group to get a response out of some attorneys general [AGs] looking for publicity. If they went to the Federal Trade Commission and couldn't get an answer about a national ad, that means this agency determined that there was nothing wrong. . . . Just because companies are knuckling under the pressure from AGs, that doesn't mean the FTC isn't doing its job."

William MacLeod, director of the FTC's bureau of consumer protection, asserts that the commission did not need to take any action on the soft drink ads, since the advertising industry's self-regulatory system was already at work on the case.

"The national advertising division of the Council of Better Business Bureaus issued its report on the matter in March 1984, before any action was taken or announced by any government entity," he says. "Shortly after that, New York announced its action with regard to Coca-Cola."

Mr. MacLeod adds that the FTC has been supportive of the self-regulatory system as an efficient monitor for industries. "If the self-regulatory mechanism can clean up advertising that we do not have to spend taxpayer dollars cleaning up, then everybody is better off."

An important aspect of rooting out false advertising, MacLeod cautions, is making sure you don't overdo it and deny consumers information that is potentially valuable to them.

He points to a case involving a Kraft ad that read: "Cheez Whiz, real cheese made easy. . . . It's a blend of Kraft cheddar and colby cheeses and other wholesome ingredients."

At the urging of the Center for Science, the attorney general for Texas challenged the ad, alleging that it falsely represented the product as real cheese and sold it at cheese prices, when it was only 51 percent cheese (the rest being whey and additives). Kraft stopped running the ad.

USEFUL INFORMATION

"I would be very interested to hear arguments as to how this Kraft advertisement was hurting consumers," MacLeod comments. "What they were trying to show in these ads is how Cheez Whiz can be heated more easily and then served as a sauce over foods, the various uses you can put it to; and this is useful information to consumers."

The U.S. Department of Transportation is so concerned about preserving information in advertising that it has threatened to sue any state attorney general who tries to enforce the NAAG guidelines for air fare ads in any way inconsistent with the department's own guidelines. The department reports that of the thousands of consumer complaints it received during 1987, only 411 were about airline advertising.

"We feel like deregulation has been extremely successful, and one reason is that there's been a great deal of competition, specifically price competition. That's the reason that there are so many, many more people flying today than there were before," says Wayne Vance, general counsel of the Transportation Department. "The first couple months of this year, after the NAAG guidelines came out, we felt like we saw, particularly in broadcast advertising, much less competition, and I think it can be attributable to concern over the NAAG guidelines."

The threat of a lawsuit doesn't seem likely to deter the attorneys general. "There's no one trembling with anxiety that some federal agency will bring a lawsuit," says Mr. Frohnmayer, the NAAG president. "If it does, it does, and we're used to advocating our position in court and presumably would do so."

In any case, a court test will probably be unnecessary, since the state attorneys general are pleased with the changes airlines have been making in their advertising, according to Frohnmayer and Abrams.

"As a result of those guidelines . . . we have seen ads suddenly overnight altered for the better," Abrams says. "Where in the past they were only giving one-way prices, they're now giving round trip prices. Whereas in the past they weren't giving all of the restrictions, they're now pointing out what some of the limits are."

Although NAAG doesn't have a specific agenda of future investigations, it is looking into airline reservation systems, for-profit vocational schools, and the cable television industry. It also plans to work for tougher federal regulation of all-terrain vehicles.

Frohnmayer says he doesn't worry that a few overzealous attorneys general could undermine NAAG's newfound clout by trying to enforce overly strict interpretations of its guidelines.

"Having devoted the time that we have to developing a common baseline understanding, there's probably a fair amount of peer group influence within our association to keep people from taking a precarious and potentially invalid legal position."

Over the seven years he has been a member of the organization, he has noticed "a growth of collegiality and communication among the various states in NAAG. I've seen a much more reflective atmosphere and also one where there's a much greater willingness to act in concert uniformly on areas of common concern.

ACTION ON MANY FRONTS[1]

Since 1987, state attorneys general have taken the following actions:

- Sued Aetna, Hartford, Allstate, and Cigna over premiums charged for insurance liability coverage.
- Won a $16 million settlement from Chrysler for owners of cars with rolled-back odometers.
- Won more than $1 million for buyers of Minolta cameras on charges that the company refused to let dealers sell its cameras at discount.
- Issued merger guidelines that are tougher than federal regulations.
- Persuaded airlines to give more explicit information in ads for bargain fares.

Meanwhile, the attorneys general are also:

- Meeting with car rental companies to make changes in their advertising.
- Examining airline reservations systems.
- Working for tougher regulation of all-terrain vehicles.
- Looking into the cable television industry.

---

[1] SOURCE: *Business Week.*

PART FOUR

International Management

In a classic poster that was popular at the peak of the environmental movement of the late 1960s and early 1970s, the earth is shown as viewed from a spaceship. To environmentalists this poster symbolized the earth as a whole system where everything is interrelated and there is no ultimate escape from the damage done to the environment. Likewise, a business person looks at the markets of the world today as a global market system. The growth of the global market and of multinational corporations (MNCs—firms headquartered in one country with subsidiaries in others) is one of the greatest challenges confronting managers and governments. The global market is increasingly complex and inescapable, ever widening in its net.

The global market is complex because it is no longer a simple matter of exporting from America to another country. It has become a vast network of consumers and multistage producers, with each stage of production possibly occurring in a separate country. In the shoe industry, for example, the old simple image of the American shoe industry losing its market share to imports from Italy simply does not fit the complexities of the global market. As Drucker notes, men's shoes sold in the United States may start out as a hide of an American cow, which is then shipped to another country, like Brazil, for tanning, then shipped, possibly with the help of a Japanese shipping company, to another country where it is made into uppers and/or soles, then shipped to yet another country where it is made into shoes, and then shipped to the United States for sale. This is happening with innumerable products from shoes to calculators.[1] Because of the globalization of industries, the basic MNC strategy has become one of producing standardized products for world markets. Thus the MNC is more responsive to consumers demanding lower-priced standardized products over those demanding higher-priced customized models.

In the context of the global market and the large chronic trade deficit of the United States, it is important to realize two things. First, although we do have indexes to measure simple international transfers, we really do not have adequate measures for the growing complexity of the global market system.

---

[1] Peter F. Drucker, *Managing in Turbulent Times* (New York: Harper & Row, 1980), pp. 96–97.

Second, over 40 percent of the imports into the United States are produced by multinational companies based in the United States. Both of these indicate the tip of a large iceberg of an international management problem that threatens to sink U.S. trade.

Because of the ongoing revolution in computers and telecommunications, the development of Third World nations, and the aggressiveness of multinational companies, the global market will certainly widen its net to include all countries, rich or poor, developed or underdeveloped. A chief executive officer headquartered in Zurich or New York can sit down at a computer terminal and know instantly not just the overall aspects of the corporation, but the minute to minute details of production in a plant in the Upper Volta.

The sad and frustrating aspect of the global market is its inescapable nature. Any American company, no matter how small, that makes a significant product cannot afford to ignore it. To do so jeopardizes its competitive position, as competitors use the advantages of what Drucker identified as production sharing, in which the elements of production are shared throughout the world in a fashion similar to laborers specializing in one task of an assembly line operation.[2]

Several possible scenarios emerge that might allow the United States to succeed in this global market. One is that American multinationals are turned loose and are allowed to roam freely in the world and in the United States, looking for locations that provide the most economically efficient production factors. This scenario ignores the social and political disruption such an approach would have on the United States. Another scenario accepts for the time being the movement of American companies overseas in their pursuit of cheaper labor markets. Years later, those companies will return to the United States to use the superior training of American technicians, engineers, and scientists and the superior American infrastructure to pursue high-level automation. This high-level automation produces a high-quality, highly customized product at near assembly line speeds and has been likened to turning out Rolls Royces at Chevy assembly line speeds and prices. This latter scenario has two profound assumptions: first, that the United States will be able to improve its educational system in order to provide the technicians, engineers, scientists, and managers needed to run these high-technology environments and second, that the United States will devote more resources to developing consumer products than it does now in relation to defense products. If either of these do not happen, then the long-term decline in the U.S.'s competitive position in the global market is likely to continue.

The ability to analyze, understand, and manage the myriad stakeholders and the sometimes subtle nuances of international environments presents one

---

[2] Ibid., p. 95.

of the greatest tests of managerial skills.[3] A firm going multinational should revise its mission statement to reflect both the new product, markets, and technology it will be dealing with, along with the new stakeholders as well. The mission statement needs to be sensitive to the subtleties of the different cultural norms it will be working within. In the United States there is a growing awareness that maximization of short-term profit is not in the best long-term interests of society and the corporation. Other countries or cultures are even more sensitive to profitability statements. Consequently some firms alter their mission statements to delete profitability statements and to highlight the importance of social responsibility.[4] This attitude is summed up by the Gulf & Western Americas Corporation:

> We believe that in a developing country, revenue is inseparable from mandatory social responsibility and that a company is an integral part of the local and national community in which its activities are based.[5]

A multinational firm is often confronted by multiple stakeholders whose activities create demands on the company by each foreign environment, principally foreign governments. The different cultural contexts make the task of coalition building to achieve effective operations much more difficult. While a firm operating in the United States may develop its operations within a relatively homogenous culture, where English is used primarily, and the political system is stable, the firm is unlikely to enjoy such an environment in many other countries of the world today. Conflicting cultural norms may confront the corporation, with different notions of time and work commitment, beliefs that the firm must provide for long-term employment and for worker participation, poorly developed financial markets, and sometimes violent and quixotic political regimes.

Tailoring the firm's mission statement and operations to the host country's cultural norms is not just a simple matter. If the firm's values stray too far from American cultural norms, then the firm becomes a target for any one of many social activist groups. And rightly so in most cases, since businesses branching out into the world do have a responsibility toward maintaining basic human values of freedom, democracy, and others that Americans hold dear.

At times, the multinational is also confronted by what seem to be insurmountable problems in corporate control. The most well-intentioned corporation still has to consider how it is going to fully implement company policy around the world in different cultures. The earlier Abbott Laboratories case

---

[3] John A. Pearce, II and Richard B. Robinson, Jr., *Formulation and Implementation of Competitive Strategy,* 3rd ed. (Homewood, Ill.: Richard D. Irwin, 1988), p. 152.

[4] Ibid., pp. 160–162.

[5] O. Williams, "Who Cast the First Stone?" *Harvard Business Review* (September–October), pp. 151–161.

dealing with the implementation of infant nutrition standards at the local organizational level is an example of such a dilemma.

The cases chosen for this section exhibit the wide range of issues confronting corporations in the global market. In the Goodyear Tire and South Africa case, a company is confronted by the political, ethical, and moral dilemmas of doing business in South Africa. In the Union Carbide and Bhopal case, one of the world's worst industrial accidents raises the question of a company's responsibility for safety and pollution standards and what controls are necessary in the global market. In the United Brands case, a company confronts internal and external threats on the international scene. The commentaries help highlight the issues raised by the cases. One deals with investing in South Africa; another addresses the effect of defense spending on our competitive position in global markets. The section concludes with "A Code of Worldwide Business Conduct" published by the Caterpillar Tractor Company. This code of conduct has served as a model for many companies.

Goodyear Tire & Rubber Company (South Africa)

OVERVIEW

In 1985 and 1986, Goodyear Tire & Rubber Company faced its most trying years in South Africa since starting operations there in 1916. Civil unrest, resulting from a system of apartheid, added to the depressed economic conditions of the country to create a troubled business environment. These problems were coupled with growing calls from social activists and political pressures in the United States for companies to divest their holdings in South Africa. Goodyear executives voiced opposition to divestiture, arguing that it would harden white segregationist attitudes and harm the workers it was supposed to help.

BACKGROUND AND OUTLOOK: GOODYEAR TIRE & RUBBER COMPANY

The Goodyear Tire & Rubber Company was incorporated in Ohio on August 29, 1898, and went on to become the world's largest tire and rubber company. By 1986, it controlled one third of the U.S. tire business and one fifth of the world market. The company produced tires and transportation products, which included new tires, retreads, wheels, rims, automotive belts and hoses, molded parts and foam cushioning, industrial rubber, and chemical and plastic products. Other Goodyear businesses provided defense systems, military aviation systems, agricultural products, and automotive accessories and repair services through 2,000 retail stores.

In the 1970s and 1980s the company faced competition from two major firms, Michelin of France and Bridgestone of Japan. To battle that competition, the company spent $43.2 billion to upgrade plants and equipment around the world, $2 billion of it tied directly to radial tires. By 1985, Goodyear controlled 20 percent of the world tire market, ahead of Michelin (13 percent) and Bridgestone (8 percent).

This case was prepared by John A. Pearce II of George Mason University and Julio O. DeCastro of the University of South Carolina. Copyright 1986 by John A. Pearce II.

In 1984, Goodyear had earnings of $411 million on sales of $10.2 billion, a record year for the company, but the value of the stock fell from $36.87 in December 1982 to $24 in November 1984. (See Appendix A; also see Exhibit 1 for data on gross revenues, operational profit margin, return on equity, net income, earnings per share, and share prices from 1975 to 1985.)

Goodyear's position in the tire business was stronger than ever in 1986, and the company was hoping to use cash from its tire business to finance its expansion into aerospace, oil, and gas. One of the biggest reasons for this newfound strength was Goodyear's highly sophisticated production methods. Some of its plants were considered at least 50 percent more efficient than major competitors' old passenger-tire plants. Goodyear had by far the largest single share of the U.S. market for tires of all types—almost 30 percent of the industry's total capacity. Firestone was a distant second with 14 percent, followed by Gencorp with 11 percent, and Goodrich and Uniroyal with 10 percent each. Exhibit 2 gives Goodyear's consolidated income statements for the years 1983 to 1985.

Goodyear executives hinted at a sales goal of $15 billion by 1989, and Chairman Robert E. Mercer also sought to boost return on sales to 5.0 percent, up from 3.1 percent in 1983, and to increase return on equity to 15 percent, up from 10.1 percent in 1983. He reportedly believed those goals could not be attained as long as the company was tilted toward the cyclical and slow-growth tire business.

As a result, in the early 1980s the company began to diversify into industries that promoted faster growth and higher profit margins. Though Goodyear wanted to keep growing market share in the tire business, Chairman Mercer said that he would like tires to constitute only one half of total corporate sales. For this reason, Goodyear acquired Celeron Corporation in 1983, which was involved in natural gas production and transmission. The other half would be evenly divided between Celeron and the aerospace division. While analysts of the industry seemed to concur that Goodyear was doing the wise thing by diversifying, they were not sure the company had the expertise to run its new businesses.

The aerospace subsidiary of Goodyear was an impressive performer. The division had sales of $617 million in 1985, representing an increase of 85 percent over the previous year, and had matched or surpassed the industry average of 15 percent return on equity for each of the past four years. However, because the company was heavily dependent on military sales (70 percent of 1985 sales), it was difficult to predict the future growth of the company. The president of the division, Robert Clark, hoped for a minimum of 10 percent growth annually throughout the second half of the 1980s.

The corporate officers had even higher expectations. They hoped that the aerospace division would contribute 25 percent of Goodyear sales by 1990, which would require a 43 percent growth rate in the last four years of the decade. Thus, the possibility of one or more related acquisitions to boost the size of the operation was frequently rumored.

EXHIBIT 1 Goodyear Financial Statistics

Year	Gross Revenues ($ millions)	Operating Profit Margin (%)	Return on Equity (%)	Net Income ($ millions)	Working Capital ($ millions)	Senior Capital ($ millions)	Shares (000s)	Earnings per Share ($)	Dividends per Share ($)	Dividend Payments (%)	Price Range	Price/Earnings	Average Yield (%)
1975	$ 5,452.5	7.4%	8.9%	$161.6	$ 987	$ 880.1	71,645	$2.24	$1.10	49%	23⅛–12¾	8.0	6.1%
1976	5,791.5	6.3	6.6	122.0	1,077	930.2	71,775	1.69	1.10	67	25¼–20¼	13.5	4.8
1977	6,628.0	8.1	10.4	205.8	1,240	1,125.8	71,466	2.85	1.20	42	23⅞–16¾	7.1	5.9
1978	7,489.1	7.9	10.7	226.1	1,496	1,418.4	71,535	3.12	1.30	42	18½–15⅜	5.4	7.7
1979	8,238.7	5.0	6.8	146.2	1,534	1,462.1	71,681	2.02	1.30	64	18⅞–11⅞	7.6	8.5
1980	8,444.0	6.2	9.0	206.7*	1,477	1,240.6	71,761	2.85*	1.30	46	18⅜–10¾	5.1	8.9
1981	9,152.9	2.2	10.3	243.9	1,527	1,157.8	72,071	3.36	1.30	39	20¼–15⅞	5.4	7.2
1982	8,688.7	8.1	10.8	247.6	1,576	1,174.1	74,142	3.35	1.40	42	36⅞–17⅞	8.2	5.1
1983	9,735.8	7.4	10.1	270.4†	1,388	665.2	105,425	2.71†	1.40	52	36⅜–27	11.7	4.4
1984	10,240.8	7.5	13.0	411.0	1,342	656.8	106,493	3.87	1.50	39	31½–23	7.0	5.5
1985‡	9,585.1	5.8	12.0	412.4	950	997.5	108,110	3.84	1.60	42	31¼–25⅛	7.3	4.9

* Before $24 million (33 cents a share) credit in 1981 and $17.2 million (24 cents a share) credit in 1982.
† Before $35.1 million (35 cents per share), extraordinary credit in 1983.
‡ Financial statistics for the year 1985 reflect changes in reporting that caused dollar figures to artifically appear depressed.
Adapted from Standard & Poor's Corporation records, 1985.

EXHIBIT 2

THE GOODYEAR TIRE & RUBBER COMPANY AND SUBSIDIARIES
Consolidated Statement of Income
(dollars in millions, except per share)

	Year Ended December 31		
	1985	1984	1983
Net sales	$9,585.1	$9,628.5	$9,031.6
Other income	118.2	85.5	61.4
	9,703.3	9,714.0	9,093.0
Cost and expenses:			
Cost of goods sold	7,635.1	7,581.9	7,073.5
Selling, administrative, and general expense	1,469.6	1,357.7	1,316.1
Interest and amortization of debt discount and expense	105.2	117.3	108.6
Plant closures and sale of facilities	(2.4)	(9.8)	73.8
Foreign currency exchange	32.7	45.8	55.6
Minority interest in net income of foreign subsidiaries	6.6	6.4	6.4
	9,246.8	9,099.3	8,634.0
Income from continuing operations before income taxes and extraordinary item	456.5	614.7	459.0
U.S. and foreign taxes on income	155.2	253.8	226.5
Income from continuing operations before extraordinary item	301.3	360.9	232.5
Discontinued operations	111.1	50.1	37.9
Income before extraordinary item	412.4	411.0	270.4
Extraordinary item—gain on long-term debt retired	—	—	35.1
Net income	$ 412.4	$ 411.0	$ 305.5
Per share of common stock:			
Income from continuing operations before extraordinary item	$2.81	$3.40	$2.33
Discontinued operations	1.03	.47	.38
Extraordinry item—gain on long-term debt retired	—	—	.35
Net income	$3.84	$3.87	$3.06

Celeron earnings declined from 1981 to 1985 after their 1981 peak of $108 million on sales of $901 million. The drops were attributed to a natural gas glut and the sale of a small electric utility subsidiary. After the company became a Goodyear subsidiary in 1985, Goodyear refused to disclose earnings, but Celeron sales in 1984 were known to have dropped to $762 million. The short-term prospects of beneficial changes in the price of natural gas were slim for 1986; however, the long-term prospects of the division looked brighter— partly because of the expected profits from its $750 million pipeline, which would carry 300,000 barrels of crude oil daily from southern California to west Texas. The pipeline was expected to be finished by 1987.

CIVIL UNREST IN SOUTH AFRICA

The white population of South Africa traced its ancestry back to 1652. A group of Dutch settlers headed by Jan Van Riebeeck landed near Cape of Good Hope. This white group of Dutch heritage did not consider themselves colonialists: they called themselves Africaners (Africans) and believed that South Africa was their country.

In political power since 1948, the governing Nationalist party tried to maintain the power and privileges in the hands of the Africaners through the policy of "Grand Apartheid." With this policy they intended to keep the Republic of South Africa as a white nation by dividing black South Africans among 10 "independent countries." In this way, whites could send the blacks not needed for low-level labor jobs to a "homeland." Given the freedom of these independent countries, blacks were thought to be less likely to cause problems in white South Africa.

The government pursued this strategy in four ways: forced resettlement, influx control, financial deprivation of the homelands, and denationalization. Forced resettlement meant the forcible transportation of blacks to the homelands. Once in the homelands, the influx control laws prevented blacks from going back to white South Africa. A passbook system was used to implement the influx laws. Only blacks with a passbook could cross the checkpoints and go into the white cities. The government introduced denationalization by stripping 7.8 million black South Africans of their citizenship when it declared 4 of the 10 homelands as financially "independent" states.

In 1960, Grand Apartheid faced its first big test. A major black protest organized by the militant African National Congress (ANC) against the passbook system resulted in the deaths of 67 blacks and the wounding of 186 others in what would become known as the Sharpeville massacre. The massacre and the ensuing economic turmoil led to the imposition of rigid exchange controls in 1961 to prevent the outflow of capital. These exchange controls prevented any foreign company from removing capital assets from South Africa without the authorization of the South African minister of finance. The controls, which were abolished in 1983, were pegged to an artificial "financial rand," which forced a company that wanted to divest from its South African holdings to forfeit as much as 30 percent of its capital.

In 1976, police assaulted unarmed demonstrators in the homeland of Soweto, resulting in 600 deaths and 6,000 arrests. To defuse tension, the government issued an initiative to allow independent black labor organizations. This was followed in the early 1980s by a climate of repression, in which union leaders were often imprisoned for weeks or months without trial.

By 1984, the African National Congress was South Africa's largest and most influential black organization; its influence was due to the fact that it was recognized by the United Nations and was thoroughly entrenched in the black townships. The ANC espoused the overthrowing of the government and the nationalization of industry. It had been underground since 1960, when it was banned after the Sharpeville massacre.

The ANC was involved in a military struggle against the South African government, but its forces numbered only 8,000. Linked to guerilla warfare that diminished after March 1984, when Swaziland and Mozambique pledged to cooperate in the elimination of ANC bases, its minimal activities consisted principally of attacks on key South African and commercial military installations.

The South African government had the most advanced military force in all of Africa. The South African Defense Force could mobilize 250,000 men, had advanced combat equipment, and was thought by some observers to possess nuclear weapons. It was widely believed that the South African Army could contain any domestic military struggle—at least for a short period of time. The power of the South African military was exemplified by its 108 combat aircraft, one light bomber squadron, two fighter squadrons with Mirage III EZ and eight III DZ aircraft, three Daphne class submarines, and two destroyers with two wasp ASN helicopters.

The year 1985 was one of the most violent in South African history. Violence in the black townships produced 700 deaths and countless numbers of detainees. The country was declared to be in a state of emergency in July by President P. W. Botha.

The most revered leader of the black movement, Nelson Mandela, who had been in prison for treason since the Sharpeville massacre in 1962 (and to whom the government made numerous unaccepted clemency offers under the conditon that he agree to renounce revolutionary methods to overthrow the government), was ailing and, in October 1985, was hospitalized. Observers agreed that his death would have triggered an explosion of violence unlike any seen before in South Arica and, in turn, more government repression.

In August 1985, highly placed South African officials hinted that the government was ready to introduce dramatic social and economic reforms. However, President P. W. Botha failed to live up to the expectations. He announced only that his government would consider (1) extending national citizenship to the 24 million blacks; (2) improving, but not abolishing, the influx laws; and (3) negotiating with unspecified black leaders. No timetable for these changes was offered.

The Botha announcements were regarded as disappointing by all but strong government supporters. They were seen as too unspecific, too mild, and generally unresponsive to the country's pressing economic and social problems. Consequently, immediately following the announcements, U.S. federal and state governments moved to adopt tougher positions on the issue of investment in South Africa.

On September 9, 1985, President Reagan, prodded by growing concerns in the U.S. Senate over the South African situation, imposed a number of sanctions on the South African government. His White House executive order included a ban on U.S. bank loans to the South African government, a prohibition of computer sales and nuclear technology to South Africa's security agencies, and a ban on the sale of South African gold krugerrands in the United States, all subject to approval by U.S. trading partners.

In an unprecedented move, a group of leading South African businessmen headed by Gavin W. H. Relly, chairman of the board of Anglo American Cooperation, flew to Luzaka, Zambia, on September 13, 1985, to begin talks with Oliver Tambo, president-in-exile of the ANC. This marked the first time that the business community had bypassed the government in an effort to resolve issues of special concern to the black population.

In mid-1986, the civil unrest and the struggle between the government of Mr. Botha and the opposing forces continued. The economic situation in South Africa was deteriorating with no relief in sight, and another new force was coming into play. The black unions boasted a growing membership of 700,000 workers, thereby constituting half of the organized labor. Even though a strike called in October 1985 by the National Union of Mineworkers had collapsed after three days, the growing power of the South African black unions was expected to pressure the South African government for social action.

Nothing had come of the September 13, 1985, meeting between a group of South Africa's leading businessmen and the leadership of the ANC. The ANC leadership reiterated its position regarding nationalization of industry and armed struggle. But the decision by the businessmen to bypass the government and to talk directly with the rebels merited attention because it opened the door to possible solutions to the problems of South Africa.

THE ECONOMIC CLIMATE IN SOUTH AFRICA

According to the Investor Responsiblity Research Center, a Washington organization backed by business, 13 U.S. companies (including General Foods, Pan American World Airways, and PepsiCo) left South Africa in 1985. However, the South African holdings of those companies were a very small percent of the total foreign investment in the country. A complete list of all U.S. companies that had left the country by October 1985 is given in Exhibit 3.

Other companies, including Ford Motor and Coca-Cola, were trying to reduce their stakes in South Africa. On January 30, 1985, Ford announced that it was merging its South African Auto Business with Amcar, a subsidiary of Anglo American Corporation, one of South Africa's biggest corporations. Ford retained 42 percent of the new company. Pursuing a similar strategy, Coca-Cola sold its controlling interest in Amalgamated Beverage Industries to South African Breweries for $36.6 million, retaining a 30 percent share.

The economic conditions in South Africa reached a low point in 1985. The rand, South Africa's official currency, lost 50 percent of its value from January to August and had an additional 35 percent plunge in September through October. Inflation was running at 16 percent, and the GNP, which had been stagnant since 1980, was forecast to fall 25 percent in 1985. It was estimated that just to maintain the current unemployment rate—which had averaged 13 percent from 1980 to 1985—the country's economy would need to grow at a 5 percent rate annually. Interest rates in South Africa in late 1985 were 20 percent, with black unemployment at 30 percent. (Refer to Appendix B for information on economic and social conditions in South Africa.)

EXHIBIT 3   U.S. Companies Disinvesting South African Holdings

Apple Computer—citing "political reasons," suspended all operations in August, with October 1 closedown date.

BBDO International—sold 75 percent ownership in South African agency to local directors in August.

Blue Bell—sold a jeans manufacturing plant on December 31, 1984.

City Investing—financial services group sold as part of corporate liquidation program.

Coca-Cola—sold a majority interest in its bottling operation; control will be transferred over two years.

Ford Motor—merged automobile operation into Anglo American Corporation's Signa Motors Corporation in February, reducing stake to 40 percent and surrendering management.

General Foods—sold 20 percent stake in Cerebos affiliate.

Helena Rubinstein—closed cosmetics sales operation in June.

International Harvester—sold truck operation in August.

Oak Industries—sold electronic components plant in April.

Pan American World Airways—closed operations in April.

PepsiCo—sold both South African bottling plants in January.

Perkin-Elmer—sold manufacturing instruments and electrical components as well as sales office, to former employees in February.

Phibro-Salomon—closed Johannesburg office in August.

Singer—sold marketing and distribution operations in April.

Smith International—sold affiliate in May as part of shift from mining and minerals to petroleum products.

Tidwell Industries—sold its home-building subsidiary to a local construction company in July.

West Point-Pepperell—sold a minority in a textile company in June.

SOURCE: *Business Week,* September 23, 1985, p. 106.

The average aftertax return on investment of the 300 American companies with direct investments in South Africa fell from 30 percent in 1980 to 7 percent in 1983 and to 5 percent in 1985.

In August 1985, after international banks refused to roll over about half of South Africa's $12 billion short-term debt, the country declared a moratorium of repaying the debt. Furthermore, to protect itself from the outflow of capital, it reimposed the exchange controls that it had lifted in 1983.

THE DISINVESTMENT ISSUE AND SOUTH AFRICA

The proponents of disinvestment wanted changes in the corporate policies of U.S. firms with operations in South Africa. Change options included adherence to the Sullivan principles, social development expenditures, and total withdrawal. Institutions engaged in disinvestment included universities, churches, unions, and state governments.

In October 1985, laws in 11 U.S. cities and 9 states required public funds to divest some or all of their stock in companies with operations in South Africa. Additional disinvestment bills were introduced in 19 states in 1985, including New York and California, which had a combined continued investment of $26 billion in corporate securities.

Some states, like Connecticut, instituted provisions that linked disinvestment decisions to compliance with the Sullivan principles. The Connecticut law required that the state divest from its holdings in any company with failing Sullivan grades. Also, in November 1985, the U.S. Congress considered legislation sponsored by U.S. Representative Stephen Solarz of New York and U.S. Representative William Gray III of Pennsylvania, which prohibited new investments in South Africa and required all companies operating in South Africa to adhere to principles similar to Sullivan's.

Banks, fund managers, and companies with state contracts were also touched by the disinvestment calls. Major New York banks saw large depositors withdrawing their funds. Fund managers, such as Kemper International Fund, were asked by clients to sell the stock of companies operating in South Africa in their portfolios. New York City had a proposal under review by which companies with operations in South Africa would be penalized when bidding for city contracts.

GOODYEAR'S SOCIAL RESPONSIVENESS IN SOUTH AFRICA

Goodyear began selling tires in South Africa in 1916. In 1946, a subsidiary, Goodyear Tire & Rubber Company (South Africa), constructed a tire plant at Uitenhage, South Africa. Throughout its 50-year history in South Africa, Goodyear had perceived itself as a positive force in the nation's racial struggle.

Goodyear was one of the original 12 charter subscribers of the Sullivan principles. The Reverend Leon H. Sullivan, a director of General Motors Corporation, developed a series of principles in 1977, to which companies operating in South Africa would voluntarily abide in an effort to reduce discrimination in South African employment. At first, 12 companies endorsed the principles; but, by 1982, 146 of the 400 American companies with subsidiaries in South Africa had signed the pact. Compliance to the principles was monitored by the consulting firm of Arthur D. Little. In 1986, the principles were especially important because investment recommendations on companies operating in South Africa had been tied to good Sullivan grades by a number of universities, pension funds, and state and local governments (see Exhibit 4 for more detailed information on the Sullivan principles).

Goodyear claimed it had a history of eliminating discrimination that predated the Sullivan principles, and it cited as an example its institutionalization of an equal-pay-for-equal-job program before the Reverend Sullivan promoted his voluntary nonsegregation code in 1977. However, Goodyear admitted that it only desegregated the company cafeteria and locker rooms as a result of preliminary discussion of the code.

EXHIBIT 4 The Sullivan Principles

The six Sullivan principles call for companies to:

1. Desegregate all eating, comfort, and work facilities.

2. Implement equal and fair employment practices for all employees and acknowledge the right of black workers to form their own unions.

3. Ensure equal pay for all employees doing equal or comparable work for the same period of time.

4. Initiate and develop training programs to prepare substantial numbers of blacks and other non-whites for supervisory, administrative, clerical, and technical jobs.

The signatories promise periodic reports on their progress in implementing these principles. According to Arthur D. Little, Inc. (the signatory companies' monitoring agency), the sixth report, published in November 1982, found:

Principle 1: All but one of the reporting units state all facilities are desegregated.

Principle 2: All but one have common medical, pension, and insurance plans for all races.

Principle 3: Black employees are receiving higher average pay increases than whites, though the average percent increase is less than the previous year.

Principle 4: The proportion of blacks participating in training programs for sales positions has continued to increase.

The monitoring organization graded as follows:

32: Making good progress (category I)
38: Making progress (category II)
37: Need to become more active (category III)

EXHIBIT 4 *(concluded)*

The six Sullivan principles call for companies to:	*The signatories promise periodic reports on their progress in implementing these principles. According to Arthur D. Little, Inc. (the signatory companies' monitoring agency), the sixth report, published in November 1982, found:*
	The monitoring organization graded as follows:

5. Increase the number of blacks and other nonwhites in managerial and supervisory positions.

Principle 5: The proportion of blacks in supervisory positions has dropped, indicating a lack of progress in this area in weaker economic times.

6. Improve the quality of employees' lives outside the work environment (e.g., housing, schooling, recreation and health facilities); provide for the right of black migrant workers to a normal family life; and assist the development of black and other nonwhite-owned and -operated businesses.

Principle 6: Contributions for community development have doubled since last year, amounting to about $11 million.

In December 1984, Reverend Sullivan revised his code. The new code included a provision that requires U.S. companies to take public, political action against apartheid.

Adapted from "Shomer, South Africa: Beyond Fair Employment," *Harvard Business Review*, May–June 1983, pp. 145–50.

After reviewing the progress in 1982, Reverend Sullivan concluded that the signatory companies were meeting their objective of improving the quality of life for black workers, but he stated that further advances ought to be made in the training and placement of black managers, the development of black-owned enterprises, and the upgrading of black educational and health services. Statistics showed that only 6 percent of the 1,450 managerial-level vacancies throughout South Africa in 1981 and 1982 were filled by blacks. Arthur D. Little found that the main black advancement was from unskilled to semi-skilled or skilled production positions, with a decline in administrative and clerical jobs.

Goodyear was one of the few companies to have been awarded top grades for its South African employment policies from Arthur D. Little since the inception of the Sullivan principles. In contrast, Firestone South African Operations, which was 25 percent owned by Firestone, had never passed the Sullivan test. Exhibit 5 gives a list of the Sullivan signatories with their rating for 1983.

EXHIBIT 5   List of Sullivan Signatories as of October 1983

Rating Categories

  I. Making good progress
  II. Making progress
 III. Needs to become more active
     IIA. Low point rating on principles 4–6
     IIB. Has not met basic requirements of
     principles 1–3
 IV. Endorsors (companies with few employees
     or little equity)
     IVA. No employees
     IVB. Fewer than 10 employees
     IVC. Less than 19 percent equity in South
     African operation
  V. New signatories
 VI. Nonreporting signatories

Alphabetical List of Signatories

AFIA Worldwide Insurance	IIA
Abbott Laboratories	II
American Cyanamid Company	I, VI
American Express Company	IVB
American Home Products Corporation	V
American Hospital Supply Corporation	II
American International Group, Inc.	IIIB
Armco, Inc.	II, IVB
Ashland Oil, Inc.	IIIA, IVA, VI
Borden, Inc.	I
Borg-Warner Corporation	II
Bristol-Myers Company	II
Burroughs Corporation	I
Butterick Company, Inc.	IIIA
CBS, Inc.	IIIA
CIGNA Corporation	II

Alphabetical List of Signatories

The Gillette Company	I
Goodyear Tire & Rubber Company	II
W. R. Grace and Company	IIIA
Walter E. Heller International Corporation	IVC
Heublein, Inc.	II
Hewlett-Packard Company	II
Honeywell, Inc.	II
Hoover Company	IIIA
Hyster Company	II
International Business Machines Corporation	I
International Harvester Company	IIIA, IVB
International Minerals and Chemicals Corporation	IIIA
International Telephone and Telegraph Corporation	I, IVC, VI
The Interpublic Group of Companies, Inc.	VI
Johnson Controls, Inc.	VI
Johnson and Johnson	I
Joy Manufacturing Company	VI
Kellogg Company	II
Eli Lilly and Company	I, II, IVA
Marriott Corporation	IIIA
Marsh and McLennan Companies	VI
Masonite Corporation	IIIB
McGraw-Hill, Inc.	I
Measurex Corporation	VI
Merck & Company, Inc.	I, II
Mine Safety Appliances Company	IIIB
Minnesota Mining and Manufacturing Company	I

EXHIBIT 5 *(concluded)*

Rating Categories		Alphabetical List of Signatories	
CPC International, Inc.	II, IVA	Mobil Oil Corporation	I
Caltex Petroleum Corporation	I	Monsanto Company	I
Carnation Company	IIIB	Motorola, Inc.	IIIA
Carrier Corporation	V	NCNB Corporation	IVB
J. I. Case Corporation	IIIA, IVA	NCR Corporation	IIIA
Caterpillar Tractor Company	II	Nabisco Brands, Inc.	II
Celanese Corporation	IIIA	Nalco Chemical Company	IIIB
The Chase Manhattan		Norton Company	II, IIIA, IVB
Corporation	II	Norton Simon, Inc.	IVA
Chicago Bridge and Iron		Olin Corporation	IIIA, IIIB, VI
Company	V	Oshkosh Truck Corporation	IVA
Citicorp	I, IVC	Otis Elevator Company	II
The Coca-Cola Company	I, II	The Parker Pen Company	II
Colgate-Palmolive Company	I	Pfizer, Inc.	I, II
Control Data Corporation	I	Phelps Dodge Corporation	IIIA, VI
Cooper Industries, Inc.	II	Phillips Petroleum Company	II
Cummins Engine Company, Inc.	IVB	Reader's Digest Association, Inc.	IIIA, IVA
D'Arcy MacManus & Masius		Rexnord, Inc.	IIIA
Worldwide, Inc.	IIIB	Richardson-Vicks, Inc.	IIIA
Dart & Kraft, Inc.	VI	Rohm and Haas Company	IIIA, IVB
Deere & Company	II, IVA	Schering-Plough Corporation	II
Del Monte Corporation	II	Sentry Insurance—A Mutual	
Deloitte Haskins & Sells	IVC	Company	IIIA
Dominion Textile, Inc.	VI	Smith Kline Beckman	
Donaldson Company, Inc.	IIIA	Corporation	II, V
The Dow Chemical Company	IV, IVB	Sperry Corporation	I
E. I. duPont de Nemours and		Squibb Corporation	IIIA
Company	II	The Standard Oil Company	
The East Asiatic Company, Ltd.	VI	(Ohio)	II, IIIA
Eastman Kodak Company	I	The Stanley Works	II
Englehard Corporation	VI	Sterling Drug, Inc.	IIIA
Exxon Corporation	I	Tampax, Inc.	I
FMC Corporation	VI	J. Walter Thompson Company	VI
Federal-Mogul Corporation	IIIA	Time, Inc.	IVB
Ferro Corporation	IIIA	The Trane Company	IIIB
The Firestone Tire & Rubber		Union Carbide Corporation	I, II, IVB
Company	IIIB, IVA	The Upjohn Company	II, IIIA
John Fluke Manufacturing		Warner Communications, Inc.	I, IIIA
Company, Inc.	IIIA	Warner-Lambert Company	II, IIIA
Fluor Corporation	II	Westinghouse Electric	
Ford Motor Company	I	Corporation	I
Franklin Electric Company, Inc.	VI	Wilbur-Elllis Company	IIIA
General Electric Company	II, VI	Xerox Corporation	I
General Motors Corporation	I		

SOURCE: Leape, Baskins, and Underhill, *Business in the Shadow of Apartheid* (Lexington, Mass.: Lexington Books, 1985).

By 1985, Goodyear had a 1.1 million-square-foot plant in South Africa, with an investment of $100 million dollars and an employee work force of 2,500 workers (64 percent black), making the company one of the top 10 American employers in South Africa (see Exhibit 6). In late 1985, the company completed a $20-million plant expansion that enabled it to produce radial truck tires, thereby further demonstrating its commitment to South Africa.

EXHIBIT 6   The 12 Largest U.S. Employers in South Africa

Company	Number of Workers
Coca-Cola	4,800
Ford Motor	4,600
General Motors	4,000
Mobil	3,300
USG*	2,600
Goodyear	2,600
Caltex Petroleum	2,200
Allegheny International	2,000
IBM	1,900
General Electric	850
Dresser Industries	800
Xerox	800

* Formerly U.S. Gypsum.

SOURCE: *Business Week,* February 11, 1985, p. 38.

The company had spent $6 million on nonwhite education in South Africa by 1986. Part of this investment was made out of self-interest. Goodyear realized that greater prosperity for South Africa's 23 million blacks, coupled with political stability, could mean greater sales in South Africa in the long run. Chairman Mercer said that they would not be making tires there if they thought of South Africa as having a market of only 4.5 million whites. A 1986 estimate was that blacks owned 430,000 of the 3 million cars operated in South Africa.

Capsulizing the corporate viewpoint, Jacques Sardas, Goodyear International president, said, "Because South Africa has always been profitable, the company has never considered leaving. Our presence there is good for our shareholders as well as South Africans—all of them."

GOODYEAR'S DILEMMA

By 1986, the company operated plants in 29 countries, and Goodyear's overseas operations were having problems in countries with high inflation and government price controls, thereby prohibiting the company from passing on increases in the price of raw materials. This caused a reduction in international profits, with foreign operating income falling 35 percent to $191 million from 1983 to 1985. Dividends from foreign operations decreased from $85 million in 1982 to $67.6 million in 1983 to $44 million in 1984. The company's net foreign assets exceeded $1.1 billion in 1985, after deducting minority shareholders' equity.

Traditionally, Goodyear's profit margins in South Africa had been among the best the corporation achieved in any country but contributed less than 1 percent of Goodyear's annual corporate profits overall. The company admitted that the South African operations dipped into red ink in 1985 for the first time in its history, though it would not disclose specific figures.

If Goodyear were to leave its South African operations, it would face the possibility of a government-mandated buyout, with the payment made in bonds denominated in deteriorating rands and stretched over a long period of time. Alternatively, Goodyear could take the best price offered from a South African or European competitor. A divestiture would, in effect, lock Goodyear out of the South African tire market that it helped develop, because the same protectionist trade barriers that helped make South Africa such a good business proposition for business already in place would prevent it from having any kind of operations there once it had ceased domestic operations.

In 1986, only 3 percent of Goodyear's 107 million outstanding shares were held by universities, pension funds, or financial institutions—the groups that might be inclined to follow calls for divestment by social activists interested in promoting black causes. Such occasional but mounting calls accused Goodyear of supporting apartheid because it paid South African taxes and sold tires to the country's police and military. However, if U.S. stockholders had been disinvesting up to mid-1986, it had been so gradual as to leave share prices unaffected.

Goodyear had a history of not giving in to political and economic pressures in the foreign countries in which it did business. The company did not want to set a negative precedent by leaving its South African operations. Douglas Hill, Goodyear International's executive vice president, told *Fortune* magazine that "leaving South Africa would send a message to other countries that Goodyear is a company that folds its tents when things get hot."

In the face of social unrest, national economic declines, uncertain business forecasts, and multifaceted political pressures, Goodyear had not publicly declared its stand on the disinvestment question by mid-1986. Surely, its strategic options were being thoroughly considered.

APPENDIX A: The Goodyear Tire & Rubber Company and Subsidiaries—
Comparison with Prior Years

(Dollars in millions, except per share)	1985	1984	1983	1982
Net sales	$9,585.1	$9,628.5	$9,031.6	$8,780.4
Income from continuing operations before				
extraordinary items and cumulative effect of				
accounting change	301.3	360.9	232.5	260.5
Discontinued operations	111.1	50.1	37.9	52.1
Extraordinary items:				
Gain on long-term debt retired	—	—	35.1	17.2
Tax benefit of loss carryovers	—	—	—	—
Cumulative effect on prior years of accounting				
change for capital leases	—	—	—	—
Net income	412.4	411.0	305.5	329.8
Net income per dollar of sales	4.3¢	4.3¢	3.4¢	3.8¢
Depreciation and depletion	$ 300.5	$ 292.3	$ 280.3	$ 250.3
Capital expenditures	1,667.6	610.9	478.7	391.4
Properties and plants—net	4,025.0	3,036.7	2,819.2	2,718.2
Total assets	$6,953.5	$6,194.3	$5,985.5	$5,885.9
Long-term debt and capital leases	997.5	656.8	665.2	1,174.5
Shareholders' equity	3,507.4	3,171.3	3,016.2	2,777.2
Per share of common stock:				
Income from continuing operations before				
extraordinary items and cumulative effect				
of accounting change	$ 2.81	$ 3.40	$ 2.33	$ 2.64
Discontinued operations	1.03	0.47	0.38	0.52
Extraordinary items:				
Gain on long-term debt retired	—	—	0.35	0.18
Tax benefit of loss carryovers	—	—	—	—
Cumulative effect on prior years of accounting				
change for capital leases	—	—	—	—
Net income*	3.84	3.87	3.06	3.34
Dividends**	1.60	1.50	1.40	1.40
Book value—on shares outstanding at				
December 31	32.44	29.78	28.61	28.09
Price range:				
High	31-1/4	31-1/2	36-3/8	36-7/8
Low	25-1/8	23	27	17-7/8
Employees:				
Average during the year	134,115	133,271	128,760	131,665
Total compensation for the year	$2,709.8	$2,623.2	$2,459.1	$2,388.1
Shareholders of record***	72,582	75,619	76,014	83,915
Common shares:				
Outstanding at December 31	108,110,085	106,492,709	105,425,079	98,866,612
Average outstanding	107,369,517	106,138,171	99,907,522	98,794,352

* Based on average shares outstanding—see note on net income per share.
** Dividends are the historical dividends paid by The Goodyear Tire & Rubber Company.
*** Includes shareholders of record of Celeron for periods prior to the merger.
The method of accounting for foreign currency translation was changed in 1981 (*SFAS No. 52*).
The method of accounting for capitalizing interest was adopted in 1979 (*SFAS No. 34*).
Financial information for 1976–1982 has been restated to include Celeron on a pooling of interests basis—see note on business combination.
Financial information for 1976–1984 has been restated to reflect the discontinued operations of the Celeron group—see note on discontinued operations.

1981	1980	1979	1978	1977	1976
$9,267.8	$8,541.7	$8,300.6	$7,500.0	$6,633.6	$5,796.2
257.2	219.0	159.8	227.9	206.5	124.9
94.8	69.4	42.0	25.2	22.5	22.0
—	—	—	—	—	—
16.4	24.0	—	—	—	—
—	—	—	—	—	(3.5)
368.4	312.4	201.8	253.1	229.0	143.4
4.0¢	3.7¢	2.4¢	3.4¢	3.5¢	2.5¢
$ 241.4	$ 234.4	$ 229.6	$ 215.1	$ 204.7	$ 195.6
377.2	291.4	378.9	423.3	298.5	243.7
2,632.7	2,558.5	2,462.4	2,280.1	2,075.3	1,968.1
$5,972.9	$6,024.2	$5,838.1	$5,565.2	$4,934.9	$4,642.7
1,245.4	1,337.3	1,531.8	1,469.0	1,168.2	1,050.0
2,647.1	2,647.5	2,400.1	2,303.3	2,126.3	2,000.0
$ 2.64	$ 2.28	$ 1.69	$ 2.46	$ 2.26	1.37
0.97	0.72	0.44	0.27	0.25	0.24
—	—	—	—	—	—
0.17	0.25	—	—	—	—
—	—	—	—	—	(.03)
3.78	3.25	2.13	2.73	2.51	1.58
1.30	1.30	1.30	1.30	1.20	1.10
27.27	27.45	25.55	24.60	23.50	22.07
20-1/4	18-3/8	18-7/8	18-1/2	23-7/8	25-1/4
15-7/8	10-3/4	11-7/8	15-3/8	16-3/4	20-1/8
138,487	144,860	154,374	154,291	153,033	151,386
$2,428.1	$2,263.1	$2,242.5	$1,979.8	$1,767.2	$1,491.0
93,731	98,421	96,169	92,547	86,952	86,073
97,056,843	96,435,863	93,944,690	93,613,834	90,468,273	90,637,740
97,375,348	96,253,559	94,642,857	92,557,520	91,283,675	91,025,235

APPENDIX B: South Africa

Area
Including homelands (larger than all Atlantic
   Coast seaboard of the United States)—   472,359 square miles
Namibia—Southwest Africa—   317,827 square miles

	Number of persons	*Percent*
Population		
African	20,084,319	72%
White	4,453,273	16
Mixed	2,554,273	9
Asian	794,369	3
Total	27,886,234	100%

1948–1976

Forced removals of blacks from white areas to black areas	2,108,000	
Labor force		
African	7,537,000	
White	1,970,000	
Mixed	1,023,000	
Asian	272,000	
Total	10,802,000	

Average wage differentials, white to black

Manufacturing	4 to 1
Mining	6 to 1

Employees of U.S. corporations

Black (African, Asian, mixed)	70,000 (estimated)
White	30,000 (estimated)

Government

Republic of South Africa established in 1961 on basis of
   voting rights for national parliament restricted to
   whites. Four states and 10 reserves or homelands.

Blacks offered vote in homelands and resident townships
   located on white land. Four homelands declared independent.

SOURCE: Adapted from "Southern Africa Perspectives," *South Africa Fact Sheet* (New York: Africa Fund), undated.

CASE

Union Carbide of India Limited

A corporation is not liable for the acts or omissions of another corporation by reason of ownership of stock.

Union Carbide Corporation lawyer

In reality, there is but one entity, the monolithic multinational, which is responsible for the design, development and dissemination of information and technology worldwide.

Indian government lawyer

We have often been promised money, but for us it was more important that those who killed our brothers and sisters should be hanged.

15-year-old survivor of the Bhopal tragedy

Life seems to be less valuable here.

Indian Supreme Court lawyer

December 2, 1984, began as a typical day in the central Indian city of Bhopal. Shoppers moved about the bustling, open-air market. Here and there a customer haggled with a merchant. Beasts of burden, donkeys and oxen, pulled carts or carried ungainly bundles through the partly paved streets. Children played in the dirt. In the shadow of a Union Carbide of India Limited (UCIL) pesticide factory, tens of thousands of India's poorest citizens milled about the shantytown they called home. A few miles away, in South Bhopal, wealthy Indians lived in elegant opulence rivaling that of the first-class districts of London and Paris.

Inside the plant, several hundred Indian workers and managers went about their duties, maintaining and operating the systems that produced the

---

This case was prepared by Arthur Sharplin and Aseem Shukla of McNeese State University and the University of Iowa, respectively. Copyright 1989 by Arthur Sharplin.

mildly toxic pesticide Sevin. The plant was running at far below capacity and most of it was shut down for maintenance.

At about 11 P.M. an operator noticed that the pressure in a methyl isocyanate (MIC) storage tank read 10 pounds per square inch—four times normal. He was not concerned, though, thinking the tank might have been pressurized with nitrogen by the previous shift. Around midnight several of the workers noticed that their eyes had begun to water and sting, a signal experience had taught them indicated an MIC leak. The leak, a slow but steady drip, was soon spotted. The operators were still not alarmed because minor leaks at the plant were quite common. It was time for tea. Most of the crew retired to the company canteen, resolving to correct the problem afterward.

By the time they returned it was too late. The MIC tank gauge was pegged. The leak had grown much larger. The entire area of the MIC tanks was enveloped in the choking fumes. The workers tried spraying water on the leak to break down the MIC. They sounded the alarm siren and summoned the fire brigade. As the futility of their efforts became apparent, many of the workers panicked and ran upwind, some scaling the chain-link and barbed-wire fence in their frantic race for survival.

By 1:00 A.M. only a supervisor remained in the area. He stayed upwind, donning his oxygen-breathing apparatus every few minutes to go check the various gauges and sensors. Pressure in the MIC tank had forced open a relief valve. The vapor could be seen escaping from an atmospheric vent line 120 feet in the air.

The cloud of deadly white gas was carried by a southeasterly wind toward the Jai Prakash Nagar shanties. The cold temperature of the December night caused the MIC to settle toward the ground. (In the daytime, or in the summer, convection currents probably would have raised and diluted it.)

As the gaseous tentacles reached into the huts there was panic and confusion. Many of the weak and elderly died where they lay. Some who made it into the streets were blinded. "It was like breathing fire," one survivor said. As word of the gas leak spread, many of Bhopal's affluent were able to flee in their cars. But most of the poor were left behind. When the gas reached the railroad station, supervisors who were not immediately disabled sent out word along the tracks and incoming trains were diverted. This diversion cut off a possible means of escape but may have saved hundreds of lives. The whole station was soon enveloped in gas. Arriving trains would have been death traps for passengers and crews.

Of Bhopal's total population of about 1 million, an estimated 500,000 fled that night, most on foot. The surrounding towns were woefully unprepared to accept the gasping and dying masses. Thousands waited outside hospitals for medical care. There was no certainty about how to treat the gas victims, and general-purpose medical supplies were in hopelessly short supply. Inside the hospitals and out, screams and sobs filled the air. Food supplies were quickly exhausted. People were even afraid to drink the water, not knowing if it was contaminated.

The second day, relief measures were better organized. Several hundred doctors and nurses from nearby hospitals had been summoned to help medical personnel in Bhopal. Just disposing of the dead was a major problem. Mass cremation was necessary. Islamic victims, whose faith allows burial rather than cremation, were piled several deep in hurriedly dug graves. Bloating carcasses of cattle and dogs littered the city. There was fear of a cholera epidemic. Bhopal's mayor said, "I can say that I have seen chemical warfare. Everything so quiet. Goats, cats, whole families—father, mother, children—all lying silent and still. And every structure totally intact. I hope never again to see it."

By the third day, the city had begun to move toward stability, if not normalcy. The plant was closed and locked. A decision was made to consume the 30 tons of MIC that remained by using it to make pesticide. Most of the 2,500 dead bodies had been disposed of, however inappropriately. The more than 100,000 injured were being treated as rapidly as the limited medical facilities would allow, although many people simply sat in silence, blinded and maimed by an enemy they had never known well enough to fear. For those who survive, doctors predict an increased risk of sterility, kidney and liver infections, tuberculosis, vision problems, and brain damage. Years after the incident newspapers reported a high incidence of still births and congenital deformities among the population that was affected by the gas. Mental health problems were another major fallout. Appendix A summarizes interviews conducted in the Bhopal area two years after the disaster.

By 1989, the death toll would exceed 3,300, with another 25,000 suffering chronic effects of MIC poisoning. And about one person a day would still be dying from causes attributable to the incident.

COMPANY BACKGROUND

The Ever-Ready Company, Ltd. (of Great Britain) began manufacturing flashlight batteries in Calcutta in 1926. The division was incorporated as the Ever-Ready Company (India), Ltd. in 1934 and became a subsidiary of Union Carbide Corporation (UCC) of New York. The name of the Indian company was changed to National Carbide Company (India), Ltd. in 1949 and to Union Carbide India Limited in 1959. The 1926 capacity of 40 million dry-cell batteries per year had expanded to 767 million by the 1960s. In 1959, a factory was set up in India to manufacture the flashlights themselves.

By the 1980s, UCIL was involved in five product areas: batteries, carbon and metals, plastics, margin products, and agricultural chemicals. Exhibit 1 provides production statistics for UCIL products. The company eventually operated 15 plants at eight locations, including the headquarters operation in Calcutta, and employed upward of 2,000. UCIL's petrochemical complex, established in Bombay in 1966, was India's first petrochemical plant.

The marine-products operation of UCIL was begun in 1971 with two shrimping ships. The business was completely export oriented and employed

EXHIBIT 1 Production Statistics

	1986 Cap.	1986	1985	1984	1983	1982	1981	1980	1979	1978
Batteries (000,000)	917	572	528	510	510	512	411	459	460	430
Flashlights (000,000)	8	8	6	7	7	7	7	7	6	6
Arc carbons (000,000)	9	8	8	7	8	7	7	7	6	6
Carbon electrodes (000,000)	3	1	1	1	1	1	1	0	1	0
Printing plates (metric tons)	1,200	416	393	376	412	478	431	399	469	506
Metal castings (metric tons)	150	18	19	17	18	13	16	15	16	18
Mn dioxide (metric tons)	4,500	4,023	3,670	3,069	3,335	3,085	3,000	2,803	2,605	2,700
Chemicals (000 metric tons)	14	3	6	6	7	6	7	8	9	9
Polyethylene (000 metric tons)	20	7	19	17	18	17	20	19	16	12
Pesticides (metric tons)	—	—	18	1,240	1,647	2,308	2,704	1,542	1,496	367
Marine products (metric tons)	—	—	—	272	424	649	642	601	648	731

15 deep-sea trawlers. Processing facilities were located off the east and west coasts of India. The trawlers harvested deep-sea lobsters in addition to shrimp. This division was closed in 1984 and the facilities were sold in 1986.

In 1979, UCIL initiated a letter of intent to manufacture dry-cell batteries in Nepal. A 77.5 percent owned subsidiary was set up in Nepal in 1982, and construction of a Rs. 18 million plant was begun. The Nepal operation was solidly profitable by 1986.

The agricultural products division of UCIL was started in 1966 with only an office in Bombay. Agreement was reached with the Indian government in 1969 to set up a pesticide plant at Bhopal. Land was rented to UCIL for about $40 per acre per year.

The initial investment was small, only $1 million, and the process was simple. Concentrated Sevin powder was imported from the United States, diluted with nontoxic powder, packaged, and sold. Under the technology-transfer provisions of its agreement with the Indian government, UCC was obligated to share its more advanced technologies with UCIL. Eventually the investment at Bhopal grew to exceed $25 million, and the constituents of Sevin were made there. Another Union Carbide insecticide, called Temik, was made in small quantities at Bhopal.

The assets of UCIL grew from Rs. 558 million in 1974 to Rs. 1,234 million in 1983. (The conversion rate stayed near 9 rupees to the dollar during this period, moving to about 12 as the dollar strengthened worldwide in 1984 and 1985, then staying near 12 until 1989.) The *Economic Times* of India ranked UCIL number 21 in terms of sales among Indian companies in 1984.

At the time of the Bhopal incident, UCC held 50.9 percent of UCIL's stock, financial institutions owned by the Indian government held 22 percent, and the remaining 27 percent or so was in the hands of about 23,000 Indian citizens. The Indian Foreign Exchange Regulation Act (see Exhibit 4) generally limits nonresident interest in multinational corporations operating in India to 49 percent. However, UCC was exempted from this provision based on its being a high-technology company.

Starting in 1967, an Indian served as chairman of the eleven-member UCIL board of directors. And foreign membership on the board was limited to four. In 1985 an expert on Indian industry affairs said, "Though the foreigners on the board are down to four from six in previous years, they continue to hold sway over the affairs of the company." However, UCC's chief litigation counsel, Robert A. Butler, wrote,

> None of Union Carbide Corporation's Directors are on the Board of the Indian Company. All of the employees and officers of the India Company, including its Chairman and Managing Director, are Indian residents and citizens.

Major capital expenditures by UCIL were required to be approved by Union Carbide Corporation. Also, the Bhopal plant submitted monthly reports to U.S. corporate headquarters detailing operations and safety procedures. And inspections of the plant were carried out from time to time by UCC technical specialists.

OPERATIONS AT BHOPAL

On the surface, the UCIL insecticide factory was a typical process plant. A wide diversity of storage tanks, hoppers, and reactors were connected by pipes. There were many pumps and valves and a number of tall vent lines and ducts. Ponds and pits were used for waste treatment, and several railway spur lines ran through the plant. Exhibit 2 is a diagram of the factory. Exhibit 3 is a schematic of just the MIC manufacturing process.

Sevin is made through a controlled chemical reaction involving alpha-naphthol and MIC. Alpha-naphthol is a brownish granular material, and MIC is a highly reactive liquid that boils and becomes a gas at usual daytime temperatures. In 1971, when plans were first made to make alpha-naphthol at Bhopal, a pilot plant was set up. A full-size alpha-naphthol plant (in fact, the world's largest) was finished in 1977.

In the meantime, work had begun on the ill-fated MIC plant. The plant was designed and mostly supplied by UCC, which sent engineers to India to supervise construction. However, an engineering company headquartered in Bombay, Humphreys and Glasgow, Pvt. Ltd., produced the detail drawings for the plant and served as general contractor. All the subcontractors were Indian firms.

Even before the MIC facility began operating, in 1980, problems began to crop up with the alpha-naphthol plant. The latter system continued in various stages of shutdown and partial operation through 1984, when the whole factory was closed permanently. V. P. Gokhale, managing director of UCIL, called the decision to make alpha-naphthol a "very large mistake." But he said the company was forced to do it to retain the operating license issued by the Indian government. The Bhopal factory was designed to produce 5,000 tons per year of Sevin but never operated near capacity; UCIL was generally the third largest producer of pesticides in India, sometimes slipping to number four.

Annual profits of several million dollars from the Bhopal operation were originally predicted by 1984. But that was not to be, for several reasons. First, an economic recession made farmers more cost conscious and caused them to search for less-expensive alternatives to Sevin. Second, a large number of small-scale producers were able to undersell the company, partly because they were exempt from excise and sales taxes. Seventeen of these firms bought MIC from UCIL and used it to make products virtually identical to Sevin and Temik. Finally, a new generation of low-cost pesticides was becoming available.

With sales collapsing, the Bhopal plant became a money loser in 1981. By late 1984, the yearly profit estimate had been adjusted downward to a $4 million *loss* based on 1,000 tons of output, one-fifth of capacity. To forestall what may have seemed inevitable economic failure, extensive cost-cutting was done. The staff at the MIC plant was cut from 12 operators on a shift to 6. The maintenance team was reduced in size. In a number of instances, faulty safety devices remained unrepaired for weeks. Though instrumentation technology

EXHIBIT 2 The UCIL Pesticide Factory at Bhopal

Administration building

Pesticide formulation plant

Storage

Methyl isocyanate-Sevin control room

Chlorine storage

Monomethylamine storage

Refrigeration unit

Methyl isocyanate storage tanks

Main evaporation pond

Railway

619

611

610

Vent gas scrubber furnace

Coal yard

Coal burner

Temik evaporation pond

Waste treatment area

Skimmer pit

Warehouse

Carbon Monoxide plant

Storage tank

Storage

Utilities office

Canteen

Sevin pesticide plant

Methyl isocyanate plant

Flare tower

Alpha-naphthol plant

Fire station

Quality control

Truck weighing station

Personnel

Shed

Fabrication and maintenance shop

Entrance

Entrance

Entrance

Medical and safety building

Office

Kali parade

Jai Prakash Nagar Shanties

N

283

EXHIBIT 3   The Methyl Isocyanate Manufacturing Process

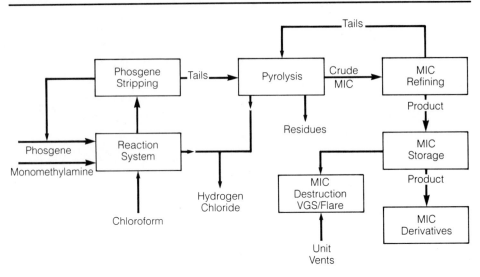

advanced at Union Carbide's other pesticide plants, the innovations were only partly adopted at Bhopal.

On the night of the disaster, five safety systems failed to work or were shut down. The flare tower, used for burning carbon monoxide, was inoperative because some of the corroded pipe needed replacing. UCC recommended maintaining MIC at temperatures below 5 degrees Celsius because it is an unstable liquid that reacts unpredictably to changes in temperature. But the refrigeration unit cooling the three MIC storage tanks had repeatedly malfunctioned and was shut down. A spare tank—designed to accept excess MIC in the event of an accident—already had one ton of liquid in it. The water curtain meant to douse leaking gas was functional on the night of the leak, but the water failed to reach the height at which the gas was escaping. Finally, the vent gas scrubber, which was designed to neutralize small leaks by flushing them with caustic soda, either could not cope with the large volume of escaping gas or, more probably, did not work at all.

The UCIL directors, like the UCC parent, disclaimed fault for the incident. The "Report of Directors," included in UCIL's 1984 annual report stated:

> At no time had any significant fault been found with the working or safety precautions taken by your company. Your company had taken all safety precautions to avoid any accident in the plant, which had been operated all along with trained and qualified operators.

In early 1985, the government of India canceled the operating license of the Bhopal plant, clearing the way for the plant's dismantlement. The like-

EXHIBIT 4   The Foreign Exchange Regulation Act

The Act was originally enacted as a temporary measure in 1947. It was made permanent in 1957, then revised in 1973. The Act covers various aspects of foreign exchange transactions, including money changing, buying or selling foreign exchange in India or abroad, having an account in a bank outside India, and remitting money abroad.

The purpose of the Act is to restrict outflow of foreign exchange and to conserve hard-currency holdings in India. One provision requires that any company in which the nonresident interest is more than 40 percent "shall not carry on in India or establish in India any branch or office without the special permission of the Reserve Bank of India." But the Reserve Bank of India has authority to exempt a company from the provisions of the Act. The 40 percent requirement was changed to 49 percent by Rajiv Gandhi's government.

High-technology companies are frequently exempted from the equity-ownership provisions of the Act. Other companies that have operated in India for many years are sometimes exempted if they agree not to expand their Indian operations.

Policies in India regarding nationalization of foreign-owned companies have varied. A number of major oil companies have been nationalized. For example, Indian Oil Corporation, Bharat Petroleum, and Hindustan Petroleum used to be, respectively, Burmah Shell, Mobil, and Stanvae (Standard Vacuum Oil Company, an Esso unit).

More typically, a multinational company is asked to reduce its holdings to 49 percent or less by offering shares to the Indian public and Indian financial institutions. Multinationals that have diluted equity to meet the 49 percent requirement include CIBA-GEIGY, Parke-Davis, Bayer (aspirin), Lever Brothers (which operates as Hindustan Lever in India), Lipton, and Brooke-Bond.

When Indira Gandhi was voted out of office in 1977, the Janata (Peoples') Party strengthened the Act. As a result, IBM and Coca-Cola pulled out of India. IBM's business in India was taken over by ICIM (International Computers Indian Manufacturers), a domestic firm. Another similar firm was set up to perform the maintenance services for the existing IBM computers.

---

lihood that this would happen provoked a Bhopal political leader to remark, "We've lost 2,000 lives, now must we lose 2,000 jobs?"

FINANCE

Exhibits 5 through 9 provide financial summaries for UCIL. Exhibit 6 gives selected comparative financial statistics for the United States and India. During the months before the Bhopal disaster, UCIL's common shares, listed on the Bombay stock exchange, hovered around Rs. 30. They dropped to a low of Rs. 15.8 on December 11, recovering only slightly in succeeding months. The shares would reach a high of Rs. 43 in January 1986 but then fall steadily to the mid teens by late 1987.

In 1975, the United States Export-Import Bank, in cooperation with First National Citibank of New York, agreed to grant loans of $2.5 million to buy equipment for the MIC project. Also, the Industrial Credit and Investment

EXHIBIT 5 Financial Statements (Rs. 000,000 except as noted)*

Balance Sheets

	1977	1978	1979	1980	1981	1982	1983	1984	1985	1986
Assets										
Cash	73	54	54	67	82	52	58	54	85	72
Sundry debtors	57	79	12	17	24	38	32	28	28	23
Inventory	190	232	293	312	349	377	369	400	419	463
Misc. CA	4	13	11	9	9	6	8	16	21	32
Total CA	324	378	480	557	704	811	750	746	802	793
P&E	518	539	493	592	603	695	722	775	569	582
Other FA	169	193	299	238	256	258	275	268	240	213
Accrued depreciation	331	363	391	425	465	503	531	579	489	504
Total FA	355	369	401	405	394	450	466	464	321	291
Subsidiaries	—	—	—	—	—	7	7	7	7	7
Intangible assets	3	3	3	3	3	3	3	3	3	3
Total assets	682	750	884	965	1,101	1,271	1,234	1,220	1,132	1,094
Claims										
Loans	117	114	120	143	142	218	54	28	11	3
Sundry creditors	106	119	154	158	208	232	218	203	219	209
Accrued taxes	13	19	50	60	63	58	52	45	37	33
Misc. CL	71	49	39	51	71	57	54	19	8	47
Total CL	308	301	363	412	485	565	378	294	275	292
Debentures	—	—	28	31	55	79	78	77	73	70
LT loans	26	33	46	40	34	31	158	163	98	34
Total LT Liability	26	33	75	72	89	130	236	240	171	104
Common Stock	184	217	217	326	326	326	326	326	326	326
Reserves	49	71	74	67	70	95	188	128	125	117
Free surplus	114	128	155	89	132	155	106	232	236	255
Total SH equity	348	416	446	482	528	575	620	686	687	698
Total claims	682	750	884	965	1,101	1,271	1,234	1,220	1,132	1,094

EXHIBIT 5 *(concluded)*

P&L Statements and Share Price Information

	1977	1978	1979	1980	1981	1982	1983	1984	1985	1986
Net sales	1,069	1,111	1,450	1,696	1,854	2,075	2,101	2,229	2,419	2,148
Stocks used	430	443	598	757	847	959	920	992	1,068	885
Wages and salaries	160	170	158	198	217	245	271	283	337	325
Manufacturing expenses	281	314	404	432	455	517	540	581	684	654
CGS	870	927	1,190	1,387	1,519	1,720	1,731	1,856	2,089	1,864
General expenses	77	55	84	103	116	137	135	129	198	153
Gross profit	121	130	176	206	220	218	235	244	132	132
Interest	26	15	19	31	31	57	63	53	35	28
Other expenses	5	10	14	24	27	27	24	12	24	26
PBT	69	91	138	161	175	147	148	153	65	90
Taxes	19	41	73	80	80	50	55	71	64	40
Net profit	50	50	65	81	95	97	93	82	1	50
Dividends	29	35	35	46	49	49	49	16	—	49
Figures below in rupees										
Share price-high	26.4	28.1	30.9	36.0	31.7	28.1	28.3	29.8	37.0	43.0
-low	18.6	19.7	25.5	22.0	24.9	23.3	21.5	18.5	17.1	20.0

* Column totals may not check and amounts less than 500,000 Rs. are shown as zero, due to rounding.

EXHIBIT 6 Comparative Financial Statistics for the U.S. and India

Year	U.S. Producer Price Index*	India Wholesale Price Index†	Conversion Rate‡
1974	161.1	169.2	8.111
1975	175.1	175.8	8.914
1976	183.6	172.4	8.985
1977	195.8	185.4	8.703
1978	197.1	185.0	8.189
1979	215.8	206.5	8.108
1980	244.5	248.1	7.872
1981	269.8	278.4	8.728
1982	280.7	288.7	9.492
1983	285.2	316.0	10.129
1984	291.1	338.4	11.402
1985	293.7	357.8	12.352
1986	289.7	376.8	12.680

* Wholesale Price Index before 1978. Arithmetic average of monthly figures. Base year, 1967.
† Arithmetic average of April–March monthly figures. Base year, 1970 (April 1970–March 1971).
‡ Arithmetic average of monthly figures (rupees per dollar).

Corporation of India (ICICI), a government agency, authorized a Rs. 21.5 million loan, part of which was drawn in 1980. Finally, long-term loans were provided by several Indian financial institutions and insurance companies. Some of these loans were guaranteed by the State Bank of India. UCC guaranteed none of the loans of UCIL.

Union Carbide Corporation stock was listed on the New York Stock Exchange. It was trading in the low fifties in the months before December 1984, having fallen back from its historical high of 74, reached in 1983. When news of Bhopal reached the United States the stock fell to the low thirties, to remain there until rumors of a takeover would propel it upward six months later.

THE GAF RAID

GAF Corporation increased its holdings of UCC stock in 1985 and announced a takeover effort. The two companies had markedly different corporate cultures. GAF had a reputation for legal toughness, if not ruthlessness, having been successfully involved in massive toxic tort litigation (related to asbestos) for decades. GAF chairman Samuel J. Heyman, an attorney, had muscled his way into control of the company in a bitter proxy fight in 1983. *The Wall Street Journal* reported a widespread belief that Heyman was likely to fire all the top managers of UCC if he ever gained control.

In contrast to what might have been expected from GAF, UCC chairman Warren Anderson had expressed extreme sympathy for the victims of Bhopal and had even gone there to try to help. Though most of his attempts at providing financial and medical aid were rebuffed, he continued to assume major responsibility for the incident, saying it would be his main concern for the rest of his working life. Anderson also admitted the MIC plant should not have been operating in its condition at the time, one of several statements he made which later complicated his company's legal defenses.

Union Carbide managers rushed to erect takeover barriers and took actions to make the company less desirable as a merger candidate. Golden parachutes worth at least $8.8 million were set up for 42 of the executives. Two separately incorporated divisions were set up, one for chemicals and plastics and the other for everything else. Various assets were written down by nearly $1 billion. The employee retirement plan was amended to free the $500 million surplus in the pension fund "for general corporate purposes." Union Carbide repurchased 56 percent of its outstanding common stock, issuing $2.52 billion in high-interest (average 14.2 percent) debt in the transaction.

The Wall Street Journal later reported 3.2 million of the shares were purchased in a private deal with Ivan Boesky. Boesky's UCC machinations figured prominently in his subsequent conviction for various securities violations. GAF, too, was later charged with stock manipulation and other offenses growing out of its efforts to take over UCC and, having failed in that, to profit from the adventure. Boyd Jeffries, also later convicted of stock manipulation, was involved in the alleged GAF crimes.

After the takeover attempt was thwarted, much of the UCC debt was repaid. Money for the repayment came from two major sources. First, the sale of Union Carbide's agricultural products and electrical carbon units and the sale and leaseback of the Danbury, Connecticut, headquarters building provided $875 million. Second, 30 million new common shares were sold for an additional $651 million. Within months Union Carbide stock recovered to predisaster levels. After a three-for-one split in 1986 the shares continued to climb, reaching the high twenties (low eighties corrected for the split) by early 1989.

PERSONNEL

Until 1982, a cadre of American managers and technicians worked at the Bhopal factory. The Americans were licensed by the Indian government for fixed periods of time. While in India they were expected to train Indian replacements. From 1982 onward, no American worked at Bhopal. Although major decisions, such as approval of the annual budget, were cleared with the U.S. parent, day-to-day details such as staffing and maintenance were left to the Indian officials.

In general, the engineers at the Bhopal plant were among India's elite. Most new engineers were recruited from the prestigious India Institutes of

EXHIBIT 7   Summary of Balance Sheets (as of December 25)

	1984 Rs. lakhs*		1983 Rs. lakhs		1982 Rs. lakhs	
Funds employed						
Fixed assets:						
Goodwill at cost	30.00		30.00		30.00	
Fixed assets	44,18.59†		41,07.55		40,51.60	
Capital expenditure in						
progress	2,23.36	46,71.95	5,50.51	46,88.06	4,43.86	45,25.46
Investments		1,37.48		92.37		96.52
Current assets:						
Stores and spares at						
cost	7,32.53		6,86.16		6,40.67	
Stocks	32,63.68		30,05.56		31,32.50	
Sundry debtors	16,27.25		23,93.25		30,00.83	
Cash and bank						
balances	5,38.88		4,23.79		5,22.05	
Loans and advances . . .	12,23.91		8,87.32		7,87.21	
Interest accrued on						
investments	0.03		0.25		0.25	
Subtotal	73,86.28		73,96.33		80,83.51	
Less: Current						
liabilities	20,53.60		21,34.92		23,36.49	
Less: Provisions	6,10.68		10,07.14		10,71.12	
Subtotal	26,64.28		31,42.06		34,07.61	
Net current assets		47,22.00		47,54.27		46,75.90
Total		95,31.43		90,34.70		92,97.88
Financed by						
Share capital and reserves:						
Share capital—issued						
and subscribed	32,58.30		32,58.30		32,58.30	
Reserves and surplus . .	35,97.32	68,55.62	29,38.97	61,97.27	24,95.43	57,53.73
Loan capital:						
Secured loans	13,53.56		14,33.75		22,32.15	
Unsecured loans	13,22.25	26,75.81	14,03.68	28,37.43	13,12.00	35,44.15
Total		95,31.43		90,34.70		92,97.88

* 1 lakh = 100,000.
† Placement of commas in numbers differs from American practice.

Technology and were paid wages comparable with the best offered in Indian industry. Successful applicants were given two years of training before being certified for unsupervised duty.

Until the late 1970s only first-class science graduates or persons with

EXHIBIT 8 Summary of Common Stock Issues

| Year | Paid-up Common Stock | | Remarks |
	Number of Shares	Total Amount (Rs. 000)	
1959–1960	2,800,000	28,000	800,000 right shares issued, premium Rs. 2.50 per share, proportion 2:5.
1964 ·	3,640,000	36,400	840,000 right shares issued, premium of Rs. 4 per share, proportion 3:10.
1965	4,095,000	40,950	455,000 bonus shares issued, proportion 1:8.
1968	8,190,000	81,900	2,047,500 right shares issued at par, proportion 1:2; 2,047,500 bonus shares issued, proportion 1:2.
1970	12,285,000	122,850	4,095,000 bonus shares issued, proportion 1:2.
1974	18,427,500	184,275	6,142,500 bonus shares issued, proportion 1:2.
1978	21,722,000	217,220	3,294,500 shares issued, premium Rs. 6 per share, to resident Indian shareholders, the company's employees, and financial institutions.
1980	32,583,000	325,830	10,861,000 bonus shares issued, proportion 1:2.

diplomas in engineering were hired as operators at Bhopal. New employees were given six months of theoretical instruction followed by on-the-job training. As cost-cutting efforts proceeded in the 1980s, standards were lowered significantly. Some persons with only a high school diploma were hired, and training was said to be less rigorous than before. In addition, the number of operators on a shift was reduced by about half, and many supervisory positions were eliminated.

The Indian managers developed strong ties with the local political establishment. A former police chief became the plant's security contractor. A local political party boss got the job as company lawyer. *Newsweek* reported that a luxurious guest house was maintained by UCIL, and lavish parties were thrown there for local dignitaries.

In general, wages at the Bhopal factory were well above those in domestic firms. A janitor, for example, earned Rs. 1,000 per month, compared to less than Rs. 500 elsewhere. Still, as prospects continued downward after 1981, a number of senior managers and the best among the plant's junior executives began to abandon ship. The total work force at the plant dropped from a high of about 1,500 to about 650. This reduction was accomplished through voluntary departures rather than layoffs. An Indian familiar with operations at Bhopal said,

> The really competent and well-trained employees, especially managers and supervisors, got sick of the falling standards and indifferent management and many of them quit despite high salaries at UCIL. Replacements were made on an 'ad hoc basis. Even guys from the consumer-products division, who only knew how to make batteries, were drafted to run the pesticide plant.

In May 1982, a team from UCC headquarters audited the safety status of the MIC plant. The team listed as many as 10 major deficiencies in the safety procedures that the plant followed. The high turnover in plant personnel was noted and commented upon. Still, the team declared it had been impressed with the operating and maintenance procedures.

MARKETING

The population of India is over 700 million persons, although its land area is only about one third that of the United States. Three fourths of India's people depend on agriculture for a livelihood. Only about one third of the population is literate. Modern communications and transportation systems connect the major cities, but the hundreds of villages are largely untouched by 20th-century technology.

English is at least a second tongue for most Indian professionals but not for ordinary Indians. There are 16 officially recognized languages in the country. The national language is Hindi, which is dominant in 5 of India's 25 states. The working classes speak hundreds of dialects, often unintelligible to neighbors just miles away.

India's farmers offer at best a challenging target market. They generally eke out a living from small tracts of land. Most have little more than subsistence incomes and are reluctant to invest what they have in such modern innovations as pesticides. They are generally ignorant of the right methods of application and, given their linguistic diversity and technological isolation, are quite hard to educate. To advertise its pesticides, UCIL had used billboards and wall posters as well as newspaper and radio advertisements.

Radio is the most widely used advertising medium in India. The state-owned radio system includes broadcasts in local languages as well as in Hindi. Companies can buy advertising time on the stations, but it is costly to produce commercials in so many dialects. Much of the state-sponsored programming, especially in rural areas, is devoted to promoting agriculture and instructing farmers about new techniques. Often the narrators mention products such as Sevin and Temik by name.

Movies provide another popular promotional tool. Most small towns have one or more cinema houses, and rural people often travel to town to watch the

EXHIBIT 9 UCIL Financial Charts

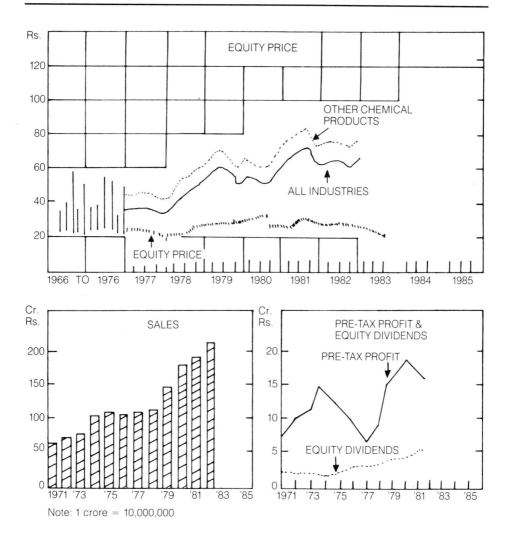

Note: 1 crore = 10,000,000

shows. Advertisements appear before and after main features and are usually produced in regional languages (though not in local dialects).

Until the 1980s, television was available only in the cities. During 1984, a government program spread TV relay stations at the rate of more than one each day, with the result that 80 percent of the population was within the range of a television transmitter by the end of the year. Still, few rural citizens had ready access to television receivers.

Pesticide sales are highly dependent on agricultural activity from year to year. In times of drought, like 1980 and 1982, UCIL's pesticide sales suffered severe setbacks. In 1981, abundant rains helped spur pesticide sales.

EXHIBIT 10   Map of India

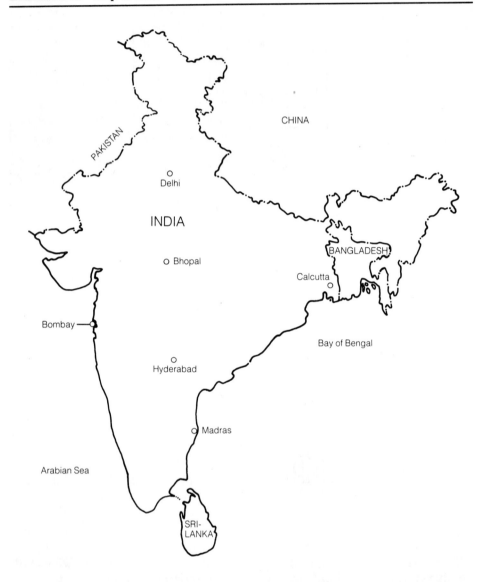

Exhibit 10 is a map of India. India has a very extensive network of railways; the total track mileage is second only to that of the USSR. The road and highway system crisscrosses the areas in between the railway lines. The railway system was especially significant to UCIL's pesticide operation because Bhopal lies near the junction of the main east-west and north-south tracks in India. An Indian familiar with the agricultural economy remarked, "Overall, physical distribution of pesticides is not too monumental a task. Getting farmers to use them and teaching them how are the real problems."

The marketing division for agricultural products was headquartered in Hyderabad, in southern India. Eight branch offices were scattered all over the country. Sales were made through a network of distributors, wholesalers, and retailers. Representatives from the branch offices booked orders from the distributors and wholesalers. Retailers got their requirements from wholesalers, who, in turn, were supplied by distributors. The distributors got their stocks from the branch offices. The branch office "godowns" (warehouses) were supplied directly from the Bhopal plant. The retailers' margin was 15 percent. Wholesalers and distributors each received about 5 percent. Most of the retailers were family or individually owned, although some of UCIL's pesticides were sold through government agricultural sales offices.

THE LEGAL BATTLE

After the Bhopal tragedy UCC and UCIL executives were charged with manslaughter and other crimes. UCC chairman Anderson, along with the head of UCIL, was briefly detained by Indian officials when he went to India shortly after the incident. Still, both companies continued for months to enjoy good relations with the Indian government. This may have been true in part because many leading Indian citizens and institutions had financial interests in UCIL. And, except for the Bhopal incident, Union Carbide had an excellent safety record in India.

Anderson said, "The name of the game is not to nail me to the wall but to provide for the victims of the disaster." He volunteered UCC to help provide funding for a hospital to treat the Bhopal victims. The company contributed $1 million to a victims' relief fund. It and UCIL set aside $20 million for relief payments. Though Anderson said the offer was unconditional, the Indian government spurned it. Anderson would retire in 1986 with $1.3 million in severance pay plus retirement and other benefits—but the gas victims would still remain essentially uncompensated.

UCIL offered to build a new plant, one that would use nontoxic inputs, on the Bhopal site. One proposal was for a nonhazardous formulation plant to be constructed by UCIL and operated by the state government. Alternatively, UCIL suggested a battery factory it would own and operate. Both ideas were turned down by the Indian government.

Within months after the incident, UCC faced lawsuits in amounts far exceeding its net worth. A dozen or more American attorneys signed up thousands of Bhopal victims and their relatives and filed suits in U.S. courts purporting to represent them. For example, famed attorney Melvin Belli brought suit for $15 billion. The Attorney General of India was authorized by his government to sue Union Carbide in an American court. He stated that compensation had to be in accordance with American standards. A Minneapolis law firm that specialized in product liability cases was retained to represent India.

The government of India issued an ordinance declaring itself the sole representative of the gas victims. In February 1985, a judicial panel in the

United States ordered 18 lawsuits pending in different courts consolidated in a single court—that of Judge John F. Keenan in Manhattan. The Indian government continued to press its lawsuit and also engaged in out-of-court negotiations with Union Carbide.

In its statement before Judge Keenan, the Government of India argued,

> Key management personnel of multinationals exercise a closely held power which is neither restricted by national boundaries nor effectively controlled by international law. The complex corporate structure of the multinational, with networks of subsidiaries and divisions, makes it exceedingly difficult or even impossible to pinpoint responsibility for the damage caused by the enterprise to discrete corporate units or individuals. Persons harmed by the acts of a multinational corporation are not in a position to isolate which unit of the enterprise caused the harm, yet it is evident that the multinational enterprise that caused the harm is liable for such harm.

As UCC struggled to recover from the disaster and restore its public image, three events thrust the company back to the forefront of international news coverage. First, in June 1985 hundreds of persons were poisoned, although not fatally, by California watermelons grown on soil to which the Union Carbide pesticide Temik had been applied (improperly applied, according to the company). Second, in August a leak of the chemical intermediate aldecarb oxime at the company's Institute, West Virginia, plant, the only U.S. facility to make MIC, sent 135 people to hospitals. West Virginia governor Arch Moore publicly criticized Union Carbide's handling of the incident and Anderson admitted the company had waited too long to warn residents. Third, a few days later another accidental discharge of chemicals at a Union Carbide plant just miles from the Institute facility caused a public health scare.

In May 1986 Judge Keenan accepted Union Carbide's plea of *forum non-conveniens*—ruling that the United States was not the appropriate place for the legal battle because most of the documents, litigants, evidence, and witnesses were in India. While victims' representatives generally expressed dismay at the decision, Union Carbide had reason to welcome it. Both the Indian and the U.S. legal systems are based on English common law. But punitive damages are almost unheard of in Indian courts and compensatory damage awards are generally much lower than in the United States. Also, the Indian judicial system is usually much slower, which could be considered either a benefit or a detriment.

In October 1986 the trial resumed in Bhopal. UCC attorneys denounced the central and state governments in India for their alleged liability for the disaster. The company's affidavit denied every charge leveled against UCC. It claimed the factory was run by UCIL and pointed out that no U.S. citizen had been employed there for two years before the disaster. UCC also stated that sabotage was responsible for the disaster and alleged that there was a conspiracy between UCIL employees and government investigators to conceal evidence after the incident. The Indian government expressed outrage at Union Carbide's position and set its damage claim at $3.1 billion.

The hearings continued concurrently with out-of-court negotiations. As 1987 drew to an end, there were rumors of a settlement. Union Carbide offered $500 million in payments over time (then present value, about $350 million). Each dependent of the 2,600 Union Carbide said were killed in the incident was to receive $2,000 a year for ten years. The chronically ill would get $1,000 annually for the same period. And those slightly injured would be given a single payment of $500. The Indian government offered to settle for $615 million in cash. When news of a possible settlement leaked out, there was a furious public outcry in India. Former Indian Supreme Court Chief Justice P. N. Bhagwati demanded that any settlement include an admission of guilt by Union Carbide.

As the settlement talks appeared to break down in January 1988, Judge M. V. Deo ordered UCC to pay $270 million in interim compensation to the gas victims. Union Carbide filed an appeal of the order, calling the idea of interim damages—before a defendant was found to owe anything at all—"unprecedented." The company continued to assert that it was confident of proving that the disaster was the result of sabotage and that it could not be held accountable in any case for the acts or omissions of UCIL, in which it claimed to only own stock.

THE SETTLEMENT

In 1987, Robert D. Kennedy, who succeeded Anderson as CEO of UCC, wrote,

> We are still committed to the idea that a just, reasonable settlement is what the victims need, and that no one is served by a prolonged legal battle. But, unfortunately, Indian authorities seem intent on continuing the litigation. Our attorneys will act accordingly.

True to his word, Kennedy continued to exercise what *The Wall Street Journal* called "fierce resolve." Altogether, UCC spent over $24 million in legal and investigative costs on the case.

Suddenly, UCC's legal odyssey ended. On Tuesday, February 14, 1989, company lawyers were presenting arguments before the Indian Supreme Court in the company's appeal of the lower court order to pay interim damages. Chief Justice R. S. Pathak interrupted the proceeding and issued an order that UCC pay $470 million by March 31 "in full and final settlement of all claims, rights and liabilities related to and arising out of the Bhopal gas disaster." Acceptance of the order had been unanimously approved by the UCC directors in a telephone poll hours earlier. The order consolidated all criminal and civil matters related to the Bhopal tragedy in the supreme court and thus was hailed as a complete settlement of the case.

UCC had previously set aside $250 million for damages and the company's insurance coverage was estimated at another $200 million. So paying the settlement would only result in an estimated $0.50 per share charge against 1988 earnings of $1.59 per share. UCC stock rose $2 a share on Tuesday and another $1.38 Wednesday, to close at $32.50, more than double the price (corrected for the three-for-one split) before the Bhopal tragedy. UCC was immediately touted as a prime takeover candidate, with an expected purchase price of about $50 a share, or $7 billion.

There was evidence some knew of the approaching settlement. A week before it was ordered, UCC stock had jumped $2 a share on volume totaling over 8 percent of all outstanding shares. That was the highest volume for any NYSE stock in five months.

It was uncertain how and when the settlement money would be distributed to victims—or even how much of it would be. Bruce A. Finzen, one of the Indian government's U.S. lawyers, said, "Even at the rate of one hour per claim, you are talking about years of court time." The Indian government had already paid some survivors $800 or so for each immediate family member who perished. Medical care and certain other benefits had also been furnished by the government.

There were immediate objections to the amount of damages and the nature of the settlement. An Associated Press report the day after the settlement was ordered said a crowd of 200 women gathered outside government buildings in Bhopal and chanted, "We want justice." Many Indians had already made it clear admission of guilt by UCC and retribution against the persons involved was more important to them than were money damages. And Indian Supreme Court lawyer Gobinda Mukhoty complained about the court's failure to "lay down guidelines." He remarked, "The court could have given an authoritative, historical judgment."

On the other hand, Kennedy called the settlement "a fair resolution of all issues." And UCC attorney Bud Holman said the negotiations were like "walking up a winding staircase in total darkness," adding "It's nice to be in the light."

APPENDIX A: EXCERPTS FROM INTERVIEWS

Gas victims and government officials in the Bhopal area were questioned in early 1987 concerning the gas incident. Excerpts from interviewee comments are presented below.

Description of the incident?

> A very thick layer of smoke caused uncontrollable tears, copious coughing, sneezing, vomiting. We ran to save our lives. We saw people in large numbers running here and there in great confusion, crushing each other, not bothering about anyone else.

> I felt chilled and soon could not see.

> I felt my eyes burning, like smoke coming from burning chilies. I was gasping for a breath of fresh air. I saw my neighbors in the same condition. A thin smoky layer was visible but its source was not known. Soon I was coughing and water was coming from my eyes and I fell unconscious.

At first I did not know what was happening because all my systems were affected. I was vomiting. My stomach was dislocated. My muscles were loose. Everyone was gasping for breath, running without any direction to find a safe place. Some of them demanded death as if it was readily available at a grocery shop.

Aftereffects?

I still do not know how bad it will get. It has become difficult to tolerate anything that is going wrong. I cannot remember like before.

I have become weak in body and mind. My memory has been affected badly. Carrying even small loads and fast walking has become a dream to me. I feel like an asthmatic patient.

The effect has subsided. But the resistance of the body is still down. My body has become allergic to muddy areas. The cough remains permanent and breathlessness occurs sometime.

Asthmatic, decreased vision, awfully unpredictable and irritable temper—future unknown, uncertain.

Loss in appetite, loss in weight, breathing trouble, uneasiness, poor eyesight, and weak memory power.

I cannot walk quickly and cannot run.

Assistance provided?

A mere Rs. 1,500 has been provided as compensation and that is only to those whose income is below Rs. 500 a year. So we have not got any assistance so far from anyone.

Symptomatic treatment is being given without knowing the cause and the disease. This should stop.

None.

After three days I was treated at the hospital with antibiotics. But there was no definite diagnosis or treatment.

So far, nil. The policies made by the local government are unbelievable. They pay by economic and social status.

For us railway officers and our families nobody has done anything.

What should be done?

The M.P. [Madhya Pradesh, the state where Bhopal is located] government with the cooperation of the government of India and aided by Union Carbide or the American government should start a fully equipped hospital basically concerned with lungs and eyes. Provision of work, housing, and education should be made.

Government should give proper treatment to the gas affected. They should rehabilitate those who lost their earner. They should stop a recurrence.

Next of kin of the deceased should be given sufficient money by UCIL. All affected people should be given suitable jobs by government. Proper treatment should be given by government out of fines imposed on Union Carbide because they have failed to give a safe design of the project and neglected all safety measures in the factory.

The affected people should be provided with good food to recoup their body. All over the world the Madhya Pradesh government has received donations for this so it must be utilized properly.

Nothing can be done now since everything is over.

Government should arrange to shift the factory to somewhere away from the town area.

The society at large, the government, and above all UCIL itself should have honorably taken to itself to soothe the sufferers. Their needs for the balance of their life span should be given gratis to them.

The government of India should pay compensation as applicable throughout the world. We are Indian nationals and all our interests are to be protected by the elected government.

What is likely to be done?

I am quite in the dark and disappointed.

It appears no one is serious to do much.

Considering the indifferent attitude of the Indian government, we are forced to compromise with our miserable lives. If anything concrete is done, it will be done only by UCIL.

Well, I wonder if anything is in store, the way it has fallen out.

Victims will be compensated and plants like this will be moved to remote places by government.

I am confident the government of India will pay compensation to all real sufferers.

Nothing.

Mostly non-affected persons and unemployed illiterate people, who chase the surveyors, get compensated.

Message for U.S. Business School Students?

Press your government not to allow multinationals like Union Carbide to operate anywhere in the world since they play with the life of people to enrich themselves.

More was expected and much better from the advanced elite in the community of nations. There is nothing but delay, tossing it from one door to another and from one country to another. It is a disgrace of the basest order to have left it to an indefinite body to compensate the sufferers, even if it was an additional burden. How can the most advanced society tolerate it?

The advanced nation like America while making any investment in developing countries should themselves ensure that all safety precautions are taken—before installing their factories. When they have already made this mistake at Bhopal, they should pressure their government and the management of Union Carbide to pay compensation without hesitation.

There is no question of talking to any other country. There is nothing to say but to blame the local administration for not arranging in a proper, methodic way in this modern world.

Multinational companies are playing with the lives of people and their property for the self-interest of earning money at any cost and by any means.

CASE

United Brands

Harvey Johnson, vice president in charge of banana operations for United Brands, looked back over the most incredible week of his business career. It was August 1974, and the company had been in the fourth month of the so-called Banana War with several of the Central American republics where United Brands grew its popular Chiquita brand bananas.

The "war" had started when Honduras, the country that supplied about 35 percent of the company's bananas, had instituted a tax of 50 cents on each 40-pound box of bananas. By the beginning of the current month, Panama and Costa Rica had also levied taxes so that the company was currently paying an average of 37 cents a box on all bananas exported from Central America. Clearly, these countries had learned some lessons from the oil-producing countries, and their policies were reflected in higher costs to the company and, ultimately, higher prices to American consumers.

Then, in the early part of the week, Mr. Johnson had been approached in Miami by the Honduran minister of the economy, Abraham Bennaton, who indicated that the tax could be rolled back if the company were willing to make a substantial payment to Honduran officials.[1] Mr. Johnson was stunned. Honduras instigated the tax; a Honduran recision would probably undermine the entire cartel. In cold economic terms, the figure mentioned—$5 million over a period of time—was a bargain. It would save the company about $7.5 million in the first year, and would probably discourage taxes in future years as well as destroy the current cartel. To Mr. Johnson, the idea of a bribe to influence government policy was unacceptable, but it was clear that Mr. Bennaton's offer would have to be reported to higher management.

Because of the magnitude of the decision involved, Mr. Johnson took the matter up directly with Eli Black, the chief executive officer of United Brands, the following day. Mr. Black rejected the demand but asked Johnson to report the offer to John Taylor. Mr. Taylor, a United Brands senior vice president, was Mr. Johnson's immediate superior.

Mr. Johnson had reason to feel that he had handled the situation quite well. He had discharged his responsibility to report the offer and the matter

---

[1] This portrayal is not intended to be a precise reflection of either the thinking or behavior of the parties involved.

was closed. He then thought about how different the outcome was from the probable workings of the old United Fruit Company, the corporation from which United Brands had sprung.

THE UNITED FRUIT COMPANY

The United Fruit Company was incorporated in 1899 and shortly thereafter bought out a number of other fruit companies whose holdings were in Central America. The Central American republics at the time were poor, weak, and governed by a few powerful families whose interest in the general welfare was minimal.

United Fruit entered the Central American countries with offers of capital benefits such as seaports, railroads, utilities, and schools in exchange for the sale or use of government land on which to grow bananas. The governments also received a one-cent-per-bunch export tax. At the time, bananas were considered a luxury fruit in the United States and Europe, because the short six-week life of the fruit after picking meant that shipment delays or inefficiencies would lead to rotten cargo. The company soon established that it was tough enough to fight back with either *la mordita* (the bribe) or physical force when its marketing timetables were threatened.[2] At the beginning of World War I, the United Fruit Company was the most powerful single force in Central America and gave the countries the nickname of "banana republics."

After World War I, the nations became very aware of the value of the concessions they had given United Fruit, and some terms were renegotiated. Nevertheless, the governments were deeply in debt and still borrowed money from United Fruit. It was claimed that government appointments were cleared through the company and that unfriendly heads of state could be removed with a phone call from United Fruit.[3] The depression period brought diseases that destroyed many plantations, but United Fruit continued its investments and social services in Central America, and brought in new, spoil-resistant and bruise-resistant varieties of bananas that were easier to harvest.

By the end of World War II, most Latin American workers had become skilled and literate. Many were operators of complex machinery. Some filled managerial positions. The standard of living was relatively high, and the banana republics bought goods and services on the world market with American currency. Still, there was pressure for local ownership of land and facilities, and for freedom from perceived foreign domination.

In response to this pressure, United Fruit developed an Associate Producer Program in the early 1960s. Company land was turned over to local growers while the company supervised cultivation and purchased bananas

---

[2] H. J. Maidenberg, "New Rules, Harsh Life in Bananas," *New York Times*, May 11, 1975, pp. 3-1, 3-9.

[3] Ibid., pp. 3-1.

from the growers. By the late 1960s, almost half of the bananas were grown under this program, but problems had arisen. Local producers had allowed working, health, and social conditions to deteriorate, unions found organization more difficult with the larger number of owners, and company qualilty standards were harder to enforce.

By this time, United Fruit had branched out into other types of operations. It acquired some petroleum and natural gas facilities in the 1950s; a Belgian fresh produce distributor in 1962; A&W Drive-Ins of Canada, Ltd., in 1966; and Baskin-Robbins, Inc., in 1967. Still, about 64 percent of corporate sales were from banana operations.

In spite of problems with the Associate Producer Program the company's overall financial position was quite strong, with some $100 million in liquid assets and no debts. While management deliberated over how to solve operational problems, they learned that controlling interest in the company had been purchased on September 24, 1968, by Eli M. Black.[4]

ELI BLACK

Eli Black was a 48-year-old former rabbi who had grown up in a poor family on Manhattan's Lower East Side. His family included 10 generations of rabbis and scholars, and he was graduated from Yeshiva University in 1940, then served a Long Island congregation for four years.

He left his congregation because he felt his ministry was not fulfilling and that his sermons had little effect on people's lives.[5] He initially joined Lehman Brothers investment house and then American Securities Corporation, where part of his responsibilities involved handling the financing for American Seal-Kap Corporation, a moderate-sized producer of milk bottle caps.

In 1954, Mr. Black became chairman and chief executive officer of American Seal-Kap Corporation. He dropped unprofitable lines, bought out other concerns, employed the corporation's funds to the fullest extent, and in 1965 renamed it AMK Corporation.

In late 1966, AMK acquired one third of John Morrell & Company, a large meat-packer in Chicago that was 20 times AMK's size. This move confirmed Mr. Black's unique ability of "uncovering value on a large scale, getting control of it, and putting it to work uncovering more assets."[6] AMK acquired the rest of John Morell & Company on the final day of 1967.

The bespectacled Mr. Black was characterized by associates as a reserved, serious, formal man who smiled frequently but seldom laughed. He main-

---

[4] "Majority" interest in a corporation is 51 percent. "Controlling" interest in a widely held firm is generally regarded as between 5 and 10 percent, since it is nearly impossible to join shareholders together who hold more than these percentages. Eli Black's AMK Corporation had purchased about 9 percent on September 24.

[5] *The Wall Street Journal,* February 14, 1975, p. 15.

[6] "United Fruit's Shotgun Marriage," *Fortune* 79, no. 4 (April 1969), p. 122.

tained tight personal control of his businesses and "wasn't comfortable with people who disagreed with his views."[7] He participated in no sports and rarely took nonbusiness vacations.

Mr. Black's hobby *was* his business, but he tried to blend it with his strong concern for social causes. His son Leon once said that his father believed that "a man's reach must extend beyond his grasp,"[8] and that he took other people's problems on as if they were his own. He was intimately involved in the economic condition of the state of Israel (as a director for PEC Israel Economics Company) and in the economic condition of the United States. Later he would send a detailed plan for steering the United States through the energy shortage to his friend, Sen. Abraham Ribicoff of Connecticut. He was confident that he could solve social problems because "he was used to being able, by the force of his intellect, to get through problems to solve them."[9]

UNITED BRANDS UNDER ELI BLACK

On February 13, 1969, Eli Black became a director of United Fruit and later that year his AMK Corporation acquired a majority interest. In June of 1970, AMK Corporation voted to merge with United Fruit, and United Brands was born.

At about the same time, the corporation began modernizing its more outdated banana installations and turned some of them over to local management. In 1970, Mr. Black personally negotiated with Cesar Chavez's United Farm Workers Union on behalf of the company's lettuce subsidiary, making United Brands the first and only major lettuce grower to sign with the union until 1975. At the signing of the contract, Mr. Black invited Mr. Chavez to his Rosh Hashanah services where Mr. Chavez read a prayer. A friend of Mr. Black said, "You should have seen it. It was something you could point out to your kids and say, 'See, business and social conscience do mix.'"[10]

This was only one example of Mr. Black's actions on social responsiveness. A portion of the *1972 Annual Report* of United Brands Company showed the depth of concern the company had developed under Mr. Black.

> Every public company has more than one constituency. Its management must answer to the shareholders, but it must also be responsive to the needs of its markets, the aspirations of its employees, and the interests of the general public. The larger the scope of the company, the more numerous those constituencies can become. In the case of an organization with the geographically widespread and varied business interests of United Brands, they can embrace a significant portion of the world.

---

[7] Mary Bralove, *The Wall Street Journal,* May 7, 1975, p. 26.
[8] *The Wall Street Journal,* February 14, 1975, p. 1.
[9] Ibid., p. 1.
[10] Ibid., p. 15.

We have very real responsibilities in each of those areas. They demand more than words; they demand substance. Companies can no longer deal with their responsibilities at the level of appearances only; they can no longer be satisfied with the treatment of effects. We must concern ourselves with causes and United Brands does.

It is because of the successful application of these principles that the *Chicago Daily News* in a story on the company last year reported, "It may well be the most socially conscious American company in the hemisphere." The company's social policies and practices have also led *The New York Times* to report in a recent front page story, "What emerges from talks with labor, management and government is a picture of a company that anticipated the changes that have swept Latin America and has quietly set about adjusting to them."

Judgments like these have been earned. They reflect substantial, long-term commitments which United Brands has made to all of the people to whom the company is responsible. In some instances, this has meant the deliberate evolution away from traditional policies and practices. And in others, it has entailed creative vigilance to unexpected needs which the company is equipped to answer.

The most recent example of this kind of responsiveness was provided by the tragedy which took place during Christmas week in Nicaragua. . . . countless thousands of men, women, and children were killed. . . . Thousands more were injured and made homeless. It was one of the most destructive earthquakes in Central American history. Within hours, your company—itself no stranger to various kinds of devastation by nature—had begun to respond.

Because one of the first requirements in dealing effectively with disaster is communication, we immediately reopened the Managua office of TRT, United Brands tropical telecommunications subsidiary. TRT remained on the air around the clock for the next several days, providing critical information on the extent of the disaster for the guidance of relief efforts, and informing concerned families and friends of the whereabouts and condition of individuals known to have been in the area at the time of the disaster. During the first frightening hours, TRT provided the only communications link between the stricken city and the outside world.

We offered the full help of our company and its personnel to the Nicaraguan government, and we began to lay out a plan of assistance. On Christmas Day we began the organization of what may be the most comprehensive relief program ever mounted by a private corporation on behalf of the people of another land. NEED, the Nicaraguan Earthquake Emergency Drive, was created by the company and officially registered later that week as a nonprofit corporation and staffed by volunteers from United Brands. . . . Thousands of dollars in contributions poured into NEED from every corner of the country. The advertisements and other announcements pledged that every cent collected will be used to aid the victims of the Managua disaster.

This is only one example of how the company discharges its obligation. The real significance of NEED is the accurate reflection it provides of a far-reaching corporate policy commitment: "to carefully examine all dimensions of our operating practices and management decisions and to measure them against their potential impact . . . on the environment, on the cultural and social climates in which we operate, on our collective consciences, and on the quality of our lives."[11]

---

[11] United Brands, *1972 Annual Report*, pp. 38–39.

Mr. Black continued to buy and sell major concerns in the 1970s. The company's Guatemala operations were sold to Del Monte in 1972. In 1973, the majority interest in Baskin-Robbins was sold as United Brands began acquiring the Foster Grant Company, a producer of sunglasses and other high-quality plastics.

Banana operations, which in 1972 had contributed about 85 percent to operating income for the corporation, began to falter in 1973 (see financial statements, Exhibits 1, 2, and 3). That year a violent windstorm had hurt production in Honduras, which had provided over one quarter of United Brand's supply. The following year, the company increased its Honduran exports, but competitors also raised shipments to the United States. Their actions resulted in a tremendous oversupply of bananas and a severe depression of prices.

At this time, seven banana republics formed a Union of Banana Exporting Countries (UBEC) and presented a plan that called for a tax of $1 per 40-pound box of bananas exported. The countries involved claimed that UBEC was necessary to offset increasing fuel costs generated in part by the Organization of Petroleum Exporting Countries (OPEC). The "Banana War" was on.

Honduras enacted a 50-cent tax per 40-pound box in April 1974, which was to begin in June. In August, with a Panamanian tax of $1 per box, a Costa Rican tax of 25 cents per box, and the Honduran tax in effect, Mr. Black wrote to shareholders that the company realized the various republics' needs for additional revenue, and said that he intended to negotiate a reasonable formula with the countries involved.

Later that month, United Brands announced it had reached an understanding with the Republic of Honduras for a tax of 25 cents per box with gradual increases beginning in 1975 depending in part on the banana market at the time.[12] In mid-September, Hurricane Fifi struck Honduras and destroyed about 70 percent of United Brands' plantations there. The $20 million loss suffered by United Brands was greater than the value of corporate net income for the previous four years. The stock price, which a year earlier had been $12 a share, dropped to $4. Faced with a third-quarter loss of $40.2 million, Mr. Black began to make arrangements to sell the company's interest in Foster Grant, an acquisition which he had called "the crown jewel of our company."[13]

While heading these negotiations, Mr. Black sent Edward Gelsthorpe to Panama to work out tax and property agreements there. Mr. Gelsthorpe had joined United Brands as senior vice president of marketing in July 1974, and his joining was what Mr. Black called "a major coup." Mr. Gelsthorpe had previously been president of Ocean Spray Cranberries, Hunt-Wesson Foods, and Gillette, all in a period of five years. After a brief period of mutual

---

[12] *The Wall Street Journal,* May 7, 1975, p. 1.
[13] "United Brands Trades More Assets for Cash," *Business Week,* January 13, 1975, p. 35.

EXHIBIT 1

UNITED BRANDS AND SUBSIDIARY COMPANIES
10 Year Summary of Operations
For Year Ended December 31
(in thousands of dollars except per share amounts)

	1975†	1974*†	1973*	1972*	1971*	1970‡	1969‡	1968‡	1967‡	1966‡
Net sales	$2,186,525	$2,020,526	$1,841,738	$1,586,747	$1,373,027	$1,447,715	$1,420,270	$815,819	$801,817	$814,811
Operating costs and expenses	2,126,013	2,018,436	1,787,126	1,546,002	1,349,610	1,418,950	—	—	—	—
Operating income	60,512	2,090	54,612	40,745	23,417	28,765	—	—	—	—
Interest and amortization of debt expense	(34,468)	(37,080)	(29,585)	(26,449)	(26,667)	(21,733)	—	—	—	—
Interest income and other income and expenses, net	2,372	2,488	7,952	7,903	6,366	3,752	—	—	—	—
Income (loss) from continuing operations before items shown below	28,416	(32,502)	32,979	22,199	3,116	10,784	—	—	—	—
Usual or infrequently occurring items	(1,048)	(26,808)	—	—	—	—	—	—	—	—
Income (loss) from continuing operations before income taxes	27,368	(59,310)	32,979	22,199	3,116	10,784	—	—	—	—
Estimated U.S. and foreign income taxes	(17,300)	(12,000)	(15,250)	(12,970)	(7,945)	(6,500)	—	—	—	—
Income (loss) from continued operations	10,068	(71,310)	17,729	9,229	(4,829)	4,284	$ 24,416	$ 12,090	$ 13,621	$ 8,770
Income from discontinued operations	—	13,768	741	1,508	3,135	—	—	—	—	—
Gains on disposals of discontinued operations	—	10,704	7,238	—	—	—	—	—	—	—
Income (loss) before extraordinary items	10,068	(46,838)	25,708	10,737	(1,694)	4,284	—	—	—	—
Extraordinary items	700	3,231	(345)	6,971	(22,318)	(6,408)	—	—	—	—
Net income (loss)	$ 10,768	$ (43,607)	$ 25,363	$ 17,708	$ (24,012)	$ (2,124)	$ 28,660	$ 12,623	$ 16,389	$ 9,190
Average number of primary shares outstanding	10,779	10,775	11,193	11,194	10,779	10,733	—	—	—	—
Primary and fully diluted income (loss) per common share:										
Income (loss) from continuing operations	$ 0.74	$ (6.82)	$ 1.42	$ 0.67	$ (0.65)	$ 0.06	2.07§	1.37§	1.60§	0.94§
Income (loss) from discontinued operations	—	1.28	0.07	0.13	0.29	0.14	.16	.07	.33	.06
Gains on disposals of discontinued operations	—	0.99	0.65	—	—	—	—	—	—	—
Income (loss) before extraordinary items	0.74	(4.55)	2.14	0.80	(0.36)	0.20	—	—	—	—
Extraordinary items	0.06	0.30	(0.03)	0.62	(2.07)	(0.59)	—	—	—	—
Net income (loss)	$ 0.80	$ (4.25)	$ 2.11	$ 1.42	$ (2.43)	$ (0.39)	$ 2.23	$ 1.44	$ 1.93	$ 1.00
Dividends per common share	0	0	0	0	$ 0.15	$ 0.30	—	—	—	—

* From United Brands, *Annual Report, 1975.*
† The 1974 hurricane loss and 1975 and 1974 gains on bond repurchases were presented as unusual or infrequently occurring items. In accordance with accounting principles applicable for prior years, similar items were presented as extraordinary items.
‡ From United Brands, *Annual Report, 1971.*
§ Fully diluted only given.

EXHIBIT 2

UNITED BRANDS AND SUBSIDIARY COMPANIES
Consolidated Balance Sheet
For Years Ended December 31
(in thousands of dollars)

Assets	1975	1974	1973	1972	1971	1970	1969	1968*
Current assets:								
Cash	$ 31,550	$ 98,976	$ 20,986	$ 18,894	$ 21,514	$ 55,620	$ 37,355	$ 12,725
Marketable securities	30,417	540	20,363	64,225	49,082	35,772	56,148	67,842
Trade receivables, less allowance for doubtful accounts of $5,230 (1974—$4,446)	131,218	125,210	170,135	119,847	92,289	92,322	120,947	45,649
Other receivables	25,225	38,355	—	—	—	—	—	—
Inventories	178,868	176,891	210,689	124,090	115,581	104,773	104,324	25,351
Materials and supplies	—	—	—	25,331	28,441	30,358	28,761	20,288
Prepaid expenses	10,572	9,223	10,876	10,997	11,593	8,546	4,915	3,167
Total current assets	407,850	449,195	433,049	363,384	318,500	327,391	352,450	175,022
Investments and long-term receivables	18,848	32,822	55,072	67,417	44,324	46,398	45,127	9,112
Property, plant and equipment, net	337,306	350,921	403,128	331,018	334,530	362,870	329,410	207,715
Other assets and deferred charges (Note 9)	7,575	10,967	23,016	26,702	36,736	14,675	30,235	49,134
Trademarks	44,931	45,031	47,004	50,249	49,882	46,071	46,174	—
Excess of cost over fair value of net assets acquired	272,190	272,146	276,639	279,069	285,255	282,112	279,508	—
Total assets	$1,088,700	$1,161,082	$1,237,908	$1,117,839	$1,069,227	$1,079,517	$1,082,904	$ 440,983

EXHIBIT 2 *(concluded)*

UNITED BRANDS AND SUBSIDIARY COMPANIES
Consolidated Balance Sheet
For Years Ended December 31
(in thousands of dollars)

	1975	1974	1973	1972	1971	1970	1969	1968*
Liabilities and Shareholders' Equity								
Current liabilities:								
Notes payable	$ 17,473	$ 70,459	$ 62,117	$ 43,419	$ 28,933	$ 48,092	$ 80,703	$ 8,069
Accounts payable	84,792	86,194	124,887	87,692	92,806	78,328	72,811	18,776
Accrued liabilities	35,764	41,561	—	—	—	—	5,569	20,600
Long-term debt due within one year	12,057	9,905	11,326	14,719	7,656	8,144	24,121	15,808
U.S. and foreign income taxes	23,037	18,994	23,511	22,820	19,874	19,166	15,309	—
Deferred U.S. and foreign income taxes	14,145	11,108	11,102	10,882	11,436	10,607		
Total current liabilities	187,268	238,221	232,943	179,532	160,705	164,337	198,513	63,253
Long-term debt	341,583	383,100	396,237	402,487	380,280	358,661	320,427	—
Accrued pension and severance liabilities	69,750	63,395	54,369	34,596	37,095	34,287	32,524	29,801
Other liabilities and deferred credits	7,784	4,819	37,600	7,689	13,158	16,478	18,275	3,278
Total liabilities	606,385	689,535	721,149	624,304	591,238	573,763	569,739	96,332
Shareholders' equity:								
$3.00 cumulative convertible preferred stock	2,649	2,715	2,723	2,738	2,769	2,876	170	3,696†
$1.20 cumulative convertible preferred stock	29,610	29,610	29,610	29,610	29,610	29,613	29,524	—
$3.20 cumulative convertible preferred stock	7,357	7,420	7,421	7,452	7,452	7,452	276	—
Capital stock, $1 par value	10,782	10,776	10,775	10,773	10,781	10,775	21,491	(20,896)‡
Warrants and options to purchase capital stock	366,498	366,375	366,367	366,322	366,303	366,192	365,518	187,876
Capital surplus	65,419	54,651	99,863	76,640	61,074	88,846	96,136	173,975
Total shareholders' equity	482,315	471,547	516,759	493,535	477,989	505,754	513,165	344,651
Total liabilities and shareholders' equity	$1,088,700	$1,161,082	$1,237,908	$1,117,839	$1,069,227	$1,079,517	$1,082,904	$ 440,983

* From United Fruit Company, *Annual Report*, 1969.
† All preferred stock less cost of reacquisition.
‡ Less cost of reacquisition.

SOURCE: Unless otherwise noted, figures taken from United Brands, *Annual Report*, 1969–75.

EXHIBIT 3

UNITED BRANDS AND SUBSIDIARY COMPANIES
Operations by Product Group
Year Ended December 31
(in thousands of dollars)

	1975*	1974*	1973*	1972*	1971*	1970†
Net sales:						
Bananas and related products	$ 657,087	$ 549,440	$ 449,971	$ 450,662	$ 397,551	$ 379,558
Meat-packing and related products	1,329,011	1,288,996	1,258,415	1,012,175	847,056	898,916
Food processing and food services	123,677	103,525	67,624	68,280	74,001	66,555
U.S. agriculture and floriculture	53,205	51,003	48,426	42,461	42,587	29,615
Other	23,545	27,562	17,302	13,169	11,832	8,961
	$2,186,525	$2,020,526	$1,841,738	$1,586,747	$1,373,027	$1,383,605
Contributions to operating income:						
Bananas and related products	$ 45,396	$ (7,523)	$ 26,323	$ 34,685	$ 11,170	$ 27,441
Meat-packing and related products	11,467	3,765	23,687	6,708	10,417	13,810
Food processing and food services	4,809	1,576	4,900	3,160	275	(1,387)
U.S. agriculture and floriculture	562	2,450	2,011	(2,473)	1,830	(11,028)
Other	3,128	5,349	1,143	1,698	3,223	2,394
	65,362	5,617	58,064	43,778	26,915	31,230
Less: Corporate overhead	(4,850)	(3,427)	(3,452)	(3,033)	(3,498)	(3,954)
Operating income	$ 60,512	$ 2,090	$ 54,612	$ 40,745	$ 23,417	$ 27,276

* From 1975 *Annual Report.*
† From 1974 *Annual Report.*

admiration, the two men began to clash when Mr. Black became deeply involved in financial problems and Mr. Gelsthorpe assumed greater operating control of the company.

As if to widen the split, Mr. Gelsthorpe was based in the old United Fruit home office in Boston, while Mr. Black stayed in the United Brands and original AMK office in New York, close to financial centers. Mr. Gelsthorpe quickly won the loyalty of the Boston group for his take-charge attitude. This group included senior vice presidents John Taylor and Donald Meltzer.[14]

When Mr. Gelsthorpe returned from Panama, he reported the Panama agreement to the board "as a fait accompli."[15] Mr. Black, however, felt that the agreement called for the forced sale to Panama of United Brands' holdings there, and he expressed his disapproval. According to one account, the report at the board meeting was the first Mr. Black had heard about the agreement, and he felt as if Mr. Gelsthorpe "had sold the company down the river in order to build up his own reputation."[16] According to Mr. Gelsthorpe, he and Mr. Black were in constant communication through Mr. Meltzer, and both said that Mr. Black had given his approval.

By either account, it was clear that increased internal communications between Mr. Black and his senior vice presidents was in order. The key challenge to Mr. Black, however, remained the financial stabilization of the company in the midst of unprecedented and unforeseeable natural disasters and political events. The resultant crushing work load had allowed little time for the types of social projects, such as the building of a new medical center in Guatemala or the distribution of over 300,000 polio doses in Costa Rica, for which he and United Brands had become well known.

FEBRUARY 1975

With these business problems on his mind, 53-year-old Eli Black read the morning paper on the way to his office on the 44th floor of the Pan American Building in mid-Manhattan. It was Monday, February 3, 1975. The key Watergate defendants had been found guilty of conspiracy to obstruct justice the previous week, and officials at 3M Corporation, Ashland Oil, and Gulf were being indicted for charges stemming from illegal political slush funds.

At 8:20 A.M., Mr. Black locked the doors to his office, smashed an outside window with his attache case, and leaped to the street below. Mr. Black left no word to explain his death. In his briefcase was a note on which he had written "Early retirement—55."

The Wall Street Journal quoted Samuel Belkin, president of Yeshiva University and a former teacher of Mr. Black's, as saying, "If it were just up to

---

[14] *The Wall Street Journal,* May 7, 1975, p. 26.
[15] Ibid.
[16] Ibid.

him he would retire, but . . . he thought of his job as a public trust." The *Journal* went on to say that "he had created that role himself by imbuing his job with his own sense of social accountability. In the end, he staggered beneath its weight and found but one possible way to retire—and took it."[17]

UNITED BRANDS AFTER ELI BLACK

The official United Brands statement issued the afternoon of February 3 said that Mr. Black had been under "great strain during the past several weeks because of business pressures. He had been working 16 to 18 hours a day and had become severely depressed because of the tension."[18]

Edward Gelsthorpe, executive vice president, expressed his opinion that "the great tragedy of Eli Black's death at this time is that under his leadership the company was on its way to overcoming several crises. We were convinced that the traumatic period was behind us."[19] Knowledgeable sources expected Mr. Gelsthorpe to be named chief executive officer.[20]

Three days after Mr. Black's death, the board met to consider the question of company leadership. A sufficient number of board members knew of the friction between Mr. Black and Mr. Gelsthorpe to block his immediate appointment as president. It was decided that two committees, executive and management, would run the company temporarily and that Dr. J. E. Goldman, a director since 1970 and a group vice president of Xerox would head each. An executive search firm would be hired to help locate a permanent successor. (The composition of the committees and the board before and after Mr. Black's death is shown in Exhibits 4–7).

During the same meeting, Mr. Gelsthorpe and Mr. Taylor explained for the first time to the full board the "Honduras Arrangement." Someone within top management had negotiated the $5 million figure down to $2.5 million, and half that amount had been paid on September 3, 1974, with the rest to follow. The Honduras government had then rolled back the banana tax to 25 cents per box.

The board meeting took place while Price Waterhouse & Co. was auditing the firm's books, and they were quoted as saying that "the matter came to our attention."[21] Acting on the advice of Price Waterhouse, the board hired counsel. Counsel then brought the matter to the attention of the Securities and Exchange Commission with the request that the matter be kept confidential. It was especially troublesome, however, since the bribe was listed as an expense for tax purposes. It therefore violated both tax laws and the SEC regulations regarding financial disclosure to stockholders.

---

[17] *The Wall Street Journal,* February 14, 1975, p. 15.
[18] Ibid.
[19] Ibid.
[20] Ibid.
[21] *The Wall Street Journal,* April 11, 1975, p. 4.

EXHIBIT 4   United Brands' Board of Directors as of January 1975

Eli M. Black (elected 1970), 53-year-old president and chairman of the board.

George F. Doriot (elected 1971), 76-year-old former assistant dean of Harvard Business School, founder of American Research and Development Corporation, and a member of several boards.

Robert M. Gallop (elected 1957, from the AMK board), 67-year-old senior vice president and general counsel for United Brands, originally from AMK Corporation.

Donald R. Gant (elected 1972), 47-year-old Harvard MBA, partner in Goldman, Sachs and Co., and member of four other boards.

George P. Gardner, Jr. (elected 1953, United Fruit), 58-year-old senior vice president of Paine, Webber, Jackson & Curtis, Inc., investment bankers, and a director of the company since its United Fruit days, as well as six others. Asked to resign by Mr. Black in November 1974, he was urged to stay by Mr. Gelsthorpe, and did.

Dr. J. E. Goldman (elected 1970), 54-year-old classmate of Mr. Black at Yeshiva and senior vice president and chief scientist of Xerox Corporation.

Maurice C. Kaplan (elected 1969, AMK), former member of the George Washington University Law School faculty, former assistant director of the SEC, the director of several firms.

Samuel D. Lunt, Sr. (elected 1956, AMK), 70-year-old partner in S. D. Lunt & Co. and director of several firms.

Joseph M. McDaniel (elected 1957, AMK), 73-year-old chairman of The Andrews-Hart Corporation, a financial consulting firm, and director of numerous firms.

Elias Paul (elected 1971), 56-year-old president and chief executive officer of John Morrell & Co. and director of three other firms.

Simon Rifkind (elected 1975), 74-year-old partner in Paul Weiss, Rifkind, Wharton & Garrison and director of several firms.

Norman I. Schafler (elected 1958, AMK), 58-year-old chairman of NRM Corporation, Condec Corporation, and director of numerous other corporations.

John A. Taylor (elected 1973), senior vice president of United Brands and president of Agrimark Group.

David W. Wallace (elected 1960, AMK), 51-year-old president of Bangor Punta, former executive vice president of AMK Corp., and director of several companies.

Jay Wells (elected 1965, AMK), 59-year-old chairman of the board of Wells National Services Corporation.

Before the February meeting, it appeared as if only five men at United Brands had known of the payment: Mr. Black; senior vice presidents Taylor, Gelsthorpe, and Meltzer (all based in Boston); and corporate counsel Robert Gallop. If there were a "Boston Plot" against Mr. Black, as some suspected, the Boston group had had heavy ammunition in its arsenal. Messrs. Gelsthorpe and Taylor remained on the board that was attempting to run United Brands by committee.

EXHIBIT 5 Changes in the Board of Directors of United Brands, January
1975–March 1976

Deletions (dates of service in parentheses):

Eli M. Black (1970–February 1975). Death by apparent suicide.

George F. Doroit (1971–February 1975). Resigned following Mr. Black's death.

Robert M. Gallop (1957–January 1975). An old friend of Mr. Black's from AMK Corporation, he resigned in January 1975 after a heated exchange with Mr. Black in a late December board meeting. He remained as corporate counsel to United Brands.

Maurice C. Kaplan (1969–late 1975). Resigned in late 1975.

Simon H. Rifkind (January 1975–April 1975). Resigned when frustrated in the role of peacemaker between board factions.

John A. Taylor (1973–late 1975). Resigned from the board, but remained senior vice president and president, United Fruit Group.

Additions (dates of election in parentheses):

Norman Alexander (February 1975), 61-year-old president of Sun Chemical Corporation and Ampacet Corporation, a member of several other boards, and an old friend of the Black family.

Wallace Booth (May 1975), 52-year-old president of United Brands.

Max M. Fisher (March 1975), 67-year-old chairman of the board of Sefran Printing Company and member of numerous boards. A major shareholder, he was elected acting chairman of the board in May 1975.

F. Mark Garlinghouse (March 1975), 61-year-old vice president and general counsel for AT&T, chairman of L. F. Garlinghouse Co., and member of several boards.

Edward Gelsthorpe (February 1975; resigned September 5, 1975), 54-year-old executive vice president and chief operating officer of United Brands.

Seymour Milstein (March 1975), private investor and largest single shareholder of United Brands stock.

C. Gilbert Collingwood (late 1975), senior vice president, finance and administration, for United Brands.

The committee approach to running United Brands was cumbersome from the beginning. The process of selecting a new chairman was probably best described by *The Wall Street Journal* reporter Mary Bralove:

> There followed a series of acrimonious board meetings. The key controversy was whether to name as United Brands chairman Norman Alexander, chairman of the Sun Chemical Corp. and an old friend of the Black family. "You could hear the shouting out in the hall," a United Brands official says of one of the sessions. At another, Mr. Goldman, who opposed Mr. Alexander, and Norman Schafler, a director who supported him, "nearly came to blows," according to more than one observer.
>
> Simon Rifkind, a board member who had tried to be a peacemaker, quit last month out of frustration. "I finally couldn't take it," he says.

EXHIBIT 6   Executive and Management Committee after Mr. Black's Death

Executive Committee	Management Committee
Dr. J. D. Goldman, Chairman	Norman I. Schafler, Chairman
George P. Gardner, Jr.	Norman Alexander
Edward Gelsthorpe	Donald R. Gant
Maurice C. Kaplan	George P. Gardner, Jr.
Elias Paul	Dr. J. E. Goldman
Simon H. Rifkind	David W. Wallace
	Jay Wells

EXHIBIT 7   The Lineup Regarding the New Management Question, February
through May 1975

For Dr. Goldman as chairman:
  Mr. Wells
  Mr. Paul
  Mr. Taylor
  Dr. Goldman

New board members pushing for an
outsider (ultimately Mr. Booth):
  Mr. Fisher
  Mr. Milstein

For Mr. Alexander as chairman:
  Mr. Lunt
  Mr. Schafler
  Mr. Alexander

Uncommitted members:
  Mr. Gant
  Mr. Gardner
  Mr. Garlinghouse
  Mr. Gelsthorpe
  Mr. Kaplan
  Mr. McDaniel
  Mr. Rifkind
  Mr. Wallace

By March 10, the board reached a strained compromise. Mr. Schafler became chairman of the management committee while Mr. Goldman remained chairman of the executive committee.

At the next board meeting, that compromise threatened to come apart. At issue, according to sources, was a proposed three-man slate to expand the board. Board member Jay Wells and others opposed the slate because they feared the new members would vote for Mr. Alexander's election as chairman. The board was deadlocked on this issue. Unknown to Mr. Wells, however, members who favored the slate had set up an elaborate telephone hookup to another director who had promised to call in from a boat in the Caribbean and vote for the slate. When the call came through, Mr. Wells was furious. In fact, he was so upset that he grabbed the phone and ripped the cord from the wall, thereby effectively ending the meeting.

During this period, the time bomb of public disclosure of the Honduran payoff was ticking in the background. Price Waterhouse had discovered payments of $750,000 that had been made to Italian officials over the last five years. Nobody seemed to know, however, why these payments were made and who authorized them.

Finally, in April 8, *The Wall Street Journal* queried United Brands about payments to a Honduran official, and in response the company publicly admitted the bribes. The secret was out, and everyone scattered to get legal help.[22]

The company statement had said that the payment to government officials in the Republic of Honduras was authorized by Eli Black and was not accurately reflected on company books and records. The Securities and Exchange Commission then formally accused United Brands of issuing false reports and suspended the trading of United Brands.

General Oswaldo Lopez,[23] president of Honduras, immediately denied the prevalent speculation that he was the official involved. He then met with his cabinet and formed a commission to investigate the allegations. Any Honduran official found to be involved was to be prosecuted to the fullest extent of the law.

The Honduran commission requested all cabinet level ministers to authorize examination of personnel financial records and accounts. All did, except for President Lopez, who was removed as president on April 22 and replaced by the new commander in chief of the armed forces, Colonel Juan Alberto Melgar.

On May 1, Costa Rica announced that it was raising its export tax to $1 per box from 25 cents per box and was asking other members of UBEC to do the same. On May 5, former President Lopez and his family were preparing for exile in Madrid, although no formal charges had been filed.

On May 7, a *Wall Street Journal* article examining the events leading to Mr. Black's suicide characterized various managers in the Boston office as saying that, since September 1974, Mr. Black had seemed "disoriented," "hooked on drugs," "cracking under the pressure," "not communicating," and "depressed." The same article, however, quoted the response of a long-time friend of Mr. Black: "They [senior Boston office executives] mutinied, and now they have to prove the captain was crazy. It's a chapter right out of *The Caine Mutiny*."[24]

On May 12, United Brands named a new president and chief executive

---

[22] *The Wall Street Journal*, May 7, 1975, p. 26.

[23] President Lopez was the closest thing to a war hero that the Honduran people had. He had led his troops in the four-day war of 1969 with El Salvador over the outcome of a soccer match. At the end of the fourth day, 2,000 lives had been lost and the El Savadorians were advancing.

President Lopez originally came to power in a 1963 coup. He was elected in 1965 for a term that lasted through 1971. He returned to power in 1972 in another coup. The week prior to the revelation of the bribe, he had been relieved of his duties of commander in chief of the armed forces in order to concentrate more fully on economic problems.

[24] *The Wall Street Journal*, May 7, 1975, p. 26.

officer. Wallace W. Booth, a 52-year-old senior vice president at Rockwell International, had spent 20 years at Ford Motor Company and had a broad background in financial management and foreign operations. Max M. Fisher, a major shareholder, was named acting chairman of the board.

One informed observer commented that:

> Booth will need the help of Gelsthorpe, who was passed over by the board in favor of Booth. Booth will have to build loyalty among the Boston staff, and he plans to spend some time on Gelsthorpe's turf. The ideal combination would be for Gelsthorpe to work in marketing, where he has most of his experience, and Booth in operations and finance, his strong suit.[25]

May 15 brought the report of the Honduran investigative commission. To the surprise of most observers, it was reported that former Economic Minister Abraham Bennaton was the official who received the $1.25 million payment. Bennaton denied his involvement.

The following day, the Honduran commission specified that John Taylor had paid the bribe money to Bennaton at a meeting on September 3, 1974, in Zurich, Switzerland. Bennaton was formally charged on May 15. Also May 16, a federal grand jury in Washington was weighing possible criminal charges against United Brands and its top executives.

Note: On September 5, Edward Gelsthorpe resigned as executive vice president, chief operating officer, and director of United Brands to become president and chief operating officer of H. P. Hood, Inc., a Boston dairy producer and distributor. The Hood appointment was the third such executive post he had held in a little over a year, and the fourth in four years.

---

[25] "Who Calls the Shots at United Brands?" *Business Week,* May 26, 1975, p. 29.

Commentaries

---

13. Dollar$ for Apartheid

James Carson
Michael Fleshman

The full extent of the American financial stake in South Africa was revealed last July with the release of a secret State Department study which put total U.S. investments in that white minority-ruled country at a staggering $14.6 billion—far in excess of the Commerce Department's official figure for direct investment of $2.6 billion or even the $6–$8 billion figure most commonly used by anti-apartheid and divestment activists.

The study, *U.S. Investment in South Africa: The Hidden Pieces,* was conducted by economic analysts at the U.S. consulate in Johannesburg and cabled to Washington. The three-page cable found its way to TransAfrica, the Washington-based black lobby for Africa and the Caribbean and was made available to *Multinational Monitor.*

Although the cable shows no dramatic new increases in the level of U.S. involvement in the South African economy, it does reveal additional types of investment that had previously gone uncounted. The revelations raise new fears about the lengths the U.S. government is prepared to go to protect U.S. investment in South Africa and seem certain to spur the growing divestment movement in the United States.

LYING WITH STATISTICS

The study suggests that a withdrawal of American investors from South Africa would be much more damaging to the apartheid economy than the business community and the State Department had been previously willing to admit.

Most assessments of U.S. financial holdings in South Africa have reported the misleading $2.6 billion Commerce Department figure for direct investment—which is defined as a single U.S. investor owning the equivalent of at

---

Multinational Monitor, November 1983, pp. 18–21.

least 10 percent of the voting shares in a South African company. But not included in the Commerce figure are investments through subsidiaries of U.S. firms based in a third country, such as that of the Ford Motor Company, which holds 88 percent of Ford Canada, which in turn owns 100 percent of Ford South Africa. Ford's $213 million investment shows up as a U.S. investment in Canada—not South Africa.

Also not included in the Commerce Department statistics are U.S. bank loans and portfolio investments by Americans in the Johannesburg Stock Exchange. "These latter transactions," the cable's author notes, "still represent U.S. investment." It is the inclusion of these investments—$3.6 billion in short-term loans from U.S. banks and over $8 billion in U.S.-owned South African stocks—together with Commerce's direct investment figure that make up the $14.6 billion total.

Significantly, the study found that the nine largest U.S. banks—Banker's Trust, Chase Manhattan, Chemical, Citibank, Manufacturers Hanover, J. P. Morgan, Continental Illinois, First Chicago, and Bank of America—accounted for 65 percent of all outstanding loans to South Africa. U.S. investors account for 57 percent of the total foreign share-holdings in South Africa's gold, diamond, and other precious metals and mineral mining houses, valued at $8.1 billion. "Most U.S. [portfolio] investment is directly in gold mining companies," the cable reports. "U.S. investors also own 25.3 percent of the platinum mines and 11.0 percent of DeBeers [the diamond mining and marketing cartel]." The cable quotes no figures for U.S. stock holdings in other sectors of the South African economy.

STOCKS AND BOMBS

It is the highly visible presence of U.S. corporate subsidiaries in South Africa that has drawn the greatest fire from human rights and anti-apartheid activists.

Since 1970, U.S. investment in South Africa has more than tripled to a point where U.S. companies now account for more than 20 percent of all foreign direct investment in South Africa. Most recently, spurred by strong expansion of the South African economy, American companies expanded their investment by almost 17 percent in 1980 and by 12 percent in 1981. By comparison, American foreign direct investment worldwide increased 14 percent in 1980 and 5 percent in 1981.

American manufacturing companies own almost 10 percent of the fixed capital stock in the manufacturing sector, and U.S. firms reportedly control 75 percent of all computer sales. What's more, U.S. petroleum companies control almost 40 percent of South Africa's petroleum sales.

Yet the gross figures for foreign direct investment do not tell the whole story. Although over 350 corporations have direct investments and more than 6,000 U.S.-based transnationals are involved in some type of arrangement with the apartheid republic, about 10 corporations—among them, Caltex,

Mobil, Ford, General Motors, Goodyear, General Electric, and U.S. Steel—control over 70 percent of the total value of United States' direct investment in South Africa. At the top of any list of American companies in South Africa are the two oil giants Caltex Petroleum Company, jointly owned by Texaco and Standard Oil of California, and Mobil Oil. Both play a key role in South Africa's energy sector.

South Africa has yet to discover any commercially exploitable petroleum reserves, and, in view of a four-year-old embargo on oil deliveries by OPEC and most non-OPEC oil producers, the government has embarked on an ambitious plan to construct synthetic fuel plants. Petroleum supplies remain a weak link in the economy, and the state goes to great lengths to ensure its supplies—including outlawing publication of information about oil supplies even by the companies themselves.

While acknowledging that apartheid is "both repugnant and indefensible," Mobil asserts its corporate responsibility to provide oil to the South African government. "Total denial of supplies to the police and military forces of a host country," the company told shareholders in response to demands that Mobil cease all sales to those institutions, "is hardly consistent with an image of responsible citizenship in that country. The great bulk of the work of both the police and military forces in every country, including South Africa, is for the benefit of all of its inhabitants."

Both Mobil and Caltex maintain that their activities in South Africa benefit black South Africans. Mobil reported to shareholders in 1981 that its subsidiaries in South Africa have "been in the forefront of community activities designed to improve the education, living conditions, and status of nonwhite South Africans."

In general, American corporations continue to argue that, while they do support the government they also provide jobs and security for large numbers of black workers who would otherwise be far worse off. But critics question this contention, noting that the 127,000 black workers that American companies employ represent less than 2 percent of the officially recognized black work force.

While some of the changes brought by the corporations—such as integrating existing facilities—are welcomed by the black workers, they can hardly be said to get at the root of the apartheid system. In 1982, average monthly wages for urban blacks in South Africa were only $271, compared with a figure for whites that stood at $1,044. And while the strength of black trade unions in South Africa has increased dramatically in the past few years, the harsh reality of apartheid as a system that encompasses the entire lives of black South Africans, on and off the workplace, cannot be erased.

The difficulties that black workers face in South Africa was illustrated in August when workers struck a Firestone-owned plant west of Johannesburg, demanding a pay raise and the elimination of incentive bonus wages in favor of straight hourly pay. As of early September, the workers, who are affiliated with the largest independent black trade union in the country, were on strike.

But even when unions successfully organize at plants, the police often step in. Thozamile Gqweta, president of the South African Allied Workers Union, was detained seven times between November 1981 and May 1982, and he has testified repeatedly about the torture he endured in prison.

The most stinging criticism of the America corporate presence is provided by the reality of apartheid. The Compensation Commissioner for Occupational Diseases on the mines recently reported that the standard payment a white mine worker receives for any "first degree compensatory disease other than TB" is $16,458. Black mine workers get $1,372. For TB compensation alone, whites receive $6,858, while blacks get $823.

COMPANIES, THE MILITARY, AND THE STATE

Corporate investment and the apartheid political system in South Africa are linked—but not in the direction of change. South African authorities are well aware of their dependence on industry—South Africa's "first line of defense" against attacks by those opposed to apartheid in the words of Defense Minister General Malan.

For example, the South African government has required companies designated as important to national security to hire armed guards and formulate plans to deal with situations of "civil unrest" by September this year. These companies, designated as "National Key Points," are defined as installations where any loss or damage could endanger South Africa's security or interests, and are generally acknowledged to include a number of American multinationals.

According to press reports, "several hundred" sites have been classified as key points, including airports, power stations, oil refineries, auto plants, and chemical installations. For those companies that might hesitate to comply, the act provides fines of up to $18,400 and possible prison terms of five years for corporate executives.

American corporate collaboration with the South African government goes back to a time long before the key points laws came into effect. In the early 1960s, the American Allis Chalmers Corporation built South Africa's first experimental nuclear research reactor. An IBM computer helps the government keep track of the black population, and GM and Ford trucks keep the police and military on the road.

More recently, in late September, the Reagan administration granted permission to seven U.S. firms to bid on a 10-year maintenance contract for South Africa's Koeberg nuclear power plant outside of Cape Town.

The South African government is clearly aware of the role U.S. multinationals can play in determining policy. This was revealed in a secret 1978 State Department cable on South African government attitudes towards multinational corporations obtained by the American Friends Service Committee. The State Department reported that "[the South African government's] stake in the multinationals is very large, not only for obvious economic reasons but because they exercise a restraining effect on policymakers abroad."

The corporate and South African lobbying effort seems to be paying off. In early October the Johannesburg *Sunday Express* reported that the Reagan administration had quietly approved a special trade promotion office in Johannesburg, the first official U.S. government–sponsored trade office for many years. The trade office, which was approved last April, is operated by the Commercial Foreign Service of the U.S. Department of Commerce and will be staffed by two Commerce officers and five local staff. "We hope to increase trade by one billion dollars annually," said Stanley M. McGeehan, the senior Commerce officer.

Codes of Misconduct

Corporate managers argue that through voluntary adherence to codes of conduct that stipulate certain minimum standards of treatment for their black work force, they can serve as a model for change. Codes such as the one designed by the Reverend Leon Sullivan, a black Baptist minister who serves on the board of directors of General Motors, stipulate that corporate facilities should not be segregated, call for equal pay for equal work, and list a number of other minimum conditions for training programs, numbers of black supervisory personnel, and the like.

The annual reports on corporate compliance with the code Sullivan introduced, however, are based on questionnaires filled out by the corporations themselves. And many unions do not agree that the Sullivan principles have improved the workers' lot. Last year one black union at Ford characterized the code as a "toothless package" that was designed as a "piecemeal reform that allows this cruel system of apartheid to survive." Most independent black trade unions regard the code as impractical.

Perhaps the most frank assessment of what the Sullivan principles are all about was provided by James Rawlings, chairman of Union Carbide Southern African Incorporated. Rawlings was asked, in an interview with the *Financial Mail* this fall, what observance of the principles entailed. "Well," he replied, "it's mainly been a matter of integrating the eating facilities and changing rooms at our plants." There was no talk of wages, additional black supervisory personnel, or of any effect beyond the workplace—just removing a few "whites only" signs.

While American officials tried to minimize the importance of the new office, the *Sunday Express* quickly saw the significance, proclaiming in its headline over the article announcing the new office: "U.S. Defies the Sanctions Lobby."

The Reagan administration and American companies argue that their presence in South Africa helps preserve American jobs by promoting trade and accelerates further change in South Africa. Yet the bottom line for corporate involvement in South Africa, as for corporate involvement worldwide, is profits. The rate of return on investment for U.S.-based corporations with direct investments in South Africa was 29 percent in 1980 and 19 percent in 1981, while average rates of return for United States direct investment worldwide were 18 percent and 14 percent for the same two years. American corporate managers, and their friends in government, can hardly be expected to work with much speed to dismantle a system that produces such large profit margins.

DIVESTMENT MOVEMENT

Recognizing the link between corporate profit margins and apartheid, black South Africans have for many years called for the complete isolation of the white minority government and for a total corporate pullout from South Africa.

The response to this call from within South Africa has been a growing international movement to isolate South Africa. In the last few years, a nationwide movement in support of a corporate pullout from South Africa has been growing. Activists on college campuses, in churches and labor unions, and in state and municipal governments have called on these institutions to sell their stocks in corporations that continue to operate in the apartheid republic—with notable success. In the past six years, according to figures compiled by the New York–based Africa Fund, colleges have been forced to sell at least $140 million in stocks in companies involved in South Africa. The Fund also reports that actions by state and municipal governments in 1982 will likely result in the sale of some $300 million in other stocks.

It is in these campaigns that activists plan to employ the secret State Department cables. "The secret cable reveals the full magnitude of the total U.S. relationship with South Africa," says TransAfrica Executive Director Randall Robinson. "It also reveals how very badly we've been deceived by this administration and by past administrations about the depth of our involvement with that country."

14. Defense Spending Is So High U.S. Falters on World Markets

Knight-Ridder News Service

WASHINGTON—American "Star Wars" research has mastered a technique for hurling a tiny projectile—the size of a tomato can—at 17,000 miles an hour through space to obliterate a nuclear-armed Soviet missile.

Japan, meanwhile, has captured the $6-billion-a-year videocassette recorder market.

The United States has developed the Stealth bomber, a batwinged bomber for the future that's invisible to radar.

Japan is leading the race to market new superconductors that could revolutionize travel as well as the giant electronics industry.

Right there, in these contrasts is why the United States is faltering in the battle to compete in world markets and losing millions of jobs, say members of Congress and economic experts.

The United States, they contend, spends so large a percentage of its research and development money on defense that its industries are having trouble developing and selling commercial products such as high-quality cars or televisions.

A Commission on Industrial Competitiveness appointed by President Reagan reported that about two thirds of the federal government's research and development money goes to defense and space, with little civilian spillover.

Meanwhile, the United States continues to pick up more than 65 percent of the check for the defense of the Free World—in effect, subsidizing its major economic competitors.

Sen. James Sasser, D-Tenn., says the nation is exporting jobs.

Japan in particular "is getting a relatively free ride," he says. "That country is able to divert its economic resources . . . to the development of its economic markets, which are crowding out American goods and resulting in lost jobs and a reduced standard of living in the United States."

Says Rep. Don Bonker, D-Wash.: "If we allow other countries to continue to plow their national resources into building up their economies while we dedicate most of our resources to maintaining this global military and strategic commitment, we are going to lose economically.

"Indeed, it could be stated of our generation that we won the security war, but we lost the economic war."

The Economic Policy Institute has estimated that more than 5 million American jobs were lost to foreign competition last year—jobs that many members of Congress believe could have been saved if America's allies shared more equally in paying the defense bills.

If the imbalance isn't corrected, members of Congress and many others say, America's competitiveness in the modern world's global economy will be imperiled.

It is an issue that strikes close to home for millions of Americans who lost jobs or have seen whole industries die because of foreign competition.

In Schenectady, Joe Cowell, of the International Union of Electrical Workers, tells of more than 32,000 jobs lost to European competition at General Electric, which once led the world in building giant turbines.

"No wonder these people can do what they are doing," he says. "We are paying for their defense."

Cowell, who worked as a machinist for 16 years, has watched a way of life die in Schenectady. "If you look at the whole picture, it's a disaster," he says.

"The community is going down hill. Taxes are going up, schools are closing. It used to be you could always get a job at GE, but that opportunity isn't there for the kids.

"It's all based on the loss of jobs, on foreign competitors who don't play fair."

John Egberg, for 27 years a Du Pont corporation executive in western Europe and now a professor at Lehigh University in Bethlehem, Pennsylvania, argues that maintaining 320,000 American troops in Europe has cost American jobs.

"The large number of U.S. units in Europe are no longer needed," he says. "If we did not have to pay the price for those troops we could put the money into research to advance American technology in the commercial sector. That would create American jobs."

Those in Congress calling for a greater allied share in defense spending believe more jobs would be created by improved American competitiveness in commercial markets than would be lost if the U.S. defense budget were cut.

President Reagan's commission on industrial competitiveness said the Japanese and the Europeans put most of their research and development effort into developing civilian products. "We find ourselves behind both Germany and Japan" in civilian research and development, the commission's report noted.

A study last year by the privately sponsored Council on Competitiveness confirmed these findings, and added: "Governments of other industrial nations emphasize the commercial applications of technology as an essential objective of their R&D programs. . . . The United States devotes a smaller share of its R&D budget to nondefense projects than Japan, West Germany, France, the United Kingdom, or Sweden."

In addition, governments of America's main competitors actively support commercial development—a no-no in America's free enterprise economy.

Many of the issues under debate come down to whether America is in economic decline.

The Commission on Competitiveness said the United States is losing its long-time world leadership in high technology, and with it millions of jobs.

In 1986, for the first time since World War II, the United States had a trade deficit in high-technology products.

The U.S. share of the consumer electronics market has dipped from almost 100 percent in 1970 to less than 5 percent today.

The United States now is in danger of losing other core industries, from semiconductors to pharmaceuticals.

"The nub of the issue is that we are subsidizing our competitors," says Larry Chimerine, chairman of the Wefa Group, an economic consulting service in Philadelphia.

"Well, once we could afford to do it. . . . But they have caught up with us. There is no justification for us to subsidize them now. . . .

"Who is hurt? . . . We're having bigger budget deficits, we're paying higher taxes, the adverse effects spread throughout the economy.

"To some extent, every American is hurt."

15. A Code of Worldwide Business Conduct—Caterpillar Tractor Co.

To Caterpillar People

Large corporations are receiving more and more public scrutiny. This is understandable. A sizable economic enterprise is a matter of justifiable public interest—sometimes concern—in the community and country where it's located. And when substantial amounts of goods, services, and capital flow across national boundaries, the public's interest is, logically, even greater.

Not surprisingly then, growth of multinational corporations has led to increasing public calls for standards, rules, and codes of conduct for such firms.

Three years ago, we concluded it was timely for Caterpillar to set forth *its own beliefs,* based on ethical convictions and international business dating back to the turn of the century.

Experience since then has demonstrated the practical utility of this document—particularly as a means of confirming, for Caterpillar people, the company's operating principles and philosophies.

This revised "Code of Worldwide Business Conduct" is offered under the several headings that follow. Its purpose continues to be to guide us, in a broad and ethical sense, in all aspects of our worldwide business activities.

Of course, this code isn't an attempt to prescribe actions for every business encounter. It *is* an attempt to capture basic, general principles to be observed by Caterpillar people everywhere.

To the extent our actions match these high standards, such can be a source of pride. To the extent they don't (and we're by no means ready to claim perfection), these standards should be a challenge to each of us.

No document issued by Caterpillar is more important than this one. I trust my successors will cause it to be updated as events may merit. And I also ask that you give these principles your strong support in the way you carry out your daily responsibilities.

Chairman of the Board
Issued October 1, 1974
Revised September 1, 1977

OWNERSHIP AND INVESTMENT

In the case of business investment in any country, the principle of mutual benefit to investor and country should prevail.

We affirm that Caterpillar investment must be compatible with social and economic priorities of host countries, and with local customs, tradition, and sovereignty. We intend to conduct our business in a way that will earn acceptance and respect for Caterpillar, and allay concerns—by host country government—about multinational corporations.

In turn, we are entitled to ask that such countries give consideration to our need for stability, business success, and growth; that they avoid discrimination against multinational corporations; and that they honor their agreements, including those relating to rights and properties of citizens of other nations.

Law and logic support the notion that boards of directors are constituted to represent shareholders, the owners of the enterprise. We have long held the view that Caterpillar board members can best meet their responsibilities of stewardship to shareholders if they are appointed solely by them—and not by governments, labor unions or other nonowner groups.

Board composition and board deliberations should be highly reflective of the public interest. We believe that is a basic, inseparable part of stewardship to shareholders.

We recognize the existence of arguments favoring joint ventures and other forms of local sharing in the ownership of a business enterprise.

Good arguments also exist for full ownership of operations by the parent company: the high degree of control necessary to maintain product uniformity and protect patents and trademarks, and the fact that a single facility's profitability may not be as important (or as attractive to local investors) as its long-term significance to the integrated, corporate whole.

Caterpillar's experience inclines toward the latter view—full ownership— but with the goal of worldwide ownership of the total enterprise being encouraged through listing of parent company stock on many of the world's major stock exchanges.

Since defensible arguments exist on both sides of the issue, we believe there should be freedom and flexibility—for negotiating whatever investment arrangements and corporate forms best suit the long-term interests of the host country and the investing business, in each case.

CORPORATE FACILITIES

Caterpillar facilities are to be located wherever in the world it is most economically advantageous to do so, from a long-term standpoint.

Decisions as to location of facilities will, of course, consider such conventional factors as proximity to sources of supply and sales opportunities, possibilities for volume production and resulting economies of scale, and availability of a trained or trainable work force. Also considered will be political and fiscal stability, demonstrated governmental attitudes, and other factors normally included in defining the local investment or business "climate."

We don't seek special treatment in the sense of extraordinary investment incentives, assurances that competition from new manufacturers in the same area will be limited, or protection against import competition. However, where incentives have been offered to make local investment viable, they should be applied as offered in a timely, equitable manner.

We desire to build functional, safe, attractive facilities to the same high standard worldwide, but with whatever modifications are appropriate to make them harmonious with national modes. They are to be located so as to complement public planning, and be compatible with local environmental considerations.

Facility operations should be planned with the long-term view in mind, in order to minimize the impact of sudden change on the local work force and economy. Other things being equal, preference will be given to local sources of supply.

RELATIONSHIPS WITH EMPLOYEES

We aspire to a single worldwide standard of fair treatment of employees. Specifically, we intend:

1. To select and place employees on the basis of qualifications for the work to be performed—without discrimination in terms of race, religion, national origin, color, sex, age, or handicap unrelated to the task at hand.

2. To protect the health and lives of employees. This includes maintaining a clean, safe work environment free from recognized health hazards.

3. To maintain uniform, reasonable work standards, worldwide, and strive to provide work that challenges the individual—so that he or she may feel a sense of satisfaction resulting from it.

4. To make employment stabilization a major factor in corporate decisions. We shall, among other things, attempt to provide continuous employment, and avoid capricious hiring practices.

5. To compensate people fairly, according to their contributions to the company, within the framework of national and local practices.

6. To foster self-development, and assist employees in improving and broadening their jobs skills.

7. To promote from within the organization—in the absence of factors that persuasively argue otherwise.

8. To encourage expression by individuals about their work, including ideas for improving the work result.

9. To inform employees about company matters affecting them.

10. To accept without prejudice the decision of employees on matters pertaining to union membership and union representation; and where a group of employees is lawfully represented by a union, to build a company-union relationship based upon mutual respect and trust.

11. To refrain from hiring persons closely related to members of the board of directors, administrative officers, and department heads. If other employees' relatives are hired, this must be solely the result of their qualifications for jobs to be filled. No employee is to be placed in the direct line of authority of relatives. We believe that nepotism—or the appearance of nepotism—is neither fair to employees, nor in the long-term interests of the business.

PRODUCT QUALITY

A major Caterpillar objective is to design, manufacture, and market products of superior quality. We aim at a level of quality which offers special superiority on demanding applications.

We define quality as the sum of product characteristics and product support which provides optimum return on investment to both the customer and Caterpillar.

Caterpillar products are designed to the same exacting standards, and manufactured to uniformly high levels of quality, throughout the world. Maximum interchangeability of components and parts is maintained—wherever they are manufactured.

We strive to assure users of timely after-sale parts and service availability at fair prices. From our experience, these goals are best achieved through locally based, financially strong, independently owned dealers committed to service. We back availability of parts from dealers with a worldwide network of corporate parts facilities.

We believe pursuit of quality also includes providing products responsive to the need for lower equipment noise levels, compliance with reasonable emissions standards, and safe operating characteristics. We continually monitor the impact of Caterpillar products on the environment—striving to minimize any potentially harmful aspects, and maximize their substantial capability for beneficial contributions.

SHARING OF TECHNOLOGY

Caterpillar takes a worldwide view of technology. We view technology transfer in a broad context—as sharing information, from many varied business functions, aimed at improved company operations everywhere.

We therefore provide design and manufacturing data and marketing and management know-how to all Caterpillar facilities, while observing national restrictions on the transfer of information. Managers are encouraged to participate in professional and trade societies. Managers are provided access, on a worldwide basis, to corporate technical competence which is appropriate to their jobs.

We seek the highest level of engineering technology, regardless of origin, applicable to our products and manufacturing processes. We locate engineering facilities in accordance with need, on a global basis. We encourage equitable relationships with investors, consultants, and research and development laboratories that have technical capabilities with our needs.

We believe the principal threat to future relationships among nations has to do with the widening gap between living standards in industrial and developing countries. Intelligent transfer of technology is a major means by which developing countries can be helped to do what they must ultimately do—help themselves.

However, technology transfer is dependent not only on the ability of people in one nation to offer it, but also in the ability of people in other nations to utilize it. We therefore encourage developing countries to create an environment of law and custom that will maximize such utilization. We support effective industrial property laws, reasonable licensing regulations, and other governmental initiatives which encourage sharing of existing technology with such countries.

Technology is property; it requires time, effort, and money to create, and has value. We believe governments can foster the spread of technology by permitting a reasonable return for its transfer.

FINANCE

The main purpose of money is to facilitate trade. Any company involved in international trade is, therefore, involved in dealing in several of the world's currencies, and in exchanging currencies on the basis of their relative values.

Our policy is to conduct such currency transactions only to the extent they may be necessary to operate the business and protect our interests.

We buy and sell currencies in amounts large enough to cover requirements for the business, and to protect our financial positions in those currencies whose relative values may change in foreign exchange markets. We manage currencies the way we manage materials inventories—attempting to have on hand the right amounts of the various kinds and specifications used in the business. We don't buy unneeded materials or currencies for the purpose of holding them for speculative resale.

INTERCOMPANY PRICING

Our intercompany pricing philosophy is that prices between Caterpillar companies are established at levels equivalent to those which would prevail in arm's length transactions. Frequently, such transactions are between Caterpillar companies in different countries. Caterpillar's intercompany pricing philosophy assures to each country a fair valuation of goods and services transferred—for tariff and income tax purposes.

ACCOUNTING AND FINANCIAL RECORDS

Accounting is called the "*universal* language" of business. Therefore, those who rely on the company's records—investors, creditors, and other decision makers and interested parties—have a right to information that is timely and true.

The integrity of Caterpillar accounting and financial records is based on validity, accuracy, and completeness of basic information supporting entries to the company's books of account. All employees involved in creating, processing, or recording such information are held responsible for its integrity.

Every accounting or financial entry should reflect exactly that which is described by the supporting information. There must be no concealment of information from (or by) mangement, or from the company's independent auditors.

Employees who become aware of possible omission, falsification, or inaccuracy of accounting and financial entries (or basic data supporting such entries) are held responsible for reporting such information. These reports are to be made as specified by corporate procedure.

DIFFERING BUSINESS PRACTICES

While there are business differences from country to country that merit preservation, there are others which are sources of continuing dispute and which tend to distort and inhibit rather than promote competition. Such differences deserve more discussion and resolution. Among these are varying views regarding competitive practices, boycotts, information disclosure, international mergers, accounting procedures, tax systems, transfer pricing, product labeling, labor standards, repatriation of profit, securities transactions, and industrial property and trademark protection laws. We favor more nearly uniform practices among countries. Where necessary, we favor multilateral action aimed at harmonization of differences of this nature.

COMPETITIVE CONDUCT

Fair competition is fundamental to continuation of the free enterprise system. We support laws prohibiting restraints of trade, unfair practices, or abuse of economic power. And we avoid such practices everywhere including areas of the world where laws do not prohibit them.

In large companies like Caterpillar, particular care must be exercised to avoid practices which seek to increase sales by any means other than fair merchandising efforts based on quality, design features, productivity, price and product support.

In relationships with competitors, dealers, suppliers, and users, Caterpillar employees are directed to avoid arrangements restricting our ability to compete with others or the ability of any other business organization to compete freely and fairly with us, and with others.

There must be no arrangements or understandings with competitors affecting prices, terms upon which products are sold, or the number and type of products manufactured or sold or which might be construed as dividing customers or sales territories with a competitor.

Suppliers aren't required to forgo trade with our competitors in order to merit Caterpillar purchases. Caterpillar personnel shall avoid arrangements or understandings prohibiting a supplier from selling products in competition with us, except where (1) the supplier makes the product with tooling or materials owned by Caterpillar or (2) the product is one in which the company has a proprietary interest which has been determined to be legally protectable. Such an interest might arise from an important contribution by Caterpillar to the concept, design, or manufacturing process.

No supplier is asked to buy Caterpillar products in order to continue as a supplier. The purchase of supplies and services is determined by evaluations of quality, price, service, and the maintenance of adequate sources of supply and not by whether the supplier uses Caterpillar products.

Relationships with dealers are established in the Caterpillar dealership agreements. These embody our commitment to fair competitive practices, and reflect customs and laws of various countries where Caterpillar products are sold. Our obligations under these agreements are to be scrupulously observed.

OBSERVANCE OF LOCAL LAWS

A basic requirement levied against any business enterprise is that it know and obey the law. This is rightfully required by those who govern; and it is well understood by business managers.

However, a corporation operating on a global scale will inevitably encounter laws which vary widely from country to country. They may even conflict with each other.

And laws in some countries may encourage or require business practices which based on experience elsewhere in the world we believe to be wasteful or unfair. Under such conditions it scarcely seems sufficient for a business manager to merely say: We obey the law, whatever it may be!

We are guided by the belief that the law is not an end but a means to an end—the end presumably being order, justice, and, not infrequently, strengthening of the government unit involved. If it is to achieve these ends in changing times and circumstances, law itself cannot be insusceptible to change or free of criticism. The law can benefit from both.

Therefore, in a world characterized by a multiplicity of divergent laws at international, national, state, and local levels, Caterpillar's intentions fall in two parts: (1) to obey the law and (2) to offer, where appropriate, constructive ideas for change in the law.

BUSINESS ETHICS

The law is a floor. Ethical business conduct should normally exist at a level well above the minimum required by law.

One of a company's most valuable assets is a reputation for integrity. If that be tarnished, customers, investors, and employees will seek affiliation with other, more attractive companies. We intend to hold to a single high standard of integrity everywhere. We will keep our word. We will not promise more than we can reasonably expect to deliver; nor will we make commitments we don't intend to keep.

In our advertising and other public communications, we will avoid not only untruths, but also exaggeration, overstatement, and boastfulness.

Caterpillar employees shall not accept costly entertainment or gifts (excepting mementos and novelties of nominal value) from dealers, suppliers, and others with whom we do business. And we will not tolerate circumstances that produce, or reasonably appear to produce, conflict between personal interests of an employee and interests of the company.

We seek long-lasting relationships based on integrity with employees, dealers, customers, suppliers, and all whose activities touch upon our own.

RELATIONSHIPS WITH PUBLIC OFFICIALS

In dealing with public officials, as with private business associates, Caterpillar will utilize only ethical commercial practices. We won't seek to influence sales of our products (or other events impacting on the company) by payments of bribes, kickbacks, or other questionable payments.

Caterpillar employees will take care to avoid involving the company in any such activities engaged in by others. We won't advise or assist any purchaser of Caterpillar products, including dealers, in making or arranging such payments. We will actively discourage dealers from engaging in such practices.

Payments of any size to induce public officials to fail to perform their duties or to perform them in an incorrect manner are prohibited. Company employees are also required to make good faith efforts to avoid payment of gratuities or "tips" to certain public officials, even where such practices are customary. Where these payments are as a practical matter unavoidable, they must be limited to customary amounts and may be made only to facilitate correct performance of the officials' duties.

PUBLIC RESPONSIBILITY

We believe there are three basic categories of possible social impact by business:

1. First is the straightforward pursuit of daily business affairs. This involves the conventional (but often misunderstood) dynamics of private enterprise: developing desired goods and services, providing jobs and training, investing in manufacturing and technical facilities, dealing with suppliers, paying taxes, attracting customers, earning a profit.

2. The second category has to do with conducting business affairs in a *way* that is socially responsible. It isn't enough to design, manufacture, and sell useful products. A business enterprise should, for example, employ people without discrimination, see to their job safety and the safety of its products, help protect the quality of the environment, and conserve energy and other valuable resources.

3. The third category relates to initiatives beyond our operations, such as helping solve community problems. To the extent our resources permit and if a host country or community wishes, we will participate selectively in such matters, especially where our facilities are located. Each corporate facility is an integral part of the community in which it operates. Like individuals, it benefits from character building, health, welfare, educational, and cultural activities. And like individuals, it also has citizen responsibilities to support such activities.

All Caterpillar employees are encouraged to take part in public matters of their individual choice. Further, it is recognized that employee participation in political processes or in organizations that may be termed "controversial" can be public service of a high order.

But partisan political activity is a matter for individual determination and action. While Caterpillar may support efforts to encourage political contributions by individual employees, the company won't make contributions to political parties and candidates even where local law may permit such practices.

Where its experience can be helpful, Caterpillar will offer recommendations to governments concerning legislation and regulation being considered. Further, the company will selectively analyze and take public positions on *issues* that have a relationship to operations, when our experience can add to the understanding of such issues.

DISCLOSURE OF INFORMATION

The basic reason for existence of any company is to serve the needs of people. In a free society, institutions flourish and businesses prosper only by customer acceptance of their products and services, and by public acceptance of their conduct.

Therefore, the public is entitled to a reasonable explanation of operations of a business, especially as those operations bear on the public interest. Larger economic size logically begets an increased responsibility for such public communication.

In pursuit of these beliefs, the company will:

1. Respond to reasonable public inquiries including those from the press and from governments with answers that are prompt, informative, and courteous.
2. Keep investors and securities trading markets informed about Caterpillar on a timely, impartial basis.

INTERNATIONAL BUSINESS

We believe the pursuit of business excellence and profit in a climate of fair, free competition is the best means yet found for efficient development and distribution of goods and services. Further, the international exchange of goods and services promotes human understanding, and thus harmony and peace.

These are not unproven theories. The enormous rise in post–World War II, gross national product and living standards in countries participating significantly in international commerce has demonstrated the benefits to such countries. And it has also shown their ability to mutually develop and live by common rules, among them the gradual dismantling of trade barriers.

One of the world's first priorities is to find more effective ways of bringing similar improvement to those developing countries whose participation in the international exchange of goods and services is relatively limited.

As a company that manufactures and distributes on a global scale, Caterpillar recognizes the world is an admixture of differing races, religions, cultures, customs, political philosophies, languages, economic resources, and geography. We respect these differences. Human pluralism can be a strength, not a weakness; no nation has a monopoly on wisdom.

It is not our aim to attempt to remake the world in the image of any one country. Rather, we hope to help improve the quality of life, wherever we do business, by serving as a means of transmission and application of knowledge that has been found useful elsewhere. We intend to learn and benefit from human diversity.

We ask all governments to permit us to compete on equal terms with competitors. This goes beyond the influence a country can exert on our competitiveness within its national boundaries. It also applies to the substantial way a government can control or impact on our business in *other* lands through domestic taxes and regulations affecting the price of products to be exported, and through "host country" laws affecting our operations outside that country.

We aim to compete successfully in terms of design, manufacture, and sale of our products, not in terms of artificial barriers and incentives.

REPORTING CODE COMPLIANCE

Each officer, subsidiary head, plant or parts department manager, and department head shall prepare a memorandum by the close of each year: (1) affirming a full knowledge and understanding of this code and (2) reporting any events or activities which might cause an impartial observer to conclude that the code hasn't been fully followed. These reports should be sent directly to the company's General Counsel; General Offices; Peoria, Illinois.

PART FIVE

Human Investment

It is often said that the most difficult challenges facing managers are "people problems." The importance of employees to organizations is readily apparent. After all, companies are composed of people: people with ambitions, fears, frustrations, grievances, illnesses, and economic needs. From top to bottom, businesses must invest in people. The effective manager is always preparing his or her successor. Managers must always seek to allow people to grow and to reach their highest possible level of development. In contrast at times with its Japanese counterpart, American management has to keep relearning this simple truth, thus reflecting poorly on how we train managers and the manner in which some firms reward managers.

In the face of an increase in mergers and acquisitions and hostile take-overs, one of the first areas hit for cost recovery is personnel. As cost-saving as this may be in the short run, management's obsessive drive to cut labor costs can be ultimately self-defeating. Recent management studies have emphasized the hidden costs of firings and layoffs. These studies have also pointed to cost reductions that can be accomplished through other means, such as plant automation and better inventory control.[1]

Given its critical importance to society as an employer of millions, it is not surprising that American business has been under particular pressure to invest well in humans: to make them productive, motivated people who work in a safe environment that is free of racial, sexual, and other forms of improper discrimination. Hence, the treatment of employees is not an "internal" issue. Human investment is as much a social/political issue as ecology or consumerism. As such, management must recognize that corporate social performance is highly influenced by human investment issues that arise external to the business environment.

Business often has little or no control over changes in the external environment, and once change starts, it may be many years before change amenable to a certain type of business occurs again. For instance, during the 1950s and 1960s the Baby Boom generation was in its youth. As more of the Baby Boomers emerged as teenagers, the fast food industry took off, driven by

---

[1] John Holusha, "Accounting in Factories Is Criticized as Outdated," *New York Times,* March 23, 1987.

a large and growing market and by a new pool of cheap labor (teenagers). Now, as we enter the 1990s, as the Baby Boom generation matures, the fast food industry is being stressed by a decline in their traditional consumer and labor markets. The number of teenagers has declined so much that fast food restaurants are having to offer premium salaries, special bonuses, and use elderly workers in order to maintain staffing levels.

Using a systems perspective enables us to study the relationships between parts of a system. Thus we can examine the impact of changes in human investment on other parts of the business. Again, in the fast food industry, some fast food giants were major contributors to the Reagan campaign with the intent to get a lowering or elimination of the minimum wage, among other things. That movement has now been made moot by the change in the population structure as the Baby Boomers mature. In most areas of the country, fast food chains are having to offer salaries far above minimum wage in order to attract enough labor.

The Civil Rights Act of 1964, the Occupational Safety and Health Act of 1970, the Employee Retirement Income Security Act of 1974, and hundreds of other pieces of federal, state, and local legislation have had a profound effect on the employer-employee relationship. The struggle for a better balance between management prerogatives and worker safety and general welfare has been a long one. Progress in this area is often hampered by seemingly arbitrary and inconsistent changes in the political environment. A business person using responsible hiring and work practices often finds that the standards for responsibility and the incentives for being responsible change from one administration to another.

Human investment also provides a further study of themes discussed in Part III, Social/Political Responsiveness. The community and political system sends signals to business regarding appropriate conduct. Over time these signals change and may be in conflict with other signals. For example, while the trend in legislation has been toward greater participation of minorities in the work force, the Reagan administration often gave business a different message. At its most benign the message was that businesses that were relatively responsive and ethical in their hiring practices would find less protection from more unethical competitors.

The cases in this section provide the opportunity to explore several human investment issues. The *Manville Corporation (1988)* case represents a growing problem in worker safety and health and liability. Labor relations is the focus of the J. P. Stevens & Co., Inc. case. It represents one of the most bitter and publicized labor/management confrontations in recent years. It highlights the impact on company operation of antiquated management attitudes toward social responsiveness. The SCA Corporation case shows a direct outgrowth of the struggles of a company to regain its competitive edge by means of productivity improvement. The complexity of the SCA productivity improvement system reflects the modern challenges facing managers in medium to large corporations. The last case, *National Savings and Loan Association and the*

Specter of AIDS, focuses on one of the most difficult challenges facing managers today and into the future. The challenge of AIDS in the workplace has profound ramifications for business operations. It raises issues of employees' rights and privacy, health and life insurance, employee testing, screening and measurement, managerial control, morale, and the company's responsibility to society at large.

The readings consider several controversial human investment topics. Peter F. Drucker, in *Workers' Hands Bound by Tradition,* considers the impact on productivity on outmoded labor practices.

Firefighters' Questionable Minority Status Went Unchallenged 10 Years raises the conundrum of how to define minority status and implement good management practices in the hiring and advancement of minorities.

The long-term issue of training workers is raised by *Workers Go Back to the Basics.* Many people believe that if America is to remain competitive, then a well-trained work force will be necessary. This piece looks at the human investment impact of high-tech work environments which are sometimes too sophisticated for a firm's employees.

More Concerns Set Two-Tier Pacts with Unions, Penalizing New Hires discusses the growing practice of negotiating two-tier employment agreements that allow companies to hire new employees at a lower compensation level (pay and benefits) than current workers enjoy. Two-tiered employment agreements have been aggressively pushed by some managers in recent airline mergers and acquisitions. The *AIDS Commission's Hidden Tax* highlights how society, through the political system, often thrusts on business the responsibility for correcting social problems. Whether one decides that individuals, the society, or the political system bears the blame for the specter of AIDS, it often falls to business to deal with the human investment fallout.

All in all, the cases and commentaries here represent the ultimate challenge to management. Without adequate attention to human investment issues, all the other issues discussed in this book are difficult or impossible to address.

CASE

Manville Corporation

Perhaps no other mineral is so woven into the fabric of American life as is asbestos. Impervious to heat and fibrous—it is the only mineral that can be woven into cloth—asbestos is spun into fireproof clothing and theater curtains, as well as into such household items as noncombustible drapes, rugs, pot holders, and ironing-board covers. Mixed into slurry, asbestos is sprayed onto girders and walls to provide new buildings with fireproof insulation. It is used in floor tiles, roofing felts, and in most plasterboards and wallboards. Asbestos is also an ingredient of plaster and stucco and of many paints and putties. This "mineral of a thousand uses"—an obsolete nickname: the present count stands at around 3,000 uses—is probably present in some form or other in every home, school, office building, and factory in this country. Used in brake linings and clutch facings, in mufflers and gaskets, in sealants and caulking, and extensively used in ships, asbestos is also a component of every modern vehicle, including space ships.

This was written by columnist Bruce Porter in 1973, just as the dangers of breathing asbestos dust were becoming widely recognized by the general public. Asbestos is a natural fiber, mined by crushing rock which contains it and sifting and blowing away the rock particles. Ingested asbestos causes mechanical injury to moving tissue, especially the lungs. The microscopic fibers are impervious to body fluids and oxygen and are almost impossible to filter out of air. The constant motion of the lungs causes tissue to be penetrated and cut by the fibers. This leads to progressive and irreversible scarring, thickening, and calcification of the lungs and their linings, a condition called asbestosis. A rare and always-fatal pleural cancer, mesothelioma, is strongly connected with asbestos exposure as are increased incidence and severity of lung cancer and many other respiratory ailments. The first outward symptoms of asbestos disease typically appear 10 to 30 years after exposure begins. But early damage is easily detectable by X rays, and some cancers and respiratory deficiencies show up after only a year or two.

This case was prepared by Arthur Sharplin of McNeese State University, Lake Charles, Louisiana, with the assistance and encouragement of the Center for Business Ethics at Bentley College in Waltham, Massachusetts, of which the author is a fellow. Copyright 1988 by Arthur Sharplin.

Annual use of asbestos in the United States rose from around 200,000 metric tons in the 1930s to a plateau of about 700,000 metric tons during the 1950s, 1960s, and early 1970s. Then it dropped sharply, to just over 100,000 metric tons in 1985.[1] Worldwide, asbestos production continued to expand rapidly until about the mid 1970s, then plateaued at about 4.6 million metric tons a year. Through 1986 world production dropped only a little, apparently because increased shipments to developing countries offset declining usage elsewhere.[2] Canada, the world's dominant marketer of asbestos in the late 1980s, sold an estimated 42 percent of its output to Asia in 1988, up from just 16 percent in 1979. Other leading producers were Russia, Canada, Zimbabwe, and Brazil.

From about the turn of the century, Johns-Manville Corporation (renamed Manville Corporation in 1981) had been the world's leading asbestos company, involved in mining and sale of the raw fibers as well as development, manufacture, and marketing of intermediate and finished asbestos products. Company executives and their cohorts in other asbestos companies knew the dangers of breathing asbestos dust during the 1930s. They took many actions to suppress research and publicity about the problem and continued into the 1980s to deny their early knowledge. Manville was the main target of a trickle of asbestos-health (A-H) lawsuits in the 1920s and early 30s which would become a flood by the 1980s.

Manville would pay little to A-H victims through 1988. But it was not able to replace the asbestos profits as they collapsed in the late 1970s. On the evening of August 25, 1982, the Manville board of directors was briefed on bankruptcy reorganization. A petition for protection from creditors under Chapter 11 of the U.S. Bankruptcy Code had already been prepared. It was approved by the board that night and filed the next day. It would be more than six years before a plan to emerge from court protection would be final. Many of the asbestos victims would die in the meantime. And the tens of thousands who had been held off by the bankruptcy court during those years would find their claims shunted to a separate trust (the A-H Trust) and effectively subordinated to those of commercial creditors as well as to other interests. Within months after paying its first A-H claim in 1989 the A-H Trust would run short of funds. But the bankruptcy judge would reaffirm his earlier ruling that no A-H victim could ever again sue Manville, its executives, or its insurers.

In the meantime, a second generation of Manville top managers would serve out their tenures and retire, many with large termination bonuses.

---

[1] Barry I. Castleman, *Asbestos: Medical and Legal Aspects* (Clifton, N.J.: Prentice-Hall Law and Business, 1987), p. 614.

[2] Ibid., pp. 636–7.

COMPANY BACKGROUND

Until the 1970s, Manville was a success by the usual standards. Incorporated in 1901, the company saw consistent growth in sales and profits. Dividends were paid every year except for the war years of 1915–1916 and the depths of the Depression in 1933–1934. Manville was one of the "Dow-Jones Industrial Thirty" for many years.

In the decades before 1970, Manville's sales grew somewhat slower than the gross national product. But the company benefited from relatively low fixed costs, due to a largely depleted and depreciated capital base and the total absence of long-term debt in the capital structure. With low operating and financial leverage, the firm was able to adapt to sales downturns in 1957, 1960, 1967, and 1970 and still earn profits in each of those years. By 1970, Manville had about $400 million ($1.2 billion in 1989 dollars) in book value net worth garnered almost entirely from the mining, manufacture, and sale of asbestos products, for which it still held a dominant market position. Appendix A describes selected pre-1970s events concerning asbestos and health.

During the 1960s, a number of the senior officials who had been with Manville since the 1930s died or retired. Compared to just the 1966 board of directors, the 1970 board had a majority of new members. In 1970, departing from a tradition of promoting from within, the board of directors installed an outsider, psychologist Richard Goodwin, as president. Thus began a prolonged effort to diversify Manville away from asbestos and to change its image.

Goodwin arranged to move the corporate headquarters from its old Madison Avenue brick building to the Denver countryside. There, he purchased the 10,000 acre Ken Caryl Ranch and planned a luxurious "world headquarters," the first phase of which was to cost $60 million.

Goodwin also led the company through more than 20 small acquisitions— in lighting systems, golf carts, irrigation sprinklers, and other products. In the process, Manville's long-term debt went from zero to $196 million and fixed costs increased several fold. A short, steep recession in 1975 cut Manville's profits in half, back to 1970 levels. U.S. asbestos consumption had begun its rapid decline, which was to accelerate and total more than 50 percent by 1982.

And Manville was suffering reverses in its fight against the asbestos tort lawsuits. In 1972, Manville and five other asbestos companies had lost the landmark Clarence Borel asbestos tort lawsuit. The appeals court in that case wrote, "The evidence . . . tended to establish that none of the defendants ever tested its product to determine its effect on industrial insulation workers. . . . The unpalatable facts are that in the twenties and thirties the hazards of working with asbestos were recognized."[3]

In an April 1976 deposition, Dr. Kenneth Smith, former Manville medical

---

[3] *Clarence Borel* v. *Fibreboard Paper Products Corporation, et al.,* 493 F. 2d. 1076–1109 (5th Cir. 1973).

director, told of his knowledge of asbestos dangers during the 1940s. He also revealed his 1950 finding that the lungs of 704 of the 708 Manville asbestos workers he studied showed asbestos damage. He went on to describe his unsuccessful efforts to get caution labels put on Manville asbestos products.[4]

Then, in April 1977, the "Raybestos-Manhattan Correspondence" was discovered by asbestos plaintiff attorneys. Included were many letters and memoranda among Manville officials and other asbestos industry executives. Most were written during the 1930s. A South Carolina judge hearing an asbestos case wrote,

> The Raybestos-Manhattan Correspondence very arguably shows a pattern of denial of disease and attempts at suppression of information which is highly probative [and] reflects a conscious effort by the industry in the 1930s to downplay, or arguably suppress, the dissemination of information to employees and the public . . .[5]

Confronted with the new and damning evidence, a growing number of juries awarded punitive damages against Manville during 1981 and 1982, as much as a million dollars per claimant. And many suits named current and former Manville executives as defendants.[6] When Manville sought bankruptcy court protection in August of 1982, asbestos-health claims against the company numbered 20,000 and new suits were being filed at the rate of three an hour every business day.[7] The average cost per case, the company said, was "sharply higher" than in prior years, averaging $40,000 per claim.[8]

The managers at Manville were particularly vulnerable to charges of conspiring to hide past sins of the company, if not for committing them. The top five executives had each been with the firm since 1952 or before. All had been senior officials since at least the early 1970s.[9]

---

[4] Dr. Kenneth W. Smith, Discovery deposition, *Louisville Trust Company, Administrator of the estate of William Virgil Sampson* v. *Johns-Manville Corporation,* File no. 164-122, (Court of Common Pleas, Jefferson County, Kentucky, April 21, 1987). A Manville attorney later claimed Smith was an alcoholic.

[5] Amended Order (Survival and Wrongful Death Actions), *Bennie M. Barnett, Administrator, for Gordon Luther Barnett, deceased,* v. *Owens-Corning Fiberglass Corp., et al.,* (Court of Common Pleas, Greenville County, South Carolina, August 23, 1978), 10 and 5.

[6] Ronald L. Motley (leading asbestos plaintiff attorney), telephone conversation with author, October 9, 1987, Charleston, South Carolina. Also see Manville Corporation, *Quarterly Report on U.S. Securities and Exchange Commission Form 10-Q,* for quarter ended June 30, 1982, II-8 (discussion of Louisiana cases).

[7] G. Earl Parker, "The Manville Decision," Paper presented at the symposium "Bankruptcy Proceedings—The Effect on Product Liability," conducted by Andrews Publications, Inc., Miami, March 1983, p. 3.

[8] Manville Corporation, "Manville Files for Reorganization," media release, August 26, 1982, p. 2.

[9] Manville Corporation, *1982 Proxy Statement,* March 25, 1982, p. 12; *Moody's Industrial Manual,* 2 (New York: Moody's Investor Service, 1971), p. 1424; (1972), p. 3222; (1973), pp. 2907–8; and (1974), p. 2040.

The outside directors were eminent in their respective fields, but they too could hardly claim noninvolvement. Among them were the deans of the School of Architecture at Princeton and the Graduate School of Business Administration at New York University. The latter had previously been chief executive of American Can Company. Also included were the chief executive of Ideal Basic Industries, Inc., who had earlier been elected three times as Governor of Colorado, the head of Phelps Dodge Corporation, and the top managers of three other companies.[10] All but 2 of the 11 directors in 1982 had over 10 years tenure, averaging 17 years on the board. Six had joined the board in the 1960s and two others, the inside directors, had worked for Manville since about 1950.[11]

Five months after the Smith deposition, the nine outside directors of Manville demanded the resignation of Richard Goodwin. According to Goodwin, the three directors who transmitted the demand refused to explain their action.[12] A later Manville chief executive would claim Goodwin had been a womanizer and an alcoholic.[13]

John A. McKinney, Manville's legal chief—who had joined the company before 1950—took over as chief executive. McKinney divested many of the Goodwin acquisitions and turned his attention to what he called "aggressive defense" of the asbestos lawsuits and the search for a "substantial acquisition." He also made plans for a $200 million expansion in the company's fiberglass operations. In his 1977 "President's Review," McKinney wrote, "[W]e do not expect asbestos fiber to dominate J-M earnings to the extent it has in the past."[14]

Ideal Basic Industries (IBI), a major producer of potash and portland cement, spurned a Manville buyout initiative in early 1978. It may have been important that the chief executive of IBI, John A. Love, was on the Manville board of directors. Next, Manville began a takeover battle (with Texas Eastern Corporation) for Olinkraft Corporation, a wood products company concentrated in paperboard and paper. Olinkraft's main assets were about 600,000 acres of prime southern timberland and several paper mills.

Manville won the contest and closed the deal in the last half of 1978. The purchase price was $595 million, 2.24 times book value and over twice recent market value. About half was paid in cash and the rest was represented by a new issue of cumulative preferred stock which was required to be repurchased beginning in 1987.

The directors and officers were guaranteed indemnification by Manville, a

[10] Manville Corporation, *1982 Proxy Statement,* March 25, 1982, pp. 4–7.

[11] Ibid., pp. 4–7.

[12] Herbert E. Meyer, "Shootout at the Johns-Manville Corral," *Fortune,* October 1976, pp. 146–54.

[13] W. Thomas Stephens, conversation with author at Seventh National Conference on Business Ethics, Waltham, Mass., October 16, 1987.

[14] Manville Corporation, *1977 Annual Report,* p. 2.

contract they had the company reaffirm in 1981.[15] The importance of such protection is illustrated by attacks by asbestos victims against the estate of Vandiver Brown, Manville vice president and secretary during the 1930s, attacks which would continue into the mid-1980s.[16]

But ordinary business problems after 1978 imperiled the managers' indemnity and rendered even their jobs insecure, not to mention the professional embarrassment failure might bring such illustrious directors and executives. That year, the company began what seemed an irreversible downward slide financially. Revenues (in 1986 dollars) fell from $2.74 billion in 1978 to a $2.18 billion annual rate for the first half of 1982. And earnings available to common stock (also in 1986 dollars) simply evaporated, going from $198 million to an $85 million annual-rate *loss*.[17] Earnings available to common stock, of course, excludes dividends on the debt-equivalent preferred stock issued in the Olinkraft acquisition. Despite its acquisitions, Manville remained intensely concentrated in construction-dependent businesses, which all suffered from the construction industry recession that began in 1979. Appendix B provides financial summaries for 1978 through the first half of 1982.

Manville's auditor, Coopers and Lybrand, qualified its opinion on the company's 1980 and 1981 annual reports.[18] Of course, Standard & Poor's and Moody's downgraded the company's debt.[19] And Manville's insurers gave the executives little solace; they stopped paying for most of the asbestos claims by 1981,[20] and generally could not pay punitive damages anyway.

The small amounts actually paid for "asbestos health costs," $13 million in 1981 and $16 million in 1982,[21] could hardly be blamed for the financial collapse. Those costs never amounted to even 1 percent of sales. But loss of asbestos profits was clearly a major factor. Until at least 1978, the immensely profitable asbestos trade was the company's mainstay. Sales of the raw fiber alone produced 41 percent of Manville's operating profit as late as 1976, though accounting for only 12 percent of revenues that year.[22] Further, many of the company's manufactured products were asbestos-based, including as-

---

[15] Manville Corporation, *1981 Proxy Statement*, September 11, 1981, Exhibit 2, pp. 5–7.

[16] "Stay Sought for Lawsuits Against Estate of Vandiver Brown," *Stockholders & Creditors News Service Re. Johns-Manville Corp., et al.* (Edgemont, Penn.: Andrews Publications, November 5, 1984), p. 3082.

[17] Manville Corporation, *1982 Annual Report and Form 10-K*, p. 7 and *U.S. Securities and Exchange Commission Form 10-Q*, for quarter ended June 30, 1982, p. I–2. Also, Johns-Manville Corporation, *1978 Annual Report*, p. 36. U.S. Consumer Price Index figures were obtained from Ibbotson Associates, *Stocks, Bonds, Bills, and Inflation: 1987 Yearbook* (Chicago: Ibbotson Associates, Inc., 1987), p. 30.

[18] Manville Corporation, *1980 Annual Report*, p. 21, and *1981 Annual Report*, p. 15.

[19] See, for example, "Manville Ratings Cut by Standard & Poor's," *The Wall Street Journal*, June 11, 1982, p. 36.

[20] Manville Corporation, *U.S. Securities and Exchange Commission Form 10-Q*, for quarter ended June 30, 1982, pp. II–11–II-14.

[21] Manville Corporation, *1982 Annual Report and Form 10-K*, p. 7.

[22] Manville Corporation, *1977 Annual Report*, p. 1.

bestos felts, papers, textiles, asbestos-cement shingles, asbestos-cement water and sewer pipe, and asbestos paper and millboard.[23]

Public awareness of asbestos-health dangers continued to increase and U.S. purchases of the substance fell by 36 percent in 1980 alone.[24] Led by lawyer McKinney, the directors voted to reorganize the company in 1981, placing the non-asbestos operations in separate corporations under the parent Manville.

By 1982, Manville's asbestos-fiber revenues were half the 1976 level. An estimated 60 percent of the fiber was sold internationally, mainly in Western Europe.[25] And each dollar of fiber sales produced markedly less operating profit, 18 cents versus 33 cents in 1976.[26]

The stock market reflected Manville's deteriorating financial condition. By mid-August 1982, the company's common stock price had dropped below $8, less than one fourth its 1977 high.

IN FULL READINESS FOR CHAPTER 11

The company was well prepared for a Chapter 11 filing. Manville was still able to pay its bills. But the 1978 bankruptcy act had removed insolvency as a requirement for filing. The Olinkraft purchase had been structured so half the cost would not come due until 1987 and later. Filing would stay that obligation. The 1981 reorganization had segregated the asbestos assets in separate corporations. Each corporation could file its own Chapter 11 petition. They could submit separate or joint reorganization plans. Management could decide which.

Manville had ready access to the best consultants and attorneys. For 50 years, the firm had been close to Morgan Stanley and Company and Davis Polk and Wardwell. Morgan Stanley was the nation's leading investment banker. Davis Polk was a top New York law firm.

And there were no rebels on the management team. Eight of the 11 directors had been with Manville since the 50s and 60s. After Goodwin took over in 1970, no senior manager came in from outside. In fact, the top five executives in 1982 each had at least 30 years tenure.

Best yet, almost none of the company's $1.1 billion debt was secured. McKinney would soon boast of "nearly $2 billion in unencumbered assets." That would prove to be a real advantage in bankruptcy. Unsecured creditors

---

[23] Johns-Manville Corporation, *1977 Annual Report,* pp. 8, 10, and 13.

[24] Raymond A. Joseph, "Problems Have Long Plagued Asbestos Firms," *The Wall Street Journal,* August 30, 1982, p. 15 (U.S. Interior Department figures in thousands of metric tons for 1976–1981 are given as 659, 610, 619, 561, 359, and 350, respectively).

[25] Manville Corporation, *1982 Annual Report and Form 10-K,* pp. 18 and 30, and Johns-Manville Corporation, *1977 Annual Report,* p. 1.

[26] Ibid.

have no claim on or control over any particular assets. And their claims can be discharged under a reorganization plan.

THE BANKRUPTCY REORGANIZATION

On August 26 that year, Manville filed its bankruptcy petition. The common stock fell from $7.875 the day before the filing to $4.625 a few days later. All legal actions against the company, including the asbestos tort lawsuits, were automatically stayed under provisions of the bankruptcy law. Appendix C summarizes the Chapter 11 process.

The company's largest division, Manville Forest Products Corporation, emerged from Chapter 11 protection in 1983. Under the court order, it was obligated to pay its commercial debt, but was free of asbestos claims.[27] Various other units, notably the main asbestos fiber subsidiaries and certain asbestos-cement pipe operations, were sold that year, also free of Manville's asbestos liabilities.[28] Appendix D provides financial summaries for several years following Manville's bankruptcy filing.

A reorganization plan for the remaining divisions was filed by Manville management in 1986. The bankruptcy judge in the case issued a confirmation order December 22, 1986. But full implementation of the plan was held up pending the outcome of two appeals from the order.[29]

The plan provided for essentially full payment of $472 million of unsecured commercial creditor claims which had not been paid earlier. Secured obligations were to be either paid in full or reinstated with payment of accrued interest. Common stockholders were to be practically dispossessed through issuance of additional shares and rights. Preferred stockholders were to receive a mixture of common and "preference" shares worth an estimated 15 percent of the face value of their preferred shares.

A trust (the A-H trust) set up to pay asbestos-health claims was to receive the following assets: (1) $615 million in expected insurance settlement proceeds, partly deferred and all contingent on the plan surviving all appeals; (2) $111 million estimated confirmation-date value in cash and receivables; (3) a zero-coupon bond worth an estimated $249 million[30]—in an October 1987 debate at the National Conference on Business Ethics, Manville chief executive W. Thomas Stephens said the value of the bond was $350 million; (4) other debt securities valued at about $45 million; (5) 50 percent of Manville's common stock, which was to be required to be voted for management's choices for

---

[27] Manville Corporation, *1983 Annual Report and Form 10K*, p. 13.

[28] Ibid., p. 15.

[29] See, for example, "Appeals Consolidated in 2nd Circuit (sic), Possible Hearing in October," *Stockholders & Creditors News Service* (Edgemont, Penn.: Andrews Publications, September 21, 1987), p. 6953.

[30] Arthur Sharplin, "Liquidation versus 'The Plan.'" *The Asbestos Litigation Reporter* (Edgemont, Penn.: Andrews Publications, November 21, 1986), pp. 13636–40.

directors for at least four years after plan consummation—sale of the stock was to be restricted for at least five years after consummation; (6) contingent claims on 20 percent of corporate earnings beginning the fourth fiscal year after consummation and on a new issue of convertible preferred stock.[31]

After the publicity surrounding the Manville bankruptcy, hundreds of property-damage (PD) claims began to be filed. They were mainly claims for estimated costs of cleaning asbestos out of the thousands of schools and government and commercial buildings where it had been used as insulation or fire proofing. By 1986 the PD claims totaled over $70 billion. Manville's plan provided that a PD trust would be set up to pay these claims. It would be initially funded with $100 million from Manville and $25 million from the A-H trust. The PD trust was also supposed to get certain extra funds the A-H trust might have.

The A-H claimants committee, consisting of 19 lawyers and one asbestos victim, endorsed the Manville plan, emphasizing the $2.5 billion nominal value of the A-H trust. However, one expert used discounted cash flow analysis to calculate the value of the proposed trust assets at $572 million.[32]

HOW THE MANAGERS FARED

Compared to the chaos which imperiled the executives' fortunes and jobs in the months before August 1982, the situation which existed thereafter must have seemed sublime. For the executives and directors, Chapter 11 brought a lightened management load, improved pay and benefits, munificent retirement for those who desired it, and bonuses and "golden parachutes" for others. The pre-filing managers and directors even arranged to continue their power over the corporation after its possible emergence from bankruptcy court protection. Finally, some of the pre-filing managers were able to control, or even own, company assets freed of asbestos claims.

Lightened Management Load

When Manville filed its Chapter 11 petition, the management burden was lightened by a surplus of cash and the ability to generate income out of avoided interest expense. The company's receivables flowed in and $627 million in unsecured liabilities were frozen, most to be paid only after conclusion of the Chapter 11 proceedings.[33] The company was not required to pay this debt, or even accrue interest on it after the filing. Consequently, Manville's cash and marketable securities balance varied from a little over $200 million in December 1982 to over $440 million December 31, 1986—compared to $27 mil-

---

[31] Ibid.

[32] Ibid.

[33] Manville Corporation, *1982 Annual Report and Form 10-K,* December 31, 1982, pp. 6 and 11.

lion on June 30, 1982, shortly before the filing.[34] The pre-filing unsecured debt, including accounts payable and other accrued liabilities, was down to $490 million by December 1986.[35] But if the avoided interest on even that amount had been accrued yearly, Manville would have suffered an overall loss for the five years 1982–1986 instead of the reported $92 million total net profit it reported.

Further, the managers were undoubtedly more comfortable in the legal/administrative milieu of the bankruptcy court than in the economic one of competitive business. Chairman/chief executive/president John A. McKinney and 4 more of the 11 directors in 1982 were attorneys (although one, William D. Tucker, Jr. had just joined the board that year). The company had been involved in asbestos-tort litigation since the 1920s. The litigation and related public affairs matters had been a dominant concern since the early 1970s. The company's success in staving off the asbestos-health claims until the 1980s contrasted with its inability to reverse the economic downslide which began in 1979.

Improved Pay and Benefits

The directors and top executives of Manville, mostly unchanged after the 60s, increased their pay and improved their benefits while in bankruptcy. For example, chief executive John McKinney's reported cash compensation went from $408,750 in early 1982 to $638,005 in 1985, his last full year of employment. Senior vice president Chester Sulewski's increased by 88 percent from 1982 to 1986. The cash compensation of W. Thomas Stephens, who became president in September 1986, was 39 percent higher that year than in 1985, the first year he appeared in the company's Compensation Table.[36]

The cash compensation of the 32 officers and directors of Manville was shown as $3.9 million in the March 25, *1982 Proxy Statement* (p. 10). The *1986 Annual Report and Form 10-K* (p. 63) reported cash compensation of $5.5 million for just the 25 executive officers during 1986.

Secure Retirement, "Golden Parachutes," and Bonuses

And the most senior pre-filing managers were able to retire in economic security, shielded by the bankruptcy court and indemnified by Manville against the asbestos victims. The Manville reorganization plan provided that the A-H Trust would be responsible for defending and paying any future asbestos claims against the company, its insurers, or the executives and

---

34 Manville Corporation, *1982 Annual Report and Form 10-K*, p. 6, *1986 Annual Report and Form 10-K*, p. 39, and *U.S. Securities and Exchange Commission Form 10-Q*, for the quarter ended June 30,1982, p. I-3.

35 Manville Corporation, *1986 Annual Report and Form 10K*, December 31, 1986, p. 45.

36 Manville Corporation, *1982 Proxy Statement*, p. 10, *1985 Annual Report and Form 10-K*, p. 79, and *1986 Annual Report and Form 10-K*, p. 63.

directors. McKinney's severance agreement, effective September 1, 1986, granted him cash payments totaling $1.3 million, two extra years of fringe benefits, and two extra years of longevity for retirement purposes. Two other managers were given severance agreements at the same time providing for payments totaling $1,030,000 and certain other benefits.

By December 1986, four of the five most highly paid executives shown in the *1982 Proxy Statement* had left the company. J. T. Hulce resigned as president in 1986, allegedly under pressure from the asbestos victims' committee, and was authorized $530,000 in severance pay.[37] G. Earl Parker, Manville's legal chief under McKinney, retired in March 1987. His severance agreement, approved by the bankruptcy court in September 1987, provided for payments of $430,000 a year through 1989, a total of $1.2 million, counting from March 1987, when he stepped down.[38] But the board of directors remained mostly unchanged from the 1982 board, with only one of the nine outside directors having departed.

The executives left behind were also reassured of large termination payments upon choosing or being asked to leave and probable bonuses in the meantime. At a special board meeting in New York held on October 11, 1985, McKinney discussed "Confidential Minute Number 13," which was said to address severance pay of up to two times annual salary for officers and other "key managerial personnel" upon any termination of employment. It was agreed that the special pay would even apply to persons terminated after any assignment of a trustee in the bankruptcy case.[39]

In mid-July 1987, Manville obtained court approval for a new executive bonus plan for that year increasing the possible bonuses for certain managers from 57.5 percent of annual salaries to 97.1 percent. The allowable bonuses for achieving less than 80 percent of goals were reduced.[40]

Post-Consummation Power

The power of the pre-filing directors and replacement senior managers promised to remain firm for at least four years after plan consummation. Two new directors were appointed at the insistence of a group of preferred share-

---

[37] Cynthia F. Mitchell, "Manville to Pay Large Severance to 2 Executives," *The Wall Street Journal,* June 24, 1986, pp. 3 and 5. Also see Cynthia F. Mitchell, "Manville President Quits After Dispute with Asbestos Plaintiff over Top Posts," *The Wall Street Journal,* April 30, 1986, p. 34.

[38] Arthur Sharplin, "Liquidation versus 'The Plan,'" *The Asbestos Litigation Reporter,* November 21, 1986, pp. 13636–40. Also see Johns-Manville Corporation et al., "Application for an Order Approving Severance Pay Agreements," *Stockholders & Creditors News Service* (Edgemont, Penn.: Andrews Publications, September 8, 1986), pp. 5569–72, and "Judge Approves Severance Pay for G. Earl Parker," *Stockholders & Creditors News Service* (Edgemont, Penn.: Andrews Publications, October 5, 1987), pp. 6988–89.

[39] "Key Manville Officers Allowed Severance in Event of Termination by Trustee," *Stockholder and Creditors News Service* (Edgemont, Penn.: Andrews Publications, April 7, 1986), p. 4995.

[40] "New Bonus Plan for Executives Approved by Court," *Stockholders and Creditors News Service* (Edgemont, Penn.: Andrews Publications, August 10, 1987), pp. 6778–9.

holders in 1984,[41] but no other new outside director appeared on the 1987 board.[42] A third director, Randall Smith, a limited partner in Bear Stearns & Co., had served briefly. Smith was appointed after Bear Stearns accumulated a large holding of Manville common stock.[43] Smith resigned his directorship in late 1985. No annual or special meetings of common shareholders, at which new directors might have been elected, were permitted after the bankruptcy filing.[44]

Further, the Manville reorganization plan provided that at least half of all common shares, those held by the A-H Trust, would be voted for management's nominees to the board of directors for four years after the consummation date.[45] While the initial post-consummation board of directors was to include seven new outside members, six of the pre-filing directors were to remain on the board, as was chief executive W. Thomas Stephens.[46]

Control of Assets Free of Asbestos Claims

Some of the executives who left the company were able to remain in control of substantial assets, assets then free and clear of asbestos claims against Manville. For example, the group which bought Manville's Canadian asbestos division on July 1, 1983, was headed by the chief executive officer of Johns-Manville Canada.[47] Aside from about $47 million apparently borrowed on the asbestos assets and remitted to Manville, the $117 million to $150 million (Canadian) selling price was payable "out of 85.5 percent of available future cash flows from asbestos fiber operations."[48] Those cash flows were so great, the bill was paid in just four years. In 1989, Peter Kyle, president of the Canadian company, said, "As far as leveraged buy-outs go, I don't think there are any as good as this one." The other divisions sold in 1983, notably certain asbestos-cement pipe operations, were presumably transferred with management in place.[49]

After leaving Manville in 1986, former president Hulce and another former Manville executive helped form a company, BMZ Materials, Inc., which

---

[41] "Manville Adds 3 to Board to Increase Shareholder Input," *The Wall Street Journal,* August 3, 1984, p. 4.

[42] Manville Corporation, *1986 Annual Report and Form 10-K,* pp. 56–59.

[43] See Dean Rotbart and Jonathan Dahl, "Manville's Common Stockholders May Have Potent Ally as Bear Stearns Bolsters Holdings," *The Wall Street Journal,* July 25, 1984, p. 51.

[44] See, for example, Manville Corporation, *1986 Annual Report and Form 10-K,* p. 33.

[45] Manville Corporation, *First Amended Disclosure Statement, Second Amended and Restated Plan of Reorganization, and Related Documents,* August 22, 1986, p. 41.

[46] Manville Corporation, *1986 Annual Report and Form 10-K,* pp. 56–61.

[47] "Hearing on Sale of J-M Canada Scheduled for August 30," *Stockholders and Creditors News Service* (Edgemont, Penn.: Andrews Publications, August 15, 1983), p. 1315.

[48] Ibid.

[49] Ibid., p. 15.

purchased several Manville plants with annual sales of $17.5 million. The purchase price was $5.5 million in cash and a $1.5 million promissory note.[50]

Several other sales of Manville assets were approved by the bankruptcy court at about the same time.[51] In all these cases, the assets involved were legally placed out of reach of the asbestos victims.

Even some of the managers who stayed with Manville, those in Manville Forest Products Corporation, controlled assets not subject to asbestos claims as early as 1983. That subsidiary accounted for more than a third of Manville's assets in 1986.[52] As previously mentioned, it emerged from bankruptcy court protection in 1983.

BENEFITS FOR ATTORNEYS AND CONSULTANTS

The Manville executives and directors found themselves able to distribute much of the largess produced by decades of asbestos production to a host of consultants and attorneys. For example, Davis Polk and Wardwell, a New York law firm which had represented Manville since 1928, was co-counsel for the Chapter 11 proceedings and charged over $200,000 a month early in the proceedings.[53] First Boston Corporation was authorized $100,000 a month in late 1984 to serve as financial adviser to certain creditor groups.[54] Through 1986, Manville had dispensed $64 million in Chapter 11 costs.[55] By October 1987, Manville chief Stephens said the number had exceeded $100 million.[56]

Leon Silverman, the "Legal Representative for Future Claimants" appointed by the bankruptcy court, submitted bills for $2.3 million for August 1, 1984, through December 31, 1986.[57] Dr. Frederick W. Kilbourne was paid

---

[50] "3 Manville Manufacturing Plants Sold to Former President Hulce," *The Denver Post,* January 5, 1988, p. 2C, and "Manville Sells Three Plants for $7 million," *Stockholders and Creditors News Service* (Edgemont, Penn.: Andrews Publications, January 11, 1988), pp. 7, 261–2.

[51] See, for example, "Court Approves Sale by Manville of 100 Acres for $22 Million," "Court Approves Sale of 14 Acres to Manville Joint Venture," and "Order Authorizing Sale of Manville, N.J. Property," *Stockholders and Creditors News Service* (Edgemont, Penn.: Andrews Publications, January 11, 1988), pp. 7261, 7262, and 7264, respectively.

[52] Manville Corporation, *1986 Annual Report and Form 10K,* p. 53.

[53] "Four Law Firms Submit Bills Totaling $1.8 Million as of December 31, 1982," *Stockholders and Creditors News Service* (Edgemont, Penn.: Andrews Publications, March 14, 1983), p. 794.

[54] In re Johns-Manville Corporation, et al., Debtors, Third Supplemental Order Approving Expanded Retention and Reduced Compensation of Investment Banker, 82 B 11656-76 (BRL) (SD NY November 16, 1984) reprinted in *Stockholders and Creditors News Service* (Edgemont, Penn.: Andrews Publications, December 10, 1984), p. 3184.

[55] Manville Corporation, *1986 Annual Report and Form 10-K,* p. 40, and *1983 Annual Report and Form 10-K,* p. 6.

[56] Debate at the National Conference on Business Ethics, Waltham, Mass., October 16, 1987.

[57] In re Johns-Manville Corporation, et al., Debtors, Statement of Compensation of the Legal Representative for Future Claimants and His Counsel, 82 B 11656-62 and 82 B 11664-76 (BRL) (SD NY August 14, 1987) reprinted in *Stockholders and Creditors News Service* (Edgemont, Penn.: Andrews Publications, September 7, 1987), p. 6945.

$73,550 for work as Manville's actuarial expert during November 1983 through April 1984.[58] The executive director of the Association of Trial Lawyers of America, Marianna S. Smith, was hired as Chief Executive Officer of the A-H Trust, at $250,000 a year.

The pattern continued into 1988. For the first six months of 1987, 22 law firms submitted bills in the Manville Chapter 11 proceeding for $5,733,983.[59] The "Provisional" trust budget for January–August 1987 provided $4.6 million to administer the A-H trust, including $194,000 for executive searches, $840,000 to pay Smith and three assistants, and $257,000 for the six trustees who were scheduled to meet only 7 times.[60] The trust rented 32,038 square feet of office space in Washington, D.C., at an annual cost of $849,007.[61] In addition to their $30,000 annual compensation, each trustee was to get $1,000 a day for meetings, intercontinental travel, and other work performed for the trust.

The managing trustee was authorized $1,500 for each day his part-time trust duties were to occupy over half his time. The trust budget for the 10 months September 1987 through June 1988 was $9.6 million, including $2.9 million for salaries and benefits. Adequate funding for such expenses was assured by the transfer of $150 million from Manville to the trust and was approved by the bankruptcy judge November 25, 1987.[62]

BENEFITS FOR THE ASBESTOS VICTIMS

By 1988, an estimated 41,500 new A-H claims were waiting to be filed against Manville[63] and, of course, many of the 20,000 1982 claimants had died. Total A-H claims filed in the United States by mid-1987 against all companies were estimated at 70,000.[64] No pre-filing A-H claim had been paid by Manville or the trust. In July 1987, the A-H trustees estimated payments from the trust could begin during the spring of 1988,[65] nearly six years after Manville's

---

[58] "Affidavit of J. Thomas Beckett in Support of the Motion of the Committee of Unsecured Creditors for an Order Authorizing and Directing Final Payment to Actuarial Experts, 82 B 11656-76 (HCB) (SD NY August 3, 1987)," in *Stockholders and Creditors News Service* (Edgemont, Penn.: Andrews Publications, August 24, 1987), p. 6819.

[59] "Firms Seek $5.7 Million in Legal Fees for Six Months Ending June 30," *Stockholders and Creditors News Service* (Edgemont, Penn.: Andrews Publications, September 7, 1987), p. 6905.

[60] "Manville Personal Injury Settlement Trust Provisional Budget/Expense Estimates (January through August 1987)," *Stockholders and Creditors News Service* (Edgemont, Penn.: Andrews Publications, August 10, 1987), p. 6800.

[61] "Terms of Lease for Personal Injury Trust Quarters Approved," *Stockholders & Creditors News Service* (Edgemont, Penn.: Andrews Publications, December 7, 1987), p. 7193.

[62] "Manville Trust Forms Being Printed; $9.2 million (sic) Interim Budget," *Stockholders and Creditors News Service* (Edgemont, Penn.: Andrews Publications, January 25, 1988), p. 7295.

[63] "Plan Protects Manville, Shortchanges Victims," *Asbestos Watch* 4, no. 1 (Fall 1986), p. 1.

[64] "JM Trust to Accept Claims in January, Negotiate Even Before Consummation," *Stockholders & Creditors News Service* (Edgemont, Penn.: Andrews Publications, July 6, 1987), p. 6681.

[65] Ibid., p. 6680.

bankruptcy filing. By January 1988, it seemed clear the bankruptcy judge's confirmation order would be appealed to the U.S. Supreme Court unless overturned by the court of appeals.[66] The estimate of when payments could begin was moved back to "April to November 1988."[67] But in March 1988 the Second Circuit U.S. Court of Appeals was still mulling one of the appeals.[68]

In addition to the delay, the asbestos victims had other reasons to despair. First, A-H representatives in the bankruptcy court had been effectively pre-empted, apparently because of Manville's threat to contest their contingent fee contracts with victims. Second, the victims were to have little control over Manville or the A-H trust for years after consummation. Third, the Manville plan provided for effective subordination of A-H claims to commercial debt, even that which was unsecured. Fourth, many of Manville's pre-filing assets had already been irrevocably insulated from potential claims against them by A-H victims. Finally, the prospective payments to the A-H trust provided for in the plan were to be substantially uncertain. In fact, the trust reported it would be unable to pay claims in the last half of 1989, having expended all its available funds.

Consummation Might Not Occur or Might Be Reversed

Some A-H victims were convinced the Manville plan offered their best hope for compensation. But there were at least two reasons to think consummation might not occur at all—or might be reversed if it did. First, there was evidence the A-H trustees were concerned Manville had made inadequate disclosure of incriminating evidence during reorganization. In March 1988, Manville and the A-H trust urgently began setting up a repository to hold 44 million pages of documents produced in two major lawsuits. The repository was to be open to "those involved in resolving health claims against the company."[69]

Second, court rulings in late 1987 and early 1988 seemed to suggest criminal indictments of Manville or its officials were possible. Such indictments could void Judge Lifland's ability to protect the company and its managers. In two Delaware cases Raymark Corporation (formerly Raybestos-Manhattan Corporation) was found liable for civil conspiracy with Manville to conceal or misrepresent the health hazards of asbestos. And a court in Washington state ruled Manville and Raymark engaged in "concert of action" to

---

[66] Marianna S. Smith, Executive Director, Manville Personal Injury Settlement Trust, "Memorandum to Attorneys with Pre-petition Cases," January 27, 1988, in *Asbestos Litigation Reporter* (Edgemont, Penn.: Andrews Publications, February 5, 1988), p. 16503.

[67] Ibid.

[68] "2nd Circuit's Delay in Kane Appeal Causes Speculation," *Stockholders and Creditors News Service* (Edgemont, Penn.: Andrews Publilcations, March 7, 1988), p. 7417.

[69] "All Manville Documents to Be Available at Repository in Denver," *Stockholders & Creditors News Service* (Edgemont, Penn.: Andrews Publications, March 7, 1988), p. 7415.

each market asbestos-containing products without warning of their potential dangers.[70]

Concerning the Delaware cases, the court later ruled the standard of proof required in civil conspiracy was "preponderance of evidence," not the "clear and convincing" test Raymark wished to impose. The court did not address whether the stronger test had been met, only that it was not required. The judge wrote, "I find no basis for singling out this type of intentional tort, or intentional torts in general, which involve a greater level of culpability than that involved in negligent conduct, for favored treatment in the proof of the wrongdoing."[71]

A-H Representatives Preempted in Bankruptcy Court

After 1984, the asbestos victims were essentially powerless to affect the outcome of the Chapter 11 process, mainly because Manville mangement was able to neutralize their committee in the bankruptcy court. The committee consisted of 19 contingent-fee attorneys and one asbestos victim. Until early 1984, the committee had aggressively confronted Manville management. For example, during September 1983 through January 1984, the committee asked the bankruptcy court to dismiss the bankruptcy filing,[72] rejected management's proposed reorganization plan,[73] requested that Manville's top management be replaced with a trustee,[74] and even petitioned the court to cut the managers' salaries.[75] But in January 1984, Manville obtained a hearing date on its motion to void the A-H attorney's contingent-fee agreements, which generally gave the attorneys one third of any settlement or judgment proceeds.[76] Manville had called the fee arrangements "completely unconscion-

[70] "Delaware Jury Awards $75 Million in Punitive Damages Against Raymark," *Stockholders & Creditors News Service* (Edgemont, Penn.: Andrews Publications, November 23, 1987), pp. 7171-2; "Delaware Jury Awards $22 Million in Punitive Damages Against Raymark," *Asbestos Litigation Reporter* (Edgemont, Penn.: Andrews Publications, March 18,1988), p. 16723; and "Washington Judge Finds Concert of Action by Raymark and J-M," *Asbestos Litigation Reporter* (Edgemont, Penn.: Andrews Publications, March 18, 1988), p. 16724.

[71] "DE Judge: Conspiracy Requires Only 'Preponderance of Evidence' Proof," *Asbestos Litigation Reporter* (Edgemont, Penn.: Andrews Publications, March 4, 1988), p. 16665.

[72] "Committee of Asbestos Related Litigants Again Asks Bankruptcy Court to Dismiss Johns-Manville Bankruptcy," *Asbestos Litigation Reporter* (Edgemont, Penn.: Andrews Publications, September 23, 1983), p. 7148.

[73] "Asbestos Claimants Committee Rejects Plan," *Asbestos Litigation Reporter* (Edgemont, Penn.: Andrews Publications, November 24, 1983), p. 7416.

[74] "Asbestos-Related Litigants Move to Have Bankruptcy Court Appoint Trustee," *Asbestos Litigation Reporter* (Edgemont, Penn.: Andrews Publications, January 6, 1984), p. 7625.

[75] "Committee of Asbestos-Related Litigants and/or Creditors Withdraws Its Motion to Reduce Salaries of Manville Officers," *Asbestos Litigation Reporter* (Edgemont, Penn.: Andrews Publications, March 16, 1984), p. 7999.

[76] "Hearing Set on Replacement for Plaintiff Contingency Fee Arrangements," *Asbestos Litigation Reporter* (Edgemont, Penn.: Andrews Publications, February 3, 1984), p. 7785.

able."[77] There seemed a high likelihood Manville could have prevailed. Judge Lifland continued to oppose the contingent fees and later expressed dismay that A-H claimants were not informed of ways to contest the fees.

In March 1984, the A-H committee withdrew its motion to decrease management salaries.[78] For the ensuing two years, the *Asbestos Litigation Reporter,* which reported legal news and filings in asbestos cases,[79] revealed no actions by the A-H committee to contest the authority or benefits of Manville management or to remove the company from bankruptcy court protection.[80] And Manville management relaxed its effort to void the contingent-fee arrangements. By July 1984, Manville was predicting quick agreement to its reorganization plan by all parties, including the A-H committee.[81] Leading asbestos attorney, and member of the A-H committee, Ronald Motley later wrote, "[The] intimation that there is some relationship between Manville's withdrawal of its objection to contingency fees in exchange for the AH Committee's not opposing certain management decisions is both false and insulting."[82]

The A-H committee became a strong management ally in seeking approval of the plan. For example, the committee sponsored promotional brochures for inclusion in the 100,000 information packets and ballots on the plan mailed in September 1986 to persons who provided evidence they had asbestos-related diseases.[83] The brochures stated, "The Asbestos Victims Committee urges you to vote in favor of the Plan. . . . Vote yes on the Manville Reorganization Plan."[84] Despite the promotional activity, including a nationwide multimedia campaign, one of the two national organizations of asbestos victims opposed the plan and the other refused to endorse it.[85] But the A-H attorneys throughout America apparently acted en masse in voting the asbestos victims' proxies for the plan. And tens of thousands of persons were allowed to vote as asbestos victims though they had never submitted an actual

---

[77] "Johns-Manville Asks Court to Void Asbestos-Claimants Attorney Fees," *Asbestos Litigation Reporter* (Edgemont, Penn.: Andrews Publications, November 25, 1983), p. 7411.

[78] "Committee of Asbestos-Related Litigants and/or Creditors Withdraws Its Motion to Reduce Salaries of Manville Officers," *Asbestos Litigation Reporter* (Edgemont, Penn.: Andrews Publications, March 16, 1984), p. 7999.

[79] Published by Andrews Publications, Edgemont, Penn. 19028.

[80] "In re Johns-Manville Corp.," *Asbestos Litigation Reporter: Eight-Year Cumulative Index, February 1979–July 1987,* (Edgemont, Penn.: Andrews Publications, August 1987), pp. 37–8.

[81] "Essentials of Consensual Plan Should Be Soon," *Asbestos Litigation Reporter* (Edgemont, Penn.: Andrews Publications, July 20, 1984), p. 8687.

[82] Letter to author, April 1, 1988.

[83] $100,000 Ballots and Information Packets Being Mailed This Week," *Stockholders and Creditors News Service* (Edgemont, Penn.: Andrews Publications, September 8, 1986), p. 5513.

[84] The Committee of Asbestos-Related Litigants and/or Creditors Representing Asbestos-Health Claimants of Manville Corporation, "Questions and Answers on Asbestos-Health Claims and the Manville Reorganization Plan" and "A Very Important Message for People With Asbestos-Related Diseases," n. d., distributed in August–October 1986.

[85] Continuing personal correspondence with the top official of each organization, 1984–1988.

claim. In any case, Manville claimed its plan received 96 percent of the 52,440 A-H votes cast.[86]

The bankruptcy judge further weakened any active opposition to the Manville plan by asbestos victims in late 1987, when he approved the transfer of $150 million into the A-H trust. Victims' hopes were undoubtedly raised because the money was not excluded from eventually being used to pay A-H claims. But the court order approving the transfer provided that if the plan failed to survive all appeals, unspent funds would go first to pay property damage claims and then to "charitable purposes."[87] So if opposition to the Manville plan from any quarter were to prove successful, an additional $150 million of Manville's assets, in this case cash, would be unavailable to pay A-H claims. Besides, much of the money would be consumed by trust administrative expenses, then running about $1 million a month.[88]

Little Control over Manville after Consummation

Even after plan consummation, if and when that were to occur, the A-H claimants would have little power over Manville or the A-H trust. As previously mentioned, six of the pre-filing directors were to remain on the post-consummation board, as was chief executive, W. Thomas Stephens. The trust would own 50 percent of Manville's common stock. But sale of the stock was to be restricted for five years and the stock was to be required to be voted for management's choices for directors for at least four years after consummation.[89]

The A-H trustees, including an investment banker, four lawyers, and a business consultant, were to have lifetime tenure. Vacancies were to be filled by the remaining trustees, after consultation with Manville and selected asbestos counsel.[90]

A-H Claims Subordinated to Those of Commercial Creditors

The plan would effectively subordinate the A-H claims to those of commercial creditors, even unsecured ones. For example, an estimated $473 million in cash was to be distributed by Manville soon after the plan's effective date.[91]

---

[86] "Manville Says Overwhelming Majority of Voters Accepted Plan," *Asbestos Litigation Reporter* (Edgemont, Penn.: Andrews Publications, December 5, 1986), p. 13677.

[87] "Manville Pays First $150 Million to Settlement Trust Mostly for Claims," *Stockholders and Creditors News Service* (Edgemont, Penn.: Andrews Publications, December 21, 1987), p. 7231.

[88] "Manville Trust Claims Forms Being Printed; $9.2 Million (sic) Interim Budget," *Stockholders and Creditors News Service* (Edgemont, Penn.: Andrews Publications, January 25, 1988), p. 7295. The budget authorized $9.6 million for the ten months September 1987 through June 1988.

[89] Manville Corporation, *First Amended Disclosure Statement, Second Amended and Restated Plan of Reorganization, and Related Documents*, August 22, 1986, p. M-41.

[90] Ibid, p. M-65.

[91] Ibid., pp. M-402 and M-407.

But only $55 million of this was to go to the victims' trust (technically, the trust would get $80 million but would have to give $25 million of that to the property damage trust).[92] In contrast, the general unsecured creditors would get $248 million in cash.[93] The rest of the general unsecured creditors' principal, with interest, would be paid within four and one half years.[94]

And much of Manville's pre-filing commercial debt had already been reinstated or paid as divisions were reorganized or sold free and clear of asbestos claims during the lengthy Chapter 11 process. As a result, the liabilities subject to Chapter 11 proceedings reported on Manville's balance sheet declined by $161 million from 1982–1986.[95]

The plan would prohibit interest on asbestos-health claims.[96] But unsecured creditors would receive 12 percent interest.[97] They would even get $114 million in debentures for interest while Manville was in bankruptcy.[98] Further, the plan provided that Manville's ability to pledge assets to the victims' trust would be limited until the unsecured creditors were paid in full.[99]

Finally, as discussed below, most payments to the A-H trust would be made from future earnings of the company, earnings which were far from certain. In contrast, general unsecured creditors would be paid from the pool of liquid assets available upon plan confirmation and within four and one half years thereafter. As the A-H trust was running out of money in 1989, Manville reported cash and marketable securities balances exceeding $270 million, providing assurance unsecured creditors could be paid.

Manville Assets Shielded from A-H Claims

The reorganization of Manville Forest Products corporation in 1983 forever insulated that division's $870 million in assets[100] from victims' claims. Another $301 million in pre-filing assets were shielded from the asbestos liabilities through the sale of Manville's U.S. pipe operations in 1982 and the asbestos fiber operations in 1983.[101] In each case, commercial creditors of the affected divisions were either paid in full or had their claims reinstated. Manville's Denver headquarters and a number of other assets were sold in 1987 and 1988, all protected from asbestos claims by the bankruptcy court. In

---

[92] Ibid., pp. M-72 and M-180.

[93] Ibid., p. M-47.

[94] Ibid., p. M-60.

[95] Annual reports, respective years.

[96] Manville Corporation, *First Amended Disclosure Statement, Second Amended and Restated Plan of Reorganization, and Related Documents,* August 22, 1986, p. M-46.

[97] Ibid., pp. M-46 and M-47.

[98] Ibid., p. M-48.

[99] Ibid., pp. M-300 and M-343.

[100] Ibid., p. M-431.

[101] Manville Corporation, *1983 Annual Report and Form 10-K,* pp. 17 and 18.

fact, Manville retained responsibility for cleaning up asbestos residue on certain of the transferred property, further decreasing the company's potential profitability.[102]

Payments to A-H Trust Uncertain

As indicated earlier, appeals from the Manville reorganization plan appeared headed for the U.S. Supreme Court in 1988. Of course, all payments to asbestos victims contemplated under the plan were contingent upon its surviving the appeals. In addition, payments under the insurance settlement agreements, which were to constitute the preponderance of A-H trust assets during the decade after consummation, were not to be paid until after the plan became final.[103]

But even if the plan were to be put into effect, little reason was given to expect the A-H trust would have the resources needed to compensate asbestos victims. The major promised source of long-term funding for the A-H trust would be an unsecured, zero-interest Manville bond. The bond would provide for semiannual payments of $37.5 million in the 4th through the 25th fiscal years after consummation.[104]

Aside from Manville's ability to pay the bond installments in the long run, reason was present for concern about the purchasing power they would represent. Using Manville's inflation assumption of 5.2 percent,[105] those payments would each be worth $29 million (consummation-year dollars) in the 5th year, $23 million in the 10th year, $17.5 million in the 15th year, and $14 million in the 20th year. If inflation were to average, say, 3 percent higher than Manville anticipated, the installments in the 20th year would each only be worth $8 million. Further, there was a provision for the payments to be reduced after the 13th fiscal year following consummation.[106]

But, Manville's ability to pay its obligations to the A-H trust seemed problematical at best. The company estimated a $473 million payout under its plan upon consummation, most to commercial creditors, and another $546 million during the ensuing five years. A capital spending program would consume another $800 million over those five years.[107] These amounts totaled $1.8 billion, compared to Manville's estimated liquidation value for all its assets of $2–2.4 billion.[108] So after paying out over 80 percent of its asset

---

[102] For example, see "Court Approves Sale by Manville of 100 Acres for $22 million," *Stockholders & Creditors News Service* (Edgemont, Penn.: Andrews Publications, January 11, 1988), p. 7261.

[103] Manville Corporation, *First Amended Disclosure Statement, Second Amended and Restated Plan of Reorganization, and Related Documents,* August 22, 1986, pp. M-55 and M-149.

[104] Ibid., pp. M-67, M-68 and M-278.

[105] Ibid., p. M-76.

[106] Ibid., pp. M-67 and M-68.

[107] Ibid., p. M-519.

[108] Ibid., p. M-399.

value—over twice its reported net worth[109]—in just five years, Manville promised to honor its further obligations under the plan. These further payments would average $108 million a year for years six, seven, and eight, including the two annual payments of $37.5 million to the A-H trust.[110]

In proving feasibility of the plan, Manville and its investment banker, Morgan Stanley and Company, "projected" the company's cash flows forward through 1991.[111] These figures were then "extrapolated" through 2011.[112] The table on page 364 shows Manville's actual sales and net earnings for 1978–1986[113] and the projections for 1987–1991. Also listed are the interest expense amounts for each of those years. As the table illustrates, Manville's net earnings declined from $121 million in 1978 to $60 million in 1981. Then, from 1982–1986 net earnings averaged only $16 million a year. Manville would have lost money for the 1982–86 period except for two nonrecurring advantages. First, the company avoided at least $50 million a year in average interest charges on liabilities subject to Chapter 11 proeedings.[114] The unsecured portions of these liabilities varied from $627 million in 1982 to $490 million in 1986. Interest expense was projected to average $85 million a year more in 1987–91 than in 1982–86. Second, other income averaged $52 million in 1982–86.[115] It was put at only $14 million a year for 1987–91.[116]

The projections and extrapolations promised an annual average of $93 million in net earnings for the five years after 1986. This despite the payment of $85 million a year more interest than in 1982–86 and the loss of $38 million a year in other income.

Manville and Morgan Stanley claimed income from operations would reach $370 million in 1990. They estimated it would *average* $283.4 million annually for the five years 1987–91.[117] That is almost exactly double the $145 million average for the preceding five years and more than Manville had ever earned in any single year.[118]

Manville issued extensive disclaimers for itself and Morgan Stanley concerning the projections. For example, the company reported, "NO REPRESENTATIONS CAN BE MADE WITH RESPECT TO THE ACCURACY OF THE PROJECTIONS OR THE ABILITY TO ACHIEVE THE PROJECTED RESULTS . . . the above pro forma and projected financial statements are unaudited . . . Morgan Stanley did not independently verify the information considered in its reviews of [the assumptions upon which the projections were

---

[109] Ibid., p. M-418.

[110] Ibid., p. M-519.

[111] Ibid., p. M-405.

[112] Ibid., pp. M-86 and M-87.

[113] Annual reports for respective years.

[114] Annual reports for respective years.

[115] Annual reports for respective years.

[116] *First Amended Disclosure Statement,* p. M-405.

[117] Ibid.

[118] Annual reports for respective years.

Actual and Projected Sales, Earnings, and Interest (millions)

	Year	Net Sales	Net Earnings	Interest
Actual:	1978	$1,648	$121	$ 22
	1979	2,276	115	62
	1980	2,267	81	65
	1981	1,895	60	72
	1982	1,685	(98)	52
	1983	1,729	67	26
	1984	1,814	77	21
	1985	1,880	(45)	23
	1986	1,920	81	20
Projected:	1987	2,043	108	112
	1988	2,239	86	114
	1989	2,411	108	116
	1990	2,636	118	115
	1991	2,480	47	106

based] and for purposes of its reviews relied upon the accuracy and completeness of all such information . . . [Under certain] PESSIMISTIC ASSUMPTIONS MANVILLE WOULD NOT GENERATE THROUGH ITS OPERATIONS SUFFICIENT CASH TO MEET ALL OF ITS OBLIGATIONS UNDER THE PLAN DURING THE PERIODS ANALYZED."[119] The presentations were accepted by the bankruptcy court as proving plan feasibility.

CONCLUSION

On October 16, 1987, Manville chief executive W. Thomas Stephens appeared in a debate before the National Conference on Business Ethics. He generally described past company managers as well intentioned but misinformed. He mentioned certain lessons he had learned: (1) Chapter 11 was the right decision. (2) "Today, it's 'Let the seller beware' and it's as it should be." (3) The industry did not tell employees and customers enough about the dangers of asbestos.[120]

On the broad question of toxic waste, Stephens said, "I think the companies and the officers of those companies should be held totally accountable for their actions. . . . Some horrible mistakes have been made in the

---

[119] *First Amended Disclosure Statement*, pp. M-75 and M-77.

[120] "Ethical Dilemmas of Chapter 11 Reorganization," transcript of session at the Seventh National Conference on Business Ethics, October 16, 1987. Reprinted in *Stockholders and Creditors News Service Re. Johns-Manville Corp., et al.* (Edgemont, Penn.: Andrews Publications, Inc.), December 7, 1987, pp. 7, 196–7, 216.

past. . . . But I think the emphasis should be on solving the problem, learning the lessons from the past, and not bashing the guys that screwed up."[121]

Later Stephens said the advantage of the asbestos victims' owning stock through the A-H trust was that they would be long-term investors looking for long-term results, not just a boost in one quarter's earnings. He expressed his hope that Manville would experience a rebirth, "like the Phoenix," when it emerged from Chapter 11. He said knowing Manville's assets and liabilities gave Manville a competitive advantage.

The cover story in the November 1987 magazine *Corporate Finance* was entitled "Miracle at Manville: How Tom Stephens Raised the Bread to Overcome Bankruptcy." The article said many considered the Manville bankruptcy "the ultimate management copout of all time." It continued, "Soon these critics will have to eat their words."[122]

In a January 1988 *Financier* article, Stephens wrote, "We have set a goal: that the new Manville will be the model of ethical corporate behavior. We have demonstrated what we can and will do. I'm proud of our record."[123]

In March 1988, Stephens took questions from a University of Montana business ethics class. He said he thought Manville's bankruptcy choice was "the most courageous and most ethical decision ever made by a Fortune 500 company."[124]

In March 1988, Manville and the A-H trust announced the creation of a depository for asbestos-related documents, mainly those produced from 1983–1987 in Manville's California lawsuit against its insurance carriers and a Washington, D.C., claims court case the company had filed against the government. That lawsuit had led to the insurance settlements which were to provide most early funding to the A-H trust. The depository, located near Manville's Denver headquarters, was opened in April 1988 and, according to Manville, was to contain over 44 million pages.

A news service reported some attorneys believed Manville and the A-H trust were anxious to avoid later claims that the full extent of the company's knowledge was hidden during the reorganization. And a person familiar with the case said certain A-H trustees became concerned about such concealment after reading a court-ordered summary of evidence in the Washington claims court case mentioned above. Some attorneys had advised the head of the Asbestos Victims of America that the inadequate disclosure which concerned the A-H trustees might necessitate a new vote by stockholders, creditors, and

---

[121] Ibid., pp. 7, 215.

[122] Stephen W. Quickel, "Miracle at Manville: How Tom Stephens Raised the Bread to Overcome Bankruptcy," *Corporate Finance,* November 1987. (No page numbers; reprint of article provided by Manville Corporation).

[123] W. Thomas Stephens, "Manville-Asbestos Ethical Issues Shaping Business Practice," *Financier,* January 1988, pp. 33–6.

[124] Patricia Sullivan, "The High Cost of Ethics: Manville Chief Defends Bankruptcy Decision," *The Missoulan* (Missoula, Montana newspaper), March 10, 1988, p. 2.

claimants on the Manville reorganization. One of Manville's attorneys wrote Judge Lifland that questions had been raised about the "breadth of the restraining provisions" which protected the A-H trustees and others involved in the trust from legal attack. Judge Lifland issued a new order on March 18, 1987, barring any action concerning "administration, enforcement or settlement of accounts" related to the trust in any court except the bankruptcy court.[125]

On March 30, 1988, the Second Circuit U.S. Court of Appeals issued its long-awaited decision on the remaining appeal from the Manville confirmation order. The other appeal had been rejected earlier and a petition for a rehearing was also rejected, setting the stage for a further appeal to the U.S. Supreme Court. Ninety days were allowed to seek review by the Supreme Court. A spokesperson for the A-H trust said if the Supreme Court refused to hear either of the appeals, consummation of the plan could occur sometime in the fall and payments to victims could begin by year end. Otherwise, consummation would slip into 1989, the seventh year after Manville's bankruptcy filing.

Appendix E contains comments on the Manville bankruptcy by executives and other principals in the case.

APPENDIX A: PRE-1970 EVENTS CONCERNING ASBESTOS AND HEALTH

1898: Manville founder and inventor of uses for asbestos, Henry Ward Johns, dies of "dust phthisis pneumonitis," assumedly asbestosis.

1929: Manville defending early lawsuits for asbestos deaths. The company claims employees assumed the risks of employment, knew or should have known the dangers, and were contributorily negligent. Legal documents in these cases bear signatures of senior Manville officials who would remain with the company until the 1960s.

1930: Dr. A. J. Lanza, of Metropolitan Life Insurance Company (Manville's insurer) begins a four-year study on the "Effects of Inhalation of Asbestos Dust upon the Lungs of Asbestos Workers."

1933: Based on interim results of his story, Dr. Lanza suggests Manville engage an outside consultant to do dust counts at company plants. A decision is made to train an insider to do this rather than bring in someone from outside the company.

1934: Asbestosis is considered for classification as a disease for workmen's compensation purposes. Manville's chief attorney writes to the company:

> In particular we have urged that asbestosis should not at the present time be included in the list of compensation diseases, for the reason that it is only within a comparatively recent time that asbestosis has been recognized by the medical and

---

[125] "Judge Lifland Bars Any Actions Relating to Administration of PI Trust," *Asbestos Litigation Reporter* (Edgemont, Penn.: Andrews Publications, April 8, 1988), p. 16798.

scientific professions as a disease—in fact one of our principal defenses in actions against the company on the common law theory of negligence has been that the scientific and medical knowledge has been insufficient until a very recent period to place on the owners of plants or factories the burden or duty of taking special precautions against the possible onset of the disease in their employees.

After reviewing a draft of Dr. Lanza's report (above, 1930), Manville vice president and corporate secretary Vandiver Brown writes Dr. Lanza, "All we ask is that all of the favorable aspects of the survey be included and that none of the unfavorable be unintentionally pictured in darker terms than the circumstances justify. I feel confident that we can depend upon you and Dr. McConnel to give us this 'break' . . ."

1935: Brown writes another industry executive, Sumner Simpson, "I quite agree that our interests are best served by having asbestosis receive the minimum of publicity." He is commenting on Simpson's response to a letter by Anne Rossiter (editor of the industry journal *Asbestos*) in which she has written, "You may recall that we have written you on several occasions concerning the publishing of information, or discussion of, asbestosis . . . Always you have requested that for obvious reasons, we publish nothing, and, naturally your wishes have been respected."

1936: Messrs. Brown and Simpson convince nine other asbestos companies to provide a total of $417 per month for the industry's own three-year study of the effects of asbestos dust on guinea pigs and rabbits by Dr. LeRoy U. Gardner. Simpson writes Gardner, "we could determine from time to time after the findings were made, whether we wish any publication or not." In a separate letter, Brown states, "the manuscript of your study will be submitted to us for approval prior to publication." Gardner will tell the companies of "significant changes in guinea pigs' lungs within a period of one year" and "fibrosis" produced by long fibers and "chronic inflammation" caused by short fibers. He will make several requests for additional funding but will die in 1946 without reporting final results.

1940: Asbestos-health lawsuits have increased in number through the 1930s, but Manville continues to successfully defend or settle them, using the same defenses as in the 1920s but adding a statute-of-limitations defense, made possible by the long latency period of asbestos diseases. The companies continue to avoid significant publicity about asbestos and health.

The war will bring spiraling sales and profits, as thousands of tons of asbestos are used in building war machines, mainly ships—resulting in exposure of tens of thousands of shipyard workers and seamen, thousands of whom will die of asbestos diseases decades later.

1947: A study by the Industrial Hygiene Foundation of America finds that from 3 to 20 percent of asbestos plant workers already have asbestosis and a Manville plant employing 300 is producing "5 or 6 cases annually that the physician believes show early changes due to asbestos."

1950: Dr. Kenneth W. Smith, Manville chief physician, has given superiors his report that of 708 workers he studied only four were free of asbestos disease.

Concerning the more serious cases he has written, "The fibrosis of this disease is irreversible and permanent so that eventually compensation will be paid to each of these men but as long as the man is not disabled it is felt that he should not be told of his condition so that he can live and work in peace and the company can benefit from his many years of experience."

1952: John A. McKinney, Fred L. Pundsack, Chester E. Shepperly, Monroe Harris, and Chester J. Sulewski, who will be Manville's top five officers as it prepares to seek bankruptcy court protection in 1982, have all joined the company in various capacities.

1953: Dr. Smith tries to convince senior Manville managers to authorize caution labeling for asbestos. In a 1976 deposition he will characterize their responses: "We recognize the potential hazard that you mentioned, the suggested use of a caution label. We will discuss it among ourselves and make a decision." Asked why he has overruled, Smith will say, "application of a caution label identifying a product as hazardous would cut out sales."

1956: The Board of Governors of the Asbestos Textile Institute (made up of Manville and other asbestos companies) meets to discuss the increasing publicity about asbestos and cancer and agree that "every effort should be made to disassociate this relationship until such a time that there is sufficient and authoritative information to substantiate such to be a fact."

1957: The Asbestos Textile Institute rejects a proposal by the Industrial Health Foundation that asbestos companies fund a study on asbestos and cancer. Institute minutes report, "There is a feeling among certain members that such an investigation would stir up a hornet's nest and put the whole industry under suspicion."

1959: An increasing number of articles connecting asbestos with various diseases have appeared in medical journals over the last few years.

1963: Dr. I. J. Selikoff, of Mt. Sinai Medical Center in New York, reads a report of his study of asbestos workers before the American Medical Association meeting. Like the earlier research, the Selikoff study implicates asbestos ingestion as the causal factor in many thousands of deaths and injuries. Selikoff will soon estimate that at least 100,000 more Americans will die of asbestos diseases this century. The study and the articles, news stories, and academic papers which follow will focus public attention on the asbestos and health issue. An estimated 100 articles on asbestos-related diseases will appear in 1964 alone.

1964: For the first time, Manville agrees to place caution labels on *some* asbestos products. The labels say, "Inhalation of asbestos in excessive quantities over long periods of time may be harmful" and suggests that users avoid breathing the dust and wear masks if "adequate ventilation control is not possible." The company's most profitable—and deadly—product, bags of asbestos fiber for distribution to other manufacturers and insulators throughout the world, will not be caution labeled for another five years.

APPENDIX B: MANVILLE FINANCIAL SUMMARIES, BEFORE AUGUST 26, 1982

Income Statements
(dollar amounts in millions)*

	1982 6 mos.	1981	1980	1979	1978
Sales	$949	$2,186	$2,267	$2,276	$1,649
Cost of sales	784	1,731	1,771	1,747	1,190
Selling, G & A expenses	143	271	263	239	193
R&D and engineering expenses	16	34	35	31	33
Operating income	6	151	197	259	232
Other income, net	1	35	26	21	28
Interest expense	35	73	65	62	22
Income before income taxes	(28)	112	157	218	238
Income taxes	2	53	77	103	116
Net income	(25)	60	81	115	122
Dividend on preferred stock	12	25	25	24	0
Net income for common stock	(37)	$ 35	$ 55	$ 91	$ 122

* Totals may not check due to rounding.

Business Segment Information
(dollar amounts in millions)*

	1981	1980	1979	1978	1977	1976
Revenues						
Fiberglass products	$ 625	$ 610	$ 573	$ 514	$ 407	$ 358
Forest products	555	508	497	0	0	0
Non-fiberglass insulation	258	279	268	231	195	159
Roofing products	209	250	273	254	204	171
Pipe products and systems	199	220	305	303	274	218
Asbestos fiber	138	159	168	157	161	155
Industrial and special products	320	341	309	291	301	309
Corporate revenues, net	12	9	11	20	12	(22)
Intersegment sales	(95)	(84)	(106)	(94)	(74)	(56)
Total	$2,221	$2,292	$2,297	$1,677	$1,480	$1,291

APPENDIX B: MANVILLE FINANCIAL SUMMARIES, BEFORE AUGUST 26, 1982   (continued)

Business Segment Information
(dollar amounts in millions)*

	1981	1980	1979	1978	1977	1976
Income from operations						
Fiberglass products	$ 90	$ 91	$ 96	$ 107	$ 82	$ 60
Forest products	39	37	50	0	0	0
Non-fiberglass insulation	20	27	27	35	28	18
Roofing products	(17)	9	14	23	14	8
Pipe products and systems	0	(5)	18	26	24	(3)
Asbestos fiber	37	35	56	55	60	60
Industrial and special products	50	55	43	36	25	19
Corporate expense, net	(23)	(38)	(23)	(23)	(24)	(49)
Eliminations and adjustments.	3	11	(2)	1	3	2
Total	$ 198	$ 223	$ 280	$ 260	$ 212	$ 116

* Totals may not check due to rounding.

Balance Sheets
(millions)*

	June 30	December 31			
	1982	1981	1980	1979	1978
Assets					
Cash	$ 10	$ 14	$ 20	$ 19	$ 28
Marketable securities	17	12	12	10	38
Accounts and notes receivable	348	327	350	362	328
Inventories	182	211	217	229	219
Prepaid expenses	19	19	20	31	32
Total current assets	$ 576	$ 583	$ 619	$ 650	$ 645
Property, plant and equipment					
Land and land improvements		119	118	114	99
Buildings		363	357	352	321
Machinery and equipment		1,202	1,204	1,161	1,043
		$1,685	$1,679	$1,627	$1,462
Less: Accumulated depreciation and depletion		(525)	(484)	(430)	(374)
		$1,160	$1,195	$1,197	$1,088
Timber and timberland, net		406	407	368	372
	$1,523	$1,566	$1,602	$1,565	$1,460
Other assets	148	149	117	110	113
	$2,247	$2,298	$2,338	$2,324	$2,217

APPENDIX B: MANVILLE FINANCIAL SUMMARIES, BEFORE AUGUST 26, 1982 *(concluded)*

Balance Sheets
(millions)*

| | June 30 | December 31 | | | |
	1982	1981	1980	1979	1978
Liabilities					
Short-term debt	$	$ 29	$ 22	$ 32	$ 23
Accounts payable	191	120	126	143	114
Employee compensation and benefits		77	80	54	45
Income taxes		30	22	51	84
Other liabilities	149	58	61	50	63
Total current liabilities	$ 340	$ 316	$ 310	$ 329	$ 329
Long-term debt	499	508	519	532	543
Other non-current liabilities	93	86	75	73	60
Deferred income taxes	186	185	211	195	150
	$1,116	$1,095	$1,116	$1,129	$1,083
Stockholders' equity					
Preferred	$ 301	$ 301	$ 300	$ 299	$ 299
Common	60	59	58	208	197
Capital in excess of par	178	174	164	0	0
Retained earnings	642	695	705	692	643
Cumulated currency transl. adj.	(47)	(22)	0	0	0
Less: cost of treasury stock	(3)	(3)	(4)	(4)	(6)
	$1,131	$1,203	$1,222	$1,196	$1,134
	$2,247	$2,298	$2,338	$2,324	$2,217

* Totals may not check due to rounding.

APPENDIX C: HOW CHAPTER 11 WORKS

The U.S. Bankruptcy Code took effect October 1, 1979, and was amended in 1984, 1986, and 1988. Chapter 11 of this law replaced various business reorganization provisions contained in chapters X, XI, and XII of the 1898 Bankruptcy Act, which provisions dated generally from the 1938 Chandler Amendment to that act (*Bankruptcy Code, Rules and Forms* 1989, pp. 290–4). The number of business reorganization filings under bankruptcy law went from about 6,000 in 1980 to an average of over 20,000 annually late in the decade (*Annual Report of the Director of the Administrative Office of the United States Courts,* various years).

Bankruptcy Reorganization Gains Respectability

Before about 1982, few large or respected firms resorted to bankruptcy and virtually all which did were insolvent. A study of 45 bankruptcies among the 2,500 largest firms in the United States during 1972–81 concluded all involved actual or imminent insolvency. But in 1982 Braniff Airlines, Wickes, Addressograph-Multigraph, Revere Copper and Brass, and Manville Corporation all filed Chapter 11 petitions. By January 1989, the list of companies which had filed also included Texaco, LTV, Wheeling-Pittsburg Steel, Allegheny International, A. H. Robins, Continental Airlines, and a host of similarly well known corporations. Several of these companies, most notably Texaco, Manville, and A. H. Robins, were far from insolvency, at least in the cash flow sense (inability to pay maturing obligations) if not in the bankruptcy sense (debts greater than assets at fair valuation) when they filed.

Not only were bigger, more prestigious companies filing, but many firms were doing so for new reasons. Some studies have concluded that a "wave" of bankruptcies after 1981 were due to attempts to escape contracts. Bankruptcy was used by Continental Airlines to abrogate a labor contract, by A. H. Robins and Manville to cope with massive toxic tort liabilities, by Texaco to delay and renegotiate a $12 billion court judgment, and by Public Service Company of New Hampshire to bring pressure for utility rate increases and regulatory restructuring.

Chapter 11 had clearly lost much of its stigma, to the extent such stigma ever existed. The stigma thesis is open to question because the primary research which concluded Chapter 11 is a discrediting label failed to discriminate between the effects of filing and those of the presumable mismanagement or misfortune which may have necessitated the filing. In some measure Chapter 11 had become merely a strategy, another way of managing the demands of various stakeholders.

The Nature and Purpose of Bankruptcy Law for Corporations

At its core, bankruptcy law is debt collection law. It is designed to solve the common pool and equitable problems which accompany creditor perceptions of actual or impending insolvency of a debtor. Some have argued that boundedly rational, self-interested creditors whose debtor appears insolvent will exercise their rights under the "grab" provisions of the Uniform Commercial Code. Those provisions generally follow a "first-come, first-served" principle and hold the first creditor acquiring and publicizing an interest in a particular asset of a debtor may be first, and fully, paid out of that asset. Only publicized interests are recognized because of a long-standing provision of Anglo-American law that secret interests in property held by another are void. Bankruptcy law respects that principle.

Because of grabbing from the common pool which occurs outside of Chapter 11, assets which are worth more together or in certain hands are separated or put in other hands; that is, the assets are not deployed to maximize their value. Thus, an insolvent debtor's owners (taken to include all holders of claims, including creditors) as a group suffer. An equitable problem exists because the first creditors in line might strip the debtor carcass bare, leaving nothing for creditors further back; that is, the assets are not distributed fairly. To avoid either result, bankruptcy law aims to substitute a process which will ensure the pool of debtor assets are *deployed* so as to maximize their value, and that such value is *distributed* to owners according to the relative values of their prebankruptcy rights.

It is probably not a purpose—although it may often be a result—of bankruptcy law to provide a "fresh start" for corporations. In addition, the discharge of prebankruptcy debts, so necessary for a financial fresh start, does not even exist for corporate debtors under Chapter 7 (liquidation). Still, the fresh start ideal for individual debtors dates at least from the "jubilee year" tradition of the Old Testament whereby all debts were forgiven every 50th year (*Leviticus* 25: 8–55). And the analogy between corporate and personal bankruptcies cannot be totally escaped.

The Chapter 11 Process

A federal bankruptcy judge assumes oversight of any firm which petitions for "reorganization" under chapter 11. As Yacos, later judge in the landmark Public Service Company of New Hampshire bankruptcy case, pointed out, all a firm needs is "the filing fee and a petition saying [the firm] wants relief." It does not have to be insolvent.

Each bankruptcy judge acts under the supervision of a federal district court, to which bankruptcy court rulings are easily appealable. This arrangement is intended to protect the bankruptcy judges, who do not have the lifetime tenures and salary protection afforded other federal judges, from political influence.

Upon filing for Chapter 11 protection, the firm becomes the "debtor in possession" (DIP) with essentially all the rights, powers, and duties of a trustee in bankruptcy. The petition itself acts as an automatic stay of all prefiling claims against the debtor. The pre-filing managers continue to operate the company in "the ordinary course of business" while a plan to emerge from court protection is being formulated, approved, and confirmed. A U.S. Trustee, often an experienced bankruptcy attorney, helps in the administration of cases under the bankruptcy court's jurisdiction. Reorganization is accomplished through the formulation and implementation of a written plan.

A committee of unsecured creditors is appointed by the U.S. Trustee to represent that stakeholder group. A committee of equity security holders may also be appointed, and usually is. Committees or advocates may be established to represent other stakeholder groups. In the Manville Corporation case, for example, a committee was set up for asbestos tort claimants and an individual was appointed as an advocate for future claimants. In the A. H. Robins case, a committee was formed to represent women who had used the company's Dalkon Shield intrauterine device. The committees are authorized to consult with the DIP in the administration of the case and to participate in the formulation of a plan of reorganization.

For the first 120 days after filing, only the DIP can submit a reorganization plan. If a plan is not submitted within 120 days and accepted by claimant groups within 180 days, any party in interest, even an individual shareholder or creditor, may file a plan. But both time limits may be extended or shortened for cause by the bankruptcy court. For example, Manville Corporation was given more than five years to prepare its plan and seek approval of it. On the other hand, Worlds of Wonder, Inc. filed for Chapter 11 protection in December 1987 and a plan submitted by the company's banks and unsecured creditors was approved by the bankruptcy court in March 1988.

Here are the main requirements for confirmation of a plan by the court: First, the plan must be proposed in "good faith" and the proponent must disclose certain specified information. Second, each holder of a claim or interest who has not accepted the plan must be allowed at least as much value, as of the plan's effective date, as Chapter 7 liquidation would provide. Third, each class of claims or interests which is "impaired" under the plan must have accepted the plan unless the judge rules the plan "does not discriminate unfairly and is fair and equitable with respect to the class." The terms *impaired* and *accepted* deserve further explanation. A class of claims or interests is unimpaired if reinstated and the holders compensated for damages or if paid in cash. Acceptance of a plan by a creditor class requires approval by over half in number and at least two thirds in amount of allowed claims in the class. Classes of interests, such as shareholders, must approve by at least two thirds in amount of such interests. The final requirement is that confirmation of the plan must not be deemed likely to be followed by the need for further financial reorganization or liquidation.

As mentioned above, all pre-filing claims are automatically stayed by the simple filing of the petition. The judge may lift the stay with regard to particular claims. Otherwise it remains in effect while the plan is being formulated, approved, and confirmed.

Executory contracts, except financial accommodations, may be assigned, assumed, or rejected by the debtor. "Executory" means neither party has completed its legal obligations under the contract. The rejection of executory contracts may create allowable claims, which are usually treated as pre-filing, unsecured claims.

Administrative costs of the proceeding and any post-filing obligations are given priority for payment. Ideally, any remaining value will be distributed to the claimant and interest groups in order of their nonbankruptcy entitlements. Thus, the allowed pre-filing claims on the debtor estate may be satisfied in this sequence: (1) secured debt (up to the value of respective collateral as of the effective date of the plan), (2) unsecured debt (including nominally secured debt above the value of respective collateral), and (3) equity interests in order of preference (e.g., preferred, then common). Claimants within each group, again ideally, share pro rata according to the value of their respective claims. The "value" may be distributed as cash, securities, or other real or personal property.

Negotiation among stakeholder representatives and court intervention often result in departures from such an "ideal" distribution. With very limited exceptions, any claim not provided for in the final reorganization plan or the order confirming it is discharged. However, the court may approve a written waiver of discharge executed by the debtor *after* the confirmation order.

Managerial Stakeholders in Chapter 11

As noted above, upon filing management becomes the "debtor in possession," with the rights and obligations of a bankruptcy trustee. In a broad sense, the debtor in possession is charged with preserving and enhancing the bankrupt estate and developing a reorganization plan which will equitably allocate the value of the estate among competing interests. Invariably, managers of bankrupt firms are bombarded with powerful, conflicting demands. Employees want their jobs assured at the same or higher pay levels. Stockholders oppose dilution of their interests and want share price to be propped up and dividends to be reinstated at the earliest possible time. Creditors seek payment or special considerations such as extra collateral, authority to "perfect" existing claims, or higher interest rates. The typical bankruptcy judge wants decorum and consensus to prevail and rapid progress to be made toward consummation of a workable plan, usually with a strong preference for a consensual one. And the community at large may fear company retrenchment and the loss of jobs, corporate giving, and economic and social activity that may bring.

The traditional Theory of the Firm, implying as it does shareholder wealth maximization as a managerial goal, provides little guidance for the managers. In fact, acting as agents for shareholders would be incompatible with their new fiduciary duty. Shareholders are usually represented by a committee in the bankruptcy court. Putting management on their side would prejudice the interests of other claimants. Besides, little or no owner's equity may be left in the debtor firm, so the court may rule there is no shareholder interest to protect. Shareholders may even be disenfranchised. For example, the judge in the six-years-long Manville case turned down several petitions to require management to conduct annual and special stockholder meetings. He even disbanded the shareholders' committee in the bankruptcy court.

Faced with such an ambiguous charter and imbued with awesome power as debtor in possession, managers may be tempted to neglect the interests of stakeholders other than themselves. Doing that implies certain strategies, some of which can be initiated before filing and others of which may follow filing. As has been indicated, compared to outright liquidation or austere survival without court protection, bankruptcy reorganization can lead to improved pay and benefits, lengthened careers, lowered job demands, and heightened respectability for the managers.

APPENDIX D: MANVILLE FINANCIAL SUMMARIES, AFTER AUGUST 26, 1982

Income Statements
(dollar amounts in millions)*

	1987†	1986	1985	1984	1983	1982
Sales	$1,541	$1,920	$1,880	$1,814	$1,729	$1,772
Other income, net	31	39	62	59	61	34
	1,572	1,959	1,942	1,873	1,791	1,806
Cost of sales	1,136	1,452	1,473	1,400	1,370	1,391
Selling, G & A expenses	166	235	246	238	224	222
R&D and engineering expenses	27	39	35	36	35	28
Operating income	243	233	188	200	161	163
Loss on dispersement of assets	(21)	47	151	0	(3)	110
Employee seperation and retirement costs						39
Asbestos health costs	6	11	52	26	20	16
Interest expense	17	20	23	21	26	52
Chapter 11 costs	8	17	9	17	18	2
Income—continued operation	233	138	(47)	135	100	(56)
Income taxes	100	57	(2)	58	40	32
Net income—continued operation	133	81	(45)	77	60	(88)
Net income—discontinued operation	0	0	0	0	7	(10)
Net income	$ 133	$ 81	$ (45)	$ 77	$ 67	$ (98)

* Totals may not check due to rounding.

† Nine months ended September 30. Sales for the year totaled $2.063 billion. Net income for 1987 was $73 million, after an extraordinary charge due to payment of $150 million to the A-H trust.

Business Segment Information
(dollar amounts in millions)*

	1987†	1986	1985	1984	1983	1982
Revenues						
Fiber glass products	$ 652	$ 809	$ 803	$ 781	$ 718	$ 609
Forest products	450	541	459	451	415	436
Specialty products	469	611	674	645	683	829
Corporate revenues-net	26	31	43	38	36	15
Intersegment sales	(25)	(33)	(37)	(42)	(61)	(82)
Total	$1,572	$1,959	$1,942	$1,873	$1,791	$1,806
Income from operations						
Fiberglass products	$ 113	$ 133	$ 106	$ 115	$ 97	$ 75
Forest products	84	68	43	63	52	48
Specialty products	45	46	33	28	19	51
Corporate expense-net	(4)	(18)	(1)	(6)	(6)	(18)
Eliminations and adjustments	5	4	7	0	0	7
Total	$ 243	$ 233	$ 188	$ 200	$ 161	$ 164

* Totals may not check due to rounding.
† Nine months ended September 30. Sales for the year totaled $2.063 billion. Net income for 1987 was $73 million, after an extraordinary charge due to payment of $150 million to the A-H trust.

Balance Sheets
(dollar amounts in millions)*

	December 31				
	1986	1985	1984	1983	1982
Assets					
Cash	$ 8	$ 7	$ 9	$ 19	$ 11
Market securities-at cost	437	314	276	240	206
Accounts and notes receivable	292	314	285	277	310
Inventories	153	153	164	141	152
Prepaid expenses	24	29	17	22	17
Total current assets	914	817	752	700	696
Property, plant and equipment					
Land and improvements	99	95	96	97	108
Buildings	312	299	308	303	332
Machinery and equipment	1,234	1,160	1,121	1,036	1,090
Less accumulated depreciation and depletion	586	538	513	472	547
	1,059	1,017	1,013	984	983
Timber and timberland-net	376	385	392	395	402
PP&E-net	1,434	1,402	1,405	1,379	1,385
Other assets	165	174	182	174	154
	$2,513	$2,393	$2,339	$2,253	$2,236

* Totals may not check due to rounding.

APPENDIX D: MANVILLE FINANCIAL SUMMARIES, AFTER AUGUST 26, 1982 *(concluded)*

Balance Sheets
(dollar amounts in millions)*

	December 31				
	1986	*1985*	*1984*	*1983*	*1982*
Liabilities and Stockholder Equity					
Short-term debt	$ 30	$ 26	$ 20	$ 94	$ 12
Accounts payable	93	84	102	65	86
Accrued employee compensation and benefits	103	94	81	14	63
Income taxes	16	12	18	9	32
Other accrued liabilities	62	69	35	26	29
Total current liabilities	304	286	256	209	221
Long-term debt	80	92	84	713	736
Liabilities—Chapter 11 proceedings	575	578	574	5	12
Other non-current liabilities	118	115	67	61	60
Deferred income taxes	161	144	162	136	140
	1,239	1,214	1,142	1,122	1,170
Preferred stock	$ 301	$ 301	$ 301	$ 301	$ 301
Common stock	60	60	60	60	60
Capital in excess of par	178	178	178	178	178
Retained earnings	749	667	713	635	568
Cumulative currency translation adjustment	(11)	(26)	(53)	(41)	(39)
Cost of treasury stock	(2)	(2)	(2)	(2)	(2)
	974	878	896	831	765
	$2,513	$2,393	$2,339	$2,253	$2,236

* Totals may not check due to rounding.

APPENDIX E: COMMENTS BY MANVILLE EXECUTIVES AND OTHER PRINCIPALS

John A. McKinney (letter to author): The suggestion that the Chapter 11 filing was for the benefit of Manville Officers is laughable . . . . The filing preserved the position of the victims as equal creditors (virtually all unsecured) in the event of a financial calamity.

John A. McKinney (letter to *Business Month*, February 1989): Shareholders were wiped out in order to provide funding to: (1) pay lawyers several hundred million dollars; (2) pay shipyard workers without ever taking testimony as to whether the government caused their injuries, as numerous trial courts and juries have held; and (3) pay whatever money remained to property-damage claimants who have yet to produce a single person made ill by occupying a building containing asbestos. . . . In my opinion, there were sufficient resources to pay deserving claimants without wiping out shareholders.

W. Thomas Stephens (letters to author): There are really only two questions. First: How do we compensate for the mistakes already made? And, second: How do we prevent another problem like that from ever arising in our society again . . . . Nothing worse could happen to the asbestos health claimants than to initiate a liquidation process . . . . There are a lot of us in this case who didn't cause this problem. As professionals, however, we were brought in to solve it . . . . Personally, I am proud that we have found a solution to a very, very complex legal, social, and financial problem.

Leading A-H Attorney Ronald L. Motley (letters to author): After four years of discussions, negotiations and consultations with our committees and investment consultants, the overwhelming majority of the AH Committee, including the representative of the Asbestos Victims of America, voted in favor of the Plan of Reorganization which was largely shaped by Leon Silverman, in consultation with myself, Stan Levy, and our counsel, Elihu Inselbuch . . . the addition of the property damage weight to the scales led many of us to view the settlement as being in the best interest of the personal injury claimants. . . .

[The] intimation that there is some relationship between Manville's withdrawal of its objection to contingency fees in exchange for the AH Committee's not opposing certain management decisions is both false and insulting.

CASE

J. P. Stevens & Co., Inc.

Whitney J. Stevens walked into the chairman's office of the J. P. Stevens & Co. headquarters located in the Stevens Tower. He walked around to the chair behind the desk and sat down. It was January 2, 1980, and he had just become the new company chairman, succeeding James D. Finley. Stevens began working for J. P. Stevens in 1947 as a trainee in one of the Greenville, South Carolina, plants. He worked with textile machinery initially and then moved into sales. By 1964 he had been appointed an executive vice president at the New York headquarters and in 1969 was made president when Finley became chairman. The 10 years Finley was chairman were the only years in the 166-year history of the company when a Stevens had not headed the firm. A Stevens was now once again moving into the office.

Stevens swiveled the chair around to the window and looked out at a torrent of rain being thrown against the glass by a winter storm and against the few people below walking down the Avenue of the Americas of New York City. To a degree, thought Stevens, the weather was appropriate since it reflected the conditions surrounding the company lately.

Stevens had inherited, from Finley, a controversial era in the company's labor history. Stevens currently faced a variety of lawsuits dealing with alleged unfair labor practices as a result of the company's resistance to organizational efforts by the Amalgamated Clothing and Textile Workers Union (ACTWU) at its southern textile mills. The union had chosen Stevens as a test case, and the outcome would set the precedent for the existence or continued absence of unions in the industry. As evidence of its determination, the union had earmarked, beginning in 1976, $1.5 million per year for the next 10 years to fight the company.

In addition to labor-mangement problems, Stevens also had other areas of concern such as rising objections to cotton dust hazards in textile mills, charges of racial discrimination, and charges of intentional mispreparation of tax returns in North Carolina.

Whitney Stevens sat and stared at the rain clouds, reflecting that since 1965 the public perception of his company had changed from one of a quiet textile manufacturer to a company many people currently viewed as a modern-day sweatshop. Stevens put his feet up against the windowsill and thought back through the last 15 years and especially about his former leader, Finley.

CHAIRMAN FINLEY

James D. Finley, chief executive officer of J. P. Stevens from 1969–1979, left his position at the beginning of 1980. Finley had insisted their antiunion stance had not harmed his company in any manner and, to the day he left, pursued a strong antiunion line. One acknowledgement he did make of union pressure occurred when he moved the annual meeting from New York to Greenville, South Carolina, in 1978 to avoid the mass demonstrations that had occurred in 1977. Past shareholder meetings witnessed resolutions ranging from investigation of labor policies to demands for accounting of the cost of the company's antiunion stance. All motions to date had been rebuffed by Finley, with the backing of his directors.

A measure of Finley's attitude in directing his company and dealing with its problems may perhaps be best seen in these exchanges with shareholders during the annual meeting. An exchange in 1977:

Finley:

This is my meeting, I'm running it.

Shareholder [politely]:

By what rules of order do you conduct this meeting, by Robert's Rules of Order?

Finley:

No. No rules.

[Uproar]

Finley:

Now just be quiet and sit down and behave. I can overrule anything. It's the J. P. Stevens rule of order here. That's the way we've been doing it for over 160 years.[1]

In 1978 during a stockholders' meeting, a shareholder told Finley:

> *The Gallagher President's Report, A Confidential Letter to Chief Executives,* names you, Mr. Finley, as one of the 10 worst chief executives for 1977 for "outdated labor practices resulting in contempt of court citation, for effort by the National Labor Relations Board to obtain a nationwide injunction against the company, for a union boycott of the company's products."[2]

In 1978, Finley announced he would not be running for reelection to a director seat on Manufacturers Hanover Trust, which held over $1 billion in union deposits. Finley said he would "not go where you're not wanted."[3]

---

[1] Mimi Conway, *Rise Gonna Rise* (Garden City, N.Y.: Anchor Press,1979), p. 123.
[2] Ibid., p. 209.
[3] "A Gathering Momentum against J. P. Stevens," *Business Week,* March 20, 1978, p. 147.

THE COMPANY

J. P. Stevens and Company was a diversified corporation, primarily concentrated in the textile industry in which it was second in sales only to Burlington Industries. In 1978, the company had sales of $1.7 billion and profits of $36 million (see Exhibit 1). Over 44,100 employees worked in the company textile mills located throughout the southeastern states. The majority of plants were located in North and South Carolina.[4]

Stevens textile divisions marketed a wide spectrum of consumer and industrial products. In the apparel area, the firm produced fabrics of wools, cotton, and corduroy, and the newer polyester blends. The company was considered to be the industry leader in home furnishings and was currently expanding in this market area. One of the carpet division's lines, Gulistan's Fervor, was recognized as the top-selling item in the industry for the second year in a row in 1978. The company also marketed bedroom fashion lines, including coordinated sheets, bedspreads, comforters, draperies, and dust ruffles. The company's line of designer sheets had been growing in popularity recently. The market for terry cloth products had been increasing and the Terry, Bath, and Kitchen Products Division was also profitable. Stevens also had an institutional division and a linen supply service, which catered to hospitals, motels, and restaurants.

In the industrial products area, Stevens produced items for industries such as synthetics and glass fabrics, which involved specialized lamination and processes, and which were used in air and water pollution control devices. Fiberglass insect screening was recently introduced and was received quite well by home builders. The automotive industry purchased fabrics for headliners, trunk liners, upholstery, and molded tufted carpeting. The U.S. government had large contracts with J. P. Stevens for uniform materials and other fabrics.

Stevens also had a printing subsidiary group comprised of Foote & Davies, Steven Graphics, and Mid-America Webbpress. They printed a wide range of material including telephone directories, periodicals, direct mail catalogs, and promotional material (see Exhibit 2). While nearly half of Stevens' sales were in apparel products, the home furnishings, industrial products, and commercial printing subsidiaries were also important contributors to total sales (see Exhibit 3).

Although J. P. Stevens company was well known in the industry, the public, for the most part, was not very familiar with the firm. Stevens did not market its products under its own name, as did Burlington and Farah. Stevens products were distributed under such brand names as J. C. Penney, Utica, and Fruit of the Loom (see Exhibit 4).

---

[4] J. P. Stevens Annual Report, 1978, p. 3.

EXHIBIT 1 J. P. Stevens & Co., Inc., and Subsidiary Companies 10-Year Financial Review (for the fiscal years 1969–1978)

	1978	1977	1976	1975	1974	1973	1972	1971	1970	1969
*Consolidated Statement of Income**										
Net sales	$1,651.4	$1,539.2	$1,421.4	$1,123.0	$1,264.1	$1,114.0	$957.7	$861.1	$892.6	$1,003.0
Less net sales from discontinued operations	—	—	—	—	—	—	10.1	37.9	90.9	96.1
Net sales from continuing operations	1,651.4	1,539.2	1,421.4	1,123.0	1,264.1	1,114.0	947.6	823.2	801.7	906.9
Cost of goods sold	1,472.9	1,369.7	1,250.1	997.6	1,094.1	968.5	848.8	740.5	716.8	791.6
Gross profit on sales	178.5	169.5	171.3	125.4	170.0	145.5	98.8	82.7	84.9	115.3
Selling, general, and administrative expenses	93.1	88.8	82.6	71.8	77.9	74.0	61.7	59.9	58.1	58.6
Interest on indebtedness	25.1	19.9	16.9	18.0	19.8	13.2	10.9	10.5	13.3	11.6
Other income	(1.6)	(.7)	(1.9)	(.9)	(1.6)	(.2)	(.3)	(1.8)	(2.1)	(2.0)
Total	116.6	108.0	97.6	88.9	96.1	87.0	72.3	68.6	69.3	68.2
Income from continuing operations before taxes	61.9	61.5	73.7	36.5	73.9	58.5	26.5	14.1	15.6	47.1
Estimated taxes on income	25.5	26.3	32.6	16.6	34.5	27.7	10.9	7.0	6.6	24.0
Income from continuing operations	36.4	35.2	41.1	19.9	39.4	30.8	15.6	7.1	9.0	23.1
Income (loss) from discontinued operations	—	—	—	—	—	—	(3.0)	(7.7)	(2.7)	3.5
Income (loss) before extraordinary item	36.4	35.2	41.1	19.9	39.4	30.8	12.6	(.6)	6.3	26.6
Extraordinary item	—	—	—	—	—	—	(6.8)	—	—	—
Net income	$ 36.4	$ 35.2	$ 41.1	$ 19.9	$ 39.4	$ 30.8	$ 5.8	$ (.6)	$ 6.3	$ 26.6
Depreciation and amortization charges	$ 44.6	$ 39.5	$ 34.2	$ 32.6	$ 31.8	$ 30.5	$ 29.6	$ 30.9	$ 31.8	$ 31.5
Per Share of Capital Stock†										
Income from continuing operations before taxes	$ 4.80	$ 4.78	$ 5.75	$ 2.85	$ .77	$ 4.51	$ 1.98	$ 1.04	$ 1.15	$ 3.19
Estimated taxes on income	1.97	2.04	2.54	1.30	2.69	2.13	.82	.52	.48	1.77
Income from continuing operations	2.83	2.74	3.21	1.55	3.08	2.38	1.16	.52	.67	1.72
Income (loss) from discontinued operations	—	—	—	—	—	—	(.22)	(.57)	(.20)	.26
Income (loss) before extraordinary item	2.83	2.74	3.21	1.55	3.08	2.38	.94	(.05)	.47	1.98
Extraordinary item							(.50)			
Net income	2.83	2.74	3.21	1.55	3.08	2.38	.44	(.05)	.47	1.98
Net income—fully diluted	2.71	2.61	3.04	1.49	2.92	2.27	.44	(.05)	.47	1.88
Cash dividends	1.09	1.09	1.00	.81¾	1.00	.73¾	.68¾	.88¾	1.09	1.09
Shareowners' equity	37.69	35.96	34.43	32.28	31.54	29.46	27.23	27.32	28.22	28.80

EXHIBIT 1 (concluded)

Condensed Consolidated Balance Sheet*

	1978	1977	1976	1975	1974	1973	1972	1971	1970	1969
Cash and marketable securities	$ 13.4	$ 18.5	$ 24.1	$ 17.1	$ 23.1	$ 23.6	$ 28.4	$ 14.7	$ 18.5	$ 15.9
Receivables—net	310.6	281.8	251.1	238.8	246.3	214.4	190.0	173.0	184.3	205.1
Inventories	328.0	311.0	282.5	252.3	251.9	249.2	219.3	218.1	221.1	234.1
Other current assets	5.9	3.6	2.8	1.8	2.6	1.3	4.3	—	—	—
Total current assets	657.9	614.9	560.5	510.0	523.9	488.5	442.0	405.8	423.9	455.1
Total current liabilities	186.5	157.5	165.0	138.6	153.7	169.4	114.7	103.3	99.5	118.8
Working capital	471.4	457.4	395.5	371.4	370.2	319.1	327.3	302.5	324.4	336.3
Fixed assets, at cost	794.2	744.7	703.5	658.2	619.3	583.7	553.9	545.2	525.2	505.9
Less: Accumulated depreciation and amortization	508.5	478.9	453.5	429.5	407.8	386.7	365.2	348.1	330.6	306.9
Net fixed assets	285.7	265.8	250.0	228.7	211.5	197.0	188.7	197.1	194.6	190.0
Other assets and deferred charges	11.5	13.5	14.7	16.8	15.2	14.6	13.6	14.8	8.3	7.8
	768.6	736.7	660.2	616.9	596.9	530.7	529.6	514.4	527.3	543.1
Long-term debt	238.2	244.0	203.4	194.5	187.4	150.0	164.0	143.3	141.9	149.5
Other liabilities and deferred credits	44.0	28.7	14.9	9.3	5.8	3.1	2.2	3.1	4.6	3.8
	282.2	272.7	218.3	203.8	193.2	153.6	166.2	146.4	146.5	153.3
Net assets	$ 486.4	$ 464.0	$ 441.9	$ 413.1	$ 403.7	$ 377.1	$ 363.4	$ 368.0	$ 380.8	$ 389.8
Represented by shareowners' equity:										
Capital stock	$ 90.7	$ 81.2	80.2	$ 79.7	$ 79.7	$ 79.1	$ 87.2	$ 88.6	$ 88.9	$ 89.6
Capital in excess of par value	80.1	73.2	73.3	73.4	73.4	73.4	73.4	73.3	73.2	73.1
Accumulated earnings	315.6	309.6	288.4	260.0	250.6	224.0	202.8	206.1	218.7	227.1
	$ 486.4	$ 464.0	$ 441.9	$ 413.1	$ 403.7	$ 377.1	$ 363.4	$ 368.0	$ 380.8	$ 389.8

* In millions of dollars.
† In dollars.

EXHIBIT 2 J. P. Stevens Subsidiaries

Stevens has 81 manufacturing plants in the United States. Of this number 35 are located in South Carolina; 26 in North Carolina; 8 in Georgia; 6 in Virginia; and the remaining 6 in Alabama, Connecticut, Massachusetts, Tennessee, and Nebraska. All the plants are owned in fee, with the exception of four plants which are leased.

The principal plants and other materially important physical properties of the company used in manufacturing and/or related operations contain an aggregate of approximately 27,300,000 square feet of floor space. All the plants are well maintained and in good operating condition. The plants, generally, have been operating on a five- to six-day week and on a two- to three-shift basis.

The executive offices and sales headquarters are located in New York City in Stevens Tower, of which Stevens is the principal tenant under a 35-year lease (running from 1970), which may be terminated at the end of 25 years under certain conditions.

Parents and Subsidiaries of Registrant	*Percentage of Voting Securities Owned by Immediate Parents as of October 28, 1978*
J. P. Stevens & Co., Inc. (Del.)	
Registrant	Parent
The Black Hawk Corporation (S.C.)	100
Foote & Davies, Inc. (Del.)	100
Foote & Davies Transport Co. (Ga.)	100
Mid-America Webpress, Inc. (Neb.)	100
Inversiones Lerma, S. A. de C.V. (Mexico)	100
Textiles Elasticos United S.A. de C.V. (Mexico)	42.5*
Stevens Beechcraft, Inc. (Del.)	100
Stevens-Bremner (N.Z.) Limited (New Zealand)	50
J. P. Stevens & Co. (Canada), Ltd.	100
J. P. Stevens & Co., Limited (Great Britain)	100
Stevens Elastomeric and Plastic Products, Inc. (Del.)	100
Stevens-Genin (France)	100
Stevens Graphics, Inc. (Ga.)	100
Books, Inc. (Ala.)	100
Carolina Ruralist Press, Inc. (N.C.)	100
Florida Printers, Inc. (Fla.)	100
Ruralist Press, Inc. (Ga.)	100
Automated Graphics Unlimited, Inc. (Ga.)	100
Superior Type, Inc. (Ga.)	100
Video Type, Inc. (Ga.)	100
J. P. Stevens International Sales, Inc. (Del.)	100
United Elastic Limited (Canada)	100

In addition to the subsidiaries listed above, there are six inactive subsidiaries having merely nominal capitalization.

* An additional 30 percent of voting securities of this subsidiary is owned by Stevens and 27.5 percent held by a trustee.

SOURCE: *1978 Annual Report.*

EXHIBIT 3   Total Sales by Product Line (1974–1977)

In years prior to fiscal 1978, the company considered itself, in all material respects, in one line of business. One customer of a subsidiary company accounts for approximately 24 percent of the sales of the commercial printing segment.

The following table shows percentage of total sales for 1977 and prior by product line:

	1977	1976	1975	1974
Apparel	47%	50%	48%	50%
Home furnishings	32	33	34	31
Industrial products	13	13	13	14
Commercial printing	5	2	2	2
Other	3	2	3	2
	100%	100%	100%	100%

Stevens's export sales of products produced in the United States amounted to less than 5 percent of total net sales. In addition, Stevens has modest investments in textile manufacturing plants in Canada, England, and France; and in joint ventures in Mexico and New Zealand.

SOURCE: *1978 Annual Report.*

EXHIBIT 4   J. P. Stevens Products

J. P. Stevens & Co. is a giant corporation with subsidiaries and associates in Canada, Mexico, France, Belgium, New Zealand, and Australia.

J. P. Stevens's subsidiaries in the United States include: Black Hawk Corporation which operates a warehouse in South Carolina; Stevens Beechcraft, which services aircraft at the Greenville-Spartanburg, South Carolina airport; Southeastern Aviation Inc.; Southeastern Beechcraft, an aircraft distributor; Stevens Graphics Inc., which prints and publishes telephone directories in the southeastern United States; Sheffield Industries, a hosiery and leisure slipper manufacturer; J. P. Stevens International Sales, Inc.; Control Top, Inc.; and Stevens Elastromeric and Plastic Products, Inc.

J. P. Stevens markets some of its unfinished products under such names as Wonder-Glass, Astroquartz, Consort, Stevenset, H20, Stevenex, Plus-X, Blen-Tempo, and Allura.

Stevens's finished products are sold as: Stevens Fabrics; Hockanum, Boldenna, Wash Ease, Wool Press, Worumbo, Forstmann, and Andover woolens and worsteds; Appelton flannels and corduroys; Twist Twill, Academy, and Lady Twist Twill cotton work fabrics; Weftamatic, 20 Below, Gesture, Coachman, Lady Consort, Carousel, Stevetex, Windsheer, and Whisper Knit synthetics and blends; Utica, Fine Arts, Beauti-Blend, Mohawk, and Beauticale sheets; Utica, Fine Arts, and Utica/Mohawk blankets; Tastemaker home furnishings, like towels, sheets, and blankets; Simtex tablecloths and table sets; Gulistan, Tastemaker, Contender, and Merryweather carpets; Finesse, Spirit, Fruit of the Loom, Hip-lets, and Big Mama women's hosiery; J. P. Stevens draperies; Kyron interfacings for apparel; and Always in Step women's slippers.

EXHIBIT 4 *(concluded)*

In addition, Stevens manufactures glass fabric insect screening; fabrics for air pollution; glass fabric for marine insulation and fishing rods; nonwoven backings for handbags, shoes, synthetic leather upholstery, and luggage; synthetic fabrics for soil erosion and flood control; and pharmaceutical stoppers for the health care industry.

SOURCE: J. G. DiNunno, "J. P. Stevens: Anatomy of an Outlaw," *American Federalist,* April 1976, p. 3.

LABOR HISTORY OF THE TEXTILE INDUSTRY

In the late 19th century an exodus was begun by textile manufacturers from the northern states into the southern region of the United States. The overall reason was lower operating costs due to low levels of employment in the South, and later, discouragement of unionization.

The owners of industrial plants found the South's manufacturing environment attractive. The southern states, ravaged by the Civil War, had to rebuild their industrial base. Heavy equipment had either been turned into useless scrap or had been carried away to the North to pay for "war damages." Southern community leaders, then, were understandably eager to entice heavy industry back into the region to begin a rejuvenation process. Northern manufacturers found the conditions "right," that is, "reasonable" wages and no unions. Thus, a basic and tacit agreement came into being throughout the region, which not only discouraged unionization but encouraged and promoted loyalty to a company that provided jobs. As the 20th century progressed, textile plants, in particular, began to migrate to the rural South. During this period it was not unusual to see what was referred to as a *company town.* In a company town, a manufacturer not only owned the plant but also the land surrounding it and all the buildings in the town. The workers rented their homes from the company, were paid in script redeemable at company stores, and sometimes were buried in company-owned cemeteries. Even if a plant did not own the real estate, the worker's dependence on the company still existed. Usually, the only work in the area to be had was at the textile mill; if a worker was fired from a plant, little recourse remained but to leave the area.

GROWTH OF UNIONISM

The Industrial Revolution made possible the existence of massive concentrations of economic power wielded by individual owners of industry. After a period of time, there came about on the part of the public a growing realization that the lone, individual worker was relatively powerless to exert any influence on his employer to secure equitable working conditions. Thus, as a response to some of the excesses committed by some industrialists against the men, women, and children employed in their plants, public policy, through the legislatures, acted to restore the economic balance of power between the worker and the employer to a more reasonable degree.

Congress enacted a series of labor laws over the years to give workers a degree of economic power to balance that wielded by employers. The intent was to create an "adversarial relationship," constrained by laws to a peaceful bargaining environment, in which dialogue could be conducted. Legislation required that wages, hours, and working conditions be discussed as well as any other topics the two parties could mutually agree on.

The operative legislation was the National Labor Relations Act (NLRA), also called the *Wagner Act,* passed in 1935. The Wagner Act guaranteed workers the right to organize, bargain collectively with their employers, and if necessary, engage in concerted activity for the purpose of collective bargaining objectives. Section 8 of the NLRA set forth guidelines for unionizing activity and listed prohibited actions, called *unfair labor practices,* on the part of both union and employer. The employer, for example, could not interfere with, restrain, or coerce employees from joining or leaving a union, or interfere with the formation or administration of a union. Employers were not permitted to discriminate against employees in hiring or firing to encourage or discourage union membership. When deciding whether to accept representation by a union, employees voted in an election administered under very strict conditions by the National Labor Relations Board (NLRB) created by the Act. The employees determined if they wished to be represented by that union when dealing with management. A simple majority vote decided, with votes counted immediately after polls were closed. If a union was defeated, it had to wait one calendar year before another attempt.

Section 8 of the NLRA also contained practices that were prohibited in the period before an election. The courts developed a particular philosophy when deciding violations in this area. If an outright violation of a rule could not be clearly proven, then subjective mental intent might be found to have a psychologically "chilling effect" on an employee so as to interfere with his or her exercise of free choice and hence destroy the desired "laboratory conditions" of a free election environment. For example, an employer might say to employees at a mass meeting: "Plant X went union last week and shut down. I'm going to be forced to do the same thing if you vote yes tomorrow for the union. Then you will all be out of a job and starving. It's your choice." Such a statement would constitute an unfair labor practice.

THE ISSUE WITH J. P. STEVENS

J. P. Stevens was founded in 1813 in Andover, Massachusetts, as a textile manufacturing plant. The company decided shortly after World War II that the South looked more inviting and began to move plants into the Southeast, particularly the Carolinas. The company concentrated most of its plants in these two states, which happened to be the least unionized states. In the mid-1970s, North Carolina had 6.8 percent, and South Carolina had 8 percent union members in the working population.[5]

In the early 1960s, organized labor decided the last bastion of nonunion companies should fall. This objective arose both from a need to increase membership and from pressure from the unions of the North to bring the southern workers into the fold, thereby equalizing wage rates and slowing the loss of industries to the South. Burlington Industries, at the time, had a strong reputation as a dedicated antiunion company; Stevens, with a more moderate union posture, was judged to be a better target by union leaders.[6]

The battle between unions and Stevens was joined in 1965 during the first unionizing attempt when an NLRB investigator found Stevens guilty at 21 plants of wholesale violations of the National Labor Relations Act. Since 1965, Stevens has been found guilty in 15 separate cases, 8 of which were upheld in federal appeals courts. Three of those cases went to the Supreme Court, which rendered decisions against the company in each case. In other instances, the Supreme Court refused to hear Stevens's appeals because of lack of merit, thereby affirming appeals courts' rulings.[7]

In the period from 1967 through 1979, J. P. Stevens was convicted of numerous violations of Section 8. In many cases, the NLRB returned to federal court to seek contempt judgment after Stevens failed to comply with federal court orders. One appeals court in New York said it could not "view with equanimity the refusal of a large employer to abide by the law of the land and refrain from interfering with the rights of its employees."[8] Another appeals court threatened to jail Stevens's officials for refusing to comply with court orders.

In one landmark case making judicial history in labor law, Stevens was found to have engaged in a continuous campaign of vigorous and pervasively illegal resistance marked by threats and actual discharge of employees, plant closings in response to union activism, discharge of employees for testifying before the NLRB, coercive interrogation, surveillance of union members and meetings, restrictions of solicitation by union members, and use of company bulletin boards to post the names of union supporters. J. P. Stevens was found by a federal appeals court to have "so grossly exceeded" the standards of the labor act that "unusual" remedies were required. Normally, a violator was required to post a notice that, in essence, says, "I violated Section 8(a), and I will not do it again." Stevens was required to: (1) post the notice in all plants in North and South Carolina; (2) mail the notice to all employees at home so they could read it in a nonhostile atmosphere so as to more appreciate the impact;

---

[5] "Boycott the Bossman," *Industry Week,* April 30, 1977, p. 99.

[6] "The Battle Heats Up at J. P. Stevens," *Industry Week,* February 28, 1977, p. 104.

[7] J. G. DiNunno, "J. P. Stevens: Anatomy of an Outlaw," *American Federalist,* April 1976, p. 1.

[8] Ibid., p. 6.

(3) convene the employees on company time and have a company officer read it to them (later modified to permit reading by a NLRB official so as not to "unduly humiliate the company"); and (4) give the union access to company premises for one year and use of company bulletin boards where notices are usually posted. Combinations of this ruling were applied not just once, but three times. The Fifth Circuit Court of Appeals stated that "never has there been such an example of such classic, albeit crude, unlawful labor practices."[9]

In another case, Stevens was found guilty of wiretapping a union motel room where leaders of a unionization effort were meeting. The company made an out-of-court settlement for $50,000 prior to trial. A later case dealt with an instance where the company arbitrarily lowered the prevailing wage scale after a pro-union vote.[10]

Between 1965 and 1976, the company had been required to pay over $1.3 million to 289 workers who were illegally fired by the Stevens company for union activity. Boyd Leedon, a former NLRB chairman, described Stevens as "so out of tune with a humane civilized approach to industrial relations that it should shock even those least sensitive to honor, justice, and decent treatment."[11]

On August 28, 1974, seven Stevens plants in Roanoke Rapids, North Carolina, voted for representation by the Textile Workers Union of America (TWUA). By law, J. P. Stevens was then required to bargain collectively with the union. By the end of 1979, no contract had been signed, and a federal appeals court had found five separate counts of "bad faith bargaining" against Stevens, and in one case, directed Stevens to reimburse the union for all past expenses.

OTHER ISSUES

J. P. Stevens's controversies were not limited to the labor relations area. A number of other accusations had been leveled at the company from various sources. In nonunion matters, Stevens entered a plea of "no contest" to government charges in 1973 that it and several other fiberglass manufacturers conspired through secret meetings to fix prices on government contract bids. Stevens paid $260,000 in damages and consented to an injunction prohibiting future practices.[12]

In 1975, a North Carolina tax official charged Stevens had not reported $75 million of taxable inventory in 22 plants going back to 1966. A secret agreement was discovered, going back to 1951, to induce Stevens to locate in

---

[9] Archibald Cox, *Labor Laws: Cases and Materials* (Mineola, N.Y.: Foundation Press, 1977), p. 271.

[10] Ibid., pp. 2 and 6.

[11] Ibid., p. 1.

[12] Ibid., p. 6.

certain counties. The agreement allowed Stevens to undervalue inventories "in perpetuity." Stevens denied any wrongdoing but began to make some back payments.

Stevens was convicted in several racial disrimination suits. Statistics in one suit indicated over a six-year period salaries for whites averaged about $670 per year more than for blacks. A judge found that there was no evidence that could explain differences due to education, previous experience or length of employment, or other factors.

A procompany organization called J. P. Stevens Employees Education Committee (JPSEEC) opposed union activities. During congressional Labor Management Relations Committee field hearings at Roanoke Rapids on August 9, 1977, a lawyer representing JPSEEC testified. The lawyer was Robert Valois, whose firm had recently successfully blocked a union organizing attempt at another company. During testimony and questioning, Mr. Valois could not supply any figures relating to a budget, annual costs, how much his firm was paid or who paid them, and where the majority of funds for the JPSEEC committee actually came from.[13]

The committee funds were, however, sufficient to send company employees to the New York headquarters to mount a counter demonstration against the union activists at the 1977 shareholders meeting. The president of the North Carolina AFL–CIO, Wilber Hobby, stated during testimony that one of Mr. Valois's associates used Sen. Jesse Helms's Senate stationery to mail literature for an organization called *Americans United Against Control of the Government*. It was stated the literature contained a poll "so biased, even I have to answer with a yes because I wouldn't want what he threatened to happen to this company."[14]

The J. P. Stevens annual report of 1978 stated that employees were "maintaining their position as among the best paid in the industry. Stevens's hourly paid textile workers earned an average of $4.77 an hour . . . 7.3 percent more than . . . industry averages . . . which was . . . $4.37. Weekly earnings were $204.02 compared to $177.42."[15]

During the company's 1978 annual meeting, an employee responded to such statements, addressing Chairman of the Board Finley in regard to wages: "We're off every other weekend. We do 56 hours' labor for about 42 hours pay. We work 12-hour shifts."[16] Some employees stated that three to five supervisors per plant received very high hourly rates, hence the average figure. According to a survey by the University of North Carolina, workers in the state averaged $21 less in wages per week than those engaged in similar jobs in other states, while profits in many North Carolina businesses were higher

---

[13] Conway, *Rise Gonna Rise,* p. 154.

[14] Ibid., p. 155.

[15] *1978 Annual Report,* p. 11.

[16] Conway, *Rise Gonna Rise,* p. 209.

than in other similar industries in other states. The study concluded that North Carolina ranked last in the nation in hourly industrial wages. New industries paid "prevailing wage rates" instead of the higher out-of-state wages. According to the Textile Workers Union of America, Southern textile workers earned $1.42 per hour less than the average rate of all manufacturing workers.[17]

The textile mill employees received one week of vacation per year although company policy stated that after five-years' service workers were entitled to two weeks of holiday pay. Employees indicated that the operative word was *entitled* and in reality was ignored. Further, if an employee insisted on the clause, he or she would be eventually discharged for various reasons. In a related area, workers often returned from sick leave to find their job taken and no work available, or they were given a less desirable job than their former one.[18]

WORKING CONDITIONS

Another area of contention concerned worker health programs. Cotton mill workers suffer from brown lung disease (byssinosis), a respiratory condition similar to black lung in coal miners. The lungs gradually lose their oxygen processing capacity through ingestion of airborne dust that coats the lung walls; the condition can be terminal. One worker had a 40 percent reduction in breathing ability and was discharged by J. P. Stevens for failure to carry out assigned duties. Occupational Safety and Health Administration (OSHA) standards limited dust per cubic meter of air to 1.0 milligram or less in cotton mills. However, studies in textile plants found as much as 2.96 milligrams per cubic meter. It was not uncommon for cotton to pile up to six inches deep on floors with dust so thick in rooms as to create a virtual fog. Stevens, since 1974, had spent over $4.2 million complying with OSHA standards, but stated in the 1978 annual report: "There is a question as to whether the technology exists" to meet requirements.[19] At the same time, the North Carolina Public Interest Research Group reported a Gaston, North Carolina, plant operating with levels of 0.1 to 0.2 milligrams of dust using modern equipment.

Perhaps chairman Finley best summed up his attitude in a statement at the 1976 shareholder meeting: "Byssinosis (brown lung) is something alleged to come from cotton dust. It is a word that's been coined, but has no meaning."[20]

At OSHA hearings, J. Davitt McAteir, an attorney with a public interest law firm, who had investigated black lung in coal miners, reviewed and

---

17 DiNunno, "J. P. Stevens: Anatomy," pp. 3, 6.
18 Conway, *Rise Gonna Rise*, p. 39.
19 *1978 Annual Report*, p. 12.
20 Conway, *Rise Gonna Rise*, p. 136.

compared cotton and coal dust standards and then made some direct parallel observations. He stated the procedure proposed by OSHA placing the responsibility

> for monitoring and notifying employees regarding noncompliance in the hands of the employer is the classic case of placing the fox in charge of security at the henhouse. Unless the monitoring program is conducted . . . by the United States . . . the possibility that fraudulent data will be forthcoming is very real. The hiring of company doctors to conduct a medical examination is a practice considered even by the coal industry as Neanderthal.[21]

In June 1976, the unions declared a national boycott of J. P. Stevens on a scale greater than that ever undertaken by the American labor movement. The AFL–CIO declared "complete, total, all-out support" for the effort including financial support. Finley referred to the boycott as "our cause, our crusade" and stated that the union was attempting to destroy "management rights."[22] A company spokesman stated that the boycott is "an improper use of the combined power of many unions."[23]

The union replied, ". . . the purpose of the boycott is not to hurt the workers, but get the company to change its position. It was the company that created the conditions of the boycott by making it impossible for us to get fair elections in the first place."[24] The American Council of Textile Workers (ACTW) president stated: "Stevens has got to create an atmosphere in all its plants that if a worker wants a union, he can join it without any pain or fear. Basically, they've got to obey the law."[25]

Through 1979, it was difficult to establish how effective the boycott had been since J. P. Stevens did not market under its own name. In addition, only 34 percent of its revenue was derived from consumer products. At the March 7, 1978, shareholders' meeting, Bob Hall, editor of *Southern Exposure* magazine, requested a special report on the impact of labor management policies on company stock. Hall's statement was printed in the Stevens proxy statement:

> Much evidence indicates that Stevens's stock performance may be affected by its policies toward labor unions. For example, on August 31, 1977, the Second Circuit Court of Appeals opened the way for the company to receive stiff fines if it continues violating the labor management laws and the Court's orders. The following week, Stevens stock fell from 16⅞ to 5⅞ while other textile stocks remained relatively unchanged.

In fact, by October 19, J. P. Stevens's stock price was 13 percent below its low price for 1976. Stevens's stock had performed worse than any other of the

---

[21] Ibid., pp. 66–67.
[22] "The All-Out Campaign against J. P. Stevens," *Business Week,* June 14, 1976, p. 28.
[23] "A Boycott Battle to Win the South," *Business Week,* December 6, 1976, p. 80.
[24] Ibid.
[25] "A Gathering Momentum," p. 148.

leading textile companies. At least one investment consultant attributed the poor performance to Stevens's labor-management problems.[26]

At the meeting, Finley noted first quarter sales in 1978 were $350.3 million, up from $334.3 generated in 1977. Profits, however, declined from $7.7 million to $7.1 million. Finley attributed the drop to rising costs and increases in foreign imports.[27]

In 1979, under the leadership of Raymond Rogers, head of ACTW's "corporate campaign," the union used financial pressure to force two directors to resign from the Stevens board.

In its boycott efforts, ACTW received endorsement from three Protestant denominations, and the National Council of Churches passed out 40,000 preaddressed postcards to mail to Avon and Manufacturers Hanover, who were represented on Stevens's board. Other unions indicated they would move over $1 billion in pension funds from Manufacturers Hanover to another bank. As a result of these pressures, the directors of Avon, Manufacturers Hanover, and New York Life resigned from the Stevens board. In the case of New York Life, Rogers organized a slate of candidates to run against the New York Life directors. Under New York law, the company would have had to mail out ballots to 6.3 million policyholders and incur the resulting expense. The New York Life director chose instead to quit the Stevens board. Rogers's basic intent was to "isolate J. P. Stevens from the mainstream of American business."

Whitney Stevens finished his mental review of recent history and wondered if his great-great-grandfather Captain Nathaniel, the founder of the company, could have even remotely imagined anything like the present size and conditions of the firm. He then recalled something he had told an interviewer from *Fortune* last October when discussing his impending change in duties. Stevens had said his appointment did not really signal a major change in company position and that everyone had become rather "thick-skinned." "The real issue is what do our people in our plants want" he had said. "Our ultimate objection is to the forcing of people into joining a union. Naturally, we'd rather not have a union. We think it is not necessary, not desirable, and certainly not in our employees' interest. This union business is unpleasant and enervating."[28]

However, Stevens mused to himself, that was back in Finley's period. One of the hallmarks of a good leader and manager is to look at all the alternatives open to him, not just those that are personally preferable. He fully intended to act as chairman in the best interests of the shareholders of his company. It was no longer what would Finley do, but what will Stevens do? It was now time to develop his own perspective on the issues that confronted his company.

---

26 Conway, *Rise Gonna Rise,* p. 209.

27 "A Gathering Momentum," p. 147.

28 "I Couldn't Be Ignored," *Fortune,* October 22, 1979, p. 23.

SCA Corporation

Founded at the turn of the century in Coventry, Pennsylvania, SCA Corporation was international in scope by the 1960s and by 1983 owned 39 plants and distribution centers in the United States, Canada, Puerto Rico, and one plant in Europe. It sold its products in over 125 countries. It had been a Fortune 500 industrial since the 1950s; its annual sales passed the $1 billion mark in 1978.

Some 14,500 people worked for SCA at the end of 1982. One third of these employees lived in Coventry, where SCA maintained its corporate headquarters, research and engineering facilities, several major plants, and a huge distribution center.

SCA had long been proud of its relationship with its employees and the city of Coventry. A 1964 company press release proudly described an incident that occurred 40 years earlier.

> [In] 1924, an incident occurred which, in itself, reflects the progressiveness and sound human relations that have governed the company's operations. A fire destroyed the entire Coventry number one plant. Six hundred and fifty employees were jobless—a situation which affected the entire community. Operations came to a complete halt. Rather than desert their people by looking elsewhere for an opportunity to relocate immediately, the SCA management made two decisions that only an administration with integrity and understanding could reach. First, it undertook to rebuild the destroyed Coventry factory in the shortest possible time. Second, it set up temporary quarters in its Coventry plant number two. It expanded operations there to the limit, transferred and gave continued employment to its workers, and continued service to its customers. Within six months both plants were going full blast.

A 1979 company brochure proclaimed:

> The superior quality of SCA's products is not the result of superior technology alone. It is, to an even greater extent, the reflection of a quality consciousness—an

---

All names, places, and other information that might identify the company have been disguised.

attitude of care and concern—on the part of the company's employees. The taproot of this attitude is embedded in the traditions and cultural values, the living standards and lifestyles of Coventry, Pennsylvania, where the nucleus of SCA employees reside. A visit to this prosperous and heritage-rich community in Pennsylvania's heartland reveals why at SCA, quality is a way of life.

SCA was the economic heart of Coventry and its 37,000 residents.

PRODUCTS

SCA Corporation offered rubber products in three industrial categories: household, industrial, and hardware (see Exhibit 1). Each of these industries was highly competitive in the area of price, service, and quality. Six to 20 major domestic firms competed in each market; in addition, imports had become a source of intensified competition in household products. SCA was among the top three competitors in each of the three industries, but its position was increasingly threatened by stronger domestic and international competitors.

EXHIBIT 1

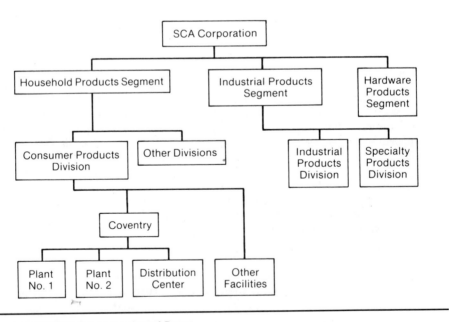

SOURCE: 1982 SCA Corporation Annual Report.

PROFITABILITY PROBLEMS

The economic recession, which began in 1981, hit SCA's household and hardware products segments particularly hard. SCA and its competitors were hurt by lower consumer spending and reductions in both distributor and retailer inventory levels. SCA's 1981 annual report had anticipated "a modest start for SCA in 1982, with improvements over the balance of the year." Instead, after 27 years of uninterrupted growth, SCA's sales declined 5 percent in 1982 to less than $1.4 billion. Net income dropped 60 percent. With its financial data adjusted for inflation, SCA lost $9.8 million in 1982. See Exhibit 2 for a summary of SCA's financial performance.

But the company's problems were not just the result of the poor economic conditions in 1981 and 1982. SCA's sales from 1979 to 1982 showed an inflation-adjusted growth rate of -3 percent (as opposed to a historical-cost growth rate of 7 percent). Moreover, SCA's inflation-adjusted profits had dropped 17 percent over the last four years, compared with the industry average of -1 percent.

The general opinion of both industry observers and SCA's management was that the company had stayed in industrial products too long. Competition had intensified in the late 1970s, and several major competitors had exited the industry. SCA picked up most of their business. As one SCA executive noted: "When everything is going great [referring to the 1960s and 70s], who looks back? An ideal manager looks retrospectively. We were too busy trying to ship things out the door and making bucks. We were going to the bank every day. We simply didn't read our difficulties as early as we should have."

Indicative of SCA's economic troubles was a stock raid, which took place in the summer of 1982. The company learned of the purchases when the raider reported his 6.2 percent stake in SCA Corporation to the Securities and Exchange Commission. He said he was prepared to buy more SCA stock and threatened to seek control of the company. To avoid the threat, SCA's board agreed to repurchase the raider's stock for $4.5 million above its market value. SCA Corporation refused to discuss the incident with either its stockholders or the press. In its 1982 annual report, the only reference to the incident was a paragraph on major investments, which included "$24.8 million for the purchase of SCA common share for treasury stock."

SCA CORPORATION'S RESPONSES TO ITS FINANCIAL PROBLEMS

SCA Corporation clearly felt threatened by its dismal performance. Foreign competitors seemed to beat them at every turn with better quality and lower prices. Many of the company's domestic competitors went out of business, and those that survived seemed intent on waging price wars. Low produc-

EXHIBIT 2 SCA Corporation Financial Summary (in thousands of dollars except per common share data)

	1982	1981	1980	1979	1978	1977	1976	1975
Operations:								
Net sales	$ 1,355,361	$ 1,430,132	$ 1,286,267	$ 1,177,784	$ 1,075,224	$ 961,995	$ 943,114	$ 740,346
Net income								
Historical cost	$ 18,482	44,450	43,193	47,448	53,850	45,135	41,061	32,556
Constant dollar	$ (9,858)	15,899	23,267	36,918				
Current cost	$ (7,911)	22,917	29,178	38,739				
Percent earned on sales	2.1%	4.7%	5.1%	6.0%	7.5%	7.1%	6.6%	6.6%
Percent earned on beginning common stockholders' equity	6.0%	15.2%	15.6%	18.5%	23.3%	21.5%	21.3%	18.0%
Per common share:								
Net income	$ 1.88	4.34	4.22	4.64	5.28	4.46	4.07	3.21
Dividends paid	$ 2.04	2.04	1.92	1.80	1.61	1.50	1.35	1.20
Other data:								
Common stockholders' equity	$ 433,799	462,129	439,194	415,116	385,569	347,360	316,254	289,112
Weighted average number of common shares outstanding	14,728,257	15,390,393	15,379,976	15,333,494	15,288,545	15,206,423	15,165,815	15,221,498
Current ratio	2.51	2.72	2.66	2.96	3.30	3.78	3.75	3.05
Number of employees	14,500	17,100	17,600	18,000	16,800	16,800	17,800	17,000

SOURCE: 1982 SCA Corporation Annual Report.

tivity and profitability emerged as the focal point for management action. They attacked the problems in several ways. Three of these actions either had, or were expected to have, a significant effect on the community of Coventry and SCA's work force.

First, SCA Corporation emphasized cost reduction and productivity improvements. Generally, the company focused on a reduction of inventory levels, investment in new equipment, realignment of production processes, energy conservation, expansion of SCA's alternate fuel capabilities, and strengthening of its energy independence. More specifically, the company emphasized a reduction of labor costs. Its 1982 annual report stated:

> A large portion of our fixed costs consists of indirect hourly plant labor and salaried costs at the plant, division, and corporate level. These costs were cut in 1982 as our work force reduction program was accelerated. Actions taken included hiring freezes, early retirement incentives, layoffs, terminations, temporary salary reductions, lower merit increases, and permanent reductions in salaried fringe benefits. Total employment was down 15 percent by year-end 1982 with more reductions planned for 1983.

Second, despite the emphasis on cost reduction and productivity improvements within the industrial products segment, SCA Corporation announced in early 1983 that it had sold its largest division within that segment. This division had accounted for one third of SCA's sales and 25 percent of its income from operations over the last five years. It employed 3,800 of SCA's 14,500 employees. It was estimated that, over the next two years, 350 nonunion SCA employees in Coventry would lose their jobs, with perhaps 100 being transferred to the divested business's new headquarters. For those left without jobs, SCA promised retraining, assistance in obtaining new jobs, and extended fringe benefits. The sale did not affect any hourly workers in Coventry.

SCA's chief executive officer, John R. Rike, told the press that the company sold the industrial division because SCA "was paying out much more in wages and benefits than we have been able to get from the customers. We had a $450 million business last year that didn't make any money." Although he did not blame the union for what happened, he said that there had been a problem getting union leaders to communicate management's concerns to the rank and file. He emphasized that management had been trying to increase productivity at all SCA plants in order to keep the corporation viable.

SCA's third response was to seek concessions (mainly in the areas of benefits and work rules) from its employees' union. Covering nearly three fourths of SCA's total hourly labor force, the union contracts were scheduled to expire soon.

The emphasis on the reduction of salaried and hourly labor costs, the sale of the industrial products division and the loss of several hundred salaried positions, consolidation of SCA's engineering groups in the spring of 1983 and the loss of additional salaried positions, and the upcoming labor negotiations created an atmosphere of tension at SCA Corporation. The focal point of this tension was a consulting firm, Management Control Systems, Inc., brought into the company in May 1982 to identify where labor costs could be cut and productivity improved. The vast majority of SCA's Coventry employees worked within its Consumer Products Division. Mostly as a result of Management Control Systems's work, this Division cut 450 hourly positions (10 percent of SCA's hourly work force in Coventry) from June 1982 to May 1983.

MANAGEMENT CONTROL SYSTEMS, INC.

Management Control Systems, founded in 1970, was a consulting firm based in New Haven, Connecticut, and specialized in savings obtained through labor productivity improvement as opposed to capital expenditures. The program by which these savings were obtained was called Productivity Improvement and Communication Systems (PICS).

Management Control Systems obtained business through mass-mailed solicitations, cold calls, and personal referrals. The organization offered to analyze a business's current operations without cost to the potential client. This audit determined whether PICS would save the client money (given the client's existing plant and equipment) and how much money could be saved. The day after an audit was finished, Management Control Systems outlined those savings to the client. The consulting firm's contractual agreement with the client specified that the latter must decide that same day whether to implement PICS. This short decision period enabled Management Control Systems to keep its audit staff on site to begin implementation of PICS.

Management Control Systems based its fixed fee on the staffing required to complete the PICS program at the client's plants. The contract guaranteed savings equal to the cost of PICS. In practice, the consulting firm looked for first-year savings of at least three times the cost of the entire PICS program. If the guaranteed savings were not obtained in the first year, Management Control Systems either refunded the difference or continued working at the client's plants until the cost of PICS was recovered. No client had ever requested a refund, although the firm had to work overtime on occasion to obtain the guaranteed savings. The contract was open-ended in that the client could terminate its relationship with Management Control Systems at any time by paying for the services rendered to date.

When the client company agreed to use Management Control Systems's services, the consulting firm required the client to appoint a liaison person. Management Control Systems trained the liaison to work as an intermediary between itself and client management, to monitor the savings obtained through PICS, and to perpetuate the programs within the firm's plants after the PICS team left.

PICS consisted of three separate programs: engineering, access, and resources. A fourth program involving energy conservation was not yet being offered by Management Control Systems. In the first program, *engineering*, Management Control Systems engineers helped analyze each task performed by a worker within a department; then company foremen and department heads established a performance norm for the task. The client used the norms to establish staffing levels. In the second program, *access*, the consulting firm provided classroom training to first-line supervisors to teach them behavioral and communication skills. In addition, consulting firm personnel worked with supervisors on the plant floor to help them develop the desired skills, advising them on how to handle specific personnel problems as they arose. *Resources*, the third program, included production and process planning, inventory control, and forecasting.

SCA Corporation's senior management first heard of the New Haven–based firm from managers of another company using Management Control Systems's services. The consulting firm was invited to conduct its audit of SCA Corporation's Consumer Products Division plants in Coventry in May 1982. Its four-week audit showed potential savings of $15 million; Management Control Systems intended to charge about $4.5 million for its services.

In selling its program to the Consumer Products Division management, Management Control Systems admitted that some of its ideas for cost savings were not novel. The consulting firm argued, however, that use of an outside team of industrial engineers to cut costs (1) would be more politically palatable to the concerned parties; (2) would preclude the division laying off a large in-house team of industrial engineers hired for the sole purpose of implementing a one-time program; (3) would be less expensive than an in-house team; and (4) would be much more objective. The division found these arguments persuasive, particularly because of its location in a small town.

THE GO-AHEAD

In early June 1982, the division gave Management Control Systems the go-ahead to implement its PICS program in its two plants and distribution center in Coventry. The entire program was expected to require 30 to 40 industrial engineers working in Coventry for 48 consecutive weeks.

The Consumer Products Division chose Pete Bolling as its liaison with Management Control Systems. Pete's formal schooling had ended with the ninth grade; yet in his 14 years with SCA Corporation, he had worked as an accountant, systems analyst, assistant plant manager, and plant comptroller. Because of this experience, he knew the people, the jobs, and the accounting systems within the division. But perhaps even more important, Pete was personable, thoughtful, and frank. He got along well with executives, supervisors, and workers alike. He seemed to possess the perfect combination of temperament, skills, and experience to ride herd on the PICS program.

Pete viewed his job both strategically and tactically. For example, he gave the following reasons for beginning PICS within the distribution center. First, the heaviest shipping within the center occurred in September and October to meet the Christmas seasonal demand. By improving productivity and cutting excess labor in a low-volume state (i.e., prior to September), increases in the work force could be minimized as volume expanded. Second, the distribution center had the greatest potential for savings. It would serve as an example of what PICS could do and a model for subsequent implementation in other departments. Third, management expected employee resistance to PICS to be highest in the distribution center (the last two SCA strikes had started there). Management felt that the center employed its most radical workers. As Pete stated, "If we can get away with PICS here, we can get away with it in any other area."

THE ENGINEERING PROGRAM

PICS engineering program required norms to be established for every job group within a department. Management Control Systems's industrial engineers and the Division's supervisors observed people at work. In practice, the supervisors themselves did about 80 percent of the observations after being trained by the consulting firm's engineers. Workers were also required to document what they did and how long it took.

Gary Hector, the personnel manager in plant 1, described the steps in the engineering program:

> The basic PICS calls for norms to be established. What is the normal time it takes to select an item, or to load a carton into a truck, or to swab oil onto a machine? What's the norm for doing that? Norms are established for all the activities in given job groups. This involves a lot of observation of people, and it also involves the people themselves keeping track of what they do. Well, you can imagine the reaction we got when we told people that you have to start keeping track of what you do and report back at the end of the day.
>
> Well, it was a combination of the people reporting back what they did plus the supervisor's observations plus the observations of the PICS engineers that helped us to develop norms: what are the normal times needed to do certain jobs. Well, these norms were all added up, and the numbers were crunched. Out of it came, on the one hand, the number of minutes or hours that are needed to perform all of the work in a department based on norms, and, on the other hand, the number of hours or minutes that are available in terms of the number of employees that work in the department. Whenever the second number exceeded the first, that meant that we had more people than we needed. It meant that there was idle time, slack time somewhere. It might mean that there were times when people were going slower than they should have. Or it might mean they had more time for coffee breaks. Or perhaps they were just plain not working as hard as they could be, based on these norms, which we state are reasonable expectations for a job. From these norms, then, came staff reductions—not always, but often.

According to management, supervisors and senior plant management discussed the norms and individualized them when necessary. Both the consultants and the company felt it was essential that the supervisor be involved in setting norms because the latter had to implement them and live with them.

Gary Hector also described how SCA Corporation dealt with the union:

Whenever we make a change of any significance, and, of course, personnel reductions are a significant change, we have to issue an official letter to the union. We then meet with the union and explain why we're making the changes, what the ramifications are, and how the changes will affect people. My job is to draft the letters, go with the department manager when the letters are issued, and sit down with the union to answer questions. After the letter is issued, there is a 30-day trial period at the beginning of which the change is implemented. During that time my job is to keep my finger on the pulse and see what the effect of the change is, kinda settle people down if need be, and then, at the end of the 30 days, meet with the union. We go through the grievance procedure, and I help convince them that the change is necessary. Sometimes we'll modify the change because they bring up points that we hadn't thought about or because things have changed during the 30 days. My role is that of communicator, trying to sell the change.

Supposedly, the department is on a 30-day trial period, during which time the methods suggested by PICS are tested. Theoretically, the grievances filed will be reviewed at the end of this time. Now that sounds fine, but anyone who has worked for SCA for very long knows that once they pull help off a job, it is practically impossible to reverse the process. Besides, to admit that these systems won't work would be, according to the [union] contract, grounds for employees who have lost work during this trial period to take action to recoup lost wages.

THE ACCESS PROGRAM

In order to minimize personnel problems, access provided first-line supervisors with classes in behavioral and communication skills and on-site coaching on how to handle employee concerns. The classroom training involved 20 hours of workshops, usually 10 two-hour sessions. These sessions taught the supervisor how to deal with people, in particular how to motivate them. The access team also worked with the managers in the plant. Management Control Systems believed that it took time to learn how to handle new supervisory tools. Access team members worked individually with each supervisor, taking into account his or her strengths and weaknesses.

Senior management praised the access program:

Access is helpful to the supervisors—a lot of them are pleased. We are teaching them how to work with people so they do not have to hit them over the head with a crowbar to get them to do the job well. In the past, the only management tool they had was muscle.

With first-line supervision, morale has never been higher. They are as positive as they have ever been about their ability to manage the business.

Another manager also felt that the access program was a worthy part of PICS. He commented, "There are 240 supervisors and 95 percent came up from the ranks. They really needed the management tools that the access program provided."

Yet one manager had a different point of view: "I don't think the access programs have been productive. If I were in total command of negotiating this contract, I would not opt for paying a lot of money for that training. The kind of comments that I've heard from people is that we've heard all of this before, that we've been through this before. I would be surprised if the foremen felt differently than I do."

Some of them did not. One said, "The access people had many ideas. I say, okay, I can manage all day long by your philosophy, but I'm not going to get anywhere. I've worked here for close to 10 years, and I've known that guy for 15, and if you don't kick him in the ass, he ain't going to move. Kindness doesn't mean a damn thing to him because he'll turn around and tell me to screw myself." The foreman concluded, "Our department is still run the same way as before access." Another foreman said, "Maybe I shouldn't say I haven't changed at all, but we were already into this before PICS ever got here— trying to pat the good man on the back. That's something our boss has always been pushing."

COMMUNICATION ABOUT PICS

Since labor cost reduction was one of the keys to the success of the PICS program, the Consumer Products Division's management had to formulate a strategy for handling layoffs. Most important, the company felt it had to remove laid-off employees quickly to prevent sabotage of expensive equipment or production. For this reason, communication about some aspects of PICS was purposefully vague.

All division employees were first notified of Management Control Systems's arrival by a memo distributed in early May (Exhibit 3). When the division signed its contract with Management Control Systems in early June, department managers and supervisors were officially notified by a memorandum (Exhibit 4), but hourly workers were not. In addition, the consulting firm briefed supervisors on the general nature of the PICS program; it did not address hourly workers, ostensibly so that the supervisors would remain the formal channel of communication with the workers. But from that point on, each level of management was left free to communicate what it felt appropriate for the next lower level to know.

Many managers approached the subject gingerly. When asked whether he "painted a clear picture" to supervisors and workers in describing PICS, one manager replied, "Normally I tell them they're a management training organization that has come at management's request, hopefully to train our management on how to be better managers. I try to stay away from labor reductions and productivity improvement." Others were more direct: "The people, of course, understood that [the PICS norms would lead to personnel reductions] because we were up front with them right from the beginning as to what we were trying to do. We had to cut costs."

EXHIBIT 3 Interoffice Correspondence

To: All Employees

From: Phillip C. Moyer, Manager, Plant 1
John F. Casseday, Processing Plants and Services Manager

Date: May 5, 1982

Subject:

We have invited Management Control Systems Incorporated, PICS, a management engineering company, into our plant to conduct a survey of our present management systems, production planning controls, scheduling systems, work flows, labor standards, and training programs. This survey will be conducted over the next four to five weeks beginning the week of May 9, 1982. During this survey the PICS personnel will be discussing our present management programs with members of supervision on all shifts and all areas of the office and plants.

This survey and evaluation of our management systems is necessary based on the current economic and business conditions and the ever increasing penetration of our competition into the marketplace. If we are to remain competitive, it is essential that we investigate every possible cost savings in order that we reduce our manufacturing costs to enable us to remain competitive.

Your assistance and cooperation during the course of this survey will be appreciated.

It will also take the efforts of all employees to implement any recommendations made at the conclusion of the program.

SOURCE: Company records.

The hourly workers were the least well-informed about PICS, but sometimes supervisors knew little more. As one supervisor lamented, "We could have done more communication early on, but we didn't know a lot about PICS." For legal reasons, communication with the union was much more open and formal, as described above. As a result, many union local officials knew more than the supervisors who supervised them.

The company gave the community of Coventry even less information on Management Control Systems and PICS than its workers received. SCA's approach to communication with its local stakeholders had been dictated by its desire to prevent its competition from duplicating production processes and machinery that it had developed in-house. In addition, since SCA was a national firm doing business worldwide, it made no special effort at local public relations. SCA did host an annual town picnic, and it sponsored several local sports teams. A local newspaper reporter summed up SCA's attitude toward the press. "In my eight and a half years at the *News Journal,* I'd never met the president of SCA Corporation. I didn't even see the inside of an SCA

EXHIBIT 4   Interoffice Correspondence

To: All Supervisors and Managers

From: S. Stasch, Vice President and General Manager, Consumer Products Division

Date: June 9, 1982

Subject: PICS

Management Control Systems Incorporated, PICS, has completed its survey of our plants and offices, and they have been engaged by our division to implement a program designed to help us improve our management system, work flow, supervisory training, production planning, and scheduling.

This program will be installed in stages over the next 48 weeks. It is critical that each one of us fully support the PICS Program so that we can strengthen our operations in view of economic and competitive situations in the marketplace.

SOURCE: Company records.

factory until last year. . . . Over the years, it has been my experience that SCA is not particularly accessible to the press. Practically all we get is press releases containing exactly what the corporation wants us to know, no more, no less."

The company was constantly fighting rumors. The arrival of the PICS team coincided with rumors that all 5,000 SCA Corporation jobs in Coventry were in jeopardy. A year later, rumors still circulated regularly; one supervisor indicated that he just heard that SCA had been acquired by Pepsi-Cola.

Stanley Stasch, vice president and general manager of the Consumer Products Divison, stated that public relations was "something we probably overlooked, especially in recent years. We didn't possess the best communication skills in the world." Another executive put it more strongly: SCA's public relations director had done "a lousy job. He is conscious of survival, too [in apparent reference to the company], and maybe he's just come awake."

Indeed, SCA Corporation suddenly started talking to the press. In March 1983, the Coventry *News Journal* began publishing articles, editorials, and letters to the editor on the events transpiring at SCA. In addition, John Rike had granted a radio interview, answering questions phoned in by listeners. (The radio station had also interviewed Rike in May 1982 when he had been promoted to chief executive officer of SCA.)

OPPOSITION TO PICS

In spite of the company's increased communication efforts, opposition to PICS was considerable. One irate employee tried to voice his opinion in a rambling letter to the Coventry *News Journal,* which refused to print it. Sections of the letter are excerpted in Exhibit 5.

EXHIBIT 5   Excerpts from an Unpublished Letter

December 17,1982
Coventry News Journal
138 W.Chestnut St.
Coventry, Pennsylvania

Attention: Managing Editor

As a citizen of Coventry, indeed as an American, with certain inalienable rights, such as freedom of speech and press, I beseech,—no, I challenge this paper to print this letter in its entirety, regardless of the editors' personal opinions. If the contents are too controversial, perhaps a more liberal publication will print it. . . . Because of my position, I must necessarily remain anonymous or surely lose my job. I swear by all that's right and just that the following revelations are true. . . .

What I wish to reveal are the events and conditions which are adversely affecting the employees (both union and nonunion) at the local SCA Corporation plants . . . understand from talking to people that these conditions are prevalent in most departments and offices. . . .

Several months ago, SCA engaged a team of production efficiency analysts, who call themselves PICS. No one seems to know where they are based, who heads them, or how long they will be here. So far, many have lost their jobs, hundreds are laid off, and those still working wonder if they can physically make it through another day. These "specialists" stand around with stop-watch, pad, and pen and watch the employees work, often following one person for a whole day or two. Every wasted motion, every idle second, every unnecessary word uttered is noted and taken into account. These sadists have no consideration of the human factor and expect employees to perform like well-oiled machines. PICS seems to have unquestioned authority to use the employees as veritable guinea pigs to test human endurance and output; to see how far people can be pushed before they crack. They have no compunctions about doing this. . . .

Meanwhile, as a result of PICS's odious invasion, people are forced to work at a pace detrimental to their health and safety, in conflict with the union contract. . . . There is as much work as ever, but fewer people are doing it. Every day, it seems, the help is cut more. In some cases individuals are doing at least twice as much work as a normal workload consisted of previously. . . .

And now, like a mighty, loud roll of thunder, I can hear the voices of all you former . . . workers and other labor-minded people yelling, "Where's your union?" Where, indeed! It seems the [union] has fumbled the ball, or has forgotten which goal needs [to be] defended; [it is] unable or unwilling to do much more for its members than go through the motions of filing grievances, and of course, collect dues. To try to fight PICS would be to impede company progress, they are told. Apparently, the employees are supposed to cooperate with these vultures who are trying to eliminate them. . . .

If SCA pulls out, Coventry is in trouble. . . . The state . . . should impose a moratorium on the operations of groups such as PICS. We don't need more people on unemployment and welfare. These efficiency experts move from factory to factory, from city to city, and like a rampant cancer they eat away at our economic foundation, destroying jobs and lives. Many plant closings have resulted from the decisions of experts such as these. Better, they think, to close a plant, open later elsewhere under another name, and hire nonunion labor. . . . Anything for more profits for the stockholders. . . .

The bottom line is, the employees want PICS out of their lives; out of the factory; out of the city; out of the state. SCA used to have a Big Brother image in Coventry; concerned with all aspects of our lives and with problems of the community. That concern has been replaced with the greed of the stockholders and the special interest groups. . . .

There are still some of us dreamers around; idealists who remember when people did things for their fellowmen out of the goodness of their hearts, not because of a tax write-off or a political ploy. Profits are not eternal; they are used, altered, distributed, or elsewise disappear. The satisfaction of knowing that you have acted fairly and equitably, and in harmony with your soul's convictions, can never be destroyed.

Thank you for reading this letter.

An SCA employee

Supervisors at SCA substantiated some of the charges in the letter. One said, "The youngest kids are the only ones able to work some jobs now. They run your butt to the bone. They're the type of job where you never finish. It used to be that a guy could go down through there and smoke a pack of cigarettes during the course of the day. Now he's lucky if he can get one."

But opposition was not limited to the hourly workers. For example, there seemed to be some confusion as to who made the actual decisions to cut personnel. Stanley Stasch said, "PICS doesn't let anybody go. Nobody gets laid off unless the supervisor signs off, his supervisor signs off, and then his supervisor signs off. They all must agree on the new norms." Supervisors were told that the initial calculations of norms and staffing reductions were not "cast in stone." While Management Control Systems may not have cast initial staff reduction estimates in stone, many department managers, eager to cut costs, apparently did.

A second supervisor commented, "There's so damn many times you can make something really look great on paper, but I don't care if you've got every person involved who's 100 percent for it, that doesn't mean it will work in reality. Management Control Systems proved that in our department." Another supervisor related, "We have one job classification that was cut in half. Now the supervisor spends half of his time trying to keep the production lines moving. I'd say this is one of the places where PICS didn't accomplish anything. They just caused more problems. And the department managers says, 'We're surviving somehow. Just do it.'"

PICS took its toll on all participants. Job-related stress and frustration among hourly workers had increased; so had absenteeism. Management Control Systems experienced high turnover among its engineers and access team. One manager stated that there had been an increase in the number of SCA executives seeking psychological counseling.

Gary Hector commented on the feelings of the work force: "There is a lot of bitterness out there, especially from people whose friends are gone now because their jobs had been eliminated or whose relatives had retired early because the work got to be too tough. This being a small town, there's a lot of family in SCA Corporation. Every time you do something involving one person, there's a relative who is affected some way too."

But after 11 months of PICS, management felt that the workers had accepted it. Gary Hector said, "Management Control Systems's PICS is known affectionately as PACMAN around here. Some of the workers have hats with PACMAN eating the plant. There's a certain gallows humor to the whole thing. Now I feel like we're over the hump. I really feel good about it." Stanley Stasch felt that morale would improve once the union contract was renegotiated and SCA had had time to rebuild its quality image.

He was not without criticism of PICS, however. "The level of assurance or reassurance that we got in the preliminary meeting was nothing compared to what actually happened once PICS became a reality. It was a much more difficult and different transition than what it had been advertised to be by their people." He had some specific suggestions for the PICS program:

> The first thing that I would do is insist that PICS have an ongoing, established public relations campaign that is part of their selling package. When they sell their programs, they should be acutely aware of the repercussions in the local market, what happens to the local community, local businesses, and people's attitudes. They should have as part of their sales repertoire a complete public relations package, including press releases to the local media, direct mail to the homes of the workers, and postings in the factories of various pieces of propaganda, literature, and material. They should also work up front selling the identified need for PICS to *all* areas of the Division.

SAVINGS FROM PICS

In its first 30 weeks, the PICS program had saved the Consumer Products Division $10,287,000 in labor reductions and productivity improvements. Pete Bolling projected that the first year's savings would be within 5 percent of the original estimate of $15 million. Exhibit 6 shows examples of projected and actual savings as of May 1982 in three departments. As a result of PICS, the Division had laid off 270 workers with 125 to 130 more to go; in addition, 52 employees had taken early retirements.

Pete Bolling and the accounting staff monitored these savings. Management Control Systems provided four or five different ways to measure savings, and SCA picked the most workable one for each department. Savings were determined by the accounting system at the end of each month.

Claims of cost savings were often met with skepticism. For example, one supervisor commented, "Mr. Stasch said that in my area SCA had a 33 percent savings. And I thought to myself, 'Where in hell did he come up with a 33

EXHIBIT 6   Selected Examples of PICS-Generated Savings

		Savings per Week		Actual Savings through 5-13/83
Department	Number of Weeks Installed	Projected during May 1982 Audit	Actual	
Distribution center	37	—	$53–68,000	$1,548,000*
Pack and select	20	$38,000	$38–60,000	$1,059,000†
Mold shop	?	$18,000	$ 150	Insignificant‡

* In the distribution center, not only was staffing cut but the productivity of the remaining workers also improved. The following data illustrate the distribution center's productivity improvements, as measured in tons shipped per person-hour.

1981	1982	Jan.–April 1983	March 1983
.403	.462	.544	.582

† The pack and select department was operating with an average of 50 fewer employees; the productivity of the workers did not change.

‡ Management Control Systems's industrial engineers had studied the mold shop four times and had been scheduled to study it a fifth time.

SOURCE: Company records.

percent savings?' Because I scheduled 84 or 85 workers before PICS got here, and I schedule 84 or 85 now." Pete Bolling responded, "PICS figures must be accurate because they're watched over by so many people, haggled over, argued about, and cussed at."

Ten million dollars in savings in one year seemed to justify hiring Management Control Systems. SCA Corporation management was obviously impressed. They planned to introduce PICS into other plants within the Consumer Products Division and in other divisions of the company.

PICS'S EFFECT ON THE UPCOMING LABOR NEGOTIATIONS

PICS and its possible use in other divisions and locations was likely to be a major issue in the union contract negotiations. SCA's senior management believed that the union had to accept the fact that companies had to maximize productivity in order to survive. Indeed, one former union president was quoted in the local newspaper as saying that SCA management had no choice but to bring in PICS despite the resulting loss of jobs. Moreover, SCA management planned to ask for some emotion-laden concessions during the contract talks, the single largest one being a change in seniority practices.

Yet management seemed confident of the outcome of the negotiations. When a local reporter asked John Rike if a strike would prompt a pullout, he replied no but that everything necessary for survival would be done. "If that means relocation, then we relocate. Nothing binds us to Coventry, except desire, tradition, and inexpensive office space." This statement was widely quoted and sent shock waves through Coventry. It was unheard of for the CEO of SCA Corporation even to hint that the company might abandon the community. The mayor responded that the people of the town had a responsibility to make sure SCA was happy in Coventry.

The workers seemed to feel somewhat differently. Morale as a result of PICS was low. Many were anxious about the upcoming negotiations. One manager noted, "People are retiring now before negotiations. Usually people retire after them, hoping to get more."

The workers felt they had their backs to the wall. The union expected the company to push for all it could get: pay reductions, rollbacks in benefits (such as vacation days, company contributions to medical benefits), and changes in work rules to allow for greater productivity. They had seen a large number of their fellow workers laid off as a result of SCA's poor performance, the divestiture, and PICS. Alternative jobs were not plentiful: unemployment in the area had averaged 14 percent over the past several months. Some asked, "After all these years of hard work and loyal service to SCA, don't we deserve better?" Others responded that the only way to preserve what they had was to draw the line and refuse to yield.

The contract was due to expire on October 31, 1983.

National Savings & Loan and the Specter of AIDS

Fred Jones was the personnel manager for the National Savings & Loan Association of Cortland located in Cortland, New York. On Thursday, May 12, 1988, Fred asked an accounting department employee, Donna Davidson, who had been with the company for almost 10 years, to talk with him in his office. This was after concerned co-workers reported that they had noticed that Donna had several bruises on her wrists, and they had also noticed Donna was in very poor spirits lately. Some friends believed that Donna was having marital problems, and, after noticing the bruises, they thought that Donna was being beaten by her husband. Fred, who prided himself on his close relationship to everyone at the main branch where the accounting department was located, decided talk to Donna to see if he could help.

During the meeting with Fred, Donna explained to him that she was not being beaten by her husband, and that her marital problems could not be remedied. Requesting that their discussion be kept confidential, Donna told Mr. Jones that her marital problems were being caused by her having been tested positive for HIV, and that doctors had recently diagnosed her as having AIDS. The purplish bruises were being caused by Kaposi's Sarcoma, also known as one of the AIDS Related Complexes (ARCs), which is an opportunistic disease of the AIDS virus.

As Fred sat in shocked silence, Donna explained what she knew about AIDS and AIDS Related Complexes and mentioned her need to feel as useful as possible for as long as possible. Consequently Donna had not told anyone at National until this moment when her need to talk about her problem was greater than her fear of reprisals.

A discussion ensued on various aspects of company policy. Donna asked questions about National's health and life insurance plans, since more than ever her job and her insurance were extremely important to her. Fred responded with what he knew about the company's medical coverage, expressed

---

This is a composite case. Although based on true incidents, the names of the participants and other identifying information have had to be changed in order to maintain confidentiality. This case is not intended to represent any particular person or savings and loan institution or bank in the Cortland County, New York area.

concern for Donna's health, but deferred on the AIDS issues since he was not familiar with how they would apply to National's situation.

Donna was worried about being fired, but stated that she wanted to keep her job at all costs. Fred told Donna that it was not the policy of the bank to terminate employees who were seriously ill and that she should probably not worry. However, since National had no policy developed on this issue, he could not promise anything except that he would have his staff look into it right away and seek a resolution of the issue as soon as possible. "Most important," said Fred, "please keep the company informed about your present health condition." Fred could not give her any answers on how they would let the rest of the employees know of her condition, but in the near future they would get together to discuss the matter further after he did some research on AIDS. Until then, he suggested to Donna that she take a week's paid vacation to give her time to work on her marital problems caused by her condition.

Later Fred held a meeting with his small staff (a secretary and one assistant personnel specialist) to review the situation and develop a plan of action. While describing the situation in general terms, he did not reveal who the AIDS victim was. His charge to the staff was to develop quickly a series of short background reports and materials on AIDS, its etiology, transmission, treatment, infectiousness, and employee related issues. The materials should also include appropriate training materials. All of this was in preparation for National's developing an AIDS policy, informing the employees of Donna's condition, and beginning an AIDS training program.

CORTLAND, NEW YORK

The Cortland area has been noted for its topography, which was shaped by ancient glaciers. The low hills and steep gorges have lent a gentle beauty to the region. The harsh winters have often been preceded by beautiful autumns. The people of Central New York have often spoken proudly of being survivors of some of the toughest winters in the continental United States. They have been a predominantly conservative, Republican group who have proudly distinguished themselves from "downstaters," or urban Democrats from New York City. At times, as has been usual with this attitude, they have felt that most of the world's problems could be solved by business and a good dose of luck and hard work. The attitude also tended to produce a certain complacency about social problems.

In 1980, Cortland had a population of 20,135, and the county had a population of 48,882. The 16–24 age group accounted for 23.8 percent of the County's population. The 25–34 age group accounted for 14.4 percent of the total population.

Occupations in Cortland County have ranged from professional and technical jobs, accounting for 15.3 percent of the work force, to private household occupations, which account for up to 8 percent of the job force. The major occupation has been within the operative occupational group making up 19 percent of the jobs in Cortland County. The major industries in Cortland have been Rubbermaid, Smith Corona, and the Pall Trinity Micro Corporation. Together, these three firms have provided 3,100 jobs for the county. Salaries within Cortland County have ranged from less than $2,500 to greater than $75,000. Only 0.9 percent of the county residents made over $75,000, and 2.8 percent of the County's residents made less than $2,500. The median income in Cortland County was $17,006 with 10.6 percent of the employees within the county making between $15,000 and $17,449.

The city of Cortland has had a large campus of the state university that, when in session, has created a major influx in the population. Cortland County also has had several commercial banks and savings and loan associations. There has been only one major county hospital with 177 beds. The county also has had a total of 80 doctors and dentists. Syracuse, New York, located near Cortland, has been a much larger metropolitan area with a greater abundance of doctors and counselors, a medical school, and several major hospitals.

The Cortland area, despite the transient student population, has not been at significantly greater risk of exposure to AIDS than other similar Central New York cities. It has been at a much lower level of risk than cities, such as New York City, which has had significant "at risk" populations (male homosexuals and intravenous drug users).

NATIONAL SAVINGS & LOAN ASSOCIATION OF CORTLAND, NEW YORK

The National Savings & Loan Association of Cortland, New York, has been one of five major banks in the city of Cortland, New York. National was chartered on December 29, 1901, as a consolidation of the Merchants Bank of Cortland (chartered under the National Bank Act in 1895) and the First Farmer's Trust Co. of Cortland (originally chartered under the National Bank Act in 1889 as the McGuire Bank & Deposit Company of Cortland. National has also been a member of the Federal Deposit and Insurance Corporation (FDIC). As a member of the FDIC, National has been subject to all laws regulating businesses with federal contracts. National has conducted general banking and trust services in the Cortland, New York, area and has several branch offices in the smaller surrounding towns and villages. National's financial health has been good (see Exhibit 1).

At the time that Donna's problem began to emerge, National had about 125 employees. National was organized as a publicly held corporation with about 499 stockholders, and the stock was traded over the counter. The structure of National was typical for most banks and savings and loan associations in that its central office and branches were organized as strategic business units and additional functional departments (finance, personnel, marketing, etc.) were located in the main office.

National has maintained good rapport with its employees who have been overwhelmingly from the city or county. Many grew up in Cortland, attended

EXHIBIT 1   First National Savings & Loan Association Financial Position
years ended December 31 ($000 omitted)

	1987	1986
Consolidated Income Account		
Interest income:		
Loan interest	$19,474	$16,885
Other interest	$1,589	$1,780
Total	$21,063	$18,665
Interest on deposits	$15,821	$13,914
Other interest expense	$83	$289
Net interest income	$5,159	$4,463
Loan loss provision	$16	$16
Non-interest income	$4,105	$3,530
Salaries, etc.	$3,560	$2,579
Other non-interest expense	$2,806	$2,710
Income taxes	$979	$893
Income before extraordinary items	$1,912	$1,796
Extraordinary items	$64	$0
Net income	$1,976	$1,796
Consolidated Balance Sheet		
Assets		
Cash & in banks	$2,769	$1,712
Short-term investments	$11,061	$16,464
Investment securities	$1,938	$4,138
Loans rec., net	$183,807	$155,782
Accrued interest rec	$1,239	$1,363
FHLB of Boston stock	$1,354	$1,250
Reserve fund	$1,238	$1,217
Prem. & equip., net	$4,117	$4,025
Other assets	$4,111	$2,288
Total	$211,607	$188,238
Liabilities		
Deposits	$193,572	$172,146
Term	$82,172	$71,996
Other	$111,400	$100,151
Advance pay	$1,610	$1,631
Accrued expenses & other	$1,372	$1,166
Income taxes	$988	$1,394
Restricted surplus	$3,796	$2,814
Surplus	$10,287	$9,085
Unrealized loss on inventory	$18	$0
Total	$211,607	$188,238
Loan loss reserve	$179	$155

state business schools, and then returned to work at National. National also has encouraged its employees in their pursuit of additional training if it relates to company needs. Many of the upper level managers have been locals who have moved up in that manner. The employees have not been unionized.

NATIONAL SAVINGS & LOAN'S RESPONSE TO DONNA

Since Donna was the first person in the company to emerge with such a problem, Fred promptly contacted Jim Boardwell, president of National, and informed him of the situation. Jim asked what National's current policy was in regard to AIDS, and Fred informed him that since this was the first time that such a question had come up there was no specific policy on AIDS. Fred did mention that he had discussed the general issues with Donna but had given her no promises. Jim then told Fred to develop a policy dealing specifically with AIDS. Jim seemed uncomfortable about the topic and terminated the discussion sooner than Fred would have preferred.

Returning to his office the next week, Fred was confronted by two of Donna's co-workers who told him that they had heard a "rumor" that someone at National might have AIDS and that they were very concerned about it. When they asked if it was true, Fred told them that he could not comment about another employee's medical condition. Angered, the employees replied that if someone else in the department got AIDS, they would hold him personally responsible if he did not tell them the truth. They demanded that if the rumor were true, he should either fire the person or give them the opportunity to transfer. They categorically stated that they would not work with an AIDS carrier. They concluded by telling him that the employees in the department had called a meeting for the end of the day and that they wanted Fred to address them concerning this situation. Fred then acknowledged the employees' concerns but explained that to have a meeting now would be inappropriate. Fred told them that at the end of the week he would call a meeting and that then everyone's concerns could be voiced. Until then, everyone had work to do.

In quick succession over the next few days, Fred received the following letters, all of which were mildly disturbing. Shortly after the round of letters, Fred also received a report on Donna's health and personal situation.

To: Fred Jones, Personnel Manager

From: William Bells, Accounting Department

Date: 17 May 1988

Subject: Resignation Intent

Mr. Jones, it is to my regret that I feel I have to resign after 20 years as head of the Accounting Department.

I do not feel that I can support the company's position in relation to that person who is rumored to have AIDS (we all know who she is). I have a family and children to think about, and I do not wish to be exposed to AIDS in any way, shape, or form.

Because of my feelings, I cannot be an effective manager to any employee with AIDS. So, if the company wishes to keep the employee with AIDS, I feel I must resign.

Effective two weeks from today, I will no longer work for the National. Thank you for your time and attention to this matter.

cc: Mr. Boardwell, President

To: Fred Jones, Personnel Manager

From: Mary Teller, Head Teller

Date: 17 May 1988

Subject: AIDS Rumor

There is a rumor that someone at National has AIDS. If this rumor is true, I no longer wish to work at the main branch.

It is my wish to be transferred to a different branch within the National structure. I have been a loyal 30-year employee who has been a head teller for 10 years.

Thank you for your time, and I hope you can approve my request.

cc: Mr. Boardwell, President

NATIONAL SAVINGS & LOAN ASSOCIATION OF CORTLAND
Office of the President

To: Fred Jones, Personnel Manager

From: Jim Boardwell, President

Date: 18 May 1988

Subject: AIDS Policy

Fred, in response to our conversation, I felt that I was a little abrupt with you. Frankly, this whole issue of AIDS disturbs me. To find out that one of our employees has AIDS is shocking. As per our conversation, please develop an AIDS policy and educational program as soon as possible.

However, what if AIDS turns out to be more contagious than people believe? Does having an infected employee on our staff put the rest of our staff and our customers in danger, as well as increasing National's exposure to liability claims?

By the way I noted that Donna Davidson has been missing a lot of work time lately. Is this grounds for terminating her or is she still within her contract?

I also wish that this issue be kept in the strictest confidence. We need not alarm other employees within National.

CONFIDENTIAL

To: Fred Jones, Personnel Manager

From: Group of Concerned Employees

Date: 18 May 1988

Subject: Get Rid of Donna

It is our feeling that Donna Davidson should be fired from her position here at National.

We, as a major employee group, feel that Donna is a risk to us as well as the general public and should not be treated with more consideration than us. She is one employee, and we are many. To lose us compared to one of her would be more costly to National.

Please act soon on our request.

cc: Mr. Boardwell, President

CONFIDENTIAL

To: Fred Jones, Personnel Manager

From: Jane Smith, Research Assistant

Date: 18 May 1988

Subject: DONNA DAVIDSON'S PERSONAL AND MEDICAL HISTORY

The following report has been complied as a result of interviews with Donna, her husband, and their family physician. A written release was obtained from Donna for permission to contact appropriate parties with the stipulation that the material obtained was to remain confidential and not to be a permanent part of her personnel file.

Donna Davidson was born in Cortland, New York, in 1958. Donna is the youngest of four children and a member of a middle-class family. Donna attended a local high school and was a member of some of the sports teams at the school. Donna never had a major illness as a child or as a teenager. Except the occasional cold or flu, or normal childhood disease, there was no illness to speak of. Donna's first sexual encounter was when she was a senior in high school. The person that Donna had her sexual encounter with was the only man she ever had sex with: she married her high school sweetheart. Her husband, on the other hand, had four sexual encounters other than the one with his wife and all while they were in high school. He claims that he always practiced safe sex, and since being with Donna he had never been with anyone else. Both Donna and her husband are from strict religious backgrounds and practice their faith regularly.

Both Donna and her husband had never been checked for AIDS until Donna started having health problems. Her current health problem started three years after the birth of their second child in 1982. Donna was 24. The birth of this child was not an easy one for Donna. During the actual birth of the baby, Donna had major complications that caused her to need a blood transfusion. Unknown to Donna and her doctor, the blood was contaminated with the AIDS virus. Except for this one time, Donna has never received blood transfusions. Donna soon recovered from her troubled birth and returned to a normal life and her job at National.

For three years after the birth of her second child, Donna had no major health problems. Then Donna started having night sweats, along with a persistent cough that could not be explained by an illness. Donna also started feeling run down and tired for no apparent reason. Unknown to her, these were AIDS symptoms. Finally, when she started to have colds and minor infections that took longer than usual to go away, she went to her doctor.

The doctor asked Donna to have an AIDS test done after she couldn't find any simple reason for Donna's problems. To Donna's surprise, the test came back positive. After finding out that she had AIDS, Donna contemplated suicide. She felt that it would be easier on her family than making them go through the ordeal of AIDS and that it would save her, as well as her family, much unneeded mental stress. This is the attitude that is causing her marital problems. Her husband wants to be supportive and help Donna because what was happening to her was not caused by something that she did. Donna's husband was lucky in that he did not have AIDS as well.

Donna's physician says that she is under so much stress at home that to lose her job now would push her over the edge. She indicates that Donna is capable of functioning at work and reassures us that the nature of Donna's work does not put other employees at risk.

During that week, Fred had continued his research and data collection on AIDS. He received information from local health officials as well as information from state and federal agencies. Fred concluded that developing an AIDS policy was a very sensitive task and that his decisions would, of course, affect more than just Donna. Other employees, National, customers, and the local community would be among those that would be impacted by National's decision on Donna. To Fred, the stakeholder list that he had quickly drawn up seemed endless, and yet he knew it was real and that the groups and individuals on it must be dealt with.

Fred was aware that his feelings about AIDS would affect the policy he designed, and, to be fair, he needed to leave out his negative personal feelings. Fred's attitude wasn't helped when he received a copy of the Surgeon General's *Understanding AIDS* pamphlet in the mail. It seemed like the AIDS issues were being pushed into the foreground, both at work and at home. He knew, objectively, that he was at little or no risk for catching AIDS, but he caught himself on several occasions beginning to fantasize the horror of him or someone in his family catching AIDS.

Depressed, he began to outline a draft AIDS policy in response to Jim's memo and a memo to the employees scheduling a meeting on Donna and AIDS for Friday. While writing, he wondered how to deal with Jim's attitude problem and the irate employees, how to draft an AIDS policy statement and devise an education program, and most of all how to deal with the sadness that rolled over him when he thought of Donna Davidson.

Commentaries

16. Worker's Hands Bound by Tradition

Peter F. Drucker

In all the hundreds of books, articles, and speeches on American competitiveness—or lack thereof—work rules and job restrictions are rarely mentioned. Such rules forbid a foreman to do any production work, whether taking the place of a worker who goes to the rest room, repairing a tool or helping when the work falls behind. They forbid workers' moving from one job to another, thus restricting them to narrow, repetitive tasks, e.g., spray-painting the door panel of a car. And they narrowly restrict what a worker may be trained for. Yet all available evidence indicates that work rules and job restrictions are the main cause of the "productivity gap" of American (and European) manufacturing industry.

To be sure, productivity is not the sum of competitiveness. But when it comes to making things, productivity is the foundation. And it is precisely those American and European industries in which making things is most hedged in by work rules and job restrictions—steel, automobiles, consumer electronics, rubber and so on—that have done the poorest against the competitors from East Asia.

"DOUBLE-BREASTING"

The best evidence for the effect of work rules and job restrictions is found in America's building industry. It alone of all major industries anywhere has—working side by side—union shops with tight job restrictions and nonunion shops without them. Both shops are often owned by the same company—it's called *double-breasting* in the industry—with the same people running them.

The Wall Street Journal, August 2, 1988. Copyrght Dow Jones & Company, Inc. All rights reserved.

Mr. Drucker is Clarke Professor of Social Sciences at the Claremont Graduate School in California.

The time it takes to do an individual job, e.g. connecting a drain pipe, is exactly the same in both. Yet the crew working under work rules and job restrictions needs two thirds more people to do the same job in the same time.

A "double-breasted" contractor recently ran a study on two nearly identical projects done by his company, one by a union crew, the other by a nonunion crew. The nonunion crew worked an average of 50 minutes out of every hour. The union crew worked 35; the rest of the time it was forced to wait—for someone to come back from the rest room or for a journeyman to become available to do work an apprentice could easily have done but was not allowed to touch. The unionized crew also had to work short-handed for 40 minutes until a man qualified to drive a truck had come back from the shop with a replacement part. When that happened on the nonunion project, the foreman ran the errand and the work continued.

The result: The unionized crew required a crew of eight, the nonunion job was done by five workers. Interestingly, the large Japanese contractors who are considered models of efficiency work with roughly the same productivity, all observers agree, as American nonunion contractors.

Work rules and job restrictions also explain in large measure the higher productivity of the Japanese-owned plants in the United States and Europe. The best documented example is an English one. In Nissan's plant in the Midlands a worker turns out 24 cars a year. At English Ford in Dagenham outside London a worker turns out six! Half of that difference may be Nissan's buying many more parts on the outside than does Ford. This still leaves a productivity differential of 2 to 1. Yet the time it takes an individual worker to do any one operation—positioning the engine on the chassis, for instance—is pretty much the same in both plants. But Dagenham has 125 job classifications, each restricting the workers to one small task; Nissan has five classifications.

Similarly, the much-publicized higher productivity of the Japanese-owned auto plants in the United States—Honda in Marysville, Ohio, for instance, or Toyota in Fremont, California—is largely, perhaps entirely, the result of their having only three to five job classifications. GM, Ford, and Chrysler are each burdened with about 60. Again, the time it takes the individual worker to do any one operation is pretty much the same all around. And yet the Japanese-owned plants turn out 30 percent to 50 percent more per worker per day.

A recent book on the productivity gap, "Tough Words for American Industry" by Hajime Karatsu, one of Japan's leading manufacturing engineers (Productivity Press, Cambridge, Mass.) predicts that the American market for manufactured goods eventually will be supplied by competition between Japanese-owned companies producing in U.S. plants, and American-owned companies importing the same goods into the United States from "off-shore" plants in Singapore or on the Mexican side of the border. In some industries (e.g. consumer electronics) this is already happening. The main—perhaps the only—reason is that the Japanese, being newcomers, are largely exempt in their American plants—even the unionized ones—from the work rules and job classifications that control the U.S. plants of their American competitors.

One of the leading multinationals recently studied its consumer electronics production in the United States, Europe, Japan, Singapore, South Korea, and Hong Kong; it also studied the productivity of its main Japanese and Korean competitors in the same areas. The time it takes to do any given task was actually somewhat shorter in its U.S. plants than it was in the best plant of its principal Japanese competitor. But, overall, its American and European plants were outproduced by the plants—both its own and those of its competitors—in East Asia. The only explanation: In the United States and in Europe the company's plants operate with more than 100 job classifications; the plants in East Asia—its own as well as those of its competitors—have at most seven.

The vehicle for work rules and job restrictions is, of course, the labor contract. But don't just blame the unions. Managements are equally at fault. One major reason for proliferation of work rules and job restrictions is the narrow focus on dollars per hour with which Western managements conduct labor negotiations—and their tunnel vision is shared by economists, politicians, and press, and the public.

As a result, managements accepted, often eagerly, tighter work rules and more restrictive job classifications in exchange against a few pennies less wages per hour. Companies that all along paid attention to the total cost of work done rather than solely to immediate wage dollars per hour—IBM is one example—do not, it seems suffer from a "productivity gap" either in their American or in their European plants.

But also Western managements typically—again IBM would be one major exception—rejected any other form of job security such as an annual wage, responsibility for retraining and "out-placing" redundant workers, and so on. This virtually forced the unions into pushing for work rules and job restrictions. In the end, of course, work rules and job restrictions have proven more costly, and in Western Europe and increasingly in the United States a good deal of expensive job security has been imposed by law on top of work rules and job restrictions, thus giving Western manufacturing companies the worst of both worlds.

But, then, conventional measurements available to both managements and unions also conceal the cost of work rules and job restrictions. It is captured neither by the industrial engineer's time-and-motion study nor by cost accounting. It shows up only in "systems" figures such as the total number of cars produced per worker per year. And until recently such figures simply did not exist. The cost of rules and restrictions were thus dismissed as "intangible" by both managements and unions.

How do we get out of the work-rule hole we have dug for ourselves? Both American managements and American union leaders—though not, so far, very many of the counterparts in Europe—increasingly realize that they must get out, and fast. U.S. Steel has more than doubled productivity per worker in the past eight years, in large measure by cutting work rules and job classifications, and is now among the world's most productive steelmakers—a few years ago it was near the bottom. And the United Steel Workers Union acquiesced in the rules and classifications cuts, even though it had to accept substantial cuts in the jobs and members.

THE ALTERNATIVES

At Ford, a joint union-management effort is under way to raise productivity by cutting job classifications in one of the company's biggest plants. Still, it is not easy for the rank and file to accept both abandonment of what for 40 years it has been taught to consider "gains" and sizable reductions in the number of jobs, especially in industries with low or no job growth to begin with.

In both a GM division in the United States and at Ford in England the membership rejected cuts in job classifications even though their own union leaders had strongly urged acceptance. But what are the alternatives? One is the disappearance of the union—America's building industry has moved pretty far down that road. Or are we going to end up with the weird paradox foreseen by Mr. Karatsu, the Japanese manufacturing engineer: Newcomers from Japan and Korea produce in the United States and Europe while American and European manufactures are being forced by work rules and job restrictions to go "off-shore" to supply their own home markets?

---

17. Firefighters' Questionable Minority Status Went Unchallenged 10 Years

BOSTON—The case of two fair-skinned firefighters who were hired under a minority preference plan after saying they were black has spawned citywide investigations of minority hiring and sparked debate.

The strange case of 33-year-old twins Phillip and Paul Malone was not challenged until this summer, though the Malones have been with the department for 10 years. They were suspended from the department without pay in August for allegedly misrepresenting their race as a minority. They are awaiting an appeal of their case in the State Supreme Judicial Court.

As a result, the racial backgrounds of 36 other firefighters have been investigated, according to department officials. Eleven firefighters, most who identified themselves as Hispanic, now face hearings but are still working.

Reprinted by permission of the Associated Press, December 19, 1988.

The Police Department was investigated as well, but no evidence of suspected minority misrepresentation was found. A review of the city School Department is ongoing.

The Malones, who live in suburban Milton, have refused to discuss their case publicly on the advice of their attorneys. They both are working at other jobs but hope to return to the Fire Department. Their wives, Marsha and Janet, have spoken briefly with reporters.

"It all comes down to who says who is black and how black do you have to be," said Marsha Malone, Philip Malone's wife, recently. "We're trying to be optimistic because they (the brothers) want their jobs back."

The twins first applied to the Fire Department in 1975, identifying themselves as white. But their scores on the state civil service exam were too low on the grading curve for acceptance into the department.

They took the test again two years later and this time identified themselves as black. They later explained that their mother told them in 1976 that their maternal great-grandmother was black. At the time, documentation was not required to back up their claim.

By 1978, when the twins got their jobs, there was a minority preference plan for hiring in effect, and their scores apparently were sufficient for them to be hired as minorities.

The controversy over their claims to be black arose earlier this year when the twins took the lieutenant's exam and scored well, said Fire Department spokesman Matthew Corbett.

When the state civil service officials returned the list of scores, the brothers were identified as black.

Corbett and Fire Commissioner Leo Stapleton, who both worked with the Malones in a station house, have said they never knew the Malones had been hired as minorities until they saw the indications on the lieutenant's exams.

"They look like . . . 6–2 white guys, Irish guys, maybe a little German because they have blond hair," said Corbett.

Boston instituted a minority preference hiring plan after a federal judge ordered the Fire Department in 1974 to bring minority representation up to levels comparable to the city's population.

At that time, just 19 of more than 2,100 city firefighters were black or Hispanic. Today, the department is 21 percent black and Hispanic, compared to 29 percent for the city's population.

"It's a very serious situation," said City Councilman Bruce C. Bolling, who is black and who represents a predominatly black section of the city. Bolling had asked Mayor Raymond Flynn to conduct a full investigation of the minority hiring after the Malone case was publicized.

Corbett said the department changed its guidelines after the Malone brothers were suspended, with incoming firefighters now required to furnish more documentation about their racial background.

The state criteria for determining who should be designated as black for minority hiring purposes involves a three-part test: visual identification, documentary evidence, and evidence that the individuals consider themselves minority in the community. Boston uses the first two parts.

---

18. *Workers Go Back to the Basics*

Meghan O'Leary

Paul Jurmo paints a grim picture of the skilled laborer in the computer age: "There's the autoworker who used to install windshields manually and could do it blindfolded. Now that the job has been automated, he can't do it because he can't read the computer printouts."

Mr. Jurmo, a program associate with the Business Council for Effective Literacy in New York, said this dilemma is typical of workers who are having trouble adapting to the more sophisticated literacy requirements imposed by computer technology.

Today, employers are finding that large groups of workers lack even the basic reading and writing skills needed to enter a command on a PC or make a selection from an on-screen menu.

"There's an emerging awareness on the part of businesses right now that illiteracy among employees exists," said Roberta Soolman, director of the Literacy Volunteers of Massachusetts, based in Boston.

Indeed, a number of employees at Onan Corp., a St. Paul, Minnesota, maker of electrical-generation equipment and engines, responded to a technology training-needs analysis with requests for courses in basic reading and writing.

"It's not a panic, but it's definitely a surprise," said Mike Bates, manager of employee relations at Onan.

"Our people are not illiterate," he added. "We're talking about functional literacy."

"Employers are suprised," said Sondra Stein, deputy director of the [Massachusetts] Commonwealth Literacy Campaign, which recently has started a program of workplace literacy initiatives. "When you have skilled people working for you, you assume that they can read and write."

DEGREES OF LITERACY SKILLS

"What we're seeing in manufacturing jobs is, as computerized applications are being used, people need higher literacy skills," she explained. "Workers who never had to be able to read and analyze printouts before now need to."

PC Week, December 15, 1987, pp. 46, 50. Reprinted with permission of Ziff-Davis Publications.

"Our assumptions about who is illiterate are so far off of reality," Ms. Stein added.

Illiteracy, agreed Mr. Jurmo, "is almost a misnomer." The problem, he said, is "a lack of basic skills . . . . It really gets down to the fact that what is functional [literacy] in one society is not functional in another."

Indeed, businesses that have acknowledged low literacy levels in the workplace take an understandably proactive approach to remedying the situation. Without exception, they de-emphasize inability, and emphasize the fact that their literacy programs are aimed at helping employees adapt to a changing workplace.

While many workplace literacy initiatives stress the relationship between technology and the need for higher levels of literacy, technology is only a catalyst in the sudden emergency of literacy problems.

"The introduction of the computer didn't create the problem," said Judy Hikes, coordinator of the Work Place Education Program for the Commonwealth of Massachusetts, based in Boston, "it just revealed it."

Thus, businesses that, in a sense, unwittingly change the requirements of the workplace by automating production processes suddenly find themselves faced with a choice. Do they replace heretofore able workers with people who are more technologically and literally adept? Or do they upgrade the skills of their existing work force?

"In the future, we'll be seeing the need for more [basic education] for employees," said Ira Tiffenberg, human-resources development manager for Nabisco Brands Inc.'s Philadelphia Biscuit Division.

Nabisco has introduced a number of "basic skills" programs for its employees on the assumption that their professional and personal educational needs will change with the advance of workplace technology.

"The more skills they have, the better prepared they'll be to meet the demands of technology," Mr. Tiffenberg said. Translated into literacy terms, this means that strong basic literacy skills will be the best raw material for employees coping with the change from manual labor to computer-driven processes.

"Companies like ours are undergoing tremendous technological change," agreed Barbara Powell, coordinator of instruction in the Technology Readiness Program at Polaroid Corp., in Boston.

"Automation of the [manufacturing] process means that there are more sophisticated requirements" for completing that process, she said.

The Polaroid program, which is voluntary and available to all of the company's 5,000 hourly employees, offers basic-to-advanced tutorials in reading, writing, math, and science, as well as courses in communication and working on a team. The company estimates about one third of its hourly employees are involved in basic literacy training.

Ms. Powell explained that her department began the basic program when it saw employees having difficulties in existing middle-level courses.

As the program developed, two realities of the work environment came into play: the new requirements placed on workers by technology and a new way of working. According to the goals of the program, Ms. Powell said, employees who operated one specialized machine for 18 years would let them learn to operate several similar [computerized] machines, she added.

Ms. Powell stresses that the courses take a job-related tack. "In order for [students] to learn to read and write, the material must be grounded in a particular context," she said.

The same principle applies to the fundamental business skills program being offered to clerical employees at John Hancock Co., in Boston. Though the program was originally customized to fine tuning the abilities of highly skilled contractual workers, it is also a nod to the problems that PC operators and other lower-level clerical workers have been experiencing in the company's "refresher" math and English program. The refresher courses are offered to any employee who wants to review mid-level skills and to upgrade his or her own job skills.

The only prerequisite for the courses is the successful completion of an entrance test. "The courses were meant to bring it all back to the employee," explained Marlene Johnson, a training consultant in the human-resources training department. "But [from the test results] we discovered that there were some people who had never learned it."

The John Hancock program provides the groundwork for future literacy-needs assessment programs.

"What we hope to do by starting the program in this area," Ms. Johnson explained, "is to [have a small success and then] offer it in areas where people are not literate."

"It's not being presented as a literacy program," she added, "but it can be adapted."

BOTTOM LINE IS FINANCIAL

While the job of literacy reeducation would seem to belong to a school system rather than a corporation, businesses like John Hancock that have invested money and time in their work forces find that they have a great deal at stake.

For many organizations, reeducation comes down to some very basic and tangible principles. "It's more of an economic process, if you want to know the truth," said Brian Murphy, president of the HRD Department Inc., a human-resource-development consulting firm in St. Paul, Minnesota.

"It used to be that you would make improvements in your business through financial means—reorganizing or buying new low-tech equipment. Now the labor element is generally more expensive than the tools. I think that most companies don't want to get into the business of educating people but that the alternatives are economically less desirable than training," he said.

Mr. Murphy has worked closely with Onan Corp. in its attempts to incorporate new technologies, such as robotics and computers, into its operations. Rather than replace longtime employees with workers who had higher-level skills, Onan Corp. opted to institute a series of specialized literacy and vocational-training courses.

Mr. Bates, the plant employee-relations manager, explained that the company did a needs-analysis study of the employees, asking them to describe their skill levels from reading, writing, and basic arithmetic to higher-level math. The employees also answered questions about what levels of proficiency they hoped to have in each category. The surveys were voluntary and anonymous. They were also surprising.

"A significant number of employees told us that they really thought they needed some basics," said Mr. Bates. "We thought they'd want to brush up on geometry or trigonometry, but people asked for refreshers in reading and writing."

Though the number of Onan employees requesting basic courses was a minority, Mr. Bates said, "it was a significant enough minority to cause concern."

Mr. Murphy said that most companies like Onan are not as surprised at uncovering the need for education as they are at how basic it has to be.

The resulting educational program—which includes courses ranging from basic reading and writing to higher math, mechanics, and electrical principles—has been up and running for over four years and since its inception has had over 1,200 enrollments from a community of 700 workers.

One of the biggest impediments to uncovering literacy problems is the employees' reluctance to help themselves by responding to offers of remedial training. In the same way that many workers feel threatened by the onslaught of automation, "there's the perception by a lot of adults that their jobs might be threatened if their illiteracy is discovered," Ms. Soolman explained.

In addition, inadequate literacy skills often go unnoticed in the computer training arena. Trouble with basic technological skills is attributed to a learning curve or "computer-phobia."

"Literacy issues are very much interconnected," Brian Murphy explained. We find that there is a strong tendency [in work-related computer classes, for example] to bypass the first levels of computer literacy. But it's important to get to the lowest common denominator of [skill]. You may find that [difficulty in learning to use] computers reveals a reading or math problem."

Beyond the human elements of re-education, however, lies the issue of adoptive responsibility. Despite its origins, the fact remains that adult illiteracy is now the problem of businesses that face the challenge of maintaining functional literacy among their employees.

Some businesses have embraced the responsibility of reeducation with understandable zeal in as much as it affects their financial well-being. In addition, there are those who feel an obligation to longtime employees.

The work force must be re-educated to each phase of technology, according to Mike Bates. "We need to deal first with the folks who are already employed here . . . to help them continue to be employable, because we're changing the rules of the games," he said.

"We're talking about people who are perfectly employable and able to do everything that has been asked of them. . . . We need to tell them what's coming down the pike, he explained.

"That's an obligation we have as an employer . . . it's eternal . . . until technology stops evolving. We look at it as a lifetime investment in the worker."

19. More Concerns Set Two-Tier Pacts with Unions, Penalizing New Hires

Roy J. Harris, Jr.

The "unborn"—workers hired after a labor agreement is signed—have been taking a beating at the bargaining table lately.

For years, unions assumed that these workers would get the same contract benefits as other employees. But increasingly, unions are accepting management proposals for two-tier wage structures, which usually increase or freeze pay for current workers but cut pay scales for newly hired employees. Many companies figure such agreements can end costly wage spirals without alienating the current work force.

Two-tier wage structures aren't new. They have been used in the past, primarily by small, ailing companies seeking concessions from unions. But for the first time relatively healthy big companies such as Boeing Co., General Motors Corp., Greyhound Corp., and American Airlines are trying the approach. Some people think the agreements could have far-reaching effects, dividing the work force, reducing productivity, and further weakening the power of organized labor.

"There's clearly going to be a lot more of this," says D. Quinn Mills, a Harvard Business School professor who follows labor trends. Two-tier agreements don't account for a large percentage of the 500 major contracts signed so far this year, but for companies trying to reduce labor costs without angering workers, "it's the only game in town," he says.

FEELING PRESSURE TO FOLLOW

The concession seems to have special allure for companies battling low-cost foreign companies or nonunion domestic competitors. And when one company in an industry signs a two-tier contract, others feel pressure to follow. Machinists at Lockheed Corp. and McDonnell Douglas Corp. recently signed two-tier agreements similar to Boeing's, for example.

Among all the wage and benefit concessions proposed by corporations, two-tier agreements seem to be the most palatable to rank-and-file union members, in part because their own incomes aren't on the line. Some union leaders have even embraced such plans. The Teamsters recently proposed a two-tier plan for the trucking industry, but it was rejected by the rank and file.

Despite the support of management and some union leaders, others have serious qualms about two-tier contracts. Such programs "usually end up with groups within groups fighting each other," says John Kerrigan, who was chief negotiator for the Transport Workers Union in March when it reluctantly accepted a lower scale for new hirees at American Airlines.

"It's a divisive force," says John Zalusky, an AFL–CIO economist. "This is a very shallow and unenlightened view on the part of management."

Mr. Zalusky predicts that productivity will plunge in future years, when companies have two distinct employee classes receiving unequal pay for equal work. Justin Ostro, a vice president of the machinists union, says some productivity problems have already shown up. At a Southwestern company that he won't identify, he says management concluded that it had created a bitter second class of workers, so the company recently narrowed the differences between the two groups.

"Any time workers are distracted by problems like that, it shows up in their work," Mr. Ostro says.

Most companies report few problems with the plans so far. GM's Delco Products division in Rochester, New York, has an agreement with the International Union of Electrical Workers that covers nearly 3,700 workers. Burdette Murphy, personnel director for the facility, says any friction caused by the two pay scales has so far been negligible.

Kohler Co., a Wisconsin maker of plumbing fixtures and other products, worried about the effect of two pay levels before it adopted its program several months ago. "But I don't think it's going to be as great a problem as had been predicted," says Kenneth Conger, vice president for administration. "No one will complain until maybe two or three years from now," when the company has more lower-paid workers.

Perhaps a more troubling prospect for union leaders is the danger that these concessions will further weaken the power of organized labor. Unions have been criticized for accepting conventional pay and benefit cuts in steel and other sick industries. And some leaders worry that young workers will interpret two-tier plans as a sellout of future generations.

The approach to wages "absolutely" challenges the idea of union brotherhood, says Mr. Ostro, although he doesn't blame workers for voting in their own interests. Rather, he says, companies have put an unfortunate choice on the table: Should workers protect their income at the expense of the unborn employee?

For companies, any worries about problems usually seem secondary to the need for cost savings. "Companies are looking down the road to a lot of competition," says Prof. Mills of Harvard. "They're just doing what they ought to do before they get into red ink."

WAGE CUTS AT GREYHOUND

At Greyhound Bus Lines, for example, Chairman John Teets says, "We need this two-tier pay structure to survive in the business." Unlike most companies installing a two-tier system, Greyhound has proposed wage cuts for both current and new employees—but the reductions would be steeper for new workers. Union leaders have recommended that the 12,700 striking employees approve a contract that includes the proposal. Employees are voting on the contract this month.

At American Airlines, "a two-tier system is the key element of our whole growth plan," says Charles Pasciuto, a vice president of AMR Corp., the holding company for American Air. Under one of the airline's contracts, the average pay for a mechanic was nearly $16 an hour; that starting rate now is $8 an hour. Pilots have also accepted a two-tier structure, and flight attendants have tentatively approved one. American hopes the plans will help it compete with new, low-cost carriers without cutting the pay of its current work force.

Both American Airlines and GM's Delco Products division say that early-retirement programs, designed to speed the turnover of high-paid people, have been popular with workers. At the Delco unit, which makes electric motors for operating automobile accessories, 642 employees have taken early retirement, more than its target under the plan.

Some labor experts suggest that fast turnover is also likely to more quickly reduce any dissension among new and old workers.

The economy may be on the side of the companies that seek two-tier concessions. For one thing, many workers now seem willing to work for less than high union scales.

And increased competition is likely to push companies in that direction. General Motors's executive vice president for finance, F. Alan Smith, recently said that GM would consider two-tier wages as a way of holding down future labor costs and staying competitive with the world auto industry. But the

United Auto Workers union has been a staunch opponent of two-tier systems and is now striking at McDonnell Douglas over the issue. At GM, a UAW official says, approval of any such plan "would be over our dead bodies."

20. The AIDS Commission's Hidden Tax

Richard A. Epstein

The president's AIDS commission, retired Adm. James Watkins in command, has issued a lengthy report calling for the vigorous enforcement of the antidiscrimination laws to protect AIDS victims. The report generally has been greeted enthusiastically. Commentators have suggested that such protection is necessary to ensure that everybody will be willing to be tested without fear of losing jobs or homes.

In the midst of the acclaim, it may seem unpatriotic, if not downright churlish, to suggest that the admiral has sent his fleet sailing in the wrong direction. But consider employment: An antidiscrimination law should form no part of the national response to the AIDS problem. Here's why.

Sound AIDS policy involves more than identifying AIDS carriers. It also requires deciding how many resources to devote to treating AIDS when these costs exceed the financial and emotional capacity of AIDS victims and their many voluntary support groups. Who makes up the shortfall? And in what amount?

THE PUBLIC MOTIVES

The obvious source of revenue is direct taxation—at the federal level from general revenues and at the state and local levels from income, sales or property taxes. Yet taxpayers may resist paying these heavy expenses in full out of their own pockets. In the end, many AIDS victims may have to make do with hospice care and forgo all heroic and costly measures.

The public motives for such a decision are not necessarily base. Taxpayers could well decide that their money is better spent on neonatal care, education for the poor, welfare, drug rehabilitation, or crime prevention. AIDS may occupy a high place on the social agenda, but it also has worthy competitors

Mr. Epstein is Hall Professor of Law at the University of Chicago.

vying for the same tax dollars. For a nation long on shortages, income re-distribution has its limits. Taxpayers who must pay for what they want are subject to an insistent reality check.

The direct funding of AIDS victims with tax dollars would also go a long way to answer the fears raised by the report. As the report notes, AIDS spreads through blood and sexual fluids. Except perhaps in highly extraordinary circumstances, there is absolutely no reason to fear its spread by casual contact. Therefore, public funding of AIDS care largely obviates the need for employers to discriminate against AIDS carriers, to test workers for AIDS, or to disclose their disease status. So long as the employer knows that the public at large will pick up the heavy medical expenses of the AIDS victim, it has strong incentives to hire any workers who can do the job.

Employers, however, do have a strong and rational incentive to discriminate if asked to make up, from their own pockets, the shortfall in funding the treatment of AIDS victims. Ironically, the antidiscrimination laws foster discrimination by imposing a selective, hidden tax on employers. The logic of insurance contracts holds the key.

Voluntary insurance is a contract whereby one person pays a fixed premium in exchange for coverage against a larger, but uncertain risk. In order for insurance to make business sense, both sides have to win when the deal is struck. In the ordinary group insurance program, they do. Workers reduce the heavy costs of uncertainty by paying a fixed premium (be it by direct contribution or wage reduction) that entitles them to medical and hospital services up to preset levels in the event of illness. Insurers, through the employers, receive premiums that more than cover their total outlays in medical benefits and administrative costs.

The AIDS carrier presents an insurance risk roughly 25 times that of a person of the same age and sex who is not an AIDS carrier. Now the deal becomes unglued. While the ordinary premiums required under the antidiscrimination policy are a matchless bargain for AIDS carriers, they don't begin to cover the extra expenses.

Rational employers naturally seek to evade systematically losing contracts. Saddled with the antidiscrimination law, employers may try to get health insurance at the usual rates, only to find the usual sources of supply have vanished, unless of course insurance companies are also coerced into entering losing transactions—an issue the commission's report does not address.

The 25-fold cost differential is too large to be covered by marginal adjustments in premiums, and most workers will balk at bearing the extra costs. Desperate firms might try eliminating health-insurance coverage, depriving workers of a vital fringe benefit, just when reformers—like Michael Dukakis—are agitating for comprehensive health insurance coverage. Firms might seek alternatives—such as switching to capital-intensive modes of production or locating new plants in places with low concentrations of AIDS carriers (Duluth, say, not San Francisco).

Why then the preference for cumbersome antidiscrimination laws over direct taxes? For AIDS activists, removing funding from the public fisc allows them to avoid direct competition with other demands of the public purse. The payoff is larger, if indirect, appropriations. Voters reluctant to spend their own money, will be more willing to make out-of-state firms and their shareholders foot the bill. Congress may prefer invisible regulation to visible taxation. But the hidden tax is every bit as burdensome as the visible one, and far more selective to boot.

There are also practical political reasons for the commission report to take so narrow a perspective on so complex a social process. The AIDS commission knows its mission—the control and treatment of AIDS. It is not charged with finding AIDS policy that minimizes distortions in other sectors. It does not labor under any budgetary constraints. It is not asked to worry about the risk of excessive expenditures on AIDS. It can write as though the redistribution of wealth by taxation and regulation does not inhibit the production of wealth to begin with.

AGE OF DEFICITS

The AIDS commission is not alone in these failings. In an age of chronic deficits, it is unpopular to raise taxes even for good causes. Astute politicians frequently opt for off-budget financing under the guise of human-rights legislation.

The commission's report champions the antidiscrimination law as a relatively painless way to make disembodied corporations pay for the medical services that all of us want to provide. But this short-term palliative is a long-term mistake. The antidiscrimination policy will first reduce companies' profits, and then the taxes they pay. A courageous insistence upon direct tax support for AIDS victims would dispel the harmful illusion that good deeds depend on national will alone. We must face the hard questions of cost and choice that the report suppresses.

PART SIX

Openness of the System

One of the major pressures on business in recent years has been the expectation that managers exercise authority and full control over those aspects of their operations that have social consequences. Ironically, the exercise of authority and control can lead to a totalitarianlike atmosphere in an organization. There is a need, therefore, for accountability but not dictatorial control.

Every major institution faces this dilemma of openness. If business is to be seen as legitimate, people must believe that it is responsive to their needs. Consequently managers must create opportunities for significant stakeholders to participate in decision making. Participation may take the form of including stakeholder representatives in the corporate governance process. Thus the role of boards of directors in governing companies has emerged as a major issue. The composition, structure, and role of the board is of great importance in determining the appropriate conduct and performance of the corporation. Openness has expanded to include not just normal managerial operational control, but includes interactions with a wide variety of stakeholders and issues.

Another major element of corporate legitimacy is the opportunity for employees to contribute to decision making and to enjoy normal constitutional rights such as free speech, privacy, and due process. The traditional notion that top-management exercises the right to control employees and to make all decisions without being questioned has given way to greater concern for human rights.

In short, the corporation cannot be viewed as a secret state protected from societal expectations about freedom. One area of particular significance has been the demand for greater financial disclosure by corporations. Largely as a result of efforts by the Securities and Exchange Commission during the 1970s, many companies are now required to provide stockholders with data on sales and earnings by major product line, research and development expenditures, and foreign sales and earnings. The passage of the Foreign Corrupt Practices Act in 1977 required corporations to establish thorough internal control systems to account for the usage of all corporate funds.

Legislation and SEC requirements have also tightened executive perquisites. Company cars, company-owned apartments and yachts, country club memberships, and the like, must be reported to shareholders. The pressure for greater openness has also resulted in demands on accountants, lawyers, and regular employees to "blow the whistle" when they discover product hazards, fraud, or other forms of improper conduct.

Not too surprisingly, the news media have echoed the demands for greater openness. Business topics have become relevant and interesting—some would say even sensational. Like it or not, executives find that the news media represent a source of increasing concern. Modern managers must learn to deal effectively with the press.

At the heart of the openness issue is the issue of corporate control. Managers are being requested and required to give up part of their traditional corporate control, calling into question the fundamental notion that an owner and his or her agents may do with the firm as they see fit. The late 1980s was a period of intense mergers and acquisitions activity, helped along by changes in the tax law making interest cheaper than equity. As a result of the outcomes of this merger activity, more people were criticizing these mergers for their social and environmental impacts. Fewer commentators were willing to accept the idea that all of the mergers were merely a restructuring of the economy to make it more efficient. More analysts saw the merger activity as a way for a few people to make a fast buck while not improving, and possibly even harming, America's productivity over the long term.

The first case in this section treats a dramatic confrontation between an Illinois utility company and the popular CBS news program, "60 Minutes." The Adolph Coors Company case focuses on a closely held, family-managed business that finds itself in a turbulent world of intense competition and social change. The Massachusetts Mutual case discusses the successful efforts of a company to draft and pass state legislation and to alter corporate bylaws to enable the company's management to fend off the challenges of a slate of dissident director candidates. The Pacific Lumber case explores the social and environmental consequences of a takeover.

The first commentary, *Privacy,* is an in-depth look by *Business Week* at privacy issues in the workplace. What management is willing to accept as the private concern of the employee and not of the corporation is always in a state of flux. Some managers are always looking for ways to extend control over their employees, and sometimes this control is extended into areas that are inappropriate. Despite the Reagan administration's challenges, the employee rights movement continues to grow. Especially problematic for managers are issues of drug and AIDS testing. However, other issues such as polygraph testing have declined in importance due to legislative initiatives and a growing consensus on the issues. Good management practices often forestall the issues raised by this commentary, and some of the practices described are the result of management failures. Yet, sometimes it is easier for irresponsible managers to blame the victim. Related to changes in privacy issues are important changes in other traditional business practices. The next commentary,

Legal Challenges Force Firms to Revamp Ways They Dismiss Workers, explores major changes in the concept of at-will employment.

In the era of mergers and acquisitions, corporate control takes on new implications as the commentary on the *Tobacco Titans Get Tough* suggests. Control over another company's responsible practices implies a significant amount of managerial responsibility. If the responsibility is not forthcoming, then companies will face more social proxy fights as the last commentary, *Talking Business with Smith of Interfaith Center: Companies Face the Social Issues,* indicates.

CASE

Illinois Power Company
and "60 Minutes"

On January 24, 1980, Harold Deakins, Illinois Power Company's manager for public affairs, leaned back in his chair and pondered the implications of a letter he had just read. The letter had been written by Robert Chandler of CBS News to Wendell Kelley, IP's chairman (see Exhibits 1 and 2). A number of areas of contention between IP and CBS News concerning a November 25, 1979, "60 Minutes" broadcast were reviewed in the letter. This broadcast, which centered around Illinois Power's construction of a nuclear power plant in Clinton, Illinois, caused IP a great deal of embarrassment. In turn, the company's response helped fuel a growing debate about the relationship between business and the news media.

Specifically, the CBS executive's letter argued that the "60 Minutes" broadcast was not guilty of errors and biases, that it was thoroughly researched, and was not unfair. While admitting two factual errors (which were to be acknowledged on the air January 27, 1980), the letter asserted that the essential thrust of the story—that the Clinton plant's cost was significantly over budget and that it was well behind schedule—was correct. The five-page letter ended with a warning that Illinois Power was guilty of infringing a CBS copyright.

PUBLIC UTILITIES

Illinois Power Company, as a public utility, operated in an unusual market situation. Whereas most industries were competitive (their profits were "regulated" by the marketplace), public utilities operated as monopolies in their markets.

Monopolistic structures, as such, lent themselves to potential abuses (i.e., overpricing and underproduction). The various state governments, having recognized this potential for abuse, attempted to reduce its occurrence through price regulation. Basically, a public utility was granted an exclusive franchise for a service area and allowed a fair rate of return in exchange for production at the levels of consumption required by society. Regulatory commissions were empowered by states to balance the needs of both the producers and consumers in setting utility rates.

The determination of utility rates was a complex task, not easily understood by most consumers. Rate structure typically had a blocklike pattern. In this structure, the higher-cost consumers would be charged a higher rate per kilowatt-hour. The largest component of electricity rates was capacity cost—which was the cost of constructing and maintaining generating facilities.

In constructing facilities, the industry typically used a cost-plus method of contracting. If there were unforeseen cost increases, the general contractor could charge the utility more, and thus, still earn an agreed on profit level. This method required a cooperative relationship between the utility and general contractor. Additionally, nuclear power plant construction was subject to inspection by the Nuclear Regulatory Commission. This safety requirement often caused delays and downtime before the plant became operational.

These delays and the high fixed costs of power plant construction caused the industry to adopt the practice of including a portion of this idle capacity in its investment base. This element, known as *construction work in progress,* enabled utilities to finance construction while raising electricity rates gradually.

Because of the construction practices of utilities, they were engaged in an adversarial relationship with consumer groups. These groups cited cost-plus contracting and construction work in progress as the villains that caused electricity rate increases.

ILLINOIS POWER

Illinois Power, a public utility that serviced a 15,000-square-mile area in northern, central, and southern Illinois, supplied electricity and natural gas to about 1.5 million people. It had revenues in 1979 of $752 million, two thirds derived from electricity sales, one third derived from natural gas sales. Of IP's $91 million net profit, about 90 percent came from electricity sales, 10 percent from natural gas sales. IP's shareholders (about 80,000) received a dividend payout in excess of 80 percent. Institutions held 40 percent of the outstanding shares of IP stock.

Illinois Power had a history of supplying electricity at rates among the lowest in Ilinois. This low cost capability was largely a result of burning coal to generate 99 percent of its electricity. Coal was plentiful, inexpensive, and its mining was a major industry in Illinois.

Although coal was cheap and plentiful, it gave off many pollutants when burned including particulates, sulphur dioxide, and nitrogen oxide. Because of the environmental damage caused by these pollutants (i.e., acid rain) the Illinois Pollution Control Board adopted new regulations limiting the emissions that could come from coal-fired power plants. These standards were considered to be unattainable by IP using the technology of the early 1970s. Despite these challenges, the company believed the future held great promise for additional growth.

THE CLINTON POWER PLANT

Based on the growth rate of electricity usage in the early 1970s, which hovered between 7.5 percent and 8.0 percent nationally, IP decided to build a nuclear power plant in Clinton. Nuclear power, it was felt, offered IP an environmentally clean way to meet the growing demand for power in the future. A summary, taken from IP's annual reports, of its progress in constructing the Clinton nuclear power plant from 1971 to 1978 follows:

1971

We are continuing the acquisition of land rights for a new major electric power plant at Clinton in Central Illinois. The plant site and adjacent lake to be used to provide cooling water for the plant require the acquisition of title to or flowage rights on about 17,000 acres. More than 40 percent of the required acquisitions have been made.

1972

In February, we announced that nuclear fuel would be used to operate the new power station near Clinton, Illinois. . . . The first unit, scheduled for operation in 1980, will have a capability of about 950,000 kilowatts. A second unit of the same size is planned for service in 1982 or 1983 . . . . The two-unit power plant is expected to cost about $800 million. The plant site and adjacent lake to provide cooling water for the plant require acquisition or land rights on about 15,000 acres. More than two thirds of the acquisitions have been made.

1973

Planning and engineering for the two nuclear units to be installed at this station are progressing satisfactorily. In October, the Atomic Energy Commission docketed for review our application for a construction permit for the plant . . . . In November, the Illinois Commerce Commission granted a certificate of public convenience and necessity for the construction of the plant . . . . We have acquired 71 percent of the 15,000 acres of land required for this project.

1974

Having in mind the reduced rate of growth that we have experienced lately, we are constantly reviewing our plans for new electrical generating capacity. The Clinton nuclear units, originally scheduled to be placed in service in 1980 and 1983, have been rescheduled for 1981 and 1984. Contributing to these deferments are delays in securing the necessary licenses, permits, and authorizations from state and federal regulatory and environmental agencies. We have acquired 85 percent of the land and land rights required for the Clinton plant site and cooling lake.

1975

Most of the delays in obtaining the necessary regulatory authorizations to proceed with construction of the Clinton nuclear station are behind us. Our application for a construction permit was docketed by the Nuclear Regulatory Commission in October 1973, and Limited Work Authorization was finally granted in October

1975 . . . . The safety hearings required before a full construction permit can be issued . . . were concluded during January 1976. We have acquired all of the required land and land rights at the Clinton site except for three small tracts.

1976

The full construction permit, received in February 1976, enabled us to start the full construction program. Progress in 1976 was good. Site development work progressed well, and lake clearing was nearly completed. Work on the dam remained on schedule with the dam closing set for early fall 1977. To meet the original commercial service date of June 1981, would, however, have required intensive and expensive construction effort. To avoid greatly increased costs, we revised the schedule six months to December 1981 . . . . The Board of Directors also decided on February 9, 1977, to defer the in-service date of Unit No. 2 from 1984 to 1988.

1977

At the site of our 950,000 kilowatt nuclear unit east of Clinton, the silolike containment structure now rises some 150 feet above the base mat. The turbine room walls, diesel generator and control room walls, and other support building walls and floors are all taking shape. A majority of earthwork was completed, and the main dam was closed . . . . Our presently scheduled construction program, including the size, type, and timing of new generating units, may change because of the many elements that can impact it. We are keeping our plans as flexible as practicable with the intention of accommodating any of those factors that may develop.

1978

Substantial progress has been made on the construction of our 950,000 kilowatt nuclear unit No. 1 located at Clinton, Illinois. Activities have been concentrated in the power block area and in completion of the earthwork. The installation of reinforced concrete walls, columns, and floors in the power block area has continued. The turbine pedestal concrete work has been completed. Structural and supporting members are being constructed in the containment building to support the reactor pressure vessel when it is lifted into place in 1979. . . . The remaining earthwork was essentially completed in 1978. This consisted of modifying drainage facilities from adjacent properties to accommodate formation of the 5,000 acre lake . . . filled by May. . . for future recreational use . . . including stocking the lake with 2.5 million fish. . . . Our station at Clinton . . . is scheduled to start producing electricity before the end of 1982.

1979 RATE CASE

The year 1979 proved to be a critical one for the Clinton project. Because of adverse economic conditions and the financial burden of its construction program, IP found it necessary to apply to the Illinois Commission for a rate increase. Wendell Kelley, chairman and president, discussed the rate increase request in IP's letter to stockholders. An excerpt from that letter follows:

We have been, and are now, a financially strong utility. We want to remain so. It is for this reason that we filed with the Illinois Commerce Commission a request for a general increase in our electric and gas rates on January 9, 1979.

The rate filing is a complete and accurate documentation of our needs. Additional revenue is needed to pay inflated costs, support needed construction, and provide adequate return to our investors.

There are two underlying public issues in the electric rate case. One is the inclusion in the rate base of some $240 million of the $500 million we have invested in the nuclear station we are building near Clinton, Illinois. This pay-as-you-go principle is indispensable to our ability to meet the energy requirements of our customers at the lowest possible costs to them in the 1980s.

The second issue is our decision to build a nuclear generating station. This is an issue in our rate case only because the antinuclear forces have chosen to make it one. Their public stand is that they are fighting our rate case to stop or delay the construction of our station at Clinton, which is scheduled to start producing electricity before the end of 1982.[1]

Illinois Power's rate increase was opposed by a number of consumer groups, conservationists, and the Prairie Alliance, an antinuclear group. The Prairie Alliance contacted CBS News about the situation, and one of "60 Minutes" producers became interested in Illinois Power's Clinton nuclear station. "60 Minutes," a top-rated television show, had evolved from network news.

TELEVISION NEWS

Television news was a product of uneven quality, which grew out of the earlier efforts of radio. Radio news, to the extent that it existed at all before 1930, had been largely corrupt. Seldom was it any better than the sensational, biased tabloids which dominated the print media in that era. Edward Klauber, a radio pioneer, began in 1930 to build a high-quality news staff at CBS: Elmer Davis, Edward R. Murrow, William Shirer, Eric Sevareid, Alexander Kendrick, Howard K. Smith, and David Schoenbrun. Most of these talented reporters made the transition to television, but there was always a struggle between the news/public service side of the business and commercial interests.

Broadcasting is a curious profession. It is the most powerful instrument in the world for merchandising soap, and it is potentially the most powerful instrument in the world for public service, and it has always been caught between the duality of its roles. . . . Over the years the instinct for merchandising has always been more powerful, particularly since most broadcasting executives in their hearts regard news and public service as a form of charity.[2]

---

[1] "Letter to the Stockholders," *Illinois Power Annual Report, 1978.*
[2] David Halberstam, *The Powers That Be* (New York: Alfred A. Knopf, 1979), p. 33.

Some would argue that the half-hour nightly network news broadcast, with reports by correspondents located worldwide, was born in 1961 as an outgrowth of the embarrassment suffered by the major networks following the revelation that certain of their popular quiz shows were fraudulent. These shows had emerged as the networks' major merchandising force.

The most popular television shows between 1954 and 1959 were quiz shows such as "The $64,000 Question," "Dotto," and "Twenty-One." "Twenty-One," in fact, was so popular that it eventually took the place of "I Love Lucy" at the top of the ratings. So enthusiastic was CBS with quiz programs that the network introduced six new ones in 1959. Five of them made their appearance on the same day. The six were "For Love or Money," "Play Your Hunch," "Lucky Partners," "Hoggis Boggis," "Anybody Can Play," and "Bid 'n' Buy," which awarded the Scottish island of Stroma as its first prize.[3] It was discovered in 1959 that many quiz shows were fixed—that contestants competing for money on these programs were often supplied, prior to the shows, with questions and answers, and that contestants were often employees of the network airing the program. One result of these revelations was that Federal Communication Commission Chairman John C. Doerfer ordered the three major networks, CBS, NBC, and ABC, to produce one hour of public affairs programming each week that did not coincide with a similar hour on another network.

The quiz scandals were also partially responsible for President John F. Kennedy's appointment of Newton Minow as chairman of the FCC. Minow, who referred to network programming as a "vast wasteland," threatened in 1961 to hold hearings to discuss direct regulation of television. It appeared that the chairman had President Kennedy's backing.

Ironically, public opinion polls in 1961 reported for the first time that a majority of Americans got their information about the world primarily from television. The networks, doubtless, were surprised by the poll results because they had not emphasized the news—news and current-affairs programs had almost completely disappeared from the networks' prime-time schedules by 1959. The networks were bound to be pleased because, as former CBS executive Fred Friendly said, "Television is the cheapest way of distributing news. Forget the immediacy, the 'I was there,' the 'Now-we'll-take-you-to-the-moon.' The fact is that TV can triple the audience, and it doesn't cost a penny more. The *New York Times* lost 50,000 circulation when it put the cost up to 15 cents. TV can make the viewers pay for its own expansion. That is the primary reason TV grew."[4] In short, networks found they could make a lot of money with the news through advertising: the perfect combination of public service and merchandising. In addition to the sensitivities of advertising sponsors, television news reporters worked within the constraints of several factors—

---

[3] Alexander Kendrick, *Prime Time: The Life of Edward R. Murrow* (New York: Avon Books, 1970), p. 456.

[4] Godfrey Hodgson, *America in Our Time: From World War II to Nixon, What Happened and Why* (New York: Vintage Books, 1978), p. 140.

the demands of their bosses, the public, and of others within their own profession.

A major issue within the reporting profession concerned the role that a reporter should play—the "mirror" or the "lamp." Advocates of the *mirror* point of view claimed journalists should only reflect the world as it is, as accurately and neutrally as possible. Advocates of the *lamp* point of view argued that journalists should instead try to learn about issues with which people were generally unfamiliar, and so help people to see what they have not seen before. Furthermore, there was a tacit internal discipline in the field of journalism that placed a high premium on such values as responsibility and objectivity.

In 1961, the competition for ratings intensified, particularly between CBS and its "CBS Reports" and NBC with its "White Papers" series. Competition was such that NBC, for example, persuaded a number of CBS top talents to move to NBC, along with a number of top-class newspaper reporters. The number of producers in the NBC news division shot up from 4 to 21 in 1961–1962. The costs of maintaining such staffs were so high that CBS expanded its evening news program from 15 to 30 minutes on September 2, 1963. NBC soon followed suit.

While nightly news programs earned high ratings and a lot of money, discussion programs, news specials, and documentaries did not. During the highly turbulent 1960s, television viewers were confronted with the loud voices of protesters each night during the news, but rarely received a detailed explanation about why these people were protesting. Viewers also watched daily updates of Americans in Viet Nam. Correspondents for the networks competed to have their stories shown on the nightly news, and they knew what type of stories would be aired—dramatic combat scenes. "Some of the correspondents kept a kind of scorecard as to which pieces were and were not used," according to CBS correspondent Mike Wallace, "and it seemed as though an inordinate number of combat pieces were used, compared with some first-rate pieces in the political area, or the pacification area, on nonbloody stories."[5]

The format of the nightly news—one- to three-minute spots—was not conducive to in-depth explanations of events. The types of news programs that could provide beneath-the-surface insight to viewers on the major issues of the day such as inflation, water and air pollution, disease, poverty, and racial oppression, were not doing so. Documentaries and news specials could have provided such insight but, as David Brinkley said in 1967 at the height of the war in Viet Nam, "Television is lacking in excitement these days. In the nonnews areas, like documentaries, we lean toward soft, pastel programs, trips through the Louvre, or up the Nile with gun and camera, that seem to me rather irrelevant to the times we live in."[6]

On Tuesday, September 24, 1968, a new type of news program, a "news

---

[5] Ibid., p. 150.
[6] Ibid., p. 148.

magazine" called "60 Minutes" took to the air on CBS. "60 Minutes" presented four correspondents—Dan Rather, Mike Wallace, Morley Safer, and Harry Reasoner—who were very polished. Each was well known for his journalistic experience in television. They dressed well, they spoke well, and they looked good on camera.

"Our purpose is to make information more palatable and to make reality competitive with make-believe," said "60 Minutes" executive producer Don Hewitt in 1980. "There are shows on TV about doctors, cowboys, and cops. This is a show about four journalists (Rather, Wallace, Safer, and Reasoner). But, instead of four actors playing these four guys, they are themselves."[7]

"60 Minutes" started off with relatively unexciting stories—the first show had Richard Nixon and Hubert Humphrey sitting before TV sets watching their respective convention nominations, along with excerpts from a film called "Why Man Creates." Such stories as "The Pope and the Pill," "Dirty Football," "What Christ Looked Like," and the "Welfare Man," however, helped the show's popularity to such an extent that, during the 1978–79 television season, "60 Minutes" became one of the 10 most popular prime-time shows on television. The show had a weekly audience of more than 24 million American households and earned CBS an estimated $25 million annually.

Each of the four "60 Minutes" correspondents had five producers, each of whom was a reporter. Once a story subject was agreed on, a producer with a team of researchers would conduct all of the research and preliminary interviews necessary to write a script and a background report for the correspondent assigned to do the story. The correspondent then traveled to the scene of the story, studied the results of the research and the script, and then conducted the necessary interviews, together with filming his reading of the script.

Critics charged that "60 Minutes" correspondents approached stories with less than objective attitudes. Rather and Wallace in particular were noted for being aggressive interviewers, seemingly leading interview subjects into trapping themselves, and then asking them questions that they could not answer without making it appear that they had done whatever the interviewer claimed they had done. Additionally, if potential interviewees refused to be interviewed, "60 Minutes" often filmed the interviewees' offices or home windows or automobiles as they sped off, while announcing that the subjects refused to be interviewed. Again, the implication was that the subjects were "guilty."

Rather commented on this issue, "Do we do a story with a point of view? If it happens, I try to stop it before it goes too far and sometimes will kill it stone

---

[7] Paul Good, "Investigating the Investigators: Why You Can't Always Trust '60 Minutes' Reporting," *Panorama*, September 1980, p. 40.

dead. We are a team operation, but I try to double and triple check everything the team does. I play the game of 'Where are the holes in the story?' "[8]

"60 MINUTES" VISIT WITH ILLINOIS POWER

In September 1979, CBS News contacted the Illinois Power Company about doing a story on nuclear power plant constuction. Since the request came near the end of their rate case hearing before the Illinois Commerce Commission, IP management was divided on the issue of cooperating with "60 Minutes." There was a general feeling that "60 Minutes" was biased toward an antinuclear point of view, which would prevent fair treatment of the Clinton power plant project.

However, IP decided to cooperate with "60 Minutes," because:

1. It gave IP the opportunity to tell its side.
2. Refusal to cooperate would mean a "guilty as charged" insinuation.
3. The visit would enable IP to gather information for a rebuttal if it were needed.

"60 Minutes" was, therefore, accommodated in every request for plant visits, interviews, and information.

"60 Minutes" paid IP a two-week visit to gather information and film. This visit culminated in a 90-minute interview with Executive Vice President William Gerstner, IP's chief quality assurance officer, conducted by "60 Minutes" correspondent Harry Reasoner. Since IP was concerned about the treatment it would receive from "60 Minutes" and since the company wanted to keep its employees informed about the visit, it was stipulated that the company would have the right to film everything "60 Minutes" did on IP property.

The show, which was broadcast on November 25, 1979, to 24 million homes, shocked IP executives because of "the use of accusations from disgruntled previous employees, disregard for factual information, and selective editing of interviews . . ."

The following day trading activity in IP stock tripled, leading to a slight drop in price. Employee morale was reported to have reached an all-time low, and hate mail started rolling in. The following excerpts were typical:

> The program (60 MINUTES) confirmed the doubts I had for a long, long time about the mismangement of the IP.

> I sold my shares 11–26–79 on the opening.

> In view of some of the things that Baldwin Associates have been "trying"

---

8 Ibid., p. 41.

to do, I would say they were a third rate outfit, not properly supervised themselves.

Yes, I think IP is well managed, but only for the directors. Whom do you think you are fooling?

I think it is so unfair to pass the cost of building this nuclear plant to the consumer.

Three days after the "60 Minutes" broadcast, the Illinois Commerce Commission decided on IP's rate request, allowing a 10.9 percent increase instead of the requested 14 percent increase ($97 million of construction work in process instead of the $240 million requested).

"60 MINUTES/OUR REPLY"

By 10 A.M. the Monday following the broadcast, a decision had been reached to rebut the broadcast with a video program. IP had the in-house capability to produce training programs, which could now be used to produce a rebuttal tape. Previous experience making training tapes had shown IP that maximum employee attention span was 40 minutes. IP attempted, therefore, to answer as many "60 Minutes" accusations as possible in 45 minutes. This would also allow employees to see the tape and ask questions in a one hour time period, cutting down on their time away from the job. The timetable for producing the tape follows.

Monday was spent viewing the "60 Minutes" tape (that IP had made) over and over, identifying inaccuracies and finding specific rebuttal information within the sworn testimony and exhibits of the rate case. Tuesday and Wednesday were spent writing and rewriting the script of the rebuttal tape and discussing ways of visually presenting the information. Thursday through Saturday were spent filming and putting the tape together. Sunday was spent putting finishing touches on the tape.

The following Monday the tape was shown to all employees. After this was completed, the tape was shown to any organized group that wished to see it (i.e., Lions and Rotary Clubs). Any time the tape was not being used before an organized group, it was set up in IP offices where customers could see it as they paid their bills. The tape was later shown to security analysts and the press. Word spread about the tape (IP did no advertising or promoting of the tape), and a flood of requests for copies began to arrive. Given the strong demand, IP decided to dub a copy of "60 Minutes/Our Reply" for anyone who sent them a blank tape and requested a copy.

Harold Deakins was proud of his involvement in the making of "60 Minutes/Our Reply." In only one week, and at an out-of-pocket cost of only $89, IP had put together a rebuttal tape. Although IP could not hope to reach 24 million homes, the rebuttal tape had been seen by all of the company's employees as well as numerous service organizations, security analysts, and other interested parties.

Yet, Deakins felt that the Illinois Commerce Commission had given IP considerably less of a rate increase than was requested, in large part, because of the "60 Minutes" program. He could not help but wonder if the company had made a mistake in cooperating with "60 Minutes" in the first place.

EXHIBIT 1

ILLINOIS POWER COMPANY   500 SOUTH 27TH STREET, DECATUR, ILLINOIS 62525

December 14, 1979

TO OUR STOCKHOLDERS:

Many of you must have seen—or heard about—the CBS 60 Minutes telecast on Sunday, November 25, 1979, on the cost and scheduling aspects of construction of our nuclear generating station at Clinton, Illinois. In our view, and in the view of many knowledgeable outsiders, this was yet another example of sensationalism in journalism at the expense of the facts of the matter.

60 Minutes became interested in the Clinton plant at the urging of a former Company employee who was fired for cause and who later became a witness for an environmental group opposing the Company in our rate case.

We told the producer of 60 Minutes that we were going to film anything that the 60 Minutes crew chose to film on Illinois Power property. This turned out to be a good idea.

With our film—which recorded in its entirety the CBS, 90-minute interview with William C. Gerstner, Company Executive Vice President—and with other documentation of the facts, we were able to compare the segments used by 60 Minutes with the actual film and facts they had to work with and choose from. We are now showing our reply in a documentary to our employees and to community leaders and other interested citizens throughout our territory.

In this letter I cannot give you our detailed response to the entire 60 Minutes show. Here is a summary of the most damaging charges and our responses.

1. Harry Reasoner stated that Illinois Power scheduled only two weeks to complete the full-system tests that on similar projects take an average of 14 months to make. He concluded by saying that we plan to accomplish in two weeks what no other nuclear builder had ever accomplished in that time period.

   In the complete interview with our Mr. Gerstner, Mr. Reasoner was told that the chart he was looking at was not a construction schedule; it was a milestone chart. Its purpose is to let the Nuclear Regulatory Commission know the approximate time during which the test is to be made. The particular test itself requires only three days to complete. In addition, the same chart Mr. Reasoner was using on camera shows that the testing of some 17 sub-systems, which precede the full-system test, are scheduled individually over a 25-month period prior to the full-system test. The fact is that our schedule is reasonable and attainable.

2. Mr. Reasoner stated that against other plants of similar design. Clinton cost overruns are well ahead of the pack.

   Mr. Gerstner showed Mr. Reasoner, on camera, a list of all seven one-unit

EXHIBIT 1   *(continued)*

---

boiling water reactor nuclear plants being built in the United States. On this list, Clinton has the lowest cost increase.

3. Mr. Reasoner made the flat statement that Clinton was the Company's first nuclear project and the first for our contractor, Baldwin Associates.

   During 60 Minutes's visit to the Company, it was explained to them that Baldwin Associates was a consortium of four major construction companies: Power Systems, Inc.; Fruin-Colnon; McCartin & McAuliffe; and Kelso-Burnett. It was pointed out to 60 Minutes that two of these companies, prior to starting Clinton, had worked on 14 nuclear projects. It would be difficult, you would think, to refer to all of that as "no nuclear experience," but that's what 60 Minutes did.

4. The major points of the 60 Minutes program were based on the comments of three former employees of either the Company or its contractor. Two of these men were fired for cause, and the third resigned because he was not satisfied with a 7 percent pay increase. All were associated with the Clinton project for short times only.

   The most vocal of these critics also appeared as an "expert" witness in opposition to our recent rate case before the Illinois Commerce Commission. After he was cross-examined in regard to his testimony, the hearing examiner ruled: "The witness has not demonstrated that he is qualified by educational experience or work experience concerning the subject matter of his testimony and should not be permitted to testify as an expert and provide opinions or arrive at all of the conclusions which are contained in his testimony." 60 Minutes knew of this ruling, yet chose to present him on camera to recite those same opinions and conclusions.

5. Lastly, it was stated on 60 Minutes that even the usual neutral staff of the Commerce Commission joined in asking that the rate increase be denied. This was not true. Just three days after the 60 Minutes telecast, the Commission, at the recommendation of its staff, granted us the major portion of the rate increase we had requested, including additional revenues to cover part of the cost of capital we have already raised and spent on the Clinton plant.

   60 Minutes was used by some of our opponents in the rate case. They used 60 Minutes to air the same irresponsible charges they had been making in recent months in our local press and in our rate proceeding. Whether 60 Minutes was willingly used, we cannot say but, in our opinion, it was no coincidence that they chose to air the program just a few days before the Commission was to rule in our rate case.

   In regards to the implications of mismanagement of our Clinton project made by 60 Minutes, it is relevant that on December 5, 1979, an official of Standard & Poor's Corporation, speaking at a public meeting on Utilities, stated:

   > Now, which managements have done a good job? Who is well positioned to meet the challenges of the 1980s? Who stands out in terms of meeting the criteria? Who benefits credit quality? For the electrics, Texas Utilities, Duke Power, Illinois Power, Southern California Edison, New England Electric are five that stand out . . . . Now, the list is clearly not all inclusive, but we do feel that some managements stand out and that their identity is warranted.

   Now, this will never get on national television. We trust, however, that our stockholders will put more confidence in the judgment of an official of Standard &

EXHIBIT 1   *(concluded)*

Poor's Corporation, than in those of the three former employees presented by 60 Minutes.

Building a nuclear unit at a time when the federal government keeps changing the rules and when inflation keeps costs rising at record rates is not an easy task; however, it will be worth it once it is completed. It is still the cheapest way to make electricity and cleanest for the environment. The changing rules and government controls may cause the cost of the plant to rise or even delay the schedule somewhat, but I assure you that our plans are reasonable and that we are dedicated to building one of the safest and best nuclear plants in the nation.

We will keep you informed of our progress. Please feel free to let us know if you have questions.

Very truly yours,

Wendell J. Kelley

WENDELL J. KELLEY
Chairman and President

EXHIBIT 2

Mr. Wendell J. Kelley
Chairman and President
Illinois Power Company
500 South 27 Street
Decatur, Illinois 62525

**CBS
NEWS**

A Division of CBS Inc.
524 West 57 Street
New York, New York 10019
(212) 975-2787

Robert Chandler Vice President
and Director Public Affairs Broadcasts

January 21, 1980

Dear Mr. Kelley:

I have had the opportunity to view Illinois Power's videotaped response to our 60 MINUTES story and to read your letter to Illinois Power's stockholders.

At the outset, I should state that neither the tape nor the letter persuades us that our story was unfair or, with two exceptions with which I shall deal below, inaccurate.

Indeed, the order of the Illinois Commerce Commission amply supports our story, both in its essential thrust and in its details. And the Commission in its order also

EXHIBIT 2 *(continued)*

rejected many of the arguments and documents you offer as "proof" in both your letter and your videotape.

I stated that we were inaccurate in two respects. They were as follows:

1. We stated that the 14 percent rate increase was attributable to the cost of the Clinton construction. We were in error; despite the Commission's assertion that "unquestionably, the driving force for the requested electric rate increase is the Company's need to generate revenue to support the construction of Clinton Unit #1," we should have said that only part of the increase was requested to pay for Clinton and the balance for general revenue purposes.

2. We also stated that the "usually neutral staff of the Commerce Commission joined in asking that the rate increase be denied." That is in error; we should have said that the staff recommended that the cost of Clinton construction not be included in the electric rate base. In short, it recommended that the part of the increase attributable to the construction be denied.

We shall, in accordance with our policy of correcting errors on the air, correct these errors on 60 MINUTES, Sunday, January 27.

But if confirmation of the overall accuracy of our story is needed, it comes in the words and actions of the Commission:

"The Commission finds it difficult to believe that the latest cost estimate for Clinton Unit #1 will be the ultimate cost of Clinton Unit #1. Therefore, the Commission is of the opinion that the Company should within 60 days . . . submit a cost estimate for Clinton Unit #1 . . . ."

We note as well that the Commission permitted only $97,000,000 of the $240,000,000 of Construction Work in Progress to be included in the rate base, and did so only because it feared that if it followed the staff recommendation not to do so "the exclusion . . . could place the Company in a financial position that could cause a further delay in the completion of Clinton Unit #1, and thus magnify extreme financial problems which have a direct adverse effect on rate-payers and investors alike."

The Commission also ordered its own "formal investigation of incentives for cost control . . . within a reasonable time after receipt of the new cost estimate," after noting that the evidence concerning cost control performance is "insufficient" but further noting "the urgency of controlling future costs."

It also ordered the Company to provide it with monthly reports for the duration of the Clinton project on schedule status, cost performance, problem areas, actual versus target dates for project activities, safety evaluation reports and monthly variance as to cost and completion dates.

It seems to us that the findings of the Commission, to say nothing of the staff, as to cost escalations and delays at Clinton more than support our report in its essentials. And as we get into the specific allegations you make, the Commission and staff recommendations again stand to refute them.

Permit me to address the issues raised in your letter to stockholders, which are also covered in the videotape:

1. Mr. Gerstner indeed took us through a 25-month cycle required to test individual components before full-systems tests can take place. We did not use that portion of the interview because it was unresponsive to our question, which dealt with suc-

EXHIBIT 2 *(continued)*

cessful completion of systems test and submission and acceptance of test results. That portion of the milestone chart we circled was "Submit applicant's test results," and it was that to which we referred in our story. Harry Reasoner said: "Even more, look at the two weeks the company says it will take to complete the full system tests, *before the Nuclear Regulatory Commission will permit the loading of nuclear fuel.* Again, Illinois Power says it will take just two weeks. But the median time for all nuclear plants for these tests is 14 months; some have done it in as little as two months; some have taken 26 months.

So, just in these several steps, Illinois Power says it will accomplish what no other nuclear builder has ever accomplished that fast before."

Indeed, the Commission's report took note of intervener testimony before the staff that "the NRC submitted to Congress a report which estimated a fuel load date of July 1984 rather than April 1982, as the Company has contended." The Commission summed up the testimony as follows: "The central theme was how can IP, who has never met industry average times for construction tasks, now beat the industry averages."

It seems perfectly obvious that we were not referring to individual component tests, as Mr. Gerstner suggests, but to the period following the testing of the entire system up to approval to load nuclear fuel. And this is the period to which the industry figures cited apply. Perhaps we should have made it clearer that in discussing the time to "complete the full system tests," we were referring to successful completion, as the rest of the sentence indicates. But, it seems to us, our meaning was clear, and Mr. Gerstner's response about the time prior to full system tests begged the question.

2. Mr. Gerstner did indeed show Mr. Reasoner a list of all seven one-unit boiling water plants being built in the United States, of which Clinton was the lowest. The fact that Mr. Gerstner offered this comparison does not make it valid. Indeed, the Commission itself rejected the list, pointing out that "all six plants are of different vintage, have a longer time period between date of original cost estimate to the date of the present costs, have been subject to longer delays, and are located in different states." The Commission suggested that a more valid comparison might have been with other Illinois plants of similar vintage and design and found the company's explanations "not sufficient to explain the difference between a 200 percent cost overrun for Clinton Unit #1 and a 106 percent overrun for Commonwealth Edison Byron Station," an Illinois plant not shown on Mr. Gerstner's list.

3. Yes, we were aware that two of the four companies constituting Baldwin Associates had worked on parts of 14 nuclear projects. What we said was that the Clinton plant is IP's "first nuclear project, and the first for their contractor, Baldwin Associates." This is accurate, and remains accurate: Baldwin has never served as the general contractor for a nuclear plant. The Commission order noted testimony challenging the company's schedule "because the required activites have never been accomplished in the time frame planned by anyone in the nuclear industry, *much less a general contractor in his first role as a nuclear project manager.*"

4. The major points in our report were not based, as you indicate, on the comments of three former employees. They were based on considerable off-camera interviews, on the testimony before the Commission, on interviews and research at the NRC on

EXHIBIT 2   *(continued)*

Clinton and other nuclear projects. The three former employees who appeared did appear as critics, but the substance of their remarks dealt with what was happening on-site and in the cost-reporting procedures that might help explain the overruns.

As to "the most vocal of these critics," as you put it, Mr. Radcliffe, you are correct—as far as you go—in citing the opinion of the hearing examiner that he should be permitted to testify as an expert witness. But it seems to us that you mislead people by failing to give the rest of the examiner's opinion. The examiner did rule that he was not an expert witness, but also ruled that his testimony should be heard. The Commission stated in its order: "Therefore, as ruled by the examiner, a large portion of his testimony and the exhibits sponsored by this witness are *relevant, material, and competent.* The Commission, therefore, has given *full* consideration to the testimony and exhibits sponsored by this witness according to such weight thereto deemed advisable."

It is noteworthy too that your videotape sought to discredit Mr. Radcliffe because he had claimed, both before the Commission and in *Who's Who in the East,* educational credentials he apparently does not possess. You did not add that in his application for employment with IP, he did not claim such credentials, yet he was hired in any case because you apparently felt he had the experience to do the job for IP. And the Commission felt his testimony was "relevant, material, and competent," despite his representations as to his educational credentials.

5. As to the question of the staff recommendation, I have dealt with that on the first page of this letter, and our statement shall be corrected. I should note again, however, that the staff recommended against inclusion of the Clinton construction costs in the rate base, and the Commission in deciding to overrule the recommendation, only allowed about 40 percent of the costs to be included in the rate base, and then because it fears further financial problems.

As to other issues raised in your videotape:

We did estimate the costs of Clinton at a million dollars a day, 30 million a month. The million a day was your figure, but you now state the monthly costs are $22 million. During our stay at Clinton, we noted a seven-day work week, and we presume your $22 million is based on a five-day week.

As to the question of whether there were sufficient written reports to senior managment and the board, first, the Commission commented that "in general, staff and intervener witnesses challenged the effectiveness of the management practices employed at the Clinton Project Unit #1." Moreover, as the Commission pointed out, your own witness, a partner in Theodore Barry & Associates, did not challenge as fact the contention that "the Company relied on oral reporting of the IP Vice President/Project Manager to the Executive Vice President and the Board of Directors." He just disagreed with the characterization of such oral reporting as poor management. Yet, your videotape insists that our report of oral reporting was inaccurate.

In sum, it should be clear that far from being "used" by your opponents in the rate case, we went to considerable lengths to get at the facts, which were and perhaps remain in dispute. In this letter I have cited at length from the Commission order because the Commission itself had access to all arguments and data, and was highly critical of the Clinton project, in terms of overruns, schedules, and the credibility of

EXHIBIT 2   *(concluded)*

your own claims. We did time our broadcast just prior to the decision and said so, because that decision was to address questions in which the entire country has a stake.

There remains one final area of concern. I note that you take pains to point out to users of your videotape that the 60 MINUTES material contained in the tape is copyrighted by CBS, and you proscribe limits on its use. While I appreciate your own concern and efforts to avoid the abuse of our rights by others, I am nonetheless obliged to point out that your own use and distribution of the material constitute in themselves an infringement of our copyright.

Sincerely,

Robert Chandler

Adolph Coors Company

There is trouble brewing at Coors, Coors Beer, which is sold in only 20 states. It used to be the third largest-selling beer in America. Now it is sixth, for sales have dropped sharply. Why? Because there are stories that the Coors Company is anti-black, anti-woman, anti-homosexual, and that's just for starters. There are also stories that Coors treats its employees shabbily, inhumanely. As a result, large blocks of people have organized boycotts against Coors Beer.

Mike Wallace, *CBS News,* "Trouble Brewing," "60 Minutes," June 5, 1983

William K. Coors, the chairman and chief executive officer of the Adolph Coors Company, smiled as he watched "60 Minutes" reporter Mike Wallace introduce the story on the Coors Company. Bill Coors had reason to smile. Although Wallace's stern, prosecutorlike opening seemed highly critical, even ominous, this segment of the popular Sunday evening TV show was a rerun of a program originally telecast on September 26, 1982, and Bill Coors knew that "60 Minutes" painted a very positive picture of his company. Indeed, the show could hardly have been more positive had Bill Coors written the script himself. Unlike many "60 Minutes" stories on business organizations, this one featured informal, friendly chats with the company's leaders; a "town meeting" hosted by Wallace for several hundred loyal, enthusiastic Coors employees; testimonials to the company, its product, its policies by numerous parties; and an unflattering interview with a union leader who was the major Coors protagonist.

At last, some positive information about the company was being brought to a large audience. And yet, Bill Coors knew that the war was far from over. His beer, which had become something of a national fad in the mid-1970s (President Ford was reported to have had cases of Coors flown from Colorado to Washington, D.C. aboard Air Force One), had suffered a serious loss of barrelage volume. Sales fell from a record high in 1980 of 13.8 million barrels to 11.9 million in 1982. The company had experienced a loss in market share every year since 1977.[1]

---

[1] "The Beer War: Heady Days End at Coors as Its Sales Pace Declines," *The Wall Street Journal,* October 6, 1982, p. 1.

Coors's problems seemed to be rooted in its negative corporate reputation and in competitive pressure resulting from a great deal of turmoil in the beer industry. In 1977, Coors's striking brewery workers organized a nationwide boycott. The AFL–CIO-initiated boycott gained widespread support among minority groups, homosexuals, and women's organizations. At the same time, the industry was being shaken by a battle between Anheuser-Busch and the Miller Brewing Company. Coors and a lot of other competitors seemed to be caught in the cross fire.

COMPANY BACKGROUND

Coors was founded in 1873 by a German immigrant, Adolph Herman Joseph Coors. Orphaned at age 15, he signed a three-year article of apprenticeship to the Henry Wenker Brewery in Germany where he was taught the art of brewing beer. Adolph ventured to America at age 21 by stowing away on a ship. In 1872, Coors opened a beer and wine bottling plant outside Denver, Colorado. He was particularly attracted to the rich Clear Creek Valley area that ran through Golden, Colorado, where clear, cool springs bubbled in abundance. Coors's dream was realized when he began brewing beer in an old tannery building in the Clear Creek Valley of Golden. After a number of years of high growth, the Coors Golden Brewery hit a major obstacle in 1916 when the state of Colorado voted in favor of Prohibition. Adolph Coors was able to keep his brewery operating during Prohibition by changing its production from beer to malted milk, cream, and near beer. Coors also sold the alcohol distilled off the near beer to drug companies and hospitals.

For over 100 years the company had been characterized by family management, rapid growth into contiguous territories, and a product reputation of the highest quality. A member of the Coors family had always been at the helm of the company. The family tradition played a major role in the evolution of the company. The family felt it was personally responsible for providing customers with the highest quality beer at a fair price. Until 1980, the distribution of Coors beer was limited to 17 western states in order to provide consumers with the freshest product possible. This commitment to quality caused the company to become dedicated to the tradition of self-sufficiency. The family was also dedicated to the tradition of developing the highest expertise in brewing technology. Investment after investment was made in operations in order to keep Coors abreast of current technology.

The Golden Years

Growth and expansion of the company continued at an impressive rate. By the mid-1970s the Coors Golden brewery was the largest single brewery in the world with an annual capacity of 15 million barrels. In 1976, the company was the third largest brewer in the nation, selling almost 12 million barrels of beer. Coors employed approximately 8,700 people.

Coors's sales had grown steadily from the end of Prohibition to 1976. The company's sales doubled between 1968 and 1973, and barrelage was growing at an annual rate of 11 percent. In 1975, Coors boasted a 50 percent market share in Colorado and similarly high shares in the rest of its 16 state distribution region. Between 1970 and 1975 the company moved from 12th to 4th place among all brewers and was the envy of the industry.

Throughout the 1960s and until 1976, the company was able to sell all the beer it could produce. Coors's management spent much of its time deciding on how to allocate its production to its distribution areas. Although it later expanded its line, during this period Coors produced only a single brand of beer—Coors Banquet—and supported it with very little advertising. In 1976, Coors spent only 25 cents per barrel on advertising compared with an industry average of approximately $1.25. The company's phenomenal success was summed up by Marketing Vice President Leland Shelton who stated, "You could have sold Coors beer in Glad bags."[2]

The company built its success on the reputation that it brewed the highest quality beer in the industry. This reputation caused a mystique to develop around the beer. Coors beer had long been associated with the mystique of the mountains and the West. Every beer label proclaimed Coors was brewed with "Pure Rocky Mountain Spring Water." This created an image of quality and freshness that proponents of the beer would go to great lengths to obtain. The mystique was further enhanced by the fact that Coors was available only in certain areas of the country.

In addition to President Ford's alleged fondness for Coors, the beer also received favorable publicity when Burt Reynolds, in the movie "Smokey and the Bandit," portrayed a madcap smuggler running cases of Coors back to a thirst-crazed Atlanta. A thriving bootlegging business actually developed in which daring entrepreneurs hauled truckloads of the beer from its Rocky Mountain home to the East Coast and sold them on an unauthorized basis at premium prices.

The mystique of Coors beer was also attributed to its unique brewing process and its stringent quality controls. Unlike most other American brewers, the Coors brewing process was entirely natural. Since all biochemical processes were allowed to occur naturally, Coors had one of the longest brewing processes in the industry, taking an average of 68 days from brewing to packaging. Absolutely no artificial ingredients, chemicals, or additives were ever used in Coors beer.

Coors's brewing process eliminated the need for pasteurization, thus avoiding beer's biggest enemy, heat. While other beers were pasteurized at temperatures reaching 140 degrees, Coors avoided this flavor-killing step by

---

[2] "A Test for the Coors Dynasty," *Business Week,* May 8, 1978, p. 69.

packaging its beer in a sterile atmosphere. They even went so far as brewing the beer in rooms with filtered air and a hospital atmosphere of sterilization.

To ensure consumers tasted Coors with brewery fresh flavor as far away as Tennessee, Coors had a refrigerated distribution process. At added expense to the brewery and to its distributors, Coors's products were shipped from the brewery in insulated rail cars or refrigerated trucks. Distributors were required to refrigerate Coors in their warehouses. On delivery to the retailers, Coors required a 60-day rotation on all of its packaged goods, by far the strictest in the industry.

Operations and Distribution

All of Coors beer came out of its single brewery in Golden, which was recognized as one of the most modern and efficient in the world. Coors used computers extensively to control and monitor many steps used in the brewing process. The use of a single brewery allowed Coors to maintain uniform quality in its beers.

Coors was a highly integrated company. The company supplied its own special barley seed to contract farmers. Coors malted almost all its own barley in company facilities. The water used in the beer came from snow-fed springs on company land in the Rocky Mountain foothills. The company had its own aluminum can and glass bottle manufacturing plants. The aluminum can manufacturing plant was the largest in the world. Coors supplied all of its energy requirements from company-owned gas wells and coal fields. Coors supplied the limestone for its bottles from company-owned mines located near its brewery. It also had its own transportation and distribution companies to provide flexibility and direct contact with retailers.

In addition, the Coors Porcelain Company, which was founded during Prohibition, was one of the world's foremost suppliers of technical ceramics, employing over 2,100 people in five states and three foreign countries. Coors also had its own engineering and construction company.

Coors's environmental philosophy encompassed the efficient uses of all recoverable products, and one of the most interesting was the transformation of brewery wastes to animal feed. Coors Food Products Company also produced Coors Cocoamost, a cocoa powder replacement that was derived from brewers yeast. Coors Golden Recycle Company was a front-runner in aluminum beverage can recovery and processing.

Coors's products were shipped by rail and truck to six company-owned distributors and 268 independent Coors wholesalers. The wholesalers were responsible for sales, merchandising, and account servicing in their local markets. They serviced bars, stores, and restaurants. One fifth of Coors's 268 wholesalers changed hands in the 1980s. More than half were selling other beers or wine to compensate for sagging Coors sales. In the 1970s, two thirds of Coors's wholesalers sold nothing but Coors.

Management and Ownership

The management style at Coors was considered unusual. In 1982, the company was run by third generation brothers. William Coors, 65, held the position of chairman and chief executive officer, while Joseph Coors, 64, was vice chairman, president, and chief operating officer. Joe also oversaw the financial and administrative functions. Bill Coors generally handled the technical side of the business and had a reputation for being a near genius within the brewing industry. There was no apparent rivalry between the brothers and no formal lines of authority. Each brother could act in any area. "People know they can talk to either one of us and get decisions," said Joe Coors.[3] Both of the brothers had engineering backgrounds.

By 1982, a fourth generation of the Coors family was also employed.[4] Joe Coors's three sons—Peter, 35, Jeffery, 37, and Joseph, Jr., 40—were all in on the family business. In 1982, the company expanded the office of the president to include Pete and Jeff Coors in order to provide the company with a more orderly transition between the two generations of management. Pete Coors took the position of divisional president of sales, marketing, and administration. He was the only family member with an MBA. Jeff Coors was promoted to divisional president of technical operations. Joe Coors, Jr., ran one of the company's porcelain operations. All members of the company's board were full-time employees of the company. Four of the seven directors were Bill, Joe, Jeff, and Pete Coors. The other three directors were senior members of Coors management.

In 1975, Coors offered its only public issue of stock. The main reason the company went public was not to raise funds for capital investment or expansion, but for estate purposes. Of the stock that was issued, the Coors family owned all of the class A common, which had full voting rights. The family also owned 41 percent of the class B common, which had no voting rights.

THE INDUSTRY

For most of its history, the brewing industry was characterized by small, regional brewers. At one time there had been as many as 750 breweries in the United States. By the early 1980s, that number had declined to fewer than 50. Traditionally, brewing companies were primarily concerned with producing a quality beer at a reasonable profit. However, in 1970, with the acquisition of the Miller Brewing Company by the Philip Morris company, the brewing industry experienced a new form of competitive strategy.

Through innovative marketing strategies, Philip Morris made Miller a dominant force in the national market (see Exhibit 1). Advertising expendi-

---

[3] Ibid., p. 69.

[4] "The Youth Movement in Coors Management," *Business Week,* May 24, 1982.

EXHIBIT 1 Top 10 Beer Brands in 1982

Rank	Brand	Brewer	Market Share	Production (millions of barrels)
1	Budweiser	Anheuser-Busch	21.6%	39.6
2	Miller High Life	Miller	11.2	20.5
3	Miller Lite	Miller	9.5	17.5
4	Coors	Coors	4.9	9.1
5	Pabst	Pabst	4.8	8.8
6	Michelob	Anheuser-Busch	4.6	8.5
7	Old Milwaukee	Schlitz	3.2	6.0
8	Old Style	Heileman	3.1	5.6
9	Stroh	Stroh	2.9	5.4
10	Schlitz	Schlitz	2.3	4.2

SOURCE: *Beverage Industry,* January 28, 1983, p. 1.

tures skyrocketed. By 1981, the competitive forces in the industry led Anheuser-Bush and Miller to spend in excess of $100 million each in advertising in an attempt to "win" market share. It began to appear that survival in this fiercely competitive industry would require a nationwide distribution system with special consideration given to demographic trends and product positioning. During the 1970s alone, 53 independent brewers went out of business. Only Miller and Anheuser-Busch were truly national in scope.

Market Growth

The U.S. beer market was the largest in the world. Although the annual growth rate peaked in the mid-1970s, 1981 beer consumption was at an all-time high of 177.5 million barrels. The decade of the 70s achieved a 4 percent average annual compound growth rate. Exhibit 2 shows growth trends for the industry.

Following steady growth in demand during the 1970s, the early 1980s witnessed a softening in demand. Indeed, it was estimated that industry volume increased only 0.43 percent in 1982. The beer industry, usually considered to be recession-proof, discovered that high unemployment could have a negative effect on sales. This slowing of market growth led to shrinking profit margins. High fixed costs due to overcapacity coupled with heavy marketing expenditures led to an intensely price-competitive situation.

Production and Distribution

Beer's principle ingredients were malt and barley. After steady cost increases in the 1970s, the cost trend flattened because of agricultural overproduction. Because of the increased costs associated with packaging the

EXHIBIT 2 Brewers' Production and Estimated Year-End 1982 Capacity (million barrels)

	1973	1974	1975	1976	1977	1978	1979	1980	1981	1982E	Year-end Capacity 1982E
Anheuser-Busch	29.9*	34.1	35.2	29.1	36.6	41.6	46.2	50.2	54.5	59.0	65.0
Miller	6.9	9.1	12.9	18.4	24.2	31.3	35.8	37.2	40.3	39.9	44.0
Stroh†	31.5	32.8‡	34.3	35.1	32.9	29.8	26.4	24.8	23.4	23.3	30.0
Heileman§	10.5	9.5	10.0	9.6	10.6	10.5	11.3	13.3	14.0	14.5	17.0
Pabst	13.1	14.3	15.7	17.0	16.0	15.4	15.1‖	15.1	13.5	12.5	17.5
Coors	10.9	12.3	11.9	13.5	12.8	12.6	12.9	13.8	13.3	12.0	15.0
Olympia#	4.7	5.3	6.6	7.3	6.8	6.7	6.0	6.1	5.7	5.2	9.0
Genesee	1.9	2.1	2.4	2.5	2.8	3.0	3.4	3.6	3.6	3.4	4.0
Others	30.9	28.1	21.5	19.7	16.5	14.4	17.4	12.4	10.9	9.6	19.4
Total	140.3	147.6	150.5	152.2	159.2	165.3	170.7	176.4	179.2	179.4	220.9

* Impacted by strike.
† Schaefer & Stroh combined for all years; Schlitz is now part of Stroh.
‡ A 40-day strike in April–May had an adverse effect on sales of Stroh.
§ Includes Carling National for all periods except first three months of 1979.
‖ Includes Blatz.
Includes certain assets of Hamm's acquired March 1975, and pro forma for Lone Star for all years. Pabst now owns 49 percent of the stock.

SOURCE: *Beverage Industry*, January 28, 1983, p. 34.

product, some brewers chose to integrate backwards and produce their own source of aluminum cans. Several brewers were involved in recycling efforts, which also decreased input costs. Thus, in 1982 the leveling of cost trends saved many brewers from what could have been disastrous profit margins.

In 1982, the top six domestic brewers—Anheuser-Busch, Inc.; Miller Brewing Co.; Stroh Brewery Co.; G. Heileman Brewing Co.; Pabst Brewing Co.; and Adolph Coors Co.—held over 88 percent of the domestic beer market (see Exhibit 3). Only Anheuser-Busch and Heileman increased production volume that year. The other industry leaders, including Coors, lost market share.

One trend in the brewing industry was the overcapacity problem that developed as the industry leaders continued to expand. In 1982, domestic brewing capacity was 220.9 million barrels, although only 179.4 million barrels were actually produced. In 1982, the major brewers operated around 85 percent of capacity. Many of the smaller brewers were not as fortunate and, as a result, profitability suffered. A high capacity utilization yielded a significant pricing edge because of the high amount of fixed costs that were associated with the modern automated packaging and brewing processes. The industry revolutionized the production process to a point where significant economies of scale existed when adequate volume was maintained. Most major brewers established production facilities in strategic locations throughout the country in an attempt to minimize shipping costs.

In 1981, over 4,600 companies competed in the beer wholesale market. Some 32 percent of the wholesalers accounted for 73 percent of the total beer sales. Survival at the wholesale level depended on reaching economies of scale

EXHIBIT 3   Brewers' Estimated Market Share

	1979	1980	1981	1982
Anheuser-Busch	26.8%	28.8%	30.0%	32.3%
Miller	20.8	20.9	22.2	21.8
Stroh	15.3	13.9	12.9	12.8
Heileman	6.6	7.5	7.7	7.9
Pabst	8.8	8.5	7.4	6.8
Coors	7.5	7.8	7.4	6.6
Olympia	3.5	3.4	3.1	2.8
Genesee	2.0	2.0	2.0	1.9
Schmidt	2.2	2.0	1.6	1.8
General	1.7	1.4	1.2	1.0
Pittsburgh	0.4	0.6	0.5	0.5
Others	4.4	3.8	4.1	3.8
Total	100.0%	100.0%	100.0%	100.0%

SOURCE: *Beverage Industry*, January 28, 1983, p 34.

EXHIBIT 4   Wholesale Establishments by Region (1981)

Region	Wholesalers	Percent of Total Wholesalers	Volume (percent)	Barrelage (percent)
New England	151	3.3%	5.4%	5.4%
Midwest	775	16.7	17.7	17.7
Great Lakes	943	20.3	18.4	18.4
Plains	552	11.9	7.5	7.5
Southeast	899	19.4	20.8	20.8
Southwest	519	11.2	11.6	11.7
Rocky Mountain	206	4.4	3.1	3.1
Far West	592	12.8	15.3	15.2
Total	4,637	100.0%	100.0%	100.0%

SOURCE: *Beverage Industry,* September 10, 1982, p. 13.

associated with a large volume and rapid turnover. Most distributors operated independently of the brewers; however, they were involved in cooperative advertising. The Southeast beer market was the most attractive for wholesalers, accounting for more than 20 percent of total industry volume in 1981 (see Exhibit 4). More than 3,000 wholesalers had annual sales of less than $3 million.

Industry Trends

Consumer Trends.   According to a number of observers, prior to 1970 the beer industry was very product oriented. There was only a vague concept of who the beer drinker was, and what influenced his or her taste. As brewers started to realize the importance of demographics, they began "targeting" different beers to different markets. In the 1970s, advertising expenditures per barrel of beer increased from $0.97 to $1.97. Beer was being marketed as an image, and themes such as "It's Miller Time," "This Bud's for You," and "Go for the Gusto" became common.

Traditionally, beer could be divided into three product categories based essentially on price and presumed quality: popular, premium, and high premium. Premium brands such as Schlitz and Budweiser were supported by national advertising and, prior to the development of their own regional brewing facilities, were shipped some distance in order to reach their widespread markets. They were priced at a higher level than local or regional brands. Thus, the local and regional brands became known as popular-priced beers. High premium beers were generally imports such as Heineken and Molson, but also included such domestic brands as Anheuser-Busch's Michelob.

A revolution in this classification scheme took place, however, when companies with national brands began constructing breweries throughout the country. No longer disadvantaged by higher shipping costs, these premium brands were now in a position to compete on a price basis with local and regional breweries. Another revolution came with the introduction of "Lite" beer by Miller in 1975. Supported by a massive, award-winning advertising campaign featuring well-known "macho" athletes, Lite struck a responsive chord with its "Less filling/Tastes great" theme. A weight-conscious society propelled Miller Lite and its imitators into a strong market position. Lite's marketing prowess was so great that it even helped push Miller's regular High Life brand into second place behind Budweiser.

Although the fitness trend increased the receptivity of the various light beer brands introduced by Anheuser-Busch, Coors, and virtually every other brewer in the industry, not all the news was good for beer companies. Many people switched consumption patterns and drank nonalcoholic beverages. There appeared to be a growing concern over alcohol abuse, which resulted in some townships becoming "dry," while others raised the drinking age. Furthermore, increased beer taxes and stricter deposit laws had a negative effect on overall consumption. The sharp recession of the early 1980s had a measurable effect on this one-time recession-proof industry. Last of all, the population decrease in 18–24 year olds, usually the heaviest beer drinkers, resulted in much less growth than in the past.

Major Geographic Trends.   During the 1970s, the beer market increased 40 percent or 50 million barrels. Of that 50 million barrels, the South Atlantic states contributed 10.5 million barrels. This region was expected to continue its rapid growth. Traditionally, the South had been a weak market for beer because of steep beer taxation, fundamentalist beliefs, higher drinking ages, and numerous dry counties. The recent influx of young people, however, made the South's demographics attractive. This population shift, in turn, led to more areas voting to become "wet." Attitudes toward beer had changed with increased female consumption and the growing acceptance of beer at social functions.

The southern regional brewer had fared much better than his northern counterpart. Southern brewers appeared more attuned with local consumer tastes, and some strong local and regional brands enjoyed considerable loyalty. Anheuser-Busch and Miller continued to make inroads into the growing Southern market, but a Stroh-Schlitz merger in 1982 created a new major competitor in this market. The South-Central market, particularly Texas and Arkansas, was predicted to be dominated by the Big Two with up to a combined 70 percent market share. But the fluctuating Southeast was not expected to be dominated by any particular brewer in the near future. Second tier brewers would continue to have significant market shares, but only in pockets in this area.[5]

---

[5] Joseph Pluta, "The South: America's Pivotal Beer Region," *Beverage World,* November 1982, p. 126.

In 1980, Texas and Florida showed strong growth in beer consumption. But seven other states (Georgia, Kentucky, Louisiana, Maryland, North Carolina, Tennessee, and Virginia) enjoyed even more phenomenal growth. Coors's 1983 planned expansion was in this area. Industry analysts expected Coors to be up against heavy competition.

Mergers and Acquisitions Trend.   In 1982, there were 44 brewing companies in operation in the United States, compared with 154 in 1970. Experts in the beer industry predicted that within three to four years, the number of major brewers could be reduced from eight to four or five.

Merger mania overtook the industry in the early 1980s. Bob Weinberger, industry consultant, gave four reasons for the sudden trend:

1. To acquire production capacity quickly rather than building new plants.
2. To acquire another brewer's barrelage so that the acquiring brewer could use some of his excess capacity for the other brewer's brands.
3. To expand into new markets.
4. To achieve a "critical mass" in order to take advantage of economies of scale. This puts the consolidated brewer in a better position to compete with the bigger brewers.[6]

As the brewing industry matured, growth was expected to slow down as the number of young people decreased. Continued mergers in the industry led some analysts to believe that in 1986 the top four brewers would hold 90 percent of the U.S. market. Regional and local brewers' profits would continue to be squeezed as the nationals took advantage of economies of scale in advertising, production, and distribution. Projected barrelage for the industry was 211 million barrels by 1985.

The Competitors

Anheuser-Busch.   Anheuser-Busch had been the number one brewer since 1967 when it overtook Schlitz. In 1981, Anheuser-Busch had sales of $3.8 billion on 54.5 million barrels, with a net income of $217.4 million. The St. Louis–based company had grown at three times the rate of the market. It believed that it could increase its market share to 40 percent by 1990 from its current share of 32 percent.

During the 1970s, demand for Anheuser-Busch products far exceeded supply; this led to dramatic capital expenditure projects. In 1982, the company allocated over $1.8 billion to increase its capacity by 50 percent (to reach 63 million barrels, annually). Anheuser-Busch planned to spend another $2 billion to increase capacity an additional 27 percent.

---

6 Bob Leaderer, "The Brewers' Survival Equation," *Beverage World,* October 1982, p. 3.

Anheuser-Busch's dominance was virtually unchallenged until Miller launched its massive marketing program. To combat the competitive forces in the industry, Anheuser-Busch committed itself to the following objectives and methods: (1) to dictate the pricing strategy in the market, (2) to cut prices to enter lucrative markets, (3) to continue its efforts to promote and support beer drinking (1982 marketing expenditures were $145 million), (4) to maintain modern, efficient breweries operating near full capacity, and (5) to maintain quality products in all three price categories as well as the light market.

Miller.   Since its acquisition by Philip Morris in 1970, Miller moved from the number seven brewer to the number two brewer in the United States. Miller had a straightforward corporate goal: "We want to be number 1." In order to accomplish this feat, Miller aggressively entered new markets by both price cutting and product line expansion. Miller Lite had become the number three beer overall and held more than 60 percent of the light beer market. In 1981, Miller sold 40.2 million barrels of beer.

Stroh, Schlitz, and Schaefer.   Stroh acquired the Schaefer Brewing Company in 1980, and it acquired Schlitz in 1982. Stroh, Schlitz, and Schaefer hoped to become the third major competitor. Schlitz was at one time a very dominant brewer. However, marketing blunders had caused market share (and profitability) to drop significantly. Schlitz had been critically acclaimed for high product quality, yet the product had a poor public image. Stroh hoped to revive some of Schlitz's old line strengths. However, the acquisitions put a tremendous strain on Stroh's resources, and experts did not predict an immediate revival.

Heileman.   Heileman followed a unique strategy. The company acquired weak regional and local brewers and turned them into strong, competitive forces. Heileman had over 30 different brands, including 11 major brands. Its main emphasis was in the northern section of the country; however, it was committed to becoming a national power.

Regionals and Locals.   It became evident that small brewers were finding it difficult to compete with the huge national firms, because of economies of scale. However, a number of regional brewers like Olympia and Genesee exhibited a strong resistance against the nationals. Local brewers, such as Hudepohl in Cincinnati, experienced local sentiment and brand loyalty, which was the driving force behind their survival. They would continue to survive as long as niches in the market could be exploited profitably. However, price differentials from the nationals would jeopardize the future of the regional and local brewer.

Imports.   In 1981, imports had 5 percent of the U.S. market. But with a 15 percent growth rate, they were expected to capture at least 10 percent of the domestic market by 1990. This rapid growth was anticipated because (1) imports were beginning to utilize American market techniques, which increased consumer awareness, and (2) imports represented a novelty item to the American consumer.

COORS'S DECLINE

Coors was getting hurt by the battle between the Big Two.[7] With industry sales growth slowing, Miller and Anheuser-Busch were putting more emphasis on regional marketing in an effort to shore up market shares in important, specific markets. The Big Two added capacity and went after a larger market share. In 11 states that used to be Coors's strongholds, the Golden, Colorado, company was able to hold the lead in only three—New Mexico, Kansas, and Oklahoma. The losses were especially critical in California and Texas, which traditionally accounted for half of Coors's sales. At its peak, Coors held about 50 percent of the California market and still had more than 40 percent as recently as 1975. By 1982, however, their share was down below 20 percent while Anheuser-Busch had 46 percent of the California market. In 1980, Coors also lost its lead to Anheuser-Busch and Miller in the Texas market.

Anheuser-Busch targeted the West, South, and Southeast as areas for growth. They expanded their Los Angeles and Houston facilities and gave serious consideration to building a plant in Colorado. Coors's market share in Colorado dropped from 50 percent to a low of 18 percent in 1981. No area was out of reach to the giants of the industry.

Marketing

Marketing Difficulties.   For decades Coors sold every drop of beer it produced. The company knew how to allocate beer, not market it. For years Coors focused on their single product, Banquet beer. They supported it with $3 million in advertising, by far the industry's lowest. Suddenly in 1977, the company had the new experience of having demand fall short of production.

The family was convinced that customers were devoted to the "Coors Mystique." The company, in turn, was committed to the legend that their Rocky Mountain spring water made the best beer. In fact, Coors relied so heavily on the selling prowess of its mystique and spring water that it did not even have a marketing department until 1975. Implementing the marketing department proved to be a difficult task for the company. Recalled one former Coors official, "It was like pulling teeth to get it done."[8] In the early years, turnover was frequent. There were three advertising directors in the first four years alone.

---

[7] "Coors Beer Stumbles in Bid to Become National Force," *The Wall Street Journal,* July 10, 1981, p. 1.

[8] "Beer War: Heady Days," p. 1.

Then Pete Coors took charge and brought in some former Schlitz marketing people. The newcomers found they were occasionally second guessed and overruled by family members. At one point Joe Coors insisted that his wife's friend Zsa Zsa Gabor tout Coors. This horrified the marketing people who felt a glamorous actress was the wrong image. The campaign did not materialize, but that sort of meddling hastened turnover in the department. Many suspected that there were more conflicts than the company admitted. Company officials conceded there were some differences over strategies. They, however, denied that the differences were dividing the company's management.

Advertising.   After 1976, when Coors spent only 25 cents per barrel on advertising compared with an industry average of $1.25, they increased advertising dramatically. By 1981, their per barrel allotment was among the highest in the industry. Being a regional brewer, Coors was unable to take advantage of better national rates (30 to 50 percent lower) on television advertising. Exhibit 5 shows Coors's advertising expenditures between 1977 and 1982.

Coors's in-house advertising division failed to make sufficient headway so Ted Bates & Company was retained in 1978 to come up with a new image for Coors. The new image urged people to "Taste the High Country—Climb Up to Coors," along with "We Are Coors." By 1982, Coors was forsaking the "High Country" look of rolling mountains and water for a more product-oriented campaign featuring traditional beer gatherings. The new themes, "Made for the Way You Really Like to Drink Beer" emphasized the beer's freshness and unique qualities. Distributors were enthusiastic over the highlighting of the natural ingredients, rather than the company and the environment. Promotional emphasis was on motor sports in 1983. Coors sponsored a professional auto racing team, certain Grand Prix events, and the Coors Bicycle Classic.

Planned Market Expansion

Coors concentrated its efforts in 11 states for many years and gradually expanded from 14 states in 1977 to 20 in 1982. Further expansion would require snatching market share from well-entrenched competition. To make

EXHIBIT 5   Advertising Expenditures, 1977–1982

	Total Advertising	Advertising, per Barrel
1977	$15,500,000	$1.23
1978	33,470,000	2.66
1979	46,400,000	3.59
1980	66,752,000	4.84
1981	85,817,000	6.49
1982	88,103,000	7.39

up for lost sales and sagging market share in its traditional territories, Coors planned to expand into the Southeast in 1983 and eventually the entire Eastern market.

Coors gave a number of reasons for the move into the Southeast: (1) the apparent vulnerability of its competitors in the area, (2) the relatively young and constantly increasing population, (3) the longer beer-drinking season resulting from the warmer climate, and (4) the increasing beer consumption in the area at a time when consumption elsewhere was declining.[9]

Financial Performance and Resources

In 1982, Coors saw its net income decline for the fourth straight year. Net income peaked at $68 million in 1979, while net income for 1982 was $40 million. (See Exhibits 6 and 7.) Net sales decreased slightly to $915 million in 1982 from a record $930 million in 1981. Most significant in 1982 was a 10.1 percent drop in barrels of beer sold to a total of 11.9 million barrels. Shipments had already decreased 3.8 percent in 1981 from 1980's record high level of 13.8 million barrels. In 1982, the company's beer business accounted for approximately 84 percent of net sales and 83 percent of operating income.

It was believed that Coors's beer shipments declined from the record volume in 1980 primarily because of intense competition rather than the boycott. This competition had the effect of narrowing the company's profit

EXHIBIT 6

ADOLPH COORS COMPANY
Income Statement
(in thousands of dollars except per share data)

	1982	1981	1980	1979	1978
Barrels sold	11,919	13,216	13,779	12,912	12,566
Net sales	$915,258	$929,916	$887,897	$740,504	$624,804
Cost of goods sold	659,033	659,623	629,758	517,748	450,439
Marketing, general, and administrative	185,076	181,348	146,293	103,679	79,369
Research and development	15,230	16,848	14,256	11,244	9,444
Other	(9,229)	(7,536)	(8,187)	(6,921)	(7,975)
Income taxes	25,000	27,633	40,800	46,305	38,753
Net income	$ 40,148	$ 51,970	$ 64,977	$ 68,449	$ 54,774
Earnings per share	$1.15	$1.48	$1.86	$1.95	$1.56

SOURCE: Annual Report, 1982, p. 24.

[9] "Coors Tries to Conquer Southeast Beer Market," *New York Times*, April 22, 1983.

EXHIBIT 7

ADOLPH COORS COMPANY
Balance Sheet
For the Year Ended December 31, 1982
(in thousands of dollars)

Assets

Current assets:

Cash and equivalents	$ 71,251
Accounts and notes receivable	64,909
Inventories	118,658
Prepaid expenses	34,614
Income tax prepayments	4,236
Total current assets	293,668

Properties:

At cost less depreciation*	702,769
Other assets	11,477
Total assets	$1,007,914

Liabilities

Current liabilities:

Accounts payable	$ 45,601
Accrued salaries and vacations	25,543
Taxes	17,252
Federal and state income taxes	2,789
Other	28,820
Total current liabilities	120,005
Deferred income taxes	95,097

Long-term liabilities:

Shareholders' equity:

Class A common stock, voting, $1 par value	1,260
Class B common stock, nonvoting, no par value	11,000
Paid-in capital	2,011
Retained earnings	795,396
Less treasury stock	(26,455)
Total shareholders' equity	783,212
Total liabilities and shareholders' equity	$1,007,914

* Accumulated depreciation in 1982 was $426,419.

SOURCE: Annual report, 1982, pp. 12, 13.

margins to less than half those the company reported in the mid-1970s. Coors's marketing, general, and administrative expenses increased significantly as the company intensified its efforts to promote sales. Coors also faced higher transportation costs as it expanded its distribution area. The company's high degree of vertical integration, however, enabled it to maintain relatively tight control over manufacturing costs.

Coors's philosophy was against borrowing, and the company always remained virtually debt free. The company planned to finance its future expansion through internally generated funds combined with available cash and short-term interest-bearing investment. Coors shied away from the recent merger activity in the brewing industry. The Coors family pointed to their unique brewing process and to the quality of their product and said there was no need to merge.

In 1980, the company allocated $1 billion for a 10-year expansion plan. The company planned to increase its capacity from 14 to 35 million barrels by the end of the decade. The plan called for the Coors Golden Brewery to be expanded to 25 million barrels. In 1982, the company purchased land options for the possible construction of a second brewery in the eastern United States. The options consisted of 2,000 acres located in Rocky Mount, Virginia, and were due to expire in 1984. The company estimated that the construction of a second brewery would take approximately four years and cost $500 million. The new brewery was expected to add 10 million barrels of annual brewing capacity.

Corporate Reputation

In addition to the challenges involved in competing in an industry in turmoil, Coors had to struggle with a serious problem of corporate reputation. In 1977, a number of issues surfaced, which played a part in reversing the favorable performance trends Coors had experienced since the end of Prohibition. The company faced major challenges from organized labor and from a number of minority groups. In addition, the political activities of the company's president, Joe Coors, became a matter of controversy. The results were a tarnished corporate image, which many felt contributed to an erosion of the company's market share and a reduced effectiveness of its marking weapon— its mystique.

Coors's union problems began in April 1977. Its employees, who at that time were represented by the Brewery Workers Union, struck over lie detector tests and periodic search and seizure raids on employees' property and over alleged racial and sexual discrimination in hiring. The union accused Coors of using its lie detector test to eliminate homosexuals from its hiring process. Coors denied these charges and defended its right to require lie detector tests. In 1960, Bill and Joe's brother, Adolph Coors III, had been kidnapped and murdered. In recent years, Joe Coors had received numerous threats. Bill Coors admitted that over the past 10 years the company's security personnel had on four occasions searched an employee's locker, lunch box, or automobile for drugs. He insisted that the practice was infrequent but could be justified in the name of worker safety and security. The company denied totally the final charge of racial and sexual discrimination.

When Coors resisted the strike, the AFL–CIO called for a boycott of Coors's products. (It should be noted that the company's union problems never involved the issue of money. The wages Coors paid its brewery workers were among the highest in the industry.) At the same time, a number of loosely allied activist groups joined the boycott. Feminists, Hispanics, gays, blacks, and other minority groups joined the boycott and contributed to a sense of shared grievances that helped to amplify the accusations against Coors. The Equal Opportunities Commission also brought minority discrimination charges against the company. Coors settled the suit, without admitting guilt, by signing an agreement promising to make future employment practices nondiscriminatory.

In December 1978, Coors won a great victory over the union. Coors's employees voted to terminate their 44-year association with the union, making Coors the only nonunionized major brewer in the nation. Seventy-one percent of the workers voted to decertify the Brewery Workers Union. Of those workers eligible to vote, 94 percent had cast ballots. The AFL–CIO attributed the one-sided result to company-applied pressure and threats.

Even before the strike, the political activities of Joe Coors had become a public issue. Some consumers apparently were offended by Joe Coors's ultra-conservative political image. He was a staunch advocate of the open shop theory and was an active supporter of the anti-union Right to Work Association. He also endorsed the John Birch Society and played an important role in Ronald Reagan's political campaigns. As a result, some consumers who had once thought it was "hip" to drink Coors, suddenly lost their taste for the brew. College students who were attracted to Coors by its mystique seemed particularly offended by Joe Coors's political affiliations, and many stopped drinking the brand.

Bill and Joe Coors were taken aback by the negative publicity. Bill Coors described the negative news stories as, "A bum rap and a smear on the company."[10] The two brothers felt the company stood for brotherhood as well as individualism. The Coors family had long supported hospitals, schools, sports organizations, patriotic groups, and various ethnic and minority organizations. The forefathers' philosophy was against self-promotion, and the Coors brothers had taken great pains not to publicize their charity. They were upset that the Coors organization was being portrayed as one that lacked compassion. As a result, the company published a pamphlet to present its side of the story (Exhibit 8).

---

[10] "Coors Tries to Conquer Southeast Beer Market."

EXHIBIT 8   Adolph Coors Company

The facts about Coors beer

- Coors beer is completely natural and contains no additives or preservatives

- All American beers served in kegs—draught beer—are not pasteurized. Only the Coors Drinkability Brewing Process makes it possible for consumers to get the flavor of draught beer in Coors cans and bottles

- Coors beer is purer than many bottled and municipal waters that have been tested. It contains the lowest asbestos fiber count of any of the common thirst quenching beverages—such as beers or soft drinks—found in the human diet that have been tested by Coors during the last five years. Coors leaves no stone unturned in its efforts to produce the finest and purest beer that can be brewed

Coors believes

- in the dignity of its employees

- that no resource is more important than its own employees

- in freedom of choice and the right to exercise that freedom

For more information write

Director of Corporate Communications

Adolph Coors Company
Dept 802
Golden Colorado 80401

Coors

Adolph Coors Company
Golden Colorado 80401

January 1982

Decide on the basis of fact . . not fiction!

Decide on the basis of fact . . not fiction!

The facts about labor relations

- In December 1978 following a 20-month strike Coors brewery workers voted by a margin of more than 2 to 1 (71% to 29%) to decertify Brewery Workers Local 366

- Until the walkout of 1977 the brewery had been strike-free for 20 years

- During the strike union officials never enjoyed the support of their own membership. More than 70% of those who left their jobs returned to work during the strike. Some never left at all

The facts about employee relations

- The average annual income in 1980 of a Coors production and maintenance worker on universal shift was $24,300. Coors consistently pays higher than average wages for the region

- Coors in addition to its stated fair hiring practices includes language in its equal opportunity policy prohibiting job discrimination due to sexual preference

- Polygraph tests initiated for security reasons are required only of job applicants as part of a pre-employment screening process. Independent firms administer the tests and ask only job related questions. No questions about sexual background or preference are asked. The polygraph tests are used ONLY in the pre-employment phase and are never required by the company for any other purpose

- More than 40,000 unsolicited applications for employment are received by Coors every year

- Coors recognizes the dignity of all its employees and recognizes them as its most important resource

The facts on affirmative action

- Coors has one of the best, if not the best, affirmative action programs of any major company in the region

- Coors has been certified as an equal opportunity employer by the United States government since 1972

- Coors contributes money and time to many organizations for the advancement of women and minorities, including NAACP, Latin American Educational Foundation, Better Jobs for Women Association, United Negro College Fund, League of United Latin American Citizens and the G I Forum

- Coors has minorities and women on its senior management team, and nine distributorships are owned by Hispanic Americans

- No court of law has ever found Adolph Coors Company guilty of an alleged discrimination charge

In 1982, producer Allan Maraynes and his staff from the television program "60 Minutes" visited Coors to investigate allegations made by the AFL–CIO that the company was still discriminating against minorities. The union also accused Coors of mistreating its employees and using its lie detector tests to pry into the private lives of potential employees.

In an interview with reporter Mike Wallace of "60 Minutes," Bill Coors claimed that the union's allegations were not valid and offered to pay anyone $10,000 if they could prove the allegations were true. He also offered to open the company's files to anyone who wanted to investigate the union's charges.

In the "60 Minutes" investigation of the union's charges, they discovered that in 1982 the Equal Employment Opportunities Commission considered Coors one of the leading affirmative action employers in Colorado. Coors had also invited gay journalists to visit its plant. The journalists concluded that there was no foundation for continuing a boycott of Coors's products on the issue of homosexuality. "60 Minutes" also discovered that many minority groups had dropped their boycott against Coors and had cited the company as a leader in minority hiring. One minority organization, the League of Latin American Citizens (LULAC), even planned to hold a testimonial dinner in praise of Coors's policies. In interviews with Coors's employees, "60 Minutes" found their morale to be very high and there was no evidence that they were being mistreated.

"60 Minutes" also interviewed AFL–CIO spokesperson David Seigler. Seigler stated that Coors was a "corporate bully" and called the praise Coors was receiving "disgusting." Seigler claimed the only reason Coors was being praised was because the company was contributing large sums of money to certain minority groups. Despite the positive publicity Coors received from the "60 Minutes" broadcast, hard feelings still lingered on between Coors and a number of minority groups. In early 1983, Coors's expansion into new markets was met by criticism from various local minority groups.

The events of 1977 and their aftermath caused some disagreement among the family members in regard to what should be emphasized in the company's advertising. Bill Coors believed the company should direct its advertising efforts toward righting what he saw as a "wronged" corporate image. Pete Coors favored a straightforward advertising strategy that stressed the quality of the company's product and price promotions. This resulted in a mixed advertising campaign in which Coors "sold a little bit of itself and a little beer instead of putting forth a massive unified advertising effort,"[11] according to an industry analyst.

Some industry observers argued that Coors's troubles indicated problems within Coors itself. Many saw the company caught in the painful transition from being a traditional family-dominated concern to becoming a sophisticated competitor. Bill Coors acknowledged, "We're on the learning curve to find out what works and what doesn't."[12]

---

[11] "Capsule Comments on America's Brewers," *Beverage World,* October 1982, p. 33.
[12] "Coors Beer Stumbles."

Coors's competitors said rough times were likely to continue until Coors decided where it would concentrate its efforts and resources. Said one competitor, "Every time they have tried to do something on the positive side to improve their image, they have either put their foot in their mouth or stepped on their own feet."[13]

The next few years at Coors would be crucial to its long-term strategy. Industry expert Bob Weinberg was unsure of where that would lead: "Coors baffles me because they're playing the game with their money . . . . I'm not sure they understand planning. I think that for a long time Coors's philosophy had been, 'We make a little beer. If we sell it, we make a little more.' Coors can still engineer a turnaround, but this will require a highly innovative strategy."[14]

---

[13] "Coors Eats Dust as the Giants Battle," *Business Week,* July 20, 1981.

[14] "Capsule Comments on America's Brewers."

Massachusetts Mutual Life Insurance Company

On April 14, 1982, the sprawling, campuslike corporate headquarters of the Massachusetts Mutual Life Insurance Company in Springfield, Massachusetts, hosted the company's annual meeting. Normally, only 200 policyholders or so would attend, but on this occasion more than 1,200 were present. The attraction was a contest between a slate of incumbent directors and a group of dissident policyholders who were seeking election to the board of directors. The contest was described by *The Wall Street Journal* as "the first big proxy fight in the mutual insurance" industry.

COMPANY BACKGROUND

The company was founded in May 1851, by George W. Rice, an agent for the Connecticut Mutual of Hartford. Operations began on August 1, 1851, in Springfield. The company was originally founded as a stock company, but in 1867 it became a mutual by retiring its capital stock and establishing the policyholders as owners.

In a mutual company, the policyholders theoretically own the company and control the management; in practice, this was true only to a limited extent. Policyholders' control of a mutual company was limited because (1) policyholders were numerous, (2) they were widely scattered geographically, (3) communication was minimal, (4) the stake of each policyholder in the company was small, and (5) many policyholders did not understand the nature of a mutual or their rights as policyholders. Insurance companies were exempt from federal antitrust laws and mutuals did not face the strictures of the Securities and Exchange Commission. Thus, the complacency of policyholders vis-à-vis their ownership rights left management with considerable latitude in conducting the affairs of mutual companies.

After completing 130 years of business, Massachusetts Mutual was the seventh largest mutual life insurance company in the nation in terms of total assets and total life insurance in force. According to *Fortune* magazine, Massachusetts Mutual ranked 74th in the top 500 U.S. corporations by total assets. The company was the 11th largest life insurance company in the United States in 1981. The A. M. Best Company, insurance industry analysts, had rated Massachusetts Mutual an A+ (excellent). According to Best, "It is purely mutual and is particularly a policyholders' institution." They continued to praise the company by adding that "it has been most ably managed and enjoys a most excellent reputation in all areas of its activities."

In 1981, the insurance industry within which Massachusetts Mutual participated had a total income of approximately $261.7 billion. Stock companies numbered 1,279 in 1981 with total income of $174.7 billion or nearly 67 percent of the industry total (see Exhibit 1). Mutual companies numbered only 129 but accounted for 33 percent of the industry total. Traditionally, companies were also classified by product line. Life/health companies accounted for 58 percent of the industry income, and property/casualty companies (auto, homeowners, and liability) were responsible for the remainder.

Massachusetts Mutual Life Insurance Company offered a complete line of ordinary life, individual annuity, and pension trust plans, as well as group life, fixed and variable annuities, pension trusts, and accident and health coverage. The company had over 4,000 agents and 6,000 employees to serve policyholders in 50 states and the District of Columbia. Business was conducted through 114 general agencies, 828 district offices, 42 group insurance offices, 20 group pension offices, and 7 regional real estate investment offices. The company had formed several investment companies in order to expand into additional financial-related areas. In the last decade, Massachusetts Mutual had also set up several wholly owned subsidiaries.

Although the insurance industry faced numerous environmental challenges in 1981, the company's total assets grew from $9 billion to $10 billion. At year-end, total premium income was $1.5 billion, and total investment income was $670 million. Life insurance in force was over $50 billion during this same period, as compared with $3 billion in 1950. Over 1.8 million policyholders were insured in 1981. Massachusetts Mutual's year-end investment portfolio totaled $7.8 billion (financial statements are provided in Exhibits 2 and 3).

According to James R. Martin, chairman of the board, the company's mission was, "to provide the maximum amount of personal financial security

EXHIBIT 1 Insurance Industry Income, 1981 ($ billions)

	Mutual	Stock	Total
Life/health	$59.3	$ 91.8	$151.1
Property/casualty	27.7	82.9	110.6
	$87.0	$174.7	$261.7

SOURCE: *Best's Aggregates and Averages* (Oldwick, N.J.: A. M. Best Company, 1982).

EXHIBIT 2

MASSACHUSETTS MUTUAL LIFE INSURANCE COMPANY
Statement of Financial Condition
As of December 31, 1981
(millions of dollars)

Assets

Securities:	
Bonds	$ 3,196.7
Preferred stocks	63.6
Common stocks	142.8
Mortgage loans	2,917.6
Real estate:	
Investment	114.0
Other	84.8
Other investments	72.9
Policy loans	2,202.2
Cash and short-term investments	173.7
Investment income due and accrued	168.9
Premiums due or deferred	269.9
Reinsurance amounts recoverable	138.7
Separate account assets	465.2
Other	11.2
Total assets	$10,022.2

Reserves and Liabilities

Policyholders' reserves and funds:	
Life and annuity	$ 7,626.2
Accident and health	95.4
Installment settlements	94.9
Dividend accumulations	200.2
Policy claims in process of settlement	33.1
Policyholders' dividends	290.7
Premiums deposited in advance	162.0
Federal income taxes	146.8
Liability for benefits for employees and agents	87.0
Mandatory securities valuation reserve	50.3
Notes payable with interest accrued	93.7
Separate account reserves and liabilities	464.6
Other	118.1
Total reserves and liabilities	9,463.0

Contingency Reserves

Required	15.5
Voluntary	16.7
General	527.0
Total contingency reserves	559.2
Total reserves, liabilities, and contingency reserves	$10,022.2

SOURCE: Annual report, 1981.

EXHIBIT 3

MASSACHUSETTS MUTUAL LIFE INSURANCE COMPANY
Summary of Operations
Year Ended December 31, 1981
(millions of dollars)

Revenue:

Premium income	$1,546.7
Net investment and other income	745.0
Total income	2,291.7

Disposition of revenue:

Cost of insurance

Policy benefits and payments	897.2
Increase in policyholders' reserves and funds	621.3
Total cost of insurance	1,518.5
Margin	773.2

Cost of operations:

Expenses	163.5
Commissions	122.1
Taxes	139.0
Total cost of operations	424.6
Net gain before dividends	348.6
Dividends	271.1
Net gain from operations	$ 77.5

SOURCE: Annual report, 1981.

at the lowest possible cost while maintaining high-quality service and safeguarding our ability to fulfill our obligations." Being a "policyholders' institution" was the guiding force at Massachusetts Mutual. A strong emphasis on service was exemplified by the fact that claim checks were processed on the day following the receipt of the paperwork for more than 99 percent of death claims. New policies were issued within 12 working days, as compared with an industry average of 30 days. A network of agency computer terminals linked directly to the company's home office facilitated "instant service" and accurate information. This concern for the policyholder was extended to both new and old policyholders. Except where forbidden by law, all important benefits and privileges that the company gave to new policyholders were also given to old policyholders on the same terms. Retroactive benefits had been granted to give new rights that were not in the original policy.

HERBERT GEIST AND THE POLICYHOLDERS COMMITTEE

One of the best paid and most successful members of the company's sales organization was Herbert Geist, a Chicago-based general agent. A member of the Massachusetts Mutual team for 25 years, he was one of the most successful agents in the company's history. For example, he received the Presidential Award, presented for having $1 million or more in policy sales, six times during his career.

Herb Geist's success could be traced to his strong personal style and keen interest in the welfare of his clients. A highly personable individual, Geist worked long hours and made a practice of staying in close contact with his clients. One of the reasons he was so enthusiastic about and loyal to Massachusetts Mutual was because it was operated solely for the benefit of its policyholders. Geist believed that

> It is the moral duty of a mutual life insurance company to take care of policyholders. The sole purpose of a mutual is to provide life insurance at the lowest possible cost. A mutual company has a sacred duty to eliminate profit margins and provide insurance at cost. There is no other reason for their existence.[1]

Geist became concerned that management had lost sight of the difference between a mutual company and a stock company. The problem was that management did not differentiate their role as a mutual, but instead followed practices found in stock life insurance companies: high executive salaries, elaborate corporate offices, multiple layers of management, large charitable contributions, and a clublike board of directors (some of whom had financial dealings with the company). Much of this ran counter to Geist's belief that a mutual company should minimize its costs and maximize its dividends to policyholders.

Tension between Herb Geist and the home office over policyholder rights was heightened in the late 1970s when the company issued a directive to general agents requiring them to discourage policyholders from borrowing against their policies. As noted above, insurance companies and other organizations offering financial services during this period faced a number of environmental challenges. Inflation was at record levels, interest rates soared, competition between different types of financial services intensified, and people sought new ways to protect their assets. One result was that owners of whole-life policies began in record numbers to exercise their rights to borrow against the cash value of their policies. These funds typically could be borrowed at 5 to 6 percent interest and invested in treasury bills or other instru-

---

[1] Personal interview with Herbert Geist, May 2, 1983.

ments at 2 to 3 times those rates. Life insurance companies were faced with loaning millions of dollars to policyholders at rates well below what those funds could earn as part of the company's investment portfolio.

Geist refused to tell his clients not to take out loans. He felt it made economic sense to borrow at the low interest rates. Indeed, one such policyholder was his wife, Millicent Geist, who borrowed $230,000 against her $1.5 million policy.

Two weeks after Mrs. Geist took out the loan, Massachusetts Mutual's vice president of agency visited Geist and asked him to resign. Geist refused and his contract as general agent was terminated immediately. Geist felt that, although the company had the legal right to terminate a general agent at will and without cause, his 25 years of service merited better treatment. Subsequently, he traveled to Springfield, negotiated a settlement, and resigned his agency.[2]

In April of 1981, the Geists attended their first annual meeting of Massachusetts Mutual policyholders. In preparation for the meeting, Herb Geist visited the office of the Illinois Insurance Commission and reviewed the annual report that the company filed with the Commission. It was the first time he had done so, and he did not like what he saw. For example, he found that the chairman of the board's income had increased in one year from $301,041 to $414,386. The report offered no explanation. Geist became all the more convinced that Massachusetts Mutual was being run for the benefit of its management, not its policyholders.

While at the annual meeting, Geist talked with some of the other policyholders about his concerns. He did not raise any questions publicly, but a number of people at the meeting with whom he talked privately said they were concerned about the welfare of the company and its policyholders. Shortly thereafter, Geist organized the Massachusetts Mutual's Policyholders Committee to explore the possibility of electing a slate of directors to the board.

IN SEARCH OF OBSTACLES

On May 28, 1981, James Martin wrote the following memorandum to A. Peter Quinn, Jr., Massachusetts Mutual's executive vice president and general counsel:

> At a recent Executive Committee Meeting [of the board of directors], Bob Mueller [outside board member and president of Arthur D. Little, Inc.] asked that we "review the obstacles that can be placed in the path of those attempting to run Mass. Mutual Director candidates who are not recommended by the Committee on Organization and Operations of the Board." He mentioned that he was thinking, of course, only in terms of those obstacles that would be legal and ethical.

---

2 Mrs. Geist filed suit on September 17, 1980, against seven officers of the company, claiming damages of $10 million for emotional distress related to her husband's termination.

This would relate to our discussions on proxies but would also pertain to the possibility of amending Bylaws so as to increase the number of nominating signatures required, etc. Please let me have your views.

In his June 5 response to the chairman's inquiry, Quinn explained that

Under existing law and our bylaws, there are several obstacles. They are as follows:

1. The directors are divided into four classes so that only one class comes up for election each year.
2. Any candidate for board membership must be a member of the Company as a life insurance policyholder or annuity contract holder.
3. Candidates must be nominated in writing by no less than 100 members of the Company, and the written nomination must be filed at least 60 days before the date of the annual meeting.
4. No member, regardless of the amount of insurance on his life, may cast more than 20 votes.
5. Group policyholders are entitled to only one vote, regardless of the number of employees insured under the group contract.
6. While members may vote by proxy, any proxies must be submitted within three months before the meeting at which it is to be voted and must be returned and recorded on the books of the Company seven days or more before such meeting. The person holding the proxy must appear in person at the meeting and may not be a Company officer.

Quinn's response was not satisfactory. On June 23, Martin sent the following memo to the general counsel:

Thank you for your June 5 memo regarding the inquiry made by Bob Mueller. However, the items you have listed do not respond to his question.

Bob wanted to know specifically what other steps could be taken to make it more difficult for dissident outsiders to nominate and elect a Director. It is important that we have a list of these steps and the reasons we have rejected them or that we are considering them.

Quinn then turned the matter over to Thomas J. Finnigan, Jr., second vice president, secretary, and associate general counsel. Finnegan's July 1, 1981, memorandum outlined eight steps.

This responds to your memorandum of June 29 in which you requested a list of steps which we might take in order to make it more difficult for dissident members to nominate and elect an outside director. I have the following items to suggest.

Nomination

1. Increase the number of members necessary to nominate a director other than one nominated by the Committee on Organization and Operations of the Board, either by increasing that number above the present number of 100 or by requiring a percentage of the company's policyholders rather than an absolute number. This, of course, is a procedure which we have been considering for some

time, and I assume that we will take steps to amend the bylaws at the next annual meeting in order to accomplish this.

2. To require the filing of nominations earlier than the present 60-day requirement found in the bylaws. This suggestion has little more than nuisance value, and would not be difficult to overcome by any group determined to make a nomination.

Election

1. Amend the law relative to proxy solicitation, either by eliminating the prohibition against the solicitation of proxies by company management or by limiting the number of votes which a member may cast at any meeting of the company either by himself or as a proxy. In view of our work on this matter, I feel that little discussion is necessary.

2. Assuming no change in the proxy laws, consider the adoption of the procedure apparently used by Boston-Arkwright whereby proxies were solicited by the corporate secretary on order of the board of directors. You will recall that Dick Baker, who advised me of this procedure, indicated that Boston-Arkwright had had this procedure "blessed" by the Massachusetts Insurance Department.

3. Assuming no change in the proxy laws, consider the adoption of a ballot procedure similar to that used by State Mutual. You will recall that we both have a question as to whether this procedure is in fact permitted by Section 94. If we are to decide to adopt such a procedure, it would no doubt give us more protection against the election of outside directors than we presently have, but would require us to include on the ballot any outside nominees. In addition, the company would have to remain "neutral" in distributing the ballot to its members and could not engage in any solicitation on behalf of its candidates.

4. Require the filing of proxies with the corporate secretary at a point in time earlier than the seven days which the bylaws presently require. In this regard, Section 94 merely states that proxies must be filed "seven days or more" before the meeting at which they are to be used. Again, this suggestion has little more to offer than nuisance value.

5. Require that a vote greater than a majority be required in order to elect a director. For instance, we might amend the bylaws to require that directors be elected by a two-thirds vote similar to the percentage required to amend the bylaws. Although I do not know of any company which requires more than a majority vote for the election of its directors, a preliminary review of the Massachusetts laws does not indicate that such a requirement is prohibited.

6. Assure that there are sufficient management nominees at each annual meeting to fill all vacancies then existing on the board. As we discussed, if management continues to nominate less than the permitted number of directors the possibility exists that both its nominees and any outside nominee could both be elected by the members.

While the exchange of memos was taking place, chairman Martin met with Massachusetts's governor Edward King and indicated that changes needed to be made in the state law that prohibited the solicitation of proxies by the management of mutual insurance companies. He explained to the governor that a change in the law would represent a significant step in the direction of democracy in the management of company affairs. Governor King responded positively, and Martin asked Quinn to draft the bill to be introduced to the legislature. The bill, which allowed mutual companies' management to solicit proxies, was passed by the legislature and signed by the governor on July 30, 1981. According to Quinn, "before the enactment of this legislation, the company was placed in the position . . . where a third party could solicit proxies to his heart's content, while at the same time the corporate officers [could not], and that represented a substantial disadvantage and vulnerability to the stability of the company."[3]

The next step in the company's campaign to create obstacles for dissident policyholders was to amend Massachusetts Mutual's bylaws. Two changes for this purpose were needed. First, it was necessary to eliminate the bylaw provision prohibiting officers from soliciting proxies. Second, a change in the provision governing the nomination of directors by policyholders was needed. In addition to nominations of directors by the board's Committee on Organization and Operations, the bylaws provided for nominations by 100 members' signatures. It was proposed to change that requirement to 1/10 of 1 percent of members, or about 1,000 signatures.

Although policyholders were guaranteed the right to vote at all meetings of the company, notice of the first emergency meeting in the history of the company was limited to an employee newsletter and a one-inch advertisement in the legal notices section of the Springfield *Daily News*. In testifying on this topic subsequently, James Martin was asked by Judge Susan Getzendanner[4]:

> Mr. Martin, does it concern you at all, as the chairman of this company, that you published that notice and, in effect, gave notice to no one?

Martin answered:

> In these things, your Honor, I rely on our general counsel to advise me if I am acting properly. In this case, I would expect him to advise me if I was acting improperly.

Some 165 policyholders attended the special meeting on November 18, 1981. Most of those in attendance were Massachusetts Mutual employees. The proposed amendments to the bylaws were adopted.

Neither Herbert Geist nor any other members of the Massachusetts Mutual's Policyholders Committee were aware of the changes in the bylaws. On February 8, 1982, Geist and five associates submitted to the secretary of the company their nomination papers with 139 signatures (see Exhibit 4 for the slate of nominees). The next day they were informed by Thomas Finnigan that the 139 signatures were insufficient under the amended bylaws.

---

[3] *William C. Stein et al.* v. *Massachusetts Mutual Life Insurance Company,* United States District Court for Northern Illinois, March 10, 1982, p. 136.

[4] Ibid., p. 66.

EXHIBIT 4   Slate of Nominees Proposed by Massachusetts Mutual's Policyholders
Committee

We apologize for making this request, but we have conducted this effort for policyholders at our expense.

If you feel it is appropriate, please include $1 or any other sum you wish in
order to help fund this cause. Make checks payable to the Policyholders Committee.

WHETHER YOU CONTRIBUTE OR NOT, PLEASE HELP US BY RETURN-
ING YOUR PROXY IMMEDIATELY, AS YOUR PROXY MUST BE IN OUR
HANDS BY APRIL 5, 1982.

PROPOSED DIRECTORS TO BE ELECTED FOR FOUR YEARS

Mr. James R. Frankel of Highland Park, Illinois	Senior Partner of law firm of Frankel, McKay & Orlikoff.
Mr. Herbert Geist of Lake Forest, Illinois	Former General Agent Mass. Mutual. Builder of one of the Company's most successful agencies. Winner of Company's top agency award six times in 25 years. Chartered Life Underwriter, Estate Planner.
Mr. Thomas Gibson of Oakbrook, Illinois	Long-time policyholder of Mass. Mutual. President of Gibson Electric Company.
Mr. Robert Gilbert Johnston of McHenry, Illinois	Professor of Law. John Marshall Law School.
Mr. David Rutenberg of Chicago, Illinois	Long-time Mass. Mutual policyholder. Prominent Chicago Attorney.
Mr. William C. Stein of Oakbrook, Illinois	CPA, MBA, Head of Wm. C. Stein Company, Accountants. Professor of Business Administration, Benedictine College. Chairman, West Alloy Corp. Chairman, Kewanee Boilers.

LITIGATION

Herbert Geist and the other five members of his directors' slate filed an
action on February 19, 1982, in the United States District Court for the
Northern District of Illinois entitled *Stein* v. *Massachusetts Mutual Life Insurance Company*. The plaintiffs asked that (1) the bylaw amendments of
November 18, 1981, be invalidated; (2) their names be placed on the ballot as
nominees for the board; and (3) company directors, officers, employees, general
agents, and agents be prohibited from soliciting proxies.

A day-long hearing was held on March 11 before Judge Susan Getzendanner. Both James Martin and Peter Quinn were called to testify. They denied
having any knowledge of the Massachusetts Mutual's Policyholders Commit-

tee or their slate of directors until January 20, 1982. They claimed that their actions with respect to changing the Massachusetts law as well as their bylaws were designed to improve the democratic processes of the company and to assure greater stability in the management of the enterprise. They were concerned that a company with long-term commitments such as life insurance benefits could be disrupted by "frivolous" and "nuisance" activities on the part of dissident policyholders. Counsel for Geist and his associates argued that Massachusetts Mutual's management not only was aware of the effort to challenge the company's slate of directors well before January 20, 1982, but that management had panicked in its effort to create obstacles to block any such efforts by Geist or other dissatisfied policyholders. Why else would the company have acted to change a 36-year-old state law? Why else would management have convened the first special meeting of policyholders in the company's history? Why else would the company have failed to notify a larger percentage of its over one million policyholders? Counsel for Geist and his associates claimed that the company officers breached their "fiduciary duty of treating all members equally."

On March 12 Judge Getzendanner ruled that the notice of the special meeting was inadequate. She required the company to place the Geist slate of directors on the ballot. Officers of the company were prohibited from soliciting proxies for that meeting. Other members, however, including directors, general agents, agents, and other policyholders were permitted to solicit proxies for the April 14, 1982, meeting. A proxy solicitation previously sent by management to policyholders was invalidated. Her order also established guidelines for the conduct of a future special meeting to be held for the purpose of amending company bylaws.

THE END OF THE STRUGGLE

Following this courtroom victory, the Massachusetts Mutual's Policyholders Committee intensified its solicitation of proxies (see Exhibit 5). Perhaps for the first time, the "dissidents" began to feel that they had a chance for victory.

The directors of the company, however, launched a major effort to reach policyholders and to solicit their proxies. Under the heading "CAUTION" the incumbent directors' proxy statement warned policyholders:

> You should be aware that Herbert Geist, an ex-general agent for the company, has threatened a disruptive proxy contest by seeking your support to elect himself and his five dissident nominees as Directors of Massachusetts Mutual Life Insurance Company . . . . Consider for yourself whether Geist and his nominees, if elected, can work in harmony with the remaining members of your Board. *Consider for yourself whether a Board consisting of different factions can continue to effectively manage over $10 billion in assets for the continued benefit and protection of our policyholders* (see Exhibit 6 for a list of the nominees for reelection as well as continuing directors).

EXHIBIT 5

MASSACHUSETTS MUTUAL'S POLICYHOLDERS COMMITTEE

Dear Mass Mutual Policyholder:

As you know, a Mutual Life Insurance Company is owned by its policyholders and its sole function is to provide insurance for them at the lowest possible cost. *Mass Mutual's 1980 financial statement indicates that dividends could possibly have been 35% to 40% higher than they were, which could have resulted in substantial reductions in insurance costs.*

As fellow policyholders and owners, we share a common interest in having the Company managed for our maximum benefit. The only way this will be accomplished is if we have representation on the Board of Directors.

The "Policyholders Committee" has been formed to achieve this goal, but we cannot succeed without your help.

WE NEED YOUR PROXY NOW. This may be your only opportunity to elect directors who share your interest.

The conflict between the interests of management and policyholders is clearly stated in the following quotes from the United States General Accounting Office report to Congress dated September 7, 1981: (Page 150)

Voting rights of policyholders

"Many life companies have accumulated large amounts of surplus, a portion of which could be paid out in the form of increased dividends. Typically, policyholders would be expected to unseat management and elect officers who would favor increasing dividends, but such activities have been conspicuously absent. This inactivity has been particularly surprising during recent periods when returns to policyholders on the savings element of life insurance policies have lagged substantially below those available elsewhere in economy. The explanation for this lack of activity may be attributed to the following conditions:

☐ the large number of policyholders, even in a medium-size mutual;

☐ the limited opportunities for communication among policyholders;

☐ the wide geographic dispersion of the policyholders;

☐ the limited stake of each policyholder in the aggregate assets of the insured; and

☐ the general lack of awareness among policyholders of their legal right to vote in elections of directors.

The enclosures present some important information about the Company's operations and the directors we hope to elect.

Please return the proxy and nomination in the enclosed self-addressed envelope. *BE SURE TO SIGN BOTH FORMS.*

If you have questions, feel free to call any of us. (312) 726-8866

Mr. James R. Frankel	Mr. Herbert Geist	Mr. Thomas Gibson	Mr. Robert Gilbert Johnston
	Mr. David Ruttenberg	Mr. William C. Stein	

EXHIBIT 5   *(concluded)*

**FACTS FROM MASSACHUSETTS MUTUAL'S
1980 FINANCIAL STATEMENT**

Company Income	$1,959,271,184
Gain from Operations	432,883,949
Dividends to Policyholders	259,911,472
Death Benefits Paid	162,899,719
Net Gain from Operations after Dividends to Policyholders	172,972,477
Federal Income Tax	107,906,764
Addition to Surplus	65,065,713

The purpose of a Mutual Life Insurance Company is *to provide insurance at the lowest possible cost.* It is not organized for profit. Excess premiums, interest earnings and savings from operation are to be returned to the policyholders as dividends.

ALLOCATION OF POLICYHOLDERS MONEY

Question: Why pay income taxes of $107,906,764 rather than increased dividends?

Question: Why add $65,065,713 to Company surplus, which will never revert to policyholders, rather than increasing dividends?

GENERAL EXPENSES OF THE COMPANY $149,301,210

Question: Why does it cost 92% of the amount paid as Death Benefits to run the Company?

Question: Why does the Company need two Executive Helicopters with crew, when less costly transportation is available?

Question: Why has Company embarked upon an expensive District Manager plan to increase sales which does not reduce cost of insurance for present policyholders?

Question: How many millions of policyholder dollars were lost financially supporting unsuccessful agents?

Question: Why does the Company require over 20 sales executives in the Home Office?

Question: Why was the income of the Chairman of the Board, who is semi-retired, increased in one year from $301,041 to $414,386?

Question: Why was $6,000,000 of policyholders money donated to charities, primarily in Massachusetts?

Question: How did policyholders benefit from the $67,000,000 investment in the unsuccessful venture known as Bay State West, whose primary objective was the rehabilitation of the business center of Springfield, Massachusetts?

These and other questions have been posed to the Company and have been ignored or inadequately answered.

Policyholders are entitled to answers to these and many more questions. There will be no answers unless policyholders interested in the basic aims of a mutual life insurance company are present on the Board of Directors.

Please sign the enclosed proxy and endorsement of directors.

EXHIBIT 6 Board of Directors of the Massachusetts Mutual Life Insurance Company

ROBERT B. ATKINSON
Partner
Bulkley, Richardson & Gelinas
Attorneys at Law
Springfield, Massachusetts

FLOYD A. BOND
Dean Emeritus and Grad-Distinguished
Professor of Business Economics
Graduate School of Business Adm.
The University of Michigan
Ann Arbor, Michigan

H. R. BRIGHT
Chairman of the Board
East Texas Motor Freight Lines, Inc.
Dallas, Texas

*WILSON BRUNEL
Chairman of the Board
Third National Bank
of Hampden County
Springfield, Massachusetts

JAMES F. CALVERT
Vice President, Operations
Combustion Engineering, Inc.
Stamford, Connecticut

WILLIAM J. CLARK
President and Chief Executive Officer

RICHARD N. FRANK
President
Lawry's Foods, Inc.
Los Angeles, California

*ROBERT J. GAUDRAULT
Retired Chairman of the Board
Friendly Ice Cream Corp.
Wilbraham, Massachusetts

WILLIAM N. GRIGGS
Senior Vice President and Economist
J. Henry Schroder Bank & Trust Co.
New York, New York

PAUL HALLINGBY, JR.
General Partner
Bear, Steams & Co.
New York, New York

*BARBARA A. HAUPTFUHRER
Director of various operations
Huntingdon Valley, Pennsylvania

J. BERKLEY INGRAM, JR.
Vice Chairman

MAURICE LAZARUS
Chairman of the Finance Committee
Federated Department Stores, Inc.
Boston, Massachusetts

*SHELDON B. LUBAR
President
Lubar & Co. Incorporated
Milwaukee, Wisconsin

DONALD F. McCULLOUGH
Chairman and Chief Executive Officer and
    President
Collins & Aikman Corp.
New York, New York

JAMES R. MARTIN
Chairman of the Board

ROBERT K. MUELLER
Chairman of the Board
Arthur D. Little, Inc.
Cambridge, Massachusetts

*BARBARA W. NEWELL
Chancellor of the State
    University System
Tallahassee, Florida

BERT E. PHILLIPS
Chairman of the Board
Clark Equipment Co.
Buchanan, Michigan

PHILIP A. SINGLETON
President
Singleton Associates International
Amherst, Massachusetts

*ALBERT E. STEIGER, JR.
President
Albert Steiger, Inc.
Springfield, Massachusetts

JOHN F. WATLINGTON, JR.
Chairman of the Executive Committee
Wachovia Bank & Trust Co., N.A. and The
    Wachovia Corporation
Winston-Salem, North Carolina

* Incumbent directors elected at annual meeting held on April 14, 1982.

EXHIBIT 7 Letter Sent by Massachusetts Mutual to Policyholders following 1982 Annual Meeting

April 15, 1982

Dear Policyholder:

Not long ago, you received requests for your proxy to vote at the Massachusetts Mutual Life Insurance Company's Annual Meeting of Policyholders which was held here yesterday afternoon. We wanted to let you know as soon as possible about the results of the meeting. Your six incumbent directors, men and women of proven service to your Company and of national reputation, were reelected to the 22-member Board by wide margins.

Six nominees from the Chicago area, led by a former General Agent of the Company, had opposed the election of the incumbents and were soundly defeated. In their proxy solicitations, these individuals raised certain questions implying poor management practices on the part of Company officers. The record shows these questions contain inaccurate information and the implications are simply not justified. Unfortunately, officers of the Company could not answer these charges because we were prohibited by federal court order from participating in the proxy solicitation process and, therefore, were unable to communicate with you.

Now that the election has been held, the prohibition no longer applies. Accordingly, we are preparing a comprehensive report for you which answers every one of these questions and details the effectivness of your Company's management practices, philosophy and performance. The report will be completed and distributed to you early next month. We are doing this because we believe that it is vital for you to know why we are considered by industry experts to be the Policyholders' Company. Let us say, for now, that A. M. Best Company, the respected industry analyst, has consistently given Mass Mutual and its management its highest rating - - "A+ (Excellent)."

A substantial majority of you supported the reelection of the six incumbent directors. We extend our sincere thanks to you. Let us assure you that Mass Mutual will continue to offer the finest service and most secure insurance protection available.

Sincerely,

James R. Martin
Chairman

William J. Clark
President

At the April 14 meeting, Herb Geist and his associates were defeated by a 2-to-1 margin. The six incumbent directors were reelected by a vote of 560,300 to 265,200. The following day the company sent a letter (see Exhibit 7) to all policyholders announcing the results. On April 30, a 14-page booklet was mailed to all policyholders presenting management's view of the controversy (excerpts are provided in Exhibit 8).

EXHIBIT 8   Massachusetts Mutual's Response to Questions Posed by Dissident Policyholders, April 30, 1982

These questions were contained in proxy material sent out by a group of policyholders made up of the former General Agent and five of his associates. The questions are designed to raise doubt about the management of the Company. Our answers should remove any doubt about whether this is a well-managed, cost-conscious Company.

Q. Why pay income taxes of $107,906,764, rather than increased dividends?
A. The income tax figure is incorrect. *In fact, the Company reported in its federal income tax return and paid income taxes of $72,399,248 for the year 1980.*

This question also incorrectly assumes that all policyholder dividends are deductible in computing our federal taxes—this is not so.

Current law imposes a limit on the amount of policyholder dividends that are deductible, and our dividends for 1980 far exceeded that limit. Therefore, an increase in dividends for that year would not reduce our federal income tax liability by a single dollar.

Q. Why add $65,065,713 to Company surplus, which will never revert to policyholders, rather than increasing dividends?
A. The $65 million is the margin remaining after paying out $1 billion 124 million in policyholder benefits and dividends.

The $65 million addition to *surplus (or "contingency reserve") is the margin needed to assure that the Company can meet its long-term obligations to policyholders* and beneficiaries. Some of our policy contracts will still be in force 50 years from now; and, in most instances, these are contracts which form the primary basis of the future security of families and businesses. Each of these rely absolutely on our ability to perform over the long-term future, no matter what contingencies occur: depression, high interest rates, wars, or other calamities.

Our present surplus amounted to 5.61 percent of total assets at the end of 1981. Experienced management and our Board of Directors feel this is the correct amount to provide for future safety, and a lesser amount would expose the Company to unnecessary risks.

A recent survey of 18 of the top mutual life companies revealed an average ratio of surplus to total assets for 1981 of 5.31 percent, with the lowest company ratio being 3.3 percent and the highest 7.91 percent. Our Company's position falls comfortably within the middle ranges of this survey group.

EXHIBIT 8 *(continued)*

Finally, this *surplus itself will not be lost to policyholders*. Last year, for example, surplus earned almost $50 million pre-tax which was available for added policyholder dividends.

Q. Why does it cost 92 percent of the amount paid as death benefits to run the Company?
A. This question compares apples and oranges and is therefore difficult to answer. The relationship between operating expenses and death claims is neither a recognized nor an appropriate measure of efficiency for a life insurance company.

What this question does do is imply that our expenses are too high and that we do not operate in a cost-effective manner. This implication is totally unjustified, and this can be demonstrated in a number of ways.

First, "Best's Report", a highly regarded, independent rating service, has rated Massachusetts Mutual "A + (Excellent)", its highest rating and further notes that the Company is "particularly a policyholders' institution" and has kept operating expenses "remarkably low."

Second, Conning & Co. of Hartford, Connecticut, a prestigious and well-known member of the New York Stock Exchange has consistently rated Mass. Mutual one of the most cost-efficient companies in the insurance industry. In Conning's yearly analysis of expense results for 1980 for the 40 largest mutual life insurers, Mass. Mutual's expense ratio of 12.3 cents per dollar of premium is fifth lowest and 34 percent better than the median. For 1981, we expect our expense ratio to be 41 percent better than the median of those same 40 companies.

Third, net cost to policyholders is the ultimate measure of operating efficiency. "Best's Review" magazine annually publishes a 20-year historical net cost comparison for Whole Life policies. In recent years, Massachusetts Mutual has ranked second among the largest 25 companies in this study.

These facts speak for themselves. We are recognized in the industry as a cost-effective Company. Even more important, we have a well-deserved reputation as being a Policyholders' Company.

Q. Why does the Company need two Executive Helicopters with crew, when less costly transportation is available?
A. Here again is a question implying Company extravagance; the facts are just the opposite.

Located as we are, 100 miles from Boston and 150 miles from New York, a helicopter has made it possible to visit either city, while avoiding the expense and delay of an overnight stay. Using 1981 figures, a Springfield to New York round trip by commercial airline, plus an overnight stay, costs a minimum of $295. By contrast, using the helicopter, which generally makes overnight stays unnecessary, the cost for this same trip with an average passenger load, is only $147—and this puts no price on employee time saved, which is considerable. In summary, *the helicopter saved the Company time and money.*

Why two helicopters? We need both of them. Even with two helicopters, we can't accommodate all employees who have business reasons to use these aircraft.

EXHIBIT 8   *(continued)*

Consider these figures: In 1981, both helicopters had combined occupied flight mileage of nearly 250,000 miles and carried approximately 2,800 passengers.

The use by different employee groups is particularly significant:

Executive Vice Presidents	2%
All other Vice Presidents	9%
Company Directors	10%
Business Guests	13%
All others, including middle management and clerical employees	66%

This breakdown clearly demonstrates that the term *Executive Helicopter* is an inappropriate description.

Q.   Why has the Company embarked upon an expensive District Manager plan to increase sales which does not reduce cost of insurance for present policyholders?

A.   Development of our District Manager plan represents our response to the rapidly escalating cost of doing business in the nation's largest cities.

Our decision was to grow through District Offices affiliated with existing General Agencies. In fact, we have found it far more economical to place District Managers in territories surrounding urban centers than to hire new General Agents. To date, our District Manager plan has had remarkable success and has already been copied by a number of our strongest competitors.

In 1981, our District Managers accounted for 47 percent of Company growth, 51 percent of new agents hired, and $2.6 billion of new production. The cost per $100 of 1981 new premium generated by a District Office was $18.80, while the cost per $100 of 1981 new premium from all sources was almost $33.00.

The plan has increased sales while decreasing expenses—an unbeatable combination.

Q.   How many millions of policyholder dollars were lost financially supporting unsuccessful agents?

A.   First, it should be noted that our results in developing and retaining successful agents far exceeds industry averages and are the envy of our competitors.

The facts are that over the five-year period between March 1977 and March 1982, we spent $3.7 million for unsuccessful agents under the Career Agents Plan approved by New York State Superintendent of Insurance. Put in perspective, this amounts to $740,000 per year, or $6,000 per agency per year. Each of these figures is only a small fraction of total expenses involved in the operation of a $10 billion corporation.

It would be great if we could pick only winners. Unfortunately, sales ability is difficult, if not impossible, to measure prior to actual performance.

Inescapably, an investment must be made in both successful and unsuccessful agents if a company is to develop and maintain a professional sales organization.

It's interesting to compare our sales organization with the industry using three common measures:

EXHIBIT 8 *(continued)*

	Industry	Massachusetts Mutual
Million Dollar Round Table	1 out of every 6 reps.	1 out of every 3 reps.
Chartered Life Underwriters	1 out of every 5	1 out of 3
National Quality Award	1 out of 10	1 out of 5

These results demonstrate better than words the professionalism of our Field Organization—there is none better.

Q. Why does the Company require over 20 sales executives in the Home Office?

A. Here again is an implication of "too many" with "too much" expense.

Results are more impressive than words, and we have the sales results to back up our need for superior executive talent. Consider these facts:

First, we have 120 General Agencies across the United States, with more than 4,000 Career Agents. This sales force in 1981 sold $9 billion of ordinary insurance, and serviced $41 billion of ordinary insurance in force, representing approximately 1.5 million policies.

Second, we have 85 Group Representatives in 46 Regional Offices throughout the United States to sell and service Group Life and Health Insurance. In 1981, they produced sales totaling $84.5 million of new annualized premium and serviced a total of $516 milion of in-force premium, which covered over 7,500 policyholders and 877,000 certificate holders.

Third, we have 28 Group Pension Sales Associates. They produced $212 million of new pension deposits and serviced over $2 billion of total assets.

Our nationally distributed products and national sales organizations require home office assistance and support in hundreds of different areas. *A selling effort of this magnitude* requires extensive home office support. It is remarkable that we can do it with only the number of sales executives we have.

Q. Why was the income of the Chairman of the Board, who is semiretired, increased in one year from $301,041 to $414,386?

A. Chairman Martin is a *full-time employee* of the Company. His schedule has never been tighter, nor his travel heavier.

Here are the facts regarding his compensation:

Since 1971, Mr. Martin has been deferring income through a deferred compensation plan in use by many others within the Company. In the year in question, 1980, he made a maximum withdrawal under the provisions of the plan of more than half of the salary increase referred to above. The deferred income had been accumulating for nine years. Therefore, *most of the apparent increase was a withdrawal of deferred income, not a salary increase.*

The salaries of the Chairman, the Vice Chairman, and the President are set by the Board of Directors after reviewing salaries of the top executives of other life companies and after comparing annual individual performance with predetermined Company goals.

EXHIBIT 8   *(concluded)*

Q.   Why was $6 million of policyholders' money donated to charities, primarily in Massachusetts?

A.   This question refers to the year 1980. *In fact, our charitable contributions that year were $710,246.*

The Company therefore did not contribute $6 million to charities in 1980. That year we established a $6 million Charitable Trust as the most tax efficient method of making future contributions.

Now—the facts:

The $6 million principal of the Trust is not used to fund contributions. It is only the income generated from the principal that is available for this purpose. The $6 million itself will revert to the Company in September of 1990.

In 1981, total charitable contributions amounted to $734,000. This included a corporate gift of $176,000 to the United Way, and $100,000 in contributions under the Company's Matching Gift Program, a national effort in which Massachusetts Mutual matches employee and agent contributions to colleges and universities located throughout the country. The remaining $458,000 was contributed to various charities.

The charitable gifts made last year represented a modest, but important, expenditure for a $10 billion corporation.

Q.   How did policyholders benefit from the $67,000,000 investment in the unsuccessful venture known as Bay State West, whose primary objective was the rehabilitation of the business center of Springfield, Massachusetts?

A.   Far from being unsuccessful, the hotel/office/retail complex known as Bay State West has proven to be the successful catalyst in the revitalization of Springfield's downtown district, precisely at a time when it was needed most. *The value of our investment—both in terms of dollars and personnel—has clearly been enhanced by this revitalization.*

As the largest private sector employer in Springfield, Massachusetts Mutual is dependent on its ability to attract the most competent personnel to Springfield from other cities and to retain a local work force of the highest caliber.

Today, because of the high degree of success realized by the close partnership between the City's public officials, federal and state government, and leading private businesses like Massachusetts Mutual, Springfield is widely known as a national model for revitalization among medium-sized cities. This has allowed the Company to continue to attract and keep a home office work force second to none in our industry.

Pacific Lumber Company's Last Stand (A)

It was a dark day in New York City in 1985, and the yellow cabs were lined up outside the terminal at John F. Kennedy airport. Julie Robards, an investment analyst for Drum, Whittier, & Drum, passed through Gate 4 as her flight to San Francisco was called. Once in San Francisco, Julie planned to catch a short commuter flight up the coast to Eureka. From there she would drive to the town of Scotia, which is the mill town for the Pacific Lumber Company (Pacific Lumber). She thought of the warm weather of California as compared to dreary New York—not that she would be anywhere near a beach or have time for any sunbathing. Nearly a week of lonely, exhausting financial detective work faced her. Luckily, the seat next to her was empty, and she placed her heavy briefcase there. The briefcase was filled with a small lap computer and information on Pacific Lumber. For the next five hours she would be reviewing information produced by her staff on Pacific Lumber and deciding how to analyze the company.

Drum, Whittier, & Drum and a major client were interested in participating in a takeover attempt of Pacific Lumber by MAXXAM Group Inc. Drexel, Burnham, and Lambert was being asked to finance the takeover, a substantial undertaking involving millions of dollars. Drum, Whittier, & Drum would gain a large commission if the deal went through. However, Drum, Whittier, & Drum prided itself on looking at all angles of a deal, including stakeholder issues. Consequently, along with the traditional financial analyses, Julie was asked to review all stakeholder issues and include them in her "bottom line" analysis and recommendation.

Julie closed her eyes for a moment and thought of a childhood trip she took with her parents through Oregon and California and of driving through Redwood National Forest. She remembered how large and majestic the trees had been and how beautiful the whole area had seemed with the trees and the Pacific Ocean in the background. The beep of the Seat Belt sign being turned on jarred her back into reality to face the magnitude of the task ahead of her.

Julie Robards and Drum, Whittier, & Drum are fictitious and not intended to represent any one person or firm.

She would report on the viability of Pacific Lumber as a takeover candidate, her first big assignment since her promotion to director of the firm's research division. The road up the corporate ladder had taken a lot of sacrifice, but it had had its rewards. There were ample salary and benefits for the 60-hour plus weeks she had put in. But the time demanded by the job had left her with little time for her personal life. With an aggressively repressed sigh, Julie began to focus on the reports in front of her.

This particular investigation had aspects different from most of the cases she had worked on before for Drum, Whittier, & Drum. The client they were investigating Pacific Lumber for was a large institutional investor who was under legislative mandate by its state government to consider social responsibility issues in its investing. Consequently, the issues involved were much more than just profitability and asset ratios, suggesting that Pacific Lumber was an undervalued company. Before Drum, Whittier, & Drum would participate in the acquisition, all significant Pacific Lumber stakeholders would be considered.

Julie decided to start her trip at Scotia rather than at Pacific Lumber's San Francisco headquarters, as a way of avoiding any biases that Pacific Lumber's executive offices might create. Seeing the site first-hand had been a hallmark of her research style. She was not content, as some investment analysts were, in just looking at the numbers and talking to the headquarters people. She insisted on examining the actual plants or production units, often in great detail. Consequently her reports had always had a depth and vividness that led people to depend on her and trust her recommendations. In this case, she also wanted to get an in-depth look at the communities that would be affected by the takeover. Her staff had prepared a series of background reports on the companies and stakeholders involved to which she turned for review.

BACKGROUND REPORT: SCOTIA, CALIFORNIA

Scotia, located about 300 miles north of San Francisco, was a small town with only about 1,200 citizens, most of whom worked for Pacific Lumber. Many were second- and third-generation employees of Pacific Lumber. While other lumber towns died, Scotia had survived and thrived. This was due, in part, to the policies of Pacific Lumber. Although many lumber towns had experienced terrible boom and bust cycles as a direct result of lumber companies' "cut-and-run" attitudes, Pacific Lumber's sustained growth philosophy had smoothed out the peaks and valleys and seemed to have created a long period of prosperity for the region.

BACKGROUND REPORT: PACIFIC LUMBER COMPANY

The Pacific Lumber Company was founded in 1905 and was incorporated in the state of Maine. Three firms—the Pacific Company, the Freshwater Lumber Company, and the former Pacific Lumber Company—merged to create the new Pacific Lumber Company. Pacific Lumber had the reputation of being good to its employees. Workers enjoyed such enviable benefits as annual bonuses and college scholarships for their children. Even after the company went public, its workers still enjoyed the same benefits as before. The company owned about 200,000 acres of redwood forest, its own mill, and its own town.

The history of the lumber industry saw most timber companies ravage the land and leave deserted towns and unemployment behind. In recent years, the old management practices and attitudes had had their greatest impact in the Pacific Northwest. In the past, many West Coast companies were guilty of cutting virgin, "old growth," stands of redwood, whereas Pacific Lumber had its loggers leave certain trees in virgin stands as residuals. Over the past 60 years, those trees had put on a lot of wood, and, in addition, a lot of young growth had developed. This was the major reason why the company had a wide variety of lumber sizes on its land and a steady supply for generations to come.

Much of this land was actually located between two large redwood preserves, Redwood National Park and Humboldt Redwoods State Park. Pacific Lumber had maintained its policy of carefully tending its resources and cutting judiciously so that in theory its supply of lumber would never run out. As a result of this careful planning, Pacific Lumber had tens of thousands of acres it had never logged.

Pacific Lumber's past performance included modernizing its existing mills, not because of performance problems but because of old age. It conducted this mill modernization at the end of 1980 and added the new machinery in a staged project that took a little over a year and that boosted production at a cost of $2.1 million. Pacific Lumber employees actively participated in the mill remodeling and helped put the new mill together. Area manager John Campbell said, "This is a conservative company; we sometimes work at the reverse end of the economic cycle. When the economy is down, we're building sawmills; when the economy is up, we're ready."

Pacific Lumber produced both rough and surfaced redwood lumber, all dried. The company harvested on a continuous yield basis as it had for decades. In addition, Pacific Lumber processed all of the harvest and bought no additional logs from outside suppliers. Production was stable, limited by the amount of annual timber growth. After harvesting and milling, redwood lumber is air-dried for six months to two years, depending on thickness and weather conditions. Then it goes to kilns for 7 to 20 days. All shipments were by truck. The mill had access to the Northwestern Pacific Railroad, but the railroad had been trying to abandon the unprofitable line. Consequently, many shippers in that region had already switched to trucks.

About 15 years ago, the company diversified by designing, manufacturing, and selling gas and plasma cutting and welding equipment. This division has generated 58 percent of Pacific Lumber's net sales and 46 percent of its operating income (see Exhibit 1). Forest products accounted for only 28 percent of sales but half of the company's 1984 income. The company also manufactured special alloy precision castings, and it operated agricultural properties

EXHIBIT 1

The Pacific Lumber Company: Forest Products and Other Products
Balance Sheet years ending December 31st
($000 omitted)

	1987	1986	1985	1984
Assets				
Current Assets:				
Cash	$456	$943	$824	$3,218
Marketable securities	$24,476	$28,587		
Receivables	$12,570	$33,175	$2,796	$6,133
Inventories	$87,646	$82,895	$9,995	$10,033
Assets held for sale	$10,382	$10,480	$19,830	$20,575
Prepaid expenses and other current				
assets	$3,114	$3,699	$14,520	$14,113
Total current assets	$138,644	$159,779	$47,965	$54,072
Property, plant and equipment, net .	$91,004	$68,437	$40,300	$37,054
Timber and timberland, at cost less				
depreciation	$507,827	$532,911	$33,843	$34,086
Deferred financing costs	$17,743	$20,249		
Long-term investments and other				
assets	$11,930	$3,454	$1,838	$1,834
	$767,148	$784,830	$123,946	$127,046
Liabilities				
Current liabilities:				
Accounts payable	$4,219	$4,854	$3,087	$1,338
Accrued liabilities	$11,938	$15,812	$8,492	$3,989
Accrued interest	$19,834	$20,120		
Margin borrowings	$2,674	$9,443		
Long-term debt, net of current				
maturities	$1,000	$2,326		$10,000
Total current liabilities	$39,665	$52,555	$11,579	$15,327
Long-term debt, net of current				
maturities	$605,993	$591,326	$32,415	$41,574
Deferred and other income taxes	$16,320	$16,650	$11,868	$9,631
Total liabilities	$661,978	$660,531	$55,862	$66,532
Total stockholders' equity	$105,170	$124,299	$68,084	$60,514
Net equity	$767,148	$784,830	$123,946	$127,046

SOURCE: Joint Proxy Statement and Prospectus, February 11, 1988, and Form 10-K, December 31, 1987.

in California's Sacramento Valley. It also owned a 140-room hotel in San Francisco. Altogether, Pacific Lumber had holdings in six states, including California, Texas, Alabama, New Hampshire, Kansas, as well as Canada.

The company mill also generated electricity which, in addition to filling its own steam and power needs, provided power for the 270 houses in the town of Scotia. Pacific Lumber had been trying to tie into Pacific Gas and Electric Company's grid so that it could sell excess electricity to the utility.

BACKGROUND REPORT: THE LUMBER INDUSTRY

Redwood has been a unique commodity with very desirable attributes as a building and decorative material. Because of its desirability, the price of the wood has been high, but processing costs have been low. Consequently, redwood lumbering has remained a very high profit margin business. All a company has had to do is cut down the trees, slice them up into planks, and sell the lumber for three or four times what Douglas fir comparatively sells for. Although it has been considered a cyclical business, its prices have not been volatile. In fact, the recession of 1981–82 was the first during which the price of top grades of lumber ever declined. This means that a company like Pacific Lumber was almost always highly profitable.

In general, the outlook for housing and the economy also had a lot to do with the earnings potential of a lumber company. Other factors that can influence lumber prices have included labor negotiations in the U.S. industry, lumber inventories, production restrictions on lumbering permits in government-owned forests, and tariffs on Canadian imports. Pacific Lumber has been attractive because it has owned the largest share of the commercial redwood acreage in the world by far. Several of the other major redwood companies, and there are only three or four of them, were clearly cutting way beyond their growth rates. Pacific Lumber was the dominant supplier and was getting progressively stronger. Pacific Lumber was virtually debt free, and since it had excess cash, it was even buying back its own stock. Pacific Lumber's book value was also considered to be low because the redwood trees on the company's books were listed at a much lower value than their actual worth.

BACKGROUND REPORT: CHARLES HURWITZ

Many felt that Charles Hurwitz, President of MAXXAM Group Inc., came across as a nice, soft spoken, warm, family man; and yet he had been accused of taking companies apart and squeezing shareholders. Although he was in his early 40s, he was in control of a $4 billion financial empire, which consisted of oil, real estate, and financial enterprises. More than other raiders of his day, like Carl Icahn and T. Boone Pickens, he was known for consolidating his control without spending any of his own money. His style was one of using the target company's own cash to repurchase stock of investors at prices below book value. Yet to all questioners he insisted that he only invested in companies with intrinsic value and where he thought his managerial skills could help to improve the company. He has stated that he buys not with the intention to sell again quickly but with the intention to build. Even though Charles Hurwitz had amassed a great amount of wealth and power, very little was known about the man. He maintained a quiet lifestyle in Houston, Texas, far from the rest of the city's business elite. He had not involved himself in local politics, although he was a staunch supporter of Israel. In 1984, he offered to set up a company to market high-tech Israeli goods in the United States. He did not surround himself with the usual trappings of the wealthy. He had neither corporate jet nor limousine, and, as of 1984, he ran his empire through an eight-person holding company. He was up at the crack of dawn every morning either riding his stationary bike or jogging. He seldom drank, and he had quit smoking. For enjoyment, he liked to play tennis in the evenings and hunt doves occassionally with his two sons.

At the age of 27, Charles Hurwitz could have been found on Wall Street managing the Summit group of mutual funds. In 1971, the Securities and Exchange Commission (SEC) charged him with violating antifraud regulations as the result of a Summit stock offering. Hurwitz signed an SEC consent decree because he wanted to complete a private financing of the group, but he signed the decree without admitting any guilt. Seven years later, a property and casualty insurance company that Hurwitz owned collapsed. The company had to be liquidated, and New York regulators charged Hurwitz with fraud and mismanagement. The charges were later dropped.

During 1973, Hurwitz's holding company, the SMR Holding Company, issued about $12.5 million of debt to take a stake in a company called *Federated Development Company*. Federated had a strong reinsurance division and some real estate holdings. After the takeover, the SMR holding company ended up defaulting on the debt with the banks receiving only 53 cents on the dollar, and SMR ended up merging into Federated. The Texas Securities Board brought inquiries later on the deal because they believed it was not fair to Federated's shareholders. It seemed that Federated's board of trustees was dominated by current or former directors of SMR. In the end, the merger was upheld.

In mid-1977, Hurwitz was part of several real estate investment trusts that were selling at below book value. One of these trusts eventually sued Hurwitz for failing to disclose his takeover ambitions in a timely fashion. The suit was eventually dropped when Hurwitz sold his shares back to the company.

Hurwitz's takover activities started in 1978 in the areas of real estate and oil. He started with the McCulloch company, the oil and real estate company begun by the inventor of the chain saw. After McCulloch's death, the company was in financial trouble with debt problems and pending litigation. Hurwitz bought a 13-percent stake in the company for $8 million. Despite opposition from McCulloch executives, Hurwitz managed to place two of his close friends on the board of directors. Within a short period of time these men were able to convince the board that the best hope for the survival of the company lay with working with Hurwitz. Hurwitz offered to help restructure their energy division and help them with their litigation problems. By 1980, Hurwitz had been named chairman of the board.

The first thing that happened was that the monthly management meetings stopped, and Hurwitz took control. He eliminated the stock option plans that the top executives used to enjoy and immediately sold McCulloch's fleet of 14 airplanes. He made the energy division independent and, during the energy boom, sold some of its coal properties, some of its biggest oil properties, and some real estate. He retired two thirds of the company's original shares and increased his voting interest to 60 percent in the meantime. All the time he reassured top management that he was doing everything for the good of the company. It took almost two years for the top managers to realize that they had lost control because he had come across as such a warm and caring individual.

The McCulloch company did return to profitability and, in the meantime, became the vehicle for Hurwitz's next acquisition target. Simplicity Patterns took two years to acquire, and once again Hurwitz placed a friend in charge. The new management changed the name to MAXXAM Group Inc., sold off the pattern making business, and turned the company into a large real estate company after a series of further acquisitions (see Exhibit 2).

In a recent filing with the SEC, Hurwitz stated that he planned to "expand and redeploy" MAXXAM's assets by acquiring non-real estate businesses with "identifiable assets and established cash flows or future earnings potential" that the market had overlooked and that were selling at "discounts to obtainable value." Hurwitz admitted that buying into companies may not end in control or acquisitions and that, given the right reasons, MAXXAM may sell its interest in a target company at any time.

The last known piece of business about Hurwitz was his attempted takeover of Castle and Cooke. Castle and Cooke was the food giant that produced Dole pineapples, BumbleBee tuna, and A & W root beer. The stock was trading at $17 a share on the open market, but it had assets that made the shares worth about $25. The management of Castle and Cooke fought Hurwitz's takeover bid by filing two lawsuits against him. One lawsuit charged that Hurwitz acquired his stake in the company illegally, while the other lawsuit charged that he used a federally insured thrift institution to finance the purchase. Hurwitz denied the charges, and Castle and Cooke ended up buying his shares back at $4 above the market price.

Julie began to think of her supervisors at Drum, Whittier, & Drum who would be reading her report when she returned to New York. Drum, Whittier, & Drum was an exciting firm to work for. It was a dynamic firm and had an environment filled with the anticipation of the next big deal. The best from her MBA program had been recruited by Drum, Whittier, & Drum. The lure was large salaries and the chance of huge commissions, while doing socially beneficial work. Julie enjoyed working for Drum, Whittier, & Drum, and the stress was duly compensated for by her generous salary. She had always been able to make clean, clear, and concise business decisions. This was especially appreciated by her superiors. She was shocked at first to realize that Drum, Whittier, & Drum meant what it said about taking stakeholders into account while making money. It turned out to be a far tougher job than she had imagined. Yet, she came to realize after a few years that such deals or opportunities were out there for the investment firm willing to look for them. Julie had developed a sense of where those deals could be found and went after them. This was in marked contrast to many other investment firms and

EXHIBIT 2

Maxxam Group Inc.
Consolidated Balance Sheet
years ending December 31st ($000 omitted)

	1986	1985
Assets		
Current Assets:		
Cash	$16,066	$38,300
Marketable securities	$147,805	$139,637
Receivables	$52,786	$46,103
Inventories	$82,895	$50,757
Assets held for sale	$40,344	$68,415
Prepaid expenses and other current assets	$6,684	$14,652
Total current assets	$346,580	$357,864
Property, plant and equipment, net	$101,829	$85,639
Real estate	$24,982	$23,605
Timber and timberland, at cost less depreciation	$520,411	$369,357
Receivables, less current portion	$10,836	$10,896
Deferred financing costs	$24,878	$17,330
Long-term investments	$17,739	$20,484
Intangible and other assets	$5,914	$4,267
	$1,053,169	$889,442
Liabilities		
Current liabilities:		
Accounts payable and accrued expenses	$30,980	$32,061
Accrued interest	$26,375	$7,223
Margin borrowings	$17,151	$29,891
Long-term debt, current maturities	$26,343	$11,192
Accrued taxes	$1,200	$37,260
Total current liabilities	$102,049	$117,627
Long-term debt, net of current maturities	$781,447	$558,508
Deferred and other income taxes	$17,788	
Other liabilities	699	3049
Total liabilities	$901,983	$679,184
Minority interests	$200	$42,108
Total stockholders' equity	$150,986	$168,150
Net equity	$1,053,169	$889,442

SOURCE: Joint Proxy Statement and Prospectus, February 11, 1988.

brokers. Thinking of that, she turned to a report on Drexel, Burnham, & Lambert.

BACKGROUND REPORT: DREXEL, BURNHAM, & LAMBERT

The past history of Drexel, Burnham, & Lambert was something of a Cinderella story, a sort of rags-to-riches fable. Looking back five years before 1984, Drexel, Burnham, & Lambert was distinctly minor league. As of 1984, however, it was one of the biggest names on Wall Street. The secret to its success was being in the right place at the right time and a man named Michael Milken.

Michael Milken had been referred to as the "junk bond" king. His rise to financial stardom and Drexel, Burnham, & Lambert's success were closely tied to this unique mode of financing takeovers. Some people call them *junk bonds* and others, especially Drexel, Burnham, & Lambert, liked to refer to them as *high-yield bonds*. By whatever name one called them, they have become extraordinarily popular. Trading in high-yield securities was someting that most brokerage firms were embarrassed about in the 1970s. This was the time Michael Milken started using them when he saw an opportunity where there was a market but no supplier.

A major reason junk bonds were so appealing was that they had an extra measure of protection. This stemmed from the 200 or so basis points in extra yield, which provided a margin of safety lacking in quality bonds. Imaginative minds at Drexel, Burnham, & Lambert had also come up with many sweetners that added value to junk bonds. For example, some junk bonds paid interest plus a share of the firm's profits, or were backed by commodities, or had springing warrants that took effect if someone tried to take over the issuer.

Thanks in part to Milken and Drexel, Burnham, & Lambert, low-rated issuers such as the Circus Corporation, Coastal Group, and Charter Medical had raised hundreds of millions of dollars by issuing junk paper through Drexel. This single firm ran at least a good half of the trading in the junk securities market. It dominated the market because of close ties with a number of major clients.

Another reason Drexel had continued to dominate a junk security market was that Mike Milken not only helped raise money and create investments for his good customers, but he also made markets in their securities. With his vast, well-maintained customer base, Milken provided the market with liquidity and stability. These qualities were once lacking in the junk bond market. He also earned his customers' loyalty because when deals went sour, he tried to help either with additional financing or in restructuring the company.

Julie was about to start outlining her report when she was interrupted by the captain announcing their impending arrival in Eureka. Julie was so involved in her review that she did not really notice the gentleman who had gotten on the plane in San Francisco. The little commuter flight to Eureka was almost full, and he had to sit next to her. She resented the interruption caused by people getting on the plane. So she barely returned his smile, before hardening for her work.

But now, as she glanced his way, she was surprised to find him reading a Moody's report on Pacific Lumber. Panicking slightly, she reviewed how she had worked with her documents. Could he have seen them? Was he a corporate spy? Gathering herself together, she made a polite inquiry as to his interest in Pacific Lumber. Introducing himself, he turned out to be an aide to one of California's state senators. The senator had taken an interest in the junk bond market and takeovers and had assigned him to develop a position paper prior to developing legislation to regulate these activities. About the time that the aide had started his research, some of the senator's constituents had asked him to intervene in the Pacific Lumber Company takeover battle. The aide was being sent to Scotia to check out the situation and touch base with the constituents. As that coincidence shocked through her, Julie began to discuss the ins and outs of merger mania and junk bonds with him.

MERGER AND ACQUISITION MANIA

Mergers and acquisitions had boomed recently, making the junk bond market grow and thrive and pushing Drexel, Burnham, & Lambert to the forefront. The wave of mergers really began in 1982, and it had been the longest and strongest in American history. The reasons were heavily debated and the results even more so. Many felt the primary reason was basic economics. The stepped up competition worldwide was forcing corporations everywhere to act. Another reason was that stock prices at that time made it cheaper to buy than to build. For those companies wishing to expand instead of consolidate, it made for an easier way to achieve their goal. Some on Wall Street felt that companies had been struck with takeover madness and that some companies felt they had to add to their size in order to ensure prosperity. In the more competitive, more global business world, they expanded any way they could. The changing values of management were also considered a reason for the merger mania. Takeovers had become much more a part of corporate strategy than ever before. The new corporate methodology was one of buying companies, breaking them up, and reselling the units for a profit instead of the old way of buying a company and keeping it. This allowed companies to make deals they could not afford in the past. Finally, it seemed the world was full of cash, and commercial banks, insurance companies, and even pension funds, among others, were trying ways of investing the cash.

The effect of these many mergers has yet to be duly determined. As corporate takeovers boomed, was the prospect of an economic bust building for the future? In 1988, more than 230 takeovers worth $73 billion were announced by March. If this pace were to continue, the value of deals would reach an incredible $439 billion at the end of 1988.

Merger opponents felt that American companies were throwing away precious energy and talent making deals or evading them instead of creating new products and new jobs. Supporters of the mergers felt that such deals made sense because they would make American companies larger and more efficient, especially in the global marketplace. Some saw it as a way to compete effectively with the Japanese. Even so, some serious concerns loomed large. One was that with this concentration of power there would be fewer and fewer jobs. Consumers might also have found that they were paying more for products because there was less competition.

It was estimated that takeover spending amounted to almost half the amount spent on capital expansion. People were wondering what this money would have accomplished if it were spent on research and development or new plant and equipment. The trend seemed to be toward acquiring already existing assets rather than on creating new assets.

Corporate restructuring left many American companies leaner in their operations but more heavily in debt. Corporate debt in default was climbing rapidly and was elevated by the recession of 1981–1982. In 1987, it reached the staggering sum of $9 billion.

The high corporate debt level had many economists worried, especially about what would happen during a future recession. Most felt that the debt level could only increase in a downturn. A key point to remember was that a company could always suspend dividend payments on stock but would go bankrupt if it could not make its debt payment. Some executives felt that even though they might have had a highly leveraged balance sheet, it was their ability to sustain cash flow that was paramount. The key was that in a downturn, if you maintained cash flow you would be all right. Some also felt that banks were looking at cash flow more closely and thus were extending credit to those they previously would have denied.

Most analysts have tended to be foreboding. They have looked at statistics, such as how much interest payments took away from profits. They have also looked at the percentage of corporate debt as compared to the gross national product. In 1987 corporate debt amounted to 40 percent. Lastly, they looked at liquidity ratios, which had also dropped.

Views were vehement on both sides. Some felt the merger and acquisitions activity was leading to better companies, and they were encouraging innovation. The other side felt they were threatening the ability of managers to take long-term views because of the fear of hostile takeovers in the short term. For every executive, economist, or business analyst a person queried, a different response would be forthcoming.

CONCLUSION

Julie watched the rain fall gently by the window of the plane as they landed. Thinking of the work ahead of her, she thought of the questions she would have to ask, the documents she would have to acquire, and the issues to be considered before arriving at a conclusion for her report.

Commentaries

---

21. Privacy

On October 29, 1987, Eastern Air Lines Inc. apparently received an anonymous tip that some in its baggage handlers at Miami International Airport used drugs. Security guards rounded up 10 workers in the plane-loading area. Then, in full view of other employees and passengers, the workers were marched down a guard-lined path to waiting vans—"like terrorists," as a lawsuit filed by the workers describes it. After questioning the men, supervisors put them aboard a bus—once again in front of onlookers—and took them to a hospital. Then came an ultimatum: Either take a urine test or be fired on the spot.

All 10 employees, members of the International Association of Machinists, tested negative. Later they filed suit in federal court, seeking at least $30,000 each on charges of invasion of privacy, defamation, and intentional infliction of emotional distress. Eastern refuses to discuss the incident. In its motion to dismiss the case, Eastern contends that the complaint should be resolved in a union grievance procedure.

Wherever this case winds up, it's a gripping example of the quintessential—and growing—American concern about privacy. The right to privacy, U.S. Supreme Court Justice Louis D. Brandeis wrote in 1928, is "the right to be let alone—the most prehensive of rights and the right most valued by civilized men." Brandeis was referring to the Fourth Amendment's guarantee against "illegal searches and seizures" by government. Today, Americans are asserting the "right to be let alone" by a different adversary: their employers. A nationwide controversy is erupting as companies probe deeper into workers' habits and health.

Unlike past labor uprisings, workers aren't mounting strikes over the privacy issue. Today's combat involves lawsuits, huge jury awards, and demands for leave-me-alone legislation. Individual employees and unions are filling court dockets with challenges to random drug testing. AIDS patients

---

By John Hoerr in New York, with Katherine M. Hafner in San Francisco, Gail DeGeorge in Miami, Anne R. Field and Laura Zinn in New York, and bureau reports, *Business Week*, March 28, 1988.

are suing employers for breach of confidentiality when co-workers learn about their condition. Employee advocates are demanding limits on electronic and telephone eavesdropping. And concern is growing over the potential for employers to delve into electronic data bases that collect the tiniest pieces of an employee's lifestyle under one neat label: the Social Security number.

SNOOPING?

The protests are being heard. Both the House and the Senate just passed bills restricting lie detector tests by private companies. Declares Paul Saffo, an expert on information technologies at the Institute for the Future: "After health care, privacy in the workplace may be the most important social issue in the 1990s."

It's not that most companies are idly snooping into their employees' lives. Behind the erosion of privacy lie pressing corporate problems. Drug use costs American industry nearly $50 billion a year in absenteeism and turnover. When employer groups opposed the lie detector bills, they cited employee theft, which is estimated at up to $10 billion annually. Moreover, in the litigious 1980s, failing to ensure a safe and drug-free work place can subject an employer to millions in liability claims when people are injured by an errant employee or faulty products.

The difficulty is maintaining a proper balance between the common good and personal freedom. It may be laudable for companies to hold down soaring medical costs by giving employees checkups and offering exercise programs. But what keeps helpful advice on high blood pressure from becoming an ominous decision on an employee's promotion potential? There are few standards to help answer such questions. "It is an era of legal uncertainty," says Robert B. Fitzpatrick, a Washington lawyer who represents both companies and employees. "In a lot of states the law is in flux, and it is unclear what the rules are any longer."

"FEAR OF ABUSE"

What is clear is that employers face a complex challenge. For years, American workers seemed to lack the body-and-soul dedication of their Japanese counterparts. Now, U.S. companies are beginning to gain the commitment of workers, who often build their private lives around the job—and the pension and health plans linked to it. But as this happens, employees also bring their off-the-job values—and demands—to work. "Increasingly," says Alan F. Westin, a Columbia University professor who has studied individual rights in the corporation since the 1950s, "Americans are coming to believe that the rights we attach to citizenship in the society—free expression, privacy, equality, and due process—ought to have their echo in the workplace."

Privacy today matters to employees at all levels, from shop-floor workers to presidents. "I don't think politicians and corporate executives realize how strongly Americans feel about it," says Cliff Palefsky, a San Francisco lawyer who handles employee lawsuits. "It's not a liberal or conservative issue, and the fear of abuse doesn't emanate from personnel policies. It's coming out of the larger, impersonal notion that workers are fungible, expendable items."

Huge jury awards in recent privacy cases reflect these concerns:

- A supervisor for Georgia-Pacific Corp. in Oregon fired a man based on an anonymous letter stating that the worker had been drunk in public. Then the supervisor repeated the allegation at a meeting of 100 employees. Concluding that such wide dissemination damaged the worker's reputation, a state appeals court upheld a $350,000 defamation award.

- A drugstore employee refused to take a lie detector test during an investigation of stock shortages at Rite-Aid of Maryland Inc. Though the company violated a state law in ordering the test, it forced a woman to resign. A state appeals court affirmed a $1.3 million award for behavior that "amounted to a complete denial of [her] dignity as a person."

These aren't isolated stories. A survey by Ira Michael Shepard and Robert L. Duston, members of a management law firm in Washington, turned up 97 jury verdicts against employers in privacy cases from 1985 to mid-1987. Damage awards averaged $316,000. Before 1980, employee suits for invasion of privacy rarely reached a jury.

They do now—largely because a decade of litigation and legislation involving employee rights has laid the groundwork. This movement has led to laws that give employees the right to know about hazardous workplace chemicals, that protect whistle-blowers, and that give workers access to medical and personnel records. Complaints of discrimination by age, race, and sex are also increasing fast. Meanwhile, nonunion workers, aided by state courts, are successfully challenging the once-undisputed employment-at-will doctrine. This gave private companies the right to dismiss employees without cause.

The erosion of the at-will concept clears the way for workers to sue employers over privacy issues. Otherwise, such cases are often difficult to file. State laws that regulate polygraph testing, for example, provide for prosecution of corporate violators but give no redress to wronged employees. But using precedents from employment-at-will cases, workers can often prove unfair dismissal—and win big awards.

TURNING POINT

All these trends are creating chaos in the rules that govern the workplace. And the changes this will bring in the employer-employee relationship could be as far-reaching as those that followed the breakthrough of industrial unionism in the 1930s. The difference is that today the courts and Congress may do much more quickly what unions would take decades to achieve. "The idea that the employment relationship cannot be regulated will never be with us again," says William B. Gould, a labor law professor at Stanford University. "In some form or another, we're going to have regulation."

The tension over privacy, in fact, marks a turning point in the cycle of management-labor relations. Starting in the early 19th century and for decades after, employers exercised wide dominion over employees' lives. Companies built and ran company towns. In 1914, Henry Ford's workers were promised a $5-a-day wage only after Ford's "sociologists" visited their homes and deemed them morally qualified. The growth of unions, the improved education of the work force, and the civil-rights and civil-liberties movements of the 1960s seemed to kill off these Big Brother policies. In the 1980s, however, the cycle is reversing—as the controversy over these major issues indicates:

AIDS Discrimination.   Employees with AIDS are already protected by federal and state laws that guarantee job rights for the handicapped. Nonetheless, some people with AIDS have been fired and in several instances not reinstated before they died.

Most companies have neither a policy nor an educational program on AIDS. Emerson Electric Co. in St. Louis has had "a couple" of employees with AIDS, says John C. Rohrbaugh, vice president for corporate communications. Those who have the disease became known "because other employees didn't want to share phones or work in the same offices," Rohrbaugh adds. Typically, "We didn't take any type of action, and eventually the employee became more and more debilitated until he was too sick to work, and frankly, he died."

For many companies, such ad hoc handling of the situation may be a costly mistake, says David Herold, director of the Center for Work Performance Problems at the Georgia Institute of Technology. In a survey conducted for the center last year, 35 percent of 2,000 workers said they didn't believe that AIDS can be transmitted only by sexual contact or blood contamination. The same percentage of workers said they'd be "concerned" about using the same bathroom as people with AIDS.

Herold believes the costs of caring for AIDS sufferers could pale by comparison with the productivity losses if healthy employees refuse to work alongside them. And he disparages the policy of many companies to treat AIDS "like any other illness." Adds Herold: "If that's what they mean by policy, that's nonsense, because other employees will not treat it like any other illness."

Some 30 of the nation's largest employers agree. IBM, AT&T, Johnson & Johnson, among others, have endorsed a 10-point bill of rights on AIDS issues. It calls for education to dispel fears, urges that medical records be kept confidential, and pledges not to test for the AIDS virus in hiring.

Polygraph Testing.   Do lie detectors tell the truth? According to recent surveys, a lot of companies think they do. Studies show that about 30 percent of the largest companies and more than 50 percent of retail businesses use lie detectors to test honesty in preemployment screening and to help investigate workplace thefts. Proponents contend that patterns of blood pressure, perspiration, and breathing recorded as a subject responds to questions reveal a liar's "internal blushes."

But many scientific and medical groups, including the American Medical Association, disagree. A strong response to a question could indicate guilt, fright, anger, "or indeed whether you artifically induced the reaction by, say, biting your tongue," says one critic. As a result, 21 states prohibit the use of tests as a condition of employment in private industry, and 10 more place restrictions on the types of questions that can be asked.

Now, after years of trying, it appears that polygraph opponents will push through a federal law. A senate bill passed on March 3 would bar most private employers from using polygraph exams in hiring process, though it permits the testing of current employees during investigations of a theft or other incident causing "economic loss or injury." It also exempts private security firms and nuclear power plants.

A stronger House bill passed last November forbids private employers to use the polygraph for any purpose, but exempts security firms and drug companies. A House-Senate committee will reconcile the two bills. Although President Reagan earlier threatened to veto a polygraph law, he may approve one if the Senate version prevails.

Defamation and Negligent Hiring.   Employees often sue when a former employer gives damaging information to a prospective employer. Because companies sometimes need to compare notes on hiring, their communications are considered "privileged." But they can lose this protection if they give information to too many people or hand out false information maliciously.

The fear of defamation suits has caused many companies, probably the majority, to refuse to say anything about a former employee except "name, rank, and serial number." But this practice is having an adverse effect on screening job applicants, which sometimes causes companies to hire people with unsavory backgrounds. Their unlawful conduct can lead to a negligent hiring suit and enormous damages. For example, in 1985 a car rental agency had to pay $750,000 in damages to atone for an employee who repeatedly hit a customer with "judo chops." In that case, a court found, the employer had ignored evidence of the worker's irascibility.

Confidentiality of Employee Records.   Considerable private information about workers exists in computer data bases kept by practically every business and government agency—and it's available to a surprisingly wide range of snoops. A crazy quilt of state and federal laws, as well as court rulings, regulates employer access to such information. Some areas, such as medical data, are highly protected. But others aren't.

Credit bureaus, for instance, sell information on employees' bank accounts, outstanding bills, and tax liens or bankruptcies, although all negative records must be purged after seven years. Only recently, TRW Inc., the largest supplier of consumer credit information, began selling such data to employers. "It didn't sound like the kind of thing we wanted to be involved in," says Edward F. Freeman, vice president and general manager of TRW's information services division. But "it's what our customers wanted, and all our competitors were doing it."

Certain employers, such as banks and nuclear power plants, can get criminal histories of prospective employees from the Federal Bureau of Investigation's Identification Division data base on more than 20 million people. In some states, other employers can get FBI information, too. Now the Bureau is considering lifting a major restriction on its criminal history data base: It may delete a rule requiring that information on people who are arrested but not convicted can't be disseminated after one year. Critics say this would add to the volume of potentially false information that employers can collect.

Many large employers have guidelines requiring managers to prove a specific business purpose before gaining access to sensitive information. But many don't. And the American Civil Liberties Union fears that voluntary guidelines won't work if the political climate changes. "What happens if society's pendulum shifts to be less concerned about personal liberty?" asks Jerry Berman, director of the ACLU's project on information technology and civil liberties.

Monitoring. Over the past decade, practically every major employer has gained the ability to monitor workers' performance through the computers and phones they use. This practice is already prevalent in service-oriented businesses such as insurance and telecommunications. And unless it's done carefully, workers resent it. "I don't think people mind having their work checked," says Morton Bahr, president of the Communications Workers of America (CWA). "It's the secretiveness of it. It's like being wired to a machine." The CWA is pushing a bill in Congress that would prohibit secret monitoring in all industries and require regular beeps when a supervisor is listening.

Worker advocates in Massachusetts are carrying the fight further in a bill that has raised strong objections by industry groups. In addition to requiring beeps, the proposal would limit the amount of monitoring and require employers to explain in writing the purpose and results of monitoring.

Genetic Screening. The most pernicious use of technology to invade privacy may be yet to come. Scientists already can identify genetic traits that indicate a predisposition to such diseases as heart disease and cancer. In 1980, Du Pont Co. came under fire for testing black employees and applicants for sickle cell anemia. The tests were given as a "service to employees," and the results were not used in hiring or career decisions, says Dr. Bruce W. Karrh, a Du Pont vice president. But because of the controversy, the company now does testing only at workers' request.

Genetic testing might be used legitimately to ensure that employees susceptible to certain occupational diseases aren't put in the wrong work environments. And as far as anyone knows, no companies now use the tests to deny employment. But Mark A. Rothstein, director of the University of Houston's Health Law Institute, believes employers eventually will try that, if only to help hold down health care costs. "Unless we have some clear indication that employers aren't going to be engaged in screening, legislation may be necessary," he says.

A preview of this issue may come as companies mount more aggressive "wellness" programs that try to push employees toward healthier lifestyles. So far these programs seem aimed at helping employees live longer—and improve their productivity. But the logical next step is mandating off-the-job behavior. "I think employers are going to get deeper and deeper into the wellness business," says Columbia's Westin. "This is going to throw up a series of profound ethical and legal dilemmas about how they should do it and what we don't want them to do."

Most workplace privacy issues pose these kinds of difficult questions. They pit the needs of the company against the worker's feelings of dignity and worth. To sacrifice much of the latter would make work life untenable. So the United States must decide which rights of a citizen in society should extend to an employee in the corporation—and in what form. If employers don't voluntarily start this process, the courts or legislatures will do it for them.

22. Legal Challenges Force Firms to Revamp Ways They Dismiss Workers

Joann S. Lublin

In the comics, the irascible Mr. Dithers regularly summons the scatterbrained Dagwood Bumstead to his office, angrily waves a finger at him, and shouts, "You're fired!"

The funnies no longer mimic reality: Firing isn't that easy anymore.

The right to sack subordinates, bosses' ultimate weapon, is coming under an unprecedented legal assault. State courts from New Hampshire to California are setting new limits on firing involving about 60 million nonunion workers. The rulings, which often provide hefty cash awards to those fired, chip away at the already-eroding "employment at will" legal doctrine allowing businesses to discharge people without cause.

In the past few years, several thousand disgruntled employees have filed suits claiming they were wrongfully discharged. Typically white male managers, they lack the federal statutory protection against arbitrary dismissal enjoyed by union members, women, minority-group members, the handicapped, and others. Those bringing unjust-discharge cases most often succeed when the firing conflicts with public policy, as in an employee's refusal to break a law against price fixing. But courts also are striking down terminations in cases where a company promised a new employee job security or didn't handle the discharge of a long-service worker fairly and "in good faith."

A partial list of companies that have lost such suits since 1980 reads like a Who's Who of American Business. Among them: International Business Machines, McGraw-Hill, Atlantic Richfield, American Airlines, and Federated Department Stores. In a much-publicized employee victory, TV anchor-woman Christine Craft last month won $500,000 from her former employer Metromedia Inc. for her demotion; she asserted she had been hired under false pretenses, a fraud claim often used in unfair-dismissal cases.

A JOB FOR LIFE?

Some corporate leaders think juries are invading management's turf and misconstruing valid firing decisions. "Are we heading for a job for life, no matter what a person's productivity is?" asks a distressed senior personnel executive for a New York company. He says the cases brought so far represent "the tip of the iceberg as far as I'm concerned."

"I think in five years you won't be able to call an employee in and fire him," predicts Jay Siegel, a Hartford, Connecticut, management attorney. Employers first will "have to go out and affirmatively make sure fair-treatment procedures are in place."

The court cases already are prompting a number of major companies to review and revamp how they hire, evaluate, discipline, and dismiss nonunion employees. In addition, "more people have been coming to us saying, 'Because of the changing employment-at-will relationship, we realize we have to have a more formal complaint system' " for nonunion workers, reports Alan Westin, a Columbia University law professor and management consultant. He estimates that 150 companies have created or formalized these systems, two thirds of them since 1978, with the greatest activity among banks, hospitals, and insurance companies.

ALTERING HANDBOOKS

The New York executive reports that his corporation hopes to ward off employee suits by altering its personnel handbooks. Even a simple reference to an employee's "permanent" status, following a probationary period, implies a degree of job security, some courts have said. Management lawyers propose that personnel manuals use the word "regular" or "full-time" instead.

That slight change might not be adequate. One plaintiff's attorney boasts that he can build a wrongful-dismissal case from help-wanted advertisements that promise "a career" or "a pension."

Blue Cross [and] Blue Shield of Michigan is putting much harsher language in its handbooks and job applications, warning people that they "can be terminated at any time without reason." A former assistant treasurer who was fired after a falling out with his boss sued the health insurer because the handbook previously had promised dismissal only for just cause. The former official won $130,000 as a result of a 1980 state supreme court ruling; his victory has triggered 20 similar suits against the insurer.

Yet some Blue Cross personnel officials fear that new wording could sour management's relations with workers. "Potential employees don't like to be told before they have a job that they might not even be there a day," observes Karen Kienbaum, the insurer's general counsel. Some labor experts say this sort of "legal armour plate" also invites unionization of white-collar staffers.

TRUTHFUL EVALUATIONS

Other companies are pressing managers to be more truthful when they evaluate subordinates, to use progressively stronger discipline for each slip-up and to document dismissals more thoroughly. Supervisors "may have personal liability if they don't give honest appraisals," cautions Frederick Brown, a San Francisco management lawyer. Unlike the winners of most sex-bias and race-bias cases, who generally collect back pay only, successful unjust-dismissal victims can collect sizable punitive and compensatory damages from their former employers. His two-year analysis of 40 California jury verdicts in such cases shows former employees won 75 percent of the cases, receiving a median of $548,000.

In the past year, Mr. Brown's law firm has trained first-line supervisors at nearly a dozen California utilities, construction firms, and high-technology concerns. The bosses learn that they will "be held to the (fairness) standard of the average person on the street," says Ralph Baxter, an associate of Mr. Brown. Some oppose the notion of franker employee evaluations and discipline, he notes. "They say, 'How can I get this guy to do a good job after I've told him he's incompetent?' "

The degree to which courts will hold management responsible for proper employee evaluations was seen in a recent case involving Bissell Inc., a maker of carpet sweepers and other home-care goods. A manufacturing executive's performance began to slip after he was passed over for a promotion to vice president. Officials told the 23-year veteran of their vague dissatisfaction, but he received neither dismissal warnings nor an opportunity to improve before his firing.

He accused Bissell of negligence. A federal judge partly agreed, saying Bissell had a duty to inform him more fully. The judge initially awarded the former manager $360,906 in lost wages, pension benefits, and mental-distress damages. Then he reduced the award to $61,354.02 because the man's poor performance made him "largely responsible for his discharge."

The July 1982 decision had led Bissell to put greater emphasis on tough, honest job evaluations. And before dismissals can occur now, the company's North American division general manager, Harry Bloem, says he asks a supervisor, "Has he been properly warned and notified? And does the file reflect the justification?"

The increasing rights of fired employees also are spurring more businesses to strengthen internal grievance procedures for their nonunion workers. A few companies even provide outside arbitration. A new catch phrase, *corporate due process,* has emerged, meaning that employee complaints will be handled more promptly and equitably. Professor Westin suspects companies could eliminate 90 percent of all terminations "by more-effective pinpointing of a problem when it arises, better counseling, and a better complaint system."

General Electric Co. adopted a new grievance system last October for 1,800 nonunion production workers at a Columbia, Maryland, electric-range plant. Several other GE facilities recently have followed suit. A five-member panel, comprising the plant manager, a personnel officer, and three specially trained hourly employees, acts as the final judge of the merits of the complaints. "The initiative for that came before the flurry of employment-at-will cases," says David Dillon, the manager of GE's employee-relations program. "But there's no question they (the cases) have sharpened our sensitivities."

CONTROL DATA APPROACH

Control Data Corp. adopted a similar "peer review" procedure companywide last February. The computer and financial-services concern uses a computer to select at random a review board including two peers of the aggrieved employee and an executive from a different division. A personnel "ombudsman" serves as the nonvoting chairman.

So far, the board has considered four cases of discharges, and it reinstated two of the workers, with back pay. The other two were fired for just cause, the board ruled.

In one case of reinstatement, the board overturned an employee's firing because he had an excusable absence. His boss had sacked him because of repeated absenteeism.

In the second instance, the board decided a professional's personality clash with his supervisor gave him little opportunity "to succeed under the difficult circumstances," recalls Fred Olson, Control Data's director of work-related problems. The board "saw it as a case of miscarriage of justice" and a case that easily could have sparked a wrongful-discharge suit.

Both employees "were ecstatic," Mr. Olson continues. "They didn't think they had a chance of getting a discharge overturned." On the other hand, some Control Data supervisors are unhappy with the new system. "It exposes them to be overruled on a crucial decision, and that doesn't leave them ecstatic," one company executive observes.

The revamped grievance systems pose another problem. Unlike Control Data, most companies use their new procedures for ordinary workers but not for managers and professionals. "There are real built-in limitations on the degree to which changes can take place" in businesses without outside pressure, contends William Gould, a Stanford University law professor. A state bar panel of which he is cochairman has tentatively agreed to push for a California law to review unjust dismissals. The measure would require arbitrators to resolve all firing disputes involving nonunion employees below the top officer level. Similar bills previously have been introduced but have gone nowhere in four other states.

CASE AGAINST IBM

Without state legislation and with more sympathetic courts, unfair-discharge litigation probably will further increase. "The only way to deter this kind of conduct is to make it expensive," insists Cliff Palefsky, a San Francisco attorney who won a $300,000 judgment against IBM. His client, a former sales manager, claimed she was coerced into resigning because of IBM's unhappiness over her dating a manager for a competitor. IBM has appealed that December 1981 ruling. Since then, Mr. Palefsky has filed 40 similar suits.

He sees heightened management resistance to lawsuits by disgruntled former employees, with companies spending up to $70,000 on pretrial maneuvers. So the lawyer tries to discourage many potential clients, telling them, "A good job is better than a good lawsuit. . . . The damage you can do to your reputation from suing your employer is irreparable."

John Harless learned that lesson the hard way. The former bank manager won an unfair-firing suit in 1978 in which he contended First National Bank of Fairmont, W.Va., had dismissed him for complaining about its alleged illegal overcharge of certain customers. The state court, in striking down his discharge, in effect upheld public policy. The victory was a bit hollow for Mr. Harless, as the $33,000 award brought him only $18,000 after legal fees.

Mr. Harless says he applied fruitlessly to every other bank in the state before landing an executive-level post at a new bank. When that job also didn't work out, he became a state banking examiner. "I didn't know if it (the litigation) was worth going through," he confesses. But he adds, "I still definitely believe in fighting for what's right."

Philip Cancellier agrees. Last October, he and two other former long-service executives of I. Magnin collected $1.9 million in damages from the department-store chain, which denied the charges. Their suit alleged unfair dismissal and age bias. But the award didn't come until nearly five years after they had lost their jobs. To survive such a protracted legal battle financially and psychologically, "you have to have a hell of a lot of money," says Mr. Cancellier, who now runs a small doll-design firm. "And people have to be really determined to fight."

---

23. Tobacco Titans Get Tough

Bonnie Liebman

Marc Mauer hates cigarette companies. "My aunt was a heavy smoker. When she died of lung cancer two years ago, it really brought home what a devastating effect the tobacco industry can have on people's lives."

What Mauer doesn't know is that each time he buys Post Grape Nuts, he's supporting Philip Morris, one of the largest tobacco companies in the country.

Cigarette companies aren't stupid. As America learns to kick the habit, they've moved to diversify. Food and alcohol aside, Saks Fifth Avenue, Marshall Field's, Ivey's, Peoples Drugs stores, Swingline staplers, Jergens lotion, Loews hotels and theaters, Regal china, Bulova watches, and Yardley cosmetics are just a few of the products or businesses affiliated with the cigarette sellers.

The spate of mergers has turned the large tobacco companies into corporate octopuses. Philip Morris spent over $1.3 billion on advertising in 1986, more than any other company except Procter & Gamble. RJR Nabisco is the fourth biggest spender (Sears is third), with an ad budget just under $1 billion.

With that stupendous size comes undeniable power. It's advertising that supports most magazines, newspapers, television, and radio. A magazine that depends on cigarette—or food—ads is going to think twice before running a story on the evils of smoking. "Advertising fees buy journalistic complacency," charges Alan Blum, a physician and cofounder of Doctors Oughta Care (DOC), an antismoking physicians' association.

Already, the tobacco titans have started to throw their weight around. Here are a few examples:

- In 1983, the American Medical Association sponsored an ad supplement on personal health in *Newsweek*. In a letter obtained by the *Chicago Sun-Times,* an AMA official admitted that the nation's largest medical association had soft-pedaled the dangers of smoking because the magazine was afraid of offending tobacco advertisers.

Reprinted from *Nutrition Action Healthletter* (September 1988) which is available from the Center for Science in the Public Interest, 1501 16th Street, N.W., Washington, D.C. 20036, for $19.95 for 10 issues, copyright 1988.

- According to Howard Wolinsky, the *Sun-Times* reporter who uncovered the scandal, the same thing happened a year later when the American Academy of Family Physicians sponsored an ad supplement in *Time*. Both groups said it would never happen again.

- In 1986, The American Heart Association approached *Reader's Digest* to run an ad supplement highlighting the dangers of tobacco. *Reader's Digest,* to its credit, is one of the few national magazines that accepts no tobacco advertising. But *Reader's Digest* does accept food advertising. The *Sun-Times* reported that pressure from General Foods (owned by Philip Morris) killed the deal.

- Last year, the Fleischmann's Margarine Division of RJR Nabisco asked the American Academy of Family Physicians to join in a $1 million antiheart-disease ad campaign. This time, the Academy insisted that the campaign warn consumers that smoking promotes heart disease.

  But when Wolinsky and a *Washington Post* reporter independently exposed the deal—pointing out that it would be the first time a tobacco company voluntarily admitted that cigarettes cause disease—Fleischmann's pulled out.

- Earlier this year, RJR Nabisco abruptly fired its longtime ad agency, Saatchi & Saatchi DFS Inc., after discovering that the firm had created a television ad for Northwest Airlines. The ad showed passengers applauding the airline's ban on smoking. According to *The Wall Street Journal,* RJR Nabisco vice chairman Edward A. Horrigan, Jr., was "furious after seeing the Northwest ad."

  Saatchi & Saatchi lost an $84 million account (for Life Savers and Nabisco cookies), sending a threatening message through the advertising world. Meanwhile, Philip Morris sent a Mailgram to thousands of its customers, urging them to call Northwest Airlines to complain.

As the cigarette-makers swallow food and other companies, they can use the best of their food products to establish ties with medical groups—and with consumers.

"The food products are powerful weapons to gain a foothold," says Blum. "Some people argue that diversification is good because it means these companies are getting out of the tobacco business. In fact, diversification just insulates the tobacco sector. And all the profit comes from tobacco. Cigarettes account for 57 percent of Philip Morris's sales but 79 percent of its profits."

Blum knows that diet is a major contributor to heart disease. But, he maintains, some tobacco-owned food companies, such as Fleischmann's, focus attention almost exclusively on diet to deflect attention from the smoking connection.

Blum has refused to buy foods made by tobacco companies for almost 10 years. For those who wish to follow his lead, we offer a list of tobacco-owned food and beverage brands. Since no one can possibly remember them all, Blum suggests checking ads or labels for the major brand names, such as General Foods, Nabisco Brands, or Del Monte.

Many see the battle against cigarette-makers as a war in which it's treason to collaborate with the enemy. Brent Blue, a physician from Jackson, Wyoming, urged that the Academy of Family Physicians cut all ties with the tobacco companies or their subsidiaries.

Says Brent, "You don't burn down villages in the morning and build orphanages in the afternoon."

---

24. Talking Business with Smith of Interfaith Center: Companies Face the Social Issues

Barnaby J. Feder

As the busiest time for corporate annual meetings arrives, scores of companies will be facing shareholder resolutions dealing with a variety of social issues.

Church groups with investments totaling $20 billion are sponsoring 157 resolutions for consideration by the shareholders of 127 companies, according to the Interfaith Center on Corporate Responsibility. Other investors, led by giant state and local pension funds with assets of more than $200 billion, have cosponsored resolutions with the church groups and filed scores of their own.

The majority deal with South Africa, but others challenge corporate involvement in weapons development and nuclear energy, press for disclosure of more information on topics such as third world debt, and attack "poison pill" measures adopted by companies without share holder approval.

The Interfaith Center, a nonprofit New York–based organization that coordinates the introduction of shareholder resolutions on behalf of more than 240 Protestant and Roman Catholic church groups, has been involved in the effort to use investments as a lever for social change since 1971, when the Episcopal Church sponsored the first resolution asking General Motors to withdraw from South Africa.

In an interview yesterday, the center's executive director, Timothy Smith, discussed the current crop of shareholder resolutions.

Q. What trends do you see in this year's shareholder resolutions?
A. The most significant is that large institutional investors have joined with the religious community to sponsor a whole range of resolutions. While not distinctly

---

different from last year, it represents a big change from five years ago. We no longer have simply the traditional gadflies. There's increasing interest in fair employment in Northern Ireland, particularly from state and local pension funds. And more companies are being asked to develop plans to convert their operations from reliance on military contracts.

Q. Shareholder activism on social issues has been heavily identified with disinvestment from South Africa. As more companies pull out, are splits developing about where pressure ought to be applied next?

A. No, I think there's a remarkable common voice on South Africa. They aren't simply asked to sell operations but to cut all ties. A perfect example would be the resolution to IBM, which sold its subsidiary and this year is being asked to end all computer sales to South Africa.

Q. What's the relationship between church groups and other shareholder activists, such as pension funds?

A. It's much more cooperative. For example, Jay Golden, the Comptroller of the City of New York, and the Interfaith Center have forged a coalition where we second each other at meetings. We do that with other institutional investors, too.

Q. What new issues do you expect to attract shareholder attention in the next few years?

A. Animal testing is a newcomer. I think we will see resolutions on political action committees and renewed interest on time-honored topics like pharmaceutical sales in the third world. Another new issue would be the domestic advertising and marketing policies of the tobacco industry.

Q. What are the limits on what you can accomplish through shareholder resolutions?

A. I think they are most effective when they are part of a combination of pressures on a corporation. For example, on South Africa, managements are facing divestment, selective purchasing by more than 35 cities and states, and the boycott of Shell Oil products. The combination goes right to the bottom line and makes them more likely to pay attention to the shareholder resolutions.

Q. What has been accomplished this year through negotiation after resolutions were introduced?

A. Black & Decker, Cigna, Sterling Drug, and Marsh & McLennan have withdrawn from South Africa. ITT agreed to make a report answering certain questions regarding their plans for the conversion of their business from reliance on military contracts. Aetna did the same on equal employment. Philip Morris agreed to do a report on tobacco sales to the third world.

PART SEVEN

Consumer Welfare

By definition, a market requires the existence of at least two parties: a seller and a prospective buyer. If sufficient value is seen in engaging in exchange, then a transaction will take place. The seller will give up his or her product or service in exchange for cash, a promise to pay, or something else of value.

This seemingly simple process involves a number of complexities. Those complexities are essentially related to *trust*. Consumer welfare depends largely on the quality of information used in making buying decisions. Sellers typically disclose information via advertising, packaging and labeling, and retail sales efforts. Misinformation and deception are possible in each of these areas. Consumer welfare is also rooted in product design, use, and post-purchase service. Product quality and safety, their effect on the environment, the range of choice they represent, and the adequacy of consumer redress are all sources of potential conflict.

The record tends to be rather clear. It is in the best interest of companies to have satisfied customers. If the market fails to produce this result, government intervention is inevitable. In general, consumer dissatisfaction tends to be widespread, and the consumer movement is perhaps the strongest evidence of this problem. Thus, it appears that managing this aspect of social responsiveness is especially challenging.

Consumers in the United States are increasingly better educated. As a result of this and the consumer movement, more consumers of all types of products are more willing to take businesses to court over purported wrongs. During the latter half of the 1980s, product liability emerged as a major concern in a variety of nontraditional management areas, such as medicine and education. Even cigarette manufacturers were being sued for the damage their tobacco products did to consumers.

Good, timely information for the consumer is vital to the operation of a free-market system. Yet in the 1980s, the Reagan administration sought to curtail the dissemination of consumer information from the government, in the name of greater government efficiency. The U.S. Government Printing Office and other federal agencies were influenced to reduce the availability of information of interest to consumers. This occurred in an administration that was purported to be the champion of free enterprise.

The concept of consumer welfare has expanded as a result of consumer movements, ethical investing, and environmental movements. Consumer welfare is no longer just concerned with the specific impact of the product on the consumer. It now encompasses everything that would or should be of concern to a consumer when purchasing a product. As indicated by the two commentaries in Part I, consumers feel their welfare includes the welfare of other people and the environment. In addition to laws requiring the disclosure of health information (as in ingredient labeling of food products or the warning labels on cigarette boxes), we may see efforts to have a wide variety of information regarding various social and personal issues disclosed at the point of sale. All of this means a more challenging environment for business.

The Johnson & Johnson/Tylenol case presents what is perhaps the ultimate challenge in consumer welfare. The case traces the events and corporate actions of Johnson & Johnson following the deaths of seven people shortly after they had taken Tylenol capsules. In contrast to many other firms, Johnson & Johnson's response is a model of responsibility. The A. H. Robins and the Dalkon Shield case presents an example of the product liability issue. While the company's behavior is not anywhere as exemplary as that of Johnson & Johnson, it deals with the implications of shifting from a *caveat emptor* (the buyer beware) to a *caveat venditor* (the seller beware) business environment.

The commentaries offer examples and perspectives on issues of consumer welfare. The first article, Debate Rages over Marketing and Alcohol Problems, reviews the social concerns and consequences of marketing alcoholic beverages. Solved: The Riddle of Unintended Acceleration is an extended discussion of the purported brake problems with the Audi 5000 where the focus is more on technological design issues and the impact of imperfect data on policy. "All-Terrain" Vehicles Spark Debate As User Deaths and Injuries Mount focuses on the interaction between consumer behavior/training and the technology of the product. In both of these, a public official must decide if a recall order should be issued, and the courts must determine liability—all of this on the basis of imperfect data and theory. Finally, Why More Corporations May be Charged with Manslaughter looks at the issue of company criminal liability for injury suffered by customers and employees. Together, the commentaries give an overview and some detailed views of current consumer welfare issues.

Johnson & Johnson/Tylenol (A): "Death in a Bottle"

SEPTEMBER 30, 1982 . . . THE INCIDENT

"Adam Janus had a minor chest pain last Wednesday morning, so he went out and bought a bottle of Extra-Strength Tylenol capsules. About an hour later, in his home in the Chicago suburb of Arlington Heights, Janus suffered a cardiopulmonary collapse. He was rushed to the Northwest Community Hospital, where doctors worked frantically to revive him."[1] The verdict was "sudden death without warning." A few hours later, his brother and sister-in-law, who happened to take capsules from the same bottle, were pronounced dead.

By the end of the week, four other residents of Chicago suffered a similar fate. The medication taken in all the seven cases was the same—Extra-Strength Tylenol, and in each case, the capsules had been laced with cyanide.

The link to Tylenol was first stumbled upon by two off-duty firemen in the area, who were monitoring their police radios and who subsequently notified their superiors. As soon as the connection was made, the whole country was alerted to the danger of the contaminated drug. Police cruisers blared warnings over loudspeakers through the streets of Chicago, while radio and television stations broadcast the details of the Tylenol-related deaths.

The public's faith in consumer packaged goods had been shaken to the core. For Johnson & Johnson (whose subsidiary, McNeil Consumer Products, manufactured Tylenol), it was the beginning of a nightmare that would have repercussions for the entire packaged goods industry.

JANUARY 1, 1982 . . . JOHNSON & JOHNSON

Johnson & Johnson was the world's most diversified health care company. The company's product lines were the result of the application of resources and technology originally designed for use in the medical industry (Exhibit 1).

---

[1] Susan Tifft, "Poison Madness in the Midwest," *Time,* October 11, 1982, p. 18.

EXHIBIT 1

Principal Domestic Operations

⋐CHICOPEE

Chicopee manufactures a wide variety of fabrics that are sold to a broad range of commercial and industrial customers, as well as being used in the manufacture of products made by other Johnson & Johnson affiliates. Chicopee also manufactures diapers for the private-label market segment.

Codman

Codman & Shurtleff, Inc. supplies hospitals and surgeons worldwide with a broad line of products including instruments, equipment, implants, surgical disposables, fiberoptic light sources and cables, surgical head lamps, surgical microscopes and electronic pain control stimulators and electrodes.

CRITIKON

Critikon, Inc. provides products used in the operating room and other critical care areas of the hospital. Intravenous catheters, infusion pumps, sets and devices for monitoring blood pressure, oxygen, respiratory and cerebral function are among its products.

⒟evro

Edible natural protein sausage casings and other collagen-based products made by Devro companies in the United States, Canada, Scotland and Australia are used by food processors throughout the world to produce pure, uniform, high-quality sausages and meat snacks, and to aid in making other products such as wine and beer.

Johnson & Johnson
BABY PRODUCTS COMPANY

The Johnson & Johnson Baby Products Company produces the familiar line of consumer baby products, including powder, shampoo, oil, wash cloths, lotion and other products. Additional products include educational materials and toys to aid in infant development and SUNDOWN Sunscreen.

Johnson & Johnson
DENTAL PRODUCTS COMPANY

The Dental Products Company serves dental practitioners throughout the world with an extensive line of orthodontic, preventive and restorative products. The company also provides dental laboratories with a broad line of crown and bridge materials, including the high-strength ceramic CERESTORE system.

Johnson & Johnson
PRODUCTS INC.

Johnson & Johnson Products Health Care Division provides consumers with wound care and oral care products. Its Patient Care Division offers hospitals and physicians a complete line of wound care products. Its Orthopaedic Division markets surgical implants and fracture immobilization products. The company also provides products to the athletic market.

McNEIL
McNeil Consumer Products Company

McNeil Consumer Products Company's line of TYLENOL acetaminophen products includes regular and extra-strength tablets, capsules and liquid; children's elixir, chewable tablets and drops. Other products include various forms of CoTYLENOL Cold Formula, SINE-AID and Maximum-Strength TYLENOL Sinus Medication.

PITMAN·MOORE

Pitman-Moore, Inc. provides veterinarians with biological and pharmaceutical products for diseases in many species of animals. It also markets the products of other Johnson & Johnson affiliates applicable to animal health.

SURGIKOS

Surgikos, Inc. markets an extensive line of BARRIER Disposable Packs and Gowns and surgical specialty products for use in major operative procedures. Other major products include sterilizing/disinfecting solutions for medical equipment, surgical and medical gloves, and a contamination control mat.

TECHNICARE

Technicare Corporation offers physicians products in four of the most important diagnostic imaging fields—computed tomography (CT) scanning, nuclear medicine systems, digital X-ray and the new field of Nuclear Magnetic Resonance.

TECHNICARE
ULTRASOUND

Technicare Ultrasound specializes in ultrasound diagnostic imaging equipment. Technicare Ultrasound equipment is used in a wide range of medical diagnoses, including abdominal, cardiovascular, gynecologic, obstetric, pediatric and neonatal applications.

SOURCE: Johnson & Johnson, 1982 Annual Report.

EXHIBIT 1   *(concluded)*

ETHICON

Ethicon, Inc. provides products for precise wound closure, including sutures, ligatures, mechanical wound closure instruments and related products. Ethicon makes its own surgical needles and provides thousands of needle-suture combinations to the surgeon.

Extracorporeal Inc.

Extracorporeal Inc. manufactures and markets products for the treatment of disease utilizing an extracorporeal circuit, including artificial kidney machines and membranes. Cardiovascular products include the INTERSEPT Blood Filters, INTERPULSE Oxygenators and HANCOCK Valves.

iolab

Iolab Corporation designs, develops and manufactures intraocular lenses for implantation in the eye to replace natural lenses after cataract surgery.

JANSSEN PHARMACEUTICA

Janssen Pharmaceutica Inc. facilitates availability in the U.S. of original research developments of Janssen Pharmaceutica N.V. of Belgium. Its products include INNOVAR, SUBLIMAZE and INAPSINE, injectable products used in anesthesiology; NIZORAL and MONISTAT i.v. for systemic fungal pathogens; VERMOX, an anthelmintic, and IMODIUM, an anti-diarrheal.

McNEIL PHARMACEUTICAL

McNeil Pharmaceutical provides the medical profession with prescription drugs, including analgesics, a major tranquilizer, anti-inflammatory agents and a muscle relaxant.

Ortho Diagnostic Systems INC

Ortho Diagnostic Systems Inc provides blood banks and clinical laboratories with products to analyze components of blood and other body fluids as an aid in medical diagnosis. Products include blood grouping and typing sera, Rh vaccine and various diagnostic tests. Its automated blood analyzers provide swift and accurate analyses of key blood components.

ORTHO PHARMACEUTICAL CORPORATION

Ortho Pharmaceutical Corporation's prescription products for family planning are oral contraceptives, diaphragms and intrauterine devices. Other products include vaginal anti-bacterial and anti-fungal agents. The Advanced Care Products Division markets non-prescription vaginal spermicides for fertility control, in-home pregnancy test kits and an athlete's foot remedy. The Dermatological Division provides dermatologists with products for professional skin treatment.

Personal Products

Products for feminine hygiene —STAYFREE Maxi-Pads and Mini-Pads, CAREFREE PANTY SHIELDS, SURE & NATURAL Maxishields, MODESS Sanitary Napkins, 'o b' Tampons and related products —are the specialty of Personal Products Company. Other consumer products include COETS Cosmetic Squares and SHOWER-TO-SHOWER Deodorant Body Powder.

XANAR

Xanar Inc. specializes in products for laser surgery. Laser surgical devices can be used in general surgery and in several surgical specialties to provide an effective, non-invasive alternative to traditional techniques. Xanar's products include surgical lasers for gynecology and otolaryngology.

The following trademarks of Johnson & Johnson and its affiliated companies appear in this report.

ABSOLOK, ACT, BAND-AID, BARRIER, CAREFREE PANTY SHIELDS, CERESTORE, COETS, CoTYLENOL, DAISY 2, DIALPACK, EXTRASENSR, FACT, HANCOCK, IMODIUM, INAPSINE, INNOVAR, INTERPULSE, INTERSEPT, J-VAC, JOHNSON'S, MODESS, MONISTAT, NEUTRALON, NIZORAL, 'o b', ORTHO-NOVUM, PDS, REACH, SHEARING, SHOWER-TO-SHOWER, SINE-AID, STAYFREE, SUBLIMAZE, SUNDOWN, SURE & NATURAL, SYNTHOGRAFT, TOLECTIN, TRIAD, TYLENOL, VERMOX, ZOMAX.

Johnson & Johnson (J&J) was established in the late 1800s by the Johnson brothers. One of the first products offered by the company was the original first-aid kit, which was developed in response to a plea from railroad workers who needed treatment as they lay tracks across America. J&J's products had long been associated with safety and gentleness, and the company's carefully cultivated image of responsibility had made it one of the most trusted companies in the United States. In 1981, J&J ranked 74th in size among the 500 largest industrials, with consolidated sales of $5.4 billion.

Corporate Structure

J&J was a family of 150 semi-independent companies manufacturing such diverse products as dental floss, blood analyzers, heart valves, and CT scanners. J&J represented the largest U.S. manufacturer of contraceptives, home bandages, and surgical sutures.

J&J led the world in painkillers with, most notably, its Tylenol line. In addition, its McNeil subsidiary had recently introduced Zomax, a prescription painkiller which was not physiologically addictive. In the first two months of 1981, doctors wrote an awesome 965,000 new prescriptions for Zomax, marking one of the most successful drug launchings ever. Thomas McGinnis, an analyst for the securities firm of F. Eberstadt & Co., estimated that by 1985, Zomax's sales would reach about $300 million annually.

Each of the 150 divisions had its own board of directors and chairman of the board. The companies were aggregated into eight groups according to geographical or product similarity. According to some observers, J&J was a "wonderful example of simplicity in form despite its size. The company represents an extreme of keeping the structure simple, divisionalized, and autonomous."[2]

Corporate Culture

"The gravitational force that keeps J&J from spinning out of control"[3] was provided by an 11 member executive committee that met almost daily for lunch in a private dining room within the corporate headquarters in New Brunswick, New Jersey. James E. Burke (chairman and chief executive officer), David R. Clare (president, chairman of the executive committee), and the vice presidents for finance and administration had corporatewide responsibility; each of the other seven members had specific product responsibility.

J&J traditionally functioned behind a "sterile gauze curtain," shunning

---

[2] Thomas J. Peters and Robert H. Waterman, Jr., *In Search of Excellence* (New York: Harper & Row, 1982).

[3] Johnson & Johnson, 1981, Annual Report.

the press and turning down most requests for interviews. Lately, however, Chairman James Burke had been pulling the "curtain" aside voluntarily. As chairman for the past five years, Burke received the external world with an openness that was liberal by most standards and revolutionary by J&J's.

Burke graduated from Harvard in 1949, spent several years at Procter & Gamble, and came to J&J in 1953 as product director for Band-Aids. Burke developed a genuine interest in health care that went beyond immediate business concerns. He frequently invited scientist-philosophers to drop by for an informal luncheon with the executive committee. A former J&J executive once described Burke as an individual who had "evolved from being a packaged-goods salesman to a man with a mission in health care."

J&J's autonomous divisions were also coordinated by a 291-word code of corporate behavior, "The Credo." The Credo was a legacy of "the General," Robert Wood Johnson, the son of one of the founding Johnson brothers, and the man who shaped the company during his long reign from 1938 to 1963 (Exhibit 2).

J&J's rigid adherence to the code of ethics had enabled the company to carve a unique niche in the field of health care. The company served customers first (especially mothers, nurses, doctors, and patients), employees second, the communities in which the company operated third, and the shareholders last of all.

The company had previously sacrificed earnings for what it perceived to be in the best interest of the consumer. For example, sunbathers independently discovered that Johnson's baby oil worked very well as a tanning agent. J&J responded to the new use with an advertising campaign directed at teenagers: "Turn on a tan, baby." However, as evidence began to accumulate to show that overexposure to the sun's rays promoted skin cancer, J&J voluntarily killed the campaign, at an estimated cost of about 15 percent of baby oil sales.

The Analgesic Market

The $1 billion a year analgesic market was comprised of two over-the-counter painkillers: acetylsalicylic acid (aspirin) and acetaminophen (non-aspirin). Milligram for milligram, aspirin and acetaminophen were identical in their effectiveness for pain and fever reduction. There were some proven side effects from aspirin usage; 2–10 percent of heavy aspirin users faced an increased risk of serious stomach bleeding.

The distinction between aspirin and acetaminophen was drawn by the marketing campaigns of the major manufacturers. The five major competitors in the analgesic market spent approximately $130 million annually on advertising, which averaged 20 percent of sales per firm. This was twice the percentage observed in most industries. Competition was severe in this market; one percentage point change in market share was equivalent to $7 million in factory sales.

EXHIBIT 2

Our Credo

We believe our first responsibility is to the doctors, nurses and
patients, to mothers and all others who use our products and services.
In meeting their needs everything we do must be of high quality.
We must constantly strive to reduce our costs in order to
maintain reasonable prices.
Customers' orders must be serviced promptly and accurately.
Our suppliers and distributors must have an opportunity
to make a fair profit.

We are responsible to our employees, the men and women who
work with us throughout the world.
Everyone must be considered as an individual.
We must respect their dignity and recognize their merit.
They must have a sense of security in their jobs.
Compensation must be fair and adequate, and working conditions
clean, orderly and safe.
Employees must feel free to make suggestions and complaints.
There must be equal opportunity for employment, development and
advancement for those qualified.
We must provide competent management, and their actions
must be just and ethical.

We are responsible to the communities in which we live and work
and to the world community as well.
We must be good citizens—support good works and charities
and bear our fair share of taxes.
We must encourage civic improvements and better health and education.
We must maintain in good order the property we are privileged to use,
protecting the environment and natural resources.

Our final responsibility is to our stockholders.
Business must make a sound profit.
We must experiment with new ideas.
Research must be carried on, innovative programs
developed and mistakes paid for.
New equipment must be purchased, new facilities provided
and new products launched.
Reserves must be created to provide for adverse times.
When we operate according to these principles, the stockholders
should realize a fair return.

Johnson & Johnson

SOURCE: Johnson & Johnson, 1982 Annual Report

COMPETITIVE ENVIRONMENT

Johnson & Johnson/McNeil Consumer Products

Tylenol, an acetaminophen pain reliever, was introduced by McNeil Laboratories in 1955.[4] J&J acquired McNeil in 1959. The company used its marketing expertise and financial resources to build Tylenol to a leadership position in the over-the-counter (OTC) pain reliever market. In 1981, sales of Tylenol products accounted for $365 million, or 34 percent of industry sales (Exhibit 4).

Tylenol was J&J's best-selling nonprescription drug; in 1981 Tylenol sales accounted for approximately 7 percent of the company's worldwide sales and 15–20 percent of the company's profits.

From 1955 to 1975, J&J followed an "ethical" marketing program, which promoted Tylenol exclusively to the medical profession. In 1975, however, Bristol-Myers introduced the acetaminophen-based "Datril," and the threat forced J&J to recognize they had a consumer business and not a quasi-ethical pharmaceutical business to defend.

J&J responded to the Datril threat by cutting prices on Tylenol products, forming a national sales force, and increasing the 1975 advertising expenditures on Tylenol to $8 million. The new multimillion-dollar advertising campaign marketed Tylenol as an "alternative pain reliever" to aspirin—one which did not promote stomach upset or other aspirin-related side effects. Tylenol's original position in the ethical drug market contributed to its success as a consumer product; 80 percent of Tylenol users purchased the product because of doctor or pharmacist referrals. Several analysts considered Tylenol to be "the best selling brand of all health and beauty products," and they believed that J&J had done "the best marketing job on Tylenol in the history of the health and beauty aids market."[5]

However, market observers questioned the integrity of J&J's strategy of initiating lawsuits against competitors. This was a common industry practice (successful litigation could delay competitors for a minimum of one to two years), and J&J had been particularly successful in the courtroom. Industry observers claimed that J&J's legal strategy shifted "the battleground from the drugstore shelf to the federal bench."[6] Market participants credited J&J with adding the "fifth P of *Plaintiff*" to the traditional marketing campaign.

J&J made a strategic marketing decision in 1976, when the results of the consumer survey showed that a significant portion of consumers concluded that Tylenol was not strong enough if it had no side effects. J&J stopped advertising the "gentleness" of Tylenol and introduced "Extra-Strength" Tylenol—the first analgesic product to contain 500 milligrams of painkiller

---

[4] Exhibit 3 contains financial statements of the company from 1972 to 1981.

[5] "A Death Blow for Tylenol?" *Business Week,* October 18, 1982, p. 151.

[6] Dennis Kueale, "Tylenol the Painkiller Gives Rivals Headache in Stores and in Court," *The Wall Street Journal,* September 2, 1982, p. 1.

EXHIBIT 3 Ten-Year Summary of Operations and Statistical Data (dollars in millions except per share figures)

	1981	1980	1979	1978	1977	1976	1975	1974	1973	1972
Earnings data:										
Sales to customers										
Domestic	$3,025.9	$2,633.6	$2,372.1	$1,991.3	$1,713.6	$1,493.2	$1,268.0	$1,138.1	$ 975.7	$ 800.2
International	2,373.1	2,203.8	1,889.5	1,506.0	1,200.5	1,029.3	956.7	799.1	636.1	437.5
Total sales	5,399.0	4,837.4	4,211.6	3,497.3	2,914.1	2,522.5	2,224.7	1,937.2	1,611.8	1,317.7
Interest income	78.8	50.0	43.3	28.7	18.9	19.3	11.8	14.8	15.2	8.6
Royalties and miscellaneous	28.6	26.4	23.1	17.2	16.8	16.7	15.6	15.9	13.6	10.3
Total revenues	5,506.4	4,913.8	4,278.0	3,543.2	2,949.8	2,558.5	2,252.1	1,967.9	1,640.6	1,336.6
Cost of products sold	2,651.3	2,427.1	2,142.9	1,743.9	1,499.8	1,335.4	1,169.5	1,044.4	829.3	681.5
Selling, distribution, and administrative expenses	2,030.6	1,794.2	1,505.3	1,258.9	1,002.3	847.9	746.6	626.1	515.0	419.1
Interest expense	60.7	37.0	21.9	13.5	8.5	6.3	8.8	7.7	5.4	3.0
Interest expense capitalized	(43.5)	(32.7)	—	—	—	—	—	—	—	—
Other expenses	23.4	12.9	16.2	12.7	7.0	7.4	8.4	2.3	2.8	1.0
Total costs and expenses	4,722.5	4,238.5	3,686.3	3,029.0	2,517.6	2,197.0	1,933.3	1,680.5	1,352.5	1,104.6
Earnings before provision for taxes on income	783.9	675.3	591.7	514.2	432.2	361.5	318.8	287.4	288.1	232.0
Provision for taxes on income	316.3	274.6	239.6	215.1	184.9	156.1	135.0	125.8	139.7	111.3
Net earnings	$ 467.6	$ 400.7	$ 352.1	$ 299.1	$ 247.3	$ 205.4	$ 183.8	$ 161.6*	$ 148.4	$ 120.7
Percent of sales to customers	8.7%	8.3%	8.4%	8.6%	8.5%	8.1%	8.3%	8.3%	9.2%	9.2%
Domestic net earnings	$ 262.2	$ 184.6	$ 172.4	$ 144.4	$ 129.3	$ 107.5	$ 90.5	$ 80.1*	$ 80.3	$ 72.8
International net earnings	$ 205.4	$ 216.1	$ 179.7	$ 154.7	$ 118.0	$ 97.9	$ 93.3	$ 81.5	$ 68.1	$ 47.9
Per share of common stock†	$ 2.51	$ 2.17	$ 1.92	$ 1.67	$ 1.41	$ 1.18	$ 1.06	$ 0.93	$ 0.86	$ 0.72
Percent return on average stockholders' equity	19.5%	18.8%	19.1%	18.8%	17.8%	16.7%	17.1%	17.3%	18.5%	17.8%

EXHIBIT 3 *(concluded)*

	1981	1980	1979	1978	1977	1976	1975	1974	1973	1972
Percent increase over previous year:										
Sales to customers	11.6	14.9	20.4	20.0	15.5	13.4	14.8	20.2	22.3	15.5
Earnings per share	15.7	12.8	15.2	18.2	19.8	11.0	13.6	8.1	20.5	18.1
Supplementary expense data:										
Cost of materials and services	$2,843.4	$2,532.4	$2,200.1	$1,803.0	$1,494.5	$1,294.4	$1,151.0	$989.7	$790.6	$640.8
Total employment costs	1,693.6	1,535.2	1,337.4	1,101.6	892.0	785.1	682.9	603.4	491.4	405.4
Depreciation and amortization	152.4	138.7	121.2	103.1	86.5	77.5	68.6	59.9	49.0	41.6
Maintenance and repairs‡	126.2	116.1	118.2	102.0	89.1	74.8	61.9	55.5	44.8	37.2
Total tax expenses§	477.0	425.3	373.2	323.0	274.9	231.1	203.7	183.4	184.9	143.8
Total tax expense per share‡§	2.56	2.30	2.04	1.80	1.57	1.32	1.17	1.06	1.07	0.85
Supplementary balance sheet data:										
Property, plant, and equipment— net investment	$1,335.6	1,161.9	947.8	788.2	652.4	568.5	528.3	467.0	365.1	301.3
Additions to property, plant, and equipment	388.5	364.0	273.3	228.5	171.7	119.2	136.0	157.6	102.5	76.4
Total assets	3,820.4	3,342.5	2,874.0	2,382.4	2,019.8	1,730.7	1,537.1	1,393.6	1,189.1	981.5
Long-term debt	91.7	70.1	69.5	52.1	37.1	26.7	39.4	43.9	40.6	31.5
Common stock information:										
Dividends paid per share†	$ 0.85	0.74	0.67	0.57	0.47	0.35	0.28	0.24	0.18	0.15
Stockholders' equity per share†	$ 13.51	12.24	10.82	9.47	8.43	7.45	6.61	5.76	5.03	4.33
Average shares outstanding (millions)†	186.4	184.8	183.3	179.4	175.2	174.6	173.7	173.1	172.2	168.6
Stockholders of record (thousands)	38.2	35.6	35.6	31.9	31.2	31.1	31.0	29.7	29.5	28.6
Employees (thousands)	77.1	74.3	71.8	67.0	60.5	57.9	53.8	54.3	49.1	43.3

* After giving effect for the adoption of LIFO in 1974.
† After giving effect for the 1981 three-for-one common stock split.
‡ Also included in cost of materials and services category.
§ Includes taxes on income, payroll, property, and other business taxes.

SOURCE: Johnson & Johnson, 1981 Annual Report.

The Analgesic Market in 1981

1981 sales for the best-selling over-the-counter analgesics, millions of dollars. Total market equals 1.085 billion.

How Tylenol was Expected to Sell in 1982

A breakdown of projected sales for over-the-counter Tylenol, millions of dollars. Total sales equal $410 million.

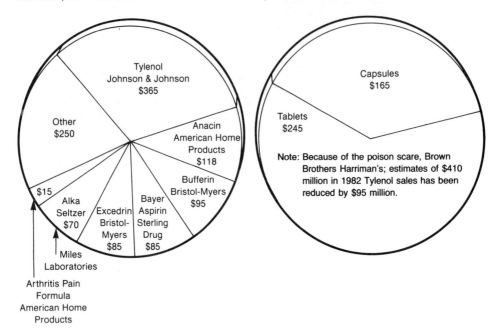

Note: Because of the poison scare, Brown Brothers Harriman's; estimates of $410 million in 1982 Tylenol sales has been reduced by $95 million.

Major Analgesic Products

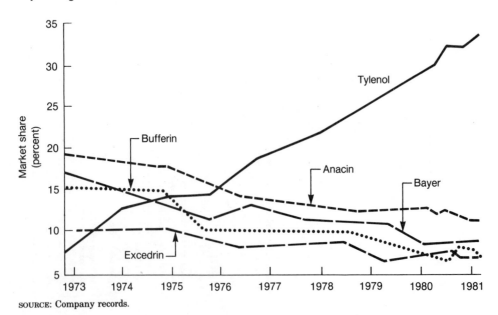

SOURCE: Company records.

per tablet (versus an industry average of 325 mg.). The new Extra-Strength Tylenol was heavily promoted as the "most potent pain reliever without a prescription." Extra-Strength Tylenol comprised approximately 70 percent of Tylenol sales in 1981.

J&J spent $43 million to advertise this Tylenol product in 1981; the amount exceeded that spent by any of their competitors. Tylenol sales were expected to reach $410 million in 1982: $165 million of capsules and $245 million of tablets. The brand was expected to achieve a 50 percent market share by 1986; the penetration was expected to come at the expense of Bayer and Bufferin.

Bristol-Myers

Bufferin's manufacturer, Bristol-Myers,[7] had sales of $3.5 billion in 1981. The company's products were primarily grouped into four industry segments: pharmaceutical and medical products, toiletries and beauty aids, nonprescription health products, and household products.

In 1981, Bristol-Myers expended approximately $144 million on research and development and $555 million on advertising. The company marketed two products in the over-the-counter analgesic market: Bufferin and Excedrin. Sales of the two products combined to make Bristol-Myers the largest marketer of aspirin-based analgesics in the United States. The combined market share for Bufferin and Excedrin was approximately 18 percent in 1981. Datril represented the company's entry in the nonaspirin pain reliever market.

American Home Products Corporation

Another competitor in this field, American Home Products Corporation (AHP),[8] manufactured and marketed prescription drugs, packaged medicines, food, and household products. Sales and earnings had increased annually for the past 29 consecutive years. Prescription drugs were the largest contributor to sales and earnings in 1981, comprising 42 percent of consolidated sales and 57 percent of operating profit before tax. Packaged medicines contributed $566 million to the corporation's $4 billion net sales.

Research and development expenditures for the three years through 1981 increased at a compound annual rate of 16 percent. The corporation marketed two aspirin-based OTC analgesics: Anacin and Maximum Strength Anacin. Anacin-3 represented AHP's only acetaminophen product. The company's share of the analgesic market was approximately 13.5 percent in 1981.

---

[7] Exhibit 5 contains 1973–1981 financial statements of Bristol-Myers.

[8] Exhibit 6 contains 1972–1981 financial statements of American Home Products Corporation.

EXHIBIT 5 Bristol-Myers, Ten-Year Financial Summary (in millions of dollars except per share amounts)

	1981	1980	1979	1978	1977	1976	1975	1974	1973
Operating results:									
Net sales	$3,496.7	$3,158.3	$2,752.8	$2,450.4	$2,233.7	$2,024.0	$1,859.3	$1,621.3	$1,387.6
Expenses:									
Cost of products sold	1,327.7	1,195.9	1,059.3	929.6	842.8	766.8	699.8	617.2	494.5
Marketing, selling, and administrative	949.0	859.9	726.4	642.4	569.4	517.3	481.5	432.9	388.9
Advertising and product promotion	553.3	513.2	457.6	423.2	407.9	379.3	348.9	297.1	270.0
Research and development	144.0	128.6	103.0	90.6	82.5	70.8	64.7	56.1	49.4
Other	(31.2)	(30.9)	(16.8)	(11.1)	2.1	1.1	6.6	(.6)	.4
	2,944.8	2,666.7	2,329.5	2,074.7	1,904.7	1,735.3	1,601.5	1,402.7	1,203.2
Earnings before income taxes	551.9	491.6	423.3	375.7	329.0	288.7	257.8	218.6	184.4
Provision for income taxes	246.1	221.0	191.8	172.7	151.3	129.0	114.2	96.3	81.2
Net earnings	$ 305.8	$ 270.6	$ 231.5	$ 203.0	$ 177.7	$ 159.7	$ 143.6	$ 122.3	$ 103.2
Dividends paid on common and preferred stock	$120.1	$105.0	$93.1	$79.6	$69.2	$59.5	$52.2	$48.7	$43.0
Earnings per common share	4.58	4.08	3.50	3.08	2.69	2.42	2.18	1.85	1.56
Dividends per common share	1.78	1.56	1.38½	1.19	1.05	0.90	0.79	0.73½	0.64½
Financial position at December 31:									
Current assets	$1,769.8	$1,587.7	$1,380.9	$1,226.9	$1,102.0	$ 991.7	$ 873.8	$ 753.2	$ 667.4
Property, plant, and equipment—net	581.8	484.9	407.5	358.5	317.6	285.0	263.8	233.5	224.5
Total assets	2,488.5	2,209.4	1,922.0	1,696.3	1,521.8	1,370.6	1,221.8	1,068.0	979.1
Current liabilities	744.0	669.2	563.7	517.1	472.5	427.2	379.6	338.3	313.2
Long-term debt	102.2	111.9	120.1	90.2	93.7	104.0	109.6	100.0	101.0
Total liabilities	924.0	837.5	728.9	645.6	598.1	556.9	516.9	458.3	443.2
Stockholders' equity	1,564.5	1,371.9	1,193.1	1,050.7	923.7	813.7	704.9	609.7	535.9
Average common shares outstanding (in millions)	66.2	65.7	65.4	65.2	65.1	64.9	64.6	64.6	
Book value per common share	$22.80	$19.85	$17.24	$15.11	$13.19	$11.51	$9.89	$8.44	$7.28

SOURCE: Bristol-Myers Company, 1982 Annual Report.

EXHIBIT 6 American Home Products, Ten-Year Selected Financial Data, Years Ended December 31, 1972–1981
(dollars in thousands except per share amounts)

	1972	1973	1974	1975	1976	1977	1978	1979	1980	1981
Year-end financial position:										
Current assets	$694,680	$739,097	$830,858	$926,773	$1,030,590	$1,114,184	$1,347,150	$1,524,683	$1,761,840	$1,944,318
Current liabilities	238,725	258,171	272,331	298,341	316,280	353,839	444,869	484,375	586,650	605,303
Ratio of current assets to current liabilities	2.91 to 1	2.86 to 1	3.05 to 1	3.11 to 1	3.26 to 1	3.15 to 1	3.03 to 1	3.15 to 1	3.00 to 1	3.21 to 1
Net current assets (working capital)	455,955	480,926	558,527	628,432	714,310	760,345	902,281	1,040,308	1,175,190	1,339,015
Total assets	1,042,004	1,125,974	1,241,596	1,390,712	1,510,862	1,611,305	1,862,181	2,090,674	2,370,262	2,588,538
Net worth (excluding goodwill)	583,347	622,269	715,015	814,161	906,335	953,036	1,094,798	1,239,315	1,391,972	1,583,475
Summary of earnings:										
Net sales	$1,587,062	$1,784,376	$2,048,741	$2,258,642	$2,471,727	$2,685,127	$3,062,633	$3,401,301	$3,798,524	$4,131,237
Other income, net	22,277	30,837	22,690	26,198	16,956	20,047	32,990	38,843	68,686	60,849
Costs and expenses	1,265,759	1,417,898	1,632,264	1,788,314	1,944,267	2,108,737	2,413,306	2,684,988	3,012,776	3,231,819
Income before income taxes	343,580	397,315	439,167	496,526	544,416	596,437	682,317	755,156	854,434	960,267
Provision for federal and foreign income taxes	163,702	189,109	204,596	238,182	258,901	281,403	323,236	346,322	393,700	455,199
Minority interests	7,175	9,051	8,929	7,655	7,584	8,867	10,659	12,795	14,845	7,736
Net income	172,703	199,155	225,642	250,689	277,931	306,167	348,422	396,089	445,889	497,332
Net income per common share	1.08	1.25	1.42	1.58	1.75	1.94	2.21	2.51	2.84	3.18
Dividends declared	94,725	99,415	122,449	142,258	157,869	180,750	207,982	234,796	265,781	295,749
Dividends per common share	0.59	0.625	0.777	0.90	1.00	1.15	1.325	1.50	1.70	1.90
Earnings retained in business	77,978	99,740	103,193	108,431	120,062	125,417	140,440	161,243	180,108	201,583

EXHIBIT 6 *(concluded)*

	1981	1980	1979	1978	1977	1976	1975	1974	1973	1972
Stockholder—outstanding shares:										
Number of common stock-holders	75,523	77,181	75,613	77,241	78,396	77,122	75,441	72,759	70,016	66,413
Number of preferred stock-holders	2,297	2,609	2,923	3,209	3,518	3,846	4,202	4,579	4,959	5,676
Average number of common shares outstanding (assuming conversion of preferred stock)	156,260,904	156,988,254	157,994,995	157,834,018	158,140,733	159,181,928	159,087,537	159,164,416	159,836,448	160,024,176
Preferred shares outstanding at year-end	176,071	205,350	243,918	277,805	324,570	370,835	426,739	498,256	573,278	713,889
Employment data:										
Number of employees at year-end	49,267	49,829	50,269	49,619	48,970	47,570	46,393	45,703	45,457	43,754
Wages and salaries	$775,972	$709,444	$657,851	581,812	524,309	480,724	436,500	405,617	363,679	323,211
Benefits (including social security taxes)	$133,036	$115,776	$101,844	87,179	71,340	66,579	62,456	56,424	53,479	42,093

SOURCE: American Home Products Corporation, 1981 Annual Report.

EXHIBIT 7 Sterling Drug Financial Statements (in thousands of dollars)

Industry Segments	1981	1980	1979
Sales:			
Pharmaceutical specialties	$ 207,375	$ 182,507*	$ 159,321*
Proprietary products	222,759	213,427*	192,264*
Household products, cosmetics, and toiletries	391,696	362,471	319,561
Chemicals and other products	145,139	136,411	130,016
Environmental control	45,036	43,206	43,696
Foreign	811,502	792,570	679,791
Intersegment sales	(30,582)	(29,159)*	(23,957)*
Consolidated sales	$1,792,925	$1,701,433	$1,500,692
Operating profit:			
Pharmaceutical specialties	$ 27,310	$ 24,242	$ 21,444
Proprietary products	41,447	40,528	37,455
Household products, cosmetics, and toiletries	66,384	56,552	55,461
Chemicals and other products	10,769	6,581	7,038
Environmental control	337	1,883	1,738
Foreign	106,396	110,854	93,227
Net unallocated expenses	(11,640)	(16,503)	(13,669)
Consolidated income before taxes	$ 241,003	$ 224,137	$ 202,694
Assets:			
Pharmaceutical specialties	$ 210,133	$ 196,357	$ 178,022
Proprietary products	101,108	85,372	71,288
Household products, cosmetics, and toiletries	112,197	108,984	99,130
Chemicals and other products	109,403	98,555	99,553
Environmental control	41,981	37,849	42,253
Foreign	649,705	663,882	598,288
Corporate	40,453	67,387	75,512
Consolidated assets	$1,264,980	$1,258,386	$1,164,046

* Restated to include certain intercompany sales.

SOURCE: Sterling Drug, 1981 Annual Report.

Sterling Drug

Sterling Drug[9] was a diversified pharmaceutical company with worldwide operations. Their businesses included the development, manufacturing, and marketing of prescription pharmaceuticals, proprietary products, household/industrial cleaners, cosmetics, and toiletries.

---

[9] Exhibit 7 contains 1979–1981 financial statements of Sterling Drug.

In the company's 1981 Annual Report, CEO W. Clark Wescare high-lighted the company's belief in research as the foundation for future growth and profitability. R&D expenditures increased to $67 million in 1981; market-ing expenditures rose to $688 million.

Glenbrook Laboratories Division of Sterling produced and marketed Bayer, an aspirin-based analgesic. Bayer held a 12 percent market share in 1981, while Sterling Drug was locked in a bitter legal battle with Tylenol's manufacturer. J&J asserted that Sterling Drug could not prove its advertising claim that Bayer was as effective as Extra-Strength Tylenol. Sterling counter-sued.

OCTOBER 1, 1982 . . . THE AFTERMATH

Stunned by the deaths linked to Tylenol, top J&J executives worked with local law enforcement agencies to bring quick resolution of the tragedy involv-ing the company's most important product.

Grappling with the gruesome events was a "nightmare, an absolute night-mare," said Chairman James Burke. He and other company officials were consumed with trying to "end the deaths, find the perpetrator, and solve the problem." Though he conceded that there was substantial concern about the damage being done to the Tylenol name, he adamantly maintained that officials "had no time to even think about reestablishing the brand."[10]

The man responsible for coordinating J&J's response was David Collins, chairman of McNeil Consumer Products. Collins had assumed his position at the helm of McNeil just one month prior to the Tylenol tragedy.

> It was a felicitous appointment for me, or so I thought at the time. Before this promotion, I had responsibility for Mexico where there had been two devaluations in one year, Central America where there had been war, and several South American countries with rampant inflation and more devaluation. I was coming from a scenario of problem upon problem to McNeil, a company with a great future and what I thought was an opportunity to win a few.[11]

The Tylenol incident became the toughest challenge Collins had faced in his career.

By the end of the first day, after the initial deaths were reported, Collins and other McNeil executives felt strongly that the company was not at fault but was being victimized by "some poor deranged person." If someone had dumped a dose of cyanide small enough to escape detection into one of the drug-mixing machines, the mixture would have been so diluted as to be nearly harmless; contaminated pills would not have been confined to Chicago's west

---

[10] Michael Waldholz, "Johnson & Johnson Officials Take Steps to End More Killings Linked to Tylenol," *The Wall Street Journal*, October 4, 1982, p. 16.

[11] Thomas Moore, "The Fight to Save Tylenol," *Fortune*, November 29, 1982, pp. 44–49.

side. Moreover, all samples from the lot reported to have poisoned the first Chicago victims showed no trace of cyanide contamination.

Regardless of their implied innocence, J&J did not take chances where public safety was concerned. The decision was made swiftly to inform the FDA and to recall the entire lot nationwide. The recall was an expensive process for which the telegrams to 450,000 hospitals, doctors, and distributors alone cost half a million dollars.

McNeil halted all commercials for Tylenol and ceased production in one of its two plants. The company posted a $100,000 reward for information leading to the arrest of persons responsible for the poisonings. Burke asserted, "It's important that we demonstrate that we've taken every single step possible to protect the public, and that there's simply nothing else that we can do."[12]

The first phase of the crisis ended when J&J learned that the sixth victim had been poisoned with Tylenol capsules manufactured at McNeil's other plant in Round Rock, Texas. This was a significant discovery because it helped to prove that the contamination had not occurred in the manufacturing process. Poisoning at both plants would have been almost impossible; it was more probable that the tampering took place in Chicago. With this information, J&J began to assess the effect that the poisonings would have on the company's image, the drug industry, and the Tylenol brand.

One of the things that was bothering Burke was the extent to which Johnson & Johnson was becoming identified with the affair. The public was learning that Tylenol was a J&J product, and the dilemma was how to protect the name and not incite whomever did this to attack other J&J products.

Company surveys supported Burke's position. Prior to the poisonings, less than 1 percent of consumers were aware that J&J was the parent company that manufactured Tylenol; this increased to 47 percent after the tragedy.

J&J's initial response had been to identify the problem and to move swiftly to contain it. Subsequent reaction was aimed at assessing the damage. At company headquarters, three task forces were developed to begin working on the image-rescue project. For internal morale, the public relations department assembled a one-hour videotape of news reports on the Tylenol tragedy and of comments by company officials. The tape was shown on the company's worldwide employee television network.

Burke evaluated the management of the crisis to the corporate level. He formed a strategic group of key executives to oversee the McNeil task forces. Reassuring as it was to have the resources of J&J at its disposal, McNeil executives did not seem altogether pleased by the new scrutiny that they were receiving from above. "Managing a crisis is one thing," said McNeil President Chiesa, "but managing all the helpful advice is another."[13]

---

[12] Waldholz, "Johnson & Johnson Officials."
[13] Moore, "The Fight to Save Tylenol."

Burke commissioned Young & Rubicam to begin polling consumer attitudes. The results of the polls would be the determining factor in assessing the future of the brand. J&J needed to monitor how the public was reacting to the crisis.

Consumer Response

During the days immediately following the poisonings, the demand for all brands of pain relievers and sleeping aids dropped 16.7 percent. Shortly after the incident, J&J was reported to have lost 87 percent of its market share with its remaining sales coming from Tylenol tablets, which had not been linked to the poisonings. According to one writer covering the poisonings and their aftermath, "Ultimately it's not the marketing experts who will determine Tylenol's fate, but a jury of millions of consumers who seek relief from pain."[14]

Surveys showed that an overwhelming number of people (94 percent of consumers polled) were aware that Tylenol had been involved with the poisonings. Of the total number of users surveyed, 87 percent said that they realized that the manufacturer was not responsible for the deaths. Yet 61 percent of these said that they were not likely to buy Extra-Strength Tylenol capsules in the future. Fifty percent intended to avoid Tylenol tablets as well as capsules, thus revealing a fear associated with the name that was not likely to dissipate soon.

The Tylenol incident was a tragic reminder of the vulnerability of the consumer to the system of mass distribution: "People have stopped buying pain relievers in capsules. They think twice about the need for nasal spray and eyedrops. Halloween candy is brought to local hospitals for X rays . . . we suddenly begin to scrutinize a product's container, wondering if it holds what it says it does, and not some anonymous death . . . an unglorified Russian roulette."[15]

The Media

In the wake of the Tylenol tragedy, J&J replaced its historically "tight-lipped" relationship with the press with a desire to be open and accessible. J&J depended on the media to keep the public informed and to gain consumer support.

The company quickly realized that the poisoning incident had created a major public relations problem. Lawrence G. Foster, vice president of communications for J&J, stated, "We decided right away to answer every single press

---

[14] Judith B. Goadner, "When a Brand Name Gets Hit by Bad News," *U.S. News & World Report,* November 8, 1982, p. 71.

[15] Peter Spiro, "Chaos by the Capsule," *The New Republic,* December 6, 1982, p. 10.

inquiry."[16] J&J did, in fact, answer nearly 300 press calls the first day after the Tylenol deaths were reported. In so doing, J&J was able to receive some of its most accurate and up-to-date information about national response from reporters calling in from as far away as Anchorage, Alaska.

The difficulty of managing the public relations issue became apparent when J&J had to reverse itself on the question of whether any cyanide was used on the manufacturing premises. Collins was originally told there was no cyanide on the premises, only to learn later that cyanide was, in fact, used in the Quality Assurance facility. This information was released to the press immediately. The reversal caused the company embarrassment, but at least J&J was signaling its openness to the media.

The Investors

By October 8, 1982, the price of J&J's stock had fallen from 46½ (as of September 29, 1982) to 42⅝; this resulted in a paper loss of $657 million to stockholders. The stock price recovered by one point on October 9, yet fell another 2⅝ on the next day of active trading. A Wall Street analyst claimed that "investors are trying to calculate what will happen to the company."

Larry Feinberg, a health products analyst for Dean Witter Reynolds, proceeded to downgrade J&J's stock ratings, since he believed that Tylenol contributed a significant amount to company earnings. J&J's sales were expected to drop, and company profitability was expected to be adversely affected by the costs involved in recalling and destroying the Tylenol capsules. Feinberg commented, "It will take a great deal of time to reestablish the brand, and J&J may never be able to reestablish its credibility fully."[17]

The Distributors

Evidence accumulated to prove that the cyanide was introduced into the capsules at the retail level. As a result, customers demanded to inspect packages and examine seals; store owners were torn between allowing customers to check the product and their need to restrict handling in order to prevent further tampering. "The sanctity of the supermarket shelf is at issue here," claimed product liability lawyer Allan Fudim.[18]

In spite of the difficulties imposed on them by the Tylenol scare, the majority of the retailing community remained loyal to J&J. Mr. James K. Jackson III, manager of a drugstore in Summerville, Georgia, did not replace the shelf space devoted to Extra-Strength Tylenol with any other product. Jackson emphatically stated, "I've got a lot of confidence in them (J&J). My

---

[16] Waldholz, "Johnson & Johnson Officials."

[17] "Death Blow for Tylenol?"

[18] "The Rush to Put the Lid on Drug Tampering," *Chemical Week*, October 13, 1982, pp. 16–17.

guess is that they'll repackage it or do something soon. I'll leave this space reserved for them."[19]

The Regulatory Reactions

The FDA worked closely with J&J immediately after the incident to discover the source of the poisoning. On October 22, the FDA officially cleared McNeil of any responsibility for the contamination of the capsules.

At first the FDA counseled Burke against recalling Tylenol, since the FDA feared that a recall would signal to the person or persons involved in the poisonings that they could cripple a major corporation and bring it to its knees. In the light of what appeared to be a "copycat" strychnine poisoning with Tylenol capsules in California, the FDA later agreed with Burke that he should recall all of the bottles of Tylenol capsules nationwide.

The Tylenol incident led to what was termed *Tylenol-induced anxiety* among other drug companies. Within days, the spokesman for the Proprietary Association, the manufacturer's trade group for OTC drug makers, asked the federal government to require sealed packages of all nonprescription drugs. It was believed that whoever tampered with McNeil's OTC pain remedy also tampered seriously with the American consumer's trust. The Proprietary Association, in acting quickly, hoped to assure the public that it would be protected from further such incidents.

In order to prevent different states and municipalities from enacting their own taper-resistant legislation, the Secretary of Health and Human Services ordered the FDA to promulgate an emergency packaging code. On October 31, 1982, the FDA submitted regulations that would require (1) tamper-resistant packaging in which consumers would see evidence of meddling and (2) a separate label drawing consumers' attention to the condition of the seal. No specific seal was mandated. Manufacturers were required to comply with the new packaging guidelines within 90 days.

Competition

The immediate response of industry competitors was to avoid exploiting Tylenol's weakness. "There was almost a gentlemen's agreement. It was surprising," said George X. Gikas, a marketing consultant. This nonaggressive phase did not last, however. Before long, according to Gikas, "They went right for the jugular."[20]

---

[19] Michael Waldholz, "J&J Can Weather Tylenol Storm—If It Hurries," *The Wall Street Journal*, October 4, 1982, p. 16.

[20] Dennis Kneale, "Rivals Go after Tylenol's Market, but Gains May Be Only Temporary," *The Wall Street Journal*, December 2, 1982, p. 31.

"Everybody who makes painkillers is trying like hell to fill the spaces on the shelves left by Tylenol," observed Vernon Brunner, the marketing vice president of Walgreen, a major drugstore chain based near Chicago. "The toppling of J&J from its number one position breathed new life into struggling competitors."[21]

American Home Products Corporation's Anacin-3 was expected to be the winner in the market share game. American Home Products began working around the clock, seven days a week, and increased production of Anacin-3 from two shifts to three to be ready for the expected increase in nationwide demand. The company was also planning chewable and liquid versions of Anacin-3 to make inroads into the Children's Tylenol market. American Home Products was pushing hard with aggressive advertisements to pick up TV time vacated by Tylenol commercials.

Bristol-Myers was expected to retaliate against J&J with a vengeance in response to previous attacks by J&J on Datril. Bristol-Myers bombarded newspapers with coupons for Bufferin and Excedrin, yet maintained a low profile with Datril, much to the surprise of industry observers.

Sterling Drug did not aggressively attempt to increase market share for Bayer aspirin. The extent to which advertisement was increased was not divulged.

Richardson-Vick had planned to enter the analgesic market with Percogesic. After the Tylenol incident, Richardson stepped up production of Percogesic and supported the introduction with national radio and coupon campaigns.

The fervor to compete with the recently weakened Tylenol had gone beyond the pharmaceutical houses. Drug chains were observed pushing their own private-label pain relievers. Walgreen's sales of their aspirin-free brand increased by 40 percent. Production was escalated, and more shelf space was allocated to these private-label brands.[22]

Larry Feinberg suggested new market share data for the major competitors:

Tylenol—7 percent (tablets)

American Home Product's Anacin-3 and other OTC analgesic products— 20 to 25 percent

Bristol-Myers's Bufferin—25 percent

Sterling Drug's Bayer Aspirin—17 to 20 percent

Feinberg added that "many less expensive brands of acetaminophen are becoming more heavily promoted now that the seemingly unpenetrable wall

---

[21] "The Race to Grab Up Tylenol's Market," *Chemical Week*, November, 3, 1982, pp. 30–33.
[22] Ibid.

surrounding the Tylenol image has been shattered, and competitive pricing is expected to become a major factor in these markets in the future."

Some analysts predicted that the market would shrink below $1 billion as more consumers decided to forego drugs to soothe mild discomfort. It was suggested that more and more products would be competing for a share of a smaller and less profitable pie.

THE DILEMMA

In spite of the adverse environment, Burke expressed confidence that Johnson & Johnson could rescue the brand. He cited reactions from the public, the medical and business communities, and government officials as the basis for his optimism. In a study conducted by Leo Shapiro, 78 percent of the consumers said that they would definitely use the product again. *Chemical Week* reported that the strongest tribute to Tylenol's appeal came in the form of reports that a black market had sprung up in Chicago since the sale of Tylenol capsules had been banned there.

"We are sensing a tremendous reservoir of good will, of trust toward J&J and the brand," Burke said. "All good consumer products develop their reservoir, but I don't know any product out there with a greater reservoir than Tylenol." He added, "People just don't blame us. They feel we are being victimized just like everyone else; it was just that J&J and Tylenol were the target."[23]

However, some marketing experts believed that Tylenol would never regain its commanding leadership among OTC pain relievers. They argued that it would be extremely difficult to overcome the amount of negative advertising that had taken place via news coverage. Some doubted that even the name could survive. "The chances are less than 50 percent," said David W. Flegal, marketing executive with Oxtoby-Smith, a New York research and consulting firm. Explained Flegal, "When a brand name is so tarred and feathered, it is difficult or impossible to ever separate the two in consumers' minds."[24]

Benjamin Lipstein, a marketing professor at New York University, summarized J&J's challenge as such: "J&J is up against the most difficult problem they've ever had to face—how to dislodge the residual elements of fear. I have a headache right now, and this time I took Bayer. I have Tylenol capsules in my house, but I'll be damned if anybody's going to take them."[25]

---

[23] Michael Waldholz, "Growing Headache: Tylenol Makes Tries to Regain Its Good Image," *The Wall Street Journal,* October 8, 1982, p. 1.

[24] Goadner, "When a Brand Name."

[25] Waldholz, "Growing Headache: Tylenol Tries," p. 1.

CASE

A. H. Robins
and the Dalkon Shield

Founded in 1866, A. H. Robins is a diversified, multinational company with base operations in Richmond, Virginia. Robins is primarily a manufacturer and marketer of two types of pharmaceuticals: those marketed directly to the consumer and those dispensed solely through the medical profession (commonly known as *ethical pharmaceuticals*). However, Robins is more than a pharmaceutical company. Pet care products, health and beauty aids, and perfumes are among the many products manufactured by the company under brand names that include Robitussin cough syrup, Sergeant's pet care products, Chap Stick lip balm, and Caron perfumes.[1]

In 1866, Albert Hartley Robins opened a tiny apothecary shop for the purpose of providing to the medical profession research-formulated, clinically proven, and ethically promoted pharmaceuticals. Over a century later, Robins is still led by members of the Robins family. Currently, the company has almost 6,000 full-time employees. Making employees feel like family has long been recognized as important to the overall success of the company. The ability to "converse as decision makers and to be treated as first class" causes Robins's employees to take great pride in their company and to demonstrate a very high degree of loyalty to the firm. As an example of this concern for the views of employees, one Robins's salesman said that "his advice often carries greater weight than that of the firm's market research department."[2]

This sense of family extends beyond work, too. The company sponsors activities that include a company softball team and company trips, and it offers employees little things that tend to make a big difference, such as free coffee and birthday holidays. Claiborne Robins believes that "his greatest assets are

---

[1] Trademarks of A. H. Robins.

[2] Quotations in this section were provided by *Product Management,* October 1972; A. H. Robins, *75th Anniversary Book;* and the *Richmond Times-Dispatch,* June 23, 1985.

the people that work for him." According to the *Richmond Times-Dispatch,* "When a person is employed by A. H. Robins, it's almost for life. Only on rare occasions do people not reach retirement with this company."

THE INTRAUTERINE DEVICE ENVIRONMENT[3]

The market for birth control devices in the1970s was very volatile. Before the inception of intrauterine devices (IUDs), several artificial methods of birth control were available to consumers. Included in this group were the diaphragm, the condom, and the pill. Each of these methods offered women significantly better birth control protection than afforded by natural measures. However, the diaphragm and the condom lacked what women seemed to want most from birth control devices—spontaneity. Thus, the pill was viewed by consumers as the ultimate form of contraception. Unquestioned, because it solved the perennial problem of birth control, the pill enjoyed a prosperous existence. The pill was convenient and safe, and it offered exceptional birth control protection.

The discovery of the pill's harmful side effects caused many women to lose confidence in oral contraceptives. The realization of problems like an increased risk of heart disease, dramatic mood swings, and excessive weight gain gave rise to a national concern over the safety of the pill. This concern was the focus of the Gaylord Nelson hearings of the early 1970s. These hearings publicly exposed the harmful side effects of oral contraceptives. "It is estimated . . . that within six months of the Gaylord Nelson hearings . . . up to 1 million women went off the birth control pills."

Since the pill was no longer viewed as the ultimate answer to birth control, women returned to traditional methods of contraception. However, they refused to sacrifice convenience and almost foolproof protection. What could have been better than a device—not a "dangerous" drug—that offered the same protection as the pill, at a comparable price, and with more convenience? The stage was set for the introduction of the IUD. Previously, IUDs had been used only on a small scale in various Planned Parenthood clinics. It was not until the harmful side effects of the pill were made public that IUDs were viewed as commercially viable.

An IUD is a "small, flexible piece of sterile plastic, which is inserted into the uterus by the physician to prevent pregnancies." The minute the device is inserted it is effective. "Once an IUD has been inserted, it entails no further costs, no daily protective procedures. It works only inside the uterus—without effects on your body, blood, or brain; it doesn't cause you to gain weight, or

---

[3] Quotations in this section were provided by Dr. Thomsen's testimony before the Committee on Government Operations, House of Representatives, June 13, 1973; and the SAF-T-COIL information pamphlet.

have headaches or mood changes. And it provides the user with a most satisfying method of contraception."

Because of the simplicity of the device, manufacturing costs are low, and profits can be high. When volume is sufficient, an IUD can be manufactured, sterilized, and packaged for 35 to 40 cents, and it can be sold for $3.00 to $3.50. Due to the size and profit potential of the birth control market, the manufacturers of IUDs were well positioned to reap a bountiful harvest, but competition was tough. The secret to success was timing, and the winners would be the first in the market. Firms competing in the market realized that "unlike most consumer products, new drugs and delivery devices must first gain acceptance among a small group of specialists. If the specialists accept this, their patients will too." Therefore, the marketing effort was directed at physicians, knowing that they would refer the device to their patients.

THE DALKON SHIELD[4]

Dr. Hugh Davis, an assistant professor of medicine at Johns Hopkins University and an expert in birth control, was instrumental in developing the Dalkon Shield. Dr. Davis conducted research on patients using the shield, and he reported a pregnancy rate of 1.1 percent (comparable with the pill).The competitive advantage the Dalkon Shield had over other IUDs was the "larger surface area designed for maximum coverage and maximum contraceptive effect." The potential of the Dalkon Shield was great, and drawing from its already-established reputation and distribution channels in the pharmaceutical industry, the IUD seemed to be a logical addition to Robins's product offerings.

On June 12, 1970, A. H. Robins paid $750,000, a royalty of 10 percent of future net sales, plus consulting fees to acquire the Dalkon Shield. At the time of purchase, Robins had no expertise in the area of birth control. Although it did hire consultants, Robins had neither an obstetrician nor a gynecologist on its staff. It assigned assembly of the shield to the corporate division of the company that manufactures Chap Stick lip balm. Before buying the product, however, Robins's medical director, Frederick A. Clark, Jr., reviewed statistical tests performed by Dr. Davis on the shield. These tests showed that in 832 insertions, 26 women became pregnant. Dr. Davis's tests, however, were done on the original shield, not the one ultimately sold by Robins. The major difference between the original shield and the one sold by Robins was the addition of a multifilament tail.

When it went to the market, Robins was excited about its product. "Possibly no other IUD has received the benefit of such ecstatic claims by its

---

[4] Quotations in this section provided by Dr. Thomsen's testimony and the *Richmond Times-Dispatch,* June 23, 1985.

developer, its manufacturer, and the admiring multitude." Robins used promotional methods that were designed especially for acceptance of the shield within the medical profession. Foremost among these promotions was a text written by Dr. Davis, *Intrauterine Devices for Contraception—The IUD*. The appendix of his book lists complications reported with the use of 10 major brand IUDs. The shield was presented in a very good light, with only 5.4 percent complication rate. The complication rate of the competition ranged from 16.9 percent to 55.7 percent.

DIFFICULTIES EMERGE

A. H. Robins began selling the Dalkon Shield on January 1, 1971. On June 22, 1971, when a doctor reported that his shield-wearing daughter suffered a septic spontaneous abortion (miscarriage caused by infection), the company was particularly concerned about the safety aspects of the shield. The main concern was the shield's unique multifilament tail, which has since been accused of actually drawing infection from the vagina into a normally sterile uterus. Ironically, the product that was thought to be the ultimate form of birth control turned sour (36 alleged deaths and 13,000 alleged injuries), and it had a devastating effect on A. H. Robins.

DIFFICULTIES WITH RESEARCH[5]

Although the text written by Dr. Davis had been accepted by the medical profession as a major textbook on IUDs, the problems with IUDs raised many concerns, and the text was referred to as a "thinly disguised promotion of the shield." Examination revealed that Robins possessed data from five formal studies based on the experience of about 4,000 shield users. Three of these five studies were performed by people with financial interests in the shield. The foremost of these studies was done by Dr. Davis. He claimed a pregnancy rate of 1.1 percent, an expulsion rate of 2.3 percent, a medical removal rate of 2.0 percent, and a total complication rate of 5.4 percent. However, another study conducted over an 18-month period and dated October 25, 1972, showed a 4.3 percent pregnancy rate.

In an interview broadcast on "60 Minutes," Paul Rheingold, a New York attorney who has represented 40 Dalkon Shield users, said that "This IUD got on the market with no animal tests, and with whatever minimal clinical . . . or

---

[5] Most of the information in this section was taken from Dr. Thomsen's testimony, May 30–31, 1973, and June 1, 12–13, 1973.

testing on human subjects . . . the company wanted to do, which turned out to be practically nothing."

FINANCIAL IMPLICATIONS[6]

Approximately 4.5 million Dalkon Shields were sold by Robins, producing an estimated profit of $500,000. "The product generated total revenues to the company of $13.7 million in four and a half years. But, during the first six months of 1985, Robins paid out $61.2 million in Dalkon-related expenses." By June 30, 1985, Robins and Aetna Life and Casualty Company (Robins's insurance company) had paid $378.3 million to settle 9,230 Dalkon Shield cases. This exhausted all but $50 million of Robins's product liability insurance. Legal fees and other costs related to the shield have totaled $107.3 million. Robins's portion of the total Dalkon claims has been $198.1 million. Robins announced an anticipated minimum cost to handle future Dalkon expenses of $685 million, excluding punitive damages.

Exhibits 1 through 11 present financial information on the company contained in its 1984 annual report.

EXHIBIT 1   Net Sales ($ millions)

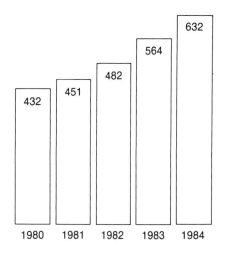

432	451	482	564	632
1980	1981	1982	1983	1984

---

[6] Information for this section was taken from the *Richmond Times-Dispatch*.

EXHIBIT 2   Net Earnings or Loss ($ millions)

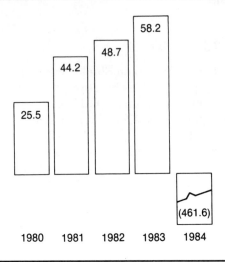

BANKRUPTCY[7]

On August 21, 1985, A. H. Robins filed for bankruptcy under Chapter 11 of the Federal Bankruptcy Code. "When it filed its request for reorganization on August 21, Robins listed $2.26 in assets for each $1 in debts and talked publicly about the strengths of the company when items related to the Dalkon Shield birth control device were excluded."

Robins noted that it had a profit of $35.3 million from net sales of $331.1 million in the first six months of 1985. What the sales and profits did not show was the extent to which Robins was having to dip into its retained earnings to pay Dalkon-related bills. "Dalkon payments have taken away only 1.7 cents for each $1 in Robins sales from 1974 through 1983, but then jumped to 12.3 cents in 1984. And when it jumped to 18.5 cents in the first six months of this year (1985), there wasn't enough left from sales to meet other expenses."

The petition in bankruptcy court stops the flow of Dalkon payments. A perceived advantage from Robins in seeking the Chapter 11 route is that the company's reorganization plan would likely stretch out Dalkon payments so that a cashflow problem wouldn't recur." The action was taken [in bankruptcy court] in an effort to ensure the economic vitality of the company, which is, of course, critical to our ability to pay legitimate claims to present and future plaintiffs."

---

[7] Quotations in this section were provided in the *Richmond Time-Dispatch* between August and September 1985, and selected October 1985 issues of *The Wall Street Journal*.

EXHIBIT 3   Earnings or Losses per Share ($)

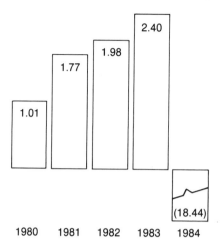

A. H. Robins's petition in bankruptcy court has been at the center of a heated debate. Those in support of the company have argued that "A. H. Robins's move into bankruptcy court could ensure that there is money for all who are suing the company instead of letting 'the first wolves who tear at the carcass' get it all." On the other hand, Aaron M. Levine, a lawyer for women filing against Robins, believes that "This is a company that's saying, 'We'll pay

EXHIBIT 4   Dividends per Share ($)

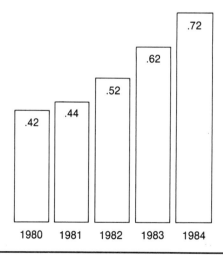

EXHIBIT 5   Worldwide R&D Expenditures ($ millions)

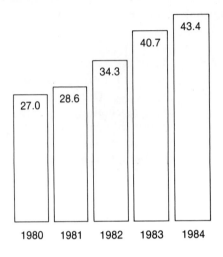

our suppliers, and we'll pay for TV ads, and we'll pay for the syrup for the Robitussin, and we'll pay our workers, but as far as this one particular group of creditors is concerned—the women we have maimed—we won't pay.' "

Levine pointed to Robins's own estimates that it has $466 million in assets and only $216.5 million owed to creditors. "Certainly this is far from the usual type of debtor who files a bankruptcy court petition." According to Levine's motion, Robins's petition was instituted not to benefit a corporation in distress,

EXHIBIT 6   Capital Additions ($ millions)

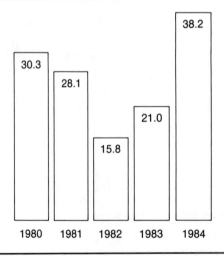

as the laws are intended, "but to enable the petitioner to escape the jurisdiction of another court when the day of reckoning for their alleged acts of misconduct was at hand." The National Women's Health Network, for instance, said at a news conference that the company is financially healthy but is trying to duck its responsibility to women who have filed lawsuits. On the other hand, Roscoe E. Puckett, Jr., a spokesman for Robins, contends that "The best hope for all concerned is for A. H. Robins to remain financially healthy. To do that, we had to stop the financial hemorrhaging that threatened to destroy the company to the detriment of everyone, including the legitimate Dalkon Shield claimants." "Other factors include our desire to ensure that all persons to whom the company has an obligation are treated fairly, to preserve the assets of the company, and maintain its current operations."

To supplement Dalkon expenses and to alleviate the tight cash flow position that Robins has experienced recently, it requested a $35 million credit limit "to meet $25 million of cash needs of its U.S. operations, $2 million in letters of credit for foreign suppliers, and $8 million of credit for its foreign units." This credit limit was the subject of heated debate among the Internal Revenue Service, the attorneys for more than 10,000 women who have filed suit against Robins, and various Robins's creditors. "The IRS contends that Robins owes about $61 million in corporate income taxes from as far back as 1978. Arguing on behalf of the agency, Assistant U.S. Attorney S. David Schiller told the judge that Robins had failed to prove that it needs the entire $35 million of credit or that it couldn't get the loans elsewhere under more favorable terms." The credit line requested by Robins was ultimately approved by a federal court judge. "Under the agreement, Robins will receive $23 million from Manufacturers Hanover Trust Company, New York, and $12 million from the Bank of Virginia. The arrangement, which was opposed vigorously by the Internal Revenue Service and others with claims pending against Robins, assigns the two banks priority for payments among all Robins's creditors."

"In approving the credit agreement, Judge Robert R. Merhige, Jr., acknowledged that some of the terms 'could be questioned.' But he said he felt compelled to 'give way to the business judgment' of the company's managers. He also expressed concern that denying the request might harm the company's prospects for obtaining credit."

THE FUTURE

In October (1984), the company filed in Federal District Court in Richmond a motion seeking a class action to resolve all punitive damage claims arising from Dalkon Shield litigation. The goal is a single trial for the purpose of determining if A. H. Robins should, in fact, be liable for punitive damages and, if so, the amount of those damages in respect to all present and future Dalkon Shield claimants. It is our view that this is the only fair means of settling this issue. In addition to the

EXHIBIT 7

A. H. ROBINS COMPANY, INCORPORATED, AND SUBSIDIARIES
Selected Financial Data
(dollars in thousands except per share and ratio data)

	1984	1983	1982	1981	1980†
Operations					
Net sales	$631,891	$563,510	$482,324	$450,854	$432,328
Cost of sales	237,508	220,628	195,008	190,759	187,496
Marketing, administrative and general	222,939	196,495	168,963	157,852	160,477
Research and development	43,352	40,686	34,279	28,572	27,033
Total operating costs and expenses	503,799	457,809	398,250	377,183	375,006
Operating earnings	128,092	105,701	84,074	73,671	57,322
Interest income	7,560	8,350	8,085	8,437	5,614
Interest expense	(3,240)	(5,441)	(10,308)	(3,564)	(4,741)
Litigation settlement income	1,205	2,256	3,135	3,379	3,590
Reserve for Dalkon Shield claims	(615,000)				
Litigation expenses and settlements	(77,950)	(18,745)	(7,091)	(3,318)	(4,616)
Provision for losses on disposition of businesses					(9,129)
Other, net	(13,190)	(144)	(3,740)	(4,997)	(4,112)
Earnings (loss) before income taxes	(572,523)	91,977	74,155	73,608	43,928
Provision for income taxes (benefits)	(110,910)	33,756	25,462	29,380	18,458
Net earnings (loss)	$(461,613)	$ 58,221	$ 48,693	$ 44,228	$ 25,470
Per Share Data					
Earnings (loss) per share	$(18.44)	$2.40	$1.98	$1.77	$1.01
Dividends per share	0.72	0.62	0.52	0.44	0.42
Stockholders' equity (deficit) per share	(5.23)	14.69	13.29	12.52	11.16
Weighted average number of shares outstanding	25,037	24,295	24,552	25,015	25,314
Balance Sheet Data					
Cash and cash equivalents	$ 91,627	$133,381	$ 79,986	$ 89,024	$ 49,705
Working capital	122,344	229,525	200,810	177,259	146,258
Current ratio	1.7 to 1	3.2 to 1	4.0 to 1	3.1 to 1	3.0 to 1
Property, plant and equipment, net	$135,685	$107,651	$ 98,079	$ 96,457	$ 80,511
Depreciation and amortization	16,310	10,253	10,384	10,096	10,950
Total assets	648,129	509,663	439,983	443,942	390,570
Long-term obligations, exclusive of Dalkon Shield reserve	25,330	48,322	51,040	48,232	35,346
Stockholders' equity (deficit)	(127,851)	355,837	321,085	310,201	280,394

(Dollars in thousands except per share and ratio data)

Amounts for 1983 and prior years have been reclassified to conform to 1984 presentation.

See Note 12 of Notes to Consolidated Financial Statements for information on litigation.

† Results preceded adoption of Statement of Financial Accounting Standards No. 52 which revised the method of translating foreign currency.

* Results were computed on a FIFO basis.

	1979†*	1978†*	1977†*	1976†*	1975†*	1974†*
	$386,425	$357,070	$306,713	$284,925	$241,060	$210,713
	157,895	146,636	122,374	108,519	89,304	71,233
	139,782	131,195	114,490	101,568	85,378	77,128
	20,522	18,951	16,107	12,729	10,690	9,568
	318,199	296,782	252,971	222,816	185,372	157,929
	68,226	60,288	53,742	62,109	55,688	52,784
	5,767	3,469	2,033	2,355	1,726	2,465
	(4,194)	(3,469)	(2,106)	(1,719)	(1,189)	(1,134)
	28,934					
	(6,005)	(9,560)	(3,331)	(1,146)	(5,065)	
	(13,539)	901	(2,675)	(2,710)	(2,518)	(1,209)
	79,189	51,629	47,663	58,889	48,642	52,906
	34,443	21,713	20,862	27,534	23,095	25,989
	$ 44,746	$ 29,916	$ 26,801	$ 31,355	$ 25,547	$ 26,917
	$1.71	$1.15	$1.03	$1.20	$ .98	$1.03
	0.40	0.34	0.32	0.30	0.27	0.26
	10.52	9.20	8.39	7.69	6.79	6.04
	26,107	26,127	26,127	26,127	26,127	26,126
	$ 69,381	$ 72,058	$ 43,611	$ 50,769	$ 41,763	$ 29,228
	153,411	156,632	128,838	126,904	100,387	89,459
	2.9 to 1	3.7 to 1	3.5 to 1	4.1 to 1	3.5 to 1	4.5 to 1
	$ 59,994	$ 55,350	$ 49,751	$ 39,066	$ 34,640	$ 30,418
	8,806	8,427	6,837	6,076	5,007	4,322
	379,597	326,073	287,045	262,668	223,544	190,263
	26,518	27,809	16,718	20,412	6,740	5,620
	272,673	240,275	219,242	200,802	177,275	157,695

EXHIBIT 8

A. H. ROBINS COMPANY, INCORPORATED AND SUBSIDIARIES
Consolidated Statements of Operations
(dollars in thousands except per share data)
Year Ended December 31

	1984	1983*	1982*
Net Sales	$631,891	$563,510	$482,324
Cost of sales	237,508	220,628	195,008
Marketing, administrative and general	222,939	196,495	168,963
Research and development	43,352	40,686	34,279
Total operating costs and expenses	503,799	457,809	398,250
Operating Earnings	128,092	105,701	84,074
Interest income	7,560	8,350	8,085
Interest expense	(3,240)	(5,441)	(10,308)
Litigation settlement income	1,205	2,256	3,135
Reserve for Dalkon Shield claims	(615,000)		
Litigation expenses and settlements	(77,950)	(18,745)	(7,091)
Other, net	(13,190)	(144)	(3,740)
Earnings (Loss) Before Income Taxes	(572,523)	91,977	74,155
Provision for income taxes (benefits)	(110,910)	33,756	25,462
Net Earnings (Loss)	$(461,613)	$ 58,221	$ 48,693
Earnings (Loss) per Common Share	$(18.44)	$2.40	$1.98
Average number of shares outstanding	25,037	24,295	24,552

* Reclassified to conform to 1984 presentation.
The Notes to Consolidated Financial Statements are an integral part of these statements.

class action, the court has been requested to establish a voluntary opt-in proceeding to dispose of claims for compensatory damages on a facilitated basis. Such a proceeding would allow those plaintiffs who so desire to advance their claims with a minimum of delay and expense.[8]

Additionally, the company initiated an advertising campaign for the purpose of persuading women using the shield to have them removed at the company's expense. As of the publication date of the company's 1984 annual report, "More than 18,250 inquiries [had] been received. . . . The company [had] paid for 777 examinations and 4,437 removals."

---

[8] A. H. Robins, *Annual Report,* 1984.

EXHIBIT 9

A. H. ROBINS COMPANY, INCORPORATED AND SUBSIDIARIES
Consolidated Statements of Stockholders' Equity (Deficit)
(dollars in thousands except per share data)

	Common Stock ($1 Par Value)	Additional Paid-In Capital	Retained Earnings (Deficit)	Cumulative Translation Adjustments	Treasury Stock (At Cost)	Total
Balance—January 1, 1982	$26,127	$700	$295,851	$ 84	$(12,561)	$310,201
Net earnings			48,693			48,693
Cash dividends—$0.52 per share			(12,696)			(12,696)
Translation adjustment for 1982				(16,559)		(16,559)
Purchase of treasury stock—644,000 shares					(8,844)	(8,844)
Issued for stock options—24,550 shares	24	266				290
Balance—December 31, 1982	26,151	966	331,848	(16,475)	(21,405)	321,085
Net earnings			58,221			58,221
Cash dividends—$0.62 per share			(14,997)			(14,997)
Translation adjustment for 1983				(9,250)		(9,250)
Issued for stock options—61,900 shares	62	716				778
Balance—December 31, 1983	26,213	1,682	375,072	(25,725)	(21,405)	355,837
Net loss			(461,613)			(461,613)
Cash dividends—$0.72 per share			(17,936)			(17,936)
Translation adjustment for 1984				(10,051)		(10,051)
Purchase of treasury stock—1,040,404 shares					(17,070)	(17,070)
Issued for stock options—20,300 shares	21	201				222
Shares reissued with acquisition—1,243,707 shares		9,427			13,333	22,760
Balance—December 31, 1984	$26,234	$11,310	$(104,477)	$(35,776)	$(25,142)	$(127,851)

The Notes to Consolidated Financial Statements are an integral part of these statements.

EXHIBIT 10

A. H. ROBINS COMPANY, INCORPORATED AND SUBSIDIARIES
Consolidated Balance Sheets
(dollars in thousands)
December 31

	1984	1983	1982
Assets			
Current Assets			
Cash	$ 1,792	$ 1,534	$ 5,792
Certificates of deposit and time deposits	13,426	57,700	14,349
Marketable securities	76,409	74,147	59,845
Accounts and notes receivable—net of allowance for doubtful accounts of $2,613 (1983—$2,560, 1982—$2,473)	111,313	112,260	107,790
Inventories	84,611	82,714	72,219
Prepaid expenses	5,643	6,674	5,136
Deferred tax benefits	15,800		3,537
Total current assets	308,994	335,029	268,668
Property, Plant and Equipment			
Land	6,313	6,552	6,940
Buildings and leasehold improvements	106,165	89,374	75,933
Machinery and equipment	90,260	70,169	68,453
	202,738	166,095	151,326
Less accumulated depreciation	67,053	58,444	53,247
	135,685	107,651	98,079
Intangible and Other Assets			
Intangibles—net of accumulated amortization	82,502	50,201	53,140
Note receivable, less current maturity			8,044
Deferred tax benefits	106,700		
Other assets	14,248	16,782	12,052
	203,450	66,983	73,236
	$648,129	$509,663	$439,983

EXHIBIT 10 *(concluded)*

A. H. ROBINS COMPANY, INCORPORATED AND SUBSIDIARIES
Consolidated Balance Sheets
(dollars in thousands)
December 31

	1984	1983	1982
Liabilities and Stockholders' Equity (Deficit)			
Current Liabilities			
Notes payable	$ 16,129	$ 7,116	$ 5,419
Long-term debt payable within one year	21,600	3,225	1,325
Current portion of reserve for Dalkon Shield claims . .	51,000		
Accounts payable	23,855	23,989	20,807
Income taxes payable	11,850	28,589	12,269
Accrued liabilities:			
Dalkon Shield costs	22,653	11,094	2,134
Other	39,563	31,491	25,904
Total current liabilities	186,650	105,504	67,858
Long-Term Debt	11,400	33,000	36,225
Reserve for Dalkon Shield Claims, Less Current Portion .	564,000		
Other Liabilities	13,930	12,270	14,022
Deferred Income Taxes		3,052	793
Stockholders' Equity (Deficit)			
Preferred stock, $1 par—authorized 10,000,000 shares, none issued			
Common stock, $1 par—authorized 40,000,000 shares .	26,234	26,213	26,151
Additional paid-in capital	11,310	1,682	966
Retained earnings (deficit)	(104,477)	375,072	331,848
Cumulative translation adjustments	(35,776)	(25,725)	(16,475)
	(102,709)	377,242	342,490
Less common stock in treasury, at cost—1,793,347 shares			
(1983—1,996,650 shares, 1982—1,996,650 shares)	25,142	21,405	21,405
	(127,851)	355,837	321,085
	$648,129	$509,663	$439,983

The Notes to Consolidated Financial Statements are an integral part of these statements.

EXHIBIT 11

A. H. ROBINS COMPANY, INCORPORATED AND SUBSIDIARIES
Consolidated Statements of Changes in Financial Position
(dollars in thousands)
Year Ended December 31

	1984	1983*	1982*
Cash Provided by Operations			
Net earnings (loss)	$(461,613)	$58,221	$48,693
Non-cash expenses			
Depreciation and amortization	16,310	10,253	10,384
Deferred tax benefit, reserve for Dalkon Shield claims	(125,933)		
Reserve for Dalkon Shield claims	615,000		
Other, net	6,140	2,477	3,201
	49,904	70,951	62,278
Operating Requirements, (Increase) Decrease			
Accounts and notes receivable	1,686	(7,212)	(18,172)
Inventories	125	(10,424)	(4,647)
Accounts payable, income taxes payable and accrued			
liabilities	(147)	36,279	(13,936)
Other, net	2,955	4,910	5,477
	4,619	23,553	31,278)
Investments			
Capital additions	(38,155)	(20,955)	(15,815)
Acquisitions	(51,809)	(5,700)	(2,035)
	(89,964)	(26,655)	(17,850)
Cash flow from operations	(35,441)	(67,849)	(13,150)
Cash Provided by (Utilized in) Financial Activities			
Notes payable and long-term debt	5,933	543	(648)
Purchase of treasury shares	(17,070)		(8,844)
Issuance of treasury shares for acquisition	22,760		
	11,623	543	(9,492)
Less Cash Dividends Paid	17,936	14,997	12,696
Net increase (decrease) in cash and cash equivalents	$(41,754)	$53,395	$(9,038)

* Reclassified to conform to 1984 presentation.
The Notes to Consolidated Financial Statements are an integral part of these statements.

1. Significant Accounting Policies

Consolidation

The consolidated financial statements include the accounts of A. H. Robins Company, Incorporated and all majority-owned subsidiaries. Accounts of subsidiaries outside the U.S. and Canada are included on the basis of a fiscal year beginning December 1 (or date of acquisition) and ending November 30. All significant intercompany accounts and transactions have been eliminated.

EXHIBIT 11   *(continued)*

Inventories
Inventories are valued at the lower of cost or market. The cost for substantially all domestic inventories is determined on the last-in, first-out (LIFO) method while cost for foreign inventories is based on the first-in, first-out (FIFO) method.

Property, Plant and Equipment
Property, plant and equipment are recorded at cost and are depreciated over their estimated useful lives. Depreciation for all companies is computed on the straight line method for assets acquired after 1979. Depreciation on assets acquired in 1979 and prior years is computed on the declining balance method for domestic companies and on the straight line method for foreign companies.

Intangible Assets
Excess of cost over net assets of subsidiaries acquired after October 31, 1970 is being amortized over a period of 40 years or less. Excess cost of $17,357,000 relating to companies acquired prior to that date is not being amortized. Expenditures for development of patents are charged to expense as incurred. Patents purchased and trademarks are being amortized over their determinable lives.

Income Taxes
The Company provides for deferred income taxes on items of income or expense reported for tax purposes in different years than for financial purposes. The investment tax credit is included in earnings in the year the credit arises as a reduction of any provision for income taxes.

The Company files a consolidated Federal income tax return with its domestic subsidiaries. Income taxes, if any, are provided for on earnings of foreign subsidiaries remitted or to be remitted. No provision is made for income taxes on undistributed earnings of foreign subsidiaries reinvested in the companies.

Retirement Plans
The Company and certain of its subsidiaries have retirement plans for their employees. Costs of the plans are funded when accrued except for the plans of certain foreign subsidiaries. Unfunded prior service costs are provided for over periods not exceeding 40 years. Certain medical and life insurance benefits are provided for qualifying retired employees. The annual costs for these programs are not material and are expensed when paid.

Earnings (Loss) Per Share
Earnings (loss) per share are based on the weighted average number of common shares and common share equivalents outstanding during each year.

2. Acquisitions and Divestitures
On January 5, 1984, the Company acquired all of the outstanding stock of Quinton Instrument Company, Inc. for which the Company issued 1,243,707 shares of its common stock valued for accounting purposes at $18.30 per share and paid $20.1 million in cash. The total acquisition cost was $42.9 million, which consisted of the assigned value of the above-mentioned shares, the cash paid and acquisition expenses. The Company accounted for the acquisition as a purchase and accordingly has included

EXHIBIT 11 *(continued)*

Quinton's results of operations in its financial statements beginning January 5, 1984. On an unaudited pro forma basis, assuming the acquisition had occurred on January 1, 1983, the Company's net sales, net earnings and earnings per share would have been $587,328,000, $56,992,000 and $2.23, respectively. The pro forma amounts reflect estimated adjustments for goodwill amortization, depreciation and interest expense. Goodwill of $27,118,000 is being amortized on a straight line basis over a period of 40 years.

On April 2, 1984, the Company acquired substantially all of the assets associated with radio stations WRQK-FM and WPET-AM in Greensboro, North Carolina. The acquisition price was $7.6 million.

In December 1984, the Company acquired all of the outstanding stock of Lode B. V., an established ergometer manufacturer located in the Netherlands. Lode B. V., an addition to the Company's Medical Instruments Division, has been accounted for by the purchase method and did not result in a significant impact on 1984 financial results.

In March 1983, the Company acquired substantially all of the assets of Scientific Protein Laboratories, a company primarily engaged in the manufacture of animal-derived pharmaceutical products.

Also in March 1983, the Company sold its Quencher cosmetics line at an after-tax gain of $801,000.

In November 1982, the Company acquired the assets of U.S. Clinical Products, Incorporated, located in Richardson, Texas. U.S. Clinical Products engages primarily in the manufacturing and marketing of tamper-resistant seals used in hospitals on intravenous containers after the manufacturer's closure has been removed.

3. Foreign Operations

At December 31, 1984, undistributed earnings of foreign subsidiaries totaled approximately $70,981,000 including amounts accumulated at dates of acquisition. Of this amount, $14,600,000 might be subject to net additional Federal income taxes if distributed currently. No provision has been made for income taxes on these undistributed earnings.

Foreign currency exchange losses included in earnings amounted to $1,187,000 in 1984 (1983—$938,000, 1982—$2,436,000). Net foreign assets included in the consolidated financial statements at December 31, 1984 were $75,098,000 (1983—$93,011,000, 1982—$101,271,000).

4. Inventories

	(Dollars in thousands)		
	1984	1983	1982
Finished products	**$41,814**	$43,462	$38,467
Work in process	**18,425**	16,186	8,221
Raw materials and supplies	**24,372**	23,066	25,531
	$84,611	$82,714	$72,219

Substantially all domestic inventories were valued on the last-in, first-out (LIFO) method while most foreign inventories were valued on the first-in, first-out (FIFO)

EXHIBIT 11 *(continued)*

method. Approximately 68% of inventories was valued under LIFO in 1984 (1983–70%, 1982—65%) and the remainder under FIFO. Current cost (FIFO method) of inventories exceeded the LIFO values by $3,281,000 in 1984; $4,424,000 in 1983; and $3,546,000 in 1982.

5. Long-Term Debt

Long-term debt, net of amounts payable within one year, is summarized as follows:

	(Dollars in thousands)		
	1984	*1983*	*1982*
8¾% promissory note due annually to 1988		$19,700	$21,025
Bonds, interest rate 55% of prime, due annually from 1984 to 1991	**11,400**	13,300	15,200
	$11,400	$33,000	$36,225

Annual maturities of long-term debt for the next five years are: 1985—$21,600,000; 1986—$1,900,000; 1987—$1,900,000; 1988—$1,900,000; and 1989—$1,900,000.

The 8¾% promissory note was redeemed at par subsequent to year end and therefore has been reclassified as long-term debt payable within one year.

Interest incurred during 1984 of $2,500,000 was capitalized and included in property, plant and equipment. No interest was capitalized in 1983 or 1982.

6. Lines of Credit

At December 31, 1984, unused lines of credit which do not support commercial paper or similar borrowing arrangements and may be withdrawn at the banks' option amounted to $12 million with domestic banks. Aggregate compensating balances were not material.

7. Stock Options

The Company has stock option plans for officers and certain key employees. The qualified stock option plan of 1973 as amended in 1982 was terminated on January 31, 1983 except as to outstanding options. A new incentive stock option plan was approved by the stockholders on April 26, 1983 under which 1,000,000 shares of common stock were made available for the granting of options. The plans are administered by a committee, subject to certain limitations expressly set forth in the plan, with authority to select participants, determine the number of shares to be allotted to a participant, set the option price, and fix the term of each option.

EXHIBIT 11   *(continued)*

Transactions of the qualified and nonstatutory stock option plans are summarized below:

	Shares Available for Option	*Options Outstanding* *Shares*	*Options Outstanding* *Price per Share*
Balance—Dec. 31, 1981	1,355,300	241,350	$10.19 to $11.38
Exercised		(24,550)	10.19 to 11.38
Canceled and expired	4,150	(4,150)	10.19
Balance—Dec. 31, 1982	1,359,450	212,650	10.19 to 11.38
Terminated—1973 Plan	(602,450)		
Exercised		(61,900)	10.19 to 11.38
1983 Plan	1,000,000		
Balance—Dec. 31, 1983	1,757,000	150,750	10.19 to 11.38
Granted	(488,500)	488,500	13.69
Exercised		(20,300)	10.19 to 13.69
Canceled and expired	13,700	(13,700)	11.38
Balance—Dec. 31, 1984	1,282,000	605,250	10.19 to 13.69

The options are exercisable at any time until their expiration dates, which are in 1986 (136,550 shares) and 1994 (468,700 shares).

8. Provision for Income Taxes

The provision for income taxes includes:

	(Dollars in thousands) 1984	1983	1982
Currently payable:			
Domestic	$ (4,061)	$13,563	$ 1,572
State	1,580	2,745	3,639
Foreign	9,234	10,947	11,859
	$ 6,753	$27,255	$17,070
Deferred:			
Domestic	$(110,009)	$ 5,917	$ 8,238
State	(8,648)	270	292
Foreign	994	314	(138)
	$(117,663)	$ 6,501	$ 8,392
Total provision	$(110,910)	$33,756	$25,462
Earnings (loss) before income taxes consist of:			
Domestic	$(590,925)	$71,613	$52,974
Foreign	18,402	20,364	21,181
	$(572,523)	$91,977	$74,155

Note 12 in the Notes to Consolidated Financial Statements discusses a minimum reserve established by the Company in 1984 for pending and future claims related to the Dalkon Shield. These claims are deductible for tax purposes as incurred by the Company. It is the Company's belief that the currently recognized claims will be fully deductible against its future taxable income. However, generally accepted accounting

EXHIBIT 11   *(continued)*

principles limit the recognition of future tax benefits to those amounts assured beyond any reasonable doubt. Accordingly, the Company has recognized for financial statement purposes only those benefits arising from the carryback of product liability expenses against income tax expenses previously recognized by the Company. At December 31, 1984, the Company had, for financial statement purposes only, unrecognized loss carryforward deductions in the amount of $138,132,000 and unrecognized foreign and investment tax credits carryforward of $86,939,000.

Should the realization of product liability claims produce a taxable loss in a future period, the Company is permitted under provisions of the U.S. Internal Revenue Code to carry such loss back as a deduction against previous taxable income for a period up to 10 years. Such loss may also be used to reduce future taxable income for a period up to 15 years.

In 1984, the Company realized net tax benefits of $5,206,000, primarily in the form of investment tax credit and depreciation, from its investment in tax benefit leases under the "safe harbor" leasing provisions enacted in 1981 and 1982. These benefits reduced the 1984 provision for domestic taxes currently payable and increased the provision for deferred taxes. As current tax benefits are realized, the Company has reduced its purchase cost of the leases and established a deferred tax liability for the leases' future taxable income. Interest income is accrued on the unrecovered purchase cost. The excess of the purchase cost and accrued interest over the cumulative tax savings expected is amortized on an interest method during the years temporary excess tax savings are produced. The interest accrued and investment amortized during the lease terms have no material effect on earnings. At December 31, 1984, the balance of unrecovered investment and accrued interest was $1,071,000.

Deferred income taxes result from tax leases and from income and expense items reported for financial accounting and tax purposes in different periods. The source of these differences and the tax effect of each is shown below:

	(Dollars in thousands)		
	1984	1983	1982
Reserve for Dalkon Shield claims	$(125,933)		
Discounted portion of installment note receivable	574	$1,106	$1,520
Tax depreciation in excess of books	2,134	1,480	1,096
Other	356	988	585
Tax benefit from tax leases	$ 5,206	2,927	5,191
	$(117,663)	$6,501	$8,392

Reconciliation of the effective rate and the Federal statutory rate is as follows:

EXHIBIT 11   *(continued)*

	Percent of Pretax Income (Loss)		
	1984	1983	1982
Statutory Federal tax rate	(46.0)%	46.0 %	46.0 %
Product liability claims in excess of amounts carried back	15.2		
Foreign, investment and other tax credits not recognized after loss carryback	11.1		
Federal tax on foreign earnings	1.4	(1.1)	(3.1)
State taxes on income, net of Federal tax benefit	(1.3)	2.8	3.6
Investment and other tax credits		(2.1)	(2.8)
Foreign earnings taxed at higher (lower) effective tax rate	0.1		0.3
Puerto Rican earnings exempt from tax	(1.1)	(6.7)	(9.0)
Tax exempt interest	(0.1)	(0.3)	(1.2)
All other, net	1.3	(1.9)	0.5
	(19.4)%	36.7 %	34.3 %

A wholly owned subsidiary in Puerto Rico operates under partial income tax exemptions granted for periods through 1999. The estimated tax saving from the Puerto Rican operation was $6,200,000 in 1984 (1983—$6,200,000, 1982—$6,700,000). Puerto Rican withholding taxes are provided on those earnings expected to be repatriated prior to expiration of the exemptions.

During 1983, the Internal Revenue Service completed its examination of the Company's tax returns for the years 1978 through 1980 and proposed a deficiency of income taxes of approximately $6,400,000. The Company is contesting the proposed deficiency which arises from a proposed reallocation of income from the Company's Puerto Rico subsidiary. It is likely that a similar deficiency will be proposed for the years 1981 and 1982.

Management believes that any additional income taxes that may result from the proposed deficiency, and from the probable proposed deficiency related to the same issues for the years 1981 and 1982, should not have a material adverse effect on the consolidated financial position of the Company.

9. Business Segment Information

Information about operations in different business segments and in various geographic areas of the world is included on page 32 of this report and incorporated herein by reference.

10. Retirement Plan

The Company and certain of its subsidiaries have retirement plans covering substantially all of their employees. The total retirement expense for 1984 was $6,908,000 (1983—$6,246,000, 1984—$5,435,000). The actuarial present value of accumulated plan benefits, assuming a weighted average rate of return of 8% in 1984 (1983—8%, 1982—6.5%), and plan net assets available for benefits of domestic defined benefit plans as of January 1, 1984, 1983 and 1982 are as follows:

EXHIBIT 11 *(continued)*

	(Dollars in thousands)		
	1984	*1983*	*1982*
Actuarial present value of accumulated plan benefits:			
Vested	$40,895	$35,601	$30,925
Nonvested	3,472	3,250	4,351
	$44,367	$38,851	$35,276
Net assets available for benefits	$55,621	$47,287	$36,017

Assets available for benefits and the actuarial present value of accumulated benefits have not been determined for several minor foreign pension plans which are not required to report such information to government agencies.

Other liabilities include $6,635,000 of accrued pensions and severance benefits in foreign subsidiaries (1983—$7,063,000, 1982—$7,100,000).

11. Commitments

Rentals of space, vehicles and office and data processing equipment under operating leases amounted to $6,718,000 in 1984 (1983—$6,428,000, 1982—$5,843,000).

Minimum future rental commitments under all noncancelable operating leases at December 31, 1984 with remaining terms of more than one year are as follows:

	(Dollars in thousands)
1985	$2,515
1986	1,804
1987	1,634
1988	1,265
1989	822
Later years	1,853
Total minimum future rentals	$9,893

The Company has agreed to repurchase, at the option of the shareholder until such time as the securities are registered, the shares of the Company issued to the former Quinton Instrument Company, Inc. shareholders. Upon tender of the shares, the Company will repurchase the shares at the current market price. At December 31, 1984, there were 1,017,103 shares subject to this agreement.

As of December 31, 1984, the Company had outstanding commitments of $8 million for the construction of plant, office and research and development facilities.

12. Litigation

Dalkon Shield—In June 1970, the Company acquired the rights to the Dalkon Shield, an intrauterine contraceptive device. Approximately 2.8 million devices were sold in the U.S. through June 1974. Approximately 1.7 million of the devices were sold abroad.

Numerous cases and claims alleging injuries claimed to be associated with use of the device have been filed against the Company in the U.S. ("Claims"). Only a few claims have been filed in foreign jurisdictions. The alleged injuries fall under the following general groups: perforation of the uterus or cervix, infection of the female reproductive system, pregnancy, ectopic pregnancy, spontaneous abortion which may be accompanied by sepsis, death, sterility, fetal abnormality and premature delivery,

EXHIBIT 11   *(continued)*

painful insertion and removal, and miscellaneous injuries. In addition to compensatory damages, most cases also seek punitive damages.

As of December 31, 1984, there were approximately 3,800 Claims pending against the Company in Federal and state courts in the U.S. The Company expects that a substantial number of new Claims will be filed against the Company in the future.

Through December 31, 1984, the Company had disposed of approximately 8,300 Claims. In disposing of these Claims, the Company and its insurer have paid out approximately $314.6 million. Prior to 1981, substantially all disposition costs (including legal expenses, but excluding punitive damages) were charged to applicable products liability insurance carried by the Company. The Company incurred costs in excess of insurance in the following amounts: 1981—$3.3 million; 1982—$7.1 million; 1983—$18.7 million; and 1984—$78.0 million (exclusive of the reserve described below).

Of the Claims disposed of prior to December 31, 1984, 50 were tried to conclusion. Of that number, 27 resulted in verdicts for compensatory damages in favor of plaintiffs and 23 in verdicts in favor of the Company. Seven of the plaintiff verdicts (involving compensatory awards aggregating approximately $5 million) and one verdict in favor of the Company are the subject of pending appeals. Eight of the plaintiff verdicts also included awards of punitive damages in an aggregate amount of $17,227,000. Six of these punitive awards aggregating $8,827,000 have been paid; two are the subject of appeals. Punitive damage awards are not covered by insurance and are payable by the Company.

The Company is unable to assess its potential exposure to additional punitive damage awards. It has recently filed a motion in the United States District Court for the Eastern District of Virginia seeking certification of a class of present and prospective claimants in both Federal and state courts for the purpose of determining and finally resolving in a single proceeding whether the Company should be liable for punitive damages by reason of the Dalkon Shield and, if so, the aggregate amount of additional punitive damages that should be awarded.

The Company had product liability insurance covering compensatory awards with respect to the Dalkon Shield for pertinent periods prior to March 1978. In October 1984, the Company settled its suit, commenced in 1979, against its insurer concerning coverage of Dalkon Shield liability. From existing coverage and some additional coverage resulting from the settlement of this suit the Company had at December 31, 1984, approximately $70 million of insurance coverage that it expects to be able to use.

In anticipation of the conclusion of the insurance coverage suit, the Company commissioned a study, the purpose of which was to provide management of the Company with data to establish a loss reserve for the future costs in compensatory damages and legal expenses of the disposition of pending and future Claims. The study estimated the amount of this future disposition cost based on the following: (1) an estimate of total injuries based on an epidemiological analysis of published literature regarding the Dalkon Shield and other IUDs; (2) a statistical analysis of all Claims filed during the period 1981 through 1983 which constitute 51% of all Claims filed since the inception of the litigation through December 31, 1983, and (3) a statistical analysis of disposition timing and costs of all Claims filed during the period January 1, 1979 through December 31, 1983 and disposed of prior to October 1, 1984. The information on claims

EXHIBIT 11 *(continued)*

filed and disposition timing and costs was extracted from a database which contains information on Claims filed through Deceember 31, 1983. The study utilized information from the periods discussed above, which was believed to be more representative of future experience, rather than the entire litigation period which would have produced a materially higher estimate of disposition cost.

Based on the study's estimate of disposition cost and a review of 1984 fourth-quarter settlement cost data, management established a reserve, net of insurance, of $615 million against 1984 earnings in the accompanying consolidated financial statements. Managment believes this represents a reasonable estimate of a minimum reserve for compensatory damages and legal expenses for pending and future Claims. The reserve does not provide for any punitive damages or damages from Dalkon Shield litigation abroad since there is no substantive basis to quantify such exposures. In taking into account 1984 fourth quarter settlement cost data, management excluded the cost of a single group settlement which management believes is reasonable to assume is not representative of the expected future disposition of Claims. If the excluded settlement cost had been factored as an increasing trend into projected future cost of disposition of Claims, the reserve would have been increased by a material amount.

Based on the study's projected schedule of disposition of pending and future Claims, the payout of the reserve will take place over many years. The Company has reduced its 1984 provision for income taxes by $125.9 million, representing the expected minimum tax benefit to be realized by loss carrybacks to 1983 and prior years, plus reductions in deferred taxes expected to turn around in the tax loss carryforward period. The net effect of the reserve, less estimated tax benefits, is $489.1 million or $19.53 per share.

Continuing uncertainties associated with the litigation preclude a determination of the ultimate cost of the Dalkon Shield litigation to the Company. There has been a significant increase in the number of new Claims filed per month and additional pressure on and a resulting increase in some settlement values which, if continued, would result in a greater Claim disposition cost than the amount estimated by the study. Whether this represents a long term trend or is, as management believes is reasonable to assume, the temporary result of publicity associated with several Dalkon Shield related events in 1984 and 1985 causing a temporary acceleration in the rate of filing of Claims with a subsequent leveling to those shown in the study will only be determined by future experience.

In addition to these uncertainties, there are other factors which could affect, either favorably or unfavorably, the ultimate outcome of the Dalkon Shield litigation and the resulting financial impact on the Company. Among them are:

- The Dalkon Shield removal campaign initiated on October 29, 1984
- The types of injuries alleged in future Claims
- The effect of the passage of time, including the effect of statutes of limitations
- The level of litigation activity relating to devices sold abroad
- The method of disposition of Claims
- The class action intended to resolve the question of punitive damages

EXHIBIT 11 *(concluded)*

Accordingly, the reserve may not necessarily be the amount of the loss ultimately experienced by the Company. It is not likely, however, that the ultimate loss will be less than the amount reserved. Further, the exposure of the Company for additional compensatory and punitive damages awards over and above this reserve, although not presently determinable, may be significant and further materially adversely affect the future consolidated financial condition and results of operations of the Company.

Other—In December 1982, the United States District Court for the Southern District of New York determined that the suit filed in 1977 by Kalman and Anita Ross, stockholders of the Company, should be certified as a class action for damages on behalf of persons who purchased the Company's Common Stock during the period March 8, 1971 through June 28, 1974. In addition to the Company, certain of its present and former officers and directors are defendants. This suit alleges dissemination of false and misleading information and failure to disclose other information concerning the Dalkon Shield. After completion of discovery, an agreement was reached under which the Company will pay $6.9 million in settlement of this class action. This agreement is subject to final judicial approval. The action against the individual defendants will be dismissed, subject to final judicial approval. A provision for this settlement has been recorded in 1984 and included in Other, Net.

In March 1980, Zoecon Corporation filed a civil action against the Company and Miller-Morton Company, a subsidiary since merged into the Company, alleging unfair competition (a claim since abandoned) and patent infringement in connection with the marketing of the Sergeant's Sentry V flea and tick collar. The Company counterclaimed alleging patent invalidity on the part of Zoecon Corporation. The case has now been disposed of by way of a settlement having no material financial impact on the Company.

Commentaries

---

25. Debate Rages over Marketing and Alcohol Problems

Kevin Higgins

In its latest salvo at the alcoholic beverage industry, the Center for Science in the Public Interest (CSPI) this month [September 1983] petitioned the Federal Trade Commission to restrict alcohol marketing practices aimed at young people, particularly promotions on college campuses and military installations.

The action follows CSPI's call for a complete ban on alcohol ads on broadcast media, elimination of advertising aimed at heavy drinkers and young people, and other measures to curb alcohol marketing.

In a related move, U.S. Rep. George E. Brown (D-Calif.) introduced two bills to require a health warning on bottles of distilled spirits and to eliminate alcohol ad expenditures as a tax deductible business expense.

Other actions advocated by CSPI in its book, *The Booze Merchants*, include:

Presentation of ads which stress health problems related to drinking.

Health warnings in print ads similar to those found in cigarette ads.

Guidelines on what information may be contained in the ads (price, taste, etc.) and a ban on imagery and "puffery."

No use of celebrities in ads.

Restrictions on the channels of distribution of beer, wine, and distilled spirits.

Accusing CSPI of presenting unsubstantiated opinions on the effects of alcohol advertising, Duncan Cameron, director of communications division, Distilled Spirits Council of the United States (DISCUS), suggested the campaign was just a way to sell copies of *The Booze Merchants*.

Reprinted from *Marketing News*, published by The American Marketing Association. Vol. 17, no. 20 (September 30, 1983), p. 1.

"There's a market for conspiracy books, and CSPI is playing to that," he said.

No one disputes that alcohol is related to a host of social problems, including alcoholism, drunk driving, and health problems. The debate really centers on a question fundamental to marketing itself.

In spending more than $1 billion a year to sell their products, are beer, wine, and spirits advertisers merely shifting sales from one brand or category to another, or are they expanding the market?

In trying to sell their products, are marketers aggravating alcohol-related problems, or are they only catering to social behavior which would occur anyway?

Citing figures from alcohol and advertising trade publications, CSPI points out alcohol ad expenditures tripled between 1970 and 1980. Per capita consumption of ethanol—alcohol sans water and other elements—increased 15 percent from 1970 to 1978.

"Only a very naive person would argue that the massive amounts of sophisticated and expensive marketing efforts do not tend to whitewash the dangers of alcohol by imbuing alcoholic beverages with an image of total harmlessness and by reinforcing drinking as the social norm," the authors of *The Booze Merchants* write.

"A tremendous amount of public awareness has been generated around the issue of alcohol advertising," observed George Hacker, *Booze Merchants* coauthor and director of CSPI's alcohol program.

"The reaction of the liquor industry has been one of recognizing that they've got problems in this area of marketing and also of denying that their advertising or marketing has anything to do with alcohol abuse.

"Every ad for alcohol is not objectionable. Some ads seem perfectly innocuous to me, although they might push somebody else's button (to drink).

"But when you look at the overall message of alcohol advertising, you realize something has to be done. No one is suggesting people stop drinking, but we would probably be a healthier society if people drank less."

Advertising codes long have been maintained by liquor industry trade groups, but CSPI dismisses them as ineffectual and a farce.

"Advertisers primarily established the codes to keep from propelling themselves into the public scorn," Hacker said, "as well as to preempt any federal intervention."

"The guidelines are generally vague and unenforceable, and they mirror the practice rather than create a standard of practice."

The guidelines do not apply to nonmembers, notably foreign manufacturers who import their products here, he added.

CSPI argues the guidelines routinely are violated. It cites a Budweiser spot prepared for cable TV's Music Television program which depicts young people quaffing brews, despite code prohibitions against showing people actually drinking, and a beer ad with a ribald limerick and the tagline, "The bottle that shows beaver."

The latter example involved an imported beer named Yukon Gold, and that ad was quickly pulled, pointed out Henry B. King, president, United States Brewers Association (USBA).

"Some brewers spill more than Yukon Gold sells," King said. "And most of the brewers who import into this country are members of the organization," which numbers 150 members.

"An independent review board made up of people with no connection with the alcohol industry review beer ads, and if they find violations of the code, they ask the advertiser to withdraw the ad," he said.

"In 20-odd years, I'm not aware of anyone not complying."

He said the ad code is necessarily voluntary and carries no sanctions because of antitrust laws. King said the Wine Institute, which represents 408 California wine growers, was forced by the FTC to drop sanctions against violators of its code because of antitrust laws.

"It's in the interest of advertisers to have ads that are in good taste," he said, adding the federal Bureau of Alcohol, Tobacco and Firearms (BATF) and the FTC can move against ads which are "obscene," "indecent," or which contain false, misleading, or deceptive statements.

"As long as the industry continues to advertise in good taste, I can't imagine any action by the Congress restricting any ads," King said, adding Rep. Brown has introduced his bills for 10 years without success.

The DISCUS code requires ads and the depiction of women in those ads to be "modest, dignified, and in good taste."

"Distillers have had a voluntary, self-imposed ban on broadcast advertising since 1936," DISCUS's Cameron said. "There have been a handful of TV ads in local markets by companies which were not DISCUS members, and in all cases those ads were stopped after a short time.

"Since 1967 distillers have spent hundreds of millions of dollars advertising their products, yet consumption is declining." He accused CSPI of using misleading figures to prove per capita alcohol consumption is increasing.

Cameron said ethanol consumption only increased 5.7 percent from 1972 to 1982 among people 18 and older, and he attributed the hike to the aging of America, arguing there are more older adults now, and those people drink more than young people.

"The average American adult drinks 2–3 drinks a day, and that amount of drinking is probably good for you," he said.

"People who have a drinking problem probably should cut down or cease drinking, but 50–60 percent could increase consumption without any problem, and some of them could even benefit" from increased consumption.

An aide to Representative Brown conceded there is little hope of Congressional action on HR 3078, which would eliminate tax deductions for liquor ads. That bill is languishing in the House Ways and Means Committee.

But a "brighter prognosis" exists for HR 3077, she said. "If enough pressure is put on the Energy and Commerce Committee, there could be hearings on the labeling bill early next year."

The bill would require beverages with more than 24 percent alcohol content to carry the warning. "Using this product too fast may cause sickness or death; may impair driving ability; may create dependence or addiction; and during pregnancy may harm the unborn. Legal age required for purchase."

The warning seems straightforward and indisputable, but DISCUS opposes it.

"Everybody knows drinking too much is not good," Cameron said, but he suggested the warning would be "harmful because it creates the impression that something meaningful has been done about the problem.

"It's a naive, symbolic kind of thing. A liquor bottle should not be the place where people turn to for medical advice."

As an alternative, he suggested public education about the problems of excess drinking and scientific research to find a cure for alcoholism.

State laws restricting alcohol advertising are on the books in Mississippi, Oklahoma, and Ohio, CSPI's Hacker said, and several other states are considering similar legislation and other measures.

Those laws are under attack by the liquor industry, he said, with free speech and states' rights issues forming the basis of legal arguments.

In Oklahoma, intrastate ads for wine and spirits are prohibited, including wine ads on cable TV shows beamed into the state. Billboard ads for liquor are banned in Mississippi, and advertisers cannot advertise in dry counties.

"On appeal the Mississippi case was reversed in favor of the advertisers," Hacker said. "But the court of appeals ruling conflicted with a similar ruling in the 10th circuit in Oklahoma," and a federal panel is expected to resolve the conflict soon.

In July a California prohibition against the giving of premiums, gifts, or free goods in connection with the distribution of alcoholic beverages, with certain exceptions pertaining to beer, was signed into law.

But state prohibitions represent a piecemeal approach, and CSPI favors federal action.

"Congress needs to subpoena and put under oath liquor industry executives, advertising executives, and marketing researchers to determine the intent of their ads," Hacker said.

"We're not suggesting the intent of the advertisers should be determinative; rather, the effect should be determinative. If an ad causes heavy drinkers or youths to drink to excess, it should not be used."

Another proposal is to hike federal excise taxes on liquor. DISCUS estimates a doubling of those taxes would increase distilled spirit prices 40 percent and result in a 25 percent drop in sales.

The Booze Merchants takes advertisers to task for alleged violations of the various ad codes.

For example, beer and wine advertisers are not to associate use of their products with risky activities, yet an ad for Riunite depicted cartoon construction workers perched on steel beams of a skyscraper and being offered a bottle of wine.

A spot for Budweiser showed a crew of lumberjacks leaning on their chain saws while "a superimposed hand seems to be offering the resting workers a drink," the authors maintain.

The most tasteless ad highlighted in the book is Yukon Gold's. Although the ad appears to violate BATF's prohibition against "indecent" statements, the agency took no action.

The book cites numerous examples of sexual double entendres, appeals to women drinkers, and appeals to college students. "No college education would be complete without Triple Sec," one ad reads.

The authors tip their hats to some advertisers. They compliment Paul Masson because "they associate drinking with eating." Seagram's emphasizes taste while advising consumers to drink in moderation.

But responsible ads, like those in bad taste or suggestive of irresponsible drinking, are not germane to the central issue: Does alcohol advertising and marketing increase consumption or merely shift spending from one category or brand to another?

CSPI cites an article in *The Lancet,* a British medical journal, which estimated a ban on alcohol advertising would cut consumption 13 percent— and 25 percent among heavy drinkers.

"There is no causal relationship between advertising and anybody drinking," maintains USBA's King, who points to studies performed at Michigan State University, East Lansing, and American University, St. Louis, which support that position.

DISCUS's Cameron notes sales of spirits have been trending downward, despite all the advertising. He suggests advertising merely allows producers to capitalize on public trends.

"Advertising doesn't cause shifts in consumption patterns," he said, "it just helps advertisers anticipate those trends and position themselves in the right place.

"The United States ranks 18th in alcoholism on a per capita basis among industrialized nations, although the exposure to alcohol advertising is probably greater here than anywhere else.

"Advertising supports the social trends rather than creates them."

But if the social trend is toward excessive drinking, then advertising must share in the guilt for the consequences, Hacker argues. He points to ads such as Miller beer's spots which urge drinkers to "bring your thirsty self right here."

"It at least infers you're going to be drinking heavily because you don't get quenched by one," he said.

"We don't believe elimination of advertising will solve society's alcohol problems, but restrictions or ads advocating a responsible lifestyle or pointing out the health risks are an important part of an overall strategy to change perceptions of alcohol."

Proposals by CSPI and Representative Brown are only part of what Hacker perceives as a grass roots movement toward less drinking and awareness of the problems connected with alcohol consumption. Related actions include community groups concerned with drunk driving, parental organizations fighting drug and alcohol use by children, and the health movement, which associates drinking light alcohol with looking good.

"Those forces, together with public health forces, are beginning to understand the enormous impact of alcohol products," he said. "It's turning into a mass movement.

"The alcoholic beverage industry is getting very serious about the threat to advertise its products as if they were wholesome and nonaddictive.

"The industry is not a pushover. It has an enormous amount of clout. But in time, as the public's voice is heard on this issue, the Congress will have to take action."

---

26. Solved: The Riddle of Unintended Acceleration

John Tomerlin

For more than 15 years, the National Highway Traffic Safety Administration (NHTSA) has been grappling with the problem of unintended acceleration. In that time it has investigated nearly 50 makes and models from 20 manufacturers and has received reports of approximately 3,000 accidents involving more than 400 injuries and 50 deaths. In spite of these efforts, and those of several auto manufacturers and independent research firms, there remains no generally accepted explanation of what unintended acceleration is, or what causes it.

Investigations are hampered because, while the behavior is widespread, actual occurrences are extremely rare. Statistically, an average driver would have to drive more than a thousand years to experience unintended acceleration in an Audi 5000—and still longer in other cars with the alleged problem.

Firsthand accounts describe sudden, full-throttle acceleration with no pedal input from the driver; in about 80 percent of the cases, the drivers report total brake failure as well. Mysteriously, no fault can be found with either the accelerator or the brakes after the incident.

The phenomenon affects cars with automatic transmissions almost exclusively, and a sizable majority of incidents occur at the beginning of the driving cycle—just after the gear lever is shifted out of Park, into Reverse or Drive.

Both the high rates of acceleration reported and the frequent claims of "brake failure" support the hypothesis of pedal error. For reasons yet to be

---

Reprinted with permission of *Road & Track* magazine. February 1988, pp. 52–59.

explained, the driver mistakes the accelerator for the brake and persists in this error until a collision occurs. Such behavior would be rare—but so is the incidence of unintended acceleration.

Some consumer groups, and most people who have experienced the problem, reject this explanation. They point instead to the complex electronic devices in modern cars, some of which are capable of opening the throttle without direct input from the driver. When the Battelle Corp. analyzed the Audi 5000, under contract to the manufacturer, it found a condition "in which a single failure within the cruise control could cause unauthorized throttle opening and result in engine racing or rapid vehicle acceleration."

This hypothetical failure could occur only if certain short circuits took place in order, only if the cruise-control switch were on, and only if the brake pedal wasn't used. Such a case had never been reported—but the theoretical possibility lends support to those who blame mechanical error.

WHY THE AUDI 5000?

Although unintended acceleration is, in NHTSA's words, "pervasive throughout the passenger car population," it has come to be associated with the Audi 5000. Hundreds of newspaper and broadcast reports have created the image of a car that, despite its excellent reputation with the motoring press, is plagued by a serious defect. What defect and why it only recently has begun to occur in such numbers aren't specified.

The 5000 has been built since 1978 with only minor changes in mechanical detail and one major body redesign in 1983. During its first four years in the United States, the 5000 was the subject of only 13 complaints of unintended acceleration involving eight accidents.

By this time, NHTSA already had investigated Mercedes-Benz, Datsun, Cadillac, Toyota, and Volvo and found no mechanical defects that might be responsible for the problem. It nevertheless opened a preliminary investigation of the Audi complaints and, in April 1982, approved a voluntary recall for correction of possible floormat interference with the accelerator pedal.

There was no apparent change in the rate of complaints as a result of this modification, and in September 1983, Audi began another voluntary recall. A spacer was installed atop the brake pedal, raising it out of the same plane as the accelerator in order to reduce the chance of pedal error.

No further action was taken until May 1986, when, with nearly a quarter of a million 5000s in service, a third recall was begun to increase the separation between the brake and accelerator pedals. The 5000's pedals were well within the range of the general automotive population (see Exhibit 1), but by this time the company was receiving increasing attention from the media and wished to be perceived as doing all in its power to respond to the problem.

Meanwhile, Audi engineers had been working on a totally different approach. If drivers were required to apply the foot brake before shifting out of Park, incidents at the start of the driving cycle could be reduced. This would be

EXHIBIT 1   Ergonomics

Lateral Distances, in Inches	Audi 5000	BMW 5-Series	Buick Skylark	Dodge 600	Mercedes-Benz 190
Center of driver's seat to right edge of brake pedal	1.1	1.6	6.2	4.4	0.8
Center of driver's seat to center of steering wheel	0.7	0.8	2.1	1.0	0.4
Right edge of brake pedal to left edge of accelerator pedal	2.4	2.3	2.6	2.5	2.4

SOURCE: Audi.

effective even if there were acceleration when shifting into gear, and the Audi's brakes will hold against full throttle.

In June 1986, the pedal-separation recall was terminated and installation of the Automatic Shift Lock (ASL) was begun.

THE PUBLICITY FIRESTORM

Only four months after it began installing the ASL, Audi initiated another recall that presumably had nothing to do with unintended acceleration. As part of a campaign to eliminate a potential fire hazard in air filters, the company began replacing the Idle Stabilizer Valve (ISV) on 1985–1986 5000s. This device controls engine speed under varying load conditions when the throttle is closed.

In response to an inquiry from NHTSA, the company explained that some defective valves had been received from its supplier, Bosch, that could cause higher than normal idle speeds under some conditions. Their replacement had nothing to do with unintended acceleration, Audi told NHTSA. This would prove to be an error.

By this time, Audi was facing a serious public relations problem. An article on unintended acceleration had appeared in the February 23, 1986, edition of the *New York Times*, dealing primarily with GM, Ford, Nissan, American Motors, and Toyota. Audi was mentioned only briefly, but this was enough to catch the eye of Long Island resident Alice Weinstein. Ms. Weinstein, who claims to have had two accidents in her Audi because of unintended acceleration, decided to contact the Center for Auto Safety (CAS), also mentioned in the article.

The CAS, which already had several complaints about the Audi 5000 on file, put Ms. Weinstein in touch with the New York Public Interest Research Group (NYPIRG). NYPIRG in turn contacted New York's Attorney General, Robert Abrams. On March 19th, Abrams held a press conference to denounce the 5000 as unsafe and to demand that the car be recalled.

Ms. Weinstein went on to found the Audi Victims Network (AVN) of about 40 drivers who claimed their cars had run away with them, and on May 28, 1986, Audi representatives met with this group. The company chose the occasion to announce its pedal-separation recall—a move that was predictably interpreted as an effort to blame drivers for unintended acceleration—and AVN left the meeting determined to force Audi to accept responsibility for its members' accidents.

Coincidentally, Illinois's Attorney General, Neil Hartigan, publicly denounced Audi on the day it was meeting with AVN. Press coverage increased again at the announcement of a recall to install the ASL in August and culminated three months later, on November 11, 1986, when the television news magazine "60 Minutes" devoted its lead story to the Audi 5000.

By January 1986, complaints of unintended acceleration for all model years of the 5000 had more than tripled—from approximately 600, at the beginning of 1986, to 1900.

There is no correlation between design and engineering changes in the Audi 5000, between 1978 and 1987, and the freqency of reports of unintended acceleration. The rate of reports for all model years remained essentially unchanged until 1986, at which point it rose over 300 percent, either coincidentally with or as a result of coverage in the media.

One point is clear: Neither the relative involvement of the 5000, nor the reasons for such involvement, can be inferred from conventional reporting after February 1986.

R&T ANALYZES THE 5000

Principal findings from the technical analyses are as follows:

1. *Throttle.*   Pedal-actuated rods link the accelerator pedal to a butterfly-type valve in the intake manifold of the Audi 5000. The throttle also can be opened by a servo mechanism governed by the cruise control or (on models built before October 1982) by reverse action of the transmission kick-down lever.

   No jamming of the throttle or the actuating rods has been reported in connection with unintended acceleration. After a collision involving extensive damage to the right-front quadrant of a 1984 Turbo 5000 in Newport News, Virgina, it was found that the engine would accelerate to full throttle because the air-intake duct had been jammed against the throttle-return arm. Apart from such isolated instances, the throttle and throttle linkage does not cause unintended acceleration in the 5000.

2. *Transmission.*   There are four methods whereby the transmission can cause throttle openings. The Battelle Corp.'s analysis of the interface between the shift lever and the throttle linkage shows that if foreign matter were to jam between them, the throttle could be opened as the shift lever was moved forward—toward Reverse, from Drive or Neutral. Because the majority of reported incidents involves shifting in the opposite direction (from Park to Reverse, or Park to Drive) and because no such jamming has ever been reported, it cannot be considered a cause of unintended acceleration.

In Audis built prior to October 1982, the kick-down lever from the transmission is capable of opening the throttle in the event of simultaneous failure of three pressure-sensing valves. Inasmuch as there is no record of failure for any *one* of these valves, it's impossible to calculate the probabilities of failure of all three.

The kick-down lever also can be actuated by introducing abnormally high pressure into the transmission from an outside source (this method was used on "60 Minutes" to simulate unintended acceleration). Spontaneous occurrence of this effect is unknown.

It is possible for the crimping that holds the spring-loaded end-connector of the kick-down lever to fail, allowing the lever to extend and open the throttle. Only one case of this sort has been reported.

Because of the extreme improbability of throttle actuation by the kick-down lever, the absence of reports of this behavior and the absence of any change in the rate of unintended acceleration after October 1982 (when the kick-down rod was redesigned to make throttle opening impossible), transmission malfunction cannot be considered a source of unintended acceleration.

3. *Cruise control.* It is theoretically possible for short circuits or voltage transients (surges) in the cruise control to cause unauthorized throttle opening. Prior to 1981, an electromagnetic coupling and a fuel-pump control circuit were designed to prevent this; after 1981, the brake pedal mechanically vented vacuum pressure from the system, allowing the throttle to return to idle.

On at least two occasions, neither involving accidents, cruise-control malfunction has resulted in spontaneous throttle openings. In both cases, use of the brake pedal disengaged the cruise control.

Two other incidents have been reported for cars sitting on hydraulic lifts—but in no case has throttle opening been reported in conjunction with failure of either the cruise-control override features or the car's brakes.

Cruise control is not a primary cause of unintended acceleration in the Audi 5000.

4. *Idle stabilizer valve.* Because engine loads and operating conditions vary at idle, so do fuel requirements. To meet these requirements without use of the main throttle, a bypass system is provided. Fuel flowing through the bypass is regulated by the idle stabilizer valve (ISV), which in modern systems is governed by a computer.

If idle speed is too high, the car can lurch when it's put into gear. It also may cause drivers to shift into neutral at stops to save wear on transmission and brakes. Both circumstances can increase the chance of pedal error, possibly leading to unintended acceleration.

In early 1984, Robert Bosch, Inc. made a minor change in the manufacture of ISV units for Audi. Instead of riveting the outer jacket to its base, Bosch began to use welds. The heat from welding hardened the jacket slightly—just enough to increase wear on the silver-plated commutators inside—causing a gradual increase in idle speed to 3,900 rpm in Park or Neutral, or 1,900 rpm in Drive or Reverse.

An additional problem has been discovered in 1984–1985 cars with VDO-manufactured idle stabilizers and control units. An intermittent short in the output transistor of the control unit can cause surges in the idle speed (no increase occurs when the unit fails completely).

FIELD TESTING THE 5000

At R&T's request, Audi agreed to provide a test car, a 1985 station wagon that had been repurchased from its owner after an accident. This particular car had accelerated in reverse along a driveway and struck the side of a neighboring house. Subsequently, its left-rear fender had been repaired, the idle stabilizer had been replaced and an automatic shift lock installed. There were 15,088 miles on the odometer.

The car was driven (without incident) from Englewood Cliffs, New Jersey, to Newport Beach, California, where it was examined and driven by several staff members. At the Audi distributorship in Culver City, under R&T's supervision, the shift lock was removed, and the ISV was replaced with a unit that could be switched on or off from inside the car.

An ignition "kill switch," also controllable from inside the car, was provided, and new tires, brake pads, and brake rotors were installed for test purposes.

To determine the role played by each system capable of opening the throttle, individual components were examined and tested. Brake tests were run and distances measured while simulating complete failure of the idle stabilizer valve, with and without full-throttle application.

To assist in analyzing test results, as well as the data obtained from outside sources, economist/statistician Dr. Charles Lave of the University of California, Irvine, was retained.

Field tests were conducted using 130 volunteers recruited from the University of California, Irvine, and Cal State Polytechnic. Males and females were used, ranging in age from 18 to 44 years and in driving experience from 2 years to more than 25 years. The tests were designed and conducted in such a way as to increase the opportunity for control errors and reveal any possible causes of unintended acceleration.

First-phase testing, including a series of forward and reverse maneuvers, was conducted at the Pomona Fairgrounds over a closed course. Test subjects were informed that they were participating in a comparison of "comfort and convenience factors" and were encouraged to complete the course in as short a time as possible.

The course was driven first in either a Mercury Sable station wagon or an Olds Delta 88, then in the Audi. During the final, reverse-gear leg in the Audi, the driver was verbally distracted, and maximum idle was secretly triggered by the observer. Pedal or control errors were noted and recorded.

Although no pedal errors were observed in any of the three cars during this series of tests, high idle speeds in the Audi were associated with an increase in control errors (more cones knocked down). It was concluded that while differences in seating position and pedal locations did not negatively influence our test group, higher than normal idle speeds did.

Second-phase tests were aimed at observing the effects of unexpectedly high idle under various driving conditions. Subjects were required to perform three consecutive driving tasks: (1) Drive forward through a serpentine of varying radius turns, maintaining a steady speed, (2) reverse through a decreasing radius curve that also became narrower, and (3) start up and proceed to the left or right, according to traffic lights.

No verifiable pedal errors were committed during the first or third tests. Drivers already in motion forward, as in test No. 1, were not troubled by minor increases in idle speed; and in test No. 3, it was not possible to tell whether an incorrect driving action was the result of pedal error or a mistake in judgment.

In test No. 2, R&T Assistant Engineering Editor Kim Reynolds, acting as observer, reported two instances of apparent pedal error. "In the first, after switching the ISV control, I glanced at the driver's feet and saw that the throttle was still depressed. The car accelerated backward and partially rotated, taking out a large number of cones. The subject finally released the accelerator and let the car slow on rolling resistance. When I asked what had happened, the subject replied that she'd been 'pushing the brake.' "

"The second incident was similar but involved less acceleration. I was unable to observe the driver's foot on the throttle, but the car moved backward much too quickly for the brake to have been used. When I asked the subject what he was doing, he answered, 'I was trying to stop.' "

These two instances appear to be the first in which pedal error resulting in unintended acceleration has been observed in controlled circumstances.

THE CASE FOR PEDAL ERROR

Technical analysis by R&T shows no way in which acceleration, regardless of cause, can lead to brake failure nor any circumstances in which the brakes are incapable of stopping the car. Transient electrical or computer malfunctions may, in theory, cause an engine to accelerate and leave little trace of the problem afterward. But mechanical parts that break stay broken, and there is no evidence of such failures in the Audi 5000.

The only explanation of unintended acceleration that is both technologically feasible and consistent with the facts is pedal error. On rare occasions, something happens to distract or confuse the driver, causing him to push the accelerator instead of the brake. In some instances, the driver fails to recognize his error and continues pushing the accelerator in an effort to stop, whereupon an accident results.

This conclusion is supported by NHTSA's investigation of more than 1,700 cases of unintended acceleration in 1973–1985 GM cars. The apparent cause was found to be, "Inadvertent and unknowing . . . application of the accelerator pedal when the driver intended to apply the brake."[1] NHTSA also cites a 1979 study in which "available facts indicate that a driver who believes he or she is pushing on the brake pedal would continue to push on the same pedal in

---

[1] *Engineering Analysis Action Report,* NHTSA, 1986.

an emergency situation, even if this belief is incorrect, and might persist in this incorrect belief even after the vehicle had crashed.[2]

The results of R&T's investigation are consistent with these findings. But it is not enough to identify pedal error as the principal cause of unintended acceleration and to ignore the causes of pedal error. Three factors are of special significance.

1. Driver familiarity with the vehicle. Lack of familiarity with the vehicle is a causal factor in accidents of all kinds. Studies by CALSPAN at Indiana University, the National Accidents Sampling System (NASS), and others show that drivers with less than 1,000 miles of experience in a vehicle are 15–25 percent more likely to be involved in an accident.[3]

Case histories submitted by Audi, as well as those in the NYPIRG survey, confirm a strong correlation between lack of driver experience in the Audi and the rate of unintended acceleration. Audi's summary shows that almost half (48.3 percent) of the drivers reporting unintended acceleration had less than 8,000 miles of experience in the subject car, while 28 percent had less than 4,000 miles. Comparable figures from NYPIRG are 46 and 37 percent (see Exhibit 2).

NHTSA'S case histories show a high percentage of involvement of parking-lot attendants, carwash personnel, and other nonowner drivers with unintended acceleration.

2. Driver age. In NHTSA's report on unintended acceleration in GM cars, older drivers had a significantly higher rate of involvement.

The highest rate in this study was for Cadillacs, which, like Mercedes-Benz, Volvo, Audi, and other upscale cars, tend to be owned by older drivers.

The mean age of Audi drivers in the NYPIRG study was 46.5 years.[4]

3. High idle speed. Every engine experiences fast idle at times, particularly at start-up when throttle mixture settings are determined automatically. A driver shifting into gear, and feeling a sudden movement of the car, may be more susceptible to pedal error (especially maneuvering in reverse gear in close quarters).

The Audi 5000 appears to have had a greater than average involvement with high idle speeds. In addition to the 1985–1986 cars with faulty Bosch ISVs, problems have been reported for some 1984–1985 cars with VDO idle control computers. Occasional high idle at start-up in R&T's test car was traced to poor adjustment of the duty-cycle computer.

Of the 96 case histories in Audi's most recent submissions to NHTSA, 41 contained references to high idle, either prior to the incident in the report or in

---

[2] Ibid.
[3] *Vehicle Familiarity and Safety*, NHTSA (DOT-HS-806-509), July 1987.
[4] *Shifting the Blame*, NYPIRG, July 1987.

EXHIBIT 2   Mean and Median Mileage at Occurrence
               (NYPIRG survey)

Miles Driven	Number of Cases	Percent
0–3,999	78	36.6
4,000–7,999	20	9.4 (median)
8,000–11,999	20	9.4
12,000–15,999	14	6.6
16,000–19,999	14	6.6 (mean)
20,000–23,999	8	3.8
24,000–27,999	7	3.3
28,000–31,999	7	3.3
32,000–35,999	12	5.6
36,000–39,999	3	1.4
40,000–43,999	11	5.1
44,000–47,999	6	2.8
48,000–51,999	3	1.4
52,000–55,999	1	0.5
56,000–59,999	0	0.0
60,000 or more	9	4.2
	213	100.0

connection with it. This rate is far too high to be dismissed as a possible cause of pedal error resulting in unintended acceleration.

It should be noted, however, that the VW Quantum and Audi 4000, both of which were equipped with the problem Bosch ISVs, are rarely cited for unintended acceleration.

R&T RECOMMENDS

Audi's automatic shift lock can reduce unintended acceleration in all cars with automatic transmissions. By bringing the driver's foot in contact with the brake long enough to shift out of Park, into Reverse or Drive, ASL addresses the most common form of unintended acceleration.

The fact that ASL doesn't protect against pedal errors that occur *after* shifting into gear in no way lessens the value of the function it does perform. Nissan already has begun installation of a similar device, and R&T recommends its adoption throughout the industry.

It is R&T's conclusion that spontaneous acceleration that is *uncontrollable by braking* cannot be demonstrated in the Audi 5000. In cases where such behavior is reported, the actual cause of acceleration is pedal error. At the same time, it is virtually certain that the drivers of some cars experience more errors than others; to the extent that such differences are inherent in the car, and not the driver, they may be extremely subtle and complex: (1) Interior sound levels may mask high idle speeds from the driver and contribute to his disorientation. (2) Obstructions of rear vision may increase the difficulty and hazards of reversing. (3) Console-mounted shift levers may produce more errors than column shifts by requiring greater head and eye deflections for their operation.

As this issue goes to press, NHTSA is investigating various models of Mercedes-Benz, General Motors, Nissan, Toyota, and Audi and has received new charges involving the Acura Legend and the Austin Rover Sterling. It is beyond the scope of this report (and R&T's resources) to investigate every car accused of unintended acceleration, but based on extensive tests and analyses of the Audi 5000, we conclude that the common factor in these cases is pedal error.

The issue now is, *What causes pedal error?* More needs to be known about the role of control location and identification. About pedal "feel," travel, and separation. About optimal seating angles, instrument layouts, and head and eye movements during control operation, to name a few.

Such information will come from better basic research and statistical analysis—not from uninformed speculation, self-serving consumer movements, or poorly researched "exposés" in the media.

---

27. "All-Terrain" Vehicles Spark Debate as User Deaths and Injuries Mount

John E. Emshwiller

"All-terrain" vehicles are small motorized contraptions with fat tires. People ride them for fun. But the ATVs—cousins of dirt bikes and snow-mobiles—have been carrying many riders, especially children, to injury or death.

Sales have boomed in the past five years, swelling riders' ranks to an estimated 5 million. At the same time, however, more than 600 people have died in ATV accidents and some 275,000 have been injured—some crippled for life. Nearly half the casualties involve children under 16.

Such grim statistics have stirred one of the biggest product-safety debates ever—and prompted hundreds of suits against ATV makers, plaintiffs' lawyers estimate. Critics charge that the makers have produced inherently unsafe vehicles and promoted their use by practically anyone not wearing diapers.

Letting a child ride an ATV "is like giving him a loaded gun," asserts Craig McClellan, a San Diego attorney for several ATV-accident victims.

Alleged design flaws include a too-high center of gravity, a solid rear axle, which can make the vehicle trickier to turn, and an inadequate suspension system. Critics also say the tripod design of three-wheeled models is inherently unstable.

SINGLED OUT UNFAIRLY?

ATV defenders deny those charges and complain that ATVs are being singled out unfairly in a world in which people find almost countless ways to maim themselves. The actual problem is the "gross misuse" of ATVs by a small minority of riders, says Paul Golde, the director of safety standards of the Specialty Vehicle Institute of America, a trade group. "There has been a horrible lack of parental supervision" in many accidents involving children, he adds.

The makers say drivers' abuses include riding with passengers, drinking and driving, driving on paved roads, driving too fast, and not wearing such appropriate accessories as helmets and boots.

The case of Wendy Molitor illustrates the debate. Miss Molitor, now of Santee, California, was an active 10-year old when she hopped onto a three-wheeled Honda ATV in 1982. Now she is a quadriplegic, living on a respirator—the result of breaking her neck when the Honda rolled over.

But was Honda Motor Co.'s U.S. unit, or the victim and her parents, at fault? The ATV rolled over while making a turn (the estimated speed was 7 to 12 miles an hour) and landed on Wendy, says Mr. McClellan, her attorney. In a lawsuit in a California state court in San Diego County, she contends that Honda designed an unsafe vehicle and then marketed it without adequate warnings about its dangers. Yet Honda isn't without defenses; Miss Molitor was riding as a passenger on an ATV driven by a 12-year-old boy. ATVs are designed to carry only one person.

Mr. McClellan says the sides have reached a settlement—but he won't comment on it, pending its approval by the court. (In a Wyoming case, a 13-year-old girl was left brain-damaged and partially paralyzed when she fell off an ATV she was a passenger on; Suzuki Motor Co. paid $2.25 million in a settlement.) A Honda spokesman says any settlement, while reflecting the severity of Miss Molitor's injury, wouldn't signify any agreement by Honda that the vehicle was unsafe.

The major makers—all Japanese—are Honda (which brought out the first ATV, in 1970, and accounts for about 60% of the market), Kawasaki Heavy Industries Ltd., Suzuki, and Yamaha Motor Co. Children's models start at $800 while ATVs for adults run as high as $3,500.

The Specialty Vehicle Institute says eight states have licensing rules for ATV drivers, while almost all states ban ATV use on paved roads and many have minimum-age rules (with minimums as low as 10 years). But most of the rules have exceptions. The age rules generally apply only on public land, for instance, or if the child isn't being supervised by an adult.

STATE BANS DISCUSSED

ATVs have bedeviled federal officials and produced strange actions. In December, the Federal Consumer Product Safety Commission, after spending 18 months and $2 million studying the matter, publicly voted to request—but not require—makers to stop producing ATVs for children under 12 and to improve safety standards.

The commission's decision outraged critics of ATV safety. Some state regulators were so upset that they discussed banding together to take the unprecedented step of trying to ban ATV sales in their jurisdictions, says Herschel Elkins, the head of the consumer-law section of California's attorney general's office.

Simultaneous to its public action, however, the federal commission voted in closed session to take a far tougher stand. By a vote of 2 to 1, it declared ATVs an "imminent and unreasonable risk" to the public—and backed a mandatory refund program that could result in makers having to repurchase hundreds of thousands of ATVs from owners. It also voted to require new public warnings about ATV dangers and free training programs.

Though word of the closed session leaked out, commission officials won't discuss those measures. Meanwhile, the commission is seeking Justice Department help in preparing a lawsuit to force makers to comply.

The repurchase would cover all three-wheeled ATVs and four-wheelers used by owners' children under 16. Four-wheelers are generally considered more stable than three-wheeled ATVs, which one commission described as having "a severe rollover problem," according to written remarks prepared in connection with the closed session, obtained from a source outside the commission. It is estimated that more than half of the roughly 2.3 million ATVs in use are three-wheelers.

Any federal effort to mandate actions by makers is likely to meet strong resistance. "We don't see a need for any kind of recall or refund program," says a Honda spokesman. He says death and injury levels plateaued last year—a sign that safety-education efforts are working.

The makers can count on the backing of many users who are fiercely loyal to ATVs. A refund program is "ludicrous," says Roy Janson, the president of the American All-Terrain Vehicle Association, which has some 10,000 members.

Like other ATV defenders, Mr. Janson concedes that riding ATVs takes "special skills." In making a turn, for example, a rider has to shift his weight away from the direction of the turn, whereas a bicycle rider leans into turns. But with proper training and care, he says, the vehicles "aren't any risk."

But critics, besides alleging design defects, say the industry bears much of the blame for any misuse—because of the way that ATVs are advertised. They say television ads have shown ATVs—the fastest of which can reach 60 miles an hour—jumping through the air and doing high-speed turns. Children, particularly, see such maneuvers and try to emulate them, these critics say.

Makers "have created a whole new sport and don't want to take responsibility for it," says Dr. Joseph Greensher, the chairman of the committee on accident and poison prevention of the Amercian Academy of Pediatrics. Dr. Greensher says ATVs are the professional group's biggest child-safety worry.

"INAPPROPRIATE ADVERTISING"

Industry spokesman Mr. Golde concedes there has been "inappropriate advertising." But he says ATV makers have accepted guidelines that "make that problem a thing of the past."

Still, some of the industry's efforts to be more responsible have met with limited success. Mr. Golde's trade group devised a four-hour, "hands-on" training course for ATV users. In nearly two years, only about 5,000 people have used it.

Not all dealers have gotten the safety message, either. Not long ago, salesmen at two Los Angeles–area ATV dealers tried to sell a prospective buyer adult-sized vehicles for use by children as young as eight, though the makers say such vehicles shouldn't be used by anyone under 14. One salesman also suggested that a child could ride as a passenger with an adult. As for training, one of the salesman said: "You can learn how to ride one in 10 minutes and then teach the kids."

Some ATV critics argue that training and experience won't solve what they see as basic instabilities in the vehicles. "I have a bunch of adult clients who operated ATVs for months," says Nicholas Patton, a Texarkana, Arkansas, attorney for ATV-accident victims in 18 suits against makers. Now, he says, his clients "are learning to operate as paraplegics."

---

28. Why More Corporations May Be Charged with Manslaughter

High on a scaffold in the California mountains, workers were installing a concrete lining in a 969-ft.-high chamber that was part of a new Pacific Gas & Electric Co. power plant. They were on a platform anchored with four cables into the overhanging rock. One cable went slack, the scaffold tilted, and a second cable broke. Seven workers plunged to their deaths. The California Occupational Safety & Health Division would rule eventually that the platform was overloaded and workers operating the hoists were undertrained.

The January 23, 1982, accident also plunged giant Granite Construction Co., the lead contractor on the job, into a legal nightmare that increasingly threatened U.S. business: The company was indicted for manslaughter. The case is the most recent example of a dramatic change now under way in rules that have long protected corporations from being charged with such crimes as murder and manslaughter.

'GROSS DISREGARD'

Last month, California's highest court let stand a decision against Granite that declared for the first time that corporations can be charged with manslaughter in that state. In other states, such corporations as Warner-Lambert Co. and Ebasco Services Inc. have faced similar charges in recent years. In the most publicized case, Ford Motor Co. was charged in Indiana with "reckless homicide" for making an unsafe fuel tank for its Pinto automobiles.

Legal experts argue about whether a corporation can have the intent that a prosecutor must prove to win a manslaughter conviction. The deputy district attorney who handled the Granite case, James Oppliger, did not share those doubts. He charges that the incident uncovered what "seemed to be a gross disregard for human life."

But business lawyers say attempts to hold companies criminally responsible for industrial accidents and product malfunctions do little more than assign blame for tragedies that cannot be prevented. That is different from other areas in which companies are vulnerable to criminal charges. Antitrust and securities laws, for example, clearly mandate what a company can and cannot do. The lawyers say that because prosecutions under general penal laws are impossible to predict, corporations are left without any way to guard themselves against the large fines and loss of business that can result. "How do businessmen protect their corporations?" asks Granite lawyer Robert L. Leslie. His answer: "They can't."

The change is due in part to modern interpretations of laws that have always talked about "persons" committing crimes. In some states the laws are being changed to encourage prosecutions of corporations. Kentucky, for instance, now declares that the word "person" in its penal code includes corporations "when appropriate."

But more important than technical legal changes is a change in social attitudes. Phillip J. Scaletta, business law professor at Purdue University, says there is increasing distrust of business and a determination to make corporations responsible for their actions. Prosecutions, he predicts, are "something we're going to see more of."

BUCKING A TREND

Granite Construction and the Fresno (California) district attorney are close to an agreement that will end that case without a trial. But the California ruling adds a new precedent to the growing list. Ten years ago in the Ebasco case, which involved a worker killed in another construction accident, New York threw out a 1909 precedent that barred manslaughter indictments of corporations. That cleared the way for the 1977 charge against Warner-Lambert for the death of six people in an explosion at a Freshen Up chewing gum plant run by Warner-Lambert's American Chicle division. That Long Island City (New York) accident, a fire marshal said, was caused by the interaction of a dry lubricant and liquid oxygen.

In 1980, Pennsylvania also approved such prosecutions. And although the Texas Court of Appeals ruled last year that existing law does not allow corporations to be charged, the judges admitted they were bucking a trend and invited the legislature to clarify the law.

Although companies have not been successful in avoiding indictments, they have done well in their cases once forced to go to court. Warner-Lambert, for example, persuaded a judge to throw out the charge against it. The company argued that its executives could not have foreseen events leading to the explosion. And Ford was acquitted in the Pinto case after a 10-week trial.

But Los Angeles lawyer Malcolm E. Wheeler, who coordinated Ford's defense, predicts that the acquittals will not stop such prosecutions. And despite the success of defense tactics, Richard Gaskins, an expert on corporate liability at Bryn Mawr College, says the threat of criminal prosecution is potent. Gaskins says companies are being threatened with indictments if they do not settle civil accident suits. "The threat of bringing a criminal case has been used as a bargaining chip," he says. Explains one of Granite's lawyers: "No one wants this kind of mark on the record."

PART EIGHT

The Environment and Energy

Management must often make decisions in the face of imperfect information and great risk. Nowhere is this as apparent as in the issues of environment and energy. The problems often seem to be so far in the distant future that a manager feels comfortable in ignoring them in making decisions for today. Scientists are also often in disagreement as to the theory and data behind some environmental problems, such as the greenhouse effect. Consequently the manager is left with no clear direction for company action. And government is often less of a help here, in setting consistent and stable priorities and in providing resources, than in any other issue area.

Environment and energy issues often represent the classic externality problems, where the costs of doing business extend to people and places not a part of the market transaction. Consequently, the prices for many products are artificially low, in that they do not reflect the cost to people and the environment of air and water pollution, solid waste disposal, noise, and resource waste.

Over the long term, there is little comfort to the manager who hopes that the problems will go away or that technology will provide a solution. While our technology to deal with pollution issues does improve, it is often outstripped by our ability to measure pollution damage. We can measure smaller and smaller amounts of pollutants (down to parts per trillion and better) and have also become more sophisticated in our ability to measure the impacts of pollutants on ecosystems. For instance, the field of toxicology used to use a crude measure of impact called LD ratios. An LD_{50} ratio indicated the amount of time it took for 50 percent of the fish in a stream to die after the introduction of a toxin. This measure is useful in spectacular instances of pollution. However, we now know that when certain common detergents and other industrial chemicals are introduced into streams on the *parts per billion* level, they disrupt the sense of smell of trout. Consequently, the trout are unable to find food or mate. They do not die as spectacularly as in a traditional fish kill, but they are wiped out just the same.

Chronic low-level forms of pollution are being studied more and more for their impact on all animals. Recent research indicates cause for concern over chronic low-level electromagnetic radiation, which is generated by such diverse products as high-voltage power lines, electric blankets, and bed pads.

There was a time when people in a few geographical areas in the United States worried about air quality (Los Angeles is probably the classic case). In that simpler era, most people assumed that energy resources were endless and that chemicals were an unquestioned blessing found along industrial-man's path of eternal progress. How different the view as we enter the 1990s. Acid rain, concerns about the hazards of nuclear power plants, toxic waste materials, war in the Persian Gulf area, all remind us of the interrelatedness and fragile nature of the world.

It is a fundamental but often overlooked truth that we are all polluters. Yet clearly much of air, water, solid waste, noise, and aesthetic pollution is directly attributable to business. Perhaps the greatest adverse environmental impact occurs in the production process, particularly in such industries as steel, oil, and paper. However, it is important to recognize that pollution occurs at all steps of the production, distribution, and consumption cycle. For instance, at the resource extraction level, oil-well leaks and acid drainage from mines can pose major pollution problems. At the other end of the economic cycle, disposal of such items as aluminum cans and mercury batteries also create environmental hazards.

According to a Council for Environmental Quality forecast, in the decade from 1974 to 1983, the United States spent $217 billion to install and operate pollution control equipment.[1] Fully two thirds of the expenditure was paid by business. Most of the expense was for water and air pollution abatement, although solid wastes, noise, thermal pollution, and land reclamation have also become significant issues.

Issues of the type cited above are evident in this section's cases. Armco Steel Corporation: The New Miami Coke Plant case graphically illustrates the problems faced by a company with a solid, well-earned reputation for social responsiveness as it is confronted with upgrading an older facility into compliance with the Clean Air Act of 1970. Metropolitan Edison Company: Three Mile Island Nuclear Plant case was compiled from the massive public record on the nuclear energy controversy and on the details of the worst commercial nuclear accident in the history of the power generation industry in America. The case is also based on Metropolitan Edison's annual and quarterly reports, which indicate that Met-Ed had 20 years of experience with nuclear energy power sources. The final case, Allied Chemical Corporation, treats management's problems at a divisional level. The president of one of Allied's divisions must evaluate a total product responsibility program planned for the company. Second, he must decide what position should be taken by the company on a bill before Congress that would place greater controls over toxic substances.

The first commentary, Utilities Face a Crisis over Nuclear Plants, in this section provides an overview of the difficulties facing the electric utility indus-

---

[1] Gladwin Hill, "The Profits of Ecology: Cleaning the Stable Makes Jobs," *The Nation* 222, no. 15 (April 17, 1979), pp. 455–58.

try in constructing nuclear power plants. It is a record of enormous costs and lengthy delays. In the aftermath of Chernobyl, the nuclear power industry seems dead again, although some advocates are trying to revive it in the context of reducing the greenhouse effect. Yet management needs to ask if there are more cost-effective methods for achieving the same ends. Free Market Environmentalists is an argument for protecting the environment via organizations like the Nature Conservancy. One should be thinking of the limits to the market model in protecting the environment, particularly with regard to externalities. Industry Waste Watchers is an example of how many firms are trying to deal with toxic chemicals. Many industries, such as the plastics industry, are active recyclers of materials. As more industry waste-exchange programs spring up, more recycling will occur. Finally, the possible financial consequences of not dealing with toxic wastes are explored in No Material Effect. Perhaps when more firms become liable for the pollution they cause, more will clean up their methods.

All-in-all, while this book ends with cases and commentaries in an extremely challenging area, we would like to leave on a note of optimism. Managers can and do make significant contributions to the clean-up of our environment. New legislation, concepts, and attitudes will help them to accomplish more. A new breadth of vision emphasizing the long-term view will help in this process.

Armco Steel Corporation:
The New Miami Coke Plant

While at home in Middletown, Ohio, on the evening of April 27, 1973, John E. Barker, director of Environmental Engineering for Armco Steel Corporation, received the news that his firm had been denied a permit to operate its New Miami coke plant beyond the July 1, 1975, deadline established by the federal Clean Air Act of 1970. The variance request had been denied across the board for 13 steelmaking plants of various manufacturers in the state of Ohio. Mr. John Trapp, the investigator for the Ohio EPA at the New Miami plant in Hamilton, Ohio, noted in his report that the coke ovens were very old and a serious source of air pollution. However, because of Armco's fine previous record at alleviating pollution in its southwestern Ohio plants, he recommended that serious consideration be given to Armco's compliance schedule, which would bring the company within the legal limits by late 1977 or early 1978. Mr. Trapp later speculated that the variance request denial had been based on the literal requirements of the law.

THE COMPANY

Armco Steel Corporation mined and processed coal and limestone for the nine steel plants that it operated in the United States and provided diversified products and services worldwide through its various divisions. The company's Metal Products Division had 45 manufacturing plants in the United States and Canada, which produced highway, drainage, and construction products; steel buildings; and other industrial products. The Machinery and Equipment Division was the world's largest supplier of oil and gas well-drilling equipment. Its drilling rigs, pumps, pipe, and other products were used worldwide at both onshore and offshore drilling installations. The International Division was responsible for the export sales of Armco products and steelmaking technology and operated steel manufacturing businesses in 18 countries. HITCO, a wholly owned subsidiary, produced high-performance, nonmetallic materials and complex composite products principally for the aerospace and defense industries. Other Armco units conducted insurance, leasing, and financing businesses on a worldwide basis.

Sales for Armco, the third largest producer and profit maker among U.S. steel manufacturers, were $1.9 billion in 1972. Net income totaled $75 million. Income was expected to be over $100 million in 1973 on the strength of almost $2.4 billion in sales.

By 1973, Armco had already spent $125 million on pollution equipment. In Middletown alone the amount was $40 million. Red smoke from the open hearths was a problem in virtually all steel towns; until recently, Middletown was no exception. However, in 1971 the company completed a 21-month project in which $10.5 million was spent on wet scrubbers for the No. 2 open hearth to clean up the smoke and another $1.5 million then to treat the scrub water and remove the solid materials. In the summer of 1969, the company started a new basic oxygen steel-making complex and installed $5.9 million worth of pollution devices on it and then retired eight old open-hearth furnaces, which were not equipped with pollution control devices. The new $16 million water treatment plant with a capacity of 144 million gallons per day was larger than the capacity of the water system for the entire city of Cincinnati. The system put the water back in the Miami River cleaner than it came out.

Mr. Barker felt that Armco probably had the best reputation for environmental effort among all steelmakers. A study conducted in 1969 by the Council on Economic Priorities (a private group) on water and air pollution in the steel industry had ranked the company tops among seven companies. Armco gave off only 4.7 pounds of particulate emissions per ton of steel produced, while National Steel, rated the worst, averaged 21 pounds per ton.[1] The CEP study also recognized the efforts of Armco in environmental cleanup, actions such as use of low-polluting electric furnaces, recent rehabilitation of older open hearths, and installation of major water reprocessing facilities. The CEP's estimated cleanup price tag of $2.8 billion for the industry was well below the $3.5 billion estimate of Thomas Barnes at the Battelle Institute, a research center in Columbus. Barnes headed a group at Battelle that did the estimates for the federal EPA.

THE PROBLEM

Upon arriving at his office in the center of Middletown the next morning, Mr. Barker found a memo from William E. Verity, Jr., chairman of the board of Armco, already on his desk with a copy of the EPA denial letter attached (see Exhibit 1). The memo requested that Mr. Barker review the company input data for the variance request and be prepared to meet the following week with the corporate comptroller, the production superintendent at Middletown, and Mr. Verity to discuss the company's strategy for the adjudication hearing. At

---

[1] *Particulate emissions* refers to any liquid or solid particles other than water which are or have been airborne.

EXHIBIT 1   EPA Denial Letter

OHIO EPA
Columbus, Ohio

30 April 1973

From: The Director of the Ohio EPA, Columbus, Ohio

To: Director, Armco Steel Corporation, Middletown, Ohio

Dear Mr. Verity:

As you know, the federal Clean Air Act has set ambient air quality standards to be met by July 1, 1975. Coke oven facilities in the state of Ohio have been the subject of extensive hearings for the past six months. Steel manufacturers were asked to submit schedules of compliance. The operators have questioned the availability of technology to bring the coke oven plants into compliance by July 1, 1975.

After extensive study it has been concluded that there is no technical obstacle to compliance with present state and federal regulations.

A sample compliance schedule is enclosed. [The EPA memo went on to describe the minimum technical modifications which would be necessary in order to bring the existing coke ovens into compliance with EPA regulations.]

At the present time the "state of the art" is the advanced technology of pneumatic or pipeline charging and is far superior to the above modifications. This office is not allowed to stipulate the method used to bring the ovens into compliance and therefore leaves the choice of technology to the company concerned.

In accordance with the law, 30 days are granted to your company to reply to this letter with a request for an adjudication hearing, should it so desire. If you desire any information or assistance in this regard, please feel free to contact Ms. Mary O'Mally at extension 266-4232 of this office.

Sincerely yours,

William T. Brandon
Director, Ohio EPA

cc: Office of Environmental Affairs
    Ohio Attorney General

---

stake was the company's competitive position and its financial condition. The denial of the variance request for the continued operation of the coke batteries at New Miami was, they felt, denying the major pollution abatement efforts made by Armco.

Mr. Barker knew that one of the most important items to be discussed at the meeting would be the disposition of Armco's huge coke ovens and the procurement of ample future supplies of coke for the steel mills.

EXHIBIT 1 *(concluded)*

OHIO EPA
Compliance Schedule

Battery location:

Plant location:

Milestones:

	Cumulative Period (months)
1. Submit final engineering designs and specifications.	3
2. Award contracts for technical modifications.	6
3. Initial on-site construction and modifications.	12
4. Completion on-site construction and modifications.	22
5. Achieve final compliance with all applicable state, federal laws, rules, and regulations.	26

Start date: May 1, 1973

Special consideration:

A. Acceptable coke charging methods employed.
B. No pushing of "green" coke.
C. Emissions not to exceed opacity* regulations.

* The *Regulations of the Ohio Air Pollution Control Board, Relative to the Control of Sulfur Oxide and Particulate Matter Emissions* (Ohio Department of Health, Columbus, Ohio) defines *opacity* as "a state which renders material partially or wholly impervious to rays of light and causes obstruction of an observer's view."

THE COKING PROCESS

Coke was the result of a process that removed gases and impurities from coal by heating it. *Coking,* as the process was called, produced a fuel that burned with a very intense heat and little smoke, making it superior to coal for iron smelting purposes. However, serious pollution problems occurred in the charging (dropping the coal into ovens), pushing (shoving the cooked coke out of the ovens by means of a "pusher" or ram), and quenching (spraying the coke with water to cool it) stages. Fugitive dust[2] escaped during the initial handling of the coal and during the charging operation. Possibly, thought Mr. Barker, modifications could keep the fugitive dust to a minimum in coal handling, and high-pressure steam jets could reduce dust created during charging.

Certain procedures used during the coking process itself led to particulate emissions. A small door had to be opened to admit a bar that leveled the coal in

---

[2] *Fugitive dust* refers to air contaminants emitted from any sources other than a flue or stack.

the ovens, and opening this door provided a natural vent from the oven. New oven construction should provide a boot to close the space around the leveling bar when the door was opened and closed, Mr. Barker noted. Since coke oven gas burned clean, visible emissions during the remainder of the cooking process had to be the result of poor combustion procedures or leaks. Leaks could be repaired but necessitated cooling the ovens, a costly process. Even to cool just one oven, a whole battery had to be shut down, which meant that none of the other ovens could be used. Also, the brick-lined oven walls often collapsed when cooled; considering that some batteries had as many as 100 ovens, shutting down an entire battery to repair only a few ovens could be expensive.

Leaking end doors were also a source of emissions and had to be scraped and cleaned regularly. The jambs also needed to be cleaned periodically. Both operations could be accomplished when oven doors were changed for repair, but maintenance was done by hand. In older 12-foot ovens the practice was relatively easy, but newer 21-foot ovens were considerably harder to clean. When repairing of door knife edges and jambs was not possible, wet clay could be used to seal doors, a method known as *luting*.

Particulate emissions occasionally occurred during the pushing process because of the thermal draft caused when the doors were opened and the coke was pushed out of the ovens into a quench car. In addition, smoke was sometimes present during pushing due to uncooked or "green" spots in the coke mass. Although coke could not be overcooked, the excess time in the oven necessary to prevent green spots could cause production slowdowns during later stages of the steelmaking process. The cooking time was determined by the width of the oven; the minimum was 16 hours, while 18 to 19 hours were required at times for old batteries.

During the quenching stage, the quench car holding the hot coke was sprayed with water, producing a plume of steam that rose in the quench tower. To prevent the steam (containing thermally drafted particulates, phenols, ammonia, and cyanides) from contaminating the ambient air, the quench towers contained *baffles,* rows of diagonally slanting metal plates on which some of the vapor condensed. It had been suggested to Mr. Barker that more baffles and sprays be added and that the openings of the tower around the quench car be sealed to reduce convection and capture more of the contaminants.

The four batteries at the New Miami plant had been built in the late 1920s. Of the four, one had 7 to 10 years of remaining life, and three had 10 to 12 years. In the environmental engineer's opinion, it was technically and economically unfeasible to reduce substantially the particulate emission of the old single gas main ovens. Additional foremen on each shift to ensure careful operation and maintenance, such as sealing cracks and doors, would help.

As Mr. Barker assessed Armco's position, three facts were foremost in his mind. First, the very process of exposing superheated material that had a tendency to flake and powder to various temperature changes created thermal drafts that naturally spawned particulate emissions. Second, limited control required major modifications of the existing ovens or construction of entirely new ones. Finally, some new technology was presently available, such as the pipeline charging mentioned in the EPA memo as the "state of the art," but it was expensive and was of marginal value at New Miami; in addition, the planning and installation horizon was so long that the deadline could not be met.

For example, installation of high-pressure charging meant that a second gas main would be needed, costing over $40 million and requiring 24 months to install. Improved quenching operations also meant completely new equipment. As a result, Mr. Barker was in essentially the same position as six months before when Armco asked for a variance from the July 1, 1975, deadline.

THE EPA REGULATORS

The EPA had designated the Butler County area where the New Miami plant was located as priority one in most categories of air pollution and held public hearings to determine the ambient air[3] quality level for the region. The industrial concentration in the Cincinnati corner of the state had eroded the air quality over the years, and the current particulate emission level was over 95 micrograms per cubic meter for the region. Mr. Barker and several others from the steel industry had been invited to give expert testimony at the hearings.

Although the present level of 95 micrograms for the region was high, the steel industry felt that with a major modification program at considerable expense, the particulate emission standard of 75 micrograms could be met by 1977 or 1978. Despite the testimony of four or five experts, the proponents of lower standards had prevailed. The ambient air quality standard was set not at 75 micrograms, but at 60 micrograms. Mr. Barker firmly believed a standard of 60 micrograms was technically impossible, even with the "state of the art" technology recommended in the EPA denial letter. Indeed, the best rural air in the state of Ohio had an ambient air quality of 45 to 50 micrograms.

The 60 micrograms ambient air standard was difficult to judge. Ambient air referred to no specific industry but was a communitywide or regional standard. The particulate regulations applicable to the steel industry came under the general heading "stationary sources." These sources gave off varying degrees of five specific pollutants measured by the Ohio EPA. Likewise, nonstationary sources gave off varying amounts of the same pollutants.[4] Although Armco was the major industrial concern in Middletown, Mr. Barker

---

[3] *Ambient air* is the outdoor air that surrounds an entire community or region.

[4] The federal EPA monitored 5 other pollutants, and a remaining balance of 20 pollutants was not monitored.

was not prepared to guess what percentage the company contributed to the overall pollution or just how far the Armco particulate emissions would have to change to bring the community standard to 60 micrograms. This issue was further clouded by the EPA's inability to control nonstationary polluters such as automobiles.

In addition, the EPA classified the efficiency of most pollution control equipment such as wet scrubbers in terms of particulate matter removed. Low efficiency meant 80 percent removal of particulates; medium, 80 to 95 percent removal; and high, 95 to 99 percent removal. The cost curve for greater efficiency followed a statistical distribution with greater efficiencies being out of the range of economic feasibility.

THE ALTERNATIVES

Later in the week at the meeting with other Armco executives, Mr. Barker explained the alternatives available to the company. First, Armco could take the matter to court and tie the issue up until beyond the 1975 deadline, maybe even beyond 1977 or 1978. Second, the company could shut the coke plant down on July 1, 1975, and go to the open market for its coke needs. Or, third, it could reapply for the variance until such time as coke oven capacity could be modified or new ovens installed in compliance with emission standards. This latter was a doubtful alternative, for it had already been rejected by the EPA and was the sole reason for the meeting.

To Mr. Barker, legal proceedings looked like the easiest and perhaps the least expensive way to delay the closure of the New Miami coke plant. Many steel companies in Ohio had chosen this route and were presently involved in court battles. In Armco's case, Mr. Barker was not sure that 60 micrograms was a viable ambient air requirement. However, Armco publicly committed itself to pollution abatement in 1966 and willingly quoted this policy to anyone who asked (see Exhibit 2 for a complete presentation of the policy). The ideal of socially responsible behavior on which the company had been founded was reaffirmed in writing by the board of directors on December 5, 1969, and distributed in booklet form to all employees. The company had worked hard at curbing air pollution and did not want to squander a hard-earned reputation in rushing a bad decision in this case.

The second alternative, to shut down the New Miami coke plant on July 1, 1975, and go on the open market for coke, was not without drawbacks. Over 50 percent of the coke ovens in the United States were in the "over 20-year-old" category of the New Miami plant, and many were faced with shutdown. In 1973, very little surplus coke was available in the United States, for nearly all coke was manufactured by steel companies for their own consumption. The maximum available monthly would be 5,000 to 10,000 tons, far short of the 50,000 tons a month needed at Middletown. At best, Armco could spot bid for a limited supply of German coke at approximately two and one half times the

EXHIBIT 2   ARMCO's Pollution Abatement Policy

The pollution of air and water in the United States has resulted from the combined abuses by the general public, municipalities, industries, and other public and private institutions over the past century when the foundation was being laid for our modern industrial economy. To reverse this trend will require both time and the cooperative planned efforts of all segments of our society.

The investment of millions of shareholder dollars in nonproductive facilities must be made in accordance with a carefully planned schedule, over a period of years, so that the financial condition of our company will not be impaired. Any broad-scale, hasty diversion of capital to nonproductive use could adversely affect our entire American economy.

We believe that both legitimate environmental needs and economic feasibility must be taken into account when pollution abatement standards are set. Those who study the massive problem of pollution in the United States realize that pollution abatement facilities are costly and generally nonproductive.

As a corporate citizen, we recognize our responsibility to cooperate fully with private and public agencies in their efforts to protect the nation's water and air resources.

Approved by Board of Directors
February 1966

U.S. price.[5] Additionally, 70 percent of the energy consumed in the production of iron and steel came from coke and coke oven gas, which was not available commercially, and coke oven by-products. Natural gas and oil were more efficient heat producers but were more expensive and currently not available.

Mr. Barker considered the technical and cost aspects alone to be sufficient arguments against the shutdown. However, the impact on jobs was sure to be on everyone's mind. The 300 employees at the New Miami plant would be immediately laid off. Because 50,000 of the 93,000 tons of coke consumed at Middletown were produced at New Miami, a shutdown would result in a cutback of about 1,000 of the 6,500 Armco jobs in Middletown. The reduction in coke needs would have a domino effect back to the coal fields and forward through the economy. Cold scrap could be used in place of hot metal in open-hearth operations, increasing heat time, and thus fuel consumption, 25 to 30 percent, and reducing production by the same amount. Because all steel companies were currently backordering and operating at capacity, the reduction would hurt such Armco customers as Frigidaire in Dayton and Fisher Body in Hamilton. Unless economic conditions changed drastically, these companies could not secure steel from other sources.

---

[5] No market prices existed on coke, but for comparative purposes Mr. Barker placed a "ficti-tious" transfer price at somewhat less than $30 per ton.

Finally, the company could reapply to the EPA for an operating permit beyond the July 1, 1975, deadline. The decision would require a $150 million capital outlay for a new plant and the best available technology. The plant could be built in Middletown to keep the jobs in Ohio and, if construction were started immediately, could be completed in 33 months, or possibly by the July 1, 1975, deadline. The new installation would be the closed pipeline type with enclosed quench car, which could reduce emissions and therefore not jeopardize the proposed ambient air quality regulation of 75 micrograms. However, Mr. Barker was doubtful that the company even then could meet the ambient air standard of 60 micrograms.

Undertaking the new plant project would mean the cancellation of a newly planned *melt shop* which had been in the works for a number of years. The capital budget had called for the installation of new electric furnace facilities at another plant location as a replacement for a number of open-hearth furnaces. In light of the world competitive situation, it was not likely that the corporate comptroller would give up "his" new furnaces easily. It was common knowledge that the American steel industry had long clung to worn out facilities and was at a competitive disadvantage with the Germans and Japanese who had retooled with the latest equipment after World War II. Further, Mr. Barker knew that to reactivate the old open hearths would require a variance request in the state in which they were located.

Metropolitan Edison Company: Three Mile Island Nuclear Plant

In early July 1979, Mr. William G. Kuhns, chairman of General Public Utilities Corporation, decided to send a letter to the stockholders of his company. He wanted to explain why the Metropolitan Edison Company, the GPU subsidiary which was the major owner and operator of the Three Mile Island Nuclear Station, should not have its operating franchise rescinded. Metropolitan Edison had been criticized for what had been called a *cover-up* during the first hours and days after a nuclear accident at the Three Mile Island near Harrisburg, Pennsylvania, which resulted in radiation emissions into the atmosphere. However, a special investigative commission ordered by President Carter concluded that there was no systematic attempt at a "cover-up" by the company. Mr. Kuhns had learned from the incident that for the public to be able to live with nuclear power, the industry must do a better job of increasing its understanding of the facts and terms associated with nuclear technology. He felt that the public must be able to sort, evaluate, and put into perspective the facts about nuclear power.

The Nuclear Regulatory Commission (NRC) would be holding hearings open to the general public at special conferences on the restart of Three Mile Island Unit 1 in the next week in Hershey and Harrisburg, Pennsylvania. In addition to oral comments, written statements could be submitted at any session or mailed to the NRC. Mr. Kuhns wanted to urge his stockholders to make known their feelings concerning the speedy return to service of Unit 1, an action which he felt was not only significant to them and the company, but to the entire country's efforts to cope with its pressing need for energy.

THE INDUSTRY

Nuclear power was introduced into commercial operation in 1957. In 1980, it supplied 14 percent of electricity production and almost 4 percent of total energy consumption nationally. These figures varied, however, according to region. In Illinois, for example, nuclear power supplied as much as 50 percent of electricity used.

In 1980, there were 72 nuclear plants operating in the United States. Prior to the Three Mile Island accident, Carter administration energy planners had projected as many as 500 by the year 2,000, producing thus 25 percent of the nation's power. Since the peak year of 1974, however, construction had turned down sharply. One explanation for this was that electric power demand was growing much more slowly than in the 1960s and early 1970s. Another reason was that nuclear construction costs had risen from $100 per kilowatt in the 1960s to $1,000 per kilowatt in the 1970s. Coal-fired plants were less expensive to construct with costs per kilowatt in the $700–$750 range. General inflation and long delays in getting a plant built were the principal causes of the cost differential. However, the industry contended that nuclear plants already in operation delivered power at a cheaper cost than those fueled by any other method. The Edison Electric Institute, a utility industry association, estimated that atomic plants produced electricity at a cost of $1.71 per kilowatt hour, versus $1.74 to $2.08 for coal-fired plants and $3.96 to $4.54 for plants burning oil.[1]

Even more pressing than the issue of cost, however, was that proven reserves of fossil fuel were rapidly becoming exhausted. According to the best estimates, total fossil fuel reserves recoverable at not over twice the 1980 unit cost were likely to run out between the years 2000–2050, if present standards of living and population growth remained constant. Oil and natural gas would disappear first; coal would last longer. Nuclear fuels, while not exactly renewable energy sources, had a tremendous capacity to breed, and moreover, had very high energy output from small quantities of fissionable material. Furthermore, such materials were abundant, placing them in a more favorable category than exhaustible fossil fuels.

Still, the nuclear industry had other limitations, most important of which was the disposal of radioactive wastes. Because of the potential for radioactive discharges, nuclear fuel could not be used directly in small machines (such as cars, trucks, or tractors) but only in large units to produce electricity or supply heating.

GENERAL PUBLIC UTILITIES CORPORATION

Founded in 1946, General Public Utilities Corporation was an electric utility holding company that provided electricity to some 4 million people living in about half the land area of New Jersey and Pennsylvania. In 1979, it served over 1.5 million customers. More than 31 billion kilowatt-hours of electricity were distributed in 1978. Of this total 34 percent went to residential customers, 23 percent to commercial accounts, and 37 percent to industry.[2]

The GPU system included three operating companies: Jersey Central Power & Light Company and in Pennsylvania, Metropolitan Edison Company and Pennsylvania Electric Company. In 1978, the system had total assets of $4.6 billion, making it the nation's 14th largest investor-owner electric utility (see Exhibit 1).

---

[1] "Nuclear Nightmares," *Time,* April 9, 1979, pp. 8–12.

[2] *General Public Utilities Corporation 1978 Annual Report,* p. 16.

EXHIBIT 1 General Public Utilities Corporation

Company	Revenues ($000)	Total Assets ($000)	Sales Mix			Customers (year-end)	Area Served (sq. mi.)	Peak Load* (mw)	Number of Employees	Fuel Mix		
			Residential	Commercial	Industrial					Coal	Oil	Nuclear
Jersey Central Power & Light	$ 591,294	$1,906,886	41%	27%	29%	677,580	3,300	2,441	3,731	16%	26%	56%
Metropolitan Edison	310,581	$1,239,803	32%	19%	40%	351,554	3,300	1,477	2,784	58%	2%	38%
Pennsylvania Electric	$ 431,753	$1,414,022	29%	21%	43%	501,983	17,600	1,980	4,253	85%	1%	13%
General Public Utilities System	$1,326,644	$4,612,683	34%	23%	37%	1,531,117	24,200	5,898	11,597	57%	9%	34%

* At time of GPU system peak.

SOURCE: *General Public Utilities Corporation 1978 Annual Report*, pp. 16–17.

The GPU companies depended primarily on coal and nuclear energy for the generation of electricity. The generation mix in 1978 was 34 percent nuclear, 57 percent coal, and 9 percent oil. The GPU companies were expected by 1985 to have a generation mix of 45 percent nuclear, 47 percent coal, and 8 percent oil, with the addition of a 1,000 megawatt nuclear plant in Forked River, New Jersey.

METROPOLITAN EDISON COMPANY

Metropolitan Edison Company was headquartered in Reading, Pennsylvania, where the company was founded in 1895. Met-Ed served residential, commercial, and industrial customers in southern and eastern sections of Pennsylvania. The company's 2,800 employees operated conventional steam plants at Titus and Portland, Pennsylvania, in addition to a nuclear-powered facility at Three Mile Island (TMI), Pennsylvania. In addition, the company was part-owner, along with Pennsylvania Electric and Jersey Central Power and Light in 13 other electrical generating plants using nuclear, coal, and oil fuel. Met-Ed had over 350,000 customers at the end of 1978.

The earnings of Metropolitan Edison had been disappointing in the mid- to late-1970s due to several factors. First, the company had spent over $1 billion from 1968 to 1978 on construction of a 1,700 megawatt nuclear generating complex at Three Mile Island. Operating income for 1978 was down over 2 percent from 1977, due principally to unrecovered costs related to construction of TMI-2, an 880 megawatt nuclear-powered generating plant which began to produce commercial power on December 30, 1978. Financial statements for 1974–1978 are shown in Exhibits 2 and 3.

Met-Ed had not been able to obtain adequate rate relief to recover increased fuel and operating costs. The company had, since 1974, been in an austerity program, including layoffs, early retirements, and reduced construction expenditures. The outlook for the future, however, was extremely favorable, with TMI-2 coming on line at the beginning of 1979. In fact, president Walter M. Creitz began the president's message in the 1978 report with:

> For Metropolitan Edison Company, 1978 will remain a memorable year, chiefly because of the completion and entry into commercial service of the second Three Mile Island nuclear generating unit. The achievement caps a decade of dedicated effort. It marks the end of a billion-dollar construction project and a significant addition to the generating capabilities of the General Public Utilities corporation of which Metropolitan Edison is a member company.[3]

These words were written on February 21, 1979, barely one month before TMI-2 failed in the most dramatic accident in the history of nuclear-powered generation of electricity.

---

[3] Ibid, p. 2.

EXHIBIT 2

METROPOLITAN EDISON COMPANY
Consolidated Statement of Income
For the Years Ended December 31, 1974–1978
(in thousands of dollars)

	1978	1977	1976	1975	1974
Operating revenues	$310,581	$305,223	$264,113	$249,525	$234,238
Operating expenses:					
Fuel	83,874	76,541	69,392	80,828	78,075
Power purchased and interchanged, net:					
Affiliates	(7,732)	(11,438)	(2,721)	(14,766)	(983)
Others	25,228	23,702	22,431	1,742	18,677
Deferral of energy costs, net	(9,989)	7,132	(12,006)	376	(3,556)
Payroll	33,770	29,635	27,419	25,537	2,617
Other operation and maintenance (excluding payroll)	41,330	33,165	33,771	29,459	24,539
Depreciation	25,485	23,910	22,176	21,198	17,354
Taxes, other than income taxes	25,290	24,176	20,654	20,171	18,218
Totals	217,256	206,823	181,116	164,545	175,941
Operating income before taxes	93,325	98,400	82,997	84,980	58,297
Income taxes	27,462	31,229	23,962	25,935	12,992
Operating income	65,863	76,171	59,035	59,045	45,305

EXHIBIT 2 *(concluded)*

METROPOLITAN EDISON COMPANY
Consolidated Statement of Income
For the Years Ended December 31, 1974–1978
(in thousands of dollars)

	1978	1977	1976	1975	1974
Other income and deductions:					
Allowance for other funds used during construction	20,882	18,929	17,249	14,138	16,269
Other income, net	78	(1,000)	291	(163)	(210)
Income taxes on other income, net	(29)	226	(213)	22	52
Total other income and deductions	20,931	18,155	17,327	13,997	16,111
Income before interest charges	86,794	85,326	76,362	73,042	61,416
Interest charges:					
Interest on first mortgage bonds	31,961	28,209	26,593	19,513	14,633
Interest on debentures	6,730	6,880	7,004	7,202	7,370
Other interest	3,818	2,397	522	2,562	4,519
Allowance for borrowed funds used during construction— credit (net of tax)	(6,665)	(5,115)	(4,439)	(3,885)	(7,213)
Income taxes attributable to the allowance for borrowed funds	(7,657)	(5,877)	(4,929)	(4,280)	(4,140)
Total interest charges	28,187	26,494	24,751	21,112	15,169
Income before cumulative effect of accounting change	58,607	58,832	51,611	51,930	46,247
Cumulative effect of accounting change	—	—	—	—	2,437
Net income	58,607	58,832	51,611	51,930	48,684
Preferred stock dividend	10,289	10,289	10,289	10,289	10,289
Earnings available for common stock	$ 48,318	$ 48,543	$ 41,322	$ 41,641	$ 38,395

EXHIBIT 3

METROPOLITAN EDISON COMPANY
Consolidated Balance Sheets
For the Years Ended December 31, 1977, and 1978
(in thousands of dollars)

	1978	1977
Assets		
Utility plant (at original cost):		
In service	$1,257,169	$ 875,685
Less: Accumulated depreciation	208,936	188,079
Net	1,048,233	687,698
Construction work in progress	19,670	327,534
Held for future use	12,561	13,151
Totals	1,080,464	1,028,291
Nuclear fuel	64,169	62,477
Less: Accumulated amortization	11,052	14,661
Net nuclear fuel	53,117	47,816
Net utility plant	1,133,581	1,076,107
Investments:		
Other physical property, net	171	172
Other, at cost	495	495
Totals	666	667
Current assets:		
Cash	6,403	4,654
Accounts receivable:		
Affiliates		476
Customers, net	16,958	14,637
Other	18,718	4,260
Inventories, at average cost or less:		
Materials and supplies for construction and operation	10,900	8,828
Fuel	15,267	18,538
Prepayments	568	718
Other	2,742	2,747
Totals	71,556	54,858
Deferred debits:		
Deferred energy costs	23,221	13,232
Other	10,779	6,659
Totals	34,000	19,891
Total assets	$1,239,803	$1,151,523

EXHIBIT 3 *(concluded)*

METROPOLITAN EDISON COMPANY
Consolidated Balance Sheets
For the Years Ended December 31, 1977, and 1978
(in thousands of dollars)

	1978	1977
Liabilities and Capital		
Long-term debt, capital stock and consolidated surplus:		
First mortgage bonds	$ 462,957	$ 404,499
Debentures	82,700	84,680
Unamortized net discount on long-term debt	(1,636)	(975)
Totals	544,021	488,204
Cumulative preferred stock	139,391	139,391
Premium on cumulative preferred stock	483	483
Less: Capital stock expense		26
Totals	139,874	139,848
Common stock and consolidated surplus:		
Common stock	66,273	66,273
Consolidated capital surplus	280,523	280,523
Consolidated retained earnings	23,019	22,701
Totals	369,815	369,497
Totals	1,053,710	997,549
Current liabilities:		
Debt due within one year	2,102	5,600
Notes payable to banks	35,500	31,250
Accounts payable:		
Affiliates	913	433
Others	17,272	13,846
Customer deposits	571	574
Taxes accrued	6,193	14,759
Interest accrued	11,027	9,341
Other	7,756	6,986
Totals	81,334	82,799
Deferred credits and other liabilities:		
Deferred income taxes	66,643	46,618
Unamortized investment credits	33,432	19,971
Other	4,684	4,586
Totals	104,759	71,175
Commitments and contingencies		
Total liabilities and capital	$1,239,803	$1,151,523

METROPOLITAN EDISON COMPANY'S INVOLVEMENT IN NUCLEAR POWER

Ironically, the accident came almost exactly 20 years from the beginning of Met-Ed's involvement with nuclear reactors. In December 1958, Met-Ed had joined with other GPU subsidiaries in a seven-and-a-half-year effort along with Westinghouse Electric Corporation to build and operate a pressurized water-type nuclear reactor at Saxton Station, Pennsylvania. The project was "aimed to give all participants first-hand knowledge of the managerial and technical problems in buying, building, operating, and maintaining nuclear plants, as well as affording an experience basis for making decisions when nuclear power technology has developed to a point where nuclear power costs are competitive with costs of power from fossil fuels."[4]

The Saxton Station project received approval from the Atomic Energy Commission in February 1960 and was completed in less than scheduled time at a lower than budgeted cost. The plant produced 20,000 kilowatts of output for a five-year period, beginning in April 1962. By the end of 1962, Met-Ed announced the project a success, ". . . serving the purpose for which it was conceived, namely: (1) to increase our knowledge about reactor technology; (2) to train personnel in the construction and operation of nuclear reactors; and (3) to provide an experimental reactor operating under actual utility conditions."

The success of the Saxton Station contributed in 1963 to the decision of GPU subsidiary Jersey Central Power and Light to construct the Oyster Creek Station. The 600,000 kilowatt facility was to be built in five years at a cost of $68 million. Met-Ed, which was to participate in the joint venture, announced to its shareholders, "This plant will be the first nuclear-fueled generating station in New Jersey and when completed will be the largest privately owned nuclear station in the world."

On March 28, 1967, exactly 12 years to the day prior to the failure of TMI-2, Met-Ed announced to its shareholders that it intended to build a nuclear generating station on Three Mile Island scheduled for an in-service date in 1971. The 840,000 kilowatt plant ". . . is the first atomic plant to be built and owned solely by Met-Ed." Application was made in 1967 to the Atomic Energy Commission and construction was scheduled to begin in 1968.

The Atomic Energy Commission granted a construction permit in May 1968. The company believed it still possible to complete the plant by fall 1971. In 1969, the completion date was revised to 1972. Also, it was decided in 1969 that a second nuclear unit would be built at Three Mile Island. The second unit, scheduled for completion in 1974 and known as TMI-2, was to be jointly owned by Jersey Central Power and Light and Metropolitan Edison.

In 1970, the completion date for TMI-1 was revised to 1973. Also, it was decided that the Three Mile Island facility would be owned 50 percent by Met-

---

[4] *Metropolitan Edison Company 1958 Annual Report*, p. 6. This section is based wholly on accounts contained in annual reports of the Metropolitan Edison Company from 1958 to 1978.

Ed, 25 percent by Jersey Central Power and Light, and 25 percent by Pennsylvania Electric. TMI-2 was still scheduled for completion in 1974. Also, in 1970, construction delays and operating problems caused an earnings decline for Metropolitan Edison, which seriously hampered financing capability in 1971.

By the end of 1971, Met-Ed announced that TMI-1 was 75 percent complete and TMI-2 was nearly 20 percent complete. No completion date was forecast because "the lack of financing capability necessary to fund our vital construction program continues to present a serious problem for the company."

By the end of 1972, TMI-1 was 95 percent complete at a cost estimated at $375 million, and the 880,000 kilowatt TMI-2 was 35 percent complete at an estimated total cost of $465 million. Med-Ed forecast that TMI-1 would be in commercial service by August 1974 and TMI-2 would be operational in spring 1976.

In 1972, the company experienced a change in top management. Frederic Cox, who had been chairman of the board and president of Met-Ed since February 1968, retired at the beginning of 1972. The board elected William G. Kuhns, chairman of the board and Walter M. Creitz as president. Both executives had spent their entire careers with Metropolitan Edison.

Up until 1973, the annual company reports had been 8-page, black and white statements without pictures and one-page narrative coverage about company progress. The *1973 Annual Report* was strikingly different. The full color 18-page brochure had an aerial photograph of the Three Mile Island plant on the front and back covers, along with an additional 35 photographs, mostly of company employees and plants. With respect to Three Mile Island, the company announced, "We look forward to 1974 for many reasons; but one of the most exciting is the expected addition of Three Mile Island Nuclear Station Unit No. 1 to the capacity of Met-Ed and the GPU System. It has been a long challenging road, and our employees and associates have contributed much to make its production a reality." The total cost of the project was now estimated at $920 million. TMI-1 was scheduled for commercial operation in October 1974; TMI-2 was to be in-service in May 1977.

Unit Number 1 went into commercial operation on Labor Day, September 2, 1974, three years later and at a total cost of $45 million more than originally planned. At the same time, due to a severe cutback in construction caused by financing problems, TMI-2 was delayed to 1978.

Austerity continued for Met-Ed in 1975 due to sharp decreases in industrial demand and unfavorable delays in rate proceedings rulings. However, TMI-1 completed its first full year in operation with an 82 percent overall capacity factor (output divided by maximum rated capacity). The company noted, "This performance is well above average for the industry's experience." Met-Ed still forecast that TMI-2 would go into commercial service in 1978.

In 1976, Met-Ed continued to feel the effects of rising costs in all aspects of doing business. While operating income was substantially the same as in 1975, the rate of return on investment declined from 9.82 percent to 8.73 percent. Met-Ed filed in 1974 for a $70.9 million annual rate increase. The action was ruled on by the Pennsylvania Public Utilities Commission in June 1976. The result was a $29.8 million increase per year with the possibility of some retroactive billing. The nuclear plant at Three Mile Island continued its fine operating record, ending the year at a cumulative capacity factor since September 1974 of 71 percent.

In 1977, TMI-1 continued to compile an impressive output record with a capacity factor of 79 percent, more than 10 points above the national average for all nuclear plants. Also in 1977 the construction on TMI-2 was completed. The operating license for TMI-2 was received in February 1978. Fuel was loaded and testing began the same month.

On September 19, 1978, TMI-2 was dedicated in an on-site ceremony. John F. O'Leary, deputy secretary of the U.S. Department of Energy, was the principal speaker. It was noted at the dedication program that TMI-1 was "one of the top 10 performing reactors in the nation. Met-Ed looks to Unit No. 2 for the same reliable, low-cost performance that is so beneficial to our customers." When TMI-2 went into commercial service on December 30, 1978, the future indeed looked bright for Met-Ed.

THE ACCIDENT

The worst accident in the history of commercial nuclear power occurred early on the morning of March 28, 1979, near Harrisburg, Pennsylvania.[5] At first, it seemed that the crew on duty at the Three Mile Island plant faced only a minor problem when part of the plant's cooling system was inadvertently shut down. Unit 2's huge turbine, which generated 880 megawatts of electricity, had shut down automatically, as it ought to when the steam that turned it somehow had been cut off. The technicians assumed that the cause would be easy to detect and remedy, but problems and mistakes multiplied quickly. A backup cooling system failed to function because sometime earlier someone had shut, apparently by accident, some key valves. As pressure and temperature began rising in the reactor, a relief valve opened automatically, but failed to close when pressure and temperature were under control. In the 10 hours it took to diagnose that problem, thousands of gallons of vital cooling water poured out of the reactor. Further complicating the situation, operators misread conditions inside the reactor and prematurely shut off emergency cooling pumps that had turned on automatically.

For the next several days, radioactive steam and gas seeped sporadically into the atmosphere from the Three Mile Island plant. While engineers struggled to cool the core of the reactor, there was tremendous threat of a "meltdown" in which the core drops into the water coolant at the bottom of its chamber, causing a steam explosion that could rupture the four-foot-thick concrete walls of the containment building; or, the molten core could burn

---

[5] Details abstracted from "Nuclear Nightmares," pp. 9–10.

through the even thicker concrete base and deep into the earth. In either case, lethally radioactive gases would be released into the environment. This would be catastrophic, considering that there were nearly 100 tons of deadly radioactive material that made up the core of the large reactor.

Reports differed greatly as to the amount of radiation emitted from the plant. However, the governor of Pennsylvania advised the evacuation of all pregnant women and young children living within five miles of Three Mile Island. Although there was no panic, thousands of residents left the area of their own volition. One woman remarked, "You hear one thing from the utility, one thing from the government, another thing from Harrisburg, and something else from civil defense." The inhabitants of the area, along with the rest of the nation, became confused about the safety of nuclear power.

THE DEBATE

Nuclear stations cost between $500 million and $1 billion to construct. In 1979, there were 72 nuclear generators in commercial operation. In the event of a nuclear shutdown, not only would this huge capital investment lie idle, but the cost of power generation of utilities would soar. For instance, Metropolitan Edison was paying $800,000 a day for supplemental power from other utilities, while TMI-1 and TMI-2 were shut down.[6] According to the Atomic Industrial Forum, without nuclear energy, the United States, in 1978, might have had to burn an additional 470 million barrels of oil to make electricity. This amount of oil could be converted to at least 12 billion gallons of gasoline, a year's supply for 17 million automobiles. If plants under construction in 1979 were allowed to go into operation, the contribution of nuclear power would triple by 1985. The oil burned in one year by a million-kilowatt electric generation plant could be used instead to produce enough gasoline for about 350,000 cars or enough heating oil for more than 400,000 homes in the northern United States. A nuclear plant such as Three Mile Island could save 10 million barrels of imported oil per year.[7]

A study by the Institute for Energy Analysis of the Oak Ridge Associated Universities estimated the direct annual economic cost of what might be called a modified limited moratorium (no new construction starts after 1980, continued operations of all reactors on line by 1985) as 1 percent of the GNP. That would be, in 1979 dollars, something like $20 billion a year. In addition to the monetary cost, the industry argued that such a moratorium would increase the principal pollutants from coal plants by 20 percent, and by any of the varying estimates of deaths from coal, that would mean thousands more deaths each year.

---

[6] *General Public Utilities First Quarter and Annual Meeting Report,* 1979.

[7] Atomic Industrial Forum, *Nuclear Info,* July 1979, p. 1.

A second study on the impact of a nuclear moratorium was conducted by National Economic Research Associates, Inc., a highly respected independent study group. The group studied the cost of several alternatives, any one of which might result from the incident.

It then was forced to make various assumptions and worked out the results under the different assumptions. In one example, it was assumed that oil prices would continue to rise, that electricity demands would grow at the low end of recent Department of Energy estimates, and that plant modifications required by the Three Mile Island experience would prove relatively inexpensive. Under those assumptions, the group determined the effect of a policy calling for stopping new nuclear power plant construction and decommissioning existing plants by 1985. The results:

1. Impose annual costs on society of $16 billion by 1985 and $22 billion by the year 2000.

2. Result in an increase in sulfur emissions of three to four million tons annually, sufficient to wipe out the alleged advantages of the 1977 amendments to the Clean Air Act.

3. Increase oil imports by two million barrels per day by 1985, falling off sharply thereafter as coal is phased in over the longer term.

4. Increase the number of human fatalities associated with the production and movement of fuel and generation of electricity by 30,000 in the next two decades.

If, in the face of nuclear cutbacks, the industry were unable to bring on line either oil-fueled capacity or coal-fueled capacity, power shortages would result. If all nuclear plants were decommissioned by 1987, and no new capacity beyond current plans were brought on line, then capacity would fall sufficiently short of projected demand so that the resultant cost to the public of power shortages would be $26 billion annually by 1987.

The generation of replacement electricity in the three-state power pool serviced by Three Mile Island (Pennsylvania, Maryland, and New Jersey) would shift sources from 46 percent to 50 percent coal fired. That change, the pronuclear advocates argued, would have inevitable health effects as sulfur dioxide and other pollutants increased in the area. Nuclear power proponents contended that nuclear reactors, routinely operated, were among the most negligible emitters of radiation, and thus the most negligible causes of radiation. Because radiation had been studied longer and more intensively, it was argued, more was known about it than the carcinogens in coal smoke. Thus, it could be measured with great precision and sensitivity.

An ad hoc group made up of technical staff members of the NRC, U.S. Department of Health, Education, and Welfare (HEW), and the U.S. Environmental Protection Administration (EPA) was chosen to assess the health impact on the approximately two million offsite residents within 50 miles of the Three Mile Island nuclear station. The study group concluded that the offsite collective dose associated with radioactive material released during the period of March 28 to April 7, 1979, represented minimal risks. The projected number of excess fatal cancers due to the accident that could occur over the remaining lifetime of the population within 50 miles was approximately one, according to the interagency team's findings. Had the accident not occurred, the number of fatal cancers that would normally be expected in a population of this size over its remaining lifetime was estimated at 325,000. The projected total number of excess health effects, including all cases of cancer (fatal and nonfatal) and genetic ill health to all future generations, was approximately two.

These figures violently clashed with those of Dr. Helen Caldicott, pediatrician and president of a national organization of doctors opposed to nuclear power, the Physicians for Social Responsibility.

> Out of a predicted 10 million people who would be exposed to radiation, there would be 3,300 prompt fatalities; 45,000 cases of respiratory impairment and burning of the lung; 240,000 cases of thyroid damage; 350,000 cases of temporary sterility in males; 40,000 to 100,000 cases of prolonged or permanent suppression of menstruation in women; 10,000 to 100,000 cases of acute radiation illness. . . . As for babies in utero: 100,000 of them would be exposed. All of them could develop cretinism. There might be 1,500 cases of microcephaly, that is, babies born mentally retarded with abnormally small heads . . . Fifteen years after the event, we could expect 270,000 cases of cancer and 28,800 thyroid tumors and genetic diseases. That all adds up to nearly one million so-called "health effects."[8]

Radiation is invisible, intangible, tasteless, odorless, and silent. It is also measured in unfamiliar units. All of these factors tend to make radiation an object of fear and mystery. Antinuclear spokespersons argued that it would take only one radioactive atom, one cell, and one gene to initiate cancer. One way of evaluating the magnitude of radiation release is to consider the maximum exposure the most exposed member of the public might have gotten. According to the NRC, this amount was 90 millirems, or the equivalent of two chest X rays. This level of radiation was only slightly less than the difference between the annual natural or background exposure in New Orleans or Denver. The average exposure to persons living within 50 miles of the reactor was 1.75 millirems, or little more than the exposure one gets each year from watching color television.[9]

THE AFTERMATH

President Carter named 11 persons to an independent commission to investigate and explore the Three Mile Island accident. The blue-ribbon commission was headed by John G. Kemeny, president of Dartmouth College,

---

[8] Katie Leishman, "Helen Caldicott: The Voice the Nuclear Industry Fears," *Ms.,* July 1979, pp. 50–93 *passim.*

[9] Atomic Industrial Forum, *Nuclear Info,* August, 1979, p. 1.

whose early career as mathematician and philosopher involved research on the Manhattan Project and a stint as an assistant to Albert Einstein. The other appointees included two critics of nuclear power.

In addition to the president's commission, at least seven other separate investigations about or related to the Three Mile Island accident were launched. The NRC conducted its own investigation. On Capitol Hill, hearings were launched immediately by Sen. Edward M. Kennedy's subcommittee on health and by Sen. Gary Hart's subcommittee on nuclear regulation. Additional hearings were planned by Rep. Morris K. Udall's energy and environmental subcommittee, by Rep. Mike McCormack's subcommittee on energy research and production, and by Sen. John Glenn's energy subcommittee of the Government Affairs Committee.

The annual shareholders meeting of General Public Utilities Corp., held on May 25, 1979, served as a forum for discussion of the TMI-2 accident. William G. Kuhns, who had been chairman of the parent corporation since 1975, addressed the shareholders and responded to their questions on the accident. The full text of chairman Kuhn's remarks and the ensuing discussion period follow.

CHAIRMAN'S ADDRESS

At 4 A.M. on Wednesday, March 28, TMI-2 was severely damaged in the worst accident in the history of America's nuclear industry.

However, despite all the damage done to the unit, I am grateful that, from all the information available, the accident has not resulted in any injury to the public health.

While we believe that the accident involved a complex interaction of equipment malfunctions, design and instrumentation shortfalls, and human response, we do not yet have a full understanding of the exact causes or sequence of events. All of our top priority efforts have been devoted to protecting the health and safety of the public and of our employees. Now, numerous investigations have been initiated, and we have pledged our full cooperation and support to them. We are determined to learn as much as we can from this unfortunate accident.

One thing that we already know is that the accident and its aftermath have had a traumatic and profound effect on the local community, on your company, and on the industry. We regret this deeply, particularly the impact it has had on the people of the Middletown, Pennsylvania area, who have traditionally strongly supported the TMI project.

I won't go into the details of the accident itself. Instead, Herman Dieckamp, president and chief operating officer, will give an explanation of the accident and TMI's current and future status.

I will not take the time to review GPU's operations in 1978. That information was covered in our Annual Report mailed to you in March. Instead, let's go right into the accident's aftermath and its ramifications for GPU.

Assessing the Impact

Shortly after the accident, as its magnitude became apparent, we began an assessment of its impact on the GPU System and of how best to deal with it.

It still is not possible to determine accurately the ultimate dollar costs. Aggravating the problem is the unavailability of TMI-1, which was not involved in the accident, but could not go back in service after its fuel reloading because of the activities on site involving TMI-2. We are identifying what must be done to return it to commercial operation.

We also expect that TMI-2 can be restored to service. Experience with the clean up and restoration activities following other nuclear accidents suggest that the problem is technically manageable. But the costs as of now are unknown, and the job may take two to four years.

The costs of the accident fall into several broad categories: namely, liability for expenses incurred by others, for example, the expenses of evacuees; physical damage to the facility; interest on money borrowed to cover costs of the accident and other related costs; and the price of replacement energy.

Insurance Coverage

Insurance will cover liability claims up to the legal limit of $560 million. The maximum GPU financial exposure in this area would be $15 million, under provisions of the Price-Anderson Act, which establishes the ground rules for liability in the event of nuclear accidents. The balance would be covered by private and federal insurance programs and assessments on other utility reactor operators.

Insurance will also cover up to $300 million of physical damage to the TMI site. We believe this insurance will pay most of the bill for clean up and repairs, but not for plant improvements or modifications.

Also not covered by insurance will be the interest costs on money we will have to borrow to see us through this emergency. Nor does insurance cover the fixed investment charges associated with TMI-2, estimated at about $8 million per month. We are currently negotiating with a group of banks for a $450 million revolving credit agreement to meet short-term needs. Discussions are in progress concerning the possible issuance of longer-term securities.

The most significant uninsured cost is that of replacement power to make up for the loss of output, about $24 million a month. It will be reduced to $10 million a month when TMI-1 comes back on line. We are aggressively exploring the means of reducing these replacement power costs.

Sharing the Costs

Because of the magnitude of these uninsured costs, we believe they must be shared by GPU's stockholders, customers, and employees. Appropriate actions have been taken, and are being planned, to implement this conclusion.

The GPU board of directors, at its April 26 meeting, voted to reduce the quarterly dividend on common stock from 45 cents to 25 cents per share.

We deeply regret the need for this action.

We recognize the importance of our cash dividend policy to our stockholders. Before reaching this decision the board held a number of extensive briefing sessions. All factors bearing on the decision were explored, including recommendations in the many letters and calls we received from shareowners.

The board also suspended the Dividend Reinvestment and Stock Purchase Plan. All funds received since the February 25 payment date will be repaid. It is our intention to reinstate the plan at an appropriate future date.

However, the dividend action does not reflect the full measure of the stockholders' share of the burden. A very significant burden is the decline in the market value of GPU shares since the accident, from just under $18 to less than $10 a share at this point. As of this morning, the shareholders have absorbed a half billion dollar decline in the value of their GPU investment.

Cutting Expenses

The system's directors, officers, and other employees are shouldering a share of the burden. A hiring freeze has been imposed, and layoffs are planned, though we hope to minimize them through attrition and incentives to encourage early retirements.

The retainers of the GPU directors have been cut from $7,500 to $6,000 annually and a $100 increase in their $300 meeting fee cancelled. The GPU system officers' scheduled 7 percent salary increase has been rescinded, returning them to April 1978 levels, and Herman Dieckamp and I are being rolled back to our April 1977 levels. To date we have avoided cutting the salaries of other employees, as we wish to retain as many of our good people as feasible.

As we announced early in April, the company, as one of the many steps to conserve cash resources, suspended all construction projects involving additional generating and transmission facilities. We also have stopped all but the most critical construction programs on existing facilities, and are postponing or reducing nonessential maintenance work.

We have reduced our 1979 construction budget by $125 million and our 1980 construction budget by $225 million. These represent cuts of nearly 30 percent and 45 percent, respectively.

The major generation projects affected are the planned 1,100-megawatt Forked River, New Jersey, nuclear unit, and the Seward-7 coal-fired plant in western Pennsylvania, both slated for operation in the middle 1980s.

Additionally, we are taking a very close look at operation and maintenance expenses, at all levels throughout the system. To date we have reduced our 1979 budget in those areas by $30 million, a 9 percent cut. We plan to reduce this further.

In addition to reducing officers' salaries and putting a freeze on hiring, we will combine a special early retirement program with a planned reduction of the work force by eliminating about 600 jobs over the next several months. This will reduce payroll costs to a level that will support a minimum construction effort and a reasonable level of service to our customers.

Further, in reducing the work force, employees whose skills and experience could be used to support the recovery operation at TMI will be offered employment there to reduce the cost of outside services over a considerable length of time.

Customers Should Participate

This brings us to our customers. We feel strongly that they also should share the burden. All the economies achieved through the operation of our nuclear plants have been passed on to them. The operation of the TMI-1 Oyster Creek nuclear facilities has already saved customers about $700 million through 1978.

None of these savings have gone to investors in GPU. The customers have been the sole beneficiaries. In light of this, it seems equitable that our customers bear some of the financial risk of nuclear power and share in the burden of the TMI-2 accident.

In proceedings now underway before the New Jersey Board of Public Utilities and the Pennsylvania Public Utility Commission, we will make it clear that the outcome of these proceedings is the key element in determining the future ability of the GPU Companies to serve their customers. We are doing everything possible to provide the agencies with the information they need in reaching their difficult and painful decisions.

The Pennsylvania PUC on April 19 initiated proceedings to determine the appropriate base rate levels for both of our Pennsylvania subsidiaries. Hearings began May 2 and will continue through this month. A decision is anticipated before the end of June. It is *most* important that this schedule be maintained.

Jersey Central Power and Light Company made a rate filing on May 4 with the New Jersey Commission to deal with the impact of the TMI-2 accident on our New Jersey customers. Here, too, we must hope for fast action.

I should add at this point that, at a price, there is adequate capacity in the GPU System and in neighboring, interconnected utilities to meet our near-term customer requirements. However, as we get further into the 1980s, there could be supply problems unless we are able to resume our construction program.

Healing Process Underway

In summary, I can only repeat what I said in my letter to you. Your company has been seriously wounded. But the healing process is underway.

During this period, the GPU stockholders have been an inspiration. There have been many letters and phone calls. We have received many expressions of support, thoughtful suggestions for dealing with the problem, including what dividend action we should take, and some criticisms.

We have received help from many other sources, especially the performance of our own people, which I can only say has been "beyond the call of duty." We are grateful for the assistance of hundreds of experts from other utilities, the nuclear industry, the academic community, and state and federal regulatory agencies.

Commitment Undiminished

Looking to the future, let me emphasize that GPU's commitment to our customers, shareowners, and employees continues undiminished.

We are committed to providing our customers with reliable electric service at the lowest cost we can achieve.

We are committed to providing our shareowners with a reasonable return on their investment.

We are committed to providing our employees with the challenge and opportunities of this highly dynamic energy business.

And to fulfill these commitments, GPU is also committed to fostering among its regulators, shareowners, customers, and employees a deeper understanding of the necessity for maintaining the financial and operational integrity of General Public Utilities Corporation.

Discussion Period

Following are some of the questions asked, and the answers given, during the meeting's discussion period.

Q. What steps were taken to keep the directors immediately and fully informed after the Three Mile Island Unit-2 accident?

Mr. Kuhns:
They received extensive briefings and were kept up-to-date by telephone calls in the intervals between sessions.

Q. Did the directors discuss management changes at Metropolitan Edison Company in light of the accident?

Mr. Kuhns:
At this point, we want to await the outcome of the many investigations now underway and our own review of the events that transpired on March 28 and subsequent events and base any subsequent actions on the evaluation of that information.

Q. Would I be correct to assume that we cannot expect any immediate rate relief, say from the next three to six months, from the regulatory agencies?

Mr. Fred D. Hafer [vice president-rate case management]:
No, the Pennsylvania Public Utility Commission has indicated that it will close hearings on the cases before them involving Metropolitan Edison Company and Pennsylvania Electric Company by the end of May, so it is reasonable that the PUC

would reach a decision during June. Both companies have also asked that the commission take some action in advance of that decision, allowing a higher billing rate beginning in June to start recovering the replacement of energy costs on a more timely basis. [Note: On May 10th, the PUC postponed action on these latter requests.]

In the case of Jersey Central, we filed our case on May 4, and we expect that sometime, perhaps this week, the commission in that state will indicate a time schedule for concluding their proceedings. I think that it is reasonable to expect some action in New Jersey within the next month or two.

Q. Let's presume a negative reaction from the regulatory agencies due to public pressure. What could we shareholders expect on the next dividend date, an increase or a decrease?

Mr. Kuhns:

It's really not productive to speculate at this point on what will happen. I think whatever the commissions do would have to be evaluated very carefully, and I am not about to suggest what they would have to do to help us accomplish certain things. I think we will have to proceed with the cases and evaluate their reaction and their response and then decide what we have to do at that point.

Q. I think we are all concerned that the dividend may drop again, or be eliminated entirely, and we would like to have some estimate of what the probability of that might be.

Mr. Kuhns:

We really can't give it to you at this point, mainly because we don't know. It depends upon what events occur between now and the dividend meeting in July and what we would recommend to the board of directors, or what the board would ultimately do. We really can't predict beyond that.

Q. Assuming you maintain the quarterly dividend of 25 cents for the rest of this year, would you anticipate that a portion of the dividend paid this year would be nontaxable for income tax purposes?

Mr. E. J. Holcombe [GPU comptroller]:

I believe that it is quite possible that a portion would be, under the assumptions we've made for planning purposes, but we cannot fix on a definite amount at this point.

Q. I notice that there was some malfunction of equipment, and I would like to know why the manufacturers, namely Babcock and Wilcox, shouldn't be approached to help spare [us] some of the effects of the accident?

Mr. James R. Liberman [GPU's general counsel]:

We have sent a letter to B&W and put them on notice that there are indications that certain equipment may have failed to meet the contract requirements, and I think that we have reserved any rights that we would have to proceed against B&W.

Several stockholders commented on GPU's public relations efforts at the time of the TMI-2 accident. Mr. Kuhns said that this had been noted by management, and that "we are very serious about examining our posture on public and customer relations, and we recognize the need to improve it."

Q. Why doesn't GPU just dispose of the Met-Ed stock at zero, write it off and get a tax benefit?

Mr. Kuhns:

Well, the problem is more than just a Met-Ed problem. It also impacts Jersey Central enormously. We don't feel that walking away from these companies would be doing the best job for the GPU stockholder. We think this is a problem that should be managed, can be managed, and that Met-Ed and Jersey Central and Penelec and the GPU System can recover from this traumatic event and continue to serve the customers and the investors as in the past.

Q. Mr. Creitz [*Walter M. Creitz, president of Met-Ed*], the newspapers accused you of holding back information that you had. May I have your comment on that please?

Mr. Creitz:

It's been our policy and practice to try to tell customers and our neighbors exactly what was going on at all times. And this is exactly what we tried to do. We understood more and more about the extent of the accident as time went on. What we saw as the situation, particularly as it related to the safety and well-being of the people who lived in the area, is the type of information that we tried to provide to the state, to the NRC people there, and to the public. Conditions did change and as this did happen, we attempted to update and relay this to the public.

Q. Can you estimate how long it will be before TMI Unit-1 will be back in operation?

Mr. Dieckamp:

If it were simply a matter of restoring the site to a state of normalcy, and of making the technical modifications to the plant that are required of similar plants, we think that could probably be accomplished in three months. There may well be some public hearings and things of that nature before the plant is allowed to go back in operation. So, for planning purposes we are thinking, realistically, the end of the year.

Q. Would someone explain what is being proposed in terms of the early retirement plan as a way of cutting costs?

Mr. Kuhns:

The board has approved a program under which employees aged 60 and above with 20 years of service would be eligible for early retirement without any actuarial reduction in their pension because of retiring before age 65.

Q. What is the status of the $450 million revolving credit that the corporation is applying for; I understand it is under negotiation, and I just wondered when the outcome might be resolved?

Mr. Verner H. Condon [GPU vice president and chief financial officer]:

Our target is prior to the end of this month. And the responses we've had from the banks to date are very supportive.

Q. What would the effect be on the corporation if the PUC were to reinstate the rate increases which were suspended for Met-Ed and Penelec?

Mr. Kuhns:

Penelec's share was $25 million and Met-Ed's was $49 million, so that totals $74 million on an annual basis.

Q. This would pretty much solve or help the problem of the $800,000 a day to buy power from other utilities, I take it?

Mr. Kuhns:

It would help, but not solve it.

Q. First, I want to thank you for having your meeting in Johnstown, and, since we are here in the coal fields, I was wondering if you could give us some of management's feelings in regard to coal?

Mr. Dieckamp:
We certainly hope to generate a significant amount of power in the future from coal. We had planned to build the next coal plant, to be located at Seward, for 1985. In our minds there is no question but that this country's and this region's demands for energy are going to require significant use of coal in the future.

While the full financial impact of the accident was still unknown, Mr. Kuhns knew that the shutdown was costing about $14 million per month. He believed that TMI-1 could be back in operation in about four months and that TMI-2 could be back in service by 1983 at a cost of about $400 million. However, the Nuclear Regulatory Commission hearings could serve as a formidable obstacle to the restart.

As Mr. Kuhns composed his letter to stockholders, he was aware that antinuclear sentiment was on the rise. In recent months, the nation had witnessed numerous organized protest marches and sit-ins at nuclear facilities. *The China Syndrome,* a movie highly critical of nuclear power, was a box office success. A recent best seller by Arthur Hailey, *Overload,* depicted the nuclear industry as poorly managed. Somehow, he must impress upon his shareholders the importance of solid support during the upcoming public hearings.

Allied Chemical Corporation (A)

In June of 1976 Richard Wagner, president of the Specialty Chemicals Division of Allied Chemical, faced two difficult decisions. He had to recommend whether Allied should support passage of the Toxic Substances Control Act pending before Congress. He also had to decide whether to implement a proposed new program, called *Total Product Responsibility,* in his division.

Wagner found these decisions especially difficult because of the variety of factors he had to consider. These included Allied's business prospects, recent developments in the chemical industry, and the increasing public and government concern about the health, safety, and environmental effects of chemical production. Another important factor was the set of problems related to Kepone, a pesticide produced until 1974 by Allied and afterwards by an outside contractor.

ALLIED CHEMICAL

Allied Chemical was a major producer of chemicals, fibers and fabricated products, and energy. The company had headquarters in Morristown, New Jersey, and operated over 150 plants, research labs, quarries, and other facilities in the United States and overseas. In 1975 Allied earned $116 million on sales of $2.3 billion. (See Exhibits 1 and 2 for Allied's organization and recent financial performance.)

Over the past eight years, Allied had changed dramatically. One company official said Allied was run as "a loose feudal barony" in the 1960s. *Forbes* called the company "a slow-moving, low-growth, low-profit producer of basic

EXHIBIT 1   Organization Chart

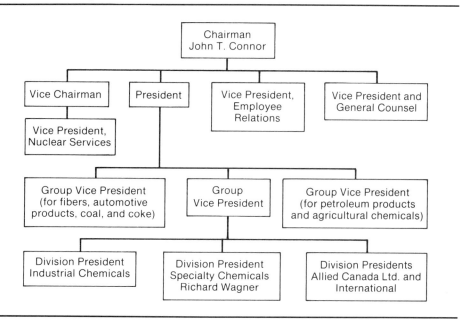

inorganic chemicals, fertilizers, and dyestuffs."[1] Changes began in 1967 when John T. Connor resigned as Secretary of Commerce and became chairman of Allied. Over the course of several years, Connor brought in 250 new executives, pruned failing businesses, established systematic planning and tight cost control, and increased corporate supervision of the divisions. At the same time, he stressed decentralized decision making and said that innovation and flexibility were crucial to Allied's future.

Connor's most important step was an $800 million commitment to find and develop oil and gas supplies throughout the world. According to Connor, this strategy was financed with new capital and with funds "from existing businesses that were losing, had poor prospects, or had severe environmental risks."[2] The largest investments were in Indonesian gas fields and North Sea oil fields. In Indonesia, Allied had a 35 percent interest in a joint venture with Pertamina, the Indonesian government petroleum agency. The British government had announced its intention to obtain a voluntary 51 percent participation in the North Sea oil fields, but the form that participation might take had not been determined.

This energy investment was very risky. Finding and developing new reserves was highly competitive, technically difficult, and very costly.

---

[1] "Risk Rewarded," *Forbes,* March 15, 1977, p. 101.

[2] Ibid.

EXHIBIT 2 Recent Financial Performance

	1975	1974	1973	1972
Sales (millions)	$2,333	$2,216	$1,665	$1,501
Aftertax income (millions)	116	144	90	64
Earnings per share	4.17	5.19	3.27	2.30
Debt/equity	0.59	0.45	0.49	0.54
Gross margin/sales	.22%	23.3%	24.6%	23.3%
R&D/sales	1.51%	1.39%	1.73%	1.89%
Pollution control facilities cost (millions)	$34.4	29.0	28.0	25.0

Line of Business Performance (millions)

Line of Business	1975		1974	
	Sales	Income from Operations	Sales	Income from Operations
Energy (petroleum, nuclear, coal & coke)	$ 581	$ 28	$ 511	$ 32
Fibers and fabricated products . .	504	46	484	81
Chemicals (inorganic, plastics, organic, agricultural)		144		135
Totals	$2,333	$218	$2,216	$248

Changes in government regulations or tax laws, either domestic or foreign, could cut profits. And problems with weather, technology, or politics in host countries could delay the start of production. These risks seemed justified as shortages of energy and chemical feedstocks occurred during the 1970s and as the potential payoff from the investment grew. Connor stated that energy could provide as much as half of Allied's profits by the early 1980s.

In mid-1976, however, the return on the energy investment was still small. In fact, it appeared that Allied's energy businesses, taken altogether, would just about break even in 1976. Allied's U.S. natural gas pipelines lost money because of federal price controls on interstate gas shipments. Its coal and coke business had chronic operating problems and, following a plea of no contest, had been fined approximately $100,000 for allegedly having failed to meet EPA air pollution requirements. Finally, obtaining government approval to operate Allied's nuclear fuel reprocessing plant could prove difficult. Company officials hoped that 1977 would bring the first profits from North Sea oil. They expected profits from Indonesian gas sales in 1978.

While Allied was investing heavily in energy, chemicals provided the foundation of company earnings. In 1976, for example, chemicals were likely to produce 75 percent of company profits, even though they were only 50 percent of total company sales. Allied produced approximately 1,500 chemicals and sold them to all major industries. These sales were primarily to other chemical manufacturers for use in making their products. Other sales were to dealers, who sometimes resold them under their own names, and to ultimate consumers. 1974 and 1975 had been the two best years in the history of Allied's chemical business. Sales were expected to weaken later in 1976 as a result of the recession that began in 1975.

Allied's fiber and fabricated products had been a steady contributor to company profits. On average, this business accounted for one fifth of total sales and profits during the early 1970s. Allied made fibers for clothing, carpeting, and auto tires. Allied was also the world's largest manufacturer of auto seat belts and shoulder harnesses.

Overall, Allied's record in the early 1970s did not compare favorably with chemical industry standards. Between 1971 and 1975, Allied's return on equity, sales growth, and return on total assets were the second lowest among the 13 major diversified chemical companies in the United States. EPS growth was exactly the average of the 13 companies. On the positive side, Allied improved its relative performance in 1974 and 1975, and its energy investment offered the prospect of major improvements in the future.

THE CHEMICAL INDUSTRY

In 1976, chemicals was one of the largest U.S. industries and had annual sales of more than $100 billion. In the 20 years after World War II, chemicals became a high-profit, glamour industry that often grew twice as fast as the GNP. In the last 10 years, however, industry growth had slowed and financial performance dimmed. Among the reasons were higher raw material costs, increased government regulation, and slowdown in U.S. economic growth, and what many considered the "maturity" of major segments of the industry. Nevertheless, the industry had continued to contribute $3–5 billion per year to the U.S balance of payments.

Roughly 80,000 chemical compounds are sold in the United States, and 500 to 1,000 new ones are added each year. More than 12,000 companies manufacture these chemicals, and most of these companies have sales of less than $5 million/year. The major customer for chemical products is the chemical industry itself. A typical chemical company will buy the product of one chemical company, process it, and sell its product to yet another chemical company. In most cases a long chain of intermediate processors connects a chemical raw material with its ultimate consumer.

The industry is highly competitive. Many chemicals are commodities and compete on price. Competition comes from both "natural" products (such as cotton fabric) and close chemical substitutes. Chemical firms also face competition from suppliers, especially oil companies, that integrate forward and from customers integrating backward. For a highly capital-intensive industry, chemicals have a low degree of concentration. The 10 largest chemical companies account for roughly 35 percent of industry shipments. Low concentration encourages competition by limiting oligopolistic pricing. The industry is also highly cyclical, lagging the business cycle by a few months, and vigorous price cutting usually occurs during recessions.

In the past, successful chemical companies tended to follow a basic pattern of growth. They made large investments in research and development. The results were new products or better processes. These innovations lowered prices and took markets from other chemicals and from natural products (like cotton fabric). In turn, new markets permitted larger scale operations, further economies, and further R&D. The R&D investments were the key to successful performance. The importance of innovation to the industry is indicated by the fact that half of all chemical products sold in 1970 were not produced commercially in the 1940s. Ammonia fertilizers, sulfa drugs, Dacron, and nylon are some of the results of chemical industry R&D.

Industry prospects were especially uncertain in 1976. The industry earned record profits in 1974 and 1975—an abrupt change from its sagging performance from 1967 to 1973. In response to these profits and to shortages in 1974, a $25 billion capital spending boom was taking place. This new capacity raised the specter of industrywide overcapacity and renewed price cutting. In fact, the new capacity was coming on line just as the economic slowdown was affecting chemical sales in 1976.

At the same time, costs were rising. Environmental laws (see Exhibit 3) and high construction costs raised the price of new plants and equipment. Companies were testing more of their products and raw materials for harmful effects, and testing costs were escalating. It was not unusual for tests on just one substance to take several years and cost $500,000. Most important, the days of cheap and plentiful oil and natural gas had ended. Chemical companies are disproportionate users of fossil fuels because they need energy to run plants and to use as feedstock for their products. Higher energy costs meant that chemical products in general lost some of their price competitiveness against nonchemical products.

EXHIBIT 3   Major Environmental Laws Affecting the Chemical Industry

National Environmental Policy Act (1970)

When a company wants to build a new plant or substantially alter an old one, it may have to prepare an "environmental impact statement," explaining how the proposed change may affect the environment.

Clean Air Act (1970)

This act establishes an intricate system of Federal-State regulation and enforcement designed to enhance the nation's air resources. Under the act, the EPA sets national ambient air quality standards for pollutants like sulfur dioxide, carbon monoxide, and lead. The states establish implementation plans with specific emission limits that will achieve the EPS standards by the end of 1982. The EPA can also set national

EXHIBIT 3 *(continued)*

emission limits for especially hazardous pollutants like asbestos, vinyl chloride, and benzene.

Clean Water Act of 1977 Amending the Federal Water Pollution Control Act of 1972

This act establishes national goals and authorizes EPA to adopt effluent standards and a national permit system. The national goals include prohibition of toxic pollutant discharges; "fishable" and "swimmable" waters by July 1, 1983; and elimination of pollutant discharges by 1985. EPA regulations cover over 250 classes and categories of existing plants, and permits require plants to apply the "best practical control technology currently available." There are also standards for over 250 classes of new plants, and these must use the "best available demonstrated control technology." Anyone building a new plant must obtain a preconstruction permit and may have to submit an environmental impact statement.

The Resource Conservation and Recovery Act of 1976 (RCRA)

This act creates a federal hazardous materials disposal program for land disposal of discarded materials. The act encourages states to create discarded waste regulatory programs while the EPA has responsibility for hazardous wastes. By April 1978, the EPA must list hazardous materials, and by July 1978, companies must file permit applications with EPA or state officials for disposal sites they operate and name any company-generated hazardous waste materials.

Federal Laws Governing the Environment

The Occupational Safety and Health Act of 1970, the Federal Coal Mine Health and Safety Act, and the Nonmetallic Mine and Safety Act are three federal laws that regulate the workplace. These laws are administered by the Department of Labor through a series of rules, regulations, and orders with very specific requirements and standards. There are frequent inspections, and citations for violations are issued. When an inspection reveals imminent danger, court orders can be obtained or administrative orders can be issued for shutting down operations. Variance from the standards are possible if an employer can demonstrate an acceptable alternative.

Other Federal Acts

These acts also deal with the environment:

The Safe Drinking Water Act of 1974 seeks to protect public and private drinking water systems and underground drinking water sources.

The Hazardous Materials Transportation Act of 1975 authorizes the Federal Department of Transportation to regulate transportation of hazardous materials affecting the interstate commerce.

Federal pesticide control laws provide for EPA regulation of pesticides.

EXHIBIT 3 *(concluded)*

The Marine Protection, Research and Sanctuaries Act of 1972 regulates waste disposal in the oceans.

Federal land use laws regulate land usage.

The Noise Control Act of 1972 authorizes the EPA to control noise pollution.

The Consumer Product Safety Act of 1972 deals with the safety of products and their parts used by consumers at home or for recreation.

The Federal Wildlife Protection Laws deal with enhancement of wildlife.

State and Local Laws

State or local governments may impose additional or tougher standards than those adopted by federal authorities, and the tougher standards normally will take precedence. State and local governments may also be the principal bodies carrying out federal programs. Local and state laws run the gamut from zoning regulations to toxic substance and board of health requirements.

Criminal and Civil Penalties

Federal and state environmental laws usually provide for a number of civil or criminal penalties or both for violations. They range from $5,000 civil penalties payable to the U.S. Coast Guard for oil spills to criminal penalties up to $50,000 per day of violation and/or imprisonment up to two years for knowing violations of the Clean Air Act, the Federal Water Pollution Control Act, or the regulations issued under these acts. False reports or inaccurate information submitted under legal reporting requirements usually involve criminal penalties.

SOURCE: Adapted from *Compliance with the Environmental Laws,* prepared by Allied Chemical Corp.

Industry executives were also concerned about an "innovation shrinkage." R&D spending in 1976 would be roughly $1.4 billion, up from $800 million 10 years before. But a higher percentage of this spending was going to modify products already on the market or into government-required health and safety research. Reduced R&D seemed to threaten future industry growth.

KEPONE

Wagner had to make his two decisions at a time when Allied was in the middle of the Kepone affair. Problems related to Kepone had preoccupied Allied executives for nearly a year and seemed to be growing rather than subsiding.

Kepone was a DDT-like pesticide used in ant and roach bait in the United States and as a banana pest killer abroad. It looks like fine, white dust and is toxic. Between 1966 and 1973, Allied made Kepone at its Hopewell, Virginia, plant or had Kepone made for it by outside contractors. Profits were under

$600,000 a year, and Allied had no health or safety problems with its Kepone production.

In early 1973 Allied needed more capacity at Hopewell for other products and sought bids from companies willing to produce Kepone for Allied. This was not unusual: twice before, outside contractors had made Kepone for resale by Allied. The lowest bid by far was submitted by Life Science Products, a new company owned by two former Allied employees. Both of them had been involved in the development and manufacture of Kepone. LSP leased a former gas station near the Hopewell plant, converted it, and began making Kepone in March 1974.

For 16 months LSP produced Kepone under conditions that might have shocked Dickens, according to most accounts. Brian Kelly, a reporter for the *Washington Post,* described the plant as

> an incredible mess. Dust flying through the air . . . saturating the workers' clothing, getting into their hair, even into sandwiches they munched in production areas.
>
> The Kepone dust sometimes blew . . . in clouds. A gas station operator across the street said it obscured his view of the Life Science Plant. . . . Two firemen in a station behind Life Science say there were times when they wondered if they could see well enough to wheel their engines out in response to a fire alarm.[3]

Two months after LSP started operations, Hopewell's sewage treatment plant broke down because Kepone allegedly killed the bacteria that digested sewage. LSP employees soon developed the "Kepone shakes." Some saw doctors, provided by "informal agreement"[4] with LSP, but were diagnosed as hypertensive. This continued until July 1975, when one worker saw a Taiwanese doctor, who sent blood and urine samples to the Center for Disease Control in Atlanta. The Kepone levels in the samples were so high that the CDC toxicologists wondered whether they had been contaminated in transit. The CDC notified the Virginia State epidemiologist.

Five days later, the epidemiologist examined several workers at LSP. He later said, "The first man I saw was a 23-year-old who was so sick he was unable to stand due to unsteadiness, was suffering severe chest pains . . . had severe tremor, abnormal eye movements, was disoriented."[5] The next day LSP was closed by the Virginia State health authorities.

In early 1976 a federal grand jury in Richmond, Virginia, was called to consider the Kepone events. In May it indicted Allied, LSP, the two owners of LSP, four supervisors at Allied, and the City of Hopewell on a total of 1,104 counts. Most of the counts were misdemeanor charges. Hopewell was indicted for failing to report the massive Kepone discharges and for aiding and abetting

---

[3] Christopher D. Stone, "A Slap on the Wrist for the Kepone Mob," *Business and Society Review,* Summer 1977, p. 4.

[4] Ibid., p. 5.

[5] Ibid., p. 6.

LSP. Allied was also indicted for aiding and abetting LSP, for violating federal water pollution laws by dumping Kepone and non-Kepone wastes into the James River before 1974, and for conspiring to conceal the dumping. These cases would be prosecuted by William B. Cummings, U.S. Attorney for Virginia. Allied faced penalties of more than $17 million if convicted.

By the end of June, there had been several more legal developments. Allied had publicly denied any wrongdoing. The city of Hopewell had pleaded no-contest to the charges against it. Allied's attorneys favored a no-contest plea on the pre-1974 dumping charges, but were confident the company would be found innocent of the other charges. The case would not come to trial until the early fall. Allied also expected suits from the LSP workers, local fishermen and seafood companies, as well as a large class action suit. These suits would claim damages of astronomical proportions—more than $8 billion.

The Kepone toll had been mounting week by week. The LSP workers were now out of the hospital, but more than 60 of them still reported symptoms of Kepone poisoning. (Mice fed high levels of Kepone had developed tumors that were characterized as cancerous.) The James River was closed to fishing because Kepone tends to accumulate in many species caught for seafood. The James had tens of thousands of pounds of Kepone in its bed, and sales of seafood from the Chesapeake Bay, into which the James flows, were hurt badly. A "60 Minutes" TV report on Kepone damaged Allied's image and reinforced a growing public view that chemicals equaled cancer. Finally, publicity about the Kepone incident increased the likelihood that the Toxic Substances Act would become law.

The impact of Kepone on Allied was traumatic. The company's reputation for environmental safety and responsibility seemed shattered. Settling the court cases could have a significant effect on earnings, and uncertainty about this cost would result in a qualified auditors' statement. Morale was low and hiring had become difficult. Problems also developed in Allied's dealings with federal regulatory agencies such as EPA and OSHA. These relations depended on good faith bargaining, and Allied met with increasing skepticism and even suspicion. The result was costly delays in getting permits for new construction (see Exhibit 3, "Clean Water Act"). Officials feared the cost of new oxime[6] production facilities at Hopewell would rise more than $10 million because of these delays.

Allied management felt a strong sense of moral responsibility to the LSP workers, their families, and the Hopewell community. The company was already funding research aimed at finding a way to eliminate Kepone from the bodies of the LSP workers. Allied also planned to establish a multimillion dollar foundation to help with the Kepone clean-up and make grants for other environmental improvements.

---

[6] *Oximes* are organic chemicals used to produce biologically degradable pesticides.

Wagner found it hard to understand how the Kepone affair happened in the first place. Allied had made Kepone without any health or safety problems, and the LSP owners should have been able to do the same. Hopewell officials knew about the discharges when the sewage facility began having trouble, yet they took no action. The Virginia Air Quality Resources Board had an air-monitoring filter within a quarter of a mile of LSP, but it was not checking Kepone emissions. Virginia's Water Quality Control Board knew there was a serious problem in October 1974. The Board did not use its authority to shut down the LSP plant but tried to use persuasion to get changes.

Federal agencies were also involved. In autumn 1974 the Occupational Safety and Health Administration received a letter from a former LSP employee, who claimed he was fired for refusing to work under unsafe conditions. OSHA responded by writing to the LSP owners. They, in turn, wrote back that there was no problem, and OSHA accepted their assurances. The Environmental Protection Agency had sent an inspector to LSP in March 1975. The inspector was uncertain whether EPA had jurisdiction over pesticides. His letter of inquiry to the EPA regional office in Philadelphia was unanswered in July when LSP was closed.

TSCA

In less than a week, Wagner would report to Allied's executive committee on the Toxic Substances Control Act. He had to recommend company support for the Act or opposition or continued neutrality. A neutral stand meant Allied would keep a low profile and issue public statements saying the company supported some features of the Act and opposed others.

TSCA was a new approach to government regulation of harmful chemicals. Past legislation aimed at remedial action. TSCA aimed at prevention. Senator James B. Pearson (R-Kan.) made this distinction:

> Existing legislation simply does not provide the means by which adverse effects on human health and the environment can be ascertained and appropriate action taken before chemical substances are first manufactured and introduced into the marketplace. At present, the only remedy available under such Federal statutes as the Clean Air Act, the Federal Water Pollution Control Act, the Occupational Safety and Health Act, and the Consumer Product Safety Act, is to impose restrictions on toxic substances after they have first been manufactured[7] [See Exhibit 3.]

TSCA was intended to *prevent* unreasonable risks to health and the environment. It gave the Environmental Protection Agency two new powers. EPA could compel companies to provide information on the production composition, uses, and health effects of the chemicals they made or processed.

---

[7] Library of Congress, *Legislative History of the Toxic Substances Control Act,* (Washington: Government Printing Office, 1976), p. 215.

Using this data, EPA could then regulate the manufacture, processing, commercial distribution, use, and disposal of the chemicals.

TSCA had three key provisions. Section 4 (Testing) authorized EPA to require testing of a chemical for any of several reasons. The reasons included clarification of health effects, toxicity, and carcinogenicity. Before requiring testing, EPA had to show that (1) the chemical could pose an unreasonable risk to health or the environment, or that human or environmental exposure to the chemical would be substantial; (2) there was insufficient data for determining the health and environmental effects of the chemical; and (3) the only way to develop this data is by testing the chemical. The manufacturer would pay for the testing.

The most controversial provision of TSCA was Section 5— Pre-market Notification. This required a manufacturer to report to EPA his intent to produce any new chemical, 90 days before doing so. A manufacturer had to make similar notice of plans to produce a chemical for a "significant new use." These reports had to disclose the chemical's name, chemical identity and molecular structure, its proposed categories of use, the amount to be made, its manufacturing by-products, and its disposal. The manufacturer was also required to submit available data on health and environmental effects.

If EPA found there was not enough information to judge the health or environmental effects, it could prohibit or limit the manufacture, distribution, or use of the chemical until adequate information was provided. This was the third key provision of TSCA. It gave EPA broad new powers to regulate the operations of more than 115,000 establishments that made or processed chemicals. TSCA also directed EPA to weigh the costs and benefits of the testing and regulations that it required under these new powers.

To make his decision, Wagner had to sort out a number of complicated issues. He had to ask whether, as a citizen, he thought TSCA was in the public interest. As an Allied executive he had to consider how support for TSCA would affect Allied's image and how the Act itself would affect Allied's chemical business. This last question was especially difficult since TSCA could help business in some ways and hurt it in others. For example, TSCA might cut the chances of another Kepone incident. The costs of testing and reporting might give large chemical companies, like Allied, a competitive edge over smaller firms. But these costs would also hurt Allied's bottom line and make chemical products, particularly new ones, less competitive against natural products.

Wagner had asked his asssistant to summarize the major arguments for and against TSCA. Here is the assistant's report.

For TSCA

1. TSCA closes gaps in current laws. The Act will require testing *before* exposure, so workers and communities will not be used as guinea pigs.
2. TSCA's cost will be low. EPA and the General Services Administration

estimate total costs to industry of \$100—\$200 million a year. Industry sales exceed \$100 billion a year.

3. TSCA will reduce national health care costs by preventing some of the health effects of harmful chemicals. Care for cancer patients alone now costs more than \$18 billion per year.

4. Under current laws, the incidence of cancer has been rising, and many chemical disasters and near-disasters have occurred.

5. The Act offers protection for the interests of chemical companies. When companies disagree with EPA regulations, they can file a timely law suit and seek a court injunction.

6. TSCA may reduce the risks of doing business in chemicals. The Act may, in effect, put a "government seal of approval" on hazardous chemicals. It could also cut the risk of a company being sued because a customer used its products in a dangerous way.

7. Public support for the Act will help restore Allied's image as a responsible community-minded company.

8. The Act is likely to pass this year, so Allied might as well get on the bandwagon. The Senate has already passed the Act, and the current version lacks several features that caused House opposition in past years. Public pressure for passage is building, especially in the wake of the Kepone headlines. The membership of the Manufacturing Chemists Association, the major industry trade group, is split over the Act.

Against TSCA

1. The industry is already sufficiently regulated. Twenty-seven major federal laws now cover almost every aspect of company operations. Large chemical companies like Allied already deal with more than 70 government agencies.

2. Companies already do extensive testing of chemicals before marketing them. The tests sometimes cost several hundred thousand dollars and take several years. They are performed by highly trained scientists working in the most modern labs. Furthermore, companies have a strong incentive to do sufficient testing: They want to avoid the many heavy costs imposed by incidents like Kepone.

3. TSCA will be extremely costly. Dow puts the costs at \$2 billion annually. The Manufacturing Chemists Association estimates \$800 million to \$1.3 billion. There will be less innovation because of excessive testing burdens on new chemicals. U.S. chemical exports will become more costly and less competitive, U.S. jobs will move overseas, and the testing and reporting requirements will hurt or even close many small companies. This will also affect large companies like Allied. We rely on many small companies as suppliers, and Allied itself is basically a composite of 60 or 70 small specialty chemical companies.

4. The Act is dangerously vague. EPA gets very broad powers with few restrictions.

5. Reporting to EPA under TSCA will require us to disclose trade secrets and other confidential data.

6. Supporting the Act to aid our image or get on a bandwagon won't fool many people. It will be taken as a public relations move and could raise even more suspicions about Allied's motives.

7. It's not even clear there's a bandwagon. The Senate passed the Act in 1972 and 1973, and the House killed it both times. Even though EPA is lobbying hard for TSCA, the Commerce Department and the Office of Management and Budget oppose it. There is as yet no indication whether President Ford will sign or veto the Act.

8. Many of the reports of chemical "disasters" have been exaggerated by the media and by environmental groups. We should not give in to pressures based on this sort of misinformation.

TOTAL PRODUCT RESPONSIBILITY

Wagner also had to decide whether to implement a new program called *Total Product Responsibility*. TPR had been developed in 1975 by the Engineering and Operations Services unit in the Specialty Chemicals Division. This 17-person staff unit developed policies and procedures related to health, safety, maintenance, and quality control (see Exhibit 4). TPR would use "tools of policy, procedure, control, and review" to help Allied "property discharge its legal and moral responsibility to protect its employees, customers, the public, and the environment from harm."

TPR was first proposed in 1975 by R. L. Merrill, vice president of Engineering and Operations Services. Merrill had come to Allied after several years with Dow Chemical and was impressed by Dow's Product Stewardship Program. According to *Business Week,* Product Stewardship meant Dow would assume "total responsibiity for how its products affect people" and Dow's products would carry "a virtual guarantee of harmlessness."[8] Dow had 600 people involved in setting up Product Stewardship in 1972. They prepared environmental and safety profiles for all 1,100 of Dow's products. Then film cassettes were made for presentations to Dow employees, customers, and distributors. In its first year Product Stewardship cost $1 million.

Merrill's original proposal was not for a program as extensive as Dow's. Merrill had suggested a survey of information currently available to Allied on the health and environmental effects of its products. This survey would be followed by whatever tests were needed to supplement existing information. But during 1975 and early 1976 an expanded TPR slowly took shape around

---

8 "Dow's Big Push for Product Safety," *Business Week,* April 21, 1973, p. 82.

EXHIBIT 4   Specialty Chemicals Division

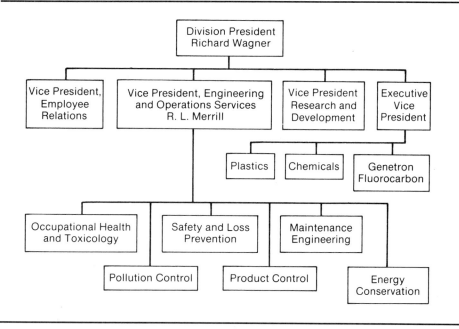

this original suggestion. If it was important to get complete health and safety information about Allied's products, it also seemed important to get similar information on raw materials, processes, and customer uses of Allied products. And, in turn, it seemed important to make sure all this information was reflected in Allied's everyday operating procedures.

The first step in implementing TPR would be for Wagner to issue a 25-page memorandum on TPR to all management personnel in his division. The memo would set out standards of operating and business practice that covered virtually every aspect of division operations. Line management would then have to make sure that operating procedures conformed to these standards.

The following are excerpts from the TPR memorandum:

Specifications: Specifications should exist for every raw material . . . and every finished product. . . . No specifications may be changed without the approval of the Director of Operations/General Manager after review with Operations Services.

Testing: All of the division's products will be reviewed on a priority basis, as determined by our toxicology specialists, to determine the known or suspected undesirable toxic effects which those products may have on our employees, customers, the public, and the environment.

Plant SOP's: Standard operating procedures will be developed by plants for each product area. Procedures will be designed by engineering, technical, and operations groups to provide capability of producing uniform product quality and to insure process continuity. Use of approved procedures will be mandatory, and revisions to accepted methods will require approval of preestablished authority levels.

Equipment Testing: Testing procedures and frequencies are to be developed to insure reliability of equipment at the 95 percent confidence level to minimize the possibility of unforeseen problems arising.

Change Procedure: Changes in R&D, product development, manufacturing, distribution, and marketing that may adversely affect the process, employees, product, customer, the public, or the environment should not be made without the approval of the Director of Operations, Director of Marketing or Research Laboratory Director, as appropriate, and after review with Operations Services.

Technical Bulletins: Technical literature and bulletins should include all safety and environmental statements necessary to protect employees, customers, the public, and the environment. Operations Services is to receive, edit, and approve all literature and bulletins to assure that all such proper statements are included.

Advertising: Advertising copy should reflect true and accurate statements about our products. Advertising copy should be reviewed by Operations Services to prevent misleading statements concerning claims in the areas of environmental products safety, health, and quality assurance.

Product End Use: Marketing departments should make every effort to determine the end use application of each product sold. Consideration should be given to the desirability of using the product in that application and the customer's understanding of the effect of such use on the operation. . . . A product should not be sold to a customer where it is known that the end use application is not proper.

Capability of Existing Customers: Marketing departments have the responsibility to establish the capability of our customers concerning their competency to handle our products in a manner that protects the customers' process, employees, the public, and the environment. Hazardous products should not be sold to customers whose capability is deemed inadequate. If it is determined that an application or end use of the product is improper . . . the sales of this product to that customer should be discontinued immediately.

New Customers: Hazardous products should not be sold to new customers until the capability of that customer is deemed adequate.

Outside Contractors: When outside contractors are to be used to process, reprocess, repackage, or manufacture materials for us, the review should include a determination of the toxicity and hazards of the materials to be handled, and an in-depth study of the contractor's capability to perform the work such as not to endanger the contractor's employees, the public, or the environment. . . . When a contractor is retained, it is the responsibility of the appropriate business area to arrange for periodic inspections and reviews of that contractor's operations by Operations Services Department.

Wagner had distributed the draft memo within SCD and discussed the program with a variety of line and staff personnel. Reaction was mixed.

Leonard Warren, director of marketing services, said:

I don't know where I come down on this. I know that chemical companies are getting burned in the newspapers and in court, and the result is more and more government people telling us how to do business. We've got to stop this, but we've also got to make money. As I read TPR, it says we're going to say no to some people who want to buy from us. We'll also be harassing our current customers and prospects by asking them how they use our products, who they sell to, and what their customers do with their products. Some of them are going to tell us to keep our noses out of their businesses. A lot of our products are virtually commodities, and they're already hard enough to sell without the burdens of TPR paperwork, TPR costs, and the mixed signals we'll be giving to our reps.

Now I'm not completely opposed to TPR in some form. After Kepone, it will make Allied's reputation a little better. There are probably some customers that we shouldn't sell to, because they're too risky, and this program will help us get rid of them. In some cases, it might even help sales because it would be a reason for our reps to have even further contacts with customers, and more information about uses of our products could be a useful kind of market research for us.

Another hesitant view came from Joe DeStefano, a production manager at the Hopewell complex:

My first reaction is that we already do a lot of the things in the TPR memo. The difference is that our current procedures are not formalized and we don't have to get as much clearance before making changes. I can't help wondering whether TPR isn't going to make business a lot more bureaucratic. It seems to me that the government already does enough of that already. Under TPR, we would have to go through Operations Services to do almost anything. We could end up with more paperwork, buck-passing, and bureaucracy. Sometimes I'm not sure what's more important: getting a good product out the door at a profit or complying with a thousand rules and restrictions.

Janet Baker, an associate corporate counsel who handled environmental cases, supported TPR.

Allied has to do something like TPR. Kepone costs are skyrocketing, and we can't afford to let another Kepone happen. TPR sends a clear message throughout the division that health and safety are top priority. We've sent the message before, but it needs vigorous emphasis. If we don't takes steps to run our business as safely as possible, the government will do it for us.

TPR does have some problems in its present form. I don't like the word *total* in the title. I don't see how a single chemical company can be totally responsible for all the ways in which its products could be used or misused. It could be very hard to persuade a jury that *total* really doesn't and couldn't mean *total*. There is some point at which the responsibility of one company ends and the responsibility of the government or other companies starts.

There are also other problems. Customers and suppliers could well resent our sanctimonious attitude when we poke our noses into their businesses. Refusals to deal have to be handled unilaterally and without publicity or else we may be liable for conspiracy allegations, antitrust, trade disparagement, or libel suits.

Despite these objections and misgivings, Merrill remained enthusiastic about TPR. Merrill argued:

Of course, TPR won't be free of problems, but it does much more good than harm. It will help our image and cut our risk of environmental and safety problems.

Besides, the government is likely to require most of what's in TPR in just a few years. By starting now, Allied can learn to do business under these inevitable new conditions.

It's also absolutely essential that the attitude of Allied managers and workers towards the government start to change. The government is going to be a major factor in the chemical industry for the indefinite future. We can either take an adversary approach and comply with regulations in a minimal, grudging way or we can recognize that the government is here to stay, learn to cooperate with federal agencies and, as a result, get better results in regulatory proceedings and lower our risks of future Kepones.

In making his decision, Wagner also had to consider the views of Allied's chairman and the executive committee. There was strong support among these executives for "some concrete steps" that would prevent another Kepone and change company attitudes towards government health and environmental rules. At the same time, Wagner could not ignore his division's earnings and performance. In the summer of 1976 sales were weakening as a result of the recession that began in 1975. Wagner wondered if this was the right time to divert managerial time and attention from the chemical business. He was also concerned about the possible impact of TPR on the flexibility, decentralized decision making, and innovation he had been trying to encourage in his division. He also wondered whether TPR would have kept the Kepone problem from happening in the first place.

RECENT EVENTS

Wagner knew that his two decisions should not be made without reference to recent regulatory actions and political trends. Wagner had kept a file of newspaper and magazine articles on government decisions, lawsuits, and political developments that seemed important to Allied and the chemical industry. These were some of the articles in his file:

VINYL CHLORIDE TIED TO HIGHER INCIDENCE OF MISCARRIAGES

Vinyl chloride, the industrial chemical that has been linked to cancer among workers who are exposed to it, apparently also causes a higher incidence than normal of miscarriages among the workers' wives, government researchers reported. They suggested the reason is that vinyl chloride may damage the sperm cells of the worker-husbands. . . .

The study wasn't released in this country until Ralph Nader's Health Research Group demanded a copy from the U.S. government under the Freedom of Information Act. The Health Research Group then distributed the report as the EPA opened hearings on proposals to limit vinyl chloride emissions from PVC plants. [*The Wall Street Journal,* February 5, 1976, p. 19.]

TRACES OF KEPONE FOUND IN BREAST MILK IN SOUTHERN STATES

The EPA said it has found small amounts of the controversial chemical Kepone in breast milk of women in Southern states. . . . EPA officials said the Kepone traces in women's milk may be linked to the Agriculture Department's program of using another controversial chemical, Mirex, as bait to kill fire ants . . . preliminary results of research indicated that "very small amounts" of Kepone are slowly formed from Mirex "under conditions of direct sunlight and moisture." . . . About 100 million acres in nine Southern states were treated with Mirex in the Agriculture Department's fire ant eradication program since 1962. . . . The EPA said the samples showed Kepone ranging from less than one part per billion to 5.8 parts per billion. [*The Wall Street Journal,* February 27, 1976, p. 16.]

HEALTH-HAZARD WATCH ON CHEMICAL INDUSTRY BOOSTED BY LABOR UNIT

The chemical industry can expect more attention from federal health inspectors, a top government official said.

Recent "shocking episodes" of serious illness among workes handling arsenic, kepone, lead, and vinyl chloride illustrate the need for increased attention to health, declared Dr. Morton Corn, Assistant Secretary of Labor for occupational safety and health.

Addressing the Manufacturing Chemists Association, Dr. Corn said the health-safety agency is improving its ability to detect "the more subtle, invisible hazards of the workplace." He said that for the next two years, "all our new hiring will be health compliance officers." The agency currently employs 1,000 inspectors, including 135 health inspectors and 113 apprentices being trained as inspectors. [*The Wall Street Journal,* March 2, 1976, p. 3.]

AFL–CIO AIDE CHARGES DELAY IN REPORTS ON EXPOSURE TO CANCER-CAUSING AGENTS

Reports on the cancer-causing properties of 150 industrial chemicals to which workers are being exposed are being held up by an information bottleneck in Washington, an AFL–CIO health and safety official charged. . . . The charge was made by Sheldon W. Samuels, director of health, safety, and environment for the AFL–CIO's industrial union department in Washington. . . .

Dr. Frank Rauscher, Director of the National Cancer Institute, said Mr. Samuels was correct but "there's nothing secret about the reports." He said the reports on the 150 compounds are being analyzed by pathologists, and the institute is extremely shorthanded of pathologists. . . .

"We don't have the most effective information system in the world," Dr. Rauscher said. He noted that many federal agencies are involved in collecting information on the toxicity and carcinogenicity of chemicals but there is little exchange of information among agencies. [*The Wall Street Journal,* March 30, 1976, p. 6.]

COURT CLEARS REQUIRING EPA TO REGULATE DISCHARGE
OF CHEMICALS IN WATERWAYS

A federal judge approved a settlement between the EPA and environmental groups to strengthen water-pollution control rules.

The agreement requires the EPA to regulate the discharge of 65 toxic chemicals, many of them cancer causing, by 21 major industries into the nation's waterways.

The approval of the settlement by U.S. District Court Judge Thomas A. Flannery ends four lawsuits brought against the EPA in 1973 and 1974 by various environmental groups, including the Natural Resources Defense Council and the Environmental Defense Fund. The suits contended that the EPA wasn't regulating the discharge into water of toxic chemicals as required by the Federal Water Pollution Control Act of 1972. [*The Wall Street Journal,* June 11, 1976, p. 8.]

Since 1976 was an election year, Wagner had been paying some attention to the positions candidates took on regulation in general and the chemical industry in particular. Senator Vance Hartke (D., Indiana), who faced a serious reelection challenge, was campaigning hard for greater regulation of chemicals. One of his recent speeches included the following remarks:

The hazards associated with chemicals like PCB's, vinyl chloride, BCME, and asbestos have all dramatically illustrated how important it is to get early warning with respect to new chemical substances. . . .

During this (last) five-year period there have been in excess of one million deaths in this country from cancer. Over a million infants have been born with physical or mental damage. . . . While many of the grave health risks to human beings have declined in recent years, cancer statistics have done just the opposite. In fact, the incidence of cancer was estimated in 1975 to be some 2.5 percent above the previous year.

It is no accident that the hot spots for cancer in this country are in close proximity to those locations where the chemical industry is most highly concentrated.

It is tragic that those who rely upon the industry for jobs have essentially become guinea pigs for discovering the adverse effects of chemical substances. It is also tragic that much of the information which has shown the cancer producing potential of many chemicals has come from death records of employees. For example, of one million current and former American asbestos workers who still survive, fully 300,000 have been projected to die of cancer. This death rate is 50 percent higher than that of the U.S. population at large.[9]

At the same time, Wagner was also aware of growing opposition to government regulation. The leading presidential contenders, Ford, Carter, and Reagan, were all sounding the theme of "too much government interference."

---

[9] Library of Congress, *Legislative History of the Toxic Substances Act* (Washington: Government Printing Office, 1976), p. 216.

Recent academic studies had documented the large indirect costs of regulation and even reformers like Ralph Nader were very critical of agencies like the FTC, which Nader said was basically a captive of the industries it regulated. Industry was joining this movement against regulation. Dow Chemical, for example, recently announced completion of its own "catalogue of regulatory horrors" and claimed it had spent $50 million in 1975 to meet regulations it considered excessive.[10]

---

[10] "Dow Chemical's Catalogue of Regulatory Horrors," *Business Week,* April 4, 1977, p. 50.

Commentaries

29. Utilities Face a Crisis over Nuclear Plants; Costs, Delays Mount

Geraldine Brooks
Ron Winslow
Bill Richards

The electric-utility industry, jolted by the 1979 accident at Three Mile Island and wounded by Washington Public Power Supply System's 1983 default, is poised on the edge of a new nuclear crisis.

Huge nuclear-power plants, long overdue and far over budget, threaten to overwhelm the utilities that are building them. Several companies face an excruciating choice: either abandon the problem plants, some of which already have cost billions of dollars, or continue to pour money into them with no assurance that they ever will operate.

Either way, grave consequences loom for the companies, their investors, and consumers. State regulators must decide whether to bail the companies out by slugging consumers with big rate increases or to refuse bailouts and perhaps push some companies into bankruptcy proceedings.

"Nobody ever thought a municipality could go bankrupt until it happened to Cleveland," says Paul R. Bjorn, a utility expert with Price Waterhouse & Co., the accounting firm. Now, he says, the once equally inconceivable prospect of a utility company's going into bankruptcy proceedings is "an increasing possibility."

HIGHER STAKES

Abandoning nuclear plants is nothing new. Although they were once viewed as the cheapest way to meet constantly growing demand for electric power, their value has grown more questionable as recession and conservation have slashed demand growth, construction costs have mounted, and prices of alternative fuels have stopped soaring. Utilities have scrapped 100 of them in

---

recent years, but most were in the planning or early construction stage. Now, however, the stakes are suddenly much higher.

In all, more than a dozen well-advanced plants are candidates for abandonment. Regulators blame mismanagement; utility officials blame excessive regulation. Whichever side is right, if regulators refuse to pass the costs of abandoned plants on to consumers, some companies would have to take write-offs that could almost wipe out their net worth.

That's where the bankruptcy threat enters. Write-offs could spawn dividend cuts, a move that would stun the utility industry's conservative investors. If the investors are turned off, some utilities could have trouble raising enough money to keep the lights on.

So far, analysts say, high yields still attract enough investors to finance the plants. But many investors have sold their holdings in troubled companies, and others are getting anxious. "Do you want me to comment with or without four-letter words?" asks an analyst at a major university that has a total of $400 million invested in two Midwest utilities with nuclear-plant problems— Cincinnati Gas & Electric Co. and Public Service Co. of Indiana.

DOMINO EFFECT FEARED

Some troubled utilities themselves are worried about other troubled utilities. At least two of them—Long Island Lighting Co. in New York State and Public Service Co. of New Hampshire—have socked away six-month contingency reserves of cash and credit, figuring that if one company goes under, the financial support that holds up the others will collapse, too.

The financial health of some utilities may be even worse than it seems, because of the way utilities count their money. Part of what they count as income is actually IOUs from ratepayers to the company for the interest and certain other expenses that the company has incurred during construction of power plants. When a plant is finished, the utility is allowed to include that accrued interest cost in its rate base.

The mechanism, called *allowance for funds used during construction,* worked fine when utilities were building modestly priced coal plants. But now many companies caught with the exploding costs of nuclear-plant construction have allowance IOUs that amount to more than half of net earnings. If the plants aren't completed, those huge IOUs might never be honored. "Nuclear plants are being built on giant Master Cards," says Irving Bupp, a specialist in utility financing at the Harvard business school.

CONSUMERS HAVE PAID

Until now, consumers have usually paid the bill when it came due. But state regulators are being urged to spare consumers the cost of plants half-finished and then abandoned. Saving the consumers now, however, might only sacrifice them in the long run if regulators allow utilities to go into bankruptcy proceedings, some experts say. Robert D. Stewart, an attorney for Oklahoma Gas & Electric Co., has developed a "worst scenario" in which a utility forced into bankruptcy proceedings by unpaid bondholders couldn't sell any more stock or bonds. It would quickly use up all its cash and soon wouldn't be able to maintain or repair its plants. Brownouts and blackouts would become common. Local industry would pack up and move, taking jobs and taxes with it.

A look at four of the most troubled plants and the utilities building them shows just how close some companies may be to testing Mr. Stewart's grim scenario.

Zimmer

For Cincinnati Gas & Electric, the next few months will be like a slow walk, blindfolded along a precipice. To keep its financial health, the company has to negotiate a slew of obstacles, including the ire of its partners—Dayton Power & Light Co. and American Electric Power's Columbus & Southern Ohio Electric Co. unit—which don't want to pay their share of the Zimmer plant's ballooning cost.

Almost everything that could go wrong at Zimmer has. The plant supposedly was 97 percent complete a year ago when the Nuclear Regulatory Commission ordered construction halted after plant workers alleged faulty welds and faked documents. But in late September, Cincinnati Gas's consultants said that Zimmer, which has already cost $1.6 billion, could cost as much as $1.9 billion more because much of it had to be reinspected and rebuilt.

Stunned officials at the utility are studying alternatives, including scrapping the plant. Their studies are expected to be finished this month, and the company's partners are pressing it for a quick decision before interest costs rise much higher.

Meanwhile, investigators from the Nuclear Regulatory Commission, the Justice Department, and the Public Utilities Commission of Ohio are examining the project for evidence of everything from mismanagement to crime. Their reports are also imminent and are certain to affect the way Ohio regulators decide to distribute the plant's costs.

If Zimmer is scrapped, the company will probably have to write off the $680 million it has already spent, because Ohio law says canceled plants can't be charged to ratepayers. But the write-off would wipe out about 80 percent of shareholder equity—enough, under the company's own regulations, to eliminate its ability to pay dividends.

If Cincinnati Gas decides to complete the plant or convert it to a gas- or coal-burning unit, its investment bankers are confident it could raise the money, assuming satisfactory treatment by regulators. But until the state regulators conclude their inquiry, that remains a big assumption.

Cincinnati Gas is delaying the sale of $15 million of pollution-control bonds, afraid of what the market might tell it. "We don't want to ask for a rating right now," says Jackson H. Randolph, the vice president of finance, but he says the company isn't having any trouble selling commercial paper or getting bank loans for its short-term needs.

A look at Cincinnati Gas's third-quarter earnings show just how inscrutable utility accounting can be. The company reported a 59 percent earnings increase, to $47.6 million from $30 million. But 40 percent of that income is Zimmer IOUs. In the 1960s, when Cincinnati Gas was building several coal plants, "allowance for funds" IOUs averaged only about 5 percent of earnings. Now they average about 50 percent. The deeper in debt the company gets for Zimmer, the better its earnings appear. The catch is that one day all the IOUs may be torn up by the state regulators.

Seabrook

Public Service Co. of New Hampshire's two Seabrook plants have blighted the company's balance sheet. In 1982, the company had to borrow money to pay not only all its common-stock dividends but about one third of its preferred dividends as well.

The utility and its 15 partners on the project recently decided to concentrate on finishing Seabrook I, which is about 85 percent complete, and to sharply curtail work at Seabrook II, which is 26 percent complete. Public Service Co., which owns 35 percent of the project and has spent $1.2 billion so far, has resisted pressure from some partners to scrap Seabrook II. The utility contends that New Hampshire needs the power from both units.

But there may be another reason for sticking with Seabrook II: It may be a lifeline for Seabrook I. If Seabrook II was abandoned, state regulators might require the company to write off the $270 million it has already invested in the unit. That would wipe out the company's retained earnings, forcing it under state law to cancel its dividends. That, in turn, would probably make it impossible to borrow the funds to complete Seabrook I.

Charles E. Bayless, the company's chief financial officer, asserts that investor confidence in Public Service Co. is still strong. But last month it took the utility's underwriters a week to sell $100 million of debentures with a 15.5 percent yield. Similar issues from financially stronger companies would sell in a matter of hours. The high-risk investor "is our niche in the market," Mr. Bayless acknowledges.

Public Service Co.'s troubles won't necessarily end when and if the plants are operating. At an estimated total cost of $5.8 billion, the company's $1.9 billion share equals 75 percent of its assets. "If something happens to that asset," says Evan Silverstein, a utilities analyst at L. F. Rothschild, Unterberg, Towbin, "the fate of the whole company is in question."

If the two units come on line for $5.8 billion, they will have cost $2,500 per kilowatt. Public Service Co.'s other plants cost an average of less than $200 a kilowatt.

Shoreham

Construction of Long Island Lighting Co.'s Shoreham plant is all but finished. But even if everything goes right, the plant won't be operating until early 1985.

For now, everything seems to be going wrong. Last week, draft findings of Gov. Mario Cuomo's Shoreham commission reinforced doubts that the plant will be economical or that Lilco will ever come up with a satisfactory emergency evacuation plan. The panel also charged that Lilco lacks the experience to operate the plant.

Such findings, disputed by the company and some panel members, increase the chances that the state will seek to prevent the plant from operating or will try to take over the company. In the meantime, Lilco is trying to repair emergency diesel generators, which cracked in tests last summer.

If repairs are unsuccessful, the generators, which provide power to shut down the reactor in an emergency, will have to be replaced, delaying start-up to 1986.

Authority to license Shoreham belongs to the Nuclear Regulatory Commission. The NRC has never denied an application to operate a plant, and in this case it has already indicated it will give Lilco permission to put uranium in the reactor and conduct preoperational tests once the diesel generators are fixed. That would be a major step toward an operating license.

With a capacity of 809,000 kilowatts and a cost estimate of $3.4 billion, Shoreham is already the country's most expensive nuclear plant—a little over $4,000 per kilowatt. In addition, Lilco acknowledges that the actual cost is likely to come close to $4 billion.

A stalled Shoreham is proving an immense drain on Lilco. The company's cash flow is negative—it is borrowing to pay dividends on its common stock and it expects to seek $700 million in external financing in 1984. Thomas P. O'Brien, Lilco's senior vice president for finance, says investment bankers have assured him the company won't have trouble raising that money. (He acknowledges, however, that such assurance may now depend on how Governor Cuomo responds to the Shoreham commissioner's findings.)

But to raise money in 1985, the company will have to obtain a rate increase in the 11 percent to 13 percent range to maintain its required ratio of earnings to bond interest payouts. Frank Herbert, the head of the accounting and finance office of the New York Public Service Commission, says regulators are under pressure to let Lilco earn enough money to stay afloat. "We clearly don't want to be the state that presides over the first major utility going under," he says. "It isn't a decision you make casually, to let a company go."

Marble Hill

When the relatively small Public Service Co. of Indiana took an 83 percent share of a nuclear-power project twice the size of Shoreham or Zimmer, it bit off more than it could comfortably chew. Now it may be choking.

In late October the company disclosed what some critics had long suspected: The two Marble Hill plants would cost $7 billion to complete, more than four times the original 1978 estimate of $1.6 billion. The company said it might have to abandon the project.

Public Service Co. already has capacity 47 percent beyond its peak-load requirement, more than double the industry's 20 percent reserve standard. With only 540,000 customers, it can't complete the Marble Hill project without hitting customers with rate increases right away.

But Indiana law won't let consumers be charged for plants under construction, so Public Service Co. is asking for exceptional treatment that might require legislation. In July it proposed rate increases of 8 percent a year until the project starts operating in 1988. Indiana's governor, Robert D. Orr, is up for reelection next year and says he opposes charging consumers for incomplete plants. However, he appointed a five-member task force to look at the project's future. Its report is expected by year-end.

"That he put businessmen on the committee reassures us," says a banker who oversees large trust holdings in Public Service Co. "We're cautiously optimistic that some solution will be worked out."

Other shareholders clearly are pessimistic. When Public Service Co. said the increased costs meant it might have to abandon the project, which had already cost $2.5 billion, its stock plunged more than 30 percent. That sent Hugh A. Barker, the chairman and chief executive officer, hurrying to New York to assure jittery securities analysts that it would continue its regular dividend. But the dividend, too, rests heavily on what Governor Orr's task force decides.

30. Corporate Donors Embrace Free-Market Environmentalism

Jo Ann Kwong

Henry Ford II's resignation from the Ford Foundation in 1977 focused attention on a growing contradiction that has taken root in America. The fortune that was earned in the profit-making sector by Henry Ford I, he noted, was increasingly used by the foundation to fund a wide array of anticorporate activities.

Reprinted by permission of *The Wall Street Journal,* Dow Jones & Company, Inc., June 23, 1988, p. 28. All rights reserved.

Ms. Kwong is a fellow in private sector, nonprofit management at the Institute for Humane Studies at George Mason University, Fairfax, Virginia.

The activities that prompted Mr. Ford's resignation have changed little in the decade since: Private-sector, profit-making corporations and their foundations widely fund antibusiness activity. Perhaps nowhere is this more evident than in the field of environmental giving. Environmental groups, which consistently and vehemently attack corporate activities, are quick to accept corporate handouts.

A major strategy for corporate giving is to support noncontroversial organizations that serve the public at large. Consequently, such groups as the Sierra Club and the Wilderness Society enjoy diverse corporate support. Because they work for a sound, healthy environment, funding them is considered a good public-relations investment. But for the most part, these groups represent proregulatory interests that look to governmental bureaucracy for regulation and management of the nation's natural resources.

Many industries and companies, torn between "social responsibility" and broader business interests, find themselves in the compromising position of giving money to groups that attack business and the market. The Atlantic Richfield Foundation, for example, has contributed to the Sierra Club and the Wilderness Society, despite those groups' clear stands against oil and gas development in areas such as the Arctic National Wildlife Refuge. Regardless of the environmentalists' well-intentioned goals, they are certainly mismatched with oil company goals.

In "Patterns of Corporate Philanthropy," Marvin Olasky cites numerous examples of corporations that fund groups that oppose them on various issues. For example, in 1985 Chevron gave to the World Wildlife Fund; Du Pont to the National Wildlife Federation; Exxon to the World Resources Institute, National Wildlife Federation, Environmental Law Institute, Resources for the Future, and Environmental Action Coalition; General Electric to Environmental Law Institute, Resources for the Future, and Conservation Foundation; Mobil to National Wildlife Federation, World Wildlife Fund, Conservation Foundation, and National Audubon Society; Monsanto to the Sierra Club and the World Wildlife Fund; and Standard Oil to Environmental Law Institute, Resources for the Future, World Resources Institute, Wildlife Conservation Fund, and National Wildlife Federation.

But the proregulatory groups are facing a growing number of competitors for corporate contributions. "Free-market environmentalists," who seek to promote environmental quality by fostering individual responsibility and private-property rights, present an alternative outlet for business giving—one that also offers benefits to the public through effective environmental management.

Free-market environmentalism is catching the eye of nature lovers as well as foundation and corporate donors. At Amoco, the company's Environmental Affairs and Safety Department suggested the corporate foundation consider the economic views of potential grant recipients for environmental funding.

For instance, to what extent does the recipient devise market solutions to environmental problems (in contrast to extra-market activities such as lobbying and adjudication)?

The Nature Conservancy, a national, nonprofit corporation dedicated to preserving rare and endangered species, is a good example of a group that works through the marketplace. It buys and sells critical plant and animal habitats in order to preserve them, rather than forcing taxpayers to bear the cost of preservation through governmental regulation and restriction. In addition to acquiring land through purchase and gifts, the Nature Conservancy also preserves natural systems through conservation easements, management agreements, and leases. With actual property rights to these resources, it directly manages the lands to achieve its goals. (It has, however, increasingly adopted strategies involving transferring lands to government ownership, thus relinquishing its control over resources.)

Cascade Holistic Economic Consultants (CHEC) in Eugene, Oregon, combines free-market economics with hardy grass-roots activism to draw attention to both problems and solutions to national-forest management. CHEC analysts argue that such management is plagued by poorly designed laws that encourage national-forest bureaucrats to increase their own budgets by selling timber below cost. Their solution? Reform policy with an eye toward markets because "markets give managers an incentive to manage the forests to produce the maximum benefits." CHEC president Randall O'Toole outlines an agenda to "marketize" the Forest Service in his new book *Reforming the Forest Service*.

Operation Stronghold also demonstrates a successful property-rights approach to environmental enhancement. With a mission to preserve and protect the nation's wildlife, Stronghold is an organization that offers expert advice and assistance about habitat preservation to private landholders. Director Dayton Hyde has much to offer to the group's 600 members: He has boosted the number of bird species on his Oregon ranch to 83 from 6 by restoring national wetlands and native prairie grasses, protecting rare wildflowers, and otherwise creating habitat diversity. In an almost preposterous irony, his bird haven, which includes endangered species such as nesting bald eagles, is being monitored by state regulatory agencies that are concerned he might adopt unsound land practices and negatively affect the birds.

By offering a better match to the foundation world, a growing number of environmental groups are finding a niche for themselves in free-market environmentalism. If corporate and foundation giving can help these groups prosper as much as the more traditional, statist groups have, there will be a chance to inject an element of property rights and markets into environmental management after all. That would not only help the environment and boost the business climate, but it would also give corporate foundation officers a grant record they can boast about to their trustees and stockholders.

31. Industry is Going on a Waste-Watcher's Diet

Eric Jay Dolin

Companies burn it, bury it, even feed it to microbes. But no matter what they do, getting rid of hazardous waste is a costly proposition that's getting more expensive all the time. So instead of focusing on fancy treatment or disposal techniques, some companies are taking a more basic approach: figuring out how not to make dangerous waste in the first place.

The benefits can be enormous. The congressional Office of Technology Assessment (OTA) estimates that, even with existing technology, U.S. industry could halve its yearly output of 300 million tons of hazardous waste. And the companies that are cutting their waste off at the source are profiting handsomely from their efforts.

"ELEGANT SOLUTION"

They have few attractive alternatives. Many companies are paying huge bills to clean up abandoned dumps where years ago they disposed of waste improperly. At the same time, safe landfill space is shrinking, and the costs of disposal are skyrocketing. Waste reduction, says Robert M. Cardillo, environmental affairs coordinator for Exxon Chemical Americas, "is the most elegant solution."

Merely condensing hazardous waste, or diluting it to reduce the danger, does not count as waste reduction. The idea is to find ways not to generate it at all. Techniques can be as simple as plugging up a leaky pipe or as complicated as designing a chemical reaction that uses up raw ingredients and leaves no waste. "Waste reduction is built up out of a lot of little things," says Environmental Defense Fund senior attorney David Roe. "It's not a cookie-cutter approach."

At 3M Co.'s Columbia (Mo.) electronics plant, workers used to clean copper sheeting by spraying it with a toxic chemical mixture. To make the process less hazardous, a group of employees designed a machine that uses an abrasive to scrub the copper clean, leaving behind a nonhazardous sludge. The new equipment, which cost only $59,000, eliminates 40,000 pounds of liquid hazardous waste annually.

Worldwide, says 3M, its waste-reduction program—called *Pollution Prevention Pays*—has saved it $400 million. A similar effort at Dow Chemical Co.,

---

which goes under the moniker of WRAP (for Waste Reduction Always Pays), is producing benefits that go beyond cost savings. Employees found that recycling solvents, and introducing better instrumentation to lower the amount of raw material not consumed in the process, cut air emissions and boosted yields at the company's Midland (Mich.) Div. That contributed to reduced air pollution from the division for each of the past three years. Dow was quick to let local newspapers in on the results. Each year the company got fewer irate calls from neighbors. After this year's news report, there were none.

So far, though, companies such as 3M and Dow are few. "What you find is an exceptional company here and there doing waste reduction," says OTA senior associate Joel S. Hirschhorn. In a study documenting industry's waste-reduction efforts, Inform, a New York environmental research group, found that 29 chemicals companies were realizing only a fraction of the potential for reduction. The poor showing "reminds me of energy conservation," says Terry Foecke, waste-reduction specialist at the Minnesota Technical Assistance Program. "Everybody says it's a good idea, but how many changed their light bulbs?"

There are many reasons for industry's tepid embrace of waste-reduction practices. Virtually all environmental laws focus on the end of the pipe—on controlling rather than preventing pollution. And companies are reluctant to fiddle with proven production processes, especially given the paucity of good data on what works. "It comes down to inertia, ignorance, and habit," says EDF's Roe.

The incentives to nip waste in the bud are becoming stronger, however. Although estimates vary, it's safe to say that the nation's yearly bill for dealing with hazardous waste tops $3 billion—and it's rising. Exxon, for one, says its disposal costs quadrupled during the past five years. And a botched disposal job can lead to huge liabilities under the Superfund environmental cleanup law.

In addition, there are simply fewer places to get rid of hazardous waste. For years the path of least resistance led to the landfill. But the environmental nightmare of toxic substances leaching into soil and water led Congress, in 1984, to ban land disposal of untreated hazardous waste. Those rules, the first of which took effect in 1986, left industry with few options: Incinerate it, treat waste to render it less dangerous, or simply stop making it.

ZEROING IN

Over the past few years, 35 states have set up programs that provide technical and, sometimes, financial assistance to industry for waste-reduction projects. But most are small: They have an average budget of $150,000 and employ just two people.

The federal government also has turned its attention to waste reduction. In 1986, Congress passed an amendment to the Superfund law that requires companies using some 300 toxic chemicals to report to the Environmental Protection Agency how much they release into the environment. Those rules, which took effect on July 1, already are having an impact. Sensitive to public pressure, Monsanto Co. accompanies its first disclosure with a pledge to chop its hazardous air emissions 90 percent by 1992 and to work from there to zero.

By late summer, the EPA will direct its officials to make waste reduction a priority. The agency also plans to award a total of $6 million to some of the state programs and is setting up a computerized clearinghouse, scheduled to come on line by autumn, that will provide states and businesses with technical information on the kinds of waste-reduction methods that work best.

There are bills before Congress encouraging waste reduction but, with elections looming, observers give them scant chance of passing during this session. In any case, many industry watchers are not sure more laws are necessary. As dealing with hazardous waste becomes more expensive, more and more companies are concluding that waste reduction is the only way to go.

---

32. SEE NO EVIL: Can $100 Billion Have "No Material Effect" on Balance Sheets?

Amal Kumar Naj, staff reporter

If Stephen King's well of weird ideas ever runs dry, he might want to dig into the weedy backyards and vacant lots of America's manufacturing industries. Bulldozing such a site in Parkersburg, West Virginia, years ago, construction workers heard the ground begin to crackle and pop. Earthmoving machinery, seemingly spontaneously, burst into flame.

It was radioactive waste that did it. Buried there—and in thousands of other industrial graveyards—is the deadly detritus of America's past manufacturing might: ordinary metals, isotopes, acids, organic compounds and solvents that can destroy men as well as machines. Among the wastes are substances that can cause leukemia, other cancers, and diseases of the heart, liver, and nervous systems.

This is real estate you won't see pictured in the annual report. Nor are you likely to find on the balance sheet the liability it now represented.

Federal law says to clean up the dumps. Companies are trying, and some smaller and weaker ones are going broke in the process. The cost? By several estimates, perhaps $100 billion or more, an amount greater than the combined 1987 profits of the Fortune 500.

The SEC Takes Notes

Manufacturers are trying to stick their insurance men with the bill, and they cite the uncertainty of their liability for their failure to account for it in their financial statements. The Securities and Exchange Commission and independent accountants, however, are beginning to have misgivings. To auditors wrestling with the question of withholding or qualifying their opinions of corporate financial statements, says a partner at Ernst & Whinney, "It's a matter of great concern."

SEC staffers have just begun examining cleanup disclosures. Although no SEC crackdown seems imminent, the staffers are unhappy with what they see—and they don't see. At least, says Howard Hodges, chief accountant for the agency's corporate-finance division, the companies should disclose the minimum cost of cleanup. Few if any are doing so.

Westinghouse Electric Corp. seems typical. A lawyer for insurance companies Westinghouse is suing says the company faces hundreds of millions of dollars in potential cleanup costs. But a Westinghouse spokesman says an estimate would be "premature." In its most recent "10-K" filing with the SEC, the company expresses its belief that the cost will have, in accounting boilerplate, no "material adverse effect." It does observe that "there can be no assurance that, by reason of future developments, the company will not hereafter incur material costs and liabilities." No figures are mentioned.

A COMPANY LIQUIDATES

Allied-Signal Inc. is even less explicit. Its most recent annual report acknowledges "environmental" claims. In its 10-K, the company says it expects actual environmental outlays of $30 million to $40 million in each of the next two years. It makes no mention of the 100 sites that give rise to unstated liabilities. The company "wouldn't know the extent of its liabilities until further down the road," a spokesman says.

The EPA figures it might cost an average of $25 million each to clean up polluted sites, but for the most troublesome, the agency says, the cost could reach $100 million each. The EPA has identified 27,000 sites—suggesting a total cleanup bill in the hundreds of billions. But EPA assistant administrator J. Winston Porter observes that "society won't be willing to spend that kind of money." He puts the ultimate cost of neutralizing the most hazardous sites at $50 billion to $100 billion.

After 30 years of manufacturing paint pigments, Bofors Nobel Inc., though profitable to the end, last year was forced to liquidate by the cost of cleaning up a single site, the 68 wooded acres behind its plant in Muskegon, Mich. The company, formerly known as Lakeway Chemical Co., was controlled by Swedish Nobel Industries. A government-ordered cleanup would have cost Bofors $60 million, more than twice its annual sales. Dozens of other small companies, in similar straits, also folded last year.

THE CLEANUP LAW

The source of the grief is the 1980 environmental "Superfund" law, tightened in 1986. Because toxic wastes from many sites are seeping into ground water, the EPA is vigorously pressing the owners to clean up. The law permits the EPA to sue to compel a cleanup, or do the job itself and force the owners to pay. "The law gives the EPA a lot of leverages, and we want to use it," says Mr. Porter.

Wall Street has yet to confront the potential damages. Few securities analysts have closely examined it. "The companies don't give the impression that the problems are insurmountable," says Robert Reitzes, who follows the chemical industry for Mabon, Nugent & Co. Leonard Bogner, of Prudential-Bache Securities Inc., says more ominously: "Companies aren't ready to share that kind of information, but I think the potential liabilities will become critical one day."

Mr. Hodges says that if he were a shareholder, "I would be peeved if I didn't know that my company had so many sites to clean up." Even disclosing the number, he says, might be inadequate, because "that wouldn't tell me how much money would be taken out of my company."

SEC staffers say it is hard to determine whether companies have knowingly withheld material information about their liabilities. "We don't go out and inspect sites," says Howard Morin, whose staff reviews management analyses in corporate annual reports. "We rely considerably on the companies' independent auditors." The SEC's current disclosure study, he says, is mainly intended to develop disclosure guidelines, but "flagrant violations" of existing disclosure rules "will be referred for enforcement action."

The site owners are spending millions of dollars in a legal effort to lay off the cost on their insurers. If they succeed, "Crum & Forster will disappear," says Leslie Cheek, senior vice president of the casualty underwriter, a subsidiary of Xerox Corp. Crum & Forster, with premiums of $4.5 billion a year, is the country's 13th largest property-casualty insurer. "Most [insurance] companies view this exposure as the most serious economic problem in the 1990s," Mr. Cheek says.

"If the insurance industry gets stuck with even a quarter of the estimated cleanup costs," says Andre Maisonpierre, president of the Reinsurance Association of America, it will cause "major insolvencies."

Shell Oil Co. and its insurers spent $40 million fighting the EPA before Shell agreed early this year to clean up the site of a Denver pesticide plant. Though Shell hasn't estimated the total cost, the Royal Dutch Petroleum unit now is obliged to pay $320 million of the first $700 million and 20 percent of the cost above that. The Army, which once made chemical weaponry on the site, will pay the rest.

Shell is seeking an out. It has sued its 300 insurers to pay the cost. Westinghouse has sued about 150 current and former insurers to force them to accept the liability for cleaning up 80 sites. United Technologies Corp. and 250 insurance companies are also in court over 150 sites. So are Allied-Signal, with its 100-plus sites, and Monsanto Co., with 40.

The insurance companies say their comprehensive liability policies now at issue cover only "sudden and accidental" events, such as the lethal gas leak from Union Carbide's plant in Bhopal, India, in 1984. If the insurers have their way, new policies will specifically exclude liability from pollution. In seven states, however, civil antitrust charges have been filed against insurers attempting to impose this exclusion.

Because of the big money at stake, and the number of insurers involved, the Shell Oil suit alone has created a small industry. Trial is taking place in the converted auditorium of an old high-school building near San Francisco. The county court was too small for lawyers from 30 firms, their support staffs, and equipment. "The cost of litigation itself, I'm confident, will exceed $50 million," says Thorn Rosenthal, a Shell attorney.

A RISK FOR BANKS

Bankers have inherited a number of sites—with liabilities attached—from improvident borrowers. Some are already getting stuck with cleanup bills, a matter of concern at the office of the Comptroller of the Currency. John Noonan, director of commercial activities for the office, has assigned bank examiners to assess the problem.

Mellon National Bank in Pittsburgh says it faced cleanup costs in 1985 in an undisclosed amount when it began to manage the affairs of a borrower in default, Turco Coatings Inc. of Phoenixville, Pennsylvania. Midlantic National Bank of New Jersey, Landmark Bank of St. Louis, and Maryland Bank and Trust Co. report similar misadventures. Mellon says it now takes an "environmental audit" of loan customers and forecloseable property.

National Bank of Fredericksburg, Virginia, last year chose to forfeit $100,000 it had lent a small firm; the company, in bankruptcy, faced a $2.2 million cleanup bill. "We don't intend to foreclose such properties," says Nancy Embrey, a senior loan officer.

Manufacturers driven into bankruptcy court denounce enforcement as uneconomic and brutal.

AN EPA RAID

"The EPA doesn't care; it's the least of their worries," says Donald Wilson, whose Denver-based Protex Industries declared bankruptcy last December after 67 years in business. The company, founded by his father, began as a purveyor of lubricating oil and grease. After World War II, it supplied chemicals to increase the durability of concrete that built the Grand Coulee Dam and many highways and airport runways.

The company packages its products in reconditioned used drums, which often arrived at the plant containing half an inch of oil or weed killer. Protex workers would dump the contents on a five-acre site behind the plant. "That was long before paved streets came into town, and before the EPA," says the 62-year-old Mr. Wilson. After the EPA came into existence in 1970, he says, his company built a holding tank for residue in the backyard.

On March 10, 1986, EPA agents, who had taken samples from the site, raided the company headquarters. Accompanied by six police cars, FBI agents and fire trucks—in all, 72 law-enforcement officials—they cordoned off the plant, Mr. Wilson says. Last December, after a lengthy trial in which he and his firm were convicted of willfully polluting the land, Protex closed its doors. The company, which had $11 million in annual sales, must still pay $7.1 million to clean up the site.

"I felt I was in Nazi Germany or communist Russia," says Mr. Wilson.

"I very strongly disagree with that kind of characterization," says Robert Duprey, EPA's director of hazardous-waste management in Denver. He adds: "The area is very heavily contaminated, and we found the company had been lying to our inspectors"—a charge Mr. Wilson denies.

Bibliography

Aaker, David A., and George S. Day. *Consumerism: Search for the Consumer Interest,* 2d ed. Homewood, Ill.: Richard D. Irwin, 1974.

Abegglen, James C. *Management and the Worker: The Japanese Solution.* Tokyo: Sophia University, 1973.

Abernathy, William J.; Kim B. Clark; and Alan M. Kantrow. *Industrial Renaissance.* New York: Basic Books, 1983.

Abt, Clark C. *The Social Audit for Management.* New York: American Management Association, 1977.

Ackerman, Robert W. "How Companies Respond to Social Demands." *Harvard Business Review* 51, no. 4 (July–August 1973), pp. 88–98.

————. *The Social Challenge to Business.* Cambridge, Mass.: Harvard University Press, 1975.

———— and Raymond A. Bauer. *Corporate Social Performance: The Modern Dilemma.* Reston, Va.: Reston Publishing, 1976.

Adams, Gordon. *The Politics of Defense Contracting.* New Brunswick: Transaction Books, 1982.

Adizes, Ichak, and Elisabeth Mann Borgese, eds. *Self-Management: New Dimensions to Democracy.* Santa Barbara, Calif.: Clio Books, 1975.

Albrandt Jr., R. S., and M. Coleman. "The Limits of Corporate Civic Responsibility." *Economic Development Review* 6 (Spring 1988), p. 40.

American Law Institute. *National Conference on Corporate Governance and Accountability in the 1980s.* Philadelphia: The American Law Institute, 1981.

Andreasen, Alan R. *The Disadvantaged Consumer.* New York: Free Press, 1975.

Andrews, Kenneth R. "Can the Best Corporations Be Made Moral?" *Harvard Business Review* 51, no. 3 (May–June 1973), pp. 57–64.

Anshen, Melvin. *Strategies for Corporate Social Performance.* New York: Macmillan, 1980.

————, ed. *Managing the Socially Responsible Corporation.* New York: Macmillan, 1974.

Aram, John D. *Managing Business and Public Policy,* 2d ed. Boston: Pitman Publishing, 1986.

Arndt, S. "Corporate Leaders Meet to Develop AIDS Policy." *National Underwriter Life & Health-Financial Services Edition,* October 19, 1987, p. 2.

Arnold, Thurman W. *The Folklore of Capitalism.* New Haven, Conn.: Yale University Press, 1938.

Aronoff, Craig E., ed. *Business and the Media.* Santa Monica, Calif.: Goodyear Publishing, 1979.

Arrow, Kenneth J. *Social Choice and Individual Values,* 2d ed. New Haven: Yale University Press, 1963.

Atkinson, L., and J. Galaskiewicz. "Stock Ownership and Company Contributions to Charity." *Administrative Science Quarterly* 33 (March 1988), p. 82.

Backman, Jules, ed. *Social Responsibility and Accountability*. New York: New York University Press, 1975.

Bacon, Jeremy. "Corporate Directorship Practices: The Audit Committee." *The Conference Board,* Report No. 766, 1979.

———— and James K. Brown. "Corporate Directorship Practices: Role, Selection and Legal Status of the Board." *The Conference Board,* Report No. 646, 1975.

Ball, George W., ed. *Global Companies: The Political Economy of World Business*. Englewood Cliffs, N.J.: Prentice-Hall, 1975.

Barach, Jeffrey. *The Individual, Business & Society*. Englewood Cliffs, N.J.: Prentice-Hall, 1977.

Barber, Richard J. *The American Corporation: Its Power, Its Money, Its Politics*. New York: E. P. Dutton, 1970.

Barnet, Richard J. "Holding Big Businesses Accountable." *Utne Reader,* January–February 1989, p. 68.

———— and Ronald E. Muller. *Global Reach: The Power of the Multinational Corporation*. New York: Simon & Schuster, 1974.

Bauer, Raymond A., and Dan H. Fenn, Jr. *The Corporate Social Audit*. New York: Russell Sage Foundation, 1972.

Beauchamp, Tom L., and Norman E. Bowie, eds. *Ethical Theory and Business,* 3d ed. Englewood Cliffs, N.J.: Prentice-Hall, 1988.

Beesley, Michael, and Tom Evans. *Corporate Social Responsibility*. Totowa, N.J.: Biblio Distribution Centre, 1978.

Bell, Daniel. *The Coming of Post-Industrial Society: A Venture in Social Forecasting*. New York: Basic Books, 1973.

————. *The Cultural Contradictions of Capitalism*. New York: Basic Books, 1976.

Bendix, Reinhard. *Work and Authority in Industry: Ideologies of Management in the Course of Industrialization*. New York: John Wiley & Sons, 1956.

Bennis, Warren G.; Kenneth D. Benne; and Robert Chine, eds. *The Planning of Change*. New York: Holt, Rinehart & Winston, 1969.

Benokraitis, Mijole, and Joe R. Feagin. *Affirmative Action and Equal Opportunity: Action, Inaction, and Reaction*. Boulder, Colo.: Westview Press, 1978.

Benston, George J. "An Analysis of the Role of Accounting Standards for Enhancing Corporate Governance and Social Responsibility." *Journal of Accounting and Public Policy* 1, no. 1 (Fall 1982), pp. 5–17.

Berg, Ivar. *The Business of America*. New York: Harcourt Brace Jovanovich, 1968.

Berenbeim, R. E. "An Outbreak of Ethics." *Across the Board* 25 (May 1988), p. 14.

Berle, Adolph A., and Gardiner C. Means. *The Modern Corporation and Private Property,* rev. ed. New York: Harcourt Brace Jovanovich, 1967.

Best, Fred, ed. *The Future of Work*. Englewood Cliffs, N.J.: Prentice-Hall, 1973.

Bishop, James, Jr., and Henry W. Hubbard. *Let the Seller Beware*. Washington, D.C.: The National Press, 1969.

Bjork, Gordon C. *Private Enterprise and Public Interest.* Englewood Cliffs, N.J.: Prentice-Hall, 1969.

Blair, John M. *The Control of Oil.* New York: Pantheon Books, 1976.

Blake, David H.; William C. Frederick; and Mildred S. Myers. *Social Auditing: Evaluating the Impact of Corporate Programs.* New York: Praeger Publishers, 1976.

————— and Robert S. Walters. *The Politics of Global Economic Relations.* Englewood Cliffs, N.J.: Prentice-Hall, 1976.

Bluestone, Barry, and Bennett Harrison. *The Deindustrialization of America.* New York: Basic Books, 1982.

Blumberg, Paul. *Industrial Democracy.* London: Constable and Co., 1968.

Blumberg, Philip I. *The Megacorporation in American Society.* Englewood Cliffs, N.J.: Prentice-Hill, 1975.

Boulding, Kenneth E. "The Economics of the Coming Spaceship Earth." In *Environmental Quality in a Growing Economy,* ed. Henry Jorrett. Baltimore: Johns Hopkins Press for Resources for the Future, 1966.

Bowman, Edward H., and Mason Haire. "A Strategic Posture Toward Corporate Social Responsibility." *California Management Review* 14, no. 3 (Spring 1972), pp. 104–106.

Boyer, Edward. "How Japan Manages Declining Industries." *Fortune,* January 10, 1983, p. 58.

Bradshaw, Thornton, and David Vogel, eds. *Corporations and Their Critics.* New York: McGraw-Hill, 1981.

Brandenberg, M. "Promoting an Awareness of Corporate Social Responsibility." *Accountancy* 99 (June 1987), p. 90.

—————. "Sustenance from the City." *Accountancy* 102 (September 1988), p. 65.

Brenner, Steven N., and Earl A. Molander. "Is the Ethics of Business Changing?" *Harvard Business Review* (January–February 1977).

Breyer, Stephen. *Regulation and Its Reform.* Cambridge: Harvard University Press, 1982.

Brookes, Warren T. *The Economy in Mind.* New York: Universe Books, 1982.

Brown, Courtney C. *Putting the Corporate Board to Work.* New York: Macmillan, 1976.

—————. *Beyond the Bottom Line.* New York: Macmillan, 1979.

Brown, M. N., and Giampetro, A. M. "The Socially Responsible Firm and Comparable Worth. (Special Issue: Business Ethics & Corporate Social Responsibility)." *American Business Law Journal* 25 (Fall 1987), pp. 467–86.

Brownlee, W. Elliot, and Mary M. Brownlee. *Women in the American Economy: A Documentary History, 1675 to 1929.* New Haven, Conn.: Yale University Press, 1976.

Bruyn, Severyn T. *The Social Economy: People Transforming Modern Business.* New York: Ronald Press, 1977.

Buchholz, Rogene A. *Business Environment and Public Policy,* 2d ed. Englewood Cliffs, N.J.: Prentice-Hall, 1986.

Bunting, John R. *The Hidden Face of Free Enterprise.* New York: McGraw-Hill, 1964.

Business Roundtable. *Statement on Corporate Responsibility.* New York: October 1981.

Caplovitz, David. *The Poor Pay More.* New York: Free Press, 1967.

Carr, Albert Z. "Is Business Bluffing Ethical?" *Harvard Business Review* 46, no. 1 (January–February 1968), pp. 145–53.

————. "Can an Executive Afford a Conscience?" *Harvard Business Review* 48, no. 4 (July–August 1970), pp. 58–64.

Carroll, Archie B. *Business and Society.* Boston: Little, Brown, 1981.

————, ed. *Managing Corporate Social Responsibility.* Boston: Little, Brown, 1977.

Carson, B. "New Developments in Corporate Responsibility." *Utne Reader,* January–February 1989, p. 54.

Chafe, William H. *The American Woman: Her Changing Social, Economic, and Political Roles, 1920–1970.* New York: Oxford University Press, 1972.

Chamberlain, John. *The Roots of Capitalism.* New York: Van Nostrand Reinhold, 1959.

Chamberlain, Neil W. *Enterprise and Environment: The Firm in Time and Place.* New York: McGraw-Hill, 1968.

————. *The Limits of Corporate Responsibility.* New York: Basic Books, 1973.

Chandler, Alfred D., Jr. *Strategy and Structure. Chapters in the History of the Industrial Enterprise.* Cambridge, Mass.: MIT Press, 1962.

————. *The Visible Hand: The Managerial Revolution in American Business.* Cambridge, Mass.: The Belknap Press of Harvard University Press, 1977.

Chandler, Marvin. "It's Time to Clean up the Boardroom." *Harvard Business Review* 53, no. 5 (September–October 1975), pp. 73–82.

Cheit, Earl F., ed. *The Business Establishment.* New York: John Wiley & Sons, 1964.

Christoffel, Tom; David Finkelhor; and Dan Gilbarg. *Up Against the American Myth.* New York: Holt, Rinehart & Winston, 1970.

Churchill, Neil C. "Toward a Theory for Social Accounting." *Sloan Management Review* 15, no. 3 (Spring 1974), pp. 1–17.

Clark, John W. *Religion and the Moral Standards of American Businessmen.* Cincinnati: South-Western Publishing, 1966.

Clinard, Marshall B., and Peter C. Yeager. *Corporate Crime.* New York: Free Press, 1980.

Cochran, Thomas C. *Business in American Life: A History.* New York: McGraw-Hill, 1973.

———— and William Miller. *The Age of Enterprise: A Social History of Industrial America.* New York: Macmillan, 1942.

Cohen, Sanford. *Labor in the United States.* Columbus, Ohio: Charles E. Merrill Publishing, 1975.

Cole, Barry, and Mal Oettinger. *Reluctant Regulators: The FCC and the Broadcast Audience.* Reading, Mass.: Addison-Wesley Publishing, 1978.

Committee for Economic Development. *Social Responsibilities of Business Corporations: A Statement on National Policy by the Research and Policy Committee of the Committee for Economic Development.* New York: Committee for Economic Development, 1971.

Commoner, Barry. *The Closing Circle.* New York: Alfred A. Knopf, 1971.

Conard, Alfred F. "Reflections on Public Interest Directors." *Michigan Law Review* 75 (1977), pp. 941–61.

"Corporations with a Conscience." *Business and Society Review,* Winter 1988, pp. 58–59.

Corson, John J. *Business in the Humane Society.* New York: McGraw-Hill, 1971.

————. "A Corporate Social Audit?" *The Center Magazine* 5, no. 1 (January–February 1972), pp. 62–65.

Corson, John J., and George A. Steiner. *Measuring Business's Social Performance: The Corporate Social Audit.* New York: Committee for Economic Development, 1974.

Congressional Quarterly, Inc. *American Work Ethic.* Washington, D.C., 1973.

Cowen, S. S.; L. B. Ferreri; and L. D. Parker. "The Impact of Corporate Characteristics on Social Responsibility Disclosure: A Typology and Frequency-Based Analysis." *Accounting, Organizations and Society* 12 (April 1987), p. 111.

Cox, Allan. *The Cox Report on the American Corporation.* New York: Delacorte Press, 1982.

Cox, Edward F.; Robert C. Fellmeth; and John E. Schulz. *The Nader Report on the FTC.* New York: Richard W. Baron Publishing, 1969.

Crew, David F. *Industry and Community.* New York: Columbia University Press, 1979.

Cross, F. B., and B. J. Winslett. " 'Export Death': Ethical Issues and the International Trade in Hazardous Products." *American Business Law Journal* 25 (Fall 1987), pp. 487–521.

Cunningham, Lynn E., et al. *Strengthening Citizen Access and Governmental Accountability.* Washington, D.C.: Explanatory Project for Economic Alternatives, 1977.

Curtiss, Ellen T., and Philip A. Untersee. *Corporate Responsibilities and Opportunities to 1990.* Lexington, Mass.: Lexington Books, 1979.

Dale, Ernest. *The Great Organizers.* New York: McGraw-Hill, 1960.

Dales, J. H. *Pollution, Property, and Prices.* Toronto: University of Toronto Press, 1968.

Dankert, Clyde E.; Floyd C. Mann; and Herbert R. Northrup, eds. *Hours of Work.* New York: Harper & Row, 1965.

Danley, J. R. "'Ought' Implies 'Can' or, the Moral Relevance of a Theory of the Firm." *Journal of Business Ethics* 7 (January–February 1988), p. 23.

Davis, Keith, and William C. Frederick. *Business and Society: Management, Public Policy, Ethics,* 5th ed. New York: McGraw-Hill, 1984.

DeGeorge, Richard T. *Business Ethics.* New York: Macmillan, 1982.

———— and Joseph A. Pichler, eds. *Ethics, Free Enterprise, and Public Policy: Original Essays on Moral Issues in Business.* New York: Oxford University Press, 1978.

Dejon, William L. *Policy Formulation.* New York: CBI Publishers, 1979.

DeMott, Deborah A., ed. *Corporations at the Crossroads.* New York: McGraw-Hill, 1980.

Denenberg, Tia Schneider, and R. V. Denenberg. *Alcohol and Drugs: Issues in the Workplace.* Washington, D.C.: The Bureau of National Affairs, 1983.

Diebold, John. *The Role of Business in Society.* New York: Amacom, 1982.

Dierkes, Mienholf, and Raymond A. Bauer, eds. *Corporate Social Accounting.* New York: Praeger Publishers, 1973.

Dill, William R., ed. *Running the American Corporation.* New York: The American Assembly, Columbia University, 1978.

Dolan, Edwin G. *TANSTAAFL: The Economic Strategy for Environmental Crisis.* New York: Holt, Rinehart & Winston, 1971.

Domhoff, William. *Who Rules America?* Englewood Cliffs, N.J.: Prentice-Hall, 1967.

Donner, Frederick G. *The World-Wide Industrial Enterprise: Its Challenge and Promise.* New York: McGraw-Hill, 1967.

Douglas, William O. *Democracy and Finance.* New Haven, Conn.: Yale University, Press, 1940.

Doz, Yves L., and C. K. Prakalad. "How MNCs Cope with Host Government Intervention." *Harvard Business Review* 58, no. 2 (March–April 1980).

Drucker, Peter F. *Technology, Management, and Society.* New York: Harper & Row, 1970.

————. *The Concept of the Corporation,* rev. ed. New York: John Day Co., 1972.

————. *Management.* New York: Harper & Row, 1973.

————. *Management: Tasks, Responsibilities, Practices.* New York: Harper & Row, 1974.

————. *Managing in Turbulent Times.* New York: Harper & Row, 1980.

Dunlop, John T. *Business and Public Policy.* Cambridge, Mass.: Harvard University Press, 1981.

Edwards, Richard C.; Michael Reich; and Thomas E. Weisskopf. *The Capitalist System: A Radical Analysis of American Society.* Englewood Cliffs, N.J.: Prentice-Hall, 1972.

Eells, Richard, and Clarence Walton. *Conceptual Foundations of Business,* 3d ed. Homewood, Ill.: Richard D. Irwin, 1974.

Eilbirt, Henry, and I. R. Parket. "The Corporate Responsibility Officer: A New Position on the Organization Chart." *Business Horizons,* February 1973.

Elbing, Alvar O.; Herman Gadon; and John R. M. Gordon. "Flexible Working Hours: It's about Time," *Harvard Business Review* 52, no. 1 (January–February 1974), pp. 18–28, 33, 154–55.

Elkins, Arthur, and Dennis W. Callaghan. *A Managerial Odyssey: Problems in Business and Its Environment.* Reading, Mass.: Addison-Wesley Publishing, 1975.

Engler, Robert. *The Brotherhood of Oil: Energy Policy and the Public Interest.* New York: Mentor Books, 1978.

————. *The Price of Power: Electric Utilities and the Environment.* New York: Mentor Books, 1972.

Epstein, Cynthia Fuchs. *Woman's Place: Options and Limits in Professional Careers.* Berkley: University of California Press, 1970.

Epstein, Edwin M. *The Corporation in American Politics.* Englewood Cliffs, N.J.: Prentice-Hall, 1969.

————. "The Corporate Social Policy Process and the Process of Corporate Governance." *American Business Law Journal* 25 (Fall 1987), pp. 361–83.

———— and Dow Votaw. *Rationality, Legitimacy, Responsibility: Search for New Directions in Business & Society.* Santa Monica, Calif.: Goodyear Publishing, 1978.

Estes, Ralph. *Corporate Social Accounting.* New York: Wiley/Interscience, 1976.

Etzioni, Amitai. *The Active Society.* New York: Free Press, 1968.

————. "Social Progress vs. Economic Progress." *Social Policy,* March–April 1980.

Ewing, David W. *Freedom Inside the Organization: Bringing Civil Liberties to the Workplace.* New York: McGraw-Hill, 1977.

————. *Do It My Way or You're Fired!* New York: John Wiley & Sons, 1983.

Fatemi, Nasrollah, and Gail W. Williams. *Multinational Corporations: The Problems and Prospects.* New York: A. S. Barnes & Co., 1975.

Fellmeth, Robert. *The Interstate Commerce Omission.* New York: Grossman Publishers, 1970.

Ferrara, Ralph C., and Mark B. Goldfus. *Everything You Ever Wanted to Know about the Future of Federal Influence in Corporate Governance.* Washington, D.C.: Financial Government and Public Affairs, 1978.

Filios, V. "Assessment of Attitudes Toward Corporate Social Accountability in Britain." *Journal of Business Ethics* 4 (June 1985), p. 155.

————. "Review and Analysis of the Empirical Research in Corporate Social Accounting." *Journal of Business Ethics,* August 1986, p. 291.

Fine, Sidney. *Laissez Faire and the General Welfare State.* Ann Arbor: The University of Michigan Press, 1956.

Finn, David. *The Corporate Oligarch.* New York: Simon & Schuster, 1969.

Fisk, George. *Marketing and the Ecological Crisis.* New York: Harper & Row, 1974.

Fox, J. Ronald. *Managing Business-Government Relations.* Homewood, Ill.: Richard D. Irwin, 1982.

Freeman, R. Edward. *Strategic Management.* Boston: Pitman Publishing, 1984.

Freeman, Roger. *The Growth of American Government.* Stanford: Hoover Institution Press, 1975.

Friedman, Milton. *Capitalism and Freedom.* Chicago: University of Chicago Press, 1962.

———— and Rose Friedman. *Free to Choose.* New York: Avon Books, 1979.

Frank, Harvey. "A Higher Duty: A New Look at the Ethics of the Corporate Lawyer." *Cleveland State Law Review* 26 (1977), pp. 337–64.

Galbraith, John Kenneth. *The New Industrial State,* 3d ed. Boston: Houghton Mifflin, 1970.

————. *Economics and the Public Purpose.* Boston: Houghton Mifflin, 1973.

————. "The Defense of the Multinational Company." *Harvard Business Review* 56, no. 2 (March–April 1978).

Garrett, D. E. "The Effectiveness of Marketing Policy Boycotts: Environmental Opposition to Marketing." *Journal of Marketing* 51 (April 1987), p. 46.

Ginzberg, Eli, and Alice M. Yohalem. *Corporate Lib: Women's Challenge to Management.* Baltimore: The Johns Hopkins Press, 1973.

Glazer, Nathan. *Affirmative Discrimination: Ethnic Inequality and Public Policy.* New York: Basic Books, 1975.

Goldman, Marshall I., ed. *Ecology and Economics.* Englewood Cliffs, N.J.: Prentice-Hall, 1972.

————, ed. *Controlling Pollution: The Economics of a Cleaner America.* Englewood Cliffs, N.J.: Prentice-Hall, 1967.

Goldston, Eli. *The Quantification of Concern: Some Aspects of Social Accounting.* Pittsburgh: Carnegie Press, 1971.

Goodpaster, Kenneth E., and John B. Matthews, Jr. "Can a Corporation Have a Conscience?" *Harvard Business Review* 60, no. 1 (January–February 1982), pp. 132–41.

Gordon, Francine E., and Myra H. Strober, eds. *Bringing Women into Management.* New York: McGraw-Hill, 1975.

Gordon, Robert A. *Business Leadership in the Large Corporation.* Berkeley: University of California Press, 1961.

Gras, Norman S. *Business and Capitalism: An Introduction to Business History.* New York: Augustus M. Kelley, 1939.

Gray, Irwin, with Albert L. Bases; Charles H. Martin; and Alexander Sternberg. *Product Liability: A Management Response.* New York: AMACOM, 1975.

Gray, R., D. Owen, and K. Maunders. "Corporate Social Reporting: The Way Forward." *Accountancy* 98 (December 1986), p. 108.

Green, Mark J., ed. *The Monopoly Makers: Ralph Nader's Study Group Report on Regulation and Competition.* New York: Grossman Publishers, 1973.

Green, Mark J.; Beverly C. Moore, Jr.; and Bruce Wasserstein. *The Closed Enterprise System.* New York: Grossman Publishers, 1972.

Green, P. "Don't Do Business with Apartheid (Disinvestment Ain't Enough)." *Nation* 246 (June 4, 1988), p. 789.

Greenberg, Edward S. *Serving the Few: Corporate Capitalism and the Bias of Government Policy.* New York: John Wiley & Sons, 1974.

————. *Understanding Modern Government: The Rise and Decline of the American Political Economy.* New York: John Wiley & Sons, 1979.

Greenwood, William T. *Issues in Business & Society,* 3d ed. Boston: Houghton Mifflin, 1976.

Gunness, Robert. "Social Responsibility: The Art of the Possible." *Business and Society Review* 12 (Winter 1974–75), pp. 94–99.

Gyllenhammer, Pehr. "Volvo's Solution to the Blue-Collar Blues." *Business and Society Review/Innovation* 7 (Autumn 1973), pp. 50–53.

Hacker, Andrew, ed. *The Corporation Take-Over.* Garden City, N.Y.: Doubleday Publishing, 1964.

_____. *The End of the American Era*. New York: Atheneum Publishers, 1970.

Hackman, Richard J.; Greg Oldham; Robert Jansen; and Kenneth Purdy. "A New Strategy for Job Enrichment." *California Management Review* 17, no. 4 (Summer 1975), pp. 57–71.

Haddad, William F., and G. Douglas Pugh, eds. *Black Economic Development*. Englewood Cliffs, N.J.: Prentice-Hall, 1969.

Hagevik, George H. *Decision Making in Air Pollution Control*. New York: Praeger Publishers, 1970.

Haider, A. K. "Measuring and Analyzing the Economic Effects of Trade Sanctions Against South Africa: A New Approach." *Africa Today* 33 (April–September 1986), p. 47.

Halberstam, David. *The Powers That Be*. New York: Alfred A. Knopf, 1979.

Harman, Willis W. *An Incomplete Guide to the Future*. New York: W. W. Norton, 1979.

Harrington, Michael. *The Twilight of Capitalism*. New York: Simon & Schuster, 1976.

Harris, Richard. *Freedom Spent*. Boston: Little, Brown, 1976.

Harte, G. "Ethical Investment and Corporate Reporting." *The Accountant's Magazine* 92 (March 1988), p. 28.

_____ and D. L. Owen. "Fighting De-industrialization: The Role of Local Government Social Audits." *Accounting, Organizations and Society* 12 (April 1987), p. 123.

Hauck, David; Meg Voorhes; and Glenn Goldberg. *Two Decades of Debate: The Controversy Over U.S. Companies in South Africa*. Washington, D.C.: Investor Responsibility Research Center, 1983.

Heald, Morrell T. *The Social Responsibilities of Business: Company and Community, 1900–1960*. Cleveland: The Press of Case Western Reserve, 1970.

Heath, R. L. "Are Focus Groups a Viable Tool for PR Practitioners to Help Their Companies Establish Corporate Responsibility?" *Public Relations Quarterly* 32 (Winter 1987), p. 34.

Heenan, David A. *The Re-United States of America: An Action Agenda for Improving Business, Government, and Labor Relations*. Reading, Mass.: Addison-Wesley Publishing, 1982.

Heibroner, Robert L. *The Future of Capitalism*. New York: Macmillan, 1967.

_____. "Rhetoric and Reality in the Struggle between Business and the State." *Social Research* 35, no. 3 (Autumn 1968), pp. 401–25.

_____, ed. *In the Name of Profit: Profiles in Corporate Irresponsibility*. Garden City, N.Y.: Doubleday Publishing, 1972.

Henry, Harold W. *Pollution Control: Corporate Responses*. New York: AMACOM, 1974.

Heyne, Paul T. *Private Keepers of the Public Interest*. New York: McGraw-Hill, 1968.

Hill, David A.; Ernest A. Chaples; Matthew T. Downey; Larry D. Singell; David M. Solzman; and Gerald M. Swatez. *The Quality of Life in America: Pollution, Poverty, Power, and Fear*. New York: Holt, Rinehart & Winston, 1973.

Hodgetts, Richard M. *The Business Enterprise: Social Challenge, Social Response*. Philadelphia: W. B. Saunders, 1977.

Holmes, Sandra L. "Adapting Corporate Structure for Social Responsiveness." *California Management Review* 21, no. 1 (Fall 1978), p. 47.

Hughes, Jonathan L. *The Vital Few: American Economic Progress and Its Protagonists.* Boston: Houghton Mifflin, 1966.

Izraeli, D. "Ethical Beliefs and Behavior among Managers: A Cross-Cultural Perpsective." *Journal of Business Ethics* 7 (April 1988), p. 263.

Jacoby, Neil H. "The Multinational Corporation." *The Center Magazine* 3, no. 6 (December 1970), pp. 37–48.

————. "The Myth of the Corporate Economy." *The Conference Board Record,* June 1971.

————. *Corporate Power and Social Responsibility.* New York: Macmillan, 1973.

Jenkins, David. *Job Power: Blue and White Collar Democracy.* Garden City, N.Y.: Doubleday Publishing, 1973.

Johnson, Harold L. "Socially Responsible Firms: An Empty Box or a Universal Set?" *Journal of Business* 39 (July 1966), pp. 394–99.

Johnson, Orace. "Corporate Giving: A Note on Profit Maximization and Accounting Disclosure." *Journal of Accounting Research* 3, no. 1 (Spring 1965), pp. 75–85.

Jones, Sidney L. *Inflation: Causes and Prospects.* New York: The Aspen Institute, 1981.

Jones, T. M., and F. H. Gautschi III. "Will the Ethics of Business Change? A Survey of Future Executives." *Journal of Business Ethics* 7 (April 1988), p. 231.

Josephson, Matthew. *The Robber Barons.* New York: Harcourt Brace Jovanovich, 1962.

Kahn, A. F. and A. Atkinson. "Managerial Attitudes to Social Responsibility: A Comparative Study in India and Britain." *Journal of Business Ethics* 6 (August 1987), p. 419.

Kahn, Herman; William Brown; and Leon Martel. *The Next 200 Years: A Scenario for America and the World.* New York: William Morrow, 1976.

Kapp, K. William. *The Social Costs of Private Enterprise.* New York: Schocken Books, 1971.

Katayama, F. H. "Ganging up for Housing (Corporate Investments in Low-Income Housing)." *Fortune* 118 (October 24, 1988), p. 12.

Kelly, M. "American Business & Professional Association (Progressive Business Organization)." *Utne Reader,* January–February 1989, p. 79.

Kelley, William T. *New Consumerism: Selected Readings.* Columbus, Ohio: Grid, 1973.

Kelso, Louis, and Patricia Hetter. *Two-Factory Theory: The Economics of Reality.* New York: Random House, 1968.

Kintner, Earl W. *An Antitrust Primer: A Guide to Antitrust and Trade Regulation Laws for Businessmen.* New York: Macmillan, 1964.

————. *A Primer on the Law of Deceptive Practices.* New York: Macmillan, 1971.

Kirkland, Edward C. *Dream and Thought in the Business Community, 1860–1900.* Ithaca, N.Y.: Cornell University Press, 1956.

————. *Industry Comes of Age: Business, Labor, and Public Policy, 1860–1897.* Vol. 6 in *The Economic History of the United States,* ed. Henry David et al. New York: Holt, Rinehart & Winston, 1961.

Klein, Thomas A. *Social Costs & Benefits of Business*. Englewood Cliffs, N.J.: Prentice-Hall, 1977.

Koch, Frank. *The New Corporate Philanthropy: How Society and Business Can Profit*. New York: Plenum Press, 1979.

Kohlmeier, Louis M., Jr. *The Regulators*. New York: Harper & Row, 1970.

Kolko, Gabriel. *The Triumph of Conservatism: A Reinterpretation of American History, 1900–1960*. Quadrangle Books, 1967.

Krasney, Martin, ed. *The Corporation and Society*. New York: The Aspen Institute for Humanistic Studies, 1979.

Kreps, Juanita. *Sex in the Marketplace: American Women at Work*. Baltimore: The Johns Hopkins University Press, 1971.

Kristol, Irving. *Two Cheers for Capitalism*. New York: Basic Books, 1978.

Krooss, Herman E., and Charles Gilbert. *American Business History*. Englewood Cliffs, N.J.: Prentice-Hall, 1972.

Kugel, Yerachmiel, and Gladys W. Gruenberg. *Ethical Perspectives on Business & Society*. Lexington, Mass.: Lexington Books, 1977.

Larson, John A., ed. *The Regulated Businessman: Business and Government*. New York: Holt, Rinehart & Winston, 1966.

Lawrence, Paul R. and Davis Dyer. *Renewing American Industry*. New York: Free Press, 1983.

Leipert, C. "Social Costs of Economic Growth." *Journal of Economic Issues* 20 (March 1986), p. 109.

Lerner, L. D. and G. E. Fryxell. "An Empirical Study of Predictors of Corporate Social Performance: A Multi-Dimensional Analysis." *Journal of Business Ethics* 7 (December 1988), p. 951.

Levitan, Sar A., and William B. Johnston. *Work Is Here to Stay, Alas*. Salt Lake City: Olympus Publishing, 1973.

Leibhavsky, H. H. *American Government and Business*. New York: John Wiley & Sons, 1971.

Light, Ivan H. *Ethnic Enterprise in America*. Berkeley: University of California Press, 1972.

Lindblom, Charles E. *Politics and Markets*. New York: Basic Books, 1977.

Linowes, David F. *The Corporate Conscience*. New York: Hawthorn Books, 1974.

————. "Corporation as Citizen." *Corporate Board,* May–June 1988, p. 6.

Lipset, Seymour Martin, and William Schneider. *The Confidence Gap*. New York: Free Press, 1983.

Littlejohn, S. E. "Competition and Cooperation: New Trends in Corporate Public Issue Identification and Resolution (Corporate Issue Management and Strategic Planning)." *California Management Review* 29 (Fall 1986), p. 109.

Litschert, Robert J., et al. *The Corporate Role & Ethical Behavior: Concepts & Cases*. New York: Van Nostrand Reinhold, 1977.

Lodge, George C. *The New American Ideology*. New York: Alfred A. Knopf, 1976.

Lovdal, Michael L.; Raymond A. Bauer; and Nancy H. Treverton. "Public Responsibility Committees of the Board." *Harvard Business Review,* May–June 1977, pp. 40–64, 178–81.

Lund, Leonard. *Corporate Organization for Environmental Policymaking.* New York: The Conference Board, 1974.

Lundborg, Louis B. *Future without Shock.* New York: W. W. Norton, 1974.

Luthans, Fred; Richard M. Hodgetts; and Kenneth R. Thompson. *Social Issues in Business,* 5th ed. New York: Macmillan, 1987.

Lydenberg, Steven D. *Bankrolling Ballots Update 1980.* New York: The Council on Economic Priorities, 1981.

Mace, Myles L. *Directors: Myth and Reality.* Boston: Division of Research, Harvard Graduate School of Business Administration, 1971.

Magaziner, Ira C., and Robert B. Reich. *Minding America's Business.* New York: Vintage Books, 1983.

Magnuson, Warren G., and Jean Carper. *The Dark Side of the Marketplace.* Englewood Cliffs, N.J.: Prentice Hall, 1968.

Manne, Henry G., and Henry C. Wallich. *The Modern Corporation and Social Responsibility.* Washington, D.C.: American Enterprise Institute for Public Policy Research, 1972.

Martyn, Howe. *Multinational Business Management.* Lexington, Mass.: D. C. Heath, 1970.

Mason, Edward S., ed. *The Corporation in Modern Society.* Cambridge, Mass.: Harvard University Press, 1959.

Mason, R. Hal. "Conflicts between Host Countries and the Multinational Enterprise." *California Management Review* 17, no. 1 (Fall 1974), pp. 5–14.

Mathews, R. "Social Accounting: A Future Need (Social Responsibility Accounting in Great Britain)." *Accountancy* 96 (December 1986), p. 139.

McCall, David B. "Profit: Spur for Solving Social Ills." *Harvard Business Review* 51, no. 3 (May–June 1973), pp. 46–56.

McClelland, David, C. *The Achieving Society.* New York: Van Nostrand Reinhold, 1961.

McConnell, Grant. *Private Power and American Democracy.* New York: Alfred A. Knopf, 1966.

McGuire, J. B., A. Sundgren, and T. Schneeweis. "Corporate Social Responsibility and Firm Financial Performance." *Academy of Management Journal* 31 (December 1988), p. 854.

McGuire, Joseph F. "The Social Responsibility of the Corporation." In *Evolving Concepts in Management,* ed. Edwin B. Flippo. Chicago: *Proceedings of the Academy of Management Meeting, December 1964.*

———. "The Social Values of Economic Organization." *Review of Social Economy* 32, no. 1 (April 1974).

McKie, James W., ed. *Social Responsibility and the Business Predicament.* Washington, D.C.: Brookings Institution, 1974.

McMenamin, Michael, and Walter McNamara. *Milking the Public: Political Scandals of the Dairy Lobby from LBJ to Jimmy Carter.* Chicago: Nelson-Hall Publishers, 1980.

Medawar, Charles. *The Social Audit Consumer Handbook: A Guide to the Social Responsibilities of Business to the Consumer.* Atlantic Highlands, N.J.: Humanities Press, 1978.

Metzger, B. L. *Profit Sharing in Perspective,* 2d ed. Evanston, Ill.: Profit Sharing Research Foundation, 1966.

Metzger, M. B. "Organizations and the Law. (Special Issue: Business Ethics & Corporate Social Responsibility)." *American Business Law Journal* 25 (Fall 1987), pp. 407–41.

Miles, Robert H. *Coffin Nails and Corporate Strategies.* Englewood Cliffs, N.J.: Prentice-Hall, 1982.

Miller, C. "Reebok Pays Cost of Human Rights Concert Tour. (Reebok International Ltd.)" *Marketing News* 22 (September 12, 1988), p. 6.

Miller, Fred D., Jr. *Out of the Mouth of Babes: The Infant Formula Controversy.* Bowling Green, Ohio: Social Philosophy and Policy Center, 1983.

Miller, P., and T. O'Leary. "Accounting and the Construction of the Governable Person. (Toward Appreciating Accounting in Its Organizational and Social Contexts, Part II)." *Accounting, Organizations and Society* 12 (June 1987), p. 235.

Miller, W. H. "Issue Management: 'No Longer a Sideshow.'" *Industry Week* 235 (November 2, 1987), p. 125.

Mills, C. Wright. *White Collar: The American Middle Classes.* New York: Oxford University Press, 1956.

————. *The Power Elite.* New York: Oxford University Press, 1957.

Millstein, Ira M., and Salem M. Katsh. *The Limits of Corporate Power: Existing Constraints on the Exercise of Corporate Discretion.* New York: Macmillan, 1981.

Mintz, Morton, and Jerry S. Cohen. *America, Inc.: Who Owns and Operates the United States?* New York: Dell Publishing, 1972.

Modic, S. J. "Movers & Shakers (Social Responsibility of America's Business Leaders; Includes a Listing, by State)." *Industry Week* 236 (January 18, 1988), p. 47.

Monsen, R. Joseph. *Modern American Capitalism: Ideologies and Issues.* Boston: Houghton Mifflin, 1963.

————. *Business and the Changing Environment.* New York: McGraw-Hill, 1973.

Morison, Elting E. *From Know-How to Nowhere: The Development of American Technology.* New York: Basic Books, 1974.

Moss, Frank E. *Initiatives in Corporate Responsibility.* Washington, D.C.: U.S. Government Printing Office, 1972.

Mueller, Robert K. *New Directions for Directors: Behind the By-Laws.* Lexington, Mass.: Lexington Books, 1978.

Murray, Edward A., Jr. "The Social Response Process in Commercial Banks: An Empirical Investigation." *Academy of Management Review* 1, no. 3 (July 1976), pp. 5–15.

Murray, K. B., and J. R. Montanari. "Strategic Management of the Socially Responsible Firm: Integrating Management and Marketing Theory." *Academy of Management Review* 11 (October 1986), p. 815.

Nadel, Mark V. *The Politics of Consumer Protection*. Indianapolis, Ind.: Bobbs-Merrill, 1971.

Nader, Ralph. *Unsafe at Any Speed: The Designed-In Dangers of the American Automobile*. New York: Grossman Publishers, 1972.

_____ and Mark J. Green, eds. *Corporate Power in America*. New York: Grossman Publishers, 1973.

_____; Mark J. Green; and Joel Seligman. *Constitutionalizing the Corporation: The Case for the Federal Chartering of Giant Corporations*. Washington, D.C.: The Corporate Accountability Research Group, 1976.

_____. *Taming the Giant Corporation*. New York: W. W. Norton, 1976.

Naisbitt, John. *Megatrends*. New York: Warner Books, 1982.

Nash, Laura L. "Ethics without the Sermon." *Harvard Business Review* 59, no. 6 (November–December 1981), pp. 79–90.

National Academy of Engineering. *Product Quality, Performance, and Cost*. Washington, D.C.: U.S. Government Printing Office, 1972.

National Industrial Conference Board. *Organizing for Effective Public Affairs*. New York, 1969.

_____. *The Consumer Affairs Department: Organization and Function*. New York, 1973.

Nelson, Ralph L. *Economic Factors in the Growth of Corporation Giving*. New York: National Bureau of Economic Research and Russell Sage Foundation, 1970.

Newcomer, Mabel. *The Big Business Executive*. New York: Columbia University Press, 1955.

Nicholson, Edward A.; Robert Litschert; and William P. Anthony. *Business Responsibility and Social Issues*. Columbus, Ohio: Charles E. Merrill Publishing, 1974.

Nicolin, Curt. *Private Industry in a Public World*. Reading, Mass.: Addison-Wesley Publishing, 1977.

Nisbet, Robert. *Twilight of Authority*. New York: Oxford University Press, 1975.

Notre Dame Law School Symposium. "The Role of Professionals in Corporate Governance." *The Notre Dame Lawyer* 56, no 5 (June 1981).

Nunan, R. "The Libertarian Conception of Corporate Property: A Critique of Milton Friedman's Views on the Social Responsibility of Business." *Journal of Business Ethics* December 1988, p. 891.

O'Connor, Rochelle. *Corporate Contributions in Smaller Companies*. New York: The Conference Board, 1973.

Orr, Leonard H., ed. "Is Corporate Social Responsibility a Dead Issue?" *Business and Society Review* 25 (Spring 1978), p. 4.

Orren, Karen. *Corporate Power and Social Change: The Politics of the Life Insurance Industry*. Balitmore: The Johns Hopkins Press, 1974.

Ostlund, Lyman E. "Are Middle Managers an Obstacle to Corporate Social Policy Implementation?" *Business and Society Review* 18, no. 2 (Spring 1978), p. 5.

O'Toole, James. *Making America Work: Productivity and Responsibility*. New York: Continuum Publishing, 1981.

Owen, James R. "The Church's Voice in the Marketplace." *United Presbyterian A.D.* 10, no. 1 (January 1981).

Palamountain, Joseph C. *The Politics of Distribution.* Cambridge: Harvard University Press, 1955.

Paluszek, John L. *Will the Corporation Survive?* Reston, Va.: Reston Publishing, 1977.

Patrick, Kenneth G., and Richard Eells. *Education and the Business Dollar: A Study of Corporate Contributions Policy and American Education.* New York: Inter-book, 1969.

Perrow, Charles. *The Radical Attack on Business: A Critical Analysis.* New York: Harcourt Brace Jovanovich, 1972.

Peters, Charles, and Taylor Branch. *Blowing the Whistle: Dissent in the Public Interest.* New York: Praeger Publishers, 1972.

Pfeffer, Jeffrey, and Gerald R. Salancik. *The External Control of Organizations.* New York: Harper & Row, 1978.

Phatak, Arvind V. *Evolution of World Enterprises.* New York: American Management Association, 1971.

Phelan, James, and Robert Pozen. *The Company State.* New York: Grossman Publishers, 1973.

Podhoretz, Norman. "The New Defenders of Capitalism." *Harvard Business Review* 59, no. 2 (March–April 1981), pp. 20–24.

Poor, Riva. *4 Days, 40 Hours: Reporting on a Revolution in Work and Leisure.* Cambridge, Mass.: Bursk & Poor Publishing, 1970.

Porter, Glenn. *The Rise of Big Business, 1860–1910.* New York: Thomas Y. Crowell, 1973.

Porter, Michael E. *Competitive Strategy: Techniques for Analyzing Industries and Competitors.* New York: Free Press, 1980.

Post, James E. *Risk and Response: Management and Social Change in the American Insurance Industry.* Lexington, Mass.: D. C. Heath, 1976.

————. *Corporate Behavior and Social Change.* Reston, Va.: Reston Publishing, 1978.

Powers, Charles W., and David Vogel. "Ethics in the Education of Business Managers." *The Journal of Higher Education* 53, no. 3 (May–June 1982), pp. 371–74.

Premeaux, S. R., R. W. Mondy, and A. L. Bethke. "The Two-Tier Wage System: Is It a Major Breakthrough in the Reindustrialization of America?" *Personnel Administrator* 31 (November 1986), p. 92.

Preston, Lee E., and James E. Post. *Private Management and Public Policy.* Englewood Cliffs, N.J.: Prentice-Hall, 1975.

————; Francoise Rey; and Meinolf Dierkes. "Company Corporate Social Performance: Germany, France, Canada, and the U.S." *California Management Review* 20, no. 4 (Summer 1978), p. 40.

Profit Sharing Council. *Guide to Modern Profit Sharing.* Chicago, 1973.

Purcell, Theodore V., and Gerald F. Cavanagh. *Blacks in the Industrial World: Issues for the Manager.* New York: Free Press, 1972.

Raelin, J. A. "An Analysis of Professional Deviance within Organizations." *Human Relations* 39 (December 1986), p. 1103.

Redman, Eric. *The Dance of Legislation*. New York: Simon & Schuster, 1973.

Reich, Robert B. *The Next American Frontier*. New York: Times Books, 1983.

Reid, T. R. *Congressional Odyssey: The Saga of a Senate Bill*. San Francisco: W. H. Freeman, 1980.

Resnikoff, Marvin. *The Next Nuclear Gamble: Transportation and Storage of Nuclear Waste*. New York: Council on Economic Priorities, 1983.

Reuschling, Thomas L. "The Business Institution: A Redefinition of Social Role." *Business and Society* 9, no. 1 (Autumn 1968), pp. 28–32.

Reynolds, John I. "Improving Business Ethics: The President's Lonely Task." *Business and Society* 19, no. 1 (Fall 1978), p. 10.

Richardson, A. J. "Accounting as a Legitimating Institution." *Accounting, Organizations and Society,* August 1987, p. 341.

Richman, Barry. "New Paths to Corporate Social Responsibility." *California Management Review* 15, no. 3 (Spring 1973), pp. 20–36.

Ridgeway, James. *The Politics of Ecology*. New York: E. P. Dutton, 1970.

Rockness, J. W. "An Assessment of the Relationship between U.S. Corporate Environmental Performance and Disclosure." *Journal of Business Finance and Accounting* 12 (Fall 1985), p. 339.

Rodewald, R. A. "The Corporate Social Responsibility Debate: Unanswered Questions about the Consequences of Moral Reform." *American Business Law Journal* 25 (Fall 1987), pp. 443–66.

Rogers, T. G. P. "Partnership with Society: The Social Responsibility of Business." *Management Decision* March 25, 1987, p.76.

Rose, Arnold M. *The Power Structure: Poliltical Process in American Society*. Fair Lawn, N.J.: Oxford University Press, 1967.

Rumelt, Richard P. *Strategy, Structure, and Economic Performance*. Boston: Division of Research, Graduate School of Business Administration, Harvard University, 1974.

Sacks, D., and R. Abratt. "The Marketing Challenge: Toward Being Profitable and Socially Responsible." *Journal of Business Ethics,* July 1988, p. 497.

Sampson, Anthony. *The Sovereign State: The Secret History of I.T.T*. New York: Stein & Day Publishers, 1973.

————. *The Seven Sisters: The Great Oil Companies and the World They Shaped*. New York: Viking Press, 1975.

Sanford, David. *Who Put the Con in Consumer?* New York: Liveright, 1972.

Savas, E. S. *Privatizing the Public Sector*. Chatham, N.J.: Chatham House Publishers, 1982.

Sawyer, George. *Business & Society: Managing Corporate Social Impact*. Boston: Houghton Mifflin, 1978.

Schiller, Z. "Doing Well by Doing Good." *Business Week,* December 5, 1988, p. 53.

Schlei, Barbara Lindemann, and Paul Grossman. *Employment Discrimination Law, 1979 Supplement*. Washington, D.C.: Bureau of National Affairs, 1979.

Schnapper, M. B. *American Labor: A Pictorial Social History*. Washington, D.C.: Public Affairs Press, 1972.

Schock, F. "Business without Morality Is Nobody's Business at All (Business Ethics)." *International Management* 43 (January 1988), p. 71.

Schon, Donald A. *The Reflective Practitioner: How Professionals Think in Action*. New York: Basic Books, 1982.

Schrag, Peter. *The End of the American Future*. New York: Simon & Schuster, 1973.

Schultze, Charles L. "The Public Use of Private Interest." *Harpers* 254 (May 1977), pp. 43–62.

Schumpeter, Joseph A. *Capitalism, Socialism, and Democracy*. New York: Harper & Row, 1947.

Securities and Exchange Commission Staff. *Report on Corporate Accountability*, presented for the use of the United States Senate Committee on Banking, Housing and Urban Affairs, September 4, 1980.

Selekman, Sylvia K., and Benjamin M. Selekman. *Power and Morality in a Business Society*. New York: McGraw-Hill, 1956.

Serpa, R. "The Often Overlooked Ethical Aspects of Mergers." *Journal of Business Ethics* 7 (May 1988), p. 359.

Serrin, William. *The Company and the Union: The "Civilized Relationship" of the General Motors Corporation and the United Automobile Workers*. New York: Alfred A. Knopf, 1973.

Sethi, S. Prakash. *Business Corporations and the Black Man: An Analysis of Social Conflict: The Kodak-FIGHT Controversy*. San Francisco: Chandler Publishing, 1970.

_____. *Japanese Business and Social Conflict: A Comparative Analysis of Response Patterns with American Business*. Cambridge, Mass.: Ballinger Publishing, 1975.

_____. *Advocacy Advertising and Large Corporations: Social Conflict, Big Business Image, the News Media, and Public Policy*. Lexington, Mass.: D. C. Heath, 1977.

_____. *Up Against the Corporate Wall*, 4th ed. Englewood Cliffs, N.J.: Prentice-Hall, 1982.

_____, ed. *The Unstable Ground: Corporate Social Policy in A Dynamic Society*. Los Angeles: Melville Publishers, 1974.

Sethi, S. Prakash, and Richard H. Holton. *The Management of the Multinationals: Policies, Operations, and Research*. New York: Free Press, 1974.

Shapiro, Irving S. "Today's Executive: Private Steward and Public Servant." *Harvard Business Review* 56, no. 2 (March–April 1978), p. 94.

Shenfield, Barbara. *Company Boards: Their Responsibilities to Shareholders, Employees, and the Community*. London: George Allen & Unwin, 1971.

Sheppard, Harold L., and Neal Q. Herrick. *Where Have All the Robots Gone? Worker Dissatisfaction in the 70s*. New York: Free Press, 1972.

Shostak, Arthur B., and William Gomberg, eds. *Blue Collar World: Studies of the American Worker*. Englewood Cliffs, N.J.: Prentice-Hall, 1965.

Silk, Leonard. "The New, Improved Creed of Social Responsibility." *Business Month* 132 (November 1988), p. 109.

_____ and Vogel, David. *Ethics and Profits: The Crisis of Confidence in American Business*. New York: Simon & Schuster, 1976.

Silverstein, D. "Managing Corporate Social Responsibility in a Changing Legal Environment." *American Business Law Journal* 25 (Fall 1987), pp. 523–66.

Simmons, John, and William Mares. *Working Together*. New York: Alfred A. Knopf, 1983.

Skoning, G. D. "Must Industry Shoulder Uncle Sam's Failures?" *Personnel Journal* 66 (September 1987), p. 52.

Smuts, Robert W. *Women and Work in America*. New York: Schocken Books, 1974.

Sobin, Dennis P. *The Working Poor: Minority Workers in Low-Wage, Low-Skill Jobs*. Port Washington, N.Y.: Kennikat Press, 1973.

Soderquist, Larry D. "Toward a More Effective Corporate Board: Reexamining Roles of Outside Directors." *New York University Law Review* 52 (December 1977), pp. 1341–62.

Solomon, Lewis D. "Restructuring the Corporate Board of Directors: Fond Hope—Faint Promise?" *Michigan Law Review* 76 (March 1978), pp. 581–610.

Sombart, Werner. *The Jews and Modern Capitalism*. New York: Free Press, 1951.

Sonnenfeld, Jeffrey A. *Corporate Views of the Public Interest*. Boston: Auburn House, 1981.

Southard, Samuel. *Ethics for Executives*. New York: Thomas Nelson, 1975.

Spence, L. D. "The Soul of the Corporation." *Utne Reader,* January–February 1989, p. 56.

Spencer, B. A., and G. S. Taylor. "A within and between Analysis of the Relationship between Corporate Social Responsibility and Financial Performance." *Akron Business and Economic Review,* Fall 1987, p. 7.

Spitzer, Carlton E. *Raising the Bottom Line*. New York: Longman, Inc., 1982.

Statement of the Business Roundtable. "The Role and Composition of the Board of Directors of the Large Publicly Owned Corporations." *The Business Lawyer* 33 (1978), pp. 2083, 2089–90.

Steade, Richard D. *Business and Society in Transition: Issues and Concepts*. San Francisco: Canfield Press, 1975.

Stein, H. "Who Decides the Private Responsibility of Business?" *Chief Executive (U.S.),* November–December 1987, p. 8.

Steiner, George A., and John Steiner, eds. *Business, Government, and Society,* 5th ed. New York: Random House, 1988.

Stern, L., and J. Goldwasser. "These Investors Take a Stand (On Social Objectives as Well as Financial)." *Changing Times* 41 (November 1987), p. 134.

Stobaugh, Robert B., and Associates. *U.S. Multinational Enterprises and the U.S. Economy*. Boston: Harvard Business School, 1972.

Stobaugh, Robert, and Daniel Yergin, eds. *Energy Future*. New York: Vintage Books, 1983.

Stone, Alan. *Regulation and Its Alternatives*. Washington, D.C.: Congressional Quarterly Press, 1982.

Stone, Christopher D. *Where the Law Ends: The Social Control of Corporate Behavior*. New York: Harper & Row, 1975.

Stroup, M. A. "Environmental Scanning at Monsanto (Monsanto, Chemical Co.)." *Planning Review (a publication of the Planning Forum),* July–August 1988, p. 24.

Sturdivant, Frederick D., and Heidi Vernon-Wortzel. *Business and Society: A Managerial Approach,* 4th ed. Homewood, Ill.: Richard D. Irwin, 1990.

Sturdivant, Frederick D., ed. *The Ghetto Marketplace.* New York: Free Press, 1969.

Subcommittee on Labor of the Committee on Labor and Public Welfare, United States Senate. *Compilation of Selected Labor Laws Pertaining to Labor Relations, Part II.* Washington, D.C.: Government Printing Office, 1974.

Sutherland, Edwin H. *White Collar Crime.* Hinsdale, Ill.: Dryden Press, 1949.

Sutton, Francis X.; Seymour E. Harris; Carl Kaysen; and James Tobin. *The American Business Creed.* Cambridge, Mass.: Harvard University Press, 1956.

Swartz, Edward M. *Toys That Don't Care.* Boston: Gambit, Inc., 1971.

Taussig, F. W., and C. S. Joslyn. *American Business Leaders.* New York: Macmillan, 1932.

Tawney, R. H. *Religion and the Rise of Capitalism.* London: Murphy, 1929.

Terkel, Studs. *Working: People Talk about What They Do All Day and How They Feel about What They Do.* New York: Pantheon Books, 1972.

Thomas, C. B., Jr. "Values as Predictors of Social Activist Behavior." *Human Relations* 39 (March 1986), p. 179.

Thomas, Ralph L. *Policies Underlying Corporate Giving.* Englewood Cliffs, N.J.: Prentice-Hall, 1966.

Thurow, Lester. *The Zero-Sum Society.* New York: Penguin Books, 1981.

Tillett, Anthony; Thomas Kempner; and Gordon Wills, eds. *Management Thinkers.* Baltimore: Penguin Books, 1970.

Toffler, Alvin. *Future Shock.* New York: Random House, 1970.

Tolchin, Susan J., and Martin Tolchin. *Dismantling America: The Rush to Deregulate.* Boston: Houghton Mifflin, 1983.

Towle, Joseph W., ed. *Ethics and Standards in American Business.* Boston: Houghton Mifflin, 1964.

Tucker, W. T. *The Social Context of Economic Behavior.* New York: Holt, Rinehart & Winston, 1964.

Tugendhat, Christopher. *The Multinationals.* New York: Random House, 1972.

Turner, James C. *The Chemical Feast: The Nader Report.* New York: Grossman Publishers, 1970.

Turner, Louis. *Multinational Companies and the Third World.* New York: Hill & Wang, 1973.

Van Tassel, Alfred J., ed. *Our Environment: The Outlook for 1980.* Lexington, Mass.: D. C. Heath, 1973.

Vaupel, James W., and Joan P. Curhan. *The Making of Multinational Enterprise.* Boston: Division of Research, Graduate School of Business, Harvard University, 1969.

Velasquez, Manuel G. *Business Ethics: Concepts and Cases.* Englewood Cliffs, N.J.: Prentice-Hall, 1982.

Vernon, Raymond. *Sovereignty at Bay: The Spread of U.S. Enterprise*. New York: Basic Books, 1973.

Vogel, David. "The Corporate Board: Membership and Public Pressure." *Executive* 3, no. 3 (Spring 1977), pp. 8–11.

————. *Lobbying the Corporations: Citizen Challenges to Business Authority*. New York: Basic Books, 1978.

————. "E pluribus capitalism." *Across the Board* 24 (September 1987), p. 34.

Votaw, Dow, and S. Prakash Sethi. *The Corporate Dilemma: Traditional Values versus Contemporary Problems*. Englewood Cliffs, N.J.: Prentice-Hall, 1973.

Wade, Michael. *Flexible Working Hours in Practice*. New York: John Wiley & Sons, 1973.

Walton, Clarence C. *Corporate Social Responsibilities*. Belmont, Calif.: Wadsworth, 1967.

————. *Ethos and the Executive*. Englewood Cliffs, N.J.: Prentice-Hall, 1969.

————, ed. *Business and Social Progress*. New York: Praeger Publishers, 1970.

Warner, W. Lloyd, and James C. Abegglen. *Big Business Leaders in America*. New York: Harper & Row, 1955.

Wartick, S. L., and R. E. Rude. "Issues Management: Corporate Fad or Corporate Function?" *California Management Review* 29 (Fall 1986), p. 124.

Wasson, Chester; Frederick D. Sturdivant; and David H. McConaughy. *Competition and Human Behavior*. New York: Appleton-Century-Crofts, 1968.

Wattell, Harold L., ed. *Voluntarism and the Business Community*. Hempstead, N.Y.: Hofstra University Yearbook of Business, 1971.

Weber, Max. *The Protestant Ethic and the Spirit of Capitalism*. New York: Charles Scribner's Sons, 1963.

Wiebe, Robert H. *Businessmen and Reform: A Study of the Progressive Movement*. Cambridge, Mass.: Harvard University Press, 1962.

————. *The Search for Order: 1877–1920*. New York: Hill and Wang, 1967.

Weinstein, James. *The Corporate Ideal in the Liberal State, 1900–1918*. Boston: Beacon Press, 1978.

Weisband, Edward, and Thomas Franck. *Resignation in Protest: Political and Ethical Choices between Loyalty to Team and Loyalty to Conscience in American Public Life*. New York: Grossman Publishers, 1975.

Welch, Patrick, J. "Social Responsibility, Semantics, and Why We Can't Agree on What We Agree On." *Business and Society* 18, no. 2 (Spring 1978), p. 38.

Wheeler, G. E. "Civic Affairs—How Deeply Should Companies Be Involved?" *Management Decision* 25 (March 1987), p. 59.

Wheelwright, Steven C. "Japan—Where Operations Really Are Strategic." *Harvard Business Review* 59, no. 4 (July–August 1981), pp. 67–74.

Whisenhunt, Donald W. *The Environment and the American Experience: A Historian Looks at the Ecological Crisis*. Port Washington, N.Y.: Kennikat Press, 1974.

White House Conference on the Industrial World Ahead. *A Look at Business in 1990*. Washington, D.C.: U.S. Government Printing Office, 1972.

Wilkins, Mira. *The Emergence of Multinational Enterprise: American Business Abroad from the Colonial Era to 1914.* Cambridge, Mass.: Harvard University Press, 1970.

————. *The Maturing of Multinational Enterprise: American Business Abroad, 1914 to 1970.* Cambridge, Mass.: Harvard University Press, 1973.

Williams, Harold M. "Corporate Accountability and the Lawyer's Role." *The Business Lawyer* 34 (November 1978), pp. 7–17.

Williamson, Oliver E. *Corporate Control and Business Behavior.* Englewood Cliffs, N.J.: Prentice-Hall, 1970.

————. *Markets and Hierarchies: Analysis and Antitrust Implications.* New York: Free Press, 1975.

Wilson, Ian H. *Corporate Environments of the Future.* New York: The President's Association, Special Study no. 61, 1976.

Woods, Barbara, ed. *Eco-Solutions.* Cambridge, Mass.: Schenkman Publishing, 1972.

Yankelovich, Daniel. *New Rules: Searching for Self-Fulfillment in a World Turned Upside Down.* New York: Bantam Books, 1982.

Yeo, M. "Marketing Ethics: The Bottom Line? (How Ethics Are Being Marketed)." *Journal of Business Ethics* 7 (December 1988), p. 929.

Yergin, Daniel, and Martin Hillenbrand, eds. *Global Insecurity: A Strategy for Energy and Economic Renewal.* Boston: Houghton Mifflin, 1982.

Zahra, S. A., and M. S. LaTour. "Corporate Social Responsibility and Organizational Effectiveness: A Multivariate Approach." *Journal of Business Ethics* 6 (August 1987), p. 59.

Zeitlin, Maurice. "Corporate Ownership and Control: The Large Corporation and the Capitalist Class." *American Journal of Sociology* 79 (March 1974), pp. 1073–1119.

Index

A. H. Robins Company, 67, 68, 374
  bankruptcy, 552–55
  Dalkon Shield, 547–72
A. M. Best Company, 478
Abbott, Wallace Calvin, 26
Abbott Alkaloid Company, 26
Abbott Laboratories, 3, 20–39
  Code of Marketing Ethics, 23–25
  Ross Laboratories, 25–28
Abelson, Alan, 105, 108, 109n
Abram, Robert, 251, 253, 578
Accola, J., 116n, 126n
Addaba, Joseph, 233–34, 237
Adams, Harkness and Hill, 108
Adolph Coors Company, 456–76
  company background, 457–60
  corporate reputation, 472–76
  decline, 468–76
  financial performance and resources,
    570–72
  union problems, 457, 572
Advertising
  alcohol, 74–75
  deceptive, 141–46, 251
  tobacco industry, 519–21
Affirmative action programs, 244
AFL-CIO, 393, 643
Africa Fund, 324
African National Congress, 263, 264
A-H Trust (asbestos-health trust), 344, 351,
  352, 356–66
AIDS
  antidiscrimination, 432–33
  insurance, 433
  president's commission, 432–34
  problems for employers, 412–19, 511
  revenue sources for treatment, 432–34
Air Holdings, Ltd., 88
Albert, Carl, 160
Alcohol problems, 373–75
  advertising, 74–75
Alden, Vernon R., 47, 48, 55

Alexander, Norman, 315, 316
Alleghany, International, 272
Allemang, Paul 41, 59
Allen, Fred T., 137
Allen, Ivan, Jr., 47
Allen, Michael, 80, 140
Allen, Robert, 114, 119
Allied Chemical Corporation, 628–47
Allied Corporation, 139
Allied Signal, Inc., 659
Allis-Chalmers Corporation, 176, 322
All-terrain vehicles (ATVs), 587–90
Amalgamated Beverage Industry, 265
Amalgamated Clothing Workers of America
  (ACWA), 9, 11, 12, 13, 380
Ambrose, James, 237
Amcar, 265
American Academy of Family Physicians,
  520
American Airlines, 88, 94, 154
  wage structure, 429, 430, 431
  wrongful discharge suits, 515
American Association of Advertising Agen-
  cies, 252
American Brands, 70
American Civil Liberties Union, 513
American Council of Textile Workers
  (ACTW), 393, 394
American Cyanamid, 117, 118, 124
American Electric Power, 650
American Heart Association, 520
American Home Products, 22, 29, 535, 545
American Investor, 103
American Medical Association, 512, 519
American SealKap Corporation (AMK), 304,
  305
American Ship Building Company, 151–60
  SEC action against, 159–60
American Stock Exchange, 103
American Telephone & Telegraph Company
  (AT&T), 147, 511
AMK Corporation, 304, 305

Amoco, 68, 654
AMR Corporation, 431
Anderson, Warren, 289, 295, 296
Anglo American Corporation, 265
Anheuser Busch, 457, 461–68
Apartheid, 263
Aponte, Angelo J., 142, 143, 144
Apple Computer, 266
Applegate, F. D., 82, 84, 85
Arkadelphia, Arkansas, 238–39
Arkus-Duntov, Yura, 108
Armco Steel Corporation, 597–605
Arthur Anderson & Co., 140
Arthur D. Little, Inc., 204–32, 267, 270
Asbestos, 343; *see also* Manville Corporation
   A-H Trust; *see* A-H Trust
   health effects, 366–68
Asbestos Textile Institute, 368
Asbestos Victims of America, 365
Ashland Oil, 154, 155
Associate Producer Program, 304
Atkins, Orkin E., 155
Atlantic Richfield, 515
Atkinson, Robert B., 490
Audi 5000, unintended acceleration, 579–87
Audi Victim's Network (AVN), 580
Augerson, William, 230, 231
Avco Corporation, 233–38
Avon, 68, 394
A & W Drive-Ins of Canada, Ltd, 304

Badaracco, Joseph L., 628
Badillo, Herman, 16
Bagamery, 114
Bahr, Morton, 513
Baker, Roger, 190
Baldo, Anthony, 209
Banana War, 302, 307
Bankers National Life Insurance company, 103
Banker's Trust, 320
Bank of America, 320
Bankruptcy, Chapter 11; *see* Chapter 11 bankruptcy
Banks, Jim, 111
Bare, Bobby, 242
Barker, Hugh A., 653
Barker, John E., 597, 598, 599, 602, 603, 604, 605
Barnes, Thomas, 598
Barnfather, Maurice, 191n
Barrons, 105
Bartels, Robert, 79

Bartlome, Robert, 156
Baruch, Wendy, 212
Baskin-Robbins, Inc., 304, 307
Baskins, 271
Basnight, Arvin O., 94, 95, 97
Bates, Mike, 425, 428, 429
Batts, Warren, 40, 43, 45, 47, 49, 59, 61, 62, 64
Baxter, William, 141
Bayer Company, 285
Bayless, Charles E., 651
BBDO International, 266
Beckett, J. Thomas, 356n
Beitzel, George B., 47, 55
Belkin, Samual, 312
Belli, Melvin, 295
Beneficial National Life, 112
Bennaton, Abraham, 302, 318
Bennie M. Barnet v. *Owens-Corning Fiberglass Corporation, Inc. et al*, 346n
Berman, Jerry, 513
Bernard, David M., 126
Bertin, J., 121n
Bhagwate, P. N., 294, 297
Bharat petroleum, 285
Bhopal, India, disaster, 277–301
   interviews with victims, 298–301
   legal battles, 292–94
   operations, 282–85
   settlement, 294–95
Bigart, Homer, 9n, 10n, 11n, 12n, 13n, 17n
Binham, Eula, 126
Bissell, Inc., 516, 517
Bjorn, Paul R., 648
Black, Eli, 302, 304–15
Black & Decker, 522
Blacks, hiring policies, 241, 242, 244
Blake, David H., 3n
Blanchard, Kenneth, 132
Blicker, Alan, 135
Block, John, 186
Bloem, Harry, 517
Blue, Brent, 521
Blue Cross and Blue Shield, 516
Blum, Alan, 519, 520
Blundell, William E., 110n
BMZ Materials, Inc., 354–55
Board of directors, 435
Boeing Corporation, 86, 89, 132, 134
   wage structure, 429
Boeing Vertel Company, 62n
Boesky, Ivan, 289
Bofors, Nobel, Inc., 659
Bogdan, Elizabeth, 547

Bogner, Leonard, 660
Bolling, Bruce C., 424
Bolling, Pete, 401, 409, 410
Bond, Floyd A., 490
Bond, William R., 47
Bonker, Don, 325
Booth, Wallace, 315, 318
Borel, Clarence, 345
Boston University Center for Applied Social
    Science, 70
Bosworth, Alfred, 26
Botha, P. W., 264, 265
Bow, Frank T., 155
Bowie, Robert, 108
Bragdon, Joseph, 70
Bralove, Mary, 305n, 315
Brandeis, Louis D., 508
Brandon, William T., 599
Braniff Airways, 154
Brewery Workers Union, 472, 473
Brewing industry, 460–68
Bridgestone, 259
Bright, H. R., 490
Brinkley, David, 445
Bristol-Myers Company, 31n, 38, 531, 535,
    545
Brocchini, Robert, 247
Brooke-Bond, 285
Brooks, Geraldine, 648
Brown, Clarence, 188, 189
Brown, Frederick, 516
Brown, Vandiver, 348, 367
Brunel, Wilson, 490
Brunner, Vernon, 545
Brunt, M., 123n
Bunker Hill Company, 80, 113, 114
Bunker Hill-Sullivan Company, 113
Bupp, Irving, 649
Burke, James E., 69, 133, 528, 529, 541,
    542, 544, 546
Burlington Industries, 382, 389
Burnham, D., 124n
Burnham and Company, 108
Business
    ethics, 79, 128–31
    ideology, 78
    media relations, 439
    openness of the system, 435
Business Council for Effective Literacy, 425
Business Roundtable, 132, 133
Business Services Package, 139
Butler, Robert A., 281
Butterfield, Alexander, 98
Byrne, John A., 80, 132

Caldicott, Helen, 619
California Farm Bureau Federation, 246,
    248, 249
California growers and illegal aliens,
    245–50
Caltex Petroleum, 272, 320–21
Calvert, James F., 490
Calvin, Geoffrey, 191n
Campbell's Soup, 251
Cancellier, Philip, 518
Cardillo, Robert M., 654
Carroll, Paul B., 192n
Carson, James, 319
Carter, Jimmy, 177, 606, 646
Carter, Ron, 197n
Cascade Holistic Economic Consultants
    (CHEC), 655
Cassedy, John F., 405
Castleman, Barry I., 344n
Caterpillar Tractor Company, 166, 177, 180,
    182, 183, 184
    Code of Worldwide Business Conduct,
    327–37
Cavanaugh, Gerald, 78
CBS News, 439–55
Celeron, 262
Centanni, Frederick, Jr., 216
Center for Auto Safety (CAS), 580
Center for Science in the Public Interest,
    251
Center for Study of Responsible Law, 143
Center for Work Performance Problems, 511
Chalfen, Melvin, 214, 215, 229, 231
Champion International Corporation, 132
Chandler, Robert, 439
The Change Masters (Kanter), 69
Chappell, Bill, 234
Chapter 11 bankruptcy
    Manville Corporation, 349–55
    reorganization under, 371–76
Chase Manhattan, 320
Chavez, Cesar, 12, 247, 305
Chavez, Paul, 247
Cheek, Leslie, 660
Chemical Bank, 133, 320
Chemical industry, 631–33
    Kepone, 634–37, 645
Chetley, Andy, 38n
Childs, Delafield, 99
Chimerine, Larry, 326
Choate, Robert, 37
Christensen, Roland, 210
Christian Century, 17
Chrysler Corporation, 134, 147

Chrysler Corporation (*Continued*)
  minority hiring problems, 242, 243
  productivity, 421
CIBA-GEIGY, 285
Cigna, 522
Cincinnati Gas & Electric Company, 649
  Zimmer plant, 650–51
Citibank, 320
City Investing, 266
Civil Rights Act of 1964, 120, 340
Clare, David R., 134, 520
Clarence Borel v. *Fibreboard Paper Products
  Corporation et al*, 345n
Clark, Arva R., 40
Clark, Frederick A., 549
Clark, Matthew, 156, 157
Clark, Ramsey, 16
Clark, Robert, 260
Clark, William J., 490, 491
Clauss, C., 121n
Clean Air Act (1970), 594, 632
Clean Water Act (1977), 633, 636
Clean Water Action Project (CWAP), 211
Clinton, Bill, 240
Coca-Cola, 251, 252, 272
  operations in India, 285
Code of Worldwide Business Conduct, Cater-
  pillar Tractor Company, 327–37
Coking process, 600–2
Cole, Robert E., 241, 242
Collingwood, C. Gilbert, 315
Collins, David, 540, 543
Commission on Industrial Competitiveness,
  325, 326
Committee for the Re-Election of the Presi-
  dent (CREEP), 153, 154, 155, 156
Committee for Responsible Genetics, 228
Commonwealth Literacy Campaign, 425
Communications Workers of America
  (CWA), 513
Compensation Commissioner for Occupa-
  tional Diseases (South Africa), 322
Condon, Verner H., 626
Conger, Kenneth, 430
Connecticut General Life, 107
Connecticut Mutual, 477
Connor, John T., 629, 630
Conservation Foundation, 654
Consumer Product Safety Act of 1972, 634
Consumer unions, 68
Consumer welfare, 523–24
  product information, 523

Conti, Leroy J., 151
Continental Airlines, 94
Continental Illinois National Bank, 186,
  191, 320
Control Data Corporation, employee dis-
  missal policies, 517–18
Convair, 82, 92, 93
Conway, Jill Ker, 210
Conway, Mimi, 381n, 391n, 392n, 394n
Coors, Adolph, III, 472
Coors, Jeffery, 460
Coors, Joseph, 460, 469, 472
Coors, Joseph, Jr., 460
Coors, Peter, 460, 469, 475
Coors, William K., 456, 475
Coors Food Products Company, 459
Coors Golden Recycle Company, 459
Coors Porcelain Company, 459
Corbett, Matthew, 424
Corn, Morton, 127, 645
"Cornell Report," 37
Corporations
  control, 436
  financial disclosure, 435
  manslaughter charges, 590–91
  social responsibility, 49
Cortese, Anthony, 222
Council for Environmental Quality, 593
Council of Better Business Bureaus, 252
Council on Competitiveness, 326
Council on Economic Priorities (CEP), 4, 70,
  598
Cowell, Joe, 325
Cox, Archibald, 390n
Cox, David O., 20, 26, 28, 31
Cox, Frederic, 615
Cox, Tracy, 547
Craft, Christine, 515
CREEP; *see* Committee for the Re-Election
  of the President
Creitz, Walter M., 609, 615, 626
Crouch, Edmund, 216
Crowell-Collier Company, 171
Crum & Forster, 660
Cull, Michael, 201n
Cummins Engine, 139
Cuomo, Mario, 652
Cushenan, Ian, 156
Cuthbertson, Eugene, 101
Curtis, M. C., 82, 85
Cyr, Ed, 212, 213, 216, 218, 219, 224, 227
Cyr, Nancy, 214

Dahl, Jonathan, 354n
Dalkin Shield, 374, 549-72
Dana Corporation, 169, 243
Daniel, Dan, 233, 236, 237, 238
D'Aveni, 371
Davis, David R., 86
Davis, Elmer, 443
Davis, Hugh, 549, 550
Davis, Milton, 239
Davis-Douglas Aircraft Company, 86
Davis Polk and Wardwell, 349, 355
Dayton Power & Light Company, 650
DC-10, 81, 82, 83, 84, 88-92
Deakins, Harold, 439, 448, 449
DeBardeleben, Newton H., 47
De Beers, 317
Deberardinis, Lou, 216
DeCastro, Julio O., 259
Deere & Company, 176, 177, 180, 182, 183
Defense spending in United States, 324-27
DeGeorge, Gail, 508
Dellums, Congressman, 38
Del Monte, 251, 521
Delta Airlines, 88
Deo, M. V., 297
Designated Engineering Representatives
    (DERs), 94
DeStefano, Joe, 641
Dibble, Robert, 156
Dickinson, Bill, 234, 236, 237
Dicks, Norm, 236, 237
Dillon, David, 517
Di Nunno, J. G., 387, 389n, 392n
Directors responsibilities, 12-76
    audit committee, 73-76
    inside, 73
    Mead Corporation, 55-57
    outside, 72
Dirks, Raymond, 99, 100, 101, 108n, 109
Divestment issue in South Africa, 266-67,
    319-24
Doerfer, John C., 444
Dolin, Eric Jay, 654
Doriot, George F., 314, 315
Double-breasting, 420
Douglas, Donald, 86
Douglas Aircraft Company, 86
Dow Chemical, 69, 640, 647, 656-57
Dresser Industries, Inc., 166, 272
Drexel, Burnham & Lambert, 497, 505-6
Drive Trust, 205
Drucker, Peter F., 255, 256, 420

Dumex, 22, 29
DuPont Corporation, 127, 513, 654
Duprey, Robert, 662
Durling-Shyduroff, Richard, 212
Duston, Robert L., 509

Eastern Airlines, 88, 508
Ebasco Services, Inc., 591
Economic Policy Institute, 325
Eddy, Paul, 82n, 98
Edens, Lloyd, 112
Edison Electric Institute, 605
Edwards and Hanley brokerage firm, 108
Egberg, John, 326
Eggert, William, 81
Elkhorn Bank and Trust Company, 239, 240
Elkins, Herschel, 589
El Paso, Texas, 10-11
Emerson Electric Company, 511
Employee discharge, 514-19
    Control Data Corporation, 517-18
Employee Retirement Income Security Act
    of 1974, 340
Emshwiller, John E., 587
Energy
    nuclear, 606-27
    oil and gas, 629-30
Environment
    air pollution, 593-605
    chemical industry, 632-47
    free-market environmentalism movement,
        654-58
    hazardous waste disposal, 656-62
    nuclear plants, 606-27
Environmental Action Coalition, 654
Environmental Defense Fund, 646
Environmental Law Institute, 654
Environmental laws, 632-34
Environmental Protection Agency (EPA)
    air pollution, 602
    Armco Steel Company, 599-605
    chemical pollution, 637-39, 646, 658
    cleanup of hazardous waste dumps,
        659-62
    nuclear power, 618-19
Epstein, Richard A., 432
Equal Employment Opportunity Commis-
    sion (EEOC), 115, 125, 241, 473, 475
Equity Funding Corporation of America,
    99-112

Equity Funding Life Insurance Company (EFLIC), 99, 104, 105, 107
Equity Growth Fund of America, 103
Esposito, Domenick, 140, 141
Ethical pharmaceuticals, 547
Ethics
    advertising, 141–46
    bottom line, 135–40
    corporations, 128–31
    codes, 23, 132–35, 327–37
    Reagan administration, 77
    small business, 140–41
Ethics Resource Center, 139, 140
Evans, Randy, 51, 59
Evans, Thomas, 158
Ever-Ready Company, Ltd., 279
Exclusionary hiring policies, 115–18, 123, 125–27
Exxon, 654
Exxon Chemical Americas, 656

Fantasia, Joseph, 216
Farah, Kenneth, 5n, 17
Farah, William F., 5, 12, 18
Farah Manufacturing Company, 3, 5–19
Feder, Barnaby J., 521
Federal Aviation Administration, 93–98
Federal Bureau of Investigation, Identification Division, 513
Federal Coal Mine Health and Safety Act, 633
Federal Election Campaign Act of 1971, 154
Federal Trade Commission (FTC), 251, 647
Federal Water Pollution Control At of 1972, 63, 646
Federal Wildlife Protection Laws, 634
Federated Department Stores, 515
Federated Development Company, 502
Feinberg, Larry, 543, 545
Fennelly, Paul, 216
Ferrarese, Joe, 96, 97
Fiat-Allis, 177
Field, Anne R., 508
Finley, James D., 380, 381, 391, 393, 394
Finnegan, Thomas J., Jr., 483
Finzen, Bruce A., 295
Firestone, 270, 321
Firing of employees; see Employee discharge
First Boston Corporation, 355
First Chicago, 320
First National Bank of Fairmont, West Virginia, 518
First National Citibank (New York), 285

Fisher, Max M., 315, 316, 318
Fitzpatrick, Robert B., 509
Flannery, Thomas A., 646
Flegal, David W., 546
Fleming, Susan, 125
Fleshman, Michael, 319
Flynn, Raymond, 424
Flynn, Thomas, 145
Foeche, Terry, 657
Ford, Gerald, 456, 458, 640, 646
Ford, Henry, 511, 653
Ford, Henry II, 653–54
Ford Foundation, 653
Ford Motor Company, 173, 175–77, 183, 242, 272
    Pinto case, 591, 592
    productivity, 421, 423
    South Africa, 265, 266, 321, 322
Foreign Corrupt Practices Act (1971), 435
Foreign Exchange Regulation Act, 285
Fort Wayne, Indiana, 161–203
    bidding war with Harvester, 188–95
    comparison with Springfield, Ohio, 169
    history and description, 168–70
Foster, Lawrence G., 542
Frank, Hillary, 211, 212
Frank, Richard N., 490
Frankel, James R., 486, 488
Franklin Research and Development, 69
Frederick, William C., 3n
Freeman, Edward F., 513
Free-market environmentalism, 595, 654–55
Freightliner, 173, 174
Frohnmayer, David, 251, 253
Frye, Paul M., 210
Fudim, Allan, 543
Fuji Heavy Industry Ltd., 242

GAF Corporation, 288–89
Gallaher, Thomas, 230
Gallop, Robert M., 314, 315
Gandhi, Indira, 285
Gant, Donald R., 314, 316
Gardner, George P., Jr., 311, 313, 314, 316
Gardner, LeRoy U., 367
Garlinghouse, F. Mark, 315, 316
Garrett Corporation, 235, 236, 238
Garza, Paul, 12, 13
Gaskin, Richard, 592
Gates, Quepec, 50, 61
Guadrault, Robert J., 490
Geist, Herbert, 481, 485, 486, 487, 488
Geist, Millicent, 482, 492

Gelsthorpe, Edward, 307, 312–16, 318
General Brewery, 463
General Dynamics Corporation, 92–93
General Electric Company, 62n, 168, 272,
    325, 517, 654
General Foods
    divestment in South Africa, 265, 266
    tobacco industry, 521
General Mills, 133, 134
General Motors Corporation, 125, 127, 173,
    175, 241, 242, 321, 322, 521
    productivity, 421, 423
    South Africa, 272
General Public Utilities Corporation, 606,
    607–9
Genesee Brewery, 462, 463, 467
Gerstner, William, 447, 449, 452, 453
Gettman, Frank, 225
Getty Oil, 147
Getzendanner, Susan, 485, 486, 487
Ghaphery, Elizabeth, 547
Gibson, Thomas, 486
Gikes, George X., 544
Ginter, James L, 1n
Glaser, Herbert, 108
Glaxo, 22, 29
Glenn, John, 620
Global market, 255
Goadner, Judith B., 542n, 546n
Goggin, Malcolm L., 214
Gokhali, V. P., 282
Gold, R., 123n
Goldblum, Stanley, 101, 102, 108, 109, 110
Golde, Paul, 588, 590
Goldman, J. D., 316
Goldman, J. E., 313, 314, 316
Goldstein, Richard, 216
Goldwater, Barry, 237, 238
Good, Paul, 446n
Goodrich, B. F., 169
Goodwin, Richard, 345, 347, 349
Goodyear Tire and Rubber company, 154,
    258, 259–76
    history of company, 259
    South African relations, 267–76, 321
Gould, William B., 511, 518
Government
    regulation, 148
    relation to business, 47–49
Gqweta, Thozamile, 322
Grace, W. R., 211, 218
Granite Construction Company, 591, 592
Gray, Paul E., 210
Gray, William, III, 267

Greany, John, 229
Great Central Life, 107
Greensher, Joseph, 590
Greiner, Ted, 37
Gresham, Samuel, 244
Greyhound Corporation, two-tier wage
    structure, 429, 431
Griggs, William N., 490
Groseclose, Everett, 153n, 158n, 160n
Gross, Leonard, 99, 101, 108
Gross, Lisa, 191n
Grossman, Dan, 212
Grzwinski, Ronald, 238, 239, 240
Gulf Oil, 154, 155
Gulf Resources, 113, 114, 118, 119
Gulf and Western Americas Corporation,
    257
Gutek, B., 113n

H. P. Hood, Inc., 318
H-2 program, 248
Hafer, Fred, 624
Hafner, Katherine, M., 508
Hailey, Arthur, 627
Halberstam, David, 443n
Hall, Bob, 393
Hall, Zedie, 239, 240
Halley, James, 115, 118, 119
Hallingby, Paul, Jr., 490
Hallisey, Robert, 218, 219, 221, 229
Hambrick, 371
Hanson, Kirk O., 134
Hardesty, Rex, 10n, 12n, 17n
Harless, John, 518
Harrington, Arthur, 16
Harris, Judith, 229, 231
Harris, Monroe, 368
Harris, Rennick, 247
Harris, Roy J., 429
Harris, W., 125
Hart, Gary, 620
Hartigan, Neil, 581
Hartke, Vance, 155, 646
Haskins & Sells, 107
Hauptfuhrer, Barbara A., 490
Hausmann, Marisa, 547
Hayden Stove, Inc., 108
Hayford, Warren, 183, 187
Hazardous Materials Transportation Act of
    1975, 633
Hazardous waste disposal, 656–57
Health Law Institute (Houston), 514
Health Research Group, 644

Hector, Gary, 402, 403, 404
Height, Dorothy, 16
Heileman Brewing Company, 147, 462, 463, 467
Helms, Jesse, 391
Herbert, Frank, 652
Herold, David, 511
Hershey, William, 201n
Hertz Corporation, 132, 134, 135
Hervey, Fred, 18
Hewlett-Packard, 139
Heyman, Samuel J., 288
Higgins, Kevin, 575
High-yield bonds, 505
Hikes, Judy, 426
Hill, Douglas, 273
Hill, G. Christian, 101
Hill, Gladwin, 594
Hill, Ivan, 140
Hindustan petroleum, 285
Hirschhorn, Joel S., 657
Hobby, Wilber, 391
Hochberg, Ann, 216
Hodges, Howard, 659
Hodgson, Godfrey, 444n
Hoeber, Amaretta, 230
Hoerr, John, 508
Hofmann, John, 243
Holcombe, E. J., 625
Holman, Bud, 295
Holusha, John, 339
Honda Motor company, 241, 243, 244
    all-terrain vehicles, 588
    minority hiring, 241, 243, 244-45
    productivity, 421
Honduras, Republec of, 302, 307, 317
Hooker Chemical Company, 225
Hopper, Pat, 111
Horrigan, Edward A., Jr., 520
Howe, Irving, 16
HRD Department, Inc., 427
Hricko, A., 122, 123n
Hubbard, David, 60
Hudepohl Brewing Company, 467
Hulce, J. T., 353
Human investment, 339-43
Humphrys and Glasgow, Pvt. Ltd, 282
Hurwitz, Charles, 501-5
Hyatt, J., 122n
Hyde, Dayton, 655
Hurt, J. B., 82, 85, 86

I. Magnin, 518
Iacocca, Lee, 134, 183

IBH Holding, 177
IBM, 67-68, 147, 272, 511
    AIDS issues, 511
    India operations, 285
    South Africa, 322
    work rules and job classification, 422
    wrongful discharge suits, 515, 518
Idaho Human Rights Commission, 117
Ideal Basic Industries, 347
Ideology, 78
Illegal aliens, 245-50
Illinois Pollution Control Board, 440
Illinois Power Company, 439-55
    Clinton power plant, 441-43
    "60 Minutes," 447-55
Illiteracy, 425, 426
Immigration and Nationality Act, 248
Imports, 256
India Institutes of Technology, 289, 291
Indian Foreign Exchange Regulation Act, 281
Indian Oil Corporation, 285
Industrial Credit and Investment Corporation of India (ICIC), 285, 288
Industrial Health Foundation, 368
Industrial Hygiene Foundation of America, 367
Industry regulation, 250-54
Infant formula, 20-39
Infant Formula Action Committee (INFACT), 20, 38
Infant Nutrition Bill of 1979, 38-39
Ingells, Douglas J., 88n
Ingram, J. Berkley, Jr., 490
Ingrassia, Paul, 183n
Inouye, Daniel K., 156, 159
Inselbuch, Elihu, 379
Institute for Energy Analysis of Oak Ridge Associated Universities, 617
Insurance industry, 477
    hazardous waste cleanup, 659-62
    restructuring, 101
Interfaith Center on Corporate Responsibility (ICCR), 20, 22, 26, 521-22
International Association of Machinists, 508
International Code of Marketing Ethics, 23
International Computers Indian Manufacturers (ICIM), 285
International Council of Infant Formula Industries (ICIFI), 22, 23
International Harvester Company, 161-203
    description of company, 172-78
        agricultural equipment, 176-77
        construction equipment, 177-78
        trucks, 173-76

International Harvester Company
(*Continued*)
disinvestment in South Africa, 266
history of company, 178
International management, 255
cultural conflicts, 257
measurement of international transfers,
255
multinational companies, 256
social responsibility, 257
International Pediatrics Association, 34
International Union of Electrical Workers,
430
Intrauterine devices (IUDs), 548
Investor Responsibility Research Center,
265
Investors Overseas Services, 103
Isuza Motors, Ltd, 243

J. C. Penney Company, 139
J. I. division of Tenneco, 176, 177
J. P. Morgan Company, 320
J. P. Stevens & Company, Inc., 380–94
subsidiaries, 382–85
union issues, 388–89
working conditions, 392–94
J. P. Stevens Employees Education Commit-
tee (JPSEEC), 391
Jackson, 374
Jackson, Brooks, 233
Jackson, Henry, 155n
Jackson, James K., III, 543
Jackson, Marlin, 240
Janson, Roy, 587
Japan, 324, 325, 326
employee-employer relations, 339
productivity, 421–23
Jeffries, Boyd, 289
Jelliffe, Derrick, 37
Jensen, Michael C., 154n
Jersey Central Power & Light Company,
607, 614, 615, 623
John Birch Society, 473
John Hancock Company, literacy programs,
427
John Morrell & Company, 304
Johns-Manville Canada, 354
Johns-Manville Corporation, 344; *see also*
Manville Corporation
Johnson, Alan, 188n, 190n, 196n, 201n
Johnson, Douglas, 38
Johnson, Harvey, 302
Johnson, Marlene, 427
Johnson, Robert, 80, 141

Johnson, Robert Wood, 529
Johnson & Johnson, 68, 69, 133, 134, 136,
511
Tylenol cyanide crisis, 525–46
Johnson Wax company, 139
Johnston, Robert Gilbert, 486, 488
Jones, Alfred W., 46
Joseph, Raymond A., 349n
Junk bonds, 505
Jurmo, Paul, 425, 426

Kahl, J. J., "Bucky," 244
Kalmbach, Herbert W., 154
Kane, Michael J., 244
Kanter, Michael, 212
Kanter, Rosabeth, 69
Kaplan, Maurice C., 314, 315, 316
Karatsu, Hajime, 421, 423
Karmin, Monroe W., 156n, 157n
Karnes, William, 191
Karrh, Bruce W., 120, 513
Kassapian, Susan, 142
Kawasaki Heavy Industries, Ltd., 588
Keenan, John F., 296
Kelley, John B., 234, 235, 236
Kelley, Wendell, 439, 442, 451
Kelly, Brian, 635
Kemeny, John G., 619
Kemper International Fund, 267
Kendrick, Alexander, 443, 444n
Kendrick, J., 114n, 118n
Kennedy, Edward, 13, 38, 153, 230, 620
Kennedy, John F., 444
Kennedy, Robert D., 297
Kentucky Central Life, 107
Kenworth, 173, 174
Kepone, 634–37, 645
Kerrigan, John, 430
Kessell, Daniel, 156
Keystone mutual funds, 102
Kienbaum, Karen, 516
Kilbourn, Frederick, 355
Kilpatrick, Bob, 141
King, Edward, 484
Kinsman Marine Transit Company, 152
Klauber, Edward, 443
Knapp, Fred, 201n
Knipe, W. Stan, 143
Koenigsberg, Paul, 142
Komatsu, 177, 187
Koten, John, 80, 141
Kotlowitz, Alex, 238
Kraft, Inc., 251, 252
Kreig, Peter, 37

Krekel, S., 122n
Krikorian, Robert, 80, 135
Krisky, Sheldon, 214, 215, 216, 231
Kristol, Irving, 80, 127n, 128
Krukewitt, Larry, 191, 196, 201
Kueale, Dennis, 531n, 544n
Kuglin, J., 117n
Kuhn, Bowie, 160
Kuhne, William G., 606, 615, 620, 624–27
Kutner, Stephen I., 70
Kwong, Jo Ann, 651
Kyle, Peter, 354

Labor unions
    Adolph Coors strike, 457, 472–73
    J. P. Stevens, 388–89
    SCA Corporation, 410–11
    two-tier hiring, 429–32
Lakeway Chemical Company, 659
Lambert, Roger, 244, 245
Lancaster, Hal, 101
Landmark Bank of St. Louis, 661
Land use laws, 634
Lanza, A. J., 366
Larwood, L., 113n
Latham, Michael, 37
Lave, Charles, 583
Lazarus, Maurice, 490
Leaderer, Bob, 466n
League of Latin American Citizens
    (LULAC), 475
Leape, 271
Leedon, Boyd, 390
Leishman, Katie, 619n
Leslie, Robert L., 591
Levine, Aaron M., 553, 554
Levy, Leonard, 9
Levy, Stan, 379
Lehman Brothers, 108
Leininger, Kevin, 203
Lennox, Donald, 161, 189, 190, 191, 200
Lepkowski, Stanley, 157
LeSoravage, Joan, 547
Lever Brothers (Hindustan Lever in India),
    285
Levin, Fred, 107, 111
Levins, Philip L., 214
Levins Laboratory, 223, 227, 229
Lewis, Arthur, 112
Liberman, James R., 625
Liebman, Bonnie, 519
Lie detectors, 510, 511–12
Life Science Products, 635

Lincoln Center for Ethics (Tempe, Arizona),
    132
Lindsay, John, 13, 16
Lipnick, Stanley, 143
Lipstein, Benjamin, 546
Lipton Company, 285
Literacy skills in the workplace, 425–29
    company programs, 426–29
    functional literacy, 425
Little, Arthur Dehon, 209
Litton Industries, Inc., 108
Lively, Robert, 78n, 147n
Livingston, Gayle, 108
Lockheed Corporation, 86, 88, 147
    wage contracts, 430
Lodge, George C., 628
Loeffler, Robert, 109, 110, 111
Long Island Lighting Company (Lilco), 649
    Shoreham plant, 652
Loomis, Carol J., 182n, 183
Lopez, Oswaldo, 317
Loud, Helen, 108
Louisville Trust Company v. Johns-Manville
    Corporation, 346
Lovdahl, Michael L., 40
Love, John A., 347
Love, Robi, 60
Lowell, Samuel B., 108
Lobar, Sheldon B., 490
Lublin, Joann S., 514
Lumber industry, 501
Lunt, Samuel D., Sr., 314, 316
Lyndenberg/Marlin/Strub 67n

M-1 tank, 233, 236
McAteir, J. Davitt, 392
McCardell, Archie, 180–83, 187, 188, 191–92
McClellan, Craig, 588
McCormack, Mike, 620
McCormick, Brooks, 180
McCormick, Bryce, 82
McCormick, Cyrus, 178–83
McCormick, Fowler, 180
McCormick, Gordon, 100, 101
McCormick Harvesting Machine Company,
    175
McCullough, Donald F., 490
McCulloch Company, 502
McDaniel, Joseph M., 314, 316
McDonald's, 251
McDonnell Douglas Corporation, 81
    two-tier wage structure, 430, 432

McGeehan, Stanley M., 323
McGinnis, Thomas, 528
McGovern, George, 12
McGowen, Jackson, 94
McGraw-Hill, 515
McJames S., 87
McKinney, John A., 347, 349, 352, 353, 368, 378
Mack Trucks, 173, 174, 175
MacLeod, William, 252
McNeil Consumer Products, 525, 526, 531, 540, 541, 544
McSweeney, Edward, 4, 72
McSwiney, James W., 40, 43, 45–50, 57, 60
Mager, John, 204, 210, 219–22, 226, 231, 232
Magnavox, 168
Maidenberg, H. J., 303n
Maisonpierre, Andre, 660
Majerus, Frank, 111
Malan, General, 322
Malley, 9n, 12n, 13n, 17n
Malone, John J., 216
Malone, Paul, 423
Malone, Phillip, 423
Maloney, Walter H., 18
Management Control Systems, Inc., 400–410
Management Horizons, 142
Mandela, Nelson, 264
Manufacturers Hanover Trust, 320, 381, 394
Manville Corporation, 343–79
    bankruptcy, 349–51
    company background, 345–49
    financial summaries, 369–71, 376–78
    managers' benefits, 351–56
    victim's benefits, 356–64
Manville Forest Products Corporation, 350, 355, 361
Marble Hill nuclear plant, 652
Margulies, Leah, 21, 22, 26, 38
Marine Protection Research and Sanctuaries Act of 1972, 634
Marlin, John A., 70
Marshall Field's, 519
Marsh & McLennan, 522
Martin, Glen L., 86
Martin, James R., 478, 482–86, 490, 491
Martin, Philip, 247, 249
Martinelli, Jack, 216
Maryland Bank and Trust company, 661
Mason, Bob, 244
Massachusetts Mutual Life Insurance Company, 477–96
    company background, 478–81

Massachusetts Mutual Life Insurance Company (*Continued*)
    proxy battle with dissident stockholders, 481–96
Massachusetts Mutual's Policyholders Committee, 482, 486–89
Massey-Ferguson, Ltd, 176, 177, 182, 183
Mautner, Henry, 216
Mavroules, Nicholas, 233, 234
Maxxam Group, Inc., 497, 503–4
Mazda Motor Corporation, 242
Mazzoli, Romano, 246
Mead, George H., 40, 41
Mead, H. Talbott, 47
Mead, Nelson S., 47
Mead Corporation, 40–76
    Corporate Responsibility Committee (CRC), 40, 46
    Operating Policy Committee (OPC), 45
Mead Johnson Company, 21, 29
Mead Pulp and Paper Company, 40
Media, 2
    relations with business, 439
    television news, 443–47
    Tylenol cyanide crisis, 542–43
Melcher, John, 157
Melgar, Juan Alberto, 317
Mellon National Bank, 661
Meltzer, Donald, 312, 314
Menk, Louis W., 191, 192
Mercedes-Benz, 587
Mercer, Robert E., 260
Merchant Marine Act of 1936, 153
Mergers and acquisitions, 436, 506–7
    beer industry, 466
Merhige, Robert R., Jr., 555
Merrill, R. L., 640, 643
Metromedia, Inc., 515
Metropolitan Edison Company, 606, 607, 609–16
    nuclear power involvement, 614–16
Metzger, Roger, 188n
Metzger, Sidney M., 13, 14, 16, 17
Metzger, William, 225
Mexican farm workers in California, 245–50
Meyer, Herbert E., 347n
Meyerson, Bess, 16
Michelin, 259
Midatlantic National Bank of New Jersey, 661
Miller, Paul F., Jr., 47
Miller Brewing Company, 457, 460–68
Milliken, Michael, 505
Mills, D. Quinn, 429, 431

Mills, Wilbur, 155n
Milstein, Seymour, 315, 316
Minimum wage, 340
Minnesota Mining and Manufacturing (3M), 154, 656, 657
Minority hiring practices, 241–45
    Boston fire department, 423–25
    Japanese auto makers, 244–45
Minow, Newton, 444
Mitchell, Cynthia F., 353n
Mitchell, John, 154
Mitsubishi Motor Corporation, 243
Mobil Oil, 272, 321
Molitor, 588
M-1 tank, 233, 236
Monsanto Company, 654, 658, 661
Moore, Arch, 293, 296
Moore, Thomas, 540n, 541n, 542n
Moran, Sharon, 212, 224, 226
Morgan Stanley and Company, 349, 363
Morin, Howard, 660
Moses, Winfield, 189, 196, 200, 201
Mosher, Charles A., 155
Moskowitz, Milton, 18n
Motley, Ronald L., 346n, 359, 379
Moyer, Phillip C., 405
Mueller, Bob, 482, 483
Mueller, Robert K., 210, 490
Mukhoty, Gobinda, 295, 298
Mullen, Nancy, 250
Muller, H. R., 32n, 33n, 36n
Muller, Mike, 20n
Multinational corporations (MNCs), 255
    corporate control, 257
    production sharing, 256
Multinational Monitor, 319
Munoz, Jesse, 17
Murai, Paul, 247
Murphy, Brian, 427, 428
Murphy, Burdette, 430
Murrow, Edward R., 443
Musselman, James, 143
Mutz, John, 189, 203
Myers, Mildred S., 3n

Nabisco Brands, Inc., 426, 521
Nader, Ralph, 644, 647
Naj, Amal Kumar, 658–62
Nakasone, Yasuhiro, 245
Nash, Bob, 240
Nash, Laura L., 134
National Accidents Sampling System (NASS), 585

National Airlines, 94
National Association of Attorneys-General, 250
National Audubon Society, 654
National Bank of Fredericksburg, Virginia, 661
National Carbide Company (India), Ltd., 279
National Coffee Association, 251
National Conference on Business Ethics, 350, 364, 365
National Economic Research Associates, Inc., 618
National Environmental Policy Act (1970), 632
National Highway Traffic Safety Administration (NHTSA), 578, 579, 585
National Labor Relations Act (NLRA) (Wagner Act), 388, 389
National Labor Relations Board (NLRB), 17, 18, 19, 388
National Steel, 598
National Transportation Safety Board (NTSB), 84, 94
National Wildlife Federation, 654
National Women's Health Network, 555
Natural Resources Defense Council, 646
Nature Conservancy, 595, 655
NBC, 445
Nederlander, James, 159
Nelson, Gaylord, 13, 548
Nestle, 21, 37, 38
Nestle Alimentana, 22, 29
Newell, Barbara W., 490
New York City, disinvestment in South Africa, 267
New York City Department of Human Affairs, 141
New York Life, 394
New York Public Interest Research Group (NYPIRG), 580, 585
New York Times, 303, 444
Nissan Motor company, 242, 243, 421, 587
Nixon, Richard, 98, 151, 153, 156
Noise Control Act of 1972, 634
Nonmetallic Mine and Safety Act, 633
North Cambridge Toxic Alert Coalition, 211
Northern Life Insurance Company, 103
Northwest Airlines, 520
Norton Company, 139
Nuclear power industry, 606–7, 648–53
    debate over future of industry, 617–19
Nuclear Regulatory Commission (NRC), 440, 606, 618–19, 652

Oak Industries, 266
Occupational Safety and Health Act of 1970, 120, 340, 633, 637
Occupational Safety and Health Administration (OSHA), 116, 117, 119, 120, 125, 126, 392
Occupational Safety and Health Review Commission (OSHRC), 117
Ocean Spray Cranberries, Inc., 132
Ochoa, Bob, 111
O'Connor, John, 211, 212, 216, 218, 219, 224, 228
Office of Technology Assessment (OTA), 656
Ogilvie & Mathes, 145
Olasky, Marvin, 654
O'Leary, John F., 616
O'Leary, Meghan, 425
Olin, John, 127
Olin Corporation, 127
Olincraft Corporation, 347, 349
Oliver, Daniel, 252
Oliver, Janet, 239, 240
Olson, Frank A., 134, 135
Olson, Fred, 517, 518
Olympia Brewery, 462, 463, 467
Ombudsman, 62, 64–66
Onan Corporation, 428
The One Hundred Best Companies to Work for in America, 69
One Minute Manager (Blanchard), 132
Operation Stronghold, 655
Oppliger, James, 591
Orr, Robert, 188, 189
Osborne, David, 239
Ostro, Justin, 430, 431
O'Toole, John, 251
O'Toole, Randall, 655
Ozonoff, David, 216, 224, 226, 228, 231

Pabst Brewing Company, 462, 463
Paccar, 173, 174, 183
Pacific Gas & Electric Co., 590
Pacific Lumber Company, 497
Page, Bruce, 82n
Palefsky, Cliff, 510, 518
Pan American World Airways, 265
Panetta, Leon, 248
Parke-Davis, 285
Parker, G. Earl, 346n, 353
Pasciuto, Charles, 431
Pastin, Mark, Jr., 132
Pathak, R. S., 297
Paul, Elias, 314, 316

Pauly, D., 120n
Peale, Norman Vincent, 132
Pearce, John A., 251n, 259
Pearson, James B., 637
Peat, Marwick, Mitchell, 109
Peeples, Porter G., 245
Penner, Gary, 188n
Pennsylvania Electric Company, 607, 615
Pennsylvania Life Insurance Company, 102, 105
People's Express, 69
PepsiCo, 251, 265, 266
Pergament, Russell, 230, 231
Perkins-Elmer Company, 266
Person, Ister, 60
Pesticide control laws, 633
Peterbilt, 173, 174
Peters, Thomas J., 528n
Phibro-Salomon, 266
Philip Morris 68, 460, 467, 519
Phillips, Bert E., 490
Phillips Petroleum, 154
Physicians for Social Responsibility, 619
PICS (Productivity Improvement and Communication Systems), 400–410
Pittsburgh & Midway Coal Mining Company, 122
Pittsburgh Brewery, 463
Placido, John Paula, 216
Platt, Raymond, 101
Pluta, Joseph, 465n
Polaroid, 67
    educational programs for employees, 426–27
Political Action Committees (PACs), 233
Polygraph testing, 510, 511–12
Porter, Bruce, 343
Porter, J. Winston, 659
Potter, Elaine, 82n
Powell, Barbara, 426–27
Prairie Alliance, 443
Presidential Life Insurance Company of America, 103, 105
Price Waterhouse, 317
Privacy, right to, 508
    AIDS discrimination, 511
    confidentiality of employee records, 512
    drug testing, 509
    genetic screening, 513–14
    monitoring, 513
Procter & Gamble, 519
Product charts, 70–71
Production sharing in international business, 256

Productivity, 420
  American compared to Japanese, 421
  job rules and restrictions, 421–23
Productivity Improvement and Communication Systems (PICS), 400–410
Product Stewardship Program (Dow Chemical), 640
Proprietary Association, 544
Protein Advisory Group (PAG), 34–36
Protex Industries, 661–62
Public Service Company of Indiana, 649
  Marble Hill plant, 652–53
Public Service Company of New Hampshire, 649
  Seabrook nuclear plant, 651
Public utilities, 439–40
  nuclear power, 440, 441–42, 646–51
  rates, 440, 442
  regulation, 439–40
Puckett, Roscoe E., Jr., 555
Pundsak, Fred L., 368

Quicksel, Stephen W., 365n
Quinn, Joe, 196n
Quinn, Peter, 482, 483, 485, 486

Rakowsky, Judy, 201n
Ramirez, Alex, 141
Randolph, A. Philip, 16
Randolph, Jackson H., 651
R&D programs, 326
Ranger National Life Insurance Company, 104, 107, 108
Ransome-Kuti, Olikoye, 33n
Rapp, Gerald D., 50, 52, 53, 55, 56, 59, 60
Rather, Dan, 446
Rating America's Corporate Conscience, 4, 67, 68, 70–71
Rauscher, Frank, 645
Rawling, James, 323
"Raybestos-Manhattan Correspondence," 346
Raymark Corporation, 357, 358
Raymond, Arthur, 86
Reagan, Ronald, 264, 322, 323, 325, 326, 340, 436, 473, 512, 523
Reasoner, Harry, 446, 447, 449, 453
Regulation of industry, 250–54
Reid, Ogden, 16
Reilly, Jack, 197
Reinsuring, 104
Reitzes, Robert, 660
Relly, Gavin W. H., 265

Resource Conservation and Recovery Act of 1976 (RCRA), 633
Resources for the Future, 654
Restructuring insurance companies, 101
Reynolds, Burt, 458
Reynolds, Kim, 584
Rheingold, Paul, 550
Rhodes, James, 189
Ribicoff, Abraham, 305
Rice, George W., 477
Richards, Bill, 648
Richards, Robert, 54, 60, 64
Richardson-Vick, 545
Rifkind, Simon, 314, 315, 316
Rike, John R., 398, 406, 410
Riordan, Michael, 101, 102, 103
Rizzo, Paul J., 134
RJR Nabisco, 519–20
Roberts, Norbert J., 120
Robertson, Wyndham, 102n, 105n, 107n, 109n
Robins, Albert Hartley, 547
Robins, Claiborne, 547
Robinson, G., 124n
Robinson, Randall, 324
Robinson, Richard B., 257n
Rocca, Earl, 247, 249
Rockwell International Corporation, 244
  ethical violations, 132
Rogers, Raymond, 394
Rohrbaugh, John C., 511
Rose, Charlie, 211, 212, 218
Rosenberger, Larry, 547
Rosendahl, Donald, 245, 246, 247, 249
Rosendahl Farms, 249
Rosenthal, Thorn, 661
Ross, Stanley, 26
Rossiter, Anne, 367
Ross Laboratories, 25, 26–28
Rotbart, Dean, 354n
Rothstein, Mark A., 514
Roulston and Company, 152
Royal Crown Cola, 251
Rubenstein, Helena, 266
Rudolph, James, 95, 96, 97
Rutenberg, David, 486, 488

Saatchi & Saatchi DFSInc., 520
Safe Drinking Water Act of 1974, 633
Safer, Morley, 446
Safo, Paul, 509
Saltzman, Marshall, 126
Samuels, Sheldon W., 645
Sardas, Jacqus, 272

Sasser, James, 325
Sawyer, Alan G., 1n
Sayre, Judson, 108
SCA Corporation, 395–410
    finances, 397
    Management Control Systems, Inc.,
        400–410
    Productivity Improvement and Commu-
        nication Systems, 400–410
    products, 396
Schaefer Brewing Company, 467
Schafler, Norman I., 314, 315, 316
Scaletta, Phillip J., 591
Schiller, S. David, 555
Schlender, B., 119n, 126n
Schlesinger, Jacob M., 241
Schlitz Brewery, 147, 462, 465, 467
Schmidt Brewery, 463
Schnapp, Steve, 212, 224, 225, 226
Schoenbrun, David, 443
Schuldt, Robert, 61
Schwope, Art, 231
Seabrook plant, 651
Sears Roebuck, 141–46
    advertising, 519
Secrist, Ronald, 106, 109
Securities and Exchange Commission (SEC),
    158, 502
    action against American Ship, 159
    financial disclosure requirements, 435–36
    United Brands, 317
Seeger, John A., 204
Seemuth, Mike, 199n
Seidman and Seidman, 107
Seigler, David, 475
Selikoff, I. J., 368
Sevareid, Eric, 443
Seven-up, 251
Seymour Warden, 52, 56
Shabecoff, P., 120n
Shaffer, John H., 94, 95, 96, 98
Shanahan, Eileen, 157n
Shapiro, Leo, 145, 546
Sharpeville massacre, 263
Sharplin, Arthur, 277, 343, 350n, 353n
Shaw, Allan, 159
Sheets, George H., 47
Shell Oil Company, 660, 661
Shelton, Leland, 458
Shepard, Ira Michael, 510
Shepperly, Chester E., 368
Shere, Dennis, 188, 189–201
Shirer, William, 443
Shomer, 269
Shoreham power plant, 652

Shriver, Sargent, 13
Shue, Harold, 241
Shukla, Aseem, 277
Siegel, Jay, 515
Siegman, Henry, 16
Sierra Club, 654
Sigler, Andrew C., 132, 133
Signal Cos, 235
Silverman, Leon, 355, 379
Silverstein, Evan, 651
Simonides, Constantine, 56
Similac, 26, 27, 28
Simpson, Alan K., 246
Simpson, Sumner, 367
Simpson Oil, 246, 248, 249
Singer Co., 266
Singleton, Philip A., 490
"60 Minutes," 439–55
    Adolph Coors Company, 475
    Illinois Power company, 475
Sliff, Richard, 95
Smith, Edward J., 225
Smith, F. Allen, 431
Smith, Howard K., 443
Smith, Kenneth, 345, 346n, 367, 368
Smith, Marianne S., 356, 357n
Smith, Randall, 354
Smith, Timothy, 521–22
Smith International, 266
SMR Holding Company, 502
Snyder, Neil H., 547
Sobel, Arnold, 159
Social responsiveness, 1
    functional area of business, 3
    strategic plan of firm, 2
Solary, Stephen, 267
Soolman, Roberta, 425, 428
South Africa
    civil unrest, 263–65
    disinvestment, 266–67, 319–24, 521–22
South African Allied Workers Union, 322
South African Breweries, 265
South Korea, productivity, 422
South Shore Bank (Chicago), 239
Soweto, 263
Spater, George, 154, 155,
Specialty Vehicle Institute of America, 586
Spencer, William M., III, 47
Spiro, Peter, 542n
Springfield, Ohio, 161–203
    bidding war for Harvester, 188–95
    compared to Fort Wayne, 169
    history and description, 170–72
Stafford, Gordon, 156
Standard Oil of California, 321

Stanley, Thomas H., Jr., 47
Stanley Furniture Company, 41n, 43
Stans, Maurice, 154
Stapleton, Leo, 424
"Star Wars," 324
Stasch, Stanley, 406, 408, 409
Stauffer Chemical Company, 114
Steiger, Albert E., Jr., 490
Steiger Tractor Company, 202
Stein, Sondra, 425
Stein, William C., 486, 488
Stein v. Massachusetts Mutual Insurance
    Company, 486
Steinbrenner, George M., 151, 152, 153, 155,
    157
Stellman, J., 123n
Stephens, W. Thomas, 347n, 350, 352, 354,
    355, 360, 364, 378–79
Sterling Drug, 522, 539–40, 545
Stevens, Whitney J., 380, 394
Stewart, Robert D., 650
Stillman, N., 121n
St. Joe's Mineral Corporation, 127
Stone, Christopher D., 635
Streitenberger, Keither, 191n
Stricoff, Scott, 223
Stroh Brewery Company, 462, 463, 465, 467
Stromberg, A., 113n
Stuart, Reginald, 170n
Sturdivant, Frederick D., 1n, 3n
Sulewski, Chester, 352, 368
Sullivan, Leon, 210n, 267, 270, 320
Sullivan, Patricia, 365n
Sullivan Principles, 210, 267–71
    signatories, 270–71
Superfund, 657–58, 655
Suzuki Motor Company, 588

Tate, C., 115n, 118n, 119n, 126n
Taub, Richard, 240
Taylor, John, 302, 312, 314–16, 318
Teamsters Union, 430
Ted Bates & Company, 469
Television news, 443–47
Tenneco, 176, 177
Texaco, 147, 321
Textile industry, labor history, 387–88
Textile Workers Union of America (TWuA),
    390
Theis, Francis W., 160
Theory of the Firm, 375
Thornton, Grant, 140
3M (Minnesota Mining and Manufacturing),
    154, 656, 657

Three Mile Island nuclear plant, 606,
    609–27, 648
Tidwell Industries, 266
Tiffenberg, Ira, 426
Tifft, Susan, 525
Tomerlin, John, 578
Tongor Corporation, 100
Total Product Responsibility (TPR) program,
    640–44
Touche Ross and Company, 109
"Tough Words for American Industry"
    (Karatsu), 421
Toyota Motor Corporation, 244, 245, 587
    productivity, 421
Toxic Alert, 211, 213, 218, 291, 221, 222
Toxic Substances Control Act (TSCA), 628,
    636, 637–40
Trans World Airlines, 88
Trapp, John, 597
Trebilcock, Ann, 122
Triner, Alma, 209, 229
TriStar aircraft, 88, 89, 90, 91
TRW Inc., 513
TSCA; see Toxic Substances Control Act
Tucker, William D., 352
Turco Coatings, Inc., 661
"Twisting" in insurance business, 101
Two-tier wage structure, 429–32
Tylenol, cyanide episode, 525–46

Udall, Morris K., 620
Underhill, 271
UNICEF, 38
Unigate Foods, 22, 29
Unintended acceleration, 578–87
    Audi 5000, 579–87
Union of Banana Exporting Countries, 307
Union Carbide Corporation (UCC), 279, 288,
    295–98
    GAF raid, 288–89
Union Carbide of India Limited (UCIL), 277
    company background, 279–82
    finance, 285–88
    insurance, 661
    interviews with victims, 298–301
    legal battle after Bhopal disaster, 295–98
    marketing, 292–95
    operations at Bhopal, 282–85
    personnel, 291–92
Union Carbide Southern African Incorpo-
    rated, 323
Unions; see Labor unions
United Airlines, 89, 94
United Auto Workers (UAW), 122, 125

United Auto Workers (UAW) (*Continued*)
Harvester strike, 169, 182, 198
minority hiring policies, 244
two-tier wage structure, 432
United Brands, 302–18
United Farm Workers of America, 246, 247, 305
United Fruit Company, 303–4
United States Export-Import Bank, 285
United Steelworkers of America, 115, 117, 124, 423
United Technologies Corporation, 235
U.S. Department of Transportation, 253
Useem, Michael, 70
USG, 272
U.S. Investment in South Africa: The Hidden Pieces, 319
U.S.-Japan International Management Institute, 244
U.S. Steel, 321
Utilities; *see* Public utilities

Valquist Company, 31
Valois, Robert, 391
Vance, Wayne, 253
Vanderbilt, Cornelius, 78
Van Riebeeck, Jan, 263
Verity, C. William, 47, 55
Verity, William E., Jr., 598
Vernon-Wertzel, Heidi, 3n
Virginia Air Quality Resources Board, 637
Virginia Water Quality Control Board, 635
Viyogi, Tarasingh, 225n
Voss, Henry, 248

Wagner, Richard, 628, 637, 641
Wagner Act (National Labor Relations Act), 388
Wagon, Gerald N., 218n
Waldholz, Michael, 540n, 541n, 544n, 546n
Walgreen's, 545
Walker, Gary, 143
Walker, Roy, 156
Wallace, David W., 314, 316
Wallace, Mike, 445, 446, 456, 475
Wall Street Journal, 130, 288, 289, 297, 312, 315, 317
Warner-Lambert Company, 591
War on Want, 34
Washington Public Power Supply System, 648

Waterman, Robert H., Jr., 528n
Watkins, James, 432
Watlington, John F., Jr., 490
Wechsler, Alfred E., 205
Weedon, D. Reid, Jr., 210, 213, 221, 222, 223, 224, 226, 228
Wefa Group, 323
Weinberg, Bob, 476
Weiner, Steve, 183n
Weinstein, Alice, 580
Weller, Edward, 146
Wells, Jay, 311, 313
Wertheim and Company, 108
Wessel, David, 238
Westin, Alan F., 509, 514, 517
Westinghouse Electric Corporation, 659, 660
West Point Pepperell, 266
Wheeler, Malcolm E., 592
White Motor Company, 173, 174
Wild, Claude C., 155
Wilderness Society, 654
William C. Stein et al v. *Massachusetts Mutual Life Insurance Company*, 485n
Williams, James, 238
Williams, Lawrence, 102
Wilson, Donald, 661
Wilson, Joe, 241, 243
Win-O'Brien, M., 122, 123n
Winslow, Ron, 648
Winthrop Rockefeller Foundation, 240
Wolfe, Ralph, 216, 218
Wolfson, Weiner Ratoff and Lapin, 107
Wolinsky, Howard, 520
Wommack, William, 45, 47
Work Place Education Program for the Commonwealth of Massachusetts, 426
World Health Organization (WHO), 20, 34, 38
Worlds of Wonder, Inc., 374
World Wildlife Fund, 652
Wyeth Company, 21

Xerox Corporation, 62n, 133, 134
Yamaha Motor Company, 588
Young, L., 114n
Yuppy, 77

Zalusky, John, 430
Zimmer nuclear power plant, 650–51
Zinn, Laura, 508